An Introduction to

PROJECTIVE TECHNIQUES

An Introduction to

PROJECTIVE

Published by

TECHNIQUES

& Other Devices for Understanding the Dynamics of Human Behavior

Edited by HAROLD H. ANDERSON

and GLADYS L. ANDERSON

Prentice-Hall, Inc.

Englewood Cliffs, N. J.

PRENTICE-HALL PSYCHOLOGY SERIES

PRINTED IN THE UNITED STATES OF AMERICA

49309

Contributing Authors

GLADYS L. ANDERSON

Associate Professor of Psychology, Michigan State College, East Lansing, Michigan; Consultant in Clinical Psychology to the Veterans' Administration.

HAROLD H. ANDERSON

Professor of Psychology and Head of the Department, Michigan State College, East Lansing, Michigan.

SAMUEL J. BECK

Departments of Psychology, University of Chicago and Northwestern University; Research Psychologist, Institute for Psychosomatic and Psychiatric Research and Medicine in Michael Reese Hospital.

RAYMOND B. CATTELL

Research Professor of Psychology, University of Illinois, Urbana, Illinois.

HELEN JANE CLARKE

Psychologist, Student Psychiatric Clinic, Associate, Department of Psychology, University of Washington, Seattle, Washington.

ROBERT BARTLETT HAAS

Head, Education Extension, University of California, Los Angeles; Consultant in Educational Sociology to the Cooperative Project in Human Relations, Los Angeles County Schools.

FLORENCE HALPERN

Assistant Professor in Medical Psychology, New York University, College of Medicine, New York City.

WILLIAM E. HENRY

Associate Professor of Psychology, Department of Psychology and the Committee on Human Development, University of Chicago, Chicago, Illinois.

v

ROBERT R. HOLT
Director of the Psychological Staff, Menninger Foundation, Topeka, Kansas.

DAVID M. LEVY
Attending Psychiatrist, New York State Psychiatric Institute, New York City.

JEAN WALKER MACFARLANE
Professor of Psychology, University of California, Berkeley, California.

KAREN MACHOVER
Senior Psychologist, Kings County Psychiatric Hospital; Associate in Clinical Psychology, Long Island College of Medicine, New York.

MARTIN MAYMAN
Research and Teaching Associate, Director, Menninger Foundation-Topeka State Hospital Psychological Interne Training Center, Topeka, Kansas.

J. ALLISON MONTAGUE
Instructor in Psychiatry, Columbia University, New York City.

J. L. MORENO
Director, Moreno Institute, Beacon, New York, and New York City.

WOODROW WILBERT MORRIS
Chief Psychologist, Psychopathic Hospital, Assistant Professor of Clinical Psychology, Departments of Psychiatry and Psychology; Assistant Dean, Colleges of Medicine and Dentistry, The State University of Iowa, Iowa City, Iowa.

PETER J. NAPOLI
Supervisor of Testing and Training, Clinical Psychology Service, Veterans' Administration Hospital, Montrose, New York; Faculty, Graduate School, Department of Psychology, Fordham University.

JOSEPH A. PRECKER
Assistant Professor of Psychology, Bard College, Annandale-on-Hudson, New York.

ALBERT I. RABIN
Associate Professor of Psychology and Director of the Psychological Clinic, Michigan State College, East Lansing, Michigan.

DAVID RAPAPORT
Research Associate, Austen Riggs Foundation, Stockbridge, Massachusetts.

Julian B. Rotter

Professor of Psychology and Director of Psychological Clinic, The Ohio State University, Columbus, Ohio.

Roy Schafer

Staff Psychologist, Austen Riggs Foundation, Stockbridge, Massachusetts; Lecturer, Clark University, Worcester, Massachusetts.

Joseph C. Solomon

Assistant Clinical Professor of Psychiatry, University of California Medical School; Associate Chief, Department of Psychiatry, Mount Zion Hospital, San Francisco, California.

Read D. Tuddenham

Associate Professor of Psychology, Research Associate, Institute of Child Welfare, University of California, Berkeley, California.

D. J. van Lennep

Professor of Diagnostic Psychology, University of Utrecht, and Director and Founder of the Netherlands Foundation of Industrial Psychology, Utrecht, Holland.

Werner Wolff

Professor of Psychology, Bard College, Annandale-on-Hudson, New York.

Rose Wolfson

Staff Psychologist, Department of Psychology, Neurological Institute of New York.

Adolf G. Woltmann

Consulting Psychologist, Lecturer, School of Education, The City College, New York City.

Editors' Preface

This book was planned to afford a general survey of the field of projective techniques by presenting the contemporary struggles of pioneers in the study of personality dynamics.

The usefulness of a projective test, like that of a bacteriologist's microscope or a surgeon's scalpel, is no greater than the training and skill of the person who uses it. Training and skill in the use of projective techniques include a consistent conceptual structure or theory of personality and behavior. Projective tests could not have been devised without the early development of such a supporting conceptual structure of personality. It is often overlooked that it was the conceptual structure, tentative as it was, and not the inkblots, as such, that constituted Rorschach's contribution to progress in psychology. Each stage in the evolution of conceptual structure must in turn be preceded by discriminating observation, by subtle differentiations in perception, and by the sorting out of finer similarities and more refined differences.

Fifty years have passed since Alfred Binet's pioneer work in the study of personality dynamics, but science is progress, and fifty years hence the struggles of future psychologists will be advancing the process of this science on new and different fronts. It is for such pioneers, in whatever particular area of the field they choose to work, that this book is intended.

The editors wish to express their appreciation to the contributors for their gracious cooperation. Each author had many other commitments, yet with only two exceptions each chapter has been prepared specifically for this book.

Acknowledgment is due the many authors and publishers who have granted permission to quote or reproduce material. The sources of quotations are individually cited in the text. The editors are grateful to Ronita Edgar, who retyped most of the manuscript and assisted in the preparation of the author index, and to Patricia Pregitzer and Claire Soppet for responsible typing assistance.

While the authors were given almost complete autonomy in the preparation of their respective chapters, the editors assume responsibility for the planning of the book and the arrangement of the chapters.

MICHIGAN STATE COLLEGE

H. H. A.
G. L. A.

ix

Foreword

This book brings us up to date with what the advanced guard of experts, the explorers and pioneers, have to say about some of the more confidently used projective techniques. Authoritative, well-organized and well-edited, it should serve our several purposes for a decade—if we are granted so long a span. Many comprehensive researches will have to be carried through, I would guess, before enough data of the right sort has been accumulated to convince us that what has been written here needs reformulation.

Up to now most of us have been more ambitious to exhibit the gold extracted from the deep earth of personality by this or that cathected technique than we have been to discover, explain, and, if possible, remedy the failures and limitations of the method. The truth is that during this first phase of our common enterprise we have not known enough about our subjects to estimate the validity of every technical rating or statement that was made, and, furthermore, we have not been disposed to criticize unseasonably. In the permissive atmosphere of curious ignorance, creative exuberance and free-for-all expansion can proceed happily and without abatement. As a result, in the realm of projective techniques today we must deal with anarchy, a state that exists in all realms that are being explored for the first time by a host of independent workers. We do not believe that the psychological phenomena we have been studying are anarchic and unlawful, but our minds have made them so, at least to the eyes of an uninvolved observer. A precisionist from Mars might wonder even whether the cognitive maps set forth in this volume—diverse as the sixteenth century maps of America—are representations of the same domain.

What we need now, I should say, are scores of subjects of both sexes, and of different ages, cultures, classes, constitutions, and backgrounds, each of whose personalities has been thoroughly investigated and classified (or rated) in respect to every variable that the procedures described in this volume are designed to measure. The projective techniques can then be administered and interpreted independently, and the results correlated with what has already been discovered about the subjects. In every case serious disagreements will call for re-investigations of the subject's early and recent experiences and behaviors, his values, aptitudes, and internal preoccupations, and, also, for re-examinations of the projective protocols in order to discover, if possible, what was overlooked or misinterpreted. Careful comparisons of this sort should lead to re-formulations of each personality, on the one hand, and, on the other, to re-estimations of the significance of each kind of test response. There is evidence in the pages before us that already some progress has been made along these lines.

Given the current situation, the editors could not have given their book a better title. For it certainly looks as if "projective techniques" had come to lodge in our minds and would be employed, for a while at least, to designate the *mélange* of methods so ably described between these covers. But the convenience of the term for this purpose should not deter us from attempting to distinguish and define the different psychological processes that are exposed by these heterogeneous procedures. "Psychology has no need for a mixture of categories," writes Dr. van Lennep, "but of sharper differentiations," *and*—I might add, in accord with our editor's spirited first chapter—significant integrations.

This is no place for me to fumble through a dissection of the phenomena described in the ensuing pages, but it does seem important to ask at the outset whether our socially integrative editor, Dr. Anderson, is justified in affirming that "most of the contributors" have used the term "projection" in its original sense. Of projection, according to Freud, I have seen, in this collection of papers, practically no evidence.

The essential criterion of projection, as Freud defined it, is: (1) The occurrence of a *veritable* delusion or misbelief (misapperception, mis-interpretation). The patient *really believes* something about another person that is not true, not justified by the observed facts; whereas in a projective test the subject is obediently playing a game of "make-believe." He is not confronted by reality, but, at most, by a representation of reality, and in few, if any, tests is he asked to report just what he perceives "out there," say, a smudge of ink on a piece of cardboard. He is encouraged instead to *imagine* something, to produce pseudo-illusions or pseudo-delusions, or, more often, to speak out or act out responses, interactions, or more extended dramas which he invents in his head as he proceeds. Thus we are dealing, in most cases, not with a real *cognitive* projection (of the Freudian type), or even with a pseudo-cognitive projection, but with an *imaginative* projection.

The other four criteria of a projection, in its original sense, are sometimes but not regularly present: (2) The subject (projector) ascribes to the object (projectee) either a tendency directed toward another object (as in pathological jealousy based on homosexuality) or a tendency directed toward himself (as in paranoid states). (3) The ascribed tendency is a significant constituent of the projector's own personality. (4) The projected constituent is unacceptable (seems shameful or blameworthy) to the subject, and is therefore repressed or suppressed. The subject is unconscious (or only half-conscious) of its existence in himself. (5) The goal of the projective process is the maintenance of self-esteem, freedom from intolerable admissions of inferiority or guilt.

Although one often concludes with some reason that certain parts of a projective protocol satisfy (in a pseudo or imaginary way) all four of these criteria, no interpreters, so far as I know, limit themselves to these definition-conforming responses. Frequently the subject is conscious of the recurrence in himself of the ascribed tendency, however unacceptable. He will tell you that *that* is the way *he* feels, or has felt, or has acted, or has been tempted to act. Furthermore, the ascribed qualities are often admirable, not in any way damaging to the subject's self-esteem. Thus common practice has extended the Freudian concept so that it now includes imaginative, make-believe projections of constituents that are unrepressed and conscious, and of constituents that are acceptable or even admirable to the subject.

I have spoken so far only of *supplementary* projection, or the projection of *self-constituents*. But most interpreters, and here we differ with Dr. van Lennep, have stretched the original conception still further in order to include *complementary* projection, or the projection of *figure-constituents*. By "figure-constituents" I mean the tendencies and qualities that characterize the *figures* (imaged objects) that people the subject's stream of thought and with which he interacts in fantasy. For the most part, these are images of significant objects (father, mother, siblings, friends, enemies) with whom the subject has been intimately related. As I conceptualize personality, it is composed not only of general (unattached) dispositions, but also of numberless more specific interaction integrates in each of which the self and an alter is represented. The tendency that the imaged alter (figure) directs toward the self may be called a *press*. It may be rejective, affiliative, expressive, aggressive, or avoidant. Anyhow, one finds these figures (members of the subject's "internal company") or constituents of these figures in great abundance in projective protocols, and the majority of interpreters seem to have agreed that these also should be called projections. In short, subjects are apt to ascribe self-constituents to one character (say, the hero) of the story that they relate or act out, and figure-constituents to other characters.

Inside the bounds of this extended definition there are a few special types of projection (such as *contrast* projection and *negative* projection), but outside these bounds, I would say, there is nothing that can be included without depriving "projection" of its unique meaning. If the term is used to denote all forms of expression—a man's characteristic postures and gestures, his style of walking, talking, and writing, the way he cocks his hat and buttons up his overcoat—then we must find a new word to stand for the process of projection as defined above. If "projection" means everything it means nothing.

A simplification that has clarified the problem for me is this: Projective techniques are ways of stimulating the imagination, of evoking and exposing single images, fantasies of interactions, and dramatic improvisations. These stimulated fictions constitute one of several forms of behavior (in the largest sense) and are of interest in themselves, especially in respect to their formal properties. But only certain parts of these representations can be called projections, *grain* for the analyst of personality. The rest is *chaff*. To call something a projection one must demonstrate that it is similar to a "relevant" constituent of the subject's personality. A relevant constituent is one that should be included in the final formulation of the personality. The distinction is important because chaff is capable of misleading us most grievously. Hence, the great question is this: By what signs can one differentiate grain from chaff? The most reasonable partial answers—contemporary knowledge permits no more than partial answers—are supplied by the contributors of this volume.

Many readers will be as thankful as I am that the editors did not confine themselves to the above-given definition of projection, but included "other devices." Exclusion of Part IV and the last half of Part III would have deprived us of excellent expositions of some revealing procedures. Call them what you will. The truth seems to be that all the methods described in this book are tests of expression, but only some of them are *also* tests of projection. In other words, all of them yield productions—perceptions, imaginations, intellections, movements—that are susceptible to formal analysis, and the variables obtained by this means are indicative of significant constituents, structures, and attributes of personality. Procedures that are restricted to such formal diagnoses are not raised in our estimation by calling them "projective techniques." They have dignity in their own right.

Not embraced in this volume is a test of unquestionable merit: Twitchell-Allen's Tri-dimensional test, and several others, promising, provocative newcomers, that might properly have been invited to join this select symposium. But there are limits to intellectual gourmandism and our editors, like ideal hosts, have taken account of them; they have stopped this side of discomforting satiation.

HENRY A. MURRAY

Harvard University

Contents

PART IV

GENERAL INTELLIGENCE TESTS IN
PERSONALITY APPRAISAL

PART V

PROJECTIVE TECHNIQUES IN THERAPY

CONTENTS

Illustrations

An Introduction to

PROJECTIVE TECHNIQUES

PART I

Introduction

CHAPTER 1

Human Behavior and Personality Growth

HAROLD H. ANDERSON, PH.D.

Projection, as originally defined by Freud [*15*], is a *defense mechanism.* It is in this sense that the word is used by most of the contributors to this book. A person is *projecting* when he ascribes to another person a trait or desire of his own that would be painful for his ego to admit. Since the act of projecting is an unconscious mechanism, it is not communicated to others nor is it even recognized as a projection by the person himself. Projection in the Freudian sense, therefore, represents a misperception or a false perception. The fault or the unsavory desire or trait is still in the person's unconscious; it is not in the person or object on whom the projection is made. Since the concept of projection is discussed at some length in the succeeding chapters, especially in Chapter 6 by van Lennep, it will not be further elaborated here.

Projection is elicited by the Rorschach Test, the Thematic Apperception Test, the Four-Picture Test, and many other methods presented in this book. It is obvious, or will easily become so, that projection as a defense mechanism, as defined by Freud, is only one kind of mental mechanism that "projective tests" today are designed to elicit. The term *projective techniques* has within very recent years acquired broad and undifferentiated meanings. Projective techniques such as the Rorschach, the TAT (Thematic Apperception Test), and many others, elicit not only projection, but also expressions of almost all other conceivable kinds of mental mechanisms and symbols of human relationships. Projective tests are, in fact, not strictly tests of projection, but tests of mental mechanisms or of personality dynamisms including projection.

It is the purpose of this chapter to examine some of the concepts of personality that can be used in understanding all personalities and that will be generally consistent with the use of all projective techniques. The succeeding chapters will also deal with general concepts of personality but will stress the methods for studying individual differences in personalities. It is not the purpose here to present a systematic review of personality theory, nor would such a presentation be appropriate or possible. In fact, psychological growth, learning, therapy, adjustment, and adaptation, like physical growth or recuperation from illness, are indeed multidimensional. The author of this chapter is aware that on almost every page there is risk of oversimplification.

A POSITIVE APPROACH IN FORMULATING A CONCEPT OF PERSONALITY GROWTH

Biological and Psychological Growth: The Confronting of Differences.[1]   There are two aspects of growth that are important both in physiology and in psychology. Growth is at once a creation of differences and an integration of differences. The truth of this observation is perhaps more readily perceived in physiology than in psychology. An illustration from biology will facilitate the definition of a number of terms applicable also to psychological growth and learning.

*Fig. 1.   A biological illustration of
the confronting of differences.*

Take as an example an unfertilized egg living in an environment in which there is a spermatozoon (see Figure 1). Each is said to be an individual organism. Each constitutes a part of the environment of the other. Each is different from the other in structure and

---

[1] The discussion of growth and of the different ways of responding to environmental stress is freely adapted and enlarged from Gladys Lowe Anderson and Harold H. Anderson, "Behavior Problems of Children," in L. A. Pennington and I. A. Berg (editors), *An Introduction to Clinical Psychology* (New York: Ronald Press, 1948), Chapter 4.   By permission.

in function. It can be said that the presence of the egg makes a difference in the behavior of the spermatozoon and the presence of the spermatozoon makes a difference in the behavior of the egg. This phenomenon is called *confronting of differences.* Confronting of differences is a relationship in which the behavior or presence of one individual or organism makes a difference in the behavior of the other. Without the egg to fertilize, the spermatozoon in due course loses its identity as a spermatozoon; it dies. Likewise, unless it is fertilized, the egg loses its form and its function as an egg. It also disintegrates.

Fig. 2.   *The yielding to differences
—biological example.*

In the process of fertilization (see Figure 2), the egg abandons its structure and its function as an unfertilized egg for a new and emerging structure and a new and emerging function. The spermatozoon also abandons its structure and function as a spermatozoon for a new and emerging structure and function. Growth comes about through the *confronting of differences, the responding to differences,* and the *abandoning* of one's self as it is for a new self in process of emerging. Growth comes about also through an *integration* of differences. There is a biological oneness of purpose implied in the act of fertilization. In the fertilization of the egg, the egg's chromosomes unite with the chromosomes of the spermatozoon. The spermatozoon and the egg integrate their differences after a pattern that is at present supposed to be determined "by chance." *There is no perfect or complete integration of differences.* So far as is known, the pattern of integration could have been different. It represents a "voluntary" or spontaneous abandoning of a momentary status quo. Growth is process. It cannot be forced or coerced; it develops only under propitious circumstances. It proceeds along a principle of participation of the parts in achieving a more highly differentiated and integrated whole.

The Criteria of Growth: Differentiation and Integration. This new integrate, the one-celled fertilized egg, is different in structure and in function from anything that has ever existed before. It is a *differentiated* and *differentiating* organism.   Growth is the creation of differences (see Figure 3).   Instead of mere reproduction of the structure and function of the original fertilized egg cell, there appear cells that become nerve tissue, cells that become muscle tissue, others that become bone tissue, and still others that become glandular tissue.   Each of these cells is different from the others and from the parent cell in structure and function.   Yet through the chromosomes they are all said to have the same biological heredity.   This is the process that is called *differentiation*.   In both the physiological family of cells and the psychological society of persons there are an infinite number of problems of individual differences.

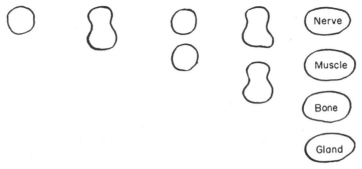

Fig. 3.   Differentiation.   Children are different from their parents and different from each other.

But as physiological growth tends to achieve an increasing development of individual differences, there is also a continued trend toward an *integration of differences* (see Figure 4).   The body lives and grows as a more or less integrated organism.   The nerves are not rigid and inflexible, but are responsive to the heart, the bones, the muscles.   The glands are flexible in their sensitivity to the needs of the other parts of the body.   There is, in fact, a common purpose among differences implied in the biologists' discovery that the individual acts as a whole.   There is an expenditure of energy by the parts in such a way that the needs of the entire body are satisfied.

There is neither a struggle of the members amongst each other in the organism, nor a struggle of the whole with the members. . . .   Only deterioration or imperfect adaptation of the organism makes members stand out abnormally.   [Goldstein: *16*, p. 423.]

It is specialization, differentiation, that has been emphasized by most writers on growth. Why is it that man boasts of being the highest form of animal life? It is because of the refinement, the specialization, the high stage of differentiation of the cells of his body. It is equally true to say that man is the highest form of animal life because of the high state of integration of the cells of his body (see Figure 4). Man, then, is the highest form of animal life because of the high stage of differentiation of his cells *and* because of the high stage of their integration. In all biological life, high differentiation is accompanied by high harmony of the parts. For millions of years biological cells have been "learning" to live harmoniously. Biologists call this evolution. It is a process of social participation of the parts, of the confronting and free interplay of differences, of the emergence of originals.

Fig. 4. Integration of differences. The child acts as a whole.

The criteria for physiological growth are two: differentiation and integration. They are not found separate in nature, and, in fact, are inseparable. *Differentiation* and *integration* of differences are different aspects of one process: growth.

The criteria for psychological growth are also two. They are, likewise, differentiation and integration, though other terms have been introduced for the same criteria. Allport [1, p. 132] has listed 14 aspects of growth, the first two being differentiation and integration. The other 12, including maturation, learning, self-conscious-

ness, and suggestion, can be subsumed under the first two. Maturation, for example, is not something apart from differentiation and
integration; maturation *is* differentiation and integration.

On these points Murray and Kluckhohn, in their, "Outline of a
Conception of Personality," have given the following elaboration:

> Furthermore, no conception of personality could be complete without
> some reference to the developments that occur, most of which can be
> adequately described in terms of differentiation and integration. "Differ-
> entiation" covers all refinements of discrimination in perception, interpre-
> tation, and conceptualization, as well as detailed specifications in laying
> out plans and exact directions and timing in action. Mental differentia-
> tion is involved in the appreciation of differences, in the intellectual process
> of analysis, as well as in the isolation and perfection of specialized action
> systems and abilities, verbal and manual. "Integration" includes the
> ability to perceive similarities, as well as different kinds of relations be-
> tween objects and events, to develop a coherent conceptual scheme, to
> resolve conflicts, to maintain loyalties, to rationalize values, to build a
> philosophy of life, to co-ordinate different plans, to think and talk in a
> logical manner, to organize dynamic systems into a unified whole. [*22,*
> pp. *30–31.*]

Growth is a positive process found in abundance in nature. It is
to some degree a characteristic of all living tissue. There is nothing
in the phenomena of differentiation and integration and of the
emergence of originals that can be meaningfully described in terms
of domination, submission, aggression, frustration, hostility, mastery,
rigidity, compensation, conflict, or even sublimation. Operationally
defined, differentiation and integration are proceeding at their
maximum under the existing conditions of the organism, of its environment, and of the nature of the interplay between them.
Rigidity, submission, mastery, aggression, conflict, hostility, pathology, and disease are terms used to designate conditions, relations,
and processes that are low in differentiation, low in integration, or
in which the growth processes are abnormally retarded. Emphasis
on mental disease and these other associated concepts constitutes a
negative approach to the understanding of personality. The very
concept of *defense mechanism* implies some answer not only to the
question, *Defense against what?* but also to, *Defense for what?*
Defense mechanisms are called into play when trouble arises, when
"something is the matter," when the environment has interfered
with the positive growth processes of differentiation and integration.
Defense mechanisms are used when the person needs to protect his

spontaneity, his autonomy, his own differentiating processes, his biological process of growing.

Optimum Growth and a Propitious Environment. Growth, like everything else the psychologist discusses, exists in degrees. Although the units of measurement or of comparison are often crude or even nonexistent, growth may be considered as faster or slower, or as more or less. Theoretically, there are absolute limits beyond which one cannot go. Practically speaking, however, it is difficult to say that anyone ever achieves this highest limit. In other words, a person is growing at his optimum, or he is growing at something less than his optimum. It is helpful to postulate a concept of optimum growth, which necessitates also a concept of propitious environment.

One child is differentiating at a more rapid rate than another of the same age. One mother permits or assists her child to emancipate (differentiate) himself faster than another mother. The units of comparison are coarse and crude, but the comparisons are possible and useful. The development of reliable, valid units for making such comparisons will be among the valued clinical research contributions of the next 20 years.

The concepts of optimum growth and propitious environment are quite acceptable in other sciences and can be equally useful to psychologists. No farmer would expect the same crop from a weedy corn field that he would get from a well-tilled field. No farmer expects the same crop of corn from a mountain field several thousand feet above sea level that he would get from a field in Iowa or Illinois. There are good reasons why cotton is not a commercially profitable crop in Minnesota. Given seed from the same stock, environment plays a determining role in the growth process.

It is no more correct to say that the cotton crop of Minnesota is characteristic of the "inherent" or "inevitable" or "predetermined" qualities of the seed used than to say that it is a product of cool nights and a short season. The cotton crop of Minnesota would be a product of the dynamic interplay between the plant and the environment. In Minnesota one cannot bring out the "best" there is in cotton no matter how "good" the seed.

Some children are indeed brought up in a chilly climate; others are literally scorched. *Man is not only a product of his environment; in a very real sense man is also a victim of his environment.*

Most children who are brought as behavior problems to the clinic are victims of their environment, and they are often brought to the clinic by older victims of other environments.

It is our hypothesis that in a fashion similar to the growth of cells in a high type of biological organism, man as a social unit becomes more and more differentiated as he learns to live harmoniously with other human beings. We assert that this is not different from the observable phenomena in biology. We do not believe that to make this assertion is to reason by analogy, but that this is a testable hypothesis and that this process can be verified in the observation of the behavior of man. Differentiation is not separate from integration of function. There is no high degree of specialization of the parts except in organisms that have worked out a high degree of harmony of function.

To say that growth is the first law of life is to make a positive but redundant statement. The test of evolution has been differentiation and integration, the creation of differences and their mutual adaptation. This is not the place to elaborate on this point, but Coker [12] has pointed out that in interpreting a law of survival, "the fittenist and the fightenist" are not identical. Aggressive behavior, which is much observed and discussed by psychologists and is brought out in many ways by projective techniques, has been seen in so many "sick" persons that some analysts have declared it to be instinctive, a basic and inescapable part of human motivation. Like Old Testament children who were born in sin and who perforce had to do something about it, man with his aggressive instinct must learn to sublimate his hate; he must channelize his innate hostility.

It is our hypothesis that to postulate aggression as instinctive is to violate the laws of parsimony. Most, if not all, aggressive behavior can be explained on the basis of learning. Some biologists have maintained that not even for Darwin was aggression as expressed in conflict a basic factor in survival of a species.

Coker has said that it is "a mischievous fallacy" to hold that "fittest to survive" and "strongest" are equivalent. Of Darwin's theory of "natural selection," which was translated by Herbert Spencer into the phrase, "the survival of the fittest," Coker writes:

According to Darwin, man owes his civilization in no small part to being social, co-operative, and kindly. We have a theory that the necessity of survival makes imperative a habit of aggression, subjugation and exploitation, and we have what may be called the Darwinian view, or the biological contention, that man has attained his present state of development primarily through his social, co-operative, and altruistic qualities. [*12*, p. 491.]

It should be apparent that under any free working of the alleged principle of survival of the strongest and most combative, there could be no survival. If the stated criterion were adhered to there would finally be one man, who could not live indefinitely. Quite obviously survival is assured only when there is agreement among a large number or a few on some policy of "live and let live." [*12*, p. 494.]

According to this interpretation, it is not aggression, not conflict, not even competition, but *co-operation* and *harmony among differences* that have constituted, for Darwin and for Coker, a propitious environment for evolution and for survival.

What, then, are the elements of the *hypothetical situation in which one is approaching his optimum?* How many different characteristics can one expect in a situation where a person is growing at something approximating the optimum of his hereditary potential in an optimum environment?

1. There is a minimum of *environmental press* or *domination.* This is consistent with the hypothesis that growth is spontaneous and with the well-demonstrated fact that growth cannot be forced or coerced. A minimum of domination is another way of saying that the setting is one in which there is a maximum of being *accepted as one is.*

2. It follows that with a minimum of environmental press or domination there is a maximum of spontaneity. Since one is accepted as he is, there can be the free expression of any ideas, activities, and impulses that occur to the individual.

3. With free expression, there is the maximum of communication to the environment, making possible a maximum of understanding of the person by the environment.

4. Since there are no threats from the environment, a maximum approximation of "true perception" would be expected. That is, perception would not be distorted by concern for what the percept meant for one's personal security. One is secure when accepted as he is. This high quality of perception would facilitate the maximum of understanding of others by the person himself.

5. Being accepted as he is, the person has no cause for attacking, dominating, or coercing another. Others would show a maximum

of spontaneity, of communication, thus facilitating a "richer" interplay of ideas and activities.

6. Because behavior is "circular" in its effects, as we shall discuss later, the relationship between the person and his environment shows a maximum of harmony, of *working with others*. (To the extent that one's spontaneity is not in harmony with the spontaneity of others, one does not continue to be accepted as he is.)

7. This situation makes for the mentally healthy person. There is a balance between the id and the superego, a well-developed relation between the ego and the id.

8. In this relation, the term "conflict with the environment" is meaningless. Projective techniques would elicit only expressive behavior; no defense mechanisms would be found.

9. As for emotional behavior, in this situation the person experiences love, ecstasy, delight, and other positive, constructive, creative, pleasant, and satisfying emotions. In this optimum environment are to be found the "inspired moments," the "insightful" flashes of the gestaltists. Here is the joy of discovery and the thrill in learning. These are moments in a positive growth relationship with one's environment. They are real in themselves. They are not a sublimation of anything under heaven.

10. But, one must now add, there is no perfection except by definition. No one is completely accepted as he is, for that would necessitate complete understanding. All things that psychologists observe are relative. There are, however, many human relationships that satisfy these criteria to a high degree, in which it is not meaningful to speak of conflict or fear of each other, of aggression or attack, of ascendance or mastery. Rousseau, it seems, had this relation in mind when, writing on the social relation of the sexes, he said:

But in the harmony which reigns between them, everything tends to the common end, and we do not know which contributes the most to it, each follows the impulsion of the other; each obeys, and both are masters. [*24.*]

LEVELS OF PERSONALITY GROWTH

We have discussed the concept of growth as the confronting and free interplay of differences, have established the criteria of growth as differentiation and integration, have hypothesized a concept of optimum growth, and have reviewed the characteristics of a propitious environment. It follows that the highest level of growth would be found in the optimum environment. We shall now distinguish six levels of growth that can have meaning to a clinical psychologist. These levels include two designated *socially integrative* behavior, and four designated *relations of conflict,* illustrated in Figure 5.

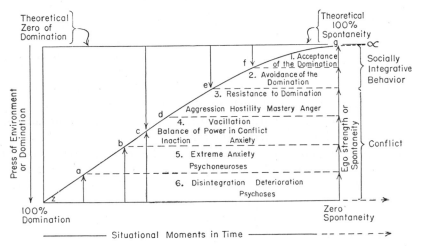

Fig. 5. Dynamic relating of individual spontaneity to environmental domination in which the levels of relating, designated socially integrative behavior, are differentiated from the levels of conflict for situational moments in time.

1. Relationships at different situational moments in time are shown along the diagonal line from points Z, through a, b, c, d, e, f, and g above the horizontal baseline and theoretically to infinity ∝.

2. The amount of Environmental Press at a given moment is indicated by the vertical distance above a point on the diagonal line; the amount of spontaneity at the same moment is shown by the vertical distance below the diagonal line.

3. The diagonal line must extend to infinity. Since spontaneity never reaches 100% and domination never decreases to zero, the diagonal line may continue indefinitely to draw nearer the top horizontal line of the graph but will never intersect it.

4. At the lower end of the diagonal line is Z for zero spontaneity, which coincides with 100% domination. Murder and capital punishment represent 100% environmental domination.

5. From our present state of knowledge about personality the range of each level, as well as the shape of the curve, appears unimportant, except that the curve must flatten off at the top into infinity.

SOCIALLY INTEGRATIVE BEHAVIOR

1. Acceptance of the Domination Without Noticeable Loss of One's Own Spontaneity. There is no perfect harmony in human relations. Perfect harmony would require perfect understanding of the desires and purposes of others as well as of one's self. Since each of us cannot be too articulate about our own desires, it would be asking too much to expect others to have a perfect understanding of us. At the highest stage of harmony in human relations (from f to infinity ∞ in Figure 5), each person causes some inconvenience to those about him; each person finds his own spontaneity somewhat restricted by the well-meaning behavior of others. Each takes a considerable amount of such inconvenience for granted. He continues to like his friends; he continues to enjoy their associations; he bears no hostility whatsoever for the minor inconveniences. He continues to show high spontaneity in his own behavior and to accept a high degree of spontaneity in theirs. Such a relationship is essentially *socially integrative*. It is basically a *working together*. Each can reveal himself to the others and not feel a need to be self-protective. Because each can be essentially himself, each can achieve a higher level of understanding of the others. This is not "adjustment"; this is creative experience [*14*].

Socially integrative behavior is possible in a relationship in which individuals may come closer and closer together in their understandings and still remain different. This is obviously an ideal relationship; for purposes of growth, differentiation can be at its highest where a person is accepted as he is. In this relationship it is meaningless to speak of conflict, aggression, attack, hostility, fear, or defense mechanisms. There is some evidence that the human being seeks and prefers this socially integrative relation. Hanfmann [*17*], reporting on the social responses of kindergarten children, found that her subjects made distinctions similar to those discovered in her psychological observations of the children. Upon being questioned by the teacher, the children were able to differentiate *dominant by force and coercion,* from *dominant by kindness, cooperativeness and understanding;* the "dominated" children actually preferred the latter form of "dominance."

Anderson [*4, 5*] and his colleagues [*7, 10*] have found among nursery school, kindergarten, and school children, higher mean frequencies of socially integrative behavior than of domination. Schilder expressed a positive view toward human behavior in his statement,

Human beings have a genuine interest in the world, in action, and in experimentation. They derive a deep satisfaction when they venture into the world. They do not experience reality as a threat to existence. Organisms, and especially human organisms, have a genuine feeling of safety and security in this world. Threats come merely from specific situations and deprivations. Even then, discomfort and danger are experienced as passing points, which finally lead to a new security and safety in touch with the world. [*25*, p. 220.]

And again:

According to our whole formulation, there is no reason to believe that the primary state of individuals is one of insecurity and danger. Individuals seek self-protection after they have been threatened, and they approach the world primarily in a spirit of interest and experimentation. . . . Genuine tendencies to help one another are present in the child as well as in the adult. [*25*, p. 217.]

Circular Behavior. Socially integrative behavior is *circular* in its effects. Manifested in one person, it tends to induce socially integrative behavior in a companion [*4, 5, 10*]. Since this behavior invites social participation, facilitates communication and understanding, and leads to further differentiation and integration, it is called the *growth circle* of dynamic interplay. The *growth circle* is contrasted with another kind of circular behavior, *domination,* which stifles dynamic interplay, obstructs communication, intensifies conflict and misunderstanding, and leads to atrophy and disintegration, and for these reasons is designated the *vicious circle* of dynamic interplay.

2. Avoidance of the Domination Without Essential Change in One's Goals or Purposes. At this second level of personality growth, the relation between domination by the environment and individual spontaneity ranges from *e* to *f* in Figure 5. It frequently happens that one person is obliged to live in some proximity to another, and finds the other an obstruction to his spontaneity, to his being himself. If he cannot accept the domination of the other person without noticeable loss of his own spontaneity, he tends to avoid the other but to continue otherwise to be himself. This manner of behavior presumes that the domination, though mild, is too great to be taken in one's stride. It presumes that the domination is great enough to warrant the taking of mild self-protective measures. Withholding information from one's parents and selective conversations with one's friends are symptomatic of such a relationship. Such behavior tells us much about the persons in the environment as well as about the individual himself.

In these two highest levels of growth in which there are responses to mild domination, the infringement on one's own spontaneity is not great enough to call forth resistance to the other person or to deflect one's energies from his own essential purposes. Behavior still reflects socially integrative relationships. But where one perceives his situation to be such that it seems desirable to withhold information or to be protectively selective in ideas, there is reduced interplay of communication and therefore less understanding. Where such behavior is found, however, it is not meaningful to say that the persons are in conflict; they are not expending energies in opposition to each other. By an adaptation of the concept of just-noticeable-differences used in laboratory psychology, the *avoiding* can be distinguished from the next lower level of personality growth, which is *resistance*.

RELATIONS OF CONFLICT

3. Resistance to Domination. One tends to resist environmental press or domination when it increases to the extent that it actively interferes with the attainment of one's goals and purposes. This is the meaning of the first part of the frustration–aggression proposition "that the occurrence of aggressive behavior always presupposes the existence of frustration."[*13*, p. 1.]

Aggression. At this third level of growth (represented from d to e in Figure 5), a part of one's energy is spent in resistance and attack. In symbolic ways this behavior takes on verbal aspects, such as the use of irony and sarcasm. The attack may be directed at the source of the domination or it may be an indirect (and ineffectual) attack on weaker if not innocent bystanders, a phenomenon known as *displacement*. Writings on personality are replete with clinical and experimental observations and theoretical formulations about aggression, frustration, hostility, and direct and symbolic variations of this kind of overt behavior. Resistance to domination will for this reason not be further elaborated here.

The Vicious Circle.   It has been pointed out elsewhere [8, 9, 11], but is not widely noted in the literature, that resistance to hostility and aggression is circular in nature.   Domination incites resistance; it intensifies conflict, reduces communication and understanding, and is behavior in a direction away from optimum growth.   It has therefore been designated a *vicious circle.*   In contrast with socially integrative behavior, which represents *working with others, expenditure of energies with others,* use of *power with others,* domination and resistance represent a *working against others, expenditure of energies against others,* and an attempt to gain *power over others.* This concept of attempting to use *power over another* is meaningless in the upper growth relations of socially integrative behavior.

It is furthermore the *directing of power against another* that is basic to a definition of conflict and that gives psychological meaning to mastery and ascendance and to all of the defense mechanisms.

Ascendance.   For example, *ascendance,* as defined by Allport [1], has no meaning except in a relation of conflict.   The writer has previously discussed an inconsistency between the test items of the Ascendance–Submission Scale [2] and the definitions of ascendance on which the scale was based, and has shown in observational studies of ascendant behavior that the concept and the definitions of ascendance include both dominative and socially integrative behavior, that is, both a *working with* and a *working against* others [4, 6]. It has been pointed out further that for this reason ascendance is an unsatisfactory concept that can now be differentiated into two psychologically different techniques of dealing with other persons.

Two general outcomes of the use of domination in human relations have been recognized: one is that domination incites resistance [4, 5]; stated another way, domination, since it constitutes frustration for another, incites aggression [13].   The other outcome is that if the domination (frustration) is sufficiently great, it induces submission; it is not safe to resist [19].   These two possibilities give full scope to the concept of ascendance–submission.   One submits when it is not feasible, discreet, or safe to resist; one waits for a more propitious moment when the balance of power over him has shifted. Actually these hypotheses state only part of the outcome of domination.   From the standpoint of the one using power over another, there are two long-range outcomes of a dictatorship: atrophy within or destruction from without; history has shown both outcomes occurring simultaneously. From the standpoint of the person dominated, the outcomes are included in the ranges shown in the four levels of relating in conflict illustrated in Figure 5. Ascendance and submission are only two of many ways of behaving in conflict. Both are properly classified with defense mechanisms.

Mastery. Mastery as a psychological concept is also meaningful only because of the concept of use of power over another. In human relations, mastery has meaning only in situations of conflict. This writer knows of no place in the psychological literature where it has been clearly pointed out that it is psychologically different to master a violin or to master one's husband, wife, or employee.

To master a violin gives power over the violin, to be sure. But psychologists have not appeared to *perceive* that that is the only relation, dynamic, static, or otherwise, in which a human being can expend energy toward or with a violin. The process ought rather to be called learning, since it is not meaningful to say that the violin has motives toward or away from the man. There is no *vicious circle;* the violin does not integrate, accept, avoid, resist, or submit to man's domination.

In mastering another person, however, the concepts of *dynamic interplay* and of *circular behavior* become meaningful. There is always some learning, let us say, but the natural laws that explain the response of the violin to mastery are not the natural laws that explain the responses of human beings, or even of other animals, to domination.

The failure of psychologists to distinguish between mastery of persons, of animals, of things, and, symbolically, of abstract experiences such as an algebra lesson, represents a perceptual limitation or lack of differentiation in psychologists. This limitation possibly stems from a long heritage of primitive magic [20]. When the distinction is made, the books on personality will be rewritten.

One can behave integratively only with persons and animals; one cannot meaningfully behave integratively with objects. One can behave only dominatively with objects; he can also behave dominatively with human beings and with animals. Without trying to oversimplify, it is suggested here that the great problems of mental hygiene and of functional mental disease stem from the failure of mankind to make a perceptual differentiation between persons and objects. In the evolution of mankind from primitive states of superstition, magic, and other confusions, it is not necessary that psychologists be the first to correct this almost universal error in perception, but it would be appropriate if they did so.

In the next grand stage of evolution men will stop pushing each other around like objects. We mentioned earlier that the individual cells of our bodies had "learned," in the course of a million years, to live integratively. By analogy, men are still psychological protozoa muddling along in the swamps. A few live integratively with others; a few achieve a high stage of mental health, poise, balance, and personality growth. But as parents and teachers, we slap our children because it takes a lower level of intelligence to behave that way than to discover some basis for common purposes. As citizens, we fight wars because we have not attained the evolutionary level of ability required to work out ways of living peacefully. We live dominatively because it takes a lower level of ability than to live integratively. It is not surprising that philosophers have concluded that all is vanity, that children are born in sin, or that aggression is instinctive. Who knows whether it will take man another million years to cease to be a vain, sinful, hostile protozoon!

The achievement of mastery over an object represents a flexibility in man's behavior, a further differentiation in the man himself; the psychological process of mastering an object is identical with the process of *learning*. But mastery of another person represents not flexibility in behavior but inflexibility; not growth as a self-abandoning, but fear as a defense of a status quo; not growth through the free interplay of differences, but rigidity through the stifling of differences.

4. Vacillation. The behavior cited above as aggressive, ascendant, negativistic, resistive, and hostile, shows evidence of a still fairly high degree of spontaneity. There is enough ego-strength to resist domination. Aggression is "common" behavior.

When domination increases still further it reaches a theoretical relationship in which the strength of the domination equals the ability of the person to resist. This is not represented by a fixed point, as shown on Figure 5 at *c;* it vacillates up and down according to the changes in one's perception of the strength and source of attack. This is the *balance of power in conflict.*

Balance of power, whether used as a concept in understanding personality or in interpreting international diplomacy, has meaning only in relations of conflict. It is meaningless in relations where either persons or nations are working with each other through socially integrative behavior. At the level of balance of power, a person's perceptions tend to become distorted. He is confused as to the source of the domination, as to its strength, or both. From his perception of his relation to the world about him, he cannot know whether to attack (and what to attack) or to run (and where to run). In children we call the hesitant, faltering, indecisive behavior at this level "excessive shyness" or anxiety. In students it is worry and nervousness. In the behavior of mice and men it can well be called "behavior without a goal" [*18*]. Although all response to frustration, including anger, is properly a fear response, aggression and hostility represent a response to a relatively highly differentiated (well-perceived) source of fear. When, however, the fear stimulus, that is, the source and strength of attack, is undifferentiated, the person is said to be in a state of anxiety or vacillation. A shy child cannot say why he is shy, nor can a student give a reason why he cannot study or concentrate. The source of anxiety in a patient is one of the diagnostic problems for which the Rorschach, the TAT, and other projective techniques are useful. Some behavior at this level is regarded as neurotic and is scarcely distinguishable from submission.

5. **Extreme Anxiety; Psychoneuroses.** A still lower level of personality growth, a still weaker ego-strength, is found in psychoneurotic behavior and other expressions of submission to environmental press. Behavior at this level is often scarcely distinguishable from that at the level of vacillation. In vacillation there is more spontaneity, more fluctuating moments when the person confronts his environment even though he then retreats.

6. **Disintegration; Psychoses.** A person who has retreated from reality into one of the several classifications of psychosis is a "sick" person indeed. There is so little confronting that he is even said to be "out of contact" with reality. There is often no discernible communication. It is to this extent meaningless to speak of learning or of differentiation, integration, ego-strength or spontaneity. This is the behavior that is found in cases of pathological fears, in persons who have lived in a tremendously oppressive environment (represented from z to a in Figure 5). Here are found persons whose perceptions, if communicated at all, are grossly distorted, even de-

lusional. It is not our purpose to attempt a detailed classification of personality disorders and mental disease. At this extremely low level of mental and emotional existence, projective techniques are frequently the only means by which communication can be reopened.

The term "personality growth" in the title of this chapter might seem to be a misnomer. A person has a physiological structure and a physiological process of functioning. He also has a psychological structure and is in process of psychological functioning. And he is a unitary being in whom these structures and functionings cannot be isolated or separated. Man is a differentiating and an integrating organism. The parts of his body and the moments of his experience are in process of refinement. As an organism he learns through his observations of the world about him and his confronting of other human beings. He expresses in greater or less degree his own spontaneity and, through the interweaving of activities with others, develops or fails to develop his ego or his own uniqueness.

If we were to submit a definition of personality, we would say that *personality is the rate at which the person is growing.* That is, personality is the rate at which one is becoming more differentiated and more integrated. Integration is usually used in the sense of something happening within the individual, as being united, devoid of internal conflicts. There is no inconsistency between this use of the term integrative and our reference in this chapter to the socially integrative relation. Persons who are conspicuously lacking in personality integration in the first sense of the term, are conspicuously out of harmony, lacking in integration with those about them. Internal personality conflicts represent in part man's struggle with environmental demands or with external conflicts. Similarly internal integration is possible only when man has achieved a fair degree of harmony in his relations with other men.

While learning represents a differentiating and an integrating of percepts, concepts, and ideas, personality is not properly the rate of this kind of growth alone. Personality is the rate of growth in a context of social learning. Personality is the rate at which the person is becoming more differentiated as an individual and at the same time living more in common purposes with other persons.

In these terms, then, a rich personality would be found in a person whose behavior was high in spontaneity and high in harmony. He would be accepted as a person and would accept others as persons. Being thus relatively freed from fear of others and relatively devoid of hostility toward others, he would be free to communicate and to listen.   He would thus be in a position to learn and to instruct. He could perceive the difference between persons and objects, treat objects as objects and treat persons with the respect and democratic regard expressed in the Golden Rule.   He could also perceive clearly the difference between a person and an idea, so that the confronting of different ideas would not necessitate a conflict of persons.   A philosopher is reported to have declared: "I disapprove of what you say, but I will defend to the death your right to say it."   A philosopher who behaves in this way is not only high in spontaneity in his own behavior but is high in his harmonious relations with others, even those with whom he disagrees.   To disagree with such a person calls for no psychological defense mechanisms, for defense is unnecessary.

In terms of the positive approach to the understanding of personality, psychotherapy would have as its general objective taking a person at whatever growth level he might be found and helping him up the scale into a higher level.   The goal of psychotherapy is to increase one's spontaneity and the harmony between this spontaneity and the spontaneities of others.   The procedures are to reduce or reconstruct environmental demands on the one hand and, on the other, to clarify and correct false perceptions, and to break the vicious circle and help the person into a dynamic relation with others characterized by the growth circle.   Spontaneity is innate and need only be released.   Harmony must be learned.

Projective techniques are devices offered without threat, unstructured materials to which a person may respond with relatively little fear.   They facilitate the expression in symbolic ways of fears and anxieties, goals and desires, fantasies and other characteristics of a private world that it is not safe otherwise to reveal.

SUMMARY

Projection, as defined by Freud, is a defense mechanism.   A person who ascribes to another person a trait or desire of his own that it would be painful for his ego to admit, is said to be projecting. Projection, being an unconscious defense mechanism, is not communicated to others and represents a false perception in the person himself. The term *projective techniques,* as it has recently been used, has acquired broad and undifferentiated meanings. Projective tests, as such, test not only projection but practically all conceivable mental mechanisms, both expressive and defensive.

Growth is a positive process found abundantly in nature. It occurs through the confronting of differences and the free interplay of differences. Growth, like learning and evolution, cannot be forced or coerced; it can only be facilitated by a propitious environment. The criteria for growth are differentiation and integration. There is nothing in the phenomena of differentiation and integration that can be meaningfully described in terms of domination, submission, aggression, frustration, hostility, mastery, rigidity, compensation, conflict, or even sublimation.

The concept of optimum growth that is proposed necessitates also a concept of propitious environment. Ten criteria of a propitious environment are listed.

Six levels of personality growth are presented. The two upper levels are designated socially integrative behavior. At these levels of relating between the person and his environment are found a maximum of personal spontaneity and of harmony with the spontaneities of others. At these levels are found expressive behavior, for it is safe to be oneself.

The four lower levels of personality growth are found only in relations of conflict between the person and other people in his environment. Defense mechanisms are, by definition, meaningful only in relations of conflict.

The six levels of personality growth are inversely related to the environmental press or domination over the individual; they are positively related to individual spontaneity, ego-strength, validity of perceptions, harmony with environment, and a state of mental health.

Two kinds of circular behavior were discussed: socially integrative behavior, and domination. Socially integrative behavior in one person tends to induce socially integrative behavior in others. Since such behavior tends to reduce conflict, increase understanding, create differences, and increase spontaneity and the confronting and free interplay of differences, it is designated as the *growth circle* of dynamic human interplay.

Domination is also circular in that it tends to incite resistance.

Since domination increases conflict, stifles differences, and reduces understanding even to the point of provoking misrepresentation and deception, the circular behavior that it represents is designated a *vicious circle* of dynamic human interplay. But domination has other outcomes: as it increases, a theoretical balance of power in conflict is reached in which a person is unable to perceive clearly the true relation between the power against him and his potentials to resist. Such a relation is found in indecision and other forms of vacillating behavior.

As domination increases further, the person is forced into the lowest levels of extreme anxiety and disintegration, where it is scarcely meaningful to speak of ego-strength, spontaneity, harmony, or personality growth.

Although this chapter is entitled "Human Behavior and Personality Growth," personality is not conceived of as something that grows. Rather, personality is conceived as a rate of growth in a context of social learning. Personality is the rate at which the person is becoming more differentiated as an individual and at the same time living increasingly in common purposes with other persons.

REFERENCES

1. Allport, G. W., *Personality*. New York: Henry Holt and Company, Inc., 1937.
2. Allport, G. W., and Allport, F. H., *The A-S Reaction Study*. Boston: Houghton Mifflin Company, 1928.
3. Anderson, G. L., and Anderson, H. H., "Behavior Problems of Children," in Pennington, L. A., and Berg, I. A., (editors), *An Introduction to Clinical Psychology*. New York: The Ronald Press Company, 1948.
4. Anderson, H. H., "Domination and integration in the social behavior of young children in an experimental play situation." *Genet. Psychol. Monogr.*, 1937, 19, 341–408.
5. Anderson, H. H., "Domination and social integration in the behavior of kindergarten children and teachers." *Genet. Psychol. Monogr.*, 1939, 21, 287–385.
6. Anderson, H. H., "An examination of the concepts of domination and integration in relation to dominance and ascendance." *Psychol. Review*, January 1940, Vol. 47, No. 1, 21–37.
7. Anderson, H. H., and Brewer, H. M., "Studies of teachers' classroom personalities: I. Dominative and socially integrative behavior of kindergarten teachers." *Appl. Psychol. Monogr.*, 1945, No. 6, 157.

8. Anderson, H. H., "Socially integrative behavior." *J. of Abn. and Soc. Psychol.*, October 1946, Vol. 41, No. 4, 379–384.

9. Anderson, H. H., "Directive and nondirective psychotherapy: the role of the therapist." *Amer. J. Orthopsychiat.*, October 1946, Vol. XVI, No. 4, 608–614.

10. Anderson, H. H., and Brewer, J. E., "Studies of teachers' classroom personalities: II. Effects of teachers' dominative and integrative contacts on children's classroom behavior." *Appl. Psychol. Monogr.*, 1946, No. 8, 128.

11. Anderson, H. H., Brewer, J. E., and Reed, M. F., "Studies of teachers' classroom personalities: III. Follow-up studies of the effects of dominative and integrative contacts on children's behavior." *Appl. Psychol. Monogr.*, December 1946, No. 11, 156.

12. Coker, R. E., "What are the fittest? I. A mischievous fallacy." *Scient. Mo.*, 1942, 55, 487–494.

13. Dollard, J., Doob, L. W., Miller, N. E., Mowrer, O. H., Sears, R. R., et al., *Frustration and Aggression.* New Haven, Conn.: Yale University Press, 1939.

14. Follett, M. P., *Creative Experience.* New York: Longmans, Green & Company, Inc., 1924.

15. Freud, S., *The Basic Writings of Sigmund Freud* (A. A. Brill, editor). New York: Random House, 1938.

16. Goldstein, Kurt, *The Organism.* New York: American Book Company, 1939.

17. Hanfmann, E., "Social structure of a group of kindergarten children." *Amer. J. Orthopsychiat.*, 1935, 5, 407–410.

18. Maier, Norman R. F., *Frustration: The Study of Behavior Without a Goal.* New York: McGraw-Hill Book Company, Inc., 1949.

19. Miller, Neal E. (with the collaboration of Robert R. Sears, O. H. Mowrer, Leonard W. Doob, and John Dollard), "I. The Frustration–Aggression Hypothesis." *Psychol. Review*, July 1941, Vol. 48, No. 4, 337–342.

20. Montague, William Pepperell, *Belief Unbound.* New Haven, Conn.: Yale University Press.

21. Murphy, Gardner, *Personality.* New York: Harper & Brothers, 1947.

22. Murray, Henry A., and Kluckhohn, Clyde, "Outline of a conception of personality," in Kluckhohn, Clyde, and Murray, Henry A. (editors), *Personality in Nature, Society, and Culture.* New York: Alfred A. Knopf, 1948, Chapter 1.

23. Pennington, L. A., and Berg, I. A., (editors), *An Introduction to Clinical Psychology.* New York: The Ronald Press Company, 1948.

24. Rousseau, Jean-Jacques, *Émile.* New York: E. P. Dutton and Company, 1925.

25. Schilder, Paul, *Goals and Desires of Man.* New York: Columbia University Press, 1942.

CHAPTER 2.

Problems in the Validation of Projective Techniques

JEAN WALKER MACFARLANE, PH.D., AND
READ D. TUDDENHAM, PH.D.

INTRODUCTION

In this volume, whose very size and scope reflect the vitality of projective techniques, the present chapter may seem to offer remarkably little solid evidence for the "scientific" validity of these devices, and to present an embarrassing number of unsolved problems in establishing their scientific worth. A clinician using projective techniques soon develops a strong conviction that they, or at least the ones with which he has had rich experience, present important data about persons and personality dynamics. Yet many workers with such strong convictions, who also have the equipment of disciplined scientific methods at their disposal, have, to their dismay, found little in their own research findings or in those of others to justify their preresearch enthusiasm. Why this ambiguity? Have we been so wrong clinically? Are our present research tools of validation inadequate to the task? Or have we failed to investigate this whole problem in a responsible and substantial fashion?

The need for a concerted methodological attack upon validation was pointed out by one of the present authors in 1942 [12]. The difficulties described then confront us still, for although the intervening years have been fat ones for the application of projective tests to new purposes and for the invention of new devices, they have been notably lean in fundamental research on the validity of these tools.

26

For example, in a recent handbook on projective tests [3], only 15 of some 798 bibliographical references on the Rorschach, and only 14 of 91 titles on the Thematic Apperception Test, are classified as being concerned primarily with validation.

Most early workers with these devices were creative artists by temperament and training, whose skills lay in synthesizing great masses of fragmentary samples of behavior and feelings. They were more concerned with coherencies meaningful in understanding the persons with whom they dealt than with the requirements of objectivity and verifiability that preoccupy the scientist. Research workers skilled in experimental design might have been expected to contribute much to a solution of these new methodological problems. However, nearly all projective techniques had been shaped to meet the exigencies of the clinical situation, and they were badly designed for evaluation by means of traditional psychometric procedures. In this situation, investigators who valued neatness and precision preferred to work with material more amenable to their available research methods, while voicing profound skepticism concerning projectivists' claims.

Disputes flourish best when the antagonists agree neither on basic premises nor on standards of evidence. Projectivists regard as incontrovertible, pragmatic proof of validity the testimony of many expert clinicians that projective devices are useful and give new clinical insights. They discount negative findings from statistical evaluations of projective tests on the ground that statistics are inadequate for revealing complex configurations in multidimensional data. Critics of projective tests reply that clinical reports of projective test validity usually confound the test and its interpreter, and are therefore not crucial to an appraisal of the test itself. They complain that the necessity for interpretation removes projective tests from the domain of science, because interpretation involves operations that are subjective and nonexplicit, and a vocabulary frequently so vague and lacking in denotative precision as to preclude either proof or disproof.

The clinical usefulness of any test is, to a clinician, adequate justification for its use. If it gives him new clues to a patient's preoccupations, anxieties, sources of strain, and methods of defense, he will and should use it. If he finds that for many patients it is a useful predictor of what he finds by longer and more time-consuming methods, and therefore, that it gives him a quick best guess as to the type of problem with which his patient is confronted, he obviously will and should use it. If with certain types of patients it adds data that help in the differential diagnosis that precedes plans for treatment, he will and should use it. Why, then, if he has a pragmatic validation for its usefulness, is he concerned with scientific objective validation?

We offer five types of answers:

1. *A social responsibility.* Too many persons of little clinical skill and maturity are using projective tests as if their validity with respect to all manner of unproved claims had been established. Worse, drastic decisions are being based upon such misuse of the tests. A body of fact that shows the degree and areas of validity should reduce rather shocking present excesses.

2. *A professional responsibility.* By determining the areas of validity and invalidity with respect to defined reference-populations, the clinician's private norms can be supplemented, thus reducing his errors of interpretation and sharpening his interpretive skills.

3. *A teaching responsibility.* Only what is communicable is teachable, and we are faced with the task of training competent clinicians.

4. *An opportunity to advance an important area of knowledge.* A responsible attack on the problems of validity with the rich materials obtained through the use of projective techniques should refine our personality theories and add to trustworthy knowledge in this important field.

5. *A challenge to research skills.* We are confronted as scientists with a challenge to see if we have enough imagination to develop research methods that will organize in a public, repeatable, objective fashion the multifactor data that the skilled clinician organizes by unpublic interpretive synthesis. To date it is clear that the clinician has already made much progress in understanding personality in spite of, or perhaps because of, the fact that he has ignored many of the contemporary scientific folkways. As scientists, we still insist that the processes by which a clinician synthesizes his material are not beyond discovery, and that eventually we shall be able to correct his subjective errors and make his methods public.

More fundamental research is mandatory if we are to avoid the inevitable reaction that will follow the present stage of enthusiasm in which projective tests are accepted uncritically by many and results are generalized far beyond the data.

The purpose of this chapter is to review the issues involved in projective test validation in the light of both clinical and conventional research orientations.

RESEARCH TRADITIONS IN PSYCHOLOGY BEARING ON THE PROBLEM OF VALIDATION

The dilemma in validating projective tests derives from the difficulty of integrating the values, methods, and research contributions of three traditions in psychology—the experimental, the statistical, and the clinical. Each is concerned with the same objective of discovering verifiable knowledge; each has impressive records of achievement; each has limitations for solving the complex problems that concern us. Future progress clearly depends upon achieving an integration of their contributions. Yet certain apparent incompatibilities of method exist between them as a product of their differing histories. These divergences are not readily bridged at the present stage of knowledge. Before turning to the specific issues of projective test validation, let us, therefore, review briefly these differing orientations upon which validation issues turn.[1]

1. The Experimental Approach. The classical experimental tradition in psychology was much influenced by developments in physical science, and readily adopted the general scientific goal of discovering and specifying relationships among variables abstracted from the complex and multiform world of nature. Its classical method is systematically to vary one condition, hold other relevant conditions as nearly constant as possible, and observe concomitant variation in a dependent variable. Although experimentation in psychology differs from that in physical science in demanding a living subject, the experimenter's interest lies in the general principles or laws and not in the individual subject per se.

The main impact from this tradition is as follows. To establish a relationship between variables, it is necessary to phrase the relationship as an explicit hypothesis to be verified. It must be set in such a way that variables may be isolated and controlled, and described so that the experiment can be duplicated and the findings confirmed by others. That is, the methods and findings must be independent of any given experimenter; hence the basic demands for objectivity, replicability, and the definite language of quantitative mathematics for specifying the nature of discovered concomitancies. This is a tradition that cannot be ignored in the research

---

[1] For a comprehensive discussion of research methods, see Brunswik, E. [5].

approach to any psychological problem. The question that all investigators in this field must face is: What aspects of this basic tradition, with its techniques so fruitful for molecular problems, are applicable to our molar and field-forces problems?

2. **The Statistical Approach.** The statisticians of differential psychology inherited the experimentalists' interest in discovering functional concomitance between abstracted variables, along with the experimentalists' insistence upon objectivity and upon defining relationships in the precise language of mathematics. This research method arose when it was recognized that many important problems do not lend themselves to classical experimental controls, and that the latter do not necesarily eliminate extraneous sources of variation among subjects. By using large numbers of subjects, and manipulating the data algebraically by such techniques as partial correlation, the statistician found he could approach the goal of isolating the variables he sought to study from the extraneous ones that interacted with them. This approach recognized both interperson and intraperson variability; indeed, one of the principal tasks it set for itself was investigating the range of such variation. However, the emphasis has remained, as in the experimental approach, upon principles rather than persons. The phrase "psychology of individual differences" has become an ironic misnomer for the statistical description of groups, in which the individual, as George Kelly once remarked, "has no function but to sit upon his continuum." Nevertheless, the statistical "individual differences" approach produced the testing movement. From this the clinician derives many of his most useful tools, particularly with respect to comparing a given individual's measured performance with that of other individuals.

The main impact of the tradition of statistical method is summarized as follows. It has given us a recognition of intraperson and interperson variability. It has given emphasis to the necessity for evaluating our tools with respect to their capacity to give us stable and reproducible measurements. It has given the related concepts of "errors of measurement" and "test reliability" and the technique for assessing them. It has forced the awareness that conclusions necessarily based upon samples of subjects cannot be generalized beyond the populations from which these samples are drawn, nor can functional relationships be established between variables unless the variables have been adequately measured. This also is a tradition that cannot be ignored. The question again to be met is: What aspects of it are applicable to our molar and field-forces problems?

3. The Clinical Research Approach. In contrast to classical experimentation and statistics, clinical research has derived its orientation not from science qua science but from attempted application of scientific knowledge, concepts, and methods to individuals. Also, it developed its own concepts and methods when "established principles" failed to help in understanding the problems met in individuals. The central focus of interest to the practicing clinician is not the abstracted variable but the individual patient for whose welfare he is responsible and whom he must understand if he is to be intelligently responsible. He can reduce the variables of this complex totality neither by statistical randomization nor by laboratory control. Indeed, he is troubled by the very notion of the "isolated variable." To him, a multiplicity of variables appear to be interacting in all life situations, and to behave very differently in different combinations. Replicability, in the sense understood by the experimentalist, is not possible, and can be approximated only by piling up cases one at a time into groups of similar congruences, syndromes, and personalities. By this method the disciplined practicing clinician strives constantly to document his conclusions, but feels he can find significant relationships in his complex data only by a process of selection and interpretive synthesis. Since this process is not *explicit* and *public*, in the manner of a mathematical operation, his procedure does not meet the basic demands made by the statistician and the experimentalist.[2] From repeated contacts with the same patients, the clinician feels he can check his interpretive syntheses with respect to both relevancy and error, and that his findings, backed up by similar findings of others, give substantial evidence relatively free from subjective bias. The clinician has small and often narrow samples of subjects, working as he does largely with disturbed patients, and has frequently committed the cardinal sin of generalizing beyond his samples. However, he feels with conviction that his data incorporate many more variables than can now be dealt with by multiple correlation or

---

[2] It is interesting to note that researchers trained in the tradition of objectivity often turn for their "criterion variables" to the clinicians, whom, for all other purposes, they regard as artists, not scientists.

analysis of variance.   Hence, he regards his findings as more real, more relevant to his molar problems, more in context, more complete than those of the other approaches.

From the clinical approach comes the tradition that the relevant personality variables are those disclosed as they operate in individuals, that the notion of "isolated" variable is not a tool but a barrier to understanding the organizational processes called personality dynamics, and that concepts and methods that take account of different patterns of interaction processes are essential to securing and ordering the data of this field.   Although his media are individuals, as in the other traditions discussed, the clinician is interested in the discovery of principles and laws.   He insists, however, that these principles must not only add to general knowledge, but must be applicable to individuals.   This too is a tradition that cannot be ignored.   The question to be faced is: Can this tradition be harnessed to objectivity?

The clinical and personality research worker, if he is to add to scientific knowledge, must somehow integrate the values, methods, and findings of these three approaches.   He must state his hypotheses in explicit and testable forms, once he has passed the exploratory stage and has relevant leads.   His methods of data-collection and analysis must be public and susceptible of duplication. Where his molar problems are not amenable to classical experimental control, he must achieve the goals of such control by other means.   Research designs using carefully planned, distributed samples of persons and domains will enable him to approach this standard.   He must appraise not only the clinical usefulness of his tools but their reliability and their contributions to basic personality theory.   He must be alert lest his tools take on a vested-interest character and seduce him into spending time in justifying them, time that could more profitably be spent devising better ones.   Few of his technical problems have been faced; fewer still have been solved, as they must be before his real research goals can be approached.   This is particularly true of projective tests that may help solve his molar problems, once they have been harnessed to the inescapable demands of scientific method.   Being multidimensional tests, and tapping perceptual thresholds and organizational processes, they offer the hope of predicting significant segments of behavior from the multidimensional complex of actual life.   This hope will be actualized or trimmed down to size only after years of responsible research.

We shall see in succeeding sections of this chapter that many problems of projective test validation grow out of failure effectively to integrate these differing research traditions. First, however, let us consider the basic assumptions that underlie the use of projective tests.

BASIC ASSUMPTIONS

The problems of validation are, to a degree, specific to the particular test under consideration and to the uses to which it is put. The range of tests that have been called projective is extremely wide, which complicates any discussion of validation. However, the fundamental common characteristic of these devices is the ambiguity of the task put to the subject, a circumstance that permits him to respond in his own way. An infinity of conceivable test situations possess this basic requisite of ambiguity, and judging by the volume of current literature, a substantial start has already been made on inventing, christening, and describing this infinity in print.

Each test raises certain unique problems. Limitation of space precludes a discussion of any but the most general issues of validation. In order to keep the discussion reasonably concrete without making it specific to any existing test, we will consider the problems of validation in serial order as they might be encountered by an inventor of a new projective device.

Since a scientist is concerned first of all with the assumptions that underlie each new method, one may begin by inquiring: What assumptions do projective tests involve?

The Assumption of Response Determination. A projectivist's explicit assumption is that every subject's responses [3] are not the consequence of sheer accident but are *determined* by psychological attributes of that subject. Few psychologists would be likely to quarrel with this, since it is a statement of the fundamental dogma of determinism upon which science rests. The typical projective test, however, involves the implicit assumption that since it offers the subject wide latitude to reveal himself, the particular sample of responses supplied by the protocol mirrors the subject's basic per-

---

[3] Throughout the discussion we shall define *response* broadly to include all aspects of test performance that are scored or utilized in interpretation.

sonality organization. There follow from this "isomorphic" assumption three corollaries that are rarely stated.

The first is the implicit *belief that a protocol is a sufficiently extensive sampling of the subject's personality to warrant formulating judgments about it.* Even if one assumes for the moment that the type of material elicited by a projective test is a valid indicator of personality, it remains to be demonstrated that the test as administered is long enough or comprehensive enough to permit personality generalizations.

The second corollary might be phrased as a *belief that the psychological determinants of each and every response are basic and general.* This point of view is implied by the common practice of utilizing each and every aspect of the subject's performance in inferring his basic personality configuration without regard for the stability or consistency with which these several aspects of performance reveal themselves. Nonprojective psychometrists were forced to recognize long ago that test behavior is in part determined by transitory or peripheral factors, which reduce the accuracy of prediction. They classified the consequences of these nonpredictive determinants as "errors of measurement" and developed methods for determining and minimizing their effects. Projectivists, finding these methods difficult to apply because of the nonquantitative nature of their data, have frequently "solved" the problem by assuming that projective responses are determined wholly by basic and central attributes, and are thus immune to a kind of error that has proved ubiquitous in all other efforts at psychological measurement.

The third corollary can be stated as the *belief that projective tests tap the durable essence of personality equally in different individuals.* This optimistic assumption does not seem to be borne out. Unpublished material of the Guidance Study [4] shows that some of the protocols of some individuals seem to summarize that which long clinical knowledge of these persons suggests are the important variables in their personality dynamics. But it is equally true that in other individuals, the protocols appear to give the periphery; in still others, to show only the protective covering. Perhaps these differences are due to the fact that some individuals spend most of

---

4 See Chapter 18, by Macfarlane [2], for a description of this investigation.

their energies in fantasy, and with them the protocols may reveal a broad segment of inner dynamics. In others who spend most of their energies in the overt perfecting of security-giving social and achievement skills, the protocols may sample a very small segment. And in still others, so much energy may be spent maintaining defenses that all we are tapping is the mechanism of defense.

The early optimistic assumption that projective tests were getting at the durable core equally in all individuals has perhaps stood in the way of investigating or seeing the need to investigate the different homeostatic functions that tests sample. The centralist philosophy, ushered in and given rich and substantial meaning by the findings of Freud, somehow got distorted into the dogma, (1) "Your unconscious is you," (2) "Your fantasy is the key to your unconscious," (3) "Your projective protocol is the key to your fantasy," (4) "Hence, your protocol is you. *Q.E.D.*" We know enough now to state with some confidence that the correlation of each of the above statements with the facts is not unity.

To summarize: adequacy of response sampling, determination of all responses by basic personality, and equal applicability to different individuals are *assumptions.* The scientific critic, while recognizing that any behavior sample possesses some intrinsic validity as an expression of personality, quite properly demands *evidence* as to the degree to which these assumptions are satisfied. Until such evidence is supplied, he will remain skeptical of the projectivist's statements.

Since a projectivist is himself usually anxious to establish the objective worth of his test on firmer ground than its face validity, he becomes inescapably involved with those Siamese twins of psychometric respectability, reliability and validity. Although fairly clear definitions and methods of measurement of these test attributes exist in the field of mental testing, their determination for a projective technique involves complex problems. Let us consider first the matter of reliability.

THE PROBLEM OF RELIABILITY

Test reliability refers to the stability with which a test yields information. Techniques for determining reliability have been developed for tests yielding quantitative scores on single dimensions. The usual type of projective test yields not a score but a nonquantitative protocol not directly susceptible of the statistical treatment suitable, for example, to achievement tests.

What are the procedures that are available for the ordering of qualitative data? There are two general methods: matching, which deals with a subject's record as a whole, and coding classifications or rating scales, which deal with selected aspects of the record. Both methods depend upon the discriminations of a judge or rater and confound the reliability of the test with that of the judge. With qualitative records this essential ambiguity is impossible to avoid, but the devices of measuring a judge against himself and against other judges yield generalizable information about the reliability of the test, when used by judges meeting the same specifications.

A further problem is, that for a judge of any given discriminative skill, the reliability of a coding, rating, or matching operation depends upon the heterogeneity of the materials to be treated. If the protocols are diverse, reliability will tend to be high, but if they are very similar, the task of discrimination is difficult and, therefore, the reliability of the ratings or matchings tends to be low.

Let us look at the two approaches in turn.

Matching Approaches.   When projective *protocols* are matched, the assessment of reliability depends upon the success with which a judge can correctly pair two sets of protocols obtained from the same group of subjects.   We are forced to admit that this may bring ambiguous results.   If the results are poor, it is possible that the fault lies with the matcher's judgments rather than with the test. If good, the results cannot guarantee the reliability of the test in other hands.   If several matchers are used and they vary with respect to matching success, the matchers are differentiated but the reliability of the protocol is not established.

Some researchers have used matching to assess the reliability of the final *interpretations* derived from projective testing, arguing that because the interpretation is what is used clinically, it is the interpretation whose reliability should be established.   Interpreters who use similar concepts and who agree upon the significance of particular kinds of responses may prepare from the same protocols interpretations similar enough to be readily matched.   This type of agreement demonstrates the reliability of the interpreters, and has been used successfully by Krugman [*11*].   This problem is distinct from that of determining the constancy and consistency with which the test qua test elicits responses from subjects.

Coding and Rating Approaches. The above considerations suggest that neither the protocols nor the interpretations easily lend themselves to establishing the reliability of a projective test itself. But since the matcher bases his pairings on cues in the records, it is possible that these cues can be classified into categories, and quantitative scores on each assigned on the basis of frequency or intensity of the cues. The reliability of the test can then be established at the score level intermediate between protocol and interpretation.

Whereas the method of matching attempts to treat materials as a whole, coding and rating approaches break down the material into parts and attempt to measure the degree of stability with which these parts can be assessed. The chief issue is deciding upon principles of analysis for ordering the protocols. One type of principle might be stated, "Stick as close to your data as possible" and see what relationships are found to exist among data organized by simple descriptive categories. This is a straightforward empirical approach and has as its goal the building up of successively more abstract and dynamic levels of description derived originally from objective classifications. The other principle states, "If you don't start with dynamic categories, you will always remain at a molecular and undynamic level. Additionally, enough is already known from the clinical personality field to use dynamic categories." Space precludes discussing the historical differences between the empirically forced theory-building and the deductive systematic approach. Obviously in each there has to be constant interplay between empirical data and theoretical concepts if theory is to evolve that leads to the pursuit of more crucial data, which in turn sharpen theory.

The various systems of analysis that have been used with projective tests emphasize one or the other of these points of departure, and range from concrete classifications of manifest content to inferential, interpretive classifications at a highly abstract level.

1. *Descriptive Content Categories.* With devices like the Dramatic Productions Test [13], where the subject's choices among test materials constitute at least one aspect of his performance, the materials of the test can be used as scoring categories (for instance, man in suit, boy in jeans). At a slightly more complex level,

descriptive action-unit or thema-unit categories (man in suit hits boy in jeans) can be used.   Analysis at the level of manifest content is relatively independent of the scorer's judgment, but it is likely to require an unmanageably large number of scoring categories, and to contribute very little to the task of condensing, organizing, and rendering comparable the protocols of different subjects. While it is possible to reduce the number of content categories by making each one more abstract and inclusive, the gain in data-reduction is likely to be offset by a loss in the agreement with which scorers can classify responses.

2. *Formalistic Categories.*   Abstract formal aspects of responses represent another classifying principle.   Examples are the form, color, and movement determinants of the Rorschach.   It is often possible to define such categories well enough to secure reasonably good agreement among scorers and to confine the scoring system to a fairly small number of such variables.   But it requires laborious trial and error to choose from among the enormous array of possibilities those formalistic categories that are not only reliably scorable but psychologically relevant.

3. *Interpretive Categories.*   Categories that involve classification in terms of inferred meanings of responses present a still more abstract level.   Thus, the descriptive statement, "man in suit hits boy in jeans," may be classified in Murray terms as "need aggression" or "need abasement," depending upon the scorer's judgment as to who is the main character.   Or quite different interpretive categories may be selected in accordance with the assumptions of particular theories of personality—"refusal to accept own immaturities," "defense against repressed homosexuality."   Since these are molar rather than molecular categories, they are theoretically better capable of expressing the organizing aspects of personality, but they depend heavily upon both the subjective judgment of the scorer and his theoretical orientation.   Critics have justifiably raised the question as to whether this type of scoring does not reveal at least as much the projections of the scorer as those of the subject.

The problem of selecting the most useful principles of analysis is a difficult one and as yet not wholly solved.   But since the publication of a projective device is usually followed by a rash of scoring systems proposed by other workers, let us pass on to a consideration of problems in establishing the *reliability* of projective test *scores.*

Methods of Measuring the Reliability of Scores. In psychometric practice, reliability is ordinarily determined by repeating the test to establish the temporal constancy with which it measures, or by giving different forms of the test to demonstrate that each form is yielding an adequate and hence stable measurement of the total domain sampled. These two kinds of operation often yield roughly equivalent results but they are not logically identical, and involve distinct problems.

Temporal Reliability. First, let us consider the meaning of a retest coefficient obtained on a scoring dimension of a projective test. Most workers adopt the view that significant aspects of personality change through time in response to internal and external pressures.[5] They may argue with considerable cogency, therefore, that the usual statistical criteria of temporal reliability do not apply to projective tests. Although a subject's test performances at different times should be congruent with each other in the sense that they reveal the more central and enduring dimensions of the subject's personality, they should not be expected to show statistical reliability because the subject himself may have changed.

The retest method of establishing reliability does not seem to meet the projectivist's needs because he cannot agree that personality is unchanging. What other procedures can he pursue to prove that his test is revealing anything stable enough to warrant generalizations about personality?

Alternate Form Reliability. To estimate the stability with which a test measures, a conventional psychometric method has been to correlate the scores on two equivalent forms of a test. With projective devices that are independent of any particular set of stimulus materials, say, handwriting, this offers no problems since another sample can easily be obtained. But in tests involving stimuli whose properties determine to a degree the range of responses that may be

---

[5] If a projectivist were to take the nativist position that the basic variables of personality which he seeks to explore are unmodifiable, and hence stable through time, he might reasonably assess the reliability of his test by the retest method popularized by mental testers. Indeed, Szondi, who has embraced a more frankly nativist position than almost any other worker, has gone even further with his test than the traditional procedure of determining its retest reliability for a group of subjects, in that he requires that *each* subject be re-examined on several occasions before an interpretation is made. In so doing, Szondi has taken advantage of the logical implications of his theory to differentiate, on the basis of their temporal constancy, between superficial responses and responses which, he asserts, reflect basic predispositions. See [6].

elicited, the test materials cannot be ignored.   Differences in card-pull on the Rorschach [*15*] and in picture-pull on the TAT [*14*] confirm this.

Many projectivists have made the assumption that their tests assess basic personality without error of measurement, and therefore, they have had no interest in creating alternative forms to determine the amount of each error.   Even if one sets out to assess reliability by this method, he must surmount very substantial difficulties in creating "equivalent forms." [6]   A psychometrician constructing a true-false achievement test can be reasonably sure of achieving equivalence between its alternate forms, because all subjects are set to respond to the same aspect of each item (that is, to its correctness) and because the items in each form can be rendered comparable with respect to difficulty and content.   In an unstructured projective test, different subjects are free to respond selectively to different qualities of the stimulus material.   The projectivist may not always be able to specify all the aspects of his test to which a subject might conceivably respond.   In this case he cannot be sure whether a second set of materials is really the equivalent of the first.   This difficulty can be met at least in part by systematic selection of the test materials to cover particular dimensions specified in advance. One may proceed either by matching the alternate forms with respect to the objective properties of their test materials, or, if one has a systematic theory of personality, by matching the materials with respect to their probable projective significance to the subject.

Surprisingly enough, not all investigators with explicit theories have selected their test materials systematically in accordance with them.   This again is probably related to the assumption that almost any material reveals central organizational processes.[7]   A case in point is the TAT.   With a well-formulated catalogue of needs available, one might have expected that the test material would be chosen systematically to elicit at least the principal ones, and thus provide the framework of a defined content area in which to determine individual variations in the degree to which different needs are

---

[6] Alternate forms of the Rorschach have been prepared by several workers, including Behn-Eschenburg [*20*] and Harrower-Erickson [*7*], although they have been criticized as not equivalent to the original cards.

[7] This centralist personality assumption is analogous to the intelligence theory of Spearman, that since "G" invests all kinds of intellectual tasks, the measurement of intelligence does not demand any specific type of test content.

emphasized. Instead, the pictures were chosen empirically for their efficiency in stimulating responses, with the result that some needs are elicited on several cards, while other needs of equal theoretical importance and probable frequency are rarely found in a protocol [*14*]. In this situation it is unreasonable to expect the relative frequencies with which a subject's various themas are elicited by the set of TAT cards to correspond even roughly to their relative importance in his total psychological organization.

In contrast stands a projective device, the Blacky Pictures [*4*], consisting of pictures of dogs on the basis of which stories are told. Although they superficially resemble the TAT, they differ in that the stimulus cards were drawn to constitute a systematic canvass of situations assumed in Freudian theory to be critical for psychosexual development. The Blacky Pictures as a diagnostic tool are conditioned by the adequacy of the theory and design upon which they rest. But since the stimulus materials were selected on a systematic rationale, alternate forms to test reliability can be constructed.

Split-half Reliability. When one lacks a basis for constructing an alternative form, a solution may be found by splitting the test into equivalent halves. Some investigators have used this method. For example, there are several published researches in which the 10 Rorschach cards have been divided into two groups and scores on the various Rorschach variables earned on one half correlated with corresponding scores on the other half. Different workers have obtained varying results, Vernon [*17, 18*] reporting low correlations, Hertz [*8*], high ones. The picture-pull and card-pull findings mentioned in connection with alternate forms also apply here.

Problems Arising from Variability in Protocol Length. In projective tests, the number of responses is determined not by the examiner equipped with a finite number of test items but by the subject. Hence protocols vary greatly in length. There is no satisfactory evidence on the general question of how many responses must be secured from a subject to justify confidence in the stability of the various scores arrived at in analyzing his protocol. For example, when a patient produces a lengthy Rorschach, one can assume that his responses approach an adequate sampling of the mode and content of his ink-blot perceptions. But when a ratio of 2:1 is regarded as nearly as safe a basis for prediction as 20:10, a question immediately arises as to the adequacy of response sampling. This is a relatively unexplored field in projective test research and merits more attention.[8]

After following the discussion this far, one's zeal for objectifying the reliability of the typical projective test may falter momentarily. We have seen that matching procedures yield ambiguous assessments because they confuse test and judge. The use of temporal indexes of reliability is precluded if one believes that personality changes through time. The use of alternate forms as a measure of the stability of a test leads to unambiguous results only if the test materials have been selected on some systematic basis. Devising a more or less unstructured test situation is simple enough. The problems encountered in proving the dependability of the technique are another matter. But since reliability is implied by validity, it is perhaps possible to circumvent the difficulties involved in measuring reliability, provided that one can demonstrate that his test makes possible valid predictions with respect to other variables. Let us, therefore, turn to a consideration of possible approaches in assessing the validity of projective tools.

VALIDITY

In the most general sense, test validity refers to the accuracy with which prediction can be made from test performances to other areas of behavior. It is customarily measured in terms of the relationship between test performance and an established criterion or set of criteria. Although all aspects of validation are interrelated, we shall for purposes of discussion treat them under four headings: (1) validation objectives, (2) scoring variables or interpretive patterns of the test to be related to criteria, (3) criteria against which to measure the validity of a given test, and (4) permissible generalizations.

1. Validation Objectives. One of the reasons that validation studies to date have been so inconclusive is that very few concise validation objectives have been specified and investigated. The shotgun approach, in which projective tests were given to all sorts of people to see what would turn up, was useful at the stage of

---

[8] There is one TAT study on this point by Tomkins [*16*], which concerns the number of stories that must be told to elicit the main themas. It uses only one case and hence is not generalizable but marks a preliminary investigation of this important point.

preliminary exploration. But enough definite hunches and clinical opinions have now been accumulated to permit defining specific validation objectives. The present need is to select and to formulate some of these objectives in terms of testable hypotheses.

There is no answer to such general questions as: Is the Rorschach a good test? Is the TAT valid? It is necessary to specify *valid with respect to what.*

Whether a specific validation question is a feasible one to investigate will depend upon discovering, among other factors, whether it can be formulated in such a way that it is susceptible of a research design that will give data necessary for an answer. Let us look at a few validation goals.

If one's purpose in prediction is a highly specific one such as: Can my graphological analysis of applications for charge accounts eliminate poor credit risks?, a design can easily be laid out because an obvious criterion of the accuracy of the predictions from the handwriting samples is available in the customers' actual payment records.

Or let us take a question of psychological rather than of tool import. Do persons characterized as spontaneous and expressive in life situations reflect this as movement responses in their Rorschach protocols, or are persons who are inhibited and inexpressive in many life situations more likely to show more movement responses? This is a question that can be formulated to be amenable to research design.

If one's purpose is seeing to what degree and with respect to what aspects a given test can predict itself over time, the problem of formulation is still simple, and once dependable scoring variables are available, the design is straightforward since it involves comparisons of scored protocols obtained with arbitrary and specified intervals of time between them.

If the question asked, however, is not specific but general, as: To what degree does the test disclose basic personality?, the investigator is thrown into a set of very complicated problems in his search for a formulation susceptible of a research design. Since this is the most pervasive type of claim made for projective tests, let us look at some of the problems it raises.

The question is inextricably bound to the many-faceted aspects of personality theory. Whatever his theory, a projectivist recognizes that personality dynamics, in which he is interested, cannot be directly equated to a brief sample of manifest behavior as secured on a test, where its total context is unknown.   Ordinary observation makes it clear that in different situations a person may perform different actions in order to achieve goals that are psychologically equivalent to one another; furthermore, apparently similar actions performed by different persons may turn out, when one discovers the total psychological context of each such action, to have been undertaken to achieve quite different goals.

However, the investigator's brand of theory, whether explicitly formulated or implicitly assumed, does affect the formulation of the validation problem.   And herein lie many of the confusions in this field.

The specific concepts, constructs, and systematic theories used to organize the empirical data of tests *and* the empirical data of criterion variables as well, are central to what validation objectives are sought and how formulations of research tasks are made.   Space does not permit discussion of the various theoretical tools.   All that can be done is to make a few general statements about them and to point up some of the outstanding issues related to them.

The laws of science derive from the discovery of verified functional relationships among empirical data obtained by methods duplicatable by others.   The concepts and constructs used are *theoretical* variables devised to reduce the complexities of empirical data (behavior, in the case of personality theories) to such a degree that functional relationships between classes of data can be determined. The scientific worth of these theoretical tools in comparison to other concepts lies in their greater utility in showing definitive functional relationships or in extending the generality of such relationships among the *empirical materials* of the domains investigated.

Constructs have to be modified continuously, as the history of science shows, in the direction of greater utility.   *Concepts and constructs are not entities but are theoretical organizational tools* concerned with functional (or dynamic) relationships.   These words are italicized because the personality and projective test literature is full of theoretical assumptions treated as established facts and constructs treated as entities.   In its extreme form this confusion has led to belief that if the protocol materials can be fitted into certain "depth constructs," validity of the test can be assumed without empirical demonstration.

The field is in a state of semantic confusion growing out of the different theoretical orientations. Let us look again at the question: To what degree does the test reveal basic personality? To certain workers of Freudian orientation who assume that basic personality is already an established reality, it would mean: How much of the "basic core" do the tests reveal? To other Freudians, it would mean: To what extent do the tests reveal dynamic materials similar to those found by long intensive psychoanalytic procedures and amenable to their theoretical constructs? To another group of different theoretical orientation, it would mean: Does the test show basic introversiveness or extrotensiveness? To others, it would mean: Does the test reveal "personal style"? To others, it would mean: Does the test adequately sample from the habit hierarchies that characterize persons? To others, it would mean: Does it predict how persons will characteristically behave in an array of situations? To others, the words "basic personality" should be reserved for those laws and principles that past, present, and future research prove to have the greatest generality.

These conceptual differences stem from the fact that a number of historically independent developments, each with its own precise and/or vague concepts, have become interested in the same field. We are confronted, therefore, with an array of overlapping concepts derived from Freudian, Jungian, Kraepelinian, psychophysicial, psychobiological, and psychosocial orientations. Further, because of the rich connotations attached to them, their users are reluctant to give them up. This makes communication and understanding difficult. It makes even more difficult a common statement of common problems amenable to research formulation, since research demands concepts that can be operationally defined and tested. The building of a denotative scientific vocabulary through the use of such operationally defined, tested, and modified concepts is a slow process, but it is the only one that will eventually meet the demands of scientific method. Progress will be achieved, in the opinion of the authors, not by global attack but by working through the lesser validation problems that can be phrased in precise and testable terms.

To return to projective tests, our validation goals, to be amenable to research, must be set in terms such that the test behavior can be demonstrated to have predictive relevance to psychologically important life situations, for instance, can ink-blot perceptions be shown objectively to bear high predictive relationships to other psychologically more important behaviors?

One of the major troubles to date in validation studies has been that a large unexplicit set of validation objectives has been sought simultaneously without regard for the fact that each objective has to have explicit formulation to be testable, and that each has to be tested against its own relevant and reliable criterion.

2. Scoring Variables.   The second factor to be considered in validation concerns the scoring variables already discussed in the section on reliability.   There we saw that it was possible to test score categories one by one and to discard or redefine those that lack stability, and that the descriptive scores and formalistic scores were most reliable but less cogent psychologically than the subjective interpretive scores.   There seem to be three possible courses of action in handling relationships among scores.   First, single score categories can be validated against simple quantitative dimensions, but this method destroys the Gestalt aspect of protocol and criterion. Second, the scores can be combined and weighted statistically, for example, in multiple regression equations, to predict quantitative criterion variables.   This appears much closer to the processes of the clinician and deserves systematic exploration as a method of organization.   Probably one of the reasons it has not been used is that the tests do not secure enough responses scorable in different categories to permit this type of manipulation.   Third, quantitative validation can be abandoned and scored categories subjectively combined into a qualitative interpretation.

There has not yet been systematic research adequate to show the relative predictive significance of these three approaches.   If it should turn out that the interpretation of certain skilled clinicians has greater predictive significance than that of the other methods, then the research attack would have to be shifted to the interpreter of the test.   Experiments would have to be designed to find the relative weights he gives to the various cues (his subjective categories) by some such procedure as having him predict at each step of an additive exposure to the protocols.

3. The Criteria.   Since criteria are the reference standards against which the protocols are to be validated, they must meet certain minimum standards.   It is obvious that unless a reliable reference standard is used, a test's predictive usefulness cannot be assessed. If the criteria are like those needed for the validation questions asked above relative to credit risks and the stability of protocols over time, good objective criteria are available.   If predictions concern overt behavior, criteria are available from observation and case materials.   By using such devices as descriptive codes, reliability can be assessed.   If, however, criteria are needed for the prediction of personality dynamics, we are dependent upon clinical interpretation and synthesis.

When we use interpretive constructs, we are caught in the same problems discussed in the section on scoring variables of tests, namely, the adequacy of sampling, the nature of the organizing constructs, and the need to evaluate the subjective judgments of the interpreters.

Adequacy of Samples.   If the criteria rest upon rich case studies planned for research purposes, there will be large samples of behavior systematically canvassed in many situational contexts.   Such studies can be planned so that the evidence, accumulated via a variety of techniques, can be cross-checked for distortion or consistency.   A substantial systematic body of evidence can be obtained.

If the materials come from service clinics, this systematic approach is more difficult to achieve, but by combining the skills of psychiatrists, social workers, and psychologists, a wide range of diagnostic tools are brought to bear on patients, which produces substantial cross-checked data.

If short-interview materials are used without adequate provisions for cross-checking and sifting evidence, the sample will probably be inadequate both in scope and in dependability of materials.

Organizing Constructs.   In a sense, the clinician is in a position to observe many concomitant changes in persons and situations that the experimentalist produces by design.   To take an extremely simple behavior variation, the clinician (or any other observer) can see that in a situation of spinach plus mother, a child merely stirs up the spinach on his plate; in a situation of spinach plus father, the child eats two or three bites, whereas the situation of spinach, father, *and* mother requires that the child eat all of it; and the situation of spinach, mother, father, and brother (whose misdeeds are receiving parental attention), means the child eats none of it. It is the interacting aspects that claim the clinician's interest. His inability to use the isolated variable as a tool derives from the fact that among his complex data the units of interaction appear to be the relevant ones. Therefore, he has developed constructs of interaction called dynamic mechanisms. Since in the rich case history he has available large cross-checked samples of behavior, he has a better base for reliably subsuming his material into interpretive variables than is available to the short-sample protocol.

Nosological categories of psychiatric diagnosis have been used frequently as criteria. Studies showing the unreliability of this type of categorizing have been available for years.[9] Further, they are syndrome descriptions and are not couched in explicit terms of dynamics. Despite this, the literature is replete with studies presenting evidence of agreement between this type of psychiatric diagnosis and classification arrived at by projective test protocols.

Organization of Materials by Judgments Made by the Clinicians. Judgments may be made in the forms of summaries, quantified codes, or ratings. Competence and skill vary. Intrajudge and interjudge reliability can be assessed when quantified codes and ratings are used. Those clinicians who have had wide sampling experience, long experience in sifting evidence and in making and revising clinical hypotheses, and long through-time contacts with the same patients to check their judgments, have developed techniques to take account of error that the experimentalist evaluates statistically. They are, therefore, our most dependable judges. The scientist's demand for evidence that is demonstrably free of the experimenter is not met by the clinician since his processes of synthesis are not public in the same sense that the experimentalist demands. But, likewise, the experimentalist assumes that *he* has controlled all relevant conditions, which the clinician often cannot accept. So long as these judgments predict important behavior better than any tools objective scientific precision has produced, we shall continue to work with them and try to objectify the processes used.

We are in the very early stages of developing a science of personality, and objective public validation criteria are not available for

9 See Ash [1] for recent reliability study.

many problems in which we are interested. As research workers, we can do several things now. We can continue to use the judgmental ratings of experienced clinicians. We can use our tests or better ones where objective reliable criteria are available, to the end that certain relationships between covert and overt behavior can be established. Or by assembling a variety of clinicians, statisticians, and research workers interested in the fields of motivation, perception, and social interaction, we can work on the problems of establishing more public objective criteria. As clinicians, we shall go on using projective tests and clinical judgment for the leads that they give us until something better is devised.

4. Permissible Generalizations. A consideration in all validation research concerns population sampling, since generalizations are limited not only by the nature of the test domains measured, but by the samples of subjects used. Frequently the clinician's concern is to assess the presence or absence of psychoneurotic, psychotic, or other abnormal personality trends in the individual patient; but except for organic conditions with a clear structural basis, the idea of abnormality is to a considerable degree defined in terms of deviation from the group to which the individual belongs.

The pattern of material elicited by projective tests appears to vary not only because of individual idiosyncracy, but as a function of age, sex, maturational status, socio-economic level, ethnic background, and many other variables. Moreover, *these variables interact and have different weightings in different combinations.* Hence, in order to assess the deviation of an individual, we need a reference population like him with respect to all these variables. For example, what general statements can be made about the significance of projective findings with adolescent subjects? Research has demonstrated sizeable age and sex differences in behavior and in protocols. Therefore, we need age-sex groups. Also, it is clear that lower-class children are allowed much more overt expression of hostility and sex than middle-class children; therefore, we might expect the patterns of covert preoccupation (as tapped by projective techniques) to be quite different, depending on class level. Intelligence may likewise be expected to influence the material elicited by a projective device. And since endocrine and growth changes that might influence projections are imperfectly correlated with chronological age (and with the changing patterns of conformity and freedom regulated in our culture in terms of chronological age), we must take account of maturity as a factor.

If we arbitrarily reduce our variables to two classifications with respect to sex, three with respect to age, three with respect to maturity level for age, three with respect to class level, and three with respect to intelligence, we discover that we require $2 \times 3 \times 3 \times 3 \times 3$, or 162 sub-groups. If 30 cases are chosen as the minimum sample size for each sub-group, we require 4,860 cases to establish reference norms even for cases drawn from a limited age range and classified crudely with respect to only a few of the relevant variables.

We are clearly not entitled to the type of generalization rampant in the current literature about this or that projective test, when data exist for only fragmentary subsamples. In fact, generalization even for the most widely used tests is legitimate only for those few population classes (largely neurotic and psychotic native-born white adults) for which adequate data have been collected. Failure to observe proper restrictions upon generalization is one factor that has led to the labeling of certain responses as constituting neurotic or psychotic "signs" before they have been checked against adequate samples of nonneurotics and nonpsychotics. Ives, McFate, and Ranzoni [15] analyzed for "neurotic signs" the Rorschach protocols of a normal group differing in age, intelligence, and social status from the group upon whom "neurotic signs" were established. Their findings show that all of their normal group also showed some "neurotic signs," and that more than one-third of them at all ages studied would be classified as neurotic on the basis of having a critical number of these signs. This means that the signs do not differentiate neurotics from normals,[10] who differ with respect to age, social status, and so on, from the original population of neurotics and controls.

Statistical Significance vs. Prediction. In choosing the research design for a validation study, an important consideration is whether one wishes to demonstrate merely that there is a nonfortuitous relationship between test and criterion or to prove that the test has practical value in predicting the criterion status of individuals.

---

[10] Even in the case of quantified tests, these sample difficulties exist. A study by Hunt et al [9] showed that scores on the Minnesota Multiphasic Inventory used in differential diagnosis failed to distinguish psychotics from nonpsychotics.

Especially since analysis of variance methods became popular, many research designs have been planned to refute the null hypothesis with respect to the association between test and criterion. However, if the samples are large enough, one may prove statistical significance when the association is a weak one.[11] Since in practice, tests are nearly always used as a basis for predictions about individuals, no test can be regarded as having satisfactory validity unless it can be shown to reduce the error of estimate enough to justify the time and effort involved in giving it.

SUMMARY

In the first paragraph of this chapter three questions were asked:

1. *Has the clinician been wrong in his judgments that projective devices disclose important materials for the understanding of person-ality dynamics,* since research findings to date do not substantiate his clinical judgments? The answer that we are forced to give in the present state of knowledge is that research attack has not proved whether the clinician is right or wrong, or to what extent. We cannot get from most currently used tests an adequate sample of scored variables to relate to adequate validation criteria for a basis of research appraisal. We feel certain, however, that all the claims made for the predictive power of a 40-minute behavior sample could not be true. We need more explicit investigations to assess those claims that are susceptible of research approach. Also, we hazard an opinion that the tests, as they are now promiscuously used, have an enormous element of predictive error, regardless of the fact that in the hands of persons relating them to other case materials they have important clinical uses. We believe that at present, inter-preter-with-his-test is the tool that should be assessed not only for the protection of the public, but in the case of the successful predictors, to investigate the weightings he gives to cues. We feel that the materials on psychological processes available from pro-jective devices are sufficiently important to psychological theory to deserve concerted research attack.

2. *Are our currently used research tools of validation adequate to the task of assessing the scientific worth of projective devices?* Our

---

[11] For example, one would regard a correlation between test and criterion of only .30 as "significant," provided $N = 100$. However, use of the correlation to predict the criterion score of an individual would reduce the standard error of estimate by only 5 per cent of the value it assumes when $r = 0.00$.

answer is that as of now we have not developed research tools that adequately handle the complex problems of interacting variables that projective tests are believed to tap, or the problems related to the complex criterion variables of personality.   The Blacky Pictures suggest a good approach for assessing the reliability with which our tests sample a domain, and this could help in establishing tests of greater adequacy than current ones in use.   We do have the tool of multiple regression equations for weighting scores, which is worth exploring.   The combination of more adequate sampling of certain aspects of protocols that seem to have real diagnostic significance with weighted scores via multiple regression should add considerably to our knowledge of dynamic interrelationships.

Systematic research on time and situation sampling offer to the clinical field rich possibilities for measuring the changing functions of a given personality variable in differing configurations.   The selection of groups distributed with respect to certain configurations of situational factors or certain combinations of overt and covert behavior patterns would permit comparisons with groups having similar configurations save for the one factor whose in-configuration function we wish to determine.   This is an approach that has not been sufficiently investigated.

3. *Have we failed up to now to attack the problems in a substantial and adequate fashion?*   Our answer is that we have failed to attack adequately the problem in its many ramifications.   Why? One of the reasons is that so much effort has gone into exploiting the diagnostic uses of projective tests in clinics and hospitals under heavy service pressure and so little effort into investigating the processes that projective devices disclose.   Too much time has been spent upon "the test" that measures a little bit of everything and not enough of anything to give dependable and quantifiable samples. What is needed, even on the level of diagnosis, is a number of tests, each designed to serve a narrow function well; when such data are in, the most stable and psychologically revealing elements can be combined into a screening device built upon an adequately sampled base.   Levy and Zubin [*19*] and others are already taking steps in this direction.

Meanwhile, normative studies of present tests already in progress could, until more adequately designed tests are possible, help to supply reference standards outside the clinician's population experience.   Studies are under way that are designed to show how much of the response is determined by the immediate situation of the clinic, by the giver of the test and his methods of administration, and by the stimulus materials, and what remains over and above these situational determinants. Studies of this sort should also help to sharpen clinical judgment.

What direction can our research efforts go that will profitably contribute to scientific knowledge and at the same time to an understanding of persons as they function? That is always the research gamble. One thing is clear, however—the design of research must be set in such a way that the findings will verify our hypotheses or force us to modify or discard them.

The larger gains in scientific terms will come, we feel certain, from smaller and more precisely formulated investigations of the perceptual and motivational processes that projective materials disclose. These studies might well begin with those variables from projective tests that experienced workers have found to have greatest diagnostic usefulness, on the assumption that their diagnostic usefulness rests upon the fact that they are expressions of important psychological functions.

The polyglot concepts from psychopathology, psychoanalysis, and traditional psychology need to be superseded, as we indicated earlier, by denotative, operationally defined and tested concepts. But since language habits change slowly, we can only ponder on what kind of action program can speed the process. At least one department of psychiatry has employed as a visiting lecturer a philosopher interested in both semantics and psychodynamics.

This chapter has raised too many issues in too little detail to be more than a point of departure for further analysis and research. We make, however, one final statement of faith: If devices that disclose projective and expressive materials are to prove their scientific or diagnostic worth, they must rest upon a strong foundation of clinical perceptiveness, of productive theory, and of research upon basic psychological processes.

REFERENCES

1. Ash, P., "The reliability of psychiatric diagnoses." *J. Abnorm. Soc. Psychol.,* 1949, Vol. 44, 272–276.
2. Barker, R. G., Kounin, J. S., and Wright, H. F. (editors), *Child Behavior and Development.* New York: McGraw-Hill Book Company, Inc., 1943.

3. Bell, J. E., *Projective Techniques.* New York: Longmans, Green & Company, Inc., 1948.

4. Blum, G. S., "A study of the psychoanalytic theory of psychosexual development." *Genet. Psychol. Monogr.*, 1949, 39, 3–99.

5. Brunswik, E., *Systematic and Representative Design of Psychological Experiments, With Results in Physical and Social Perception.* Berkeley, Calif.: University of California Press, 1947.

6. Deri, S., *Introduction to the Szondi Test, Theory and Practice.* New York: Grune and Stratton, 1949.

7. Harrower-Erickson, M. R., and Steiner, M. E., *Psychodiagnostic Inkblots, a Series Parallel to the Rorschach Blots* (Manual). New York: Grune and Stratton, 1945.

8. Hertz, M. R., "The reliability of the Rorschach ink-blot test." *J. Appl. Psychol.*, 1934, 18, 461–477.

9. Hunt, H. F., Carp, A., Cass, W. A., Jr., Winder, C. L., and Canter, R. E., "Differential diagnostic efficiency of the MMPI." *J. Consult. Psychol.*, 1948, 12, 331–344.

10. Ives, V., McFate, M. Q., and Ranzoni, J. H., "The 'neurotic' Rorschachs of normal adolescents" (In press. *J. Genetic Psychol.*)

11. Krugman, J. I., "A clinical validation of the Rorschach with problem children." *Rorschach Res. Exch.*, 1942, Vol. 6, 61–70.

12. Macfarlane, J. W., "Problems of validation inherent in projective methods." *Amer. J. Orthopsychiat.*, 1942, Vol. 12, 405–410.

13. Murray, H. A., *Explorations in Personality.* New York: Oxford University Press, 1938.

14. Radsliff, E., and Sanford, R. N., "Picture-pull on the Thematic Apperception Test" (unpublished manuscript), Institute of Child Welfare, Berkeley, Calif.

15. Ranzoni, J. H., McFate, M. Q., and Ives, V., "Rorschach 'card-pull' in a normal adolescent population." *J. Projective Techniques,* March, 1950, Vol. 14, 2, 107–133.

16. Tomkins, S. S., "The limits of material obtainable in the single case study by daily administration of the Thematic Apperception Test." *Psychol. Bull.*, 1942, Vol. 39, 490.

17. Vernon, P. E., "The Rorschach ink-blot test." *Brit. J. Med. Psychol.*, 1933, Vol. 13, 89–118.

18. Vernon, P. E., "The Rorschach ink-blot test. III." *Brit. J. Med. Psychol.*, 1933, Vol. 13, 271–295.

19. Zubin, J., "Personality research and psychopathology as related to clinical practice." *J. Abnorm. Soc. Psychol.*, 1949, Vol. 44, 14–21.

20. Zulliger, H., *Einführung in den Behn-Rorschach Test.* Bern: Huber, 1941.

CHAPTER 3

Principles of Design in "Projective" or Misperception Tests of Personality

RAYMOND B. CATTELL, PH.D., D.Sc.

DEFINITION IN RELATION TO OTHER PERSONALITY TESTS

The first tests explicitly and deliberately employing the design of projection were published in 1936 and 1937 independently by Cattell [6] in England and by Murray [34] and Sears [44] in America.[1] Since that time a considerable number of psychologists have been content to use or to "sell" projective devices with inadequate research justification. The fact that projective devices have become so widely used in such a short span of time should not blind us to the salutary truth that their scientific design remains in its crudest infancy. Indeed, the partial purpose of this chapter will be to call for a far greater research effort from those who use these devices. It is desirable, first, that scientific work be more nearly proportional to the amount of clinical activity, and second, that the research that does get done should be more systematically planned in the light of relevant psychological hypotheses. For if these tests continue to be

---

[1] Tests employing free association to words, colors, inkblots, and pictures, or free drawing and construction with toys, have been in use since the beginning of psychology, for example, the tests of Galton, Jung, Wertheimer, Stern, Jaensch, Roemer, Rorschach, the Lowenfeld mosaic test, and others. But these did not involve the psychoanalytic conception of projection, nor, with the exception of the Jung and Bleuler experiments, did they invoke any specific hypothesis as to the quantitative relation that should exist between test responses and dynamic mechanisms.

left to sporadic, desultory, amateur, and inconsequential research attention, they threaten to make this branch of clinical psychology egregious—"the little boy who never grew up" among psychological techniques.

A first helpful step consists in recognizing that the term *projective* is a serious misnomer. The pioneer scientific interest in this field [*6, 34, 44*], impressed by certain profound clinical principles that we shall shortly examine, was focused on employing the *ego defense mechanism* of projection, as defined by Sigmund Freud [*19*], and later by Anna Freud [*18*] and others, to investigate personality structure. However, it was soon recognized that other ego defense dynamisms like fantasy and reaction formation might be used in precisely the same way, to slip past the guard of self-awareness and reveal important facts about the ego and the dynamics of the total personality. The correct title for this class of clinical instrument— and one that can be used consistently in research, clinical practice, and design, as the present label cannot—should therefore be *ego defense dynamism tests,* which may be conveniently shortened to *defense test* or *dynamism test.* This at least would be less misleading to research design and clinical diagnosis. However, the clarification of terms is best taken up again after some discussion of the tests themselves.

Three Classes of Observation in the Assessment of Personality. A brief glance at the position of ego defense dynamism personality tests generally will help to clarify their role. The assessment of personality is made broadly through three classes of observation:

1. *Life-record* data, in which observations or measurements are in terms of behavior *in situ,* that is, in the everyday life of the subject. Life-record data may be gathered by various methods, such as time sampling, behavior rating by persons living with the subject, and examination of life records for frequencies of, say, mental disorder, accidents, and social activities.

2. *Self-rating* data, as in questionnaires, opinionnaires, and the like, in which the subject makes statements about himself that are accepted as evidence. Self-rating data yield "mental interiors," pictures of how the person sees himself introspectively, rather than evidence of behavior.

3. *Objective-test* data, which, unlike self-rating data, do not depend on the correctness of the subject's self-estimate or on his

willingness to communicate such knowledge honestly, but which infer personality from actual behavior in a defined, reproducible, artificial or laboratory situation. In the laboratory situation, research has to demonstrate the predictive relation that exists between performance in the test and performance in other, real-life situations. For example, the psychologist may discover that performance on an analogies "intelligence" test is highly correlated with performance in engineering, or that a high ratio of color to form in a sorting test is associated with proneness to cycloid rather than schizoid mental disorder. Usually both objective-test and self-rating data are externally validated against life-record data, though they may also need to be internally validated against some pure factor measure in the objective-test or self-rating data.

Until recent years most personality measurement, except in the special region of abilities, has had to depend in practice on life-record or self-rating data and methods. Both are unsatisfactory in applied psychology. Life-record data, as found in their principal form of behavior ratings, are unsatisfactory because the nice conditions for truly dependable ratings [8, 44] can rarely be met in the given, restricted work situation. Self-rating data fail because the validity and scoring pattern of questionnaires are apt to vary sharply with changes in the level of education and social background of the readers. Moreover those qualities of self-insight, honesty, and cooperativeness, which with university student research subjects can to some extent be depended upon, are rarely found in the situations in which the practicing psychologist wishes to apply the questionnaire, namely, in competition for occupational positions, in the disturbed populations of clinics, and perhaps among the inmates of prisons.[2]

The enthusiasm with which the practicing psychologist greeted defense or "projective" techniques arose from a correct appreciation of the fact that they offered an escape from this unsatisfactory state of affairs. They promised genuine objective-test data with no more trouble than the self-rating questionnaire—in fact, without the

---

[2] It is perhaps unnecessary to reiterate that not all questionnaires in form are *self-rating* devices in essence. But, until recently [12], no one had demonstrated that the unitary traits in questionnaires correspond to any unitary traits in behavior and it has been customary for psychometrists to describe the personality of an individual high on a given questionnaire scale in terms of what the individual says about himself in that scale.

individual test apparatus or elaborate control of miniature situations that had so frequently accompanied the use of objective tests.

A closer examination of the field of objective personality tests will reveal in what context of research opportunities the ego defense dynamism techniques stand.   Research on objective personality tests is at the moment in so lively a state of creative flux, and is so replete with half-formed, intuitive, and unexplicit assumptions, that no classification of such techniques can be offered whose categories will preserve much permanence. However, the relations of the ego defense type of test to the techniques of other types can be sufficiently indicated by considering five major categories of objective personality test.

1. *Miniature Test Situations.*   A method of attempting to devise tests to represent in miniature the situation in which the important behavior occurs in real life has had its empirical triumphs and failures, but its guiding principles have still not fully emerged.   A good deal of research and thought has been applied, notably through the work of Downey [*16*], Brogden [*4*], Ryans [*40*], Hartshorne and May [*21*], Cummings [*15*], O'Neil [*35*], Rethlingshafer [*37*], Crutcher [*14*], and others.

2. *Expressive or Stylistic Behavior.*   A second section of the objective-test field is that concerned with *expressive* or *stylistic* behavior, as in handwriting or speech, in which an attempt is made to measure and validate the subtle thing we call *style*.   This approach has been promoted by German psychologists, notably Klages [*25*], has received some scientific advance from the work of Allport and Vernon [*1*] and Pascal [*36*], and is treated in its recent scientific aspects by Precker and Wolff (Chapter 16), and Wolfson (Chapter 15), in this volume.

3. *Pure Process.*   A third objective-test approach using its own techniques and goals is that which seeks first to isolate by factor analysis the dimensions of personality with which it is concerned. It seeks the functionally unitary personality processes behind test performances and aims to set up valid measures of these "pure processes."   The *pure-process* approach was first exemplified in the study of abilities by Spearman's conception of intelligence as "relation perception" and by Thurstone's search for primary abilities. This approach has now some successes to show also in the field of personality tests.   It is evident in the work over the past 30 years on

measuring perseveration and disposition rigidity [9], and perhaps in the recent attempts to measure *surgency* (or extraversion) by *fluency of association* tests. The factor-analysis method is now being applied to new fields of personality response [8].

4. *Miscellaneous.* A large section of "miscellaneous" and tentative new approaches may be mentioned from which distinct branches of method may soon emerge.

5. *Misperception Tests.* As will be seen below, defense tests belong in the wider category of tests that measure differential perception of a situation (against a true perception, or norm). The recognition that such tests are an integral part of an *objective-test approach* to personality is essential if progress is to be made in this field. Defense tests require the same scientific standards, the same attention to techniques of design and validation, and the same integration with hypotheses in systematic psychology as has been aimed at in the four other objective-test approaches.

MISPERCEPTION, AUTISM, DYNAMISM AND DYNAMIC APPERCEPTION TESTS

Closer examination of what have loosely been called projective tests shows that the essential thing they have in common is observation of the deviation of a cognitive activity, commonly a perception, from some norm. In fact, they can be brought under the operational formula of *distortion* [3] *of a perception, or misperception,* though this stretches perhaps with a little difficulty to include fantasy. Whether or not the formula of misperception has *precisely* the same boundaries as those defining the miscellany of tests now called projective is not of great importance. It *does* fix meaningful boundaries, and the few so-called projective tests that fall outside it will be found, on closer inspection, to belong in their design to other branches of objective personality tests.

Although all of these tests essentially involve observations of *the departure of the meaning and associations of a percept from some standard of reality or of social or statistical normality,* they are not concerned with *all* kinds of cognitive aberration. A person asked to

---

[3] It may be necessary to point out that "distortion" is used here in its ordinary sense and without value judgment. A man hungrier than the average may see *more* food items in an unstructured picture and a surfeited man may see *fewer*. The "distortion" is from a convenient norm or standard adopted for purposes of measurement reference.

interpret a picture may depart from the mode through (a) differences of intelligence or other abilities, even sensory abilities; (b) differences of reproductive (memory) capacity due to different past *cognitive* experiences and powers of retention; and (c) differences of past *emotional* experience and present dynamic structure. Since we are not interested in the first of these, and since differences in intelligence can generally be eliminated from these perception tests by suitable design, we are left with (b) and (c), which together constitute what have always aptly been called in psychology *apperception* differences. It seems then that the correct designation for this class of personality tests is *misperception tests,* or *apperception tests,*[4] as Murray has conservatively called his own test in this realm. If we wish to distinguish (c) from (b), that is, tests in which the distortion is due to emotional causes from tests in which it is due to differences in memory, the c-group can be called *dynamic distortion,* or *dynaception* tests and the b-group, *cognitive misperception tests.* (*Dynaception* is suggested simply as a thoroughly convenient and nonmisleading abbreviation of *dynamic apperception.*) However, although we are more interested in the dynamic distortions than in the cognitive apperception aberrations, it will be evident from the discussion below, first, that our existing tests cannot readily separate them, and second, that even the purely cognitive misperception process throws light on some important aspects of personality.

Before focusing attention exclusively on misperception tests, we may summarize in the following diagram their relation to personality testing as a whole, and thus bring perspective to the definitions reached above.

Personality tests that depend on observation of the apperception process, as indicated above, are likely to throw light on both cognitive experience and on dynamic, emotional needs, even when the influences due to abilities are suitably canceled or extracted. Since the beginning of experimental psychology, occasional observations have been made relating distortions of perception to the combined action of these influences. For example, it is nearly

---

[4] It might be more closely operational to call them perceptual tests, but this term has already been pre-empted for an important class of culture-free intelligence tests [6]. In any case, the degree of abstraction from the operation implied in the well-tried concept of apperception, or the unmistakable term *misperception* or *misperceptive,* is not great.

half a century since Kretschmer discovered that schizoid, leptoso-
matic individuals placed more emphasis than pyknics upon form,
relative to color, in tachistoscopically exposed shapes [27]. The
Rorschach is now the most typical and widely employed test in this
area, but apparently, no attempts have been made to split the two
sources of differential interpretation or to present definite hypotheses
as to the way in which specific cognitive experience backgrounds,
unitary temperament traits, or dynamic needs operate to produce the
specific distortions measured.

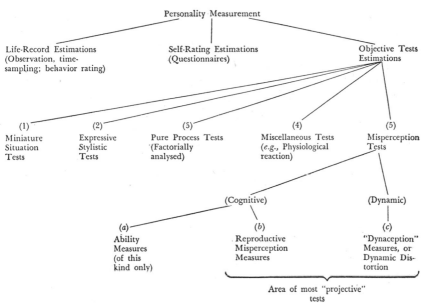

Fig. 1. Personality measurement.

It would be a contribution to personality study to examine for
evidence of the specific effects of cognitive apperceptive processes,
not only the Rorschach data but also the general experimental
psychological literature of the past 50 years. In the absence of such
a survey, however, we are bound to conclude that nothing is
systematically known as yet about the role of personality differences
of memory or "mental furniture" (or of differential temperamental
reactivities) in determining perception. Our effective study turns,
therefore, to *dynamic distortion* tests, that is, to that section—(c)—

of misperception tests that deal with distortions through dynamic traits and emotional states.

By analytical reasoning, one can see that distortions of this kind could arise from three major kinds of dynamic traits or states:

1. Transient emotional states or appetitive conditions.
2. Permanent dynamic traits integrated in the conscious personality.
3. Permanent dynamic traits that the individual is unable and unwilling to integrate and that are therefore in some degree unconscious.

Dynamic traits could, undoubtedly, be further subdivided but it is enough, at present, to expose them separately to experimental investigation.   It seems likely, moreover, that these *divisions according to personality source* would be less differential in their effects than would the *modes of operation* that cut across them, and must now be considered.   Granted a certain dynamic need (temporary or permanent), in a state of nonsatisfaction, in what way will it affect perception?   First, it may do so by what has been called *naive projection* [7], discussed below, causing the individual to imagine that others feel as he does.   It is probable that Sears' important demonstration [44] that projection is inversely related to self-insight refers largely to this projection.   *Naive misperception,* as we may call it in the wider context, actually belongs largely to the realm of cognitive apperception effects, in that it is the individual's cognitive perception of his dynamic nature which is insufficiently matured in cognitive perception of his differences from other people, that permits him to make this misperception.   Dynamic traits share this naiveté distortion along with cognitive and temperamental traits.

Second, the individual's dynamic condition may distort his perception by causing the perception to approach nearer to what would satisfy his desires.   This may be called the misperception of *autism,* in the accepted meaning of that word.

Third, it may cause him to misperceive the situation so as to make it fit in better, logically and psychologically, with his emotional state, not by giving greater satisfaction to the desire, but by making the consciously perceived desire more acceptable to his self-sentiment and his need for "logic."   As illustrated below, this *press compatibility misperception* takes the form of an angry man seeing a situation as more irritating and obstructive than it really is (to justify his anger), or a depressed man seeing people as colder and more unfriendly than they are.

Fourth, we encounter a set of modes of operation upon the percepts that are peculiar to unconscious, rejected dynamic forces. These may seem to have some relation to the third category above, in that the search for compatibility is again the source of distortion. But, as argued in the fuller illustration below, the need for compatibility in the third category is a comparatively superficial logical and security need and operates consciously, whereas here we deal with more drastic needs, operating with the illogic of the unconscious.

These modes of operation involve essentially the various ego defense dynamisms, but most discussion so far has centered upon the action of one mechanism only—projection—defined now in the sense of true psychoanalytic projection.

It will be seen from the above that any dynamic distortion or dynaception test measures a complex response, from which the clinician needs to tease out what is due to emotional state, what is due to conscious trait, and what is due to unconscious need. Before he can get this information about the strength of various personality structures, however, he needs some device either in the test construction or in the analysis of scores that will separate the three sources and, moreover, undo the overlapping reinforcement and cancelation of the various modes of operation in the distortion of the percept.

These needs of analysis—if our general hypotheses are correct—are summarized by Figure 2, in which the single Dynaception Test division of Figure 1, 5 (c), is expanded into consideration of all its parts. These parts cover four major modes of operation, each operating upon one of the main dynamic condition varieties.

Incidentally, the trend of both research and practice in this area for some time has been toward recognition of an analysis of the above kind. Sears [45, 46], for example, has already pointed out very cogently that the underlying theory of test construction, where any theory can be perceived, is essentially that *perception and judgment are changed by dynamic, motivational conditions,* which is in accord with our designation of dynaception tests as the principal subvariety of misperception tests. Let us now examine the four above-defined *modes of operation* of dynamic distortion, with extended illustration.

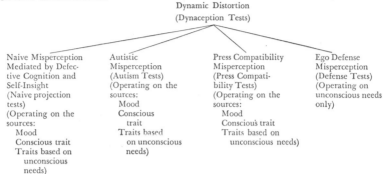

Fig. 2. Modes of operation of distortion in tests designed for dynamic influences only.

EXPANDED DESCRIPTION AND ILLUSTRATION OF THE CHIEF MODES OF OPERATION

The typical percept involved in misperception tests is an individual in the *field,* or *environment,* which may itself consist of inanimate objects or of one or more persons. This individual we shall call the *principal*; it is usually the object of the test-designer and artist to get the subject to identify himself with the principal, for otherwise there are too many degrees of freedom in the test for it to count as the same test for different people. Even when the subject identifies with, or is specifically asked to describe, what is happening in the mind of the principal, his misperception of the motivation of the principal is partly determined by any misperceptions he may make independently regarding the field. Thus, if the principal is depicted sitting before a heap of oysters, and the subject has never seen oysters, his interpretation of the principal's motivation is likely to be different from that of a more informed person. This complication cannot be followed up further here and it can obviously be lessened by making the presentation picture or story as vague as is compatible with realism, but it should be kept in mind in studying the following modes of operation.

Naive Misperception. Assuming that intelligence is little involved, the chief cognitive source of distortion of dynamic perceptions is that of limited information and experience. The opposite situation would produce complete self-insight, which supposes that the subject knows a lot about other personalities and is prepared to recognize and remember constantly that his own standards and conditions are not everyone's standards.

The most commonly observed of all forms of projection would seem to be this naive misperception, rather than the psychoanalytically observed phenomenon of projection, for the present phenomenon has been noted down the ages. The Bible, for example, has many references to the process and assigns a relation of likeness to perceiver and percept, as in, "A lying tongue hateth those that are afflicted by it." (*Proverbs,* 26:28), and "As in water face answereth to face, so the heart of man to man." (*Proverbs,* 27:19). Thomas à Kempis observed, "What a man is inwardly, that will he see outwardly," and it is hard to find a developed culture that does not have some aphorism to this effect. Primitive animism, in which physical objects share in the misperception, is the most generalized of all projections. Shakespeare frequently used projective techniques, as when Hamlet used a play to bring out the covert guilt of his uncle. One may note particularly the more recent instance in which leading scholars explained Freud's preoccupation with the sexual roots of neurosis as due to projection of his own personal interests!

In general, in the mode of operation now being studied, which has been distinguished earlier as NIPE projection—*Naive Inference from (Limited) Personal Experience*—the individual deduces (perhaps consciously and explicitly, but more often automatically) that the depicted behavior of the principal springs from the trait that would operate in himself if he were reacting in the same situation. His error is the naive one, arising from youth, thoughtlessness, or inexperience, of not recognizing the possible existence or the signs of other personalities and traits in action.

This can operate with respect not only to dynamic traits but also to temperament traits and to abilities—and even to physique. For example, a person who solves a quantitative problem by visual imagery will be astonished, as Galton found, when told that others obtain the answer without recourse to such imagery. Naive projection thus involves not only dynamic distortion effects but also, extensively, the errors studied in *cognitive apperception* tests of personality. We should expect naive inference from limited personal experience, that is, naive misperception, to decline with age, intelligence, and experience.

We shall see in later discussion of other misperception mechanisms that any successfully designed test has not only to meet the difficulty of confusing trait sources of misperception but also to adapt to and to discount the above differences in experience, age, and intelligence, in which the action of naive misperception runs through all other misperception operations.   One of the very first selective answer tests directed explicitly to measuring naive misperception (as naive projection) may be illustrated by the following example from a battery for children [6].

Item 1. When John was hurt he always wanted to
    (a) show how brave he could be
    (b) be left alone
    (c) run to his parents

Underlining the (c) alternative would on this hypothesis indicate a dependent and timid disposition.

A second design, which does not employ naive projection so obviously but may be classified as a more sophisticated utilization of the same essential process, is as follows. *It consists in making statements about the inner connections in a certain type of personality on the assumption that the individual who is most near to the type will most confidently endorse the existence of these connections, while the individual most remote will be more doubtful of their reality.*

Thus if we say, "A person who is nervously exhausted is likely (a) to have inordinate difficulty in making decisions even over trifles; and (b) to experience strange feelings of unreality," the statement that (a) and (b) go together will be more "self-evident" to a neurasthenic than to a person who is remote from any such experience.   A conversion hysteric, who would not confidently endorse the truth of the above, might be more likely to recognize the inner unity in the juxtaposition of traits offered in the following item: "A person who (a) tends to walk or talk in his sleep is likely (b) to crave and be inclined to seek constant attention and sympathy." The question may be raised whether identification, as a defense mechanism, is not also operative here.   Identification may help concentration on the given qualities, but apart from that, it does not seem necessary to the apperception concerned.

The item-construction that most readily utilizes the second naive misperception test principle above is that in which two "insights" (each on a pair of traits) are contrasted, one of which would naturally be perceived as a unity by an individual at one pole of the trait dimension while the other would be a self-evident pairing to the person at the opposite extreme of the trait. In choosing the parts (a) and (b) that go together in the pattern at one extreme, we have the guidance both of pathological syndromes and of the correlation studies [8] showing patterns of surface traits and source traits in normal individuals.

A test employing naive projection can almost certainly be used for temperamental and ability traits as well as for dynamic traits and tendencies. Thus, in the following example an insight into schizothyme behavior is contrasted with one into the cyclothyme make-up (trait-indicators taken from Source Trait *A* [8, 10]), to obtain a measure on this temperament dimension. It is probable, however, that intelligence and general life experience, both of which we desire to rule out of this type of apperception test, intrude unduly into such items.

Item 2. Which of the following statements seems to you more certainly true?
(a) That a man who is easy-going will be optimistic on most issues, or
(b) That a man who is emotionally cold and unresponsive will tend to be secretive?

Autistic Misperception. Little has yet been done to bring autism systematically within the range of practicable tests. The nearest approach has occurred, almost inadvertently, in a number of attitude tests in which the subjects' beliefs are taken as indications of their wishes.

Thus, the generalized hostility of the schizothyme *A*-factor might be measured by readiness to check as true or probable, statements that the world will shortly be devastated by warfare (compare the world-catastrophe theme frequently found in true schizophrenics). Or the strength of dominance might be measured by autistic willingness to believe the proposition that the majority of men are slaves by nature and naturally seek dominating individuals to take charge of them. Again, the high general emotionality and instability of the *C*-individual would show itself by willingness to believe incompatible things about one and the same object, according to the emotional mood of the moment. It might also show itself in a generalized Dionysian, as opposed to Apollonian, set of beliefs, that is, beliefs in the efficacy of emotion to achieve its ends by "magical" means.

Autistic misperception has been remarkably little employed in tests, considering the ease of design. Its effectiveness is perhaps already sufficiently indicated by the excellent correlations obtained between *C*-ratings and measures of fluctuation of beliefs [*8, 9*].

Press Compatibility Misperception. Austistic misperception, in which "normal" or abnormal distortions occur to bring the external world nearer to the heart's desire, must be distinguished from another form of misperception also likely to arise with strong emotional states or needs; we have defined it above as a need to make the external percept *compatible with* the need. Fortunately this form of need to make the external world appear more appropriate to the prevailing emotion has already received some experimental investigation and confirmation, though more varied and quantitative research is still needed. Murray [*33*] found that of five frightened girls, four read more maliciousness into faces shown to them than they did at other times. Johnson [*23*] found that in depressed moods, her subjects rated their associates significantly less friendly than when in more elated moods. Sanford [*41*] found that as subjects became more hungry, their associations had significantly more food references.

The mechanism here is not wish-fulfillment (for it is not satisfying to see danger when one is afraid or a lot of obstinate people when one is aggressive), but the need for consistency. However, this need *may* be based on certain wish-fulfillments, among other things. For example we may seek rationality in order to escape fear of the unknown or to satisfy our self-regard as rational persons. And what is "rational" will depend on past experience; for although a person in a self-assertive mood in our culture may show it by claiming that people are being obstinate, it is possible that an Eastern potentate, used to seeing people cringe at his rage, would reveal an aggressive mood by imagining people to be unduly cowering and submissive.

Test items can be constructed in a form adapted to this process of press projection by requiring endorsement of statements about the environment that are very closely related to and derivable from subjective states of the person tested, as follows.

Item 7. Do you feel that:
    (a) in your walk of life you meet a lot of important, awe-inspiring
        people?
    or
    (b) you never seem to meet anyone very important?

Item 8. Do you think that the prospects of peace and prosperity for the
    next generation (those just growing up) are
    (a) bad?
    (b) good?

Item 9. Do you find in your present group a sufficiency of people who
    are stimulating in conversation and capable of maintaining a witty
    exchange?
    (a) Yes.
    (b) No.

Item 7 is put together on the assumption that through projection of press required by emotional state the person of low dominance will be more impressed by the number of important people he meets, submissiveness engendering an exaggerated idea of "importance." *Items 8* and *9* are measures of the factor, Surgency-vs-Desurgency.[5] The desurgent (depressed, pessimistic, worrying) person will tend to take a less optimistic attitude toward affairs generally. (Response on *Item 8*—a). In *Item 9,* the desurgent person should give the (b) response, because he will interpret his failure to have lively conversation as due to a lack of sufficient stimulation in his environment.

Ego Defense Misperception. The distortions of ego defense mechanisms, as Figure 2 reminds us, differ from those of the first three modes of operation in applying only to dynamic traits that are in conflict with and assail the security of the ego, and that are therefore in the unconscious. Thus, in the defense of projection, the clinician observes that without any consciously perceivable intermediate process, a drive that it would be painful to the ego to own, is regarded as coming from the external world, usually from another person. This form of escape by externalizing the drive so that it can be avoided or attacked less painfully, belongs to the active peripheral forms of ego defense. It is one of the earliest defenses of the child and persists in dreams of normal people and in the pathological processes of phobias, hysterias, hypochondria, depres-

---

[5] The *F*-factor referred to later in this chapter.

sion, and especially, paranoia. It is an attempt to gain psychic reward, based on the pleasure principle and therefore foredoomed by its rashness to be partly maladjustive in the light of later reality requirements.

In true projection we may assume that there is always some element of the unpleasant, the unwanted, and the morally undesirable about the projected trait. There is too much of it, as the reiterated *too* in the test items below indicates. This presents us with an opportunity to make some differentiation of the test form from that of naive projection, but the forms remain sufficiently similar to require in many cases some supplementary evidence to permit an interpretation as to which variety of projection is responsible for the answer. The test from which the following items are taken masquerades as a test of social judgment on undesirable trends in modern society. The examples are taken from a test [29] intended to involve true projection, but further defense mechanisms will be illustrated later.

Item 3. Most people tend to get unpopular socially through being
    (a) oversociable and too familiar.
    (b) too "stuck up" and aloof.

Item 4. One of the worst faults in friends is being
    (a) too tyrannical and bossy.
    (b) too quiet, dependent, and dull.

Item 5. When people get into difficulties over their work, it is most often due to being
    (a) too lazy, easy-going, and sociable.
    (b) too much given to shy daydreaming.

Item 6. One of the commonest faults in young men and women is being
    (a) too conceited.
    (b) too shrinking and sensitive.

Items 3 and *5* are intended measures of the cyclothyme-schizothyme or A-factor dimension already mentioned, the two (a) alternatives being indicators of projected cyclothyme "faults."

Items 4 and *6* are intended measures of the dominance-submission source trait, the (a) alternatives being indicators of projected high dominance or self-assertion. A priori, one might expect intelligence to intrude into this apperception, as into naive-projection items.

FURTHER DYNAMISM TEST DESIGNS: FANTASY, IDENTIFICATION, REACTION FORMATION, RATIONALIZATION, AND REPRESSION

Fantasy. Some of the most complex theoretical and practical issues arise in connection with dynaception tests employing fantasy. First, fantasy is not quite in line with the other defense dynamisms, for it may operate *before* repression as conscious fantasy, whereas all the others presuppose a condition of repression. We do not know enough about these differences and the differences between conscious and unconscious fantasy (except in regard to degree of symbolism) to set up tests in the best possible form. At least, however, it is clear that the wish-fulfillment in fantasy is going to operate to reveal both conscious and unconscious dynamic traits. Further, the content may be determined by more than simple wish-fulfillment under the pleasure principle—in fact, by the repetition compulsion attempting to solve, in play, a traumatic problem, whence the pattern of drives as well as the drive strengths themselves will become evident. Under fantasy, of course, we shall include all test situations that employ play, dramatization, and playful creativity.

The test employing fantasy differs from that designed for projection (in any one of the above three senses) in that it is not necessary to present a fully defined (even though "empty") situation. In projection, the stimulus situation to which "the person in the story," the principal, is subjected, is fixed as completely as possible in order to facilitate interpretation of the response; in some forms of test, the relative effectiveness of which is still speculative, even the response is given, the subject being asked to decide only the motive behind the response.

One of the most valuable of ego defense tests, Murray's Thematic Apperception Test [20, 34, 49], is, by its design and administration, largely a fantasy test, not a projection test. The pictures may invoke an initial projection, but thereafter the individual develops his fantasy in a free manner just as a patient does in a chain of free associations that may have begun with the recounting of a dream but soon pass far beyond it. The same is true of Shakow and Rosenzweig's use of the tautophone [47].

There are, it is true, moments in purely unrestricted fantasy where motives are imputed to other individuals, but this cannot be called a misperception since no data are given the subject whereby the true motive to be assigned to the principal could be decided.   Though this is not projection, it is the assignment of a motive and, as such, has some relation to the motives of the subject.   The relation is the primary one of wish-fulfillment operative in all fantasy—if the individual needs to satisfy self-display, the drive he will invent in the creatures of his fantasy will be admiration.   However, where he, himself, or someone with whom he identifies himself, is depicted in the fantasy, the dynamic traits described will be those that he himself falls short of satisfying.

Fantasy can be studied in an extraordinarily wide array of media —the dream, free association, word association, sentence completion, drawings, plays, and so on [*2, 20, 28, 43, 51, 52*], some of which are discussed by Montague, Moreno, Napoli, Solomon, and Wolt- mann in other chapters of this book.   The problem has to be faced here, however, of greatly improving the objectivity of the experi- menter's evaluation of the meaning of the subject's fantasies.   In- deed, it is necessary to broach here, where it is most crucial, a question that has hitherto been avoided—the relative desirability of *selective* and *inventive* answer forms.

The question of selective or inventive answer forms is a thorny issue, particularly in projection, fantasy, and free play devices for diagnosis; it is provocative of very diverse views throughout all misperception and dynaception test practice.   Admittedly, some diagnostic devices such as diagnosis from free drawings, fantasies, and free associations must at present, in practice, be left at the level of arts rather than sciences.   But it is the aim of scientific psychology to reduce the chance of error in the diagnostic art, just as it is the aim of scientific medicine to develop laboratory techniques that leave less scope for wild clinical guesswork.

Consequently, the progressive psychometrist will always seek to shift from inventive to selective answer forms.   In all other person- ality tests, the improvement of reliabilities and validities has been accompanied by successful progression from inventive to selective responses.   Even in fluency tests [*6*], where the highest degree of freedom is necessary, it has been possible to use an objective score. Some clinicians have clung to the inventive answer in misperception and dynaception tests as if it were the essence of the test, where in fact it is only a secondary, unavoidable by-product of the primary test design and a measure of the clinician's lack of ingenuity.   Worse still, it remains a measure of the clinician's naiveté; for how many clinicians have attempted to investigate the reliability of interpretations by different diagnosticians of the same fantasy or dream or free association?   What little evidence exists on this matter is dismally discouraging.   In misperception tests, it does not seem to have been squarely faced that the free interpretation of the subject's inventive answers by a single clinical psychologist is a compounding of two sets of projections (though the same diagnosticians will freely admit that an unanalysed psychiatrist is incapable of judging the analytical problems of a patient).

We are scarcely so scientifically advanced today in interpreting one person's apperceptions that we can lightly undertake to disentangle the superimposition of *two* persons' projections or fantasies.   The crucial need in misperception tests, therefore, is the development of sufficiently ingenious selective forms, which may lose a little of the flexibility of "free" forms but which can raise reliability to a level where it means something.   Many of the items illustrating this chapter, incidentally, may be too "all-or-nothing" in character to get the best results by selective means; but this crudity is likely to give way to possibilities of more subtle grading as selective tests pass beyond the experimental stage.

The demand for the freedom of inventive answers is most hard to meet in selective designs where the projection or fantasying of *emotional situations* rather than single traits or drives in the unconscious is concerned.   In free association, the individual indicates not only the repressed drives but also their setting in the situation of his inner mental conflicts and external life situation.   Rotter's use [*39*] of word associations and incomplete sentences, as described in a later chapter, offers an intermediate degree of control that may give a useful practical compromise at present, but eventually it would seem desirable, as indicated in the section below on questions and hypotheses, to include both situations and traits in selective answer devices.

One form of the selective answer fantasy test that has been particularly promising in preliminary experiments on reliability and validity is that in which the subject chooses the books or plays that he would most enjoy seeing.   These must not be real books or plays, which would be unevenly familiar to different subjects, but must be invented items described by truly indicative titles and a brief resume of the themes concerned. These themes can be designed either with respect to classifications of needs or, if the diagnosis is concerned more with personality structure, conflict, and problems, with respect to classifications in terms of common problem situations. The first two items below aim to measure a dynamic trait, the strength of the drive of self-assertion or aggression, as shown in dominance, while the second pair illustrate the use of this mechanism to measure a temperament dimension, namely, surgency-vs-desurgency.

Check the book title from each pair presented that you would prefer to read. They are not actually published books but the title and subtitle indicate the general nature of the story.

Item 10. (a) *Saint Francis.* An account of a life of service in humble poverty.
or
(b) *Charles the Bold.* The story of a genius of battle, who saved his own country in war and dominated a continent by his diplomacy.

Item 11. (a) *The Invincible Frigate.* The life of Captain Black, a daring pirate who swept all before him with his invincible ship.
or
(b) *The Fugitive.* The story of a man who took all the blame upon himself for the crime of his father and sacrificed his own ambitions.

Item 12. (a) *The Gay Lady.* The story of an actress whose life was full of color.
or
(b) *The Pit.* The story of a man, outwardly respectable, who lived in mental torment over a crime that he imagined he had committed.

Item 13. (a) *Souls in Torment.* An account of the life of a group of drug addicts.
or
(b) *Beau Daniels.* The story of a famous wit who added greatly to the entertainment of his society.

In scoring these, the dominance direction in *Items 10* and *11* is obvious, while in *Items 12* and *13*, surgency is connected respectively with responses (a) and (b).

Introjection and Identification. These two defense mechanisms can be considered together because the type of test construction to which they lead is very similar. As is well known, introjection leads to adoption by the subject of some qualities of the object, or, at least, to the belief that the subject has those qualities. Since assertion that he has the same qualities as another person may take the form of asserting that the other person has the same qualities as himself, the process can be considered with identification. In identification, the subject experiences an emotional unity with the object that causes him to share, more than sympathetically, the responses of the object to the environment and therefore some of the traits of the second personality. Thus, a woman in love (and therefore identifying) with a musician may believe that she shares all his sensibilities—as well as that he experiences her own tastes in other directions. In any case, the individual will love the other's qualities as his own.

Although we cannot, in a test, tap the line of communication to a specific beloved object, discovering what person is being introjected, we can assume that the introjected qualities are themselves admired and from following what is admired, decide what has been introjected. Parenthetically, the weakness remains that though what has become part of the personality must be what has been admired, not all that is in personality has been admired and not all that has been admired has been incorporated in the personality.

On the main hypothesis, however, the tests of the following type may be set up, which, on the surface, look like tests of values, or, at least, of compatibilities.

Check the quality (a) or (b) in each of the following that you consider more desirable, that is, more admirable, socially valuable, and *worthwhile,* in any individual.

Item 14. (a) to be relatively forceful, headstrong, and assertive.
       (b) to be relatively self-critical, modest, and submissive.
Item 15. (a) to have a high opinion of oneself, not easily squashed.
       (b) to be meek, obedient to authority and to conventions.

Here it is assumed that the individual who is self-assertive and dominant will value the (a) qualities, while the individual at the opposite end of the scale in the factor of Dominance-Submissiveness (Factor E) will underline the (b) choices.

Reaction Formation. This defense leads to character traits that are the exact reverse of those that would naturally have developed from the unfettered expression of the individual's primary nature. The "purpose" of such traits in the total personality is to make doubly sure that the ego is not disturbed or the superego outraged by manifestations of the dynamic tendency now largely thrust into the unconscious.   The individual conjures up for himself a picture of something as different as possible from the temptation and develops the corresponding response with obsessional concentration and rigidity.   Thus come traits of marked asceticism, pedantry, or overscrupulousness.   Frequently, as in prudery, the overcompensation at the same time gives an oblique, unrecognized satisfaction to the drive at fault.

Whatever the detailed structure of the reaction formation, whether it be overcompensation for defects or excessive inhibition of powerful drives, we may expect the consciously approved formation to be strongly supported by "oughts" and appeals to social norms.   This implies also a somewhat excessive indignation against other people who fail in this particular respect.   Consequently, the type of test called for is one in which moral judgments are involved in relation to the self and others and in which the subject is asked to indicate the relative importance and desirability of certain inhibitions.   In the experiments to be described below, items of the following kind were used:

Item 16. The best type of individual is one who keeps his emotionality always firmly in hand and gives as little outward display of emotion as possible.   Agree   Disagree

Item 17. A person who is naturally very stable, stolid, and phlegmatic can and should aim to be more vivacious and to share the emotional upsets of others.   Agree   Disagree

These were designed as measures of General Emotionality-vs-Emotional Stability (Factor C), an "agree" response on *Item 16* and a "disagree" response on *Item 17* being scored as indications of naturally high emotionality, requiring a reaction formation toward calmness and control.

Rationalization.   The suppression of certain logical connections and the acceptance of false ones are involved in rationalization. The wider manifestations of this lack of reality in thinking, in assisting the other defense mechanisms, are perhaps not sufficiently appreciated.   It is possible to construe many other defenses as operating formally through rationalization.   Lundholm [32], in particular, has attempted to show that repression is a form of rationalization.   Taking the process at its face value, however, it is relatively easy to employ it in test forms. It suffices to take a trait—in a degree departing from an approved norm—and to see whether the individual will endorse rationalizations supporting such behavior. Naturally this has certain presuppositions, say, that the individual knows that he departs from the approved norm; that he is not given to rationalizing *all* eccentricities, his own and those of others included; that he does not approve his own behavior and that in consequence he *does* find it necessary to rationalize it.

The simplest form of test item may be illustrated by the following:

Item 18. Sarcasm and ridicule are sometimes the best methods to employ in making a lazy person "toe the line."

$\qquad\qquad$ Agree $\qquad\qquad\qquad$ Disagree

Item 19. When people tell one not to worry, one has to remember that unless *someone* worries many of the most important and necessary things in society would never get done.

$\qquad\qquad$ Agree $\qquad\qquad\qquad$ Disagree

Item 18 is from a scale [29] for measuring the dominance factor (correlation shows sarcasm to be heavily loaded with the dominance factor [8]), the "agree" answer being scored positively. *Item 19,* rationalizing a tendency to excessive worry and depression, scores negatively on the F-factor—in the direction of desurgency.

Repression. Like fantasy, though in a different sense, repression is unique among defense mechanisms. It is also, in the opinion of some writers [32] specifically related to rationalization, as the extreme end-result of that process. Further, and partly because of this characteristic, it does not lend itself to direct observation in a test situation. It is not safe to presume that preferential forgetting in a short-term memory test will involve the same mechanism as in a longer-term personality process of irreversible repression. At least on a first exploration, it has seemed more promising to investigate *existing* repressions by the employment of wit and humor tests. This test design is based on the assumption that the individual will enjoy most those jokes that depend on the dynamic tendency that is most repressed by his own ego [11].

For example, the following joke, with its sexual levity and breakdown of normal guilt sense, might be expected, on the above hypothesis, to be rated above the average for most people by those who have either excessive guilt about irresponsible and perverse sexuality generally, or especially strong sex interests.

Item 20. "Do you have a fairy godmother?"
     "No, but I have an uncle I'm not so sure about."

Dominance or aggression, unusually strong constitutionally or excessively repressed, might be expected to lead to unduly high satisfaction with the following:

Item 21. He: "I'll go to the end of the Earth for you."
     She: "Fine, but will you stay there?"

EXPERIMENTS ON RELIABILITY AND VALIDITY OF DYNAMISM TESTS

The investigation of that section of misperception tests that may be called defense tests, and that includes most approaches loosely termed "projective," must be along experimental lines dictated by several alternative and supplementary hypotheses.   Initially, how-ever, it would seem desirable to determine the extent to which their scores correlate with *observable behavior* as estimated in overt personality traits.   Such an investigation does not pledge us to the hypothesis, evidently implicit in much of the practical use to which projective tests are now put, that these tests will significantly predict personality traits.   But it enables us to investigate whether this holds in certain simple cases and it permits us to know where we stand when we come to design the experiments necessary to check on the more complex hypotheses.

Investigation of the relation of defense test scores to overt person-ality traits, if it is to be of maximum value in clearing the founda-tions for more specific research, must begin with a broad sweep, in which the relations are investigated for a sample of all kinds of traits—ability, temperamental, and dynamic.   It should also, as in a Latin Square design, investigate each kind of trait for each kind of defense mechanism, since a mechanism would conceivably work with one kind of trait when it would not work with another.

The research now to be described is a preliminary inquiry to illustrate possible designs and to throw light on the question of whether there is any value at all in defense tests employing misper-ception.   Seven different defense or dynaception operations were tried out with respect to four different primary personality traits.

Before validating any test against personality ratings and clinical judgments, it is necessary at least to show that its component items are pulling in the same direction, to make some form of item analysis. In this case, a collection of 30 items was put together for each primary trait with respect to each of the defense operations. This work, by Lowry [29], set out to put the items together by straightforward but skillful application of a clear general principle and to test the truth and consistency of the principle by seeing whether items thus chosen would in practice have good mutual consistency coefficients. To carry out this test, the items devised a priori on the principles stated above were tried out on a normal range population, and tetrachoric correlations were calculated between each item and the pool of all items in the measure.

Obviously, items can fail for two reasons: either because the misperception operation conceived to represent the defense mechanism has been applied by an incorrect principle, or because, despite correct conception of the mechanism, the conception of the particular source trait being tested has failed.

In view of these two signal possibilities of failure, it is striking that Lowry's results show the great majority of the items to have every indication of effectively measuring the same trait and by the same mechanism. With a population of the size tested (124), an r of .21 is the minimum to exceed thrice its standard error. With the three defense operations—true projection, identification, and fantasy—and the four factors—Source Traits A, C, E, and F—there were 12 distinct tests each with 30 items. Three hundred and five of the resulting 360 correlations were significant by the above test. The mean r of all individual accepted items with the pool was 0.52.

This proof of the capacity of the principles of defense to yield empirically consistent items when applied to established personality source traits, still leaves unanswered the question of whether these consistent responses significantly relate themselves to overt or covert personality as assessed by other means.

The experimental test of this second proposition, unfortunately, could not be made at the date of writing on the full-length tests above, which at that time were not "groomed." Instead, two items were taken at random from each of the above lists before reliability had been measured and they turned out by accident to be the poorer items in an undue number of cases! The 70 items so obtained—two for each of five source traits (A, C, E, F, and I), with respect to seven types of defense mechanism (see Table 1)—were administered to 358 undergraduate students (118 men, 240 women).

These subjects were then rated on behavior by 15 sorority or fraternity members living in the same house, under rating conditions described elsewhere, on 35 defined personality traits [6]. In assessing each of the source traits, four or five of these contributary traits-values were added together to get the value for the general source trait, as follows:

(1) *Factor A.   Cyclothymia-vs-Schizothymia.*   Presumably a temperament dimension.   This was estimated from a pool of four trait ratings.

Readiness to cooperate-*vs*-Obstructiveness
Goodnatured, easy-going-*vs*-Spiteful, grasping, critical
Mild, self-effacing-*vs*-Self-willed, egotistical
Attentive to people-*vs*-Cool, aloof

(2) *Factor C.   Emotionally Stable Character-vs-General Emotionality.*   Presumably a factor defining soundness of total dynamic integration.   Estimated from a pool of three trait ratings.

Absence of neurotic fatigue-*vs*-Neurotic fatigue
Calm, phlegmatic-*vs*-Emotional
Emotionally stable-*vs*-Changeable

(3) *Factor E.   Dominance-vs-Submissiveness.*   Presumably a dynamic factor of disposition: the strength of the assertive-aggressive drive.   Estimated from a pool of three trait ratings.

Assertive, self-assured-*vs*-Submissive
Independent-minded-*vs*-Dependent, immature
Depressed, solemn-*vs*-Cheerful

(4) *Factor F.   Surgency-vs-Desurgency.*   Almost certainly a temperament factor.   Estimated from ratings of four traits.

Energetic, alert-*vs*-Languid, slow
Cheerful-*vs*-Depressed, solemn
Adventurous, bold-*vs*-Cautious, retiring, timid
Talkative-*vs*-Silent, introspective

(5) *Factor I.   Sensitive Emotionality-vs-Mature Poise.*   A factor having something to do with neuroticism, but of unknown cause despite its repeated confirmation as a pattern.   Estimated from five trait ratings.

Demanding, impatient-*vs*-Emotionally mature
Dependent, immature-*vs*-Independent-minded
Esthetically fastidious-*vs*-Lacking artistic feeling

Frivolous-*vs*-Responsible

Sensitively imaginative-*vs*-Practical, logical

The reliabilities of the ratings of the single traits in each of the above factors range from 0.4 to 0.9, so we need have little doubt that the factor estimates derived from a pool of these have a very satisfactory reliability.   (These factors, incidentally, were also estimated by questionnaires and objective tests.)   But before correlating them with the defense tests, it is necessary to know the reliability of the latter.

Here we encounter a difficulty that must be kept in mind in all later interpretations of the promise of these tests.   There are no fewer than eight distinct defense mechanisms to be tried out above, each with respect to five different source traits, making 40 distinct validities to be calculated.   In this exploratory study, we deemed it sufficient to test each validity with only two items, except in repression (humor), where five were employed.   Even so, this required testing, correlation and analyses with respect to over 80 items.[6]

But the reduction to two items per test meant that if we missed the mark with one of these items the split-half reliability would be unsatisfactory and the further possibility of testing validity would vanish.   Now, as Table 1 shows, the split-half reliabilities—the tetrachoric correlations of the first with the second test item—are in many cases very poor.[7]   But it must be remembered that the agreement of any two single items in a test can be very low—as low as 0.1— while the split half for 50 items against another 50 items is very high indeed (so much do chance, irrelevant influences enter into the stark single item).   And in this case we know from the preliminary internal consistency analysis presented above that in every 100 items designed deliberately according to the present principles, no fewer than 85 of them have individually significant correlations with the pool, while the mean correlation therewith is around $+ 0.52$.

---

[6] The 80 items were presented to the subjects in thoroughly mixed order and in four distinct tests, masked by such titles as Social Judgments Test, Test of Reading Preferences, Judgment of Motives, etc.   There seemed to be, among these non-psychological students, no awareness of the tests being directed to ego defense mechanisms.

[7] The eight double-starred *r*'s are significant at the one per cent level; 12 are significant *at least* at a five per cent level; 24 out of 35 are positive.   As will be seen from Table 3, the incompleteness of certain ratings and, especially, the incompleteness of certain tests, reduced the initial population of 358 by one-third to two-thirds in various tests.

TABLE 1 [8]

RELIABILITY OF ITEMS REPRESENTING VARIOUS DEFENSE OPERATIONS
FOR VARIOUS TRAITS

1. True Projection				2. Projection due to Press Compatibility Misperception			3. Projection Through Naive Inference from Limited Personal Experience		
(3)	(5)	Factor A	.18**		Factor A	.04	(2)	Factor A	.02
		Factor C	.09		Factor C	.15*		Factor C	.05
(4)	(6)	Factor E	.18**	(7)	Factor E	.10		Factor E	.05
		Factor F	.09	(8) (9)	Factor F	—.16*		Factor F	.01
		Factor I	.10		Factor I	.12		Factor I	.05

4. Identification			5. Reaction Formation			6. Rationalization		
	Factor A	—.10		Factor A	—.01		Factor A	.15*
	Factor C	—.05	(16)(17)	Factor C	.22**		Factor C	—.05
(14)(15)	Factor E	.30**		Factor E	—.10	(18)	Factor E	.02
	Factor F	—.04		Factor F	—.07	(19)	Factor F	—.05
	Factor I	—.02		Factor I	.10		Factor I	.15*

7. Fantasy		
	Factor A	.40**
	Factor C	—.15
(10)(11)	Factor E	.20**
(12)(13)	Factor F	.48**
	Factor I	.45**

The numbers in parentheses refer to the test item numbers in this chapter. Where there are no numbers, the items have not been used in illustration in the text.

* Significant at the five per cent level.
** Significant at the one per cent level.

Even so, it has seemed desirable to proceed further only with respect to those items of Table 1 that, as shown by an asterisk, have reliability coefficients that are of adequate validity in this exacting situation. These eight tests of two-item length are picked out in Table 2, which, for the sake of comparison with other types of test, shows what reliability would be gained by extending the test to 20 items; i.e., a split half r between two 10-item divisions.

The calculation of the validities of these eight sufficiently reliable tests was considered best undertaken by Chi square, for at this exploratory stage our object is to find whether any validity exists rather than to estimate its exact level by a correlation coefficient.

---

[8] The figures in Tables 1, 2, and 3 are from Cattell and Pitluk [*12*].

TABLE 2

COEFFICIENTS OF RELIABILITY FOR ONE-ITEM TESTS RAISED BY SPEARMAN-BROWN
FORMULA TO TEST-LENGTH OF TEN ITEMS

Test and Factor (from Table 1)	r for One-item Test	Spearman-Brown r for Ten-item Test
Fantasy A	.40	.87
Fantasy E	.20	.71
Fantasy F	.48	.92
Fantasy I	.45	.89
Identification E	.30	.81
Reaction Formation C	.22	.74
True Projection A	.18	.69
True Projection E	.18	.69

The distribution of the three possible scores, 0, 1, and 2, on each of the tests is shown for those who were above and those who were below average on the corresponding factor estimates. As Table 3 indicates, the Chi square criterion shows that only the identification test of dominance had clearly significant validity, though some promise exists for the fantasy test of surgency and the "true projection" test of cyclothymia-vs-schizothymia.

Before discussing and summarizing in regard to these defense test findings, let us consider findings in regard to one more defense test—that employing repression, diagnosed by humor response, as described above.

Among the humor tests of repression, the failures were not so high, perhaps because the tests were longer. In this case, as described elsewhere [11, 30], reliability was assured by grouping together some four to eight jokes that correlated positively in all mutual relationships, forming a cluster; the validity of the cluster was then tested by correlating the individual's scores on the cluster with estimates of personality factors made by the Guilford-Martin questionnaires. These results cannot be fitted into quite the same categories as those of the other defense tests, though the *A, C, E,* and *F* personality factors in the behavior ratings are known through recent work [12] to be matchable with the Guilford questionnaire factors.

However, the outcome of this analysis of humor responses, reported separately in three articles [11, 13, 30] by Luborsky, Saunders, and the present writer, is that significant correlations arise between the dynamic tendency, as it has been perceived and described previously by psychologists examining the joke cluster, and the *overt* personality traits of the subject. Thus, high appreciation of the cluster containing the Joke 21, above, labeled on inspection, "irony and dominance," correlates $+0.43$ with Guilford's I-factor, described as "self-confidence and lack of inferiority feelings." Similarly, high score on the cluster containing Joke 20, above, labeled "debonair sexuality," correlates $+0.49$ with Guilford's R-factor, described as "happy-go-lucky liveliness and impulsiveness," and now known to be the same as the Surgency (F) factor in behavior ratings, in which "debonair" has always been a descriptive term [*8*].

TABLE 3

VALIDITIES AGAINST RATINGS FOR TEST ITEMS OF ADEQUATE RELIABILITY

True Projection Test

Items (3)(5)	Score	2	1	0	Total
Factor A rating	(+)	14	53	40	107
	(−)	12	25	17	54
Total		26	78	57	161

$$\chi^2 = 2.27$$

True Projection Test

Items (4)(6)	Score	2	1	0	Total
Factor E rating	(+)	34	31	9	74
	(−)	37	41	8	86
Total		71	72	17	160

$$\chi^2 = .52$$

Identification Test

Items (14)(15)	Score	2	1	0	Total
Factor E	(+)	12	72	49	133
	(−)	18	58	82	158
Total		30	130	131	291

$$\chi^2 = 9.10*$$

Reaction Formation Test

Items (16)(17)	Score	2	1	0	Total
Factor C	(+)	34	43	26	103
	(−)	22	25	12	59
Total		56	68	38	162

$$\chi^2 = .76$$

Fantasy Test

(Items not Set out in Text.)	Score	2	1	0	Total
Factor A rating	(+)	19	27	16	62
	(−)	10	10	5	25
Total		29	37	21	87

$$\chi^2 = .96$$

Fantasy Test

Items (10)(11)	Score	2	1	0	Total
Factor E rating	(+)	10	14	9	33
	(−)	9	24	17	50
Total		19	38	26	83

$$\chi^2 = 1.13$$

Fantasy Test

Items (12)(13)	Score	2	1	0	Total
Factor F rating	(+)	14	18	11	43
	(−)	10	13	22	45
Total		24	31	33	88

$$\chi^2 = 4.19$$

Fantasy Test

(Items not Set out in Text.)	Score	2	1	0	Total
Factor I rating	(+)	9	11	12	32
	(−)	16	19	20	55
Total		25	30	32	87

$$\chi^2 = .05$$

* Asterisk after χ^2 denotes a significant result.

Wherever defense tests have been happily enough chosen to give good reliability, therefore, there has been a tendency to validity, and the validity has taken the form of a *positive* relation between the vector measured in the defense reaction and the overt, over-all personality trait. This seems to be true both for dynamic traits like disposition to dominance and emotional integration, and for temperamental (perhaps constitutional) patterns like cyclothymia-vs-schizothymia and surgency-vs-desurgency.

QUESTIONS AND HYPOTHESES ON THE OPERATION OF DEFENSE TESTS

The present demonstration that only *low* correlations exist despite the existence of a generally significant, real relationship, is in accord with the failure to obtain useful validities in the first exploratory study [6] as well as with whatever scattered research can be found in between. Before examining hypotheses, let us try to decide what the value of the test-trait correlation really is, bearing in mind the influence of test mechanics and statistical conditions.

The lowness of the correlations cannot be ascribed to accidentally starting with traits that happen to be unsuitable for assessment by this instrument, since greatly *varied* traits were taken and the valid instances are spread pretty evenly among them. To the extent that the devices work with dynamic traits, they work also with temperament dimensions. The low validities cannot be ascribed to poorness of the traits estimates, since these could be well-defined from previous study and were known to have high reliabilities. However, many of the defective validities could be due to failure to incorporate the trait process correctly in the items, for this would show itself also in poor reliability of items, and it is here in fact that about 90 per cent of the loss is found.

Where the tests were really "long" (four to eight items) and had demonstrably good reliability—namely, in the humor clusters —there was never complete failure of validity. That failure occurred in several of the tests, which, though only *two* items long, had very fair reliability, could be due to the fact that this degree of reliability arose from those two particular items having something in common other than the process that they were *planned* to have in common. One cannot be certain just what the reliability of two items means, or what degree of reliability should be expected to make possible good validities. It would be interesting to know how the reliabilities of single pairs of items in any normally good questionnaire or intelligence test distribute themselves relative to those found here. Obviously, however, the next research step in defense tests is to investigate whether these apparently uneven levels of validity are in fact due to different levels of reliability. This can now be done by returning to the finished Lowry tests described above, using for each trait and mechanism a test some 30 to 50 items long, as with practicable tests in other fields that give a known and satisfactory reliability with a sufficiency of items. For the results of the present exploration sufficiently indicate that the lengthened tests obtained at such a cost of item analysis have every prospect of substantial validity.

Meanwhile, insofar as a rough estimate for our present theoretical discussion can be made from the data on the above seven defense mechanism experiments and the experiments on humor, it would seem that the validities run at about one-half of the reliabilities, or a little more. This indicates (through the correction for attenuation) that with good tests the correlation between defense mechanism measure and overt personality trait would be, say, 0.6. If so, what is the meaning of this figure for test theory and interpretation? Why, in fact, does the correlation, while being positive and appreciable, fall significantly short of unity?

Theory of Proportionality of Overt to Covert Deviation. If the defense test is actually measuring the strength of the repressed, unconscious drives, we should expect a zero correlation between the test and overt, rated behavior—unless there are psychological or statistical reasons for the latter's being related to repressed drive.

Let us see what quantitative relations might exist between covert, that is, unconscious, repressed drive-strengths on the one hand, and overt strength, as obtained by behavior rating, on the other. In Figure 3 are represented a general case and three specific individuals. The drive in question is measured from a zero strength (Z) at the left to a position O that marks its overt strength and a position C that marks the extent of its covert strength, that is, the strength that it naturally possesses but that the individual is not willing to express. The line N represents an approved social norm, and it is assumed that in this case the social norm approves an almost average amount, as, say, with dominance-submission, so that either extreme excites disapproval.

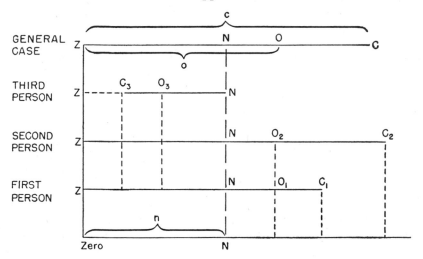

Fig. 3. Proportionality of overt to covert personality deviation.

Now the obtained correlation is between the test score and the length ZO—which we will call o. Actually, the only correlation we should expect is between the test and ZC minus ZO, that is, $(c - o)$, on the assumption that the difference between the overt and the covert represents the amount of repression going on. For if we accept the standard psychoanalytic conception of defense mechanisms, the score on a defense test—the amount of the dynamic tendency demanding expression—will be a function of the distance $(c - o)$ or the difference between the way the person behaves and the way he wants to behave.

The above positive and significant correlation (estimated at $+0.6$) between o and, by hypothesis, $(c - o)$, that is, between overt personality and the difference of overt and covert personality, is therefore very surprising. For if c is unrelated to o in any systematic fashion, the correlation should be negative, though it should always remain well below unity in proportion to the variance contributed by c.

A positive correlation is possible only on the assumption that $(c - o)$ tends to be proportional to o. One can see no psychological reason for this, but one *can* see from our understanding of adjustment that $(c - o)$ is likely to be proportional to $(o - n)$. The reason for this is that the social pressure upon the individual to conform to the norm is not likely to carry the individual the whole way, and, if we assume a fairly constant disposition rigidity (a kind of psychological coefficient of elasticity), the fraction of the distance that the individual is carried will be about the same for all people.   A naturally highly aggressive person will never approach our culture pattern of "blessed are the meek" quite so well as one fortunately less endowed with aggressiveness.   This is the essence of our theory of *proportionality of overt and covert personality deviation,* which, of course, may be derivable from more basic propositions about social pressures and about disposition rigidity [*8, 9*].

Now, even if the fraction $\frac{c-o}{o-n}$ were perfectly constant, as is intended to be illustrated by the second and third persons in the diagram, where the constant equals 2, the correlation of test and overt behavior would not be perfect, for the overt behavior is o, not $(o - n)$.   (A rank-order correlation would be unity, but a product moment would not.)   Whether this suffices to account for our estimate that the correlation departs considerably from unity or whether other attenuating influences must be brought in is a question we have no space to pursue further here.   However, the attenuation due to the present effect would decline to zero as n declines to zero, so that the effect can be investigated by comparing studies in which n is high, for example, on sociability, which can go a long way before society begins to frown, with personality trait studies for which it is practically zero, for instance, sex in some culture patterns.

RESEARCH QUESTIONS CONCERNING THE OPERATION OF PROJECTION AND OTHER DEFENSE MECHANISMS

Although this theory of codeviation of overt and covert traits suggests the above and many other interesting and clear-cut issues for investigation, it also reminds us that a good deal of the failure to get positive results in research is likely to be due to failure to take note of and control certain "extra" conditions.   Let us therefore systematically list some of the more important questions that remain unanswered and that indicate variables to be taken account of, investigated, and, where possible, controlled.

1. Does the individual *know* (and if so, with what degree of accuracy) how much he deviates from the norm in overt behavior? If this awareness is lacking, presumably no need for adjustment and, later, defense, is felt. The relative poorness of defense tests for certain traits may be due to the self-concept being usually vaguer with respect to these traits.

2. If and when he knows, are there other conditions of the personality that qualify (intruding, as a separate variable, to a different extent in different persons) the extent of the defense response? A person may feel so secure that he does not care. Certainly there is evidence that the dominance factor (*E*-factor) is correlated with unconventionality [*7, 8*]. Further, the individual with a strong ego and a general absence of neuroticism who takes steps to conform to the norm succeeds in doing so with less need for the props offered by defense mechanisms. Here are two factors, therefore, Dominance (*E*-factor) and Emotional Maturity or freedom from general neuroticism (*C*-factor), that existing research already indicates are likely to be disturbing influences on the above correlation and in the measurement of personality by defense tests.

3. What differences in personality are due to differences in the sociological situation? These concern three aspects of *N*, as follows:

(a) What are the differences due to *N* being far below, equal to, and far above the population average in the trait concerned?

(b) What are the differences due to the different degrees of insistence of society upon conformity to a norm? Sex, aggression, and emotional instability are usually under comparatively strong pressure, whereas differences in schizothymia (introversion) or intelligence are only under slight pressure, and some personality factors may be under none at all. Presumably the last cannot be brought under surveillance by defense tests, but the data in this chapter show no marked trend among traits differing in degree of social pressure.

(c) Are there differences in the psychological effects of moral norms, explicit conventional norms, and unspoken, unrealized norms upon the internal conflict engendered in the individual and the resultant defenses? The questions (a), (b), and (c) will be related in various ways—moral norms, say, may prove to be systematically more urgent than others and systematically more deviant from the population average.

4. Do all individuals make about equal use of the various defense mechanisms or would some, despite great $(o - c)$ discrepancy, show this need only in certain kinds of test?   Only at a comparatively late stage of research, with adequate tests and dependable correlations, can this question of "generality" be answered.

5. To what extent are measures of particular dimensions such as strengths of drives affected by the well-known tendency of subjects to project and fantasy not only single traits but whole emotional *situations*?

It is likely that the most potent objection to be raised to the selective as opposed to the inventive test is that it will not in any case permit detection of the total situations over which the individual is in conflict.   These situations are perhaps quite as important in clinical diagnosis and personnel assessment as are personality traits, and our concentration on traits has been due to the fact that more objective experimentation exists there, and that in discussing the methodology for them, we are doing the same for situations.   But these last should be separately investigated.

It is a mistake to assume that selective answer methods cannot be applied to situations just as they are applied to disposition and temperament traits.   The regularities in the culture pattern are as definite as those in the biological constitution, and common patterns applicable to all subjects can be found in both.   For example, the emotional situations in the family pattern—a mother attachment, a situation of jealousy and conflict with respect to an older brother—are sufficiently universal to be set up as standard selective "answers" in fantasy and other tests.   The admittedly greater demands made by this method on the psychometrist's ingenuity and clearness of conception are more than compensated for by the shortening of scoring time and the greater objectivity of diagnosis.

Consequently, the answer to the above question seems to be that the projecting, fantasying, identifying, and so on with respect to situations does not, as far as any present knowledge goes, preclude or interfere with analysis in terms of personality traits.   In fantasy situations as in real-life situations, a trait estimate is obtained as a *mean* of the strength of certain kinds of behavior, in a number of occasions and times. It is an abstraction, with greater predictive value than the observations on any one situation. As such, it can be obtained as a mean from defense tests designed to give emphasis to assessing particular situations, though it can be more readily evaluated from tests such as those illustrated above, in which the narrower situations are specifically chosen for high factor situations, that is, to give the maximum involvement of a particular trait.

6. A last and most important question for further research is whether, in a defense test, we are to conceive ourselves to be testing a defense process occurring at the moment of the test, in respect to the test situation, or merely reactivating and sampling a defense that has already long taken place and that has established, perhaps over the course of years, a definite defense mechanism structure in the personality. For example, in *Item 3,* above, employed for true projection, does the individual meet for the first time the opportunity of projecting his tendency to be excessively familiar and over-sociable, or has he long adopted this defense as a habit of thinking, so that he is addicted to reminding people sententiously that "there is such a thing as being too sociable"?

The possibility has to be considered that the mechanism will not operate proportionately in an *ad hoc* "test" situation, away from the life situation in which it is embedded, or that it will even show an inverse action because of the reduction of the need in the special test situation resulting from the magnitude of the successful discharge elsewhere. For example, if an individual has successfully projected his aggression upon, say, his wife, will he need as much to project it upon people in general in *Items 4* and *6,* above?

Although this cannot be answered in any quantitative and specific fashion, there seems no reason to believe that defense mechanisms will operate differently from other dynamic traits in this respect. Narrow directions of discharge *do* tend to reduce the discharge over wider fields, but an individual of aggressive disposition will *tend* to be aggressive in many situations, and it is the task of the test designer to sample the area of expression of the average person as thoroughly as possible. Nevertheless, a source of attenuation of possible validity coefficients will always exist here, and the work of Luchins [31] and others shows that the specific attitudes of the subject to the test and the tester as well as the fixations of his personal background can have an appreciable effect upon the scores in projective tests. The quantitative investigation of the relative effectiveness of items sampled from different areas of behavior, together with clinical observations on the effects of strong, specific, inveterate defense mechanisms upon the reliability of items in these areas is much needed.

A further unsettled issue regarding the design of defense tests is the extent to which different mechanisms operating on the same given item might produce conflicting answers, that is, the possibility of the response from the operation of the mechanism that the experimenter *intended* to invoke in the item becoming confused by the operation of a mechanism he had not contemplated.   The better results from certain dynamisms should also be examined to see how far they are caused by common action.   For example, as *Items 3, 4, 5* and *6,* above, show, it is difficult to devise tests of true projection that do not also operate to some extent as measures of reaction formation.

THE CANCELLATION AND REINFORCEMENT OF MISPERCEPTION AMONG VARIOUS DEFENSE MECHANISMS

The interaction of various defense mechanisms in any given type of misperception test cannot be systematically investigated in this space.   But some of the outstanding possibilities can be sufficiently illustrated by taking a particular trait as an example and studying the action upon it of several defense mechanisms.

If we take the case of a highly dominant individual, and assume that high dominance conflicts with the culture, we shall find the following distortions arising from each of the eight mechanisms discussed above: (1) Naive projection: that people generally are dominating; (2) True projection: that people are dominating; (3) Press projection: that people are submissive; (4) Fantasy: that the interesting theme is domination; (5) Identification: that dominating people are admirable; (6) Reaction formation: that dominance is a trait to be eschewed; (7) Rationalization: that domination is often essential; (8) Repression, humor: that successful dominance is amusing.   If the reader constructs a table with various other personality extremes on factors like *A, C, E, F,* and *I* labeled at the tops of columns and the eight mechanisms labeled down the side he will find that this same pattern runs through socially suppressed extremes (inverted, of course, for submissiveness, and so on), and is similar for more socially neutral traits like surgency, except that true projection, reaction formation, rationalization, and repression probably have very slight action.

This pattern reveals that naive and real projection tend to agree in their direction of distortion, which is opposite to that of press projection. Fantasy, if we equate "overinteresting" with "overprevalent," distorts as in press projection. Identification and rationalization make the trait respectively more admirable and more necessary than it is, while reaction formation makes it unjustly censurable and repression makes it more amusing. A test response should therefore permit a trait to be rated more admirable while permitting it to be censurable, to be more prevalent while yet more undesirable, and so on. Evidently, unless items are chosen and designed with a nice sense of the different distortions, the distortions in a given test-item response are in danger of cancelling one another. And in the case of press projection, the effect is bound to be diametrically opposite to that of the two other forms of projection unless some quite special device can be introduced to prevent it.

It is perhaps not surprising, therefore, that many of our test items from the beginning lacked reliability. An examination of the more and less reliable items, even among the few used to illustrate this chapter, might help in demonstrating the exact slant of meaning that it is necessary to give and the contaminations of meaning that it is desirable to avoid. The best defense tests in general (for most traits) have turned out to be true projection, identification, and fantasy. It is perhaps significant that the first two of these are the two that are reinforced by other defenses (naive projection and rationalization, respectively), so that a slight error in slanting the question does not result in its being completely invalidated by the possible opposing distortions.[9] Fantasy succeeds perhaps because it distorts in a dimension practically untroubled by others, namely,

---

[9] Thus, *Items 3* and *5*, above, pull together and have some validity as measures of cyclothymia-vs-schizothymia, because both naive and true projection work the same way, and the usually opposed press projection is in this case neutral or assistant. For an individual in a sociable mood is probably more inclined to think others sociable to account for his mood. On the other hand, the press projection *Item 7* may have its ineffectiveness explained by the tendency of the submissive (who think by press projection that there are many important people) to think by true and naive projection, as well as by identification, perhaps, that the people they meet are as unimportant as themselves.

that of being "interesting."   An action can be good, bad, admirable, necessary, or censurable and still be interesting.

SUMMARY

1. The test methods with which we are here concerned constitute one class among several classes of *objective tests of personality.* Objective tests themselves constitute only one of three approaches to personality estimation, the remaining approaches being *self-rating* (true questionnaires) and *life-record observation* (including behavior ratings by observer).

2. The present tests have in common the operation of measuring the difference between the subject's perception of a situation and some standard perception, and are therefore most accurately called *Misperception or Apperception Tests.*   The psychologist studying personality, however, is mainly interested in that large class of misperception tests that may be called *dynaception tests,* because they deal with distortions due to dynamic needs, rather than with those due to cognitive (intelligence and reproductive power) effects.   Dynaception tests in turn break down into those operating through *naive misperception, autistic misperception, press compatibility misperception,* and *ego defense misperception.*

3. Most of the situations set up for dynaception tests are likely to be affected by both conscious and unconscious dynamic needs. The problem of test design and analysis is to separate effects from these two sources, as well as from the several distinct kinds of misperception operation that are likely to work even on a single source.

4. The problem is studied here with particular regard to the varieties of ego defense operations, though autistic and other operations of misperception are illustrated by examples.

Defense tests can be set up for the defense dynamisms of projection, reaction formation, identification, introjection, rationalization, fantasy, and repression.   True projection effects are liable to be modified by the action of naive projection, varying sensitively with age and intelligence, and press compatibility projection, which is also partly dependent on individual differences of experience.   The existing degree of insight into design does not give very high reliability to the construction of dynamism test items, and when reliability is attained, validity does not always follow.   However, reliabilities equal to the best tests in other fields and validities of clear significance have been attained with brief tests of *identification, fantasy, true projection, and repression.*

5. Correlations of the defense test scores with *overt* trait strengths are consistently positive, and if corrected for attenuation, would probably run at about 0.6. If these tests are truly measuring the defense dynamism effect, only then the supplementary hypothesis must be invoked that the deviation of the overt trait from the norm is proportional to the deviation of the covert trait. Alternatively, it may be that defense tests as now constructed are really general dynaception tests, mixing a misperception effect from the defense dynamism with a misperception measure from the overt dynamic trait.

6. A number of questions and hypotheses are raised with respect to the design and operation of autism and dynamism tests. These include questions of the effect of the accuracy of self-awareness, of the degree of ego strength, of the specificity and overlapping of defense activities, of the extent to which the projection of situations can be broken down into the projection of drives, of the influence of transient appetites, and of the relative modes of action of conscious and unconscious dynamic traits. These hypotheses indicate many urgent experimental research designs.

7. It is evident that even without disentanglement of the various dynamic, ability, and temperament actions in perception, apperception tests can be expected on theoretical grounds to show certain consistent empirical relations to personality. Every statement that an individual makes about (his perception of) the real world is the end of a chain argument at one or several stages of which personality traits intrude as "hidden premises." This occurs even if the individual is entirely realistic and logical; but if in addition he adopts neurotic defenses, rationalizations will enter in, which may operate on inductive or deductive conclusions either by suppression of (his awareness of) facts or by various well-known errors of logic. The examination of both beliefs and of lines of reasoning will therefore throw light on both basic personality (the hidden premises) and on the structure of defenses. Factor analysis of the attitude measurements has already shown certain groupings of beliefs that cannot be due to logical connections and must therefore be due to deeper premises in personality, especially temperament.

REFERENCES

1. Allport, G. W., and Vernon, P. E., *Studies in Expressive Movement*. New York: The Macmillan Company, 1933.

2. Balken, E. R., and Masserman, J. H., "The language of phantasy: 3. In conversion hysteria, anxiety state and obsessive compulsive neuroses." *J. Psychol.*, 1940, Vol. 10, 75–86.

3. Bellak, L., "The concept of projection: an experimental investigation and study of the concept." *Psychiatry*, 1944, Vol. 7, 353–370.

4. Brogden, H. E., "A factor analysis of forty character tests." *Psychol. Monog.*, 1940, 52, No. 3, 39–56.

5. Burt, C. L., "The assessment of personality." *Brit. J. Educ. Psychol.*, 1945, 15, 107–121.

6. Cattell, R. B., *A Guide to Mental Testing*. London: University of London Press, 1936 (Revised 1946).

7. Cattell, R. B., "Projection and the design of projective tests of personality." *Char. and Person.*, 1944, 12, 177–194.

8. Cattell, R. B., *The Description and Measurement of Personality*. New York: World Book Company, 1946.

9. Cattell, R. B., *Personality: A Systematic Theoretical and Factual Study*. New York: McGraw-Hill Book Company, Inc., 1950.

10. Cattell, R. B., "The main personality factors in questionnaire, self-estimate material." *J. Soc. Psychol.*, 1950, 31, 3–38.

11. Cattell, R. B., and Luborsky, L. B., "Personality factors in response to humor." *J. Abn. and Soc. Psychol.*, 1947, 42, 402–421.

12. Cattell, R. B., and Pitluk, M. J., "A note on the reliability and validity of some projective or misperception tests of personality." *J. Clin. Psychol.* (In press for 1951)

13. Cattell, R. B., and Saunders, D. R., "Inter-relation and matching of personality factors from behavior rating, questionnaire, and objective test data." *J. Soc. Psychol.*, 1950, 31, 243–260.

14. Crutcher, R., "An experimental study of persistence." *J. Appl. Psychol.*, 1934, 18, 409–417.

15. Cummings, J. D., "Variability of judgment and steadiness of character." *Brit. J. Psychol.*, 1939, 29, 4, 345–370.

16. Downey, J. E., *The Will-Temperament and Its Testing*. New York: World Book Company, 1923.

17. Eysenck, H. J., "General social attitudes." *J. Soc. Psychol.*, 1944, 19, 207–227.

18. Freud, A., *The Ego and the Mechanisms of Defense*. London: Hogarth, 1937.

19. Freud, S., *New Introductory Lectures on Psychoanalysis*. New York: Garden City Press, 1933.

20. Harrison, R., "Studies in the use and validity of the thematic apperception test. II and III." *Char. and Person.*, 1940, 9, 122–138.

21. Hartshorne, H., May, M. A., and Shuttleworth, F. K., *Studies in the Organization of Character*. New York: The Macmillan Company, 1930.

22. Hertz, M. R., "Rorschach twenty years after." *Psychol. Bull.*, 1942, 39, 529–572.

23. Johnson, W. B., "Euphoric and depressed moods in normal subjects. I and II." *Char. and Person.*, 1937 and 1938, 6, 79–98 and 188–202.

24. Junger, E., *The Storm of Steel*. London: Chatto and Windus, 1929.

25. Klages, L., *Handschrift und Charakter*. Leipzig: Barth, 1932.

26. Klein, M., "Personification in the play of children." *Internat. J. Psychoanalysis*, 1929, 10, 37–58.

27. Kretschmer, E., *Korperban und Charakter* (8th ed.). Berlin: Springer, 1929.

28. Levy, D., "Use of play technique as experimental procedure." *Amer. J. Orthopsychiat.*, 1933, 3, 266–277.

29. Lowry, N. D., "Item validation of some ego defense dynamism tests," Thesis, University of Illinois Library, 1950.

30. Luborsky, L. B., and Cattell, R. B., "The validation of personality factors in humor." *J. Person.*, 1947, 15, 283–291.

31. Luchins, A. S., "Situational and attitudinal influences on Rorschach responses." *Amer. J. Psychiat.*, 1947, 103, 780–784.

32. Lundholm, H., "Repression and rationalization." *Brit. J. Med. Psychol.*, 1933, 13, 23–50.

33. Murray, H. A., "The effect of fear upon estimates of the maliciousness of other personalities." *J. Soc. Psychol.*, 1933, 4, 310–339.

34. Murray, H. A., "Techniques for a systematic investigation of phantasy." *J. Psychol.*, 1937, 3, 115–143.

35. O'Neil, W. M., Dept. of Labor and Industry, Vocational Guidance and Juvenile Employment Section, Sydney, Australia. Personal communication of results to the present writer, 1936.

36. Pascal, G. R., "The analysis of handwriting: a test of significance." *Char. and Person.*, 1943, 12, 123–144.

37. Rethlingshafer, D., "The relation of tests of persistence to other measures of continuance of action." *J. Abn. and Soc. Psychol.*, 1942, 37, 71–82.

38. Rosenzweig, S., "The picture association method and its application in a study of reactions to frustration." *J. Person.*, 1945, 14, 3–23.

39. Rotter, J. B., and Willerman, B., "The incomplete sentences test." *J. Consult. Psychol.*, 1947, 11, 43–48.

40. Ryans, D. G., "The meaning of persistence." *J. Gen. Psychol.*, 1938, 19, 79–96.

41. Sanford, R. N., "The effect of abstinence from food upon imaginal processes: a preliminary experiment." *J. Psychol.*, 1936, 2, 129–136.

42. Sanford, R. N., and others, "Physique, personality and scholarship," Vol. 8, *Monog. Soc. for Res. in Child Devel.* Washington, D. C.: Nat. Res. Council, 1943.

43. Sargent, H., "Projective Methods," in Pennington, L. A., and Berg, I. A. (editors), *An Introduction to Clinical Psychology.* New York: Ronald Press, 1948, Chapter 17.

44. Sears, R. R., "Experimental studies of projection: I. Attribution of traits." *J. Soc. Psychol.*, 1936, 7, 389–398.

45. Sears, R. R., "Experimental studies of projection: II. Ideas of reference." *J. Soc. Psychol.*, 1937, 8, 389–401.

46. Sears, R. R., "Survey of objective studies of psychoanalytic concepts." *Soc. Sci. Res. Council Bull.*, 1943, No. 51.

47. Shakow, D., and Rosenzweig, S., "The use of the tautophone as an auditory apperceptive test for the study of personality." *Char. and Person.*, 1940, 8, 216–226.

48. Symonds, P. M., *Diagnosing Personality and Conduct.* New York: D. Appleton-Century, 1931.

49. Tomkins, S. S., *The Thematic Apperception Test: The Theory and Practice of Interpretation.* New York: Grune and Stratton, 1948.

50. Vernon, P. E., "The Rorschach ink-blot test." *Brit. J. Med. Psychol.*, 1933, 13, 89–118, 179–200, 271–291.

51. Waehner, T. S., "Interpretation of spontaneous drawings and paintings." *Genet. Psychol. Monogr.*, 1946, 33, 3–70.

52. White, R. W., "Interpretation of imaginative productions," in Hunt, J. McV. (editor), *Personality and the Behavior Disorders.* New York: Ronald Press, 1944.

PART II

The Rorschach Test

CHAPTER 4

The Rorschach Test:
A Multi-Dimensional Test of Personality

SAMUEL J. BECK, PH.D.

INTRODUCTION

In 1921, when Hermann Rorschach published the *Psychodiagnostik* [14], a monograph describing his test, psychoanalysis was just about one generation old. So also was clinical psychology, if we date its inception from the time when Binet tried some "mental tests" on his two young daughters. An experimental psychology, including much study of perception, was already relatively venerable, dating back three-fourths of a century and more to Wundt, Helmholtz, Fechner, and Müller; its roots were even deeper in philosophical speculations, principally those of Kant, as to knowledge. Comparatively young, however, was the newest of the experimental approaches to the psychology of perception, Gestalt psychology, which started in papers by Wertheimer a mere decade earlier. This is the setting that must be kept in mind if we are to understand how it happened that the Rorschach test appeared when it did, and the interest it has held among students of personality. These are the facts that disclose, for one thing, the intellectual matrices within which the test derives its particular form. These facts also make clear what the intellectual forces were that dictated the invention of an objective instrument having a potential for penetrating into the whole person, in his several psychological dimensions.

This chapter is an exposition of the Rorschach test as a multi-dimensional instrument in the study of personality. As such, the test is only one among many techniques, groups of tests, individual tools, and organized scales with which psychologists are currently experimenting. This experimenting is a phase that psychology, as a science of personality, has been approaching in the normal course of its progress. It is well that it is doing so, since the assignment is also being imposed on it from fields outside its own limits, strictly defined. These fields are, however, closely related to it. They are clinical psychiatry, psychiatric social work, and certain disciplines of the social sciences, such as education and delinquency.

Several movements in psychology itself are dictating the psychologist's thinking of personality in multi-dimensional terms. Currently there is, for one thing, the resurgent interest in perception and its relation to the perceiver, that is, to his emotions, and to unconscious forces, using the term "unconscious" in the Freudian sense. The use of psychometrics for obtaining perspective insight into personality is a comparatively old approach. The most notable systematic efforts in this direction are those of Rapaport [13] and his co-workers (Chapter 19); Rosenzweig [16], and the earlier efforts of Jastak [9] deserve mention here. Wells has been contributing to this thinking for a generation, in shorter articles too numerous to mention. His one book [17] anticipates some of these briefer writings. Then there is Gestalt theory, which has been vigorously effective for a generation. Its critical hypotheses place emphasis on the whole as shaping the part. Implicit in this concept is the need to think in more than one dimension of the personality as a whole, in clarifying any of its manifestations. The writings of Koffka [11], especially, come to mind in this connection. Older still, and too frequently omitted in psychological exposition, are the hypotheses of Hughlings Jackson. They provide the neurologic rationale for the proposition that any individual is at any moment one whole functioning unit, manipulating his then available psychologic equipment. To quote from Jackson:

All mental states, healthy or morbid, are the survival of the then fittest states. [They are] the positive mental symptoms, survival . . . on the lower, but then highest level of evolution. . . . [A mentally disturbed person] ceases to be his highest self and at once or soon becomes his lower self . . . in the strictest sense another person differing . . . from his ante-epileptic self. . . . Illusions, hallucinations, delusions, and extravagant conduct are the outcome of activity of nervous elements untouched by any pathological process; they arise during activity on the lower level of evolution remaining. [8]

A direct corollary of this thinking is the postulate that an individual's manifestations, healthy or pathological, are resultants of brain tissue activities at several levels, corresponding to the psychological forces in the several dimensions that make up that personality. Levels or dimensions that need to be understood are a person's conscious intellectual activity, reasoning, abstraction, judgment, recognition, and perception; his immediate affect-dictated responses; and those responses shaped by older emotional influences —repressions and conflictual, anxiety-dictated behaviors, that is, those subsumed in the term "unconscious" as that term is now commonly used in psychological science.

Mention of the unconscious necessarily leads to the name of Freud and to those explorations associated with his name, explorations into personality as *depth* phenomenon. The term "depth" itself directly connotes a three-dimensional concept, and so we find again the roads leading to the hypothesis of personality as multi-dimensional.

A multi-dimensional phenomenon requires a multi-dimensional instrument for its investigation. The most stable instrument so far developed for probing into the human personality at its several levels is that made up by Rorschach's ten ink-blot figures. Hermann Rorschach, a psychiatrist, was living and working in or near Zurich during the 10 years when he devised this test. Thus, he was at the very nucleus of the energetic psychiatry that includes the names of Forel and Bleuler; he was at the center of the Jungian school. Practicing psychoanalysis, he was living the Freudian doctrines. Not too far away were the then great schools of psychology in Marburg and Würzburg, not to mention the influences of Berlin and Vienna. How all these influences entered into the test is made clear by a knowledge of its actual working. But some hints are gleaned from a remark here and there by Rorschach himself in the *Psychodiagnostik*. They add up to this: as a psychoanalyst, Rorschach was at home in the field of depth psychology, and he knew the value of free association. Fortunately, too, he possessed an experimental bent, appreciated the advantages of objectivity, and was gifted also with creative insight. All of these merged in the idea of a fixed stimulus, the free association to which would be a depth instrument sunk into the personality, a fluoroscope into the psyche to enable one to observe it without trauma to the personality.

THE TEST

It took Rorschach about 10 years to complete the test that now bears his name.   Concerning his earlier trials and errors, he himself says:

Originally the plan of experimentation followed along theoretical lines. It was on a purely empirical basis, without our seeking it, that the experimental results showed themselves as having diagnostic value.   It was only so that the experiment became a test.   As our next step, clinical application was used as control of the findings.   Attempts followed, to work out diagnoses, from response records, obtained by my colleagues with subjects unknown to me.   The more accurate the diagnoses so obtained,— without any indication to me as to the age or sex of the subject, and whether in good health, neurotic, or psychotic—the more certainly must the method be accurate.   [*14*, p. 128.]

He also comments, *passim:* he engaged in "a large number of trials, with earlier pictures."   "The problems, from which the first trials of this kind emerged, in 1911, were essentially of another kind than those which forced themselves more and more to the fore with continued investigation."   He emphasizes throughout that he considered his findings tentative, but he insists that "the conclusions arrived at in the experiment are to be considered findings rather than theoretical derivations."   He experimented with other blots, parallel series; he attempted control experiments.   His *Psychodiagnostik* is his only publication on the test.   The article published after his death in 1922 by Oberholzer [*15*] is the one other paper in which Rorschach reports his own experience with the test.

While the test figures are by now well known, especially to students, a brief description follows.   The test consists of 10 symmetrical ink-blot designs, printed on white paper 8 by 10¾ inches in size. All the figures are centered on the paper, which is mounted on stiff cardboard.   They are always presented in exactly the same order. Five of the cards are gray, in varying amount of saturation.   These are Figures I, IV, V, VI, VII.   In Figures II and III, bright red blotches are present, but no other color.   Three are constituted of color blots only, Figures VIII, IX, X (some minor details in X are grayish). The order in which the figures are presented is itself important diagnostically, having effects in inducing neurotic shock and anxiety shock.

The devising of the test figures, according to Rorschach, was simple. But certain conditions had to be fulfilled by the figures used, and the achievement of a series that worked was, therefore, not really so simple. He tells us:

> The construction of the blots consists only in throwing some blots of ink on a sheet of paper, folding it in the center, and smoothing the folded paper with the finger. But the forms must be relatively simple since complicated designs greatly enhance the difficulties in evaluating the experimental factors. The arrangement of the design on the card must fulfill certain conditions of spatial rhythm. When that is not the case, the design lacks pictorial unity, with the result that many subjects put the design off as "merely blots," without offering interpretations. Asymmetrical designs are rejected by a large number of subjects. Their symmetry gives the designs a large portion of their needed rhythm. It also has somewhat of a stereotyping effect on the interpretations. But on the other hand the conditions are made identical for right-handed and left-handed. The symmetry also makes it easier for some inhibited and conflicted persons to react. It promotes interpretations of scenes as a whole. [*14*, pp. 15–16.]

Now, whether or not Rorschach consciously intended a multi-dimensional test, the fact is that one can use the test only by constantly keeping in mind the several dimensions that it is measuring at once. Implicit in such operations is, conversely, the concept of the substance measured, the personality as multi-dimensional.

The three major dimensions along which the test measures personality operations have long been known. They are essentially elucidated by Rorschach himself. These are: conscious intellectual activity, the externalized emotions, and internalized emotional living. Each of these, however, emerges on further study as a structure that is itself measurable along more than one dimension; they are crystals, with many facets. Rorschach himself recognized some of these. The others have been patterned out by later workers.

INTELLECTUAL ACTIVITY

Perception of Form, $F+$. Referring first to the intellectual sphere, the most important variable described by Rorschach is $F+$. When *form* is accurately perceived, it is scored $F+$. Cumulative work with the test confirms Rorschach in his recognition of the importance of $F+$. In fact, it accents its value. Rorschach's description of $F+$ emphasizes:

The ability to center the attention, making possible clear perception; possession of clear mental pictures [*Engramme*]; power to bring these clear memory pictures into consciousness; ability to select from among the memory pictures which present themselves the one most nearly resembling the stimulus—a process that again depends on control of the perception activity and on critical interpretation.   [*14,* pp. 60–61.]

$F+$ is thus the measure of clearness of perception, along a continuum from rigid accuracy (high $F+$ per cent) to clouded or indefinite perception (low $F+$ per cent).   More critical significance of this variable emerges as we inspect the varying amounts of $F+$ per cent characteristic of different clinical types or syndromes.   Implicit in these differentials are always certain theories as to the structure of the several illnesses.   Thus, high $F+$ per cent in depression is assumed to represent the need for rigid, undeviating, obsessive caution in observing the world's proprieties.   This, in turn, bespeaks the apprehension, the anxiety, the guilt consciousness that is so dynamic a factor in depression.   On the other hand, a lowered $F+$ per cent is expected in the hypomanic, and in a number of unstable emotional conditions.   In these, we see the result of the affects so dominating the individual as to produce the flighty behavior that prevents concentration.   This, in turn, lowers precision in perception and permits the regressive thinking that is found in these mental states.

It follows that $F+$ per cent is itself a function of three variables. It involves clear perception, recognition, and discrimination. These, in turn, vary along a continuum from a low level found in the feeble-minded to the high degree seen in the very superior.   It requires the inner need or wish to be accurate—an ego factor—which breaks down most notably in schizophrenia.   It is also dependent on emotional pressures that heighten or lower one's "normal" level of accuracy.   Thus, the behavior projected in $F+$ (clear, accurate perception), and in $F-$ (vague or inaccurate perception) is a product of three other psychologic activities, each measurable along its own dimensions.

Perception of the Whole, W.   In measuring height of intelligence, Rorschach lays accent on the *whole* response (*W*).   He reports this as a sign of the abstracting or theoretical behavior.   But the very fact that there are individuals whose Rorschach test protocols are notable for their *W*'s highlights the fact that other persons emphasize the *D,* or major *detail* in the blot stimulus; and there are those who accent the *Dd,* or fine *detail.* The *D* individual is traditionally the one with the concrete, practical approach. Yet it does *not* follow that subjects with the *D* approach, or practical intelligence, are inferior in their endowment to those who distinguish themselves by more *W.* The differential is in *kind* of intelligence, not height. Two persons may resemble each other closely in the Rorschach test variables that point to any given level of intelligence, and not differ significantly in respect to *W,* especially the difficult or "superior" *W*'s (chiefly in Figures III, IX, X of the test; less so, but still significant *W* in Figures II and VIII). Again, Rorschach, in his *approach (Erfassungstypus),* is dealing with a different dimension of intelligence from that which he finds projected in the absolute number of *W.*

Organization, Z. Beck [2] has extended the *W* concept in his *organization* variable, which he has designated *Z.* This measures the ability to grasp new, meaningful relations between portions of the figures not usually so organized. Other writers have studied the *organization* variable. It appears consistently related to intelligence in the *height* dimension. More recent observations lead to the conclusion that its principal value is that of indicating the degree of *liberated* intellectual energy. A superior person, when depressed, anxious, or guarded, organizes relationships far below expectancy.

Sequence. Discussion of the *Erfassungstypus* necessarily dictates our focusing also on the *Sukzessionstypus,* generally translated in English as the *sequence.* Both of these are derived from the same variables, *W-D-Dd,* but they differ materially in what is projected. The *Sukzessionstypus* bears in fact a closer relation to *F+.* From *sequence,* one interprets the level of intellectual control, which is a central directive function of personality. Its sensitivity as such is clearly demonstrated in the more disturbed schizophrenic conditions. There, *Sukzessionstypus* is notably confused. Here, then, is an entirely intellectual operation, the distortions in which bear closest relation to factors in other spheres of the personality, chiefly those identified with the ego—which is itself a multi-dimensional psychological organ.

Animal Content, A.   At least four other variables in the test are intellectual products, each projecting its own facet of the personality.   Two of these are really extremes of the same continuum.   At one end, the per cent of *animal content, A,* is an index to the sterility of thought process.   The fact is that animal forms are most easily seen in the test; the more common ones are: bat, butterfly, bear, dog, wolf, cat, tiger, and birds.   Animal skins are also classified in this content group.

Originals.   At the other extreme are the *originals,* which Rorschach identified as evidence of superior and "differentiated" intelligence.   As he uses the latter term, it denotes the many-sided mind, that capable of benefiting by exposure to cultivation.   Examples of originals: embryonic chickens, where chickens are normally seen; a keystone, for the butterfly detail of Figure III; a lunar moth, for the butterfly of Figure V; a cello, for Figure VI; an abstract form of modern architectural art, for the upper half of Figure VIII; a scarab, for the usual beetle of Figure X; a test tube, for the upper tubular detail of Figure X.   I have myself abandoned the original as not a quantitatively derived finding.   But I take account of this differential by inspecting the various categories within which the contents of a subject's responses can be grouped.   In this way I arrive at a judgment on the qualitative richness of the responses.   The judgment has to be to some extent subjective.   The finding is again one in a different dimension from that obtained out of the sheer quantity of content categories.   This is evident in the considerable variability of content among individuals in the same kind of clinical group, ranging from the very stereotyped to the highly individualized original.   In schizophrenia, especially, the findings in this respect are bimodal.   But some clinical groups are identifiable by a uniform absence of richness.   These include most of the feeble-minded, the more deteriorated among patients with brain pathology, and those in advanced old age.   But even in these groups, exceptional individuals are continually found.

Content.   The great variety of content is almost endless.   Beck [2] has grouped content into the following categories: abstraction, alphabet, anthropology, antiquity, architecture, art, astronomy, botany, clothing, clouds, death, fire, food, geography, household, implement, landscape, mineral, music, mythology, nature, personal, recreation, religion, rural, science, sex, travel, vocation.   These are in addition to the five most common categories: humans, parts of humans, animals, parts of animals, and anatomy.

Popular Response, P. Another variable in the intellectual sphere is *P*, the *popular response*, Rorschach's *vulgär*. He does not treat this in the *Psychodiagnostik*, but he does note it in the posthumous paper published by Oberholzer [15]. This measures a more conscious, less deeply dictated, attention to the world's proprieties than does *F+*. It represents a surface interest, not necessarily a sincere wish, to be in conformity, sometimes to adapt at the Yes level. Both in low and in excessive quantity, it can be a critical finding. Low *P* expresses rebellion against conventionalities or indifference to them. The finding is a lead, in some patients, to their homosexual components. When *P* is in excess, it is an index to a passive knuckling under, still at the conscious level, the Uriah Heep complex. The dimension measured is not the ego-tense effort of *F+*, nor of a controlled or rigid *Sukzessionstypus*. *P* is the obeisance that we all make to the fact that we are part of a social group with which we want to identify.

Productivity of Response, R. One other variable that shows correlation with intelligence is *productivity, R*. It measures a raw intellectual productivity, or responsivity, that may also be interpreted as liberated associated potential. This, of course, is a very important dimension in personality. But the term *intellectual energy* connotes a significant aspect of mental health not necessarily projected by a high *R*. The fact is that productivity may result from the nervous need of the obsessional to be thorough, or from the narcissistic self-display of the latent schizophrenic, as well as from the exuberance of the superior in healthy spirit. Quality of the productivity, and the general integration of the individual, are always to be appraised before *R* can be judged as evidence of high intelligence.

One other variable that Rorschach names in connection with high intelligence is the *movement* response, *M*. But this is so identified with the subject's inner world, that I am saving it for discussion under that heading. In addition, evidence currently emerging is raising serious question whether *M* is necessarily identified with the artistic or the inventive potential that Rorschach saw in it, and by inference ascribed to high intelligence.

THE INNER PSYCHOLOGICAL OPERATIONS

The dimensions measured along the *color* continuum (*C*)—those measured by the gray-black responses, including the manifestations identified by *shading responses* (*Y*), *Vista* (*V*), and *Texture* (*T*); and the *movement* responses (*M*)—are keys to the inner psychological operations.

Man's externalized emotions are, together with verbal expressions, his most direct way of communicating with his world, that is, with the world of other men. The emotional communications are frequently more impressive than the verbal, even if they are not always so overtly clear in their significance. But the keen percipient grasps their meanings. Freud comments somewhere that women are always performing psychoanalysis on one another. He is referring to the accuracy with which, in social settings, women understand the unverbalized, emotionally nuanced behaviors. It is hard to see, however, why Freud restricted it to the one sex. The behavior forms include, in fact, a large battery constantly being employed: gestures, looks, screened language, and the meaningful silences. Cicero, in his passionate denunciation of the conspirator, Catiline, repeatedly and accurately identified this non-vocal manner of self-expression. The City's, and the Senators', silences are condemnations, the louder for their being mute. *Quae tacita, loquitur. Patiuntur, tacent. Cum tacent, clamant.* (Her [Rome's] silence, speaks. Their [the Senators'] speechlessness, confirms me. Their silence shouts.)

The battery of emotional communications has long been known. It forms a technique often used by novelists and dramatists. Examples that come to mind: Eugene O'Neil's *Strange Interlude;* Meredith's *The Egoist;* and those vignettes in Proust's *A la recherche du temps perdu* that are essentially intense psychological analysis.

Color Responses, C, CF, and FC. In the color responses, *C*, Rorschach recognized the test's medium for projecting the exciting, and usually pleasurable, externalized feelings. So, all color-determined responses project one great dimension of personality reaction. But this, too, turns out to be a structure in more than one plane. Color-determined responses vary in respect to whether color is the sole element or whether a form element contributes. At the one extreme are responses like, "ocean," "sky," "blood," which are usually dictated entirely by the color of the selected detail. An intermediate response is one in which color predominates, but form is present, like, "a splattered egg," "an orchid," "a sunset." The color response at the other extreme of this dimension is one in which color is present but of secondary importance to form. Examples: "a fir tree," "a flag," "a butterfly," all in Figure VIII; "masquerade costume," in Figure IX.

The *pure color* responses, *C,* and the *color-form* responses, *CF,* measure something different from what is projected in the *form-color* responses, *FC.* When *C* is of extreme quality, it represents something different even from what is projected by *CF.* The more unmixed the *C,* the more egocentric, self-gratifying, the experience. The reactions more disregardful of socially tempered, and of learned, attitudes are projected at the *C, CF,* end of the color response dimension. This is so whatever may be the clinical dynamics behind the failure to learn, whether it be through inability, as in the feeble-minded, through excess structural domination by the feelings, as in the elated and manic, through breakdown of the older learned behavior, as in the aged and in patients with brain pathology, or through solution of stressful conflict through indifference to social values, as in schizophrenia. It is in these groups that color responses, when found, regularly crowd the *C, CF,* statistics.

The *form-color* response, *FC,* appears when emotional growth has reached the stage of ability to sympathize with the other. It is allocentric behavior, as contrasted with the egocentric behavior projected in *C* and *CF.* The trait projected in *FC* is thus characteristic of another plane of behavior, qualitatively different from that indicated in *C* and *CF.* Characterologically and structurally, it is behavior in another dimension.

The Light-determined Responses, Y, V. The painful emotions, those related to anxiety, depressed attitudes, and inadequacy feelings, are projected in the test in the shading-determined responses, especially those in which the varying amount of light influences the blot stimuli along the gray-black continuum. Rorschach had become sensitive to the possible significance of this light-determined factor. But its fuller inspection, and detection of the significance in the several new answers involved, was the work of later students. Principal contributions have been made by Binder [5], on shading as such; by Oberholzer [12], on both shading and vista; and by Klopfer [10], on texture. Examples of simple shading responses are:

"smoke," "fog," "x-rays," "a dark curtain," "a nebulous form of a ship." Texture responses are related principally to the sense of touch. The most common ones are the fur associations. There are others in which the subject describes a tactual element, for instance, smooth, hard, or rough. It may be noted here that the shadow-dominated responses still provide the most unexplored areas of the Rorschach test terrain. Knowledge is still hazy as to the psychological significance of a number of light-nuanced associations. Experience has, however, established the meanings in at least two of the dimensions.

The Shading Response, Y. That which is projected by the darkness of the blot stimulus in itself (a "gathering storm," a "black vampire") is the determining factor in the shading response.

The Vista Association, V. This is a percept of the blot stimulus selected as if in three dimensions. The vista associations include perceptions of distance, architecture, and islands. Examples are: "a mountain pass, with a bridge"; "promenade . . . a flight of stairs"; "a tree, and like a precipice"; "a lake, and reflection in the water."

The common denominator in the stimulus quality of both the Y and the V responses is the gray-black variation. The common denominator psychologically is the unpleasant or distressing quality of the experiences projected.

Shading responses and *vista* associations are found blending with varying degrees of *form* (Y, YF, FY, V, VF, FV). But the evidence so far does not point to any shift in quality to a new plane of behavior (comparable to the gradations in C, CF, FC associations). FY measures psychological experience on the same plane as YF and Y. The difference, insofar as is known at present, consists in the intensity of the unhappy experience. Similarly, FV is on the same dimension with V and VF. There may be some exceptions here. Thus, $FV+$ in a framework of intact and healthy personality may represent a healthy self-appraisal. As such, it differs from the mordant inferiority feeling of the neurotic. The surmise is in order that in a few rare individuals, a momentary inferiority feeling can become an asset that the ego uses constructively. When this is so, it measures a dimension of personality other than the restrictive one that the V nuances project in neuroses and in schizophrenia. But this point requires much follow-up and systematic study.

Texture Response, T. The texture response owes its identity as a separate determinant to Klopfer [*10*], who interprets it as an expression of vague, uncertain anxiety. Should further study verify this interpretation, the texture response would be equivalent to the *Y* nuance; in this case, a separate scoring symbol would appear unnecessary. Yet, it would be important to keep *texture* as a precision technique, since the association set off is more closely related to a sense modality other than that usually indicated by *Y*. That is, *T* stems from a contact experience.

This writer is experimenting with the interpretation of *T* as stemming from affect hunger and from the sense of deprivation of gratifying affects, usually love.

The White Space Response, S. It was pointed out above that *detail, D,* and *rare detail, Dd,* represented certain intellectual approaches or mental activities of the subject. Response to a *white space* on the Rorschach test is one variety of *D* or *Dd*. The *white space* response, *S*, however, represents a projection of resistiveness. This technical fact would indicate that the measurement of resistiveness is obtained along one of the dimensions of the intellectual sphere *(Erfassungstypus)*. Yet, psychologically, resistiveness must requisition intense emotional experiences, and in large quantity. This is another dimension of personality than that projected in the *Erfassungstypus*.

How, then, does *S* cross over into the emotional sphere? The fact is that *S* has been subjected to no analytical study in the experimental field. It does arrest much attention in clinical reports because of its significance in hostility. But in this field, too, it has not, to this writer's knowledge, been analyzed into its psychologic components. Resistiveness has just been taken for granted, and *S* has been accepted as its Rorschach test manifestation because it gives valid findings: the more *S*, the more stubborn or negativistic the individual. A hint as to the rationale for *S* as equivalent to the opposition trait is afforded by Gestalt theory. Structurally, *S* is a reversal of figure and ground, but does it follow that such reversal in perception argues for an obverse, or opposed, attitude in the perceiver? The hypothesis may be set up as a deductive point of departure. Its verification is a task still awaiting some eager, and curious, young psychologist.

THE FANTASY RESPONSE

The Movement Response, M. A variable *sui generis* in the Rorschach test, and in psychology as an objective science, is the activity projected in the *movement* response, *M*, Rorschach's *Bewegung, B.* It penetrates to a dimension in personality whose existence psychology had long been denying, much less attempting to measure. Rorschach, in grasping the significance of *M*, disclosed the fruitful effect of his experience as psychoanalyst and also a flash of the genius' insight. This can be said even though newer investigations are questioning Rorschach's surmise with reference to *M* as an index to artistic creativity.

Rorschach's description of *M* centered on seeing the blot figure, or some portion of it, as if in movement or action. But he emphasized that this apparent movement is *M* chiefly when it is humans that are seen in movement. Also, the converse is not always true. Many human responses are not *M*. But he did not exclude the possibility of true *M* in animals, or even in inanimate objects. He did, however, accent the need for careful questioning of the subject in order to establish that the association is psychologically *M* in Rorschach's sense.

What is most important is that Rorschach accented *M* as *strongly felt wish experience*. Students of the test have tended to overlook the term "strongly felt" in interpreting *M*. The crux of the matter is that the motion in the *M* response represents a fantasy in which the subject is strongly involved, an activity in which he is engaged, either toward something he deeply desires or away from something he would urgently avoid. The present writer sees this association as representing internalized emotion, just as the color response is the index to externalized emotional reaction. This would explain, too, why Rorschach set *M* and *C* against each other in his all-important *experience balance (Erlebnistypus)*.

M penetrates inward, into the personality, to the wishful living. The depth of penetration by any one Rorschach test protocol varies. In some, it goes to very early layers of the personality, exposing the individual's most primitive desires, ontogenetically speaking.

Among the methods of measuring this depth are: (a) the number of movement responses; (b) their structure, as $F+$ or $F-$; (c) the individuality of the content in them; and (d) true *M* in animal content.

With regard to the *number* of *M,* it should be noted that quantity of these associations does not in itself necessarily project wishful living of very deep variety. Certain *M's* occur so regularly that they do not differentiate. They may be set down as the stock *M* of the test, and as representing a conventional, and personally not significant, fantasy life. Should any one test record yield a large number of this common, garden-variety *M,* the high quantity for the entire protocol would still not be a depth penetration.

Examples of the more common *M* responses are: in Figure II, "Two clowns playing patty cake"; in Figure III, "Two waiters bowing"; in Figure VII, "Two women talking to each other"; and in Figure IX, "Two witches staring at each other."

When the *form structure* of the moving figure is an erratic, distorted perception (scored as *M—*), personal needs have entered into the production. The source of the *M* in those instances is always deep. In *M—*, incidentally, we measure again along two dimensions in the one association, that of accurate, critical perception, and that of wish, or fantasy living.

Examples of *M—* are: in Figure VI, "ghosts holding on to a pole"; in Figure VIII, the center skeletal detail, with the white space, "a man upside down, shinnying down a rope."

It is in the *highly individualized M* responses that the innermost wishes and fears of the personality are laid open. Here the test gives its most critical information as to the nuclei of the individual's conflict. The *M—* are also among samples of highly unique *M*. Here, too, belong the *M* in animal content, described in the paragraph following. Examples of *M* in animals, some of which are *M—*, are: in Figure X, the low brown outer details are "two little bunnies, as though someone is holding them up, someone's hands"; in the same figure, the inner blue, "two animals reaching out to touch each other . . . trying to escape, uncomfortable and straining"; in Figure IV: "a big gorilla reaching for you"; in Figure II: "two bull dogs, standing at a bonfire, carrying on secret societies"; this latter is an example of a deeply regressed, psychotic fantasy. Similar was "a butterfly dance" in response to the whole of the first figure. But the very original can also be healthy as, for example, in Figure VII, "two children, with caps on, on top of two piles of snow." Space does not, of course, permit citing full case records, but the finding of *highly individualized M* is known to everyone who has used the test in any broad range of clinical groups. The intimate significance of such *M* is obvious in the responses of many psychotics. At less regressed levels, the significance depends for its clarifying on the patient himself. This is a task in which the Rorschach test as such is weakest, as will be noted again below.

Comment is in order, first, on *M* in *animal content*. Although Rorschach emphasizes *M* as found in human content, he does not restrict it to humans. His caution is that the perceived movement must be one in which humans engage. Our researches [1] with the test in schizophrenia in both children and adults, make it clear that there are many true *M*, of the kind Rorschach describes, in animal associations. By true *M*, is meant *movement in human activity*. That is, Rorschach's description of *M* in the *Psychodiagnostik* still sets the pattern. The great importance of *M* in animal content is the thicker screening of the subject's wish that it entails. The projected fantasy is one that the individual must disguise that much more, must keep that much farther from the conscious thinking; hence the animal actors. It is apt to be a dream quality association.

ASSOCIATIONAL CONTENT

This chapter, so far, has treated *structural* factors in the personality: $F+$, W, Z, C, Y, and M. We can take these measures of a person and so know what he is in terms of clinical structure—whether he is in neurotic conflict, mild or severe, and what kind of neurosis, whether depressed or schizophrenic; or whether he is in disintegrated psychosis. That is, from the Rorschach test structure, we can describe the patient for purposes of nosological grouping. We may still not know what his personal needs are, nor the outside presses on him—to borrow from the language of that other very busy projective test, the TAT. We do not know what causes the conflict. It is here that the content in the patient's record should give us leads. Does the conflict stem from a homosexual urge unpalatable to the ego? Does it arise from antagonism to a parent? Is envy of a sibling the source of basic repressed emotions? The

[1] These research projects are supported by United States Public Health Service Grants Nos. 63 and 64.

content should lead us to the answers to these questions. To the extent that it does, it explores along a totally new dimension of personality, one not at all touched in structural findings.

Two or more records may closely resemble each other in respect to $F+$, M, C, and any of the other structural variables. Yet they may show nothing in common in content (aside from the usual stereotyped animals and humans). It is in the differing content that persons project their different personal experiences; in a few instances, the factors in the premorbid personality are revealed. The factors of intelligence, of potential for fantasy living or for emotional self-expression, and the amount of depressing emotional experience may be constant for any two or more individuals. Yet their personal histories have been different. It is this dimension, that into which his own personal life has been kneaded, that the content in the Rorschach test etches out—when it does.

The qualification, "when it does," states one of the weak spots in the Rorschach test today. It is a weakness that, as far as this writer can see, the test has in common with all other free association methods—tests or clinical. I refer to the absence of systematic study of symbolism in associational content, by whatever technique obtained. The one valid method in use for detecting significance of a patient's production, whether dream or other, is that employed by the psychoanalysts. Their technique amounts to having the patient himself penetrate to the significance. This avenue is open also to the user of the Rorschach test. The therapist, knowing the individualized associational content in his patient's Rorschach test protocol, will be alert for the emergence of its meaning, as the therapy proceeds, and as the patient verbalizes related significant material. The content he will watch for will be the very original fantasy associations and the original associations structured in C, V, and Y. In addition, he will, of course, observe all other markedly original content.

Should general laws of symbolism be developed, it will be possible to interpret association directly for its meaning to the patient. Again, the analysts have gone farther in this direction, validating by clinical experience. Among the examples of psychoanalytical symbolism that come to mind are the following: tooth, water, ship, tree, and horse. But lack of universal significance is still attested to by the fact that the analysts do look to the patient for confirmation.

So we are still far from having any established generalizations according to which any one symbol can be immediately interpreted for its meaning to the person producing it. It is in the sphere of content, therefore, that important research in the Rorschach test still lies before us. The structural dimensions give us a measure that tell us what the person is. The content, when we know more about it, will tell us where he has been, and to what he has been exposed.

OTHER PERSONALITY MEASURES

So much for the principal dimensions in the personality as projected in the Rorschach test. Some other directions of measurement have been followed by sundry investigators. These do not provide major outlines of the personality, but they do help to etch out certain features. Among these other measures are: time for first response, fluctuation of productivity, fluctuation of time for first response, and quality of W. The many variables into which Klopfer [10] has broken up Rorschach's original test factors are now well known. To the extent that any of these variables, developed since the time of Rorschach, have been shown validly to identify psychological operations, they represent the smaller dimensions in which the test measures personality.

The problem of validation has, of course, been a major one from the moment the test was published. Hertz [6, 7] was one of the first, and has been among the most persistently vigorous, in testing out the Rorschach concepts by statistical techniques. As a result, she has brought to light additional nuances on some of the personality dimensions. The sum total of all the work, clinical, statistical, and experimental, has by now reached very great proportions. A survey of recent validation studies is presented in chapter 5 in this volume.

Experience Balance, EB. One other of Rorschach's concepts was very important to him. It has not gripped the interest of other workers in the same degree. This is the *experience balance (Erlebnistypus)*. Rorschach's fascination with it is gauged by his devoting about one-fourth of his monograph to it alone.

This factor is obtained as a quantitative relation between the M and the total C scores. Each M is given a value of 1.0; the C responses are valued as follows: pure C, 1.5, CF, 1.0, FC, 0.5. C, in experience balance, is the sum of the values of all C responses in the record. In this index, the Rorschach is estimating the balance between introversive and extratensive living; the internalized emo‹ tions, as offset by the externalized. Concerning his *Erlebnistypus,* Rorschach says:

> [It] shows only the manner in which the individual experiences [*erlebt*], but not how he actually lives [*lebt*]. . . . The psychologic apparatus through which the individual experiences, is a much broader, more exten- sive one than the equipment with which he lives. . . . The experience type discloses how extensive the equipment is with which the individual could live. [*14,* p. 94.]

To this writer, the real significance of the *Erlebnistypus* is in representing a balance of psychologic operations or forces, a constant give and take of stresses. The emotions press outwardly, and then turn inwardly. The focus, therefore, is on personality dynamics. This is the essence of the *Erlebnistypus.* The fact is that the test projects stresses and balances other than those indicated in the *Erlebnistypus.* In fact, the entire test is a projection of forces con- stantly in balance and check, one against the other. Rorschach saw this balance only between *M* and *C,* an understandable emphasis in view of his geographical proximity to Jung, and the prominence of the extraversion-introversion hypothesis at the time Rorschach was writing.

Ego Strength. The principal psychological force (in addition to *M* and *C*) effective in structuring the personality is that measured along the dimension $F+$. The evidence seems dependable that this is the major index in the test to the ego's developmental level and firmness. The balances represented by the proportion of $F+$ to *M,* and the proportion of $F+$ to the sum of *C* values, assume significance of critical importance. Through regard for reality, they are the ego's check against wishful living on the one hand, and against the pressure of the feelings, on the other. When first publishing this thinking [*3*], the present writer included the operations measured along the *W-Z* dimensions as of equal importance with those held by *M, C,* and $F+$. Subsequent experience leaves him in doubt on this point, a doubt not yet resolved. *W-Z* is an index to the height of intelligence, and this can be a potent force in altering a direction taken by the whole person. But we see subjects in whom it is entirely impotent. It is likely that for the personality as a whole, the issue is settled by these stresses represented in the planes *M, C,* and $F+$. That is the writer's present, even if not fully decided, view, arrived at from observing a very extensive number of Rorschach test protocols in what seems to be never-ending variety. The wonder, nevertheless, is how constant in all these records the underlying structures can be from human to human, and how seemingly infinite the finer differentials. They constantly exemplify the human potential and the conflict in Hamlet's exuberant and ironic apostrophe:

What a piece of work is a man! how noble in reason! how infinite in faculty! in form and moving how express and admirable! in action how like an angel! in apprehension how like a god! the beauty of the world! the paragon of animals! and yet, to me, what is this quintessence of dust? man delights not me; no, nor woman neither, though by your smiling you seem to say so.

Whether the major stresses are three or four, and whatever the contributions from the stresses measured along the smaller dimensions, the fact is that the test is constantly demonstrating a theory of personality as a system of psychological forces in constant strain and check one against the other.

Insofar as these test factors validly indicate the psychological activities claimed for them, they are quantitative statements of stress relations between these processes. Of course—as this writer has pointed out before [3]—when we speak of "quantity," we must remember that we may get any quantity of the other factors. And that, in fact, is what we have. The infinitely fine gradation in character between personality and personality is evidence of it. But for purposes of scientific classification, this possibility of infinite combinations is no serious difficulty. In actual experience, and for purposes of social concern, differences in quantity do not become differences in quality until they have passed certain thresholds. Many a person is "queer" but never becomes schizophrenic. There are, in a word, limited numbers of stable personality patterns recognizable in human society, the observed groups. And though the precise quantity of any of the psychological processes within any individual in that group may vary from the quantity in any other individual in that group, it is not until the variation has passed a certain threshold, resulting in a changed equilibrium, that we classify him in another group. The number of possible combinations or balances may be infinite, but the number of thresholds with which society is concerned is definite.

The thinking here outlined can, the writer believes, be shown to be consistent with the theory resulting from the Gestalt experiment in perception, especially in Angyal's exposition [*1*]. It is consistent with the dynamics of personality as brought to light in psychoanalysis. It can be shown to have rationale in the knowledge now available concerning functions of the higher brain centers, including the frontal lobes, the knowledge relative to the inter-relating and integrating functions of the higher mental processes. That is, this notion of the whole personality as a system of equilibria has its foundations in the neurological substratum of which the psychological operations are functions.

SUMMARY

The Rorschach test was introduced by Hermann Rorschach, in 1921, in the form of ten ink blots.   It is essentially a test of perception to which a person responds by reporting what he sees in the ink blot. This chapter discusses the test as a measure of dimensions in personality. The dimensions are grouped under *intellectual activity, inner psychological operations,* and *fantasy living.* Under intellectual activity, the most important dimension stressed by Rorschach was $F+$, good perception of form. Other dimensions of an intellectual nature are perception of the whole, organization of perception, sequence of responses through the entire test, animal content in the responses, originals, other content, popular responses, and productivity of responses.

Measures of inner psychological operations are found in pure color responses and in responses in which form is secondary to color.   Still another dimension is shown where color is secondary to form.   Inner psychological operations are revealed also in light-determined responses, which include shading and vista responses. Also included are perceptions of texture and responses to white spaces.

Fantasy living is revealed in movement responses.   Rorschach originally reported movement as essentially human movement or movement in animals that is mainly characteristic of human behavior.

This chapter includes also a discussion of associational content and of other personality measures, including Rorschach's *experience balance,* and a brief discussion of ego strength as revealed by the test.

REFERENCES

1. Angyal, A., *Foundations for a Science of Personality.* New York: Com, monwealth Fund, 1941.

2. Beck, S. J., "Configurational tendencies in Rorschach responses." *Am. J. Psychol.,* 1933, 13, 519–532.

3. Beck, S. J., "The Rorschach method and personality organization. Balance in personality." *Am. J. Psychiat.,* 1933, 13, 519–532.

4. Beck, S. J., *Rorschach's Test, Vol. I, Basic Processes.* New York: Grune and Stratton, 1944.

5. Binder, H., *Die Helldunkeldeutungen im Psychodiagnostischen Experiment von Rorschach.* Zürich: Füssli, 1932.

6. Hertz, M. R., "Personality patterns in adolescence as portrayed by the Rorschach ink-blot method: III. The 'Erlebnistypus,' a normative study." *J. Gen. Psychol.,* 1943, 28, 225–276.

7. Hertz, M. R., "Personality patterns in adolescence as portrayed by the Rorschach ink-blot method: IV. The 'Erlebnistypus,' a typological study." *J. Gen. Psychol.,* 1943, 29, 3–45.

8. Jackson, H., *Selected Writings* (2 vols.). London: Hodder and Stoughton, 1931.

9. Jastak, J., "Variability of psychometric performance in mental diagnosis." Delaware State Hospital, 1934.

10. Klopfer, B., and Kelley, D. M., *The Rorschach Technique.* Yonkers, N. Y.: World Book Company, 1942.

11. Koffka, K., *The Growth of the Mind* (R. M. Ogden, trans.). London: Kegan Paul, Trench, Trubner & Co., 1925.

12. Oberholzer, E., in DuBois, C., *The People of Alor.* Minneapolis: University of Minnesota Press, 1944, Chapter 22, "Rorschach's Experiment and the Alorese."

13. Rapaport, D., Gill, M., and Schafer, R., *Diagnostic Psychological Testing* (2 vols.). Chicago: Year Book Publishers, 1945.

14. Rorschach, H., *Psychodiagnostik: Methodik und Ergebnisse eines wahrnehmungs-diagnostischen Experiments* (second edition). Bern and Berlin: Huber, 1932. (Translated by P. Lemkau, and B. Kronenberg, New York: Grune & Stratton, 1942.)

15. Rorschach, H., and Oberholzer, E., "Zur Auswertung des Formdeutversuchs." *Ztsch. f.d. ges. Neurol. u. Psychiat.* 1923, 82, 240–74. (Transl., *J. Nerv. & Ment. Dis.,* 1924, 60, 225–48, 359–79, in Rorschach's *Psychodiagnostics,* pp. 193–227. (Transl., pp. 184–216).

16. Rosenzweig, S., *Psychodiagnosis.* New York: Grune and Stratton, 1949.

17. Wells, F. L., *Mental Tests in Clinical Practice.* Yonkers, N. Y.: World Book Company, 1924.

CHAPTER 5

Validating and Experimental Studies with the Rorschach Method

ALBERT I. RABIN, PH.D.

INTRODUCTION

The method published by Hermann Rorschach in 1921 is still primarily an empirical one. Rorschach did not present his test to the scientific public as a finished experimental product, but as a tentative clinical diagnostic tool that was merely a phase of development in a larger projected research program. Unfortunately, this larger project was not carried out because of Rorschach's early death. Among numerous other qualifications and words of caution, Rorschach stated that "The conclusions drawn . . . are to be regarded more as observations than as theoretical deductions. The theoretical foundation for the experiment is, for the most part, still incomplete." [25, p. 13.]

Not only was the creator of the Rorschach method aware of the theoretical limitations of his experiment, but he was also conscious of the *qualitative* aspects of this type of examination. He was dissatisfied with the insufficient *quantitative* basis for the test and its interpretation, stating that "experience and practice" even play a significant role in the evaluation of the "quantitative importance of symptoms." These realizations led him to the conclusion and hope that it would be possible to increase the conclusiveness of the quantitative aspects of the test by means of "control experiments taking up each symptom individually. Other psychological methods might also be used in control research." [25, p. 121.]

Since the introduction of the Rorschach test into American psychiatric and psychological circles, the reactions have been widely divided. On the one hand, there arose a group of devoted Rorschach workers who more or less unquestioningly accepted Rorschach's hypotheses and proceeded to apply his test to a variety of clinical situations. Much useful research was produced by this group. However, the research was primarily of the practical, clinical variety, in which the relationships and magnitudes of a variety of Rorschach factors were studied in sundry psychiatric classifications and different age groups. In their experiments, they did not question the basic foundations and principles of the test. On the other hand, the Rorschach early met with considerable hostility from the large group of "experimental," general, and nonclinical psychologists. Those workers who had been reared in the tradition of psychometric and nomothetic approaches to personality investigations, or in the traditional experimental approaches in which single factors were varied in otherwise controlled situations, found it difficult to accept the claims of Rorschach and his supporters.

In recent years, however, a rapprochement between these two camps has taken place. The Rorschach method has proved its usefulness in clinical situations, in personality description and diagnosis. Those working with it are aware of the numerous unexplored frontiers of ignorance in the use of the test and of the need for research and investigation. Other psychologists not in the clinical field are now impressed by the test's potentialities and are no longer willing to throw out the baby with the bath water.

In an effort to learn the attitudes of psychologists toward the Rorschach test, Faterson and Klopfer sent a questionnaire to a large number of nonclinical psychologists. They reported, in part, that "the majority of the group indicated a positive attitude to the Rorschach method. . . . Only a few psychologists expressed a consistently skeptical attitude." [8, p. 29.]

A further analysis of these data by Munroe [19] did not indicate uncritical acceptance. Most of those who responded with qualitative comments expressed "the need for scientific standards." The fulfillment of such a need would bridge the gap between the area of Rorschach clinical psychodiagnosis and the field of psychology in general.

The present discussion will be concerned with a review of pertinent critiques of the Rorschach method and with attempts at solutions of the problems posed by them.

CRITIQUES OF THE RORSCHACH METHOD

Most of the critiques of the Rorschach method and expressions of the need for further investigation have come from soul-searching Rorschach workers themselves. Thus, Rickers pointed out in 1943 that "theoretical and systematic formulation have been lagging too far behind the impressive accumulation of empirical data." [23, p. 42.] Beck, the foremost pioneer in the Rorschach method in this country, also stated more specifically that "the Rorschach investigator must . . . subject his separate factors to the necessary controls so that he will be able to solidify the scientific foundations of the test." [3, p. 103.] Hertz [11] and other workers have made similar comments and suggestions.

A constructive critique of the Rorschach method has been offered by Zubin [37],who has outlined a program for research and understanding of the basic psychological principles underlying the test. His hope is that an experimental approach such as he has suggested will eliminate the intuitive or "mystery" aspects of Rorschach interpretation. Furthermore, he speculates that ". . . when the experimental and psychopathological roots of the response are laid bare, it is possible that actual interpretation may be independent of the present type of scoring and may turn out to be simply a reflection of long-established psychological and psychopathological facts which have thus far been related to the Rorschach test." [37, p. 5A–1.] Zubin suggested that in Rorschach interpretation, there are a number of factors that are significant in any standard psychological experimental situation and around which research might be oriented:

1. The subject
2. The experimenter
3. Rapport between the subject and the experimenter
4. Acceptance of the task set by the examiner
5. The final performance

These factors, however, should be subjected to experiment rather than left on the descriptive level.

Along with Baumgarten-Tramer [2], Zubin has pointed out a

number of "unrecognized factors," such as "the completion tendency, shift ability, associational trends, shading, etc.," that need further study.   He feels that his criticism of the intuitive aspects of the Rorschach is not a negation of the test, but a stimulus for finding "experimental analogues" of some of the Rorschach scores that presumably often have an intuitive basis for their determination. Zubin's critique was not written with a predisposition for a seg-mental or molecular approach in research—molar, or global, aspects are implicit and are definitely taken into consideration.   The unity of the personality and its idiomatic uniqueness are not being sacri-ficed on the altar of "scientific" elementism.

In a sense, the pleas and suggestions for further experimentation with the Rorschach are simply indications of the felt need for better validation of the method and its several components.   Does the Rorschach permit correct diagnosis?   Do the personality descriptions based on this method agree with those obtained from clinical study and observation of behavior?   Are the various factors and com-binations of factors actually measures or indices of the traits and characteristics that they purport to measure?

As long ago as 1941, Hertz [*11, p.* 531], in an analysis of the problem of validity, outlined four approaches that have been ap-plied in investigations of the Rorschach method:

1. Direct experimentation, giving the test under experimentally changed conditions.   Examples of this approach would be administering the test to patients under hypnosis [*28*], or under sodium amytal narcosis [*13*]. Work in direct experimentation with the Rorschach has been extremely limited.

2. Comparison of Rorschach categories with other objective criteria by means of correlational technique.   The various correlational techniques, though useful in some instances, yielded low coefficients of correlation. Various Rorschach workers have protested against this method, since it abstracts certain traits out of their context and neglects their setting, which is the total personality Gestalt or configuration presented in the Rorschach record.

3. Comparison of groups of varying intelligence and personality pictures, to detect characteristic differences in Rorschach categories and patterns. This approach has been employed quite extensively by many investigators, including Rorschach himself.   However, it does not really strike at the heart of the matter since mere concomitance of certain Rorschach characteristics with certain groups of varying intelligence and personality pictures leaves the conclusions on a purely phenomenological plane.

4. Case studies including comparison with clinical data, psychoanalytical material, and so on. The case-study approach, though quite fruitful, remains a "clinical," qualitative approach rather than a quantitative, "scientific" one. It may be that new statistical devices will be created that will be able to place this approach, through a quantitative analysis of the clinical material itself, in a position of good validation. At present, much of Rorschach personality description does not coincide with clinical description and analysis. The differences in frame of reference are responsible for this situation. A more precise definition of these frames of reference would make possible the study of parallel personality evaluation and, consequently, would make the validation of the Rorschach a less formidable task.

Despite the numerous lacunae described above, a great many investigations have attacked the problem of validation in recent years with added vigor and greater scientific and clinical sophistication. In the following pages, an attempt will be made to present validating and experimental evidence.

In view of the weaknesses in the last three approaches mentioned above, this chapter will be concerned mainly with the first one, the direct experimental approach, and only secondarily with the others. The following types of investigation will be considered through some of their most representative examples.

1. Validation by means of comparison of "total personality" pictures—*the molar approach.*

2. Attempts at validation of individual Rorschach factors—*the molecular approach.*

3. A more direct experimental approach that does not accept, implicitly or explicitly, any of the Rorschach hypotheses, but tests some of them by means of: (a) placing the subject under special, varying, experimental conditions; (b) varying one or more factors in the test procedure itself; (c) measuring organismic or physiological correlates within the subject. It is understood that these methods or approaches are not mutually exclusive.

THE MOLAR APPROACH

In a sense, the molar approach is being used in daily practice by the clinician, validating the Rorschach diagnosis against that of the psychiatrist, therapist, or clinical interviewer. Several investigations, because of their extensive control, may be reported here as experimental validations of the molar variety.

In 1938, Benjamin and Ebaugh [*4*] compared the diagnoses of 50 patients representing a variety of disorders with the diagnoses based on the Rorschach test. These patients were examined psychiatrically by one of the authors. The other author administered the Rorschach test, personally, to 34 of the cases; the remainder of the Rorschach examinations were interpreted "blindly," that is, the test was administered by an examiner other than the interpreter. Four of the cases were eliminated from the calculations because the Rorschach examiner was somewhat acquainted with them outside the test situation. Complete agreement of diagnoses occurred in 39 of the remaining 46 cases (84.7 per cent). In five others, there were some minor disagreements. If the minor disagreements were to be discounted and only the rough classificatory diagnoses were to be considered, the agreement would be almost 100 per cent (97.8 per cent). Eleven of the blind diagnoses showed complete agreement, even in details. There was greater agreement between the final psychiatric diagnoses and the Rorschach than between the Rorschach and the preliminary diagnoses. Thus, the Rorschach diagnoses from the start offered more penetrating insights as to the course of the illness of the patients involved.

A similar study, but with a different type of population, was reported by Siegel [*29*]. This investigator administered the Rorschach to 26 children and re-examined them with the same technique about a year later. The children had been referred to a child guidance clinic for a variety of problems and represented several diagnoses (primary behavior disorders, psychoneurosis, psychopathic personality, and incipient schizophrenia). At the time of the first examination, there was only 61.5 per cent agreement between the Rorschach and psychiatric diagnosis. A year later, however, at the time of the re-examination and psychiatric re-evaluation of the cases, the percentage of agreement rose to 88.5, approaching that reported by Benjamin and Ebaugh. It is worthy of note that all the shifts in diagnosis responsible for the increased percentage of agreement were made by the psychiatrists. Thus, in both instances, the Rorschach was in better agreement with the final than with the preliminary psychiatric diagnoses.

Siegel's study also attempted to correlate Rorschach findings with "improvement." Four gradations in rating improvement—from "considerable improvement" to "worse"—were employed. Refusals,

FC, W per cent, *Fc, H,* Testing the Limits, *O,* and *F+* per cent are the indices of improvement in descending order of importance. It may be noted that at least two of these items (Refusals and Testing the Limits) are among the nonscorable Rorschach factors that, as Zubin pointed out, are part of the standard experimental situation.

A classic experiment involving both the reliablity and validity of the Rorschach method was reported by Hertz and Rubenstein [*12*]. Hertz administered the Rorschach to one case and interpreted it without any knowledge of the clinical findings. The other author collected clinical material in a series of 14 interviews. The verbatim Rorschach record was sent out for "blind" interpretation to two trained Rorschach workers (Beck and Klopfer). A comparison of the three interpretations obtained shows a high degree of agreement between them (reliability) and also a high degree of agreement with the clinical description (validity). The authors concluded that the Rorschach method was thus shown "to have a high degree of diagnostic validity." [*12,* p. 312.] Of course, they were not unmindful of the fact that the conclusion was drawn from a single case and that it alone did not prove the Rorschach method to be reliable and valid. Many more such studies need be undertaken if such proof is to be secured. Moreover, these results were obtained with experienced Rorschach examiners. The question arises whether such results could be obtained by less experienced interpreters. If not, there is a definite need of reducing that subjectivity of experience to more objective criteria.

It may be added that although close perusal of the three interpretations and the presentation of clinical material showed few disagreements, some interpreted items did not have their parallels in the interpretations of the other examiners, or in the case-history material. Thus, perfect correlation was not obtained mainly because of the different frames of reference of the examiners and the clinicians. Here, too, the tendency of some aspects of personality description not to coincide with one another and not to overlap makes perfect comparison and validation impossible.

One study that lies somewhere in the border zone between the molar and molecular approaches deals with behavior checks on the Rorschach method (36). Twenty-one unstable boys, ages 10–15, were observed closely in a psychiatric summer camp. The following aspects of the children's personalities as observed in the camp were checked against their Rorschach findings: intellectual functioning, emotional factors, anxiety, neurotic, and psychotic tendencies, and interests. To be sure, no scales were devised for these items, and the comparison was largely in the nature of "clinical" qualitative validation. In 16 of the 19 cases in which the intellectual levels had been determined by means of tests (Stanford-Binet), the Rorschach estimates of intelligence were supported. Mere examination of emotional Rorschach factors failed to correlate with observations of emotionality, though *Fc* was "very sensitive in predicting social adjustment." Since reaction to shading (and chiaroscuro) was missing in many tests, the relation of this type of response to anxiety was not clearly supported. The content of the Rorschach responses, however, was frequently a clue to sexual anxiety. Color shock was insufficient as a sole indicator of neurosis. The predominance of animal movement over human movement was a consistant neurotic "sign." Great sensitivity of the Rorschach to psychiatric trends was demonstrated in the two cases in which they were manifest. With the exception of aesthetic and sexual preoccupation, the content of the Rorschach records was an inadequate index of the children's dominant interests.

Thus, partial validation through consistent observation of behavior was obtained. One would wish for more adequate control and for clearer definition of the behavior patterns, including quantitative measures, for a more rigorous study of the relationships involved. These would be especially important since this study was not altogether a molar diagnostic study, but in some respects a molecular one as well.

A similar study, but experimentally and statistically well-designed, was reported by Krugman [15]. This investigation dealt with both reliability and validity. We shall concern ourselves mainly with the latter.

The Rorschach personality descriptions of 25 problem children were matched in groups of five with the abstracts of the clinical charts of those cases, by five judges. As a result of these 125 matchings, an average coefficient of contingency of .850 ± .022 showed a highly significant relationship between the Rorschach and clinical descriptions. The average percentage of correct matching for the five judges was 84. Only one judge had less than 80 per cent agreement in his matching. The same judges later rated the agreement between the Rorschach interpretations and case-study abstracts in respect to the following four broad categories:

1. Intellectual aspects
2. Personality, emotional aspects
3. Diagnosis
4. Total picture

The summary of percentages of agreement showed an average of 73.0 per cent of "essential agreement"; 21.2 per cent, "fair agreement"; and the remainder, "slight agreement." The highest percentage of essential agreement was achieved in the judgment of intellectual aspects, and the lowest, in diagnosis.

The results justify Krugman's conclusion that there is high validity in the Rorschach method in clinical situations of the type described above. One may also agree with the author that it is probable ". . . that results may even be better when the terminology and concepts used in the various aspects of the clinical study become more uniform and objective." [*15*, p. 68.]

In concluding this section, it must be emphasized that in the hands of trained examiners, the Rorschach has demonstrated a high degree of diagnostic validity. One should not lose sight of the fact that psychiatric diagnoses are far from being "scientific" and, consequently, a comparison with them does not necessarily establish the Rorschach as a thoroughly valid instrument of personality diagnosis. It does prove to be a *useful tool* in clinical diagnosis, considering the status of present-day knowledge of personality and its deviations. In order to avoid a lack of congruence or lack of overlapping in validating studies, it would be well to adopt Rosenzweig's [*26*] suggestions concerning a comparison of controlled psychiatric reports with Rorschach interpretations. Only then can we establish the validity of the Rorschach in terms of personality structure and dynamics rather than in terms of diagnostic labeling. The last two studies reported in this section are beginnings in the right direction. Though the case studies were not systematized, an attempt to relate them to several aspects of the Rorschach was made.

THE MOLECULAR APPROACH

Studies employing the molecular approach attempt to investigate the validity of single Rorschach variables or combinations of them against certain aspects of the subject's behavior.   These studies may be subdivided into two groups: direct, validating studies and indirect factor validation.

To the first group belongs the study of Ruesch and Finesinger [27] on the relationship between color responses in the Rorschach and the use of color in drawing.   Fifty-five psychiatric patients (21 of whom were feeble-minded) and five normal adults constituted their experimental population.   In addition to the regular administration of the Rorschach, the subjects were asked to sketch two drawings.   One, with ordinary pencil, "in response to a suggestion of sadness"; the other, with color crayons, "in response to a suggestion of joy."   Color "scores" for the drawings were devised on the basis of type of color and size of drawing.   These scores correlated very highly with the number of color responses on the Rorschach.   A correlation between color responsiveness on the Rorschach and use of color in drawing was thus demonstrated, constituting a behavioral check on Rorschach behavior and a demonstration of consistency.

The authors were not content with this operational relation. They proceeded on another level, that of interpolation of the meaning of interpretation.   They concluded that ". . . extratensive type of Rorschach used much larger areas in the color drawings than did the introversive type of the Rorschach."   [27, p. 387.]   The extratensive-introversive dichotomy refers to the direction of the *experience balance (Erlebnistypus)* described by Rorschach himself. There was demonstrated not only a relationship between color in both situations (drawing and Rorschach), but also the expansiveness of the extratensive type (based on Rorschach) in the use of color in drawing.   Another behavioral correlate was the relationship between high color scores (drawings and Rorschach) and high values for the use and selection of red.

As part of a study of the reliability of *Erlebnistypus,* Thornton and Guilford [30] correlated Rorschach factors such as M, M per cent, C, C per cent, and log M/C with scores on the Nebraska Personality Inventory, which purports to measure introversion-extraversion, among several other characteristics.   The Rorschach was administered to two groups of college students totaling 100.   The instructions and time limits imposed upon the subjects actually varied from the standard Rorschach procedure.   No significant relationship between the above-mentioned Rorschach variables and the Nebraska Personality Inventory were noted. The variations in experimental procedure and the doubtful validity of the Personality Inventory itself make questionable the value of studies of this type and their contribution to further understanding of the Rorschach test. Moreover, as pointed out by Piotrowski, Rorschach definitions of introversion and extraversion are quite different from those used in questionnaires; for this reason the results are not comparable [20, p. 444].

Gustav [10] set herself the task of determining the relationships between the Rorschach variables and items on several personality scales. In the first step of the experiment, she correlated inventory items with some 20 Rorschach variables in responses from a group of 15 female college students. Thirteen variables showed some relationship with some items, and a combined inventory of 284 items was devised on this basis. A second group of students was used in order to devise inventory scores by means of which the 13 Rorschach variables might be estimated. Later, the scoring method was employed in the investigation of a third group of subjects. Statistically significant estimates were obtained for factors W per cent, D per cent, Fc, H, FM and Total C. One would wish that the investigator had been able to list the inventory items that corresponded to these predicted variables. Only then might the validity of the interpretation of those variables in Rorschach work be checked and examined. As an initial research step, Gustav's procedure is a contribution, but it does not go far enough. Mere correlation is not indicative of rationale. However, Gustav implicitly accepted the Rorschach hypotheses and was mainly interested in devising an inventory that would predict, on a large scale, the variables of the test.

Wishner [35] made a correlational study of intellectual indicators with 42 neurotic patients. Some 17 "reputed intelligence indicators" were correlated with the various subscores of the Wechsler-Bellevue test. The three most significant intelligence indicators on the Rorschach turned out to be R (number of responses), W, and Z (Beck's organization score). Contrary to expectations, $F +$ per cent, in this group, did not seem to be an adequate index of intelligence. It must be borne in mind that this was a special, selected group of subjects (neurotics). The obtained results must be considered as strictly applicable to this type of patient. No broad generalizations for the Rorschach as a whole can be made. All that can be said is that some of the clinically used indicators of intelligence in the Rorschach have been validated, for this group, against a psychometric tool that purports to measure intelligence.

As for the molecular approach, it may be said that although it lifts certain factors out of their context in the Rorschach, some worth-while validating data have been obtained. Though some of the studies have been unclear and inadequate in the conclusiveness of their results, others have added validity to the Rorschach method. We note the need to define the concepts of the Rorschach as well as of the measures (say, introversion-extraversion) against which an attempt is made to validate it. More knowledge and investigation of larger populations, within the normal range, and at various age levels are needed as a backdrop against which the results of mildly and severely pathological groups, as well as those of other selected groups, may be projected.

THE DIRECT EXPERIMENTAL APPROACH

Special Experimental Conditions. By varying the conditions of the subjects themselves in an experimental situation, it is possible to estimate the effects of the altered condition or conditions upon the remaining variables of that situation. Following this reasoning, Rorschach examinations have been administered to subjects under hypnosis, under the influence of drugs, and in other special conditions. A considerable amount of data concerning validity can be obtained by this method.

One of the earliest researches of this type was executed by Sarbin [28] by placing a single subject under hypnosis. Four Rorschach records were obtained; one, while the subject was in a waking state, and the three others under hypnosis (as self, Madame Curie, and Mae West). All that can be said concerning the results of this study is that considerable change in a number of the factors occurred from one state to another. It is difficult, however, to relate the changes to the self-identifications of the subject. The only striking changes were noted in the content of the Rorschachs when under the suggestions of being Mae West and of being Madame Curie (clothing vs. scientific content). Moreover, we agree with the author that a single case should not be used as a basis for generalization. The *method* is suggestive.

Another single case study [*17*] dealt with the effects of hypnotically suggested mood changes on the Rorschach performance. The original Rorschach record of the subject in a waking state was compared with her response under a variety of moods suggested while under hypnosis. The induced moods were reactive depression, elation, hypochondria, simple depression, anxiety caused by sexual conflicts, and a state of panicky fear. These states were suggested with a view of duplicating some of the commonly found disturbances in mental disorder. An analysis of the various records indicated shifts and changes in the expected direction (observed in actual psychopathology) and resulted in ". . . validation of some of our interpretive and diagnostic 'signposts'." [*17*, p. 144.] Again, this is a report on a single case. The results are *suggestive*.

The administration of sodium amytal ordinarily changes patients who are resistive and withdrawn into cooperative, friendly, communicative persons. The effects of sodium amytal were observed in 14 cases where the patients had not given adequate Rorschach records under ordinary conditions of administration [*13*]. The patients who had rejected five or more of the cards responded to nearly all of them while under the effects of sodium amytal. In addition to the production of adequate records (that is, more responses), accurate diagnosis on the basis of the Rorschach (previously impossible) was made on 12 of the cases, when compared with the previous clinical diagnosis. Thus, no important changes in the qualitative aspects of the records were caused by the sodium amytal, though some changes did occur. The main effect was that of baring the accurate and undisturbed personality structure.

Taking advantage of the amnesic condition following electric shock treatment (EST), Kelley and co-workers [*14*] compared the pre-shock Rorschach records with the post-shock records, obtained two hours later. Of 30 cases, 12 were chosen who had "complete amnesia without confusion." These cases represented a variety of disorders: circular psychoses, schizophrenia, and psychoneuroses. The subjects, after EST, were unable to remember the cards, the instructions, the examiner, or the test in general. This special condition gave the authors the opportunity to check the reliability of the test by re-examination without involving the memory factor. They concluded ". . . that all areas and determinants are essentially stable . . . a change of only an occasional single response, except for . . . *R. .D. .F%*, the per cent of responses in cards VIII, IX and X and the popular *(P)* responses." [*14*, p. 42.] No statistical measures of variablity were reported, but it *is* notable that changes did occur in the aforementioned variables. These changes may not necessarily have been due to the instability of the Rorschach as a measure, but to certain cerebral changes that certainly must have occurred during EST, though the amnesia was apparently "without confusion." This critique does not detract from the stability of the Rorschach determinants but focuses needed attention upon the effects of EST upon personality variables.

Williams [*33*] reported an experiment in which he attempted to study the effects of stress on intellectual control and associated Rorschach factors. Intellectual control was defined as ". . . that degree to which an individual may efficiently utilize his mental processes in the face of strong emotional demands." [P. 23.] *F*+ per cent and the color reaction are the two Rorschach factors most concerned with this type of control. After having administered the Rorschach to his 25 subjects (male students), Williams had them practice the Digit Symbol subtest of the Wechsler-Bellevue Scale. Then, he established a basal performance level in this test, under optimal conditions. The final step consisted in performance on the Digit Symbol test under extremely trying and stressful situations (physical discomfort, noise, social scrutiny and disapproval, and so on). The decrement in the stressful performance period (as compared with performance under optimal conditions) showed an $r = -.724$ with *F*+ per cent in the color cards. Both correlations are highly significant and establish the validity of these two Rorschach factors in intellectual control as originally defined by the investigator. From the viewpoint of methodology, this study demonstrates that Rorschach variables can be well selected and defined for experimental validation.

The excellent study on color shock by Brosin and Fromm [*6*] is somewhat different in design from the others discussed here. The altered or controlled conditions of the subjects were not produced experimentally, but were inherent in their organic makeup. However, the study does meet the criterion of a changed variable.

Twelve subjects with different types of color blindness were examined by means of the Rorschach test. A clinical evaluation of each case as to the presence of neurosis or psychosis was made. The presence or absence of color shock in each Rorschach record was also determined. Despite the fact that the subjects were color-blind, color shock occurred to a considerable degree in those whose clinical diagnosis was that of neurosis. "It was found that the presence of a *significant amount of color shock* corresponded to the independent clinical diagnosis of neurosis." [*6*, p. 51.] These findings left the authors compelled to advance three hypotheses regarding the cause of color shock in the color-blind subjects:

1. Sufficient retention of color vision caused the shock.

2. The possibility of a physical stimulus causing a physiological response in the central nervous system, without consciousness on the part of the subject.

3. Color perception of the color-blind as "psychological grey" may have different characteristics from the black-white variety of grey.

These hypotheses need further proof. Doubtlessly, this crucial experiment has raised the important question as to whether the color shock phenomenon is actually due to color perception or to some additional factors. Further doubts and some insight into the concept may be obtained from other experiments to be cited below.

Variation of Test Procedure or of the Stimulus Itself. Rabin and Sanderson [*22*] administered the Rorschach to two groups of subjects, 17 in each group (student nurses). The order of presenting the cards was reversed in one of the groups, beginning with Card X and ending with Card I. Thus, instead of beginning with an achromatic card (I), according to the usual procedure, a chromatic one (X) was presented first. In the second group, the usual order of presentation was followed. The order of presentation of the first test was reversed upon retest for both groups some two months later. The authors then set themselves the task of investigating the effects of the change of the "temporal gestalt" of card presentation on the productivity, response time, shock, and other Rorschach factors. The problem of shock was subjected to a particularly crucial test, since by changing the order of the cards, the element of surprise and suddenness of shift from noncolored to colored cards had been eliminated. The evidence was that some cards were "objectively" more difficult and less productive than others. The hypothesis was advanced that the constricted productivity and prolonged time (shock indicators) may actually have been due to the greater difficulty of association to the more formal aspects of the blots. The authors stated, in part, that color shock may ". . . be due to actually greater difficulty of certain cards and lesser potentiality of others to evoke responses." [22, p. 225.] Additional analysis of the response times at crucial "shift" points (from achromatic to chromatic and vice versa) did not substantiate Baumgarten-Tramer's [2] hypothesis concerning their importance in Rorschach performance. As a by-product, evidence was given that the $M:C$ ratio (experience balance) was ". . . a highly stable index in the large majority of individuals, regardless of the order in which the test is presented." Few changes in this index, from test to retest were observed, despite the change in procedure.

A study by Wallen, primarily concerned with the nature of color shock [31] had for its basic assumption the relationship between dislike for a card and shock. A total of 419 subjects (in military training) was employed in this experiment. It consisted of seven subgroups, representing the seven steps of the experiment. The first three steps consisted in presenting the Rorschach cards to three groups of normal subjects in different temporal order, one by one, and asking them ". . . just tell me whether you like it or whether you dislike it." First, the order was the usual one (I–X); the second step reversed the order (X–I); still a different order constituted the third step (X, I, II, and so on). The results showed that the order of presentation of the cards had an effect on their being liked: ". . . if they appeared late in the series, they were more popular . . ."

The fourth step was to test the effect of position of the cards upon their being liked or disliked. The 58 subjects of another group were shown the cards in an inverted position. Obtained results revealed that the position had little effect on likes or dislikes. The cards were also presented to a group of 30 unstable (mostly neurotic) men who showed a general trend of less liking for color than was found with normal men. A reliable difference between unstable and normal men was obtained only for chromatic cards II and IX and for achromatic card VI.

For the two final steps, the cards were photographed so that all became achromatic. The achromatic cards were presented to a group of unstable subjects and to a group of normal subjects. A significant decrease in the popularity ("liked") of the last three cards was found in the normal group. This was not true of cards II and III, however. In the unstable group, card VI remained quite unpopular. Cards III, IX, and X were reliably less popular with this group than with the normals. It appeared, therefore, that some of the color cards aroused unpleasant affects even when they were achromatic. It was the investigator's hypothesis, therefore, that ". . . the contour and organization of a blot is an outstanding determiner of affective reaction." [*31*, p. 352.]

A supplementary study with two more groups (normal and unstable) to whom pairs of cards II, III, VIII, IX, and X were presented in the ordinary (chromatic) and achromatic versions, showed that with the exception of cards VIII and X, the chromatic members of the pairs were "markedly less popular" with the unstable than with the normal group.

Thus, if the assumption of the relationship between dislike and color shock is to be accepted, the critique of color shock as presented here is quite valid; that is, not only is the color responsible for the "shock," but an objective difference in the affective reactions to color between stable and unstable persons has been demonstrated.

Lazarus [*16*] also attacked the problem of color shock by means of an achromatic reproduction of the Rorschach series. His two groups of subjects (high school seniors) totaling 100 were given the group Rorschach. One group was given the ordinary series of slides (representing the Rorschach cards) first, followed by the noncolor version six weeks later. The order was reversed in the second group. When the Rorschach scoring categories for the color and noncolor administrations were compared, the only significant difference was seen in an increased F per cent in the latter. This was to be expected, since the opportunities for variability in response determination had been reduced. The comparison of the records of 30 of the subjects who showed color shock also indicated an increase in P in the noncolor series.

The obtained records were also scored for 12 indices of color shock (response time was omitted, since it was a group examination). Only one of the indices, lowest response total, was significantly higher in the color series for the entire population. In the 30 color shock subjects, the index "appearance of poor form answers" decreased in the noncolor series. This was mainly due to a reduction of *CF-* and *FC*-responses, present in the color series. Since the first index also appeared mostly in the chromatic cards, the author believed that "the term color shock may be a misnomer." Finally, each of the slides of the series was ranked for each of the shock indices. When a correlation between the frequencies of the indices for the color and noncolor series was obtained, it was quite significant statistically; thus, it was concluded "that color played a minimal role, if any, in producing the 'color shock' indices." [*16*, p. 7.] A difference in "difficulty" of the slides was also hypothesized.

Despite the objections that may be raised against this study on the ground that the results were obtained with the group Rorschach, which is really a different test, the criticism of our present thinking in relation to color shock is well taken. It is in line with some of the problems raised by Brosin and Fromm [*6*], Rabin and Sanderson, and others [*22, 31*] mentioned above.

Organismic and Physiological Correlates. The few studies to be described in this section are not concerned primarily with the investigation or validation of Rorschach categories, but with an objective description of somatic events concomitant with Rorschach performance. The evidence obtained, however, may indirectly and by inference be applied to a more thorough understanding of the psychophysiological processes underlying the test.

Blake [*5*] photographed the eye movements of 20 college students during Rorschach administration. The head of the subject and the stimulus rack for the cards were fixed at a standard distance. The eye movements for each card were photographed from the time of presentation to the time of production of the first response. The mean number of fixations per card and the mean of their durations correlated positively with the standard order of their presentation. The tendency of the majority of the fixations was to center above the horizontal axes of the design and to deviate from the center as time went on. Areas receiving later fixations after early centering seemed to be determined by the characteristics of the card involved. Early fixations facilitated the perception of the blot as a total gestalt. Finally, the early fixations were shorter in duration than the final ones, indicating an early ". . . inspectional, while later ones show a more reflecting attitude." [5, p. 169.]

Autonomic changes in the body during Rorschach performance were reported in some studies and projected in others. A briefly reported investigation [24] of changes in palmar skin resistance (30 normal and psychoneurotic subjects) stated that "the autonomic-electrical response differed significantly." Particular differences were evidenced in cards I and VII.

A more extensive study carried out by Frost [9] set for its purpose the investigation of the relationship between the galvanic skin responses and Rorschach responses in normalcy and schizophrenia. A continuous GSR record during Rorschach administration was obtained for 20 normal males and 20 male schizophrenics. Both groups were well matched for age, education, socio-economic status, and so on. The accumulative shift from the bodily resistance level was used as a measure of the ". . . organism's adaptive mobilization and autonomic involvement . . ." The most significant findings concerning the relationship between the GSR and the Rorschach were as follows:

1. The greater number of Rorschach responses in the normal subjects was associated with their significantly greater GSR. Conversely, the lower verbal production of the schizophrenics was correlated with their lower GSR.
2. Greater GSR in normals was associated with their form-dominated Rorschach responses, and less GSR with the "form-subordinated" responses. The exact reverse was true in the schizophrenics.
3. The schizophrenic GSR at the first Rorschach response to each card was greater than the mean GSR of all the responses of that card; the reverse was true in the case of the normal subjects.

The parallel interpretations of the chief findings enumerated above were suggested by Frost as follows:

1. Normal subjects showed greater participation and involvement in the test situation.
2. The normal subjects were capable of better control, while the schizophrenics showed a breakdown of the control when "more meaningful" stimuli were involved (that is, form-subordinated responses).
3. Schizophrenic subjects were not able to delay "their impulse to respond to the most meaningful stimulus as are the normal subjects."

Additional studies involving autonomic functions during Rorschach performance may be mentioned. Balloch [1] has attempted to determine the effects of varying the degree of shading contrast in ink blots upon productivity, shading responses, pulse rate, blood pressure, and rate of respiration. Wishner's project [34] on the relationship between physiological tension and Rorschach estimation of anxiety includes, in addition to the autonomic measures mentioned, electrocardiographic, electoencephalographic, and several myographic measurements. These and other studies show that direct experimentation with the Rorschach and its somatic correlates is a research area of high potential.

The direct experimental approaches described in the last few pages offer considerable confirmatory evidence as to the validity of a number of Rorschach determinants and Rorschach interpretations. Particularly convincing is the type of experiment that deals with circumscribed areas of the test, defines them well, and checks them against well-defined behavioral situations. Since interpretation of Rorschach production is independent of the intent of the subject involved, its relationship to measurements of autonomic involuntary processes is of particular interest. Thus far, unfortunately, data in this area are still meager and limited. However, the data that are available at present seem to confirm some of the claims of the Rorschach workers. The experimental critiques to which such a cardinal concept as color shock has been subjected suggest the need for a more careful definition of this aspect of the test and still greater care of its application in interpretation. The critiques are not yet conclusive, but raise considerable doubt and should alert the thoughtful and scientific Rorschach worker.

DISCUSSION AND SUMMARY

From the foregoing, it may be noted that many are the roads that lead to Rome. The molar, molecular, and direct experimental approaches have made valuable contributions to the Rorschach test on its gradual path of transformation from an empirical and practical procedure to a scientifically and experimentally founded method of personality analysis.

Basically, research with the Rorschach method has been and will be carried on in two directions. The vast majority of the several hundred publications on the Rorschach test deal with concomitance of individual or aggregate phenomena of the test with clinical and nonclinical groups of known general characteristics. These are mainly, in a way, "descriptive" studies. Unfortunately, as was pointed out elsewhere [21], our present statistical methods are inadequate for making the various "concomitances" or combinations of "signs" fool-proof and convincing. Such studies as that of Buhler and others, [7] in which they expressed faith "that typical personality pictures in Rorschach terms can be described statistically," may be worthwhile. However, as suggested in a critique of the same study [18], there is a need for adherence to the strict and experimental conditions of the administration and scoring of the test. Neither should there be an admixture of "clinical experience" interpolated in purely quantitative data. Even if various "signs" and scores based on them are absolutely indicative of a certain diagnosis, little contribution is made to the understanding of the underlying processes that make the test diagnostic. To be sure, this type of study serves a practical clinical purpose, but it does not lead to ultimate scientific enlightenment concerning the instrument. The hundreds of studies that represent this or similar methods are making but one small step beyond Rorschach's original empiricism.

The comparatively small number of studies cited in the present chapter, with few exceptions, represent another direction, new and relatively recent. This direction is mainly characterized by the experimental rather than the correlational and "diagnostic concomitance" approach. When diagnoses are validated, they are validated not descriptively, but by means of "blind" interpretations, rating of judges, and so on. Conditions within and without the test are noted and varied experimentally. When psychological concomitance is involved, it is sufficiently well circumscribed and accurately measurable. Considerable promise is to be found in these methods. Further desirable accomplishments may be mentioned, though the list is by no means exhaustive:

1. More "blind" validating diagnostic studies involving minor differences of subgroups within a larger general diagnostic group (that is, subgroups within the general psychoneurotic group, and so on).

2. "Controlled" clinical descriptions with which Rorschach interpretations may be compared; this means that care should be taken that the clinical material deals with the same factors as the Rorschach interpretation, so that congruence of interpretation is possible.

3. Ingenious experimental designs that would by the performance involved define clearly certain activities corresponding to clearly defined Rorschach hypotheses represented by certain determinants.

4. Statistical methods to represent quantitatively the gestalt of the Rorschach pattern and the dynamic and modifying relationships between its various constituent factors.

REFERENCES

1. Balloch, J. C., "An experimental investigation of the effect of the degree of shading contrast in ink-blots on verbal and physiological responses." East Lansing, Mich.: Michigan State College Library, Ph.D. thesis, 1950.

2. Baumgarten-Tramer, F., "Der Rorschach-Test in Lichte der experimentellem Psychologie." *Schweiz. Arch. Neurol. Psychiat.*, 1944, 54, 3–41.

3. Beck, S. J., "Error, symbol, and method in the Rorschach test." *J. Abn. & Soc. Psychol.*, 1942, 37, 83–103.

4. Benjamin, J. D., and Ebaugh, F. G., "The diagnostic validity of the Rorschach test." *Am. J. Psychiat.*, 1938, 94, 1163–1178.

5. Blake, R. R., "Ocular activity during administration of the Rorschach test." *J. Clin. Psychol.*, April, 1948, 4, 159–169.

6. Brosin, H. W., and Fromm, E. O., "Rorschach and color blindness." *Rorschach Res. Exch.*, 1940, 4, 39–70.

7. Buhler, C., Buhler, K., and Lefever, D. W., *Development of the Basic Rorschach Score with a Manual of Directions.* Rorschach Standardization Study. 1948. Los Angeles. Published by the authors.

8. Faterson, H. F., and Klopfer, B., "A survey of psychologists' opinions concerning the Rorschach method." *Rorschach Res. Exch.*, 1945, 9, 23–29.

9. Frost, C. F., *The Relationship Between the Verbal and Galvanic Skin Responses to the Rorschach Test for Schizophrenic and Normal Subjects.* Worcester, Mass.: Clark University, doctoral dissertation, 1948.

10. Gustav, A., "Estimation of Rorschach scoring categories by means of an objective inventory." *J. Psychol.*, 1946, 22, 253–260.

11. Hertz, M. R., "The validity of the Rorschach method." *Am. J. Orthopsychiat.*, 1941, 11, 512–520.

12. Hertz, M. R., and Rubenstein, B. B., "A comparison of three 'blind' Rorschach analyses." *Am. J. Orthopsychiat.*, 1939, 9, 295–314.

13. Kelley, D. M., and Levine, K., "Rorschach studies during sodium amytal narcoses," (abstract). *Rorschach Res. Exch.*, 1940, 4, 146.

14. Kelley, D. M., Margulies, H., and Barreva, S. E., "The stability of the Rorschach method as demonstrated in electric convulsive therapy cases." *Rorschach Res. Exch.*, 1941, 5, 35–43.

15. Krugman, J. I., "A clinical validation of the Rorschach with problem children." *Rorschach Res. Exch.*, 1942, 6, 61–70.

16. Lazarus, R. S., "The influence of color on the protocol of the Rorschach test." *J. Abn. & Soc. Psychol.*, 1949, 44, 506–516.

17. Levine, K. N., Grassi, J. R., and Gerson, M. J., "Hypnotically induced mood changes in the verbal and graphic Rorschach: a case study." *Rorschach Res. Exch.*, 1943, 7, 130–144.

18. Molish, Herman. (Review of Reference 7, above). *Am. J. of Psychotherapy*, 1949, 3, 130–135.

19. Munroe, R. L., "Considerations on the place of the Rorschach in the field of general psychology." *Rorschach Res. Exch.*, 1945, 9, 30–40.

20. Piotrowski, Z., "The reliability of Rorschach's Erlebnistypus." *J. Abn. & Soc. Psychol.*, 1937, 32, 439–445.

21. Rabin, A. I., "Statistical problems involved in Rorschach patterning." *J. Clin. Psychol.*, Jan. 1950, VI, 1, 19–21.

22. Rabin, A. I., and Sanderson, M. H., "An experimental inquiry into some Rorschach procedures." *J. Clin. Psychol.*, 1947, 3, 216–225.

23. Rickers-Ovsiankina, M., "Some theoretical considerations regarding the Rorschach method." *Rorschach Res. Exch.*, 1943, 7, 41–53.

24. Rockwell, F. V., Welch, L., Fisichelli, V., and Kubis, J., "Changes in palmar skin resistance during the Rorschach experiment." *Am. Psychologist*, 1946, 1, 287.

25. Rorschach, H., *Psychodiagnostics* (translation by P. Lemkau and B. Kronenburg). Berne: Verlag Hans Huber, 1942.

26. Rosenzweig, S., "Outline of a cooperative project for validating the Rorschach test." *Am. J. Orthopsychiat.*, 1935, 5, 121–123.

27. Ruesch, J., and Finesinger, J. E., "The relation of the Rorschach color response to the use of color in drawings." *Psychosom. Med.*, 1941, 3, 370–388.

28. Sarbin, T. R., "Rorschach patterns under hypnosis." *Am. J. Orthopsychiat.*, 1939, 9, 315–318.

29. Siegel, M. G., "The diagnostic and prognostic validity of the Rorschach test in a child guidance clinic." *Am. J. Orthopsychiat.*, 1948, 18, 119–133.

30. Thornton, G. R. and Guilford, J. P., "The reliability and meaning of Erlebnistypus scores in the Rorschach test." *J. Abn. & Soc. Psychol.*, 1936, 31, 324–330.

31. Wallen, Richard, "The nature of color shock." *J. Abn. & Soc. Psychol.*, 1948, 43, 346–356.

32. White, Robert W., "The Interpretation of Imaginative Productions," in Hunt, J. M., *Personality and the Behavior Disorders,* Vol. I. New York: Ronald Press, 1944, Chapter 6.

33. Williams, Meyer, "An experimental study of intellectual control under stress and associated Rorschach factors." *J. Consult. Psychol.,* 1947, 11, 21–29.

34. Wishner, J., "The relationship between physiological measures of tension and Rorschach estimation of anxiety" (in preparation).

35. Wishner, J., "Rorschach intellectual indicators in neurotics." *Am. J. Orthopsychiat.,* 1948, 18, 265–279.

36. Young, R. A., and Higginbotham, S. A., "Behavior checks on the Rorschach method." *Am. J. Orthopsychiat.,* 1942, 12, 87–94.

37. Zubin, J., *Manual of Projective and Cognate Techniques.* Madison, Wis.: College Typing Company, 1948 (Mimeographed). (Printed edition: *Quantitative Techniques and Methods in Abnormal Psychology.* New York: Columbia University Press, 1950.)

PART III

Varieties of Tests of Personality Mechanisms

CHAPTER 6

The Four-Picture Test

D. J. VAN LENNEP, PH.D.

A THEORY OF PROJECTION

Nowadays in America, *projection* is used to include all kinds of utterances and expressions of the subject as far as these are *personal* and not decided by the rules of his society. This is definitely a broadening of the concept of projection as Freud [8] first used it as a technical term in 1894. He meant principally the tendency, under certain circumstances, to attribute to other persons characteristics, emotional structures, and social relationships that might be more relevant to the critic himself than to the other persons. Since then, however, the term has also been used for entirely different utterances, which are phenomena of a quite different structure. The concept has thus acquired at least five different meanings, and because of this, the typical characteristics of the phenomenon that Freud called projection have somewhat faded into the background. We think that this is not a gain, but a loss. Psychology has no need of a mixture of categories; the need is for sharper differentiation. Therefore, we should prefer the term to retain its original denotation.

In my book on projection phenomena [15], we have discussed the various meanings of the concept of projection more thoroughly; in this chapter we will limit ourselves to the demarcation of the original meaning as compared with two meanings in which the word is nowadays used, especially in American writings.

In the first place, *projection* is also used when the *affect* itself is not attributed to another person, but when it deforms the outside world to such a degree that it finds its correlate again there. When I am frightened, for instance, it may be that I ascribe fear to

149

another's face.   According to us, that is a real projection phenomenon in the true sense of the word.   But it may also be that I call
that other face *frightening*.   In that case, my fear-affect has created
its correlate object in the outer world.

In this connection I would draw attention to the well-known
experiments of Sanford [23] in 1936 and 1937, and to that of Murray
[19] in 1933, both of which I believe to be relevant to the fact
that our affects, especially when they are very strong, have a
tendency to deform the outer world so greatly that the affect can
find its correlate there.

Sears [25] speaks of motivationally determined perception and
very rightly distinguishes this from projection in the sense of
attributing characteristics to others.   But unfortunately few have
followed Sears' example.   This distinction has not escaped most
European psychologists, but few have come to the necessary conclusions for the concept of projection.   Piaget introduced the very
unfortunate term *projection de réciproque* [21].   When a child is
afraid of fire, he says somewhere, then it is not the fear-affect
that is projected, but the feeling is objectified and the child projects
the reciprocal state of that fear into the fire: angriness.   This
explanation, of course, is really no explanation at all, and makes
this particular phenomenon no clearer.

The human being, however, is forever seeking the correlates of
his affect, indeed, the most adequate correlates.   Sometimes, as a
result of an unusually strong affect, an illusory change-over of the
outside world occurs: a chance object is regarded as the right correlate of the affect.   But this psychological happening is certainly
not comparable with assigning the affect itself to another.   When
I am frightened and unjustly call another's face frightening, my fear
finds its motive in the fear-inspiring face.   Consciousness is always
conscious of something: being afraid of John is the same as finding
John frightening.   Now, it is doubtless true that I may get to know
something of someone's affect if I know what the correlate of that
affect is.   If somebody takes a loaf of bread from among a thousand
objects, the chances are that he is hungry.   In the selection of the
loaf he will certainly reveal himself.   But this is not therefore a
projection.   It is, of course, quite natural to construct tests based
on this phenomenon, to try to get the subject to choose the most

adequate correlates for his affects from a large number of possibilities. The Szondi test is partly founded on this principle. But from our point of view, the Szondi test is not really a projection test in the strict sense of the word.

Application of the principle becomes more dubious, however, when analysis of handwriting is included among the projection techniques. For then, by degrees, every utterance, every revelation, every expression, is called a projection. The concept of projection becomes so diluted that it is of no more use to us and we might as well do without it altogether.

For every projection is indeed utterance, but each utterance is certainly not a projection, and particularly not that which is called a person's expression. Each expression supposes a partnership, a reciprocity, and it is just this reciprocity that must be denied to the projective utterance. In nothing is the nature of a projection more clearly shown than in contrast with real self-expression. This contrast has been remarked by various authors, among others, Bellak [3], who distinguishes between adaptive, expressive, and projective behavior. Perls, too, in his *Ego, Hunger and Aggression* [20], has devoted a chapter to projection, in which he divides projection from expressive utterances: "A healthy mental metabolism requires development in the direction of expression and not projection. The healthy character *expresses* his emotions and ideas, the paranoid character projects them." In his conception, however, an important criterion for all true expression is lacking, namely, that every expression presupposes communication. Expression is not merely the way in which I do something (Bellak), but it certainly concerns the content of what I express, and the fact that in expressing it, I impart it to another, consciously or unconsciously. In other words, expression only makes sense in behavior that may be seen as *communicative*. Expression, unconscious as well as conscious, is a *means* of communication, and this concerns both the how and the what of expression.

Now we come to the projection itself, at least that which we think ought to come under the heading of a true projection. It is not, therefore, a projection if, when we are frightened, we really express this fear, in whatsoever way, to a fellow being; it is not a projection either when we, looking for a motive, call a person frightening, as this still implies a certain form of communication; it is projection when we say he is frightened. That is our own private fear projected into him.

For we now use the outer world not as correlate of our affect, but as the analogon of our own affective structure. The other person becomes the bearer of our own affect, he becomes completely separated from his own subjectivity (which to us is unpredictable) and is used as object, as a "stooge" for our own longings and thoughts or a peg to hang them on. As Aeppli so aptly says: "Der Andere ist in der Projektion nicht ein Anderer, sondern ein Symbol, ein Inhaltstrager personlicher seelischer Gegebenheiten." (The other is not another in the projection, only a symbol, a container of personal data of one's own soul [1].)

This use of the outer world as an analogon of ourselves is well known to us all from daily life. It stands to reason that not everything can be used as an analogon of ourselves or of partial structures of ourselves, although choice of analogon is not limited to people or to objects like people. Everything that can serve in any way as a representation of categorical anthropological forms may become a screen for projection. In this way, a solitary tree with some branches stretched up to heaven may be to the lonely man a suitable symbol of his loneliness. A symbol, says Jaspers, "ist eine analogische Anschauung," (is an analogous percept [14]). A distant landscape in a bluish mist may become the symbol of an especially disconsolate frame of mind, but on the other hand, we know from Heidegger [11] that our moods are never free from our views of the things of our world. The mood is actually already "being-in-the-world," says Heidegger. We must note the difference between this tie with the world and the use we make of special aspects of the world to hang our moods and longings on—to project onto. This means that only those objects of the outer world can serve as a screen for projection, that in some measure symbolize an individual projection of being. "That is why," says Freud in another place, "we do not project into the blue" [9]; but in the first instance, we project from a stimulus that arouses in us the feeling to be projected. This, then, is the necessary limitation of every projection test, which, however polyvalently constructed it may be, must always be stimulating, and because of this can never be universal. But I shall refer to this later. The person projecting therefore makes an analogous use of the outer world. He is not "open to the world," but he repeats himself on a world that can give him nothing new. He *does not communicate* with another, because this means being open to the difference of another. He uses the other as an analogon of himself, and in so doing, *places himself at a distance* from the other. Proceeding from this fact, we have repeatedly shown in our studies on the psychology of projection that *projection is noncommunicative behavior.* One must therefore pay constant attention to the difference between the outer world that touches him, himself, and by which it is possible, so to say, to read off his mood on the objects from the outer world; and the outer world of which the objects might be symbols according to a chance analogy that makes them serve as representations for the effective creations of the beholder.

It was Ferenczi [6], we believe, who first pointed out that the analogy need be only very slight. An analogy is something the same (resembling something) in strange surroundings, in a strange context. We shall return to this subject shortly, because we believe that it is just the strange surroundings that are necessary to set projection working.

The projecting person makes an analogon completely identical with himself, or with some part of himself, and, of course, this is a method of intercourse with the outer world, which must run parallel to the way of intercourse with oneself.

One can, therefore, be sure that he who projects onto another also, in a certain sense, projects onto himself; that is to say, he is not dealing with himself in the true sense of the word, but distances himself (projects his traits, attributes, or moods) from himself in a false manner. It is our relation to ourself that we repeat in the projection on another. It is not because we have repressed something that we throw it out, but because we remove ourself from it by treating it as quality, objectively. The repression is rather the effect than the cause.

This fixation in "matter"-qualities is what also happens in repression. He who has fixed himself as a whole of qualities, who has diagnosed himself and has stated himself as being this or that, has deprived himself of his freedom, which is necessary to a truly dialectical intercourse with himself. He has divided himself into roles, as Binswanger [5] puts it, and can now do nothing else but repeat this playing of roles in the outer world. The repressed attribute, structure, affect, cannot longer take part in the free development of the personality, not because it is unconscious, but because it is fixed in a special phase and the deprojection begins then, when the emotion or the affect concerned is once more questioned by the ego, and it can once more be taken into intercourse with itself and therefore changes its meaning again and again.

With the human being, the "I" is not completely identical with the "Me" because man is an ex-centric being, (Plessner [22]). The tiresome clinging to oneself that everyone continually feels, and chiefly feels painfully if he has diagnosed himself as guilty or wicked, he endeavors to make good by projection on himself and on others. Thus, we find in someone's projection responses on a projection test, for instance, the way in which he has determined that he sees himself with regard to himself expressed implicitly or explicitly.

This point of view completely agrees with that which Freud developed from the beginning, which regarded the projection mechanism as a defense mechanism. By diagnosing myself (this is, owing to the ex-centric position, already a sort of outer world) as being something or other in the way of *being-what-I-am,* I already feel that *I* am not that. However much I push it away afterwards, or forget it, keep it silent, suppress it, is of no importance. Also, he who is afraid of being something or other and who projects this quality on to the outer world, has by implication made himself the object, he has already projected a quality on to himself and is already thereby shut off from true communication with another, in which he forgets himself in quite a different way, namely by living "ecstatically" in that other. It has over and over again become apparent to us through our projection test, that the degree of consciousness, of knowledge of ourself, has no direct connection with the degree of projection, and that it is definitely incorrect to say, as Jung is never tired of repeating, that only repressions are projected.

Therefore we do not believe that it is true, as Freud at first believed, that projection is outward because the external danger is easier to avoid than the internal. Also, this idea does not appear with the behavior of the paranoid. He feels himself threatened all the time. Finally, he can never escape the danger because he has cut off every possibility of communication. One may really just as well (as, for instance, Fleischman [7] does) explain the "repression" genetically as an analogon of the flight from exterior stimuli.

If a person can be brought to deprojection, for example by psychoanalysis, then he can once more hold intercourse with himself and with others; he accepts himself and others in freedom; he has no more fixation; he is *belehrbar* (teachable), open to change, spontaneous, creative, and there is an actual dialectical contact with others. He is not afraid of himself or of others, he does not consider his qualities congealed, but he *is becoming,* in the true sense, what he *is not.*

These fixations of qualities can also be caused by others. If a parent constantly holds before a child a quality that one should have in the ordinary way of being what one is, a fixation takes place, which among all sorts of other possible consequences may lead to projection of this quality, because, for example, the child learns to deal with himself as if he were untidy, and then also sees the analogon of an untidy person in another, that is to say deals with the other as if the other were untidy.

In this connection it is significant, as Werner Wolff has found out by his remarkable experiments, that a person usually projects into the unrecognized form of his own expression his wish-image or his fear-image. "Thus it was difficult to separate the positive and the negative trend in the wish-image" [26]. (We are reminded in this connection of what Freud wrote about the *"Gegensinn der Urwerte"* [10], and the phenomenon that, as a result of our own experiments, we have named *negative projection.*) The subject expresses this by speaking of himself either in extremely favorable terms or in extremely unfavorable ones. This tendency to extreme qualification is nothing else than the distancing of the ego from itself, which will unavoidably reflect itself in the intercourse with others to whom we shall ascribe both our negative and our positive values.

The projection-urge is nothing else than this distancing-urge, and the consequence is that at the same time we distance ourselves from others. Mounier rightly says, in his *Traité du Caractère (Treatise on Character)*: "Pour nous connaitre nous-même, il faut d'abord nettoyer le monde de cette projection de nous-même, qui nous masque le visage d'autrui et le notre." (In order to know ourselves we must rid the world of this projection of ourselves, which masks for us the face of others and our own [18].)

So also, positively valued qualities are projected. This is in opposition to many authors, among them Freud himself, who saw projection above all as the admission of negatively valued structures. That this is incorrect has already been noticed by v. d. Hoop [*12*], in 1924, and Janet too, gives voice to it in *l'Hallucination du Persécuté*: "Le malade n'attribue pas uniquement aux autres des actions méprisables, qu'il aurait honte d'avoir faites, on le voit souvent attribuer à autrui des actions honorables dont il pourrait être fier." (The sufferer does not attribute to others alone despicable actions that he would be ashamed of doing himself, he is often seen to attribute to others honorable actions of which he might be proud [*13*].)

We must mention briefly a special form of projection that is apparently more complicated than that already named—those cases where the affect aimed at another is not only projected onto that other, but at the same time is again working on the subject himself; for example, a women patient who has erotic feelings toward her doctor thinks via a projection of her feelings that the doctor is in love with her. These complications are not difficult to explain if we take into account the sort of affects that are projected in each separate case. Always with love feelings, the wish for reciprocity is inherent. Loving someone, rightly, says Sartre [*24*], is wishing that the other loves me; that is to say: wishing that the other wished that I loved him, and so on ad infinitum. There is thus no introduction of a separate mechanism for reversion necessary to explain this special case of projection. Allport [2] speaks here of a complementary projection, but this term is superfluous. It is not because the woman patient represses her love for the doctor that this appears outside; the imagined love of the doctor for her gives her an opportunity to motivate her quasi-repellent attitude: she is pursued by the attention of the doctor, as she is also pursued by her own need of love. In the end she treats the doctor as she treats herself. Also where paranoia is based on a so-called latent homosexuality, we see a similar case taking place. It is our relation to ourself that mirrors itself in our relation to our fellow men. Through the fact that the ex-centric position of the human being only implies a *scheinbare Spaltung*, (nonreal split), we are perforce pursued, pressed, haunted by that part of ourself that we, by fixation of it as a quality, try to remove. By denying the homosexuality to himself, the paranoid fixes just this as his own quality with all its consequences. As van den Berg has lately summarized it: "There is indeed nothing of a psychic nature of which a human being is not aware in one way or another" [4]. This knowledge need not be discursive. The relation to the outside world clearly betrays the knowledge, which is so-called unconscious.

From the foregoing, it can now be stated roughly what will work unusually well to further projection—that is, everything that causes fixations, and especially, so-called *frustration*. As soon as we are hampered, blocked, hindered in the attainment of an affective goal, we feel frustrated. The results of frustration have been accurately examined by Maier [17], among others. He names aggression, regression, resignation, but chiefly fixation. His experiments on rats in this connection are impressive and convincing.

But as soon as there is question of fixation with people, the danger of projection is present in a high degree. And we also observe that with experimentally produced projections, the content of the projection is very often connected with fixations that have arisen through frustration in the life history of the patient. Fixations, however, are certainly not the exclusive source of content of projections. Everything can be projected of which the patient, owing to his ex-centric position, has knowledge in one way or another and from which he has tried to distance himself, it may be, by making it ego-inimical, ego-ideal, or ideal-ego. Seeing that one can speak of a projection-urge, a projection-need, the adequate correlate in this case is the person who can be projected onto. And it could be said with some truth that a person consciously or unconsciously seeks for another onto whom he can project himself. In this capacity, the last-named may be envied or feared. Thus, we see that in daily life as well as in projection tests, the true projection often goes hand-in-hand with the search for the correlate of the affect. Naturally, this has contributed greatly to the confusion of the two phenomena. We only have to watch international politics to see that as soon as a power isolates itself, it immediately begins to project itself more.

HISTORY OF THE FOUR-PICTURE TEST

The Four-Picture Test (FPT) came into being in 1930 after various experiments inspired by the projection test of Dr. G. A.

Roemer, of Stuttgart, a pupil and personal assistant of Rorschach. Roemer's test consisted of a complex picture, put together as a photograph montage containing a number of cuttings from photographs, stuck pell-mell onto a piece of cardboard. At first we imitated this method, but the results were not satisfactory; the cut-out pictures were too haphazard, and it was not possible to create sufficient order. After various other attempts, it occurred to us to start from a definitive principle, and to have some pictures drawn to portray just human situations in general, and thus the FPT was made.

The object of this test was to discover a subject's general attitude toward life as quickly as possible, as far as this was determined by his personality structure, by the dynamics of his personality, and, above all, as far as these were set in motion in social situations.

THE RATIONALE OF THE FOUR-PICTURE TEST

Each projection test represents a piece of "world," and however polyvalent this may be by itself, it is also necessarily limited. If one uses a projection test for some time, one learns the extent and possibilities of the test little by little, and one becomes the more convinced that no single test is so universal that it might claim a monopoly. The world of FPT is limited, too, and yet many dynamics can exist in it: love relationships, jealousy, social jars, social ambitions, vengeful feelings, the desire for death for oneself or extinction for one's surroundings, fears, wanderlust, mistrust, longing for one's mother, narcissism, neurotic fatigue, and so on. How is this possible? The underlying idea of the author was this: the polyvalency can be achieved in various ways. The most usual way is to give pictures that cover as large a field as possible, that is to say, those of which experience has taught us, or of which we believe, that they will be the stimuli for as many different dynamics as possible. The method we have followed with the FPT, however, is more or less the opposite: a small number of pictures, which have, however, been kept so general that they can be combined in many different ways. For this purpose, the figures on the pictures must naturally remain vague, show no definite physiognomy, and be presented solely as human figures, so that the characters in the story constructed by their aid might easily be carried over from one picture to the next. As will be shown later in the instructions for FPT, the point is not to make a story from each separate picture, but to tell a story in which all four pictures appear; the choice of the order in which the pictures come is left to the subject. Since only four pictures are used, the choice of the pictures had not only to be kept very general but had also to represent four principal situations. This led of itself, as it were, to the choice of the four pictures shown in Figure 1:

I   II

III   IV

Fig. 1. The Four-Picture Test.

I. *Being together with one other person;* II. *Being personally alone;* III. *Being socially alone;* IV. *Being together with many others in a group.*

The way in which these situations are represented is, of course, somewhat haphazard and may attract criticism. Many will be inclined to suppose that the picture showing the first situation will be taken by everybody to be a conflict situation. Study of the manual will, however, convince the reader that the polyvalency of this picture is especially great, and that it most certainly is not interpreted exclusively as a conflict situation.   The most difficult choice for portrayal is that of the group, because a group is always strongly determined by class.   Therefore, a situation involving a game was chosen, because this is relatively more neutral with regard to class (though not entirely, of course).   The tennis court was taken because it gave the possibility of drawing both players and onlookers; the latter, however, often are interpreted to form a small companionable group by themselves, in which eroticism plays a greater part than interest in the play of others.

The bed was drawn in such a way that it is uncertain whether there are one or more persons lying in it, or nobody at all.   Being alone with oneself is therefore not quite indicated in the picture itself.   In experiments in which a bed was shown with somebody *clearly* sleeping in it, the polyvalency of all four pictures was seen to diminish, and so the vaguer portrayal was kept.

The man by the lamp post symbolizes social loneliness.   The situation is a street, a section of the community, therefore, but this street is empty: the man has temporarily no link with society. This is accentuated by the streaming rain, which makes the situation even more dreary.

In contrast with TAT, for instance, the FPT pictures are colored. This has a twofold aim.   In the first place, the affective value of a colored picture is greater than that of an uncolored one.   It has a stronger appeal.   In the second place, there was the possibility of unifying the mood of the four pictures somewhat by using the same range of colors, which would lighten the intellectually difficult demand of combining them into one story via the affect. The similar colors incline one to see in the four pictures a certain coherence affectively, and thus the intellectual opposition to combining things that have nothing to do with one another is weakened. The artist has been very successful in creating a contrast between the bright, sunny weather on the tennis court and the more or less somber atmosphere of the other pictures; thus, in spite of the same palette, there is contrast and at the same time pictorial unity when the pictures are looked at simultaneously.

In the construction of this projection test, we have also striven to make it as real a test of projection per se as possible.   For, according to us, not everything that presents itself is suitable to produce real projections; but this remark is, of course, connected with the theory concerning the essence of projection, which we have discussed above.

INSTRUCTIONS FOR THE FOUR-PICTURE TEST

If direct observation of the subject is preferred, the technique is as follows. The examiner places before the subject, on a table 60 x 60 cm, or about two feet square, the four pictures, close together as in Figure 1, in this order: I–II above, with III–IV directly below them, giving the impression of a whole. The table must be otherwise bare, so that no distracting objects can influence the total impression. The following instructions are then given: "Here you see four totally unrelated pictures. Try to build up a story that combines these four pictures and brings them into relation with one another. You can choose the order in which they are to appear, starting and finishing where you like. You can start here, or here" (pointing to the pictures in an arbitrary order). From here on, the examiner writes down all the utterances of the subject, even those remarks that have no connection with the subject's story.

If the examiner is in doubt as to whether the instructions have been clearly understood, and in all cases where young people are under test, he can repeat them, or add: "Illustrations are usually drawn for an existing story, but I want you to do exactly the opposite; make a story out of these pictures." The investigator, avoiding any appearance of pressing for a quick answer, concludes with: "Look at the pictures as long as you like; there is plenty of time."

In the manual there is further detailed instruction about the other ways in which the instructions can be given. Every psychologist can choose from these the best method for his purpose. As with similar projection tests, the FPT can be taken orally, or the subject can write down the story himself after receiving the instructions. With the FPT, the latter method has great advantages, although it is a pity that the subject cannot then be so well observed during his composition. With the written method, the pictures are shown to the subject for one minute in the usual order and then taken away. The test then becomes a complete imagination test and the memory works as a filter as well.   Also the written method takes practically no time from the examiner and the subject can set down his ideas on paper without being inhibited by the presence of the examiner.   If there is time, a combination of the two methods is very fruitful.   In that case the subject should write the story, say, in the morning, and at the end of the day, or the following day, he should be asked:

"Do you remember what you wrote about those four pictures this morning? Tell me the outline of it." Then he is asked to construct an *entirely different* oral story from the same pictures.

If necessary, one might continue and get the subject to relate the possible connections of different pairs of pictures with a prescribed sequence.   This whole oral procedure is of course best recorded electrically.   With some subjects the pictures turn out to have changed significantly in their memory in a comparatively short time.

Comparison of the written story with the synthesis made later by the subject himself, and comparison of these two stories with a possibly quite new story from the subject, often produces points of contact for those passages that are most important because of what they reveal.   The subject thus helps to interpret his own story. It also facilitates a talk with him about his own interpretation. Such a conversation is very often possible, though this naturally depends on the case, and again and again it reveals startlingly that many subjects were indeed implicitly or explicitly conscious that they were projecting themselves while telling their story.

As with similar projection tests, the analysis of the protocols divides into a formal analysis and an interpretation of the contents.   Shape and contents, however, are never to be completely separated in the psychic.   An extensive summary of the headings under which we have placed the formal categories may be found in the manual.   The trouble that must be taken in the making of a formal analysis is never wasted: it is the only way to avoid overlooking points that would otherwise have been passed over in reading, since the story keeps our attention away from formal structures by its own logic.   It will be seen from the manual with what frequency a particular category occurs.   Although, in general, the rule, "the fewer the more personal," and "the more general the more impersonal," is valid, in practice there are exceptions, since, owing to the great number of categories in a single story, originality can be expressed in combination and nature of the use of generally applied categories.

It is not without significance that with normal subjects, the sequence in which the pictures are used most often is as follows: IV–I–III–II. In other words, the subject goes from the group, to the situation with a single partner, to social solitude, to personal loneliness. Since the sequence of the pictures is very closely connected with the dynamics that stand out from the story, it is a good thing always to note this sequence. Neurotics who feel themselves repulsed or lonely, in any case not accepted, often begin with III. From III as a beginning, it is difficult to find the right connection with Group IV, unless in a contrast. Anyone who begins with III will seldom put the hero, the principal character, in a social situation. Generally speaking, one may say that the beginning as well as the end of the story is very significant. The beginning is mostly the introduction of the subject: is the hero herein connected with the group, or exchanging conversation with the partner, or isolated, or dreaming of lost chances, or something else? Very often, it immediately gives a surprising interpretation of the attitude of the subject toward his surroundings. One need only reflect on what it means if somebody begins by saying, "Two good friends were playing cards together" (I), or, "Mr. Smith accuses Mr. Brown of cheating." Reversed, we have noticed that the end of the story gives a sign of the attitude of the subject toward his immediate future. It is nearly always suspect when no clear ending is made, but everything is left vague.

As has already been noticed, the intellectual level of the story is important as an indication of mental originality, but a projection test is not an intelligence test, and we shall not go into the matter further. We should like to remark only that the pictures can be connected with very extreme levels. The lowest level of composition is by a simple relation of time: "and then they did this, and then they did that." There is a higher level that reveals itself in a more inward connection made between the pictures, and by which, in the interpretation of the one picture, the meaning of another is concerned; for example, when someone begins his story by saying: "Two organizers of a tennis match. . . ."

When making use of the pictures, we always distinguish among the meanings given to the place-situation (I, for example, a study or police office), to the figures, and to the action. By this, a great number of different combinations is possible.

The meaning of the people on Picture I may be classified as to whether the narrator uses categories concerned with a relation that indicates a certain tie (blood relationship, friendship, love, work, ideology) or a relation of division, distinction, distance between the two people, as, for example, father and son, or manager and employee. Further, it depends on the use of the standing figure if there is question of submission, rightful protest, or rebellion.

Also, with the meaning that is attached to the action, the answers may be divided into those of cooperation, need for freedom, aggression, subjugation and submission, and so on.

Here are a few examples of the above categories from stories that began with Picture I.

1. A boy pours out his heart to a friend who appears not to understand him.
2. Two friends make plans to go on a journey over the holidays.
3. An assistant is accused of theft on his arrival at the office.
4. Two businessmen who run a big factory together; one bangs the table with his fist, saying that this and that must be done.
5. Mrs. Johnson is upset at the prospect of another winter on its way and she is saying to her husband, "Do you remember how high the snow was?" (She demonstrates with her hand.)
6. The people are two parts of one and the same personality, of which the one part preserves the other part from stupidities . . . and then the empty chair: one would like to put a person on that who had been sent away.
7. Someone gets a few days' leave from his boss.
8. This makes me think of an old mother who is asked by her son for advice, and who says to him that he must not throw his money away.
9. As director of a big business I had unpleasant experiences on this day.
10. I came home in a fuss, because I had tipped over a tray with glass on it in an expensive shop.

Of the use made of Picture II (the bed), I will mention, besides the meanings that have to do with sexuality, chiefly the consideration of social relationships, or the ending or lack of them.

With all the pictures, it is important to note where they enter the story. Neurotics often use the bed as a refuge or to seek rest for their deadly fatigue. In such a case, it comes at the end of the story. On the other hand, it is often placed at the beginning by neurotics, to let the hero mull over plans for the next day. Schizophrenics sometimes make a deathbed of it, or a bed of prostitution, and now and then they are attracted by the details of the drawing, a thing that hardly ever happens with normal people. The meaning given to the picture is then generally a misinterpretation, like, "A flag lies on the bed."

Sometimes Picture II is completely ignored; this is called bed-shock.

The bed often plays the role of a mother-symbol. This room is the place where the hero turns inward to himself, is alone with himself and with his unconscious strivings. The narcissistic tendencies have free play here. An unslept-in bed may be a sign of a feeling of lack of protection.

Some examples of interpretations from protocols:

1. John lay at home on the bed and thought over all that he had done.
2. He worried at night over sexual feelings.
3. Then the two boys went and slept together in the big bed.
4. He no longer dares to go into the room, fearing to be fetched out of his bed.
5. The man in the rain would be better lying in his bed, that is more comfortable.
6. He remained lying in his bed, in order to be well rested for the tennis match.
7. To forget all his misery he went to bed and quickly fell asleep.
8. At night in bed he thought over how he could tell it to his boss.
9. The four walls of his room became too small for him, and he strolled up the street.
10. That night the bed was not slept in.

Picture III is seldom used at the beginning of the story, but then, just as when used at the end, it is a neurotic symptom. It is often given the meaning of someone waiting in the rain for another who does not come, or of someone who is just standing in the rain because he had to live without one or other form of companionship. Sometimes it is on the hero's own initiative, some-times also because he feels himself rejected, or has been dismissed, or has been jilted. The feeling of being rejected, if present, is mostly projected onto this picture. Occasionally the individual against the lamp post is completely ignored, and the subject relates that the hero is walking through a lonely street in the rain. Or also the man is *seen,* but he is taken for a beggar with whom one has nothing to do.   This last solution is often found with people in whose social contact there is something wrong.

Stories do occur where the hero remains standing by the lamp post during the whole story, and all the action takes place there.

A patient tested with FPT after administration of 300 milligrams of veronal, related the following: "I had no home, no bed, nothing, and had to stand in the rain leaning against a lamp post.   Opposite me I saw a room where two people were quarreling.   I thought, what are those people getting excited about; a minute later tennis players came by soaking wet, and I thought, *they* at least have a house where they can change, and a warm bed to sleep in."

With persons whose basal metabolism is very low, such stories also occur, where all dynamics are lacking in the hero.

The feeble-minded are sometimes unable to free the man from the lamp post because their observation is not sufficiently differentiated, and thus they say, "There stands a man with a lamp on his head."

Examples of the use of Picture III from the protocols:

1. He walked angrily out of the house and went and reflected, leaning against a lamp post.
2. When he was dismissed, he did not know what to do and stood leaning against a lamp post.
3. There he stood at the appointed time leaning against the lamp post, but the girl did not turn up.
4. He was sent out as a spy to see what was happening in the house.
5. Every evening a dreary man took up his position in front of my door.
6. Then they tied him firmly to the lamp post.
7. As he had forgotten his latch key, he had to wait for the others in the rain.
8. This street corner is the symbol of conflict.
9. I saw from the window an old friend of mine who had fallen upon bad times.
10. Coming home we passed a man who looked darkly at us.

The use that is made of plate IV must be judged, in the first place, with regard to whether or not the hero of the story has placed himself in the group.   If he has not, he may be present on the tennis court, but yet, one way or another, not be joining in the society, because he inwardly remains apart.   If this goes further, he remains *literally* outside, and walks alone past the field "where he does not belong," or goes nowhere near the field, but only thinks of it with melancholy and rancor. If he *is* included in the society, this can naturally happen in many different ways. Often this picture is the beginning of an erotic intrigue. A youth with strong homosexual tendencies began his story with the words, "The boy on the extreme left will not talk to the woman next to him, not because she is a girl. . . ." All sorts of motives can come to light: ambition, sportsmanship, vanity, love of company, and so on. The picture, it is true, is not often very strongly differentiated in observation, but it serves as a peg for many attitudes and can thus serve as a beginning for the story.

Examples of the use of picture IV in the protocols:

1. Two friends fall out on the tennis court, because the one finds that the other is cheating.
2. This figure attracts me, it is the server, but he is in a bad position with regard to the net.
3. The longer that he thought of the tennis court where he used to enjoy himself so with the others, the more hopeful the situation appeared to him.
4. He walked past the tennis club of which he could not become a member.
5. On the tennis court two gentlemen are playing tennis and they are admired by two ladies and two gentlemen who are sitting on chairs.
6. He dreamed that he was going to play tennis, but that he had no balls and no racquets.
7. He is very little interested in the game, but actually in the girl who is sitting next to him.
8. Just go to the tennis court, there are people who can help you to find employment.
9. They met each other on the tennis court and looked deeply into each other's eyes while their better halves played a set.
10. He dreamed of an unbelievably successful tennis match.

About the other formal factors of which question arises when analyzing the protocols of the FPT, we can be brief in this chapter. They are extensively described in the manual and much resemble those described with regard to the protocols of the TAT and other projection tests. We will only remark that the structure of the principal figure is often *actually* to be found in the teller, while the dynamics of the secondary figure denote more the teller's *unrealized* tendencies. The remaining formal factors, such as the atmosphere and mood of the hero; the different kinds of conflict (between individuals and within individuals); the subjects and objects from the story; and the make-up and verbal structure and the amplitude and manner of the story, will not be gone into further here.

A variant of the protocols of the FPT, that occurs less clearly with other projection tests, because no story with several pictures at once must be made, is the time and space quality of the story. By this is meant the qualitative determination of time and space, in which the hero pursues the events of his life. The hero times himself in a different way from one story to another. Thus, it is important for the diagnosis whether the happenings result from each other in an after-each-other way (a man starts wandering after a quarrel with a girl), or whether the events happen in order to achieve a particular aim (he goes to the tennis court to show his girl how well he can play). The first form will be found with depressive patients, the second with hysterics.

With regard to the space qualities, these can cover a huge compass spreading over different widely scattered areas (sometimes a symptom of independence), or the whole story can take place on almost the same ground (a symptom of fear).

From the formal analysis, conclusions may be drawn with regard to a very great number of dynamics and personality structures: superficiality, egocentricity, aggressiveness, conflicts, soberness, sensitivity, emotionality, impulsiveness, passivity, evasion of difficulties, dependence, need of contact, downheartedness, fear, suspicion, lightheartedness, domination, need to make oneself count, ambition, vanity, sensuality, inferiority feelings, carefulness, consideration, perseverence, fantasy, intelligence, and differentiation. Other indications occur less often, but can have more value, such as indications of jealousy, narcissism, dependence upon the father, or the need for self-punishment.

We give below the outlines of some stories, to give an idea of some of the different attitudes toward life which have come to light with the FPT.

Paranoid attitude	Two organizers of a tennis match have noticed something suspicious. They send a spy to see what happens in a particular room, but the room is empty.
Depression	He lost all the games on the tennis court through his own fault, and at the office he made such stupid mistakes that he felt compelled to ask for his dismissal. Then he had to sell everything and become a homeless tramp.

Neurotic ambition   At first he was a poor man, who wandered along the streets and earned money by acting as a ball-boy on the tennis court. He did this so well that one of the players noticed him and took him into his office. Here he worked himself up to co-director, and slept only in luxurious hotel bedrooms.

Social conflict   Director dismisses worker in the presence of the manager. While the first man went off happily to play tennis, the second remained restless and searched until he found the dismissed man leaning against a lamp post, after which he provided him with a bed and a new job.

Laziness   There was once a boy, and he didn't feel like working any more, and then he went to watch a tennis match and then he was tired and went to bed, and . . . I can't bring the lantern into it.

Psychopathic   Youth wants to be rich and successful. Won't go the hard way, no will, does nothing, thinks back to his happy childhood, and finally of the scene when father turns him out of the house. Completely on his beam-ends, he considers the possibility of taking his own life.

Lack of independence   Gets a scolding from his boss which he has not deserved. Rebellious, resigns. By lamp post in contact with another man, who says: go to the tennis court, there I can help you to another job. He had lost his room (this owned by first boss), but the friend has a double bed and they can both sleep there.

Homosexual   Youth has to speak to a girl on the tennis court, has more interest for young man, is invited by this young man to his room, where he tries to make friends with him by means of a discussion about the violin on the table, but without success; goes to his room where he can't sleep. Gets up to go outside and come to himself.

Lack of activity   I stood against a lamp post in the pouring rain and thought: if the sun was shining it would be lovely weather for tennis. But it is not so, it's cold and wet here and I am so shivery. It would not be a bad idea to go to bed, I should peep out from the snug warmth.

Flight from hard reality   Jack got the sack from his boss; to forget misery, he played tennis with friends. Dared not go home at night. Luckily it begins to rain, so that he must find shelter and has a valid excuse not to go home, so that he only has to meet his father on the morrow.

Autism

Figure X got a scolding from his boss, because he was absent-minded (thinking of the tennis court), thence dismissal; result, disconsolate walking the streets; the thought of his gloomy room prevented him from going home.

Feeling of nonacceptance

Man is blackballed by the tennis club he lives near. On a rainy day he lets the ladies shelter in his house while he himself goes out. Shortly afterwards the club president nevertheless invites him to become a member. He refuses with the remark that he has already joined another club.

Neurotic aggression

Three men have a discussion after having been admired on the tennis court; a quarrel; one hits the other so that he knocks his head off, two others quarrel so in the street that the one nails the other to the lamp post. The third man now dares not go home for fear of being arrested.

Uncomplicated optimism

John, naughty at school, must stay in. He didn't mind a bit because it was raining hard, and so he couldn't play anyhow. At 6 o'clock he might go home, and then he quickly changed into dry clothes. Next day, lovely weather and he went with father and mother and won the game.

Weak-willed

Herman had to begin at the beginning to get anywhere. But he didn't like the work, and he sat all the time thinking of his girl, with whom he always played tennis. At last the manager said, when are you going to work decently (it would be for the first time), you ought to have a hard life and have to earn your money in wind and weather.

Insufficiency feelings, masochistically colored

My brother had coaxed me to go with him with beautiful words and beautiful girls. As I am not companionable or a tennis player, I felt myself the fifth wheel on the coach. Forced to do so by a shower, we went to the house of a friend of my brother's. This friend wanted to show his hypnotic tricks on us. I didn't want to, but when I lay on the table all began to laugh. I wished something would happen to me, namely that I should be taken into the game, and I laughed with them. On the way home I thought over my blunders, and in bed I thought over what I ought to have done in these circumstances.

Naturally, in the unabridged story that sometimes is one to one and a half pages in writing, many more dynamics come to light. Above, only one of the most important has been mentioned.

For the formal analyses we use a form like the one in Figure 2.

After the formal analysis, there follows the psychological analysis of the contents of the story itself. Making these content analyses demands great psychological experience, a feeling for and knowledge of the psychology of personality and psychopathology, and so, as a matter of course, great experience with the FPT itself. Further, it will depend on psychological ideology, on the special psychological construction of the personality, with what methods one attacks the protocols. He who wishes, for example, to use the Freudian categories of ego and superego finds very rich material chiefly in Picture I, for possible interpretations.

To illustrate this, we give below an example of a protocol with the formal and content analysis. A protocol of the FPT is not always especially significant, but an important aspect of the life history is usually projected. Above all, the fact that the combination of the four pictures encourages a story that plays continuously through different phases, gives the possibility of dramatizing, an advantage over other projection tests.

Because of the short time taken by administration, the FPT lends itself exceedingly well to a rapid orientation of the subject's general attitude toward life and to a repeated application during a therapeutic treatment.

Chiefly in Picture I, the patient easily projects his actual attitude to the therapist. We have also observed that a change in the self-concept of the patient is accompanied by the possibility of composing a new story on the FPT.

EXAMPLE OF PROTOCOL ANALYSIS

Ronald, a 28-year-old certified public accountant, is a youthful type, sensitive, accessible, and very conscientious. Although he is intelligent (IQ, 135) and also has great need of control, he does not excel in his work. Perhaps this is connected with the fact that he has more interest in persons than in dry numbers. Meanwhile, this interest is embedded in a strongly paranoic structure, which appears, besides in distrust, in a great need for control where the human relationships in his immediate surroundings are concerned.

He forms his own opinions fairly slowly, and they are then not unreal, but still, he is too slow and at the moment too neurotic, and not sufficiently energetic for business life. He does reflect on all kinds of vital questions, and is very much preoccupied by erotic

Four-Picture Test — *Testblank*

Name:.., oral/written

Chosen order: ....

Span of combination: (e.g., combination of 2 pictures) ....|.....

Quality of combination: (e.g., coherent story)..|.....

I	II
III	IV

Use made of picture (I)
- extent: (e.g., differentiated) ....
- quality: (e.g., normal meaning given)...
- room: (e.g., living-room) ....
- persons: (e.g., two friends) ....
- action: (e.g., quarrel) ....

Use made of picture (II)
- extent: (e.g., global) ....
- quality: (e.g., normal meaning given)...
- action: (e.g., go to sleep)...

Use made of picture (III)
- extent: (e.g., differentiated) ....
- quality: (e.g., normal meaning given)...
- action: (e.g., waiting)..

Use made of picture (IV)
- extent: (e.g., differentiated) ....
- quality: (e.g., normal meaning given)...
- action: (e.g., recreation) ....

Identification of subject with actors in the story : (e.g., with principal figure as real-ego)...

....

....

Form of identification: (e.g., hidden) ....

Depth of identification: (e.g., part is assimilated)..

Principal figure of the story: (e.g., man) ....

(I) principal figure: (e.g., standing figure)..

(II) bed is of or for: (e.g., principal figure) ....

(III) leaning against lamp post: (e.g., principal figure)..

(IV) principal figure: (e.g., tennis player) ....

Appearance of the principal figure: (e.g., active)..

Time quality: (e.g., consecutive) ....

Space quality: (e.g., daily surroundings) ....

Life of principal figure: (e.g., homely) ....

Mood of the story: (e.g., sensitive)...

Fig. 2(a).

172

Conflicts in the story

types: (e.g., inter-individual) ....

starting conflict: (e.g., difference of opinion) ....

following conflicts: (e.g., doubt)..

chief conflict: (e.g., quarrel) ....

Themes: (e.g., amusement)..

Objects not included in pictures { things: (e.g., tram).............................
{ persons: (e.g., policeman) ....

Make-up: (e.g., remained close to pictures)...

Structure: (e.g., plausible) ....

Amplitude: (e.g., story kept short)..

Manner: (e.g., ease of expression of subject) ....

Behaviour of subject towards examiner: (e.g., inhibited)......................

Indications from formal analysis: (e.g., superficiality) ....

U 4002 - H 175 p 13 (905)

Fig. 2(b).

173

problems.　Behind a certain forced lightheartedness there is undeniable depression.　With other persons he is friendly, as he is also with his colleagues (inside the boundaries laid down by his mistrust), but he is also fairly easily intimidated and hurt.

Protocol of the Four-Picture Test.　On the tennis court a bank director whispers to his wife his misgiving that his chief accountant is cheating.　He has become suspicious because the accountant often works late at night.　He means to go to the bank that night to make sure.　With the excuse that he is undermining his health, he will send him away and then see what's up.

One of the bank employees nearby has heard the drift of this conversation; he hatches a plan in his head.　At night he waits disguised near the bank, waits till the sent-away chief accountant comes out, goes in, murders the director, and vanishes with an important sum in securities. . . .　The director's wife waits vainly in bed that night for her husband.

Formal analysis
   Name: Ronald　　　　　　　　　　　written
   Chosen order: IV-I-(IV)-III-(I)-II
   Span of combination: Combination of 3
     pictures (IV-I-III)
   Quality of combination: Coherent story
     with return to a picture already used

Use made of picture I

  Extent:　differentiated
  Quality:　normal meaning given
  Room:　office
  Persons:　(a) employer (left) and employee
     (right)
    (b) murderer (left) and employer
     (right)
  Action:　(a) persuade the other
    (b) murder

Use made of picture II

  Extent:　differentiated
  Quality:　normal meaning given
  Action:　remain waiting

Use made of picture III

  Extent:　differentiated
  Quality:　normal meaning given
  Action:　waiting

Use made of picture IV

  Extent:　differentiated
  Quality:　original meaning given
  Action:　(a) explain plan
    (b) eavesdrop

Identification of subject with actor in the story: With principal figure (employer) as superego and with secondary figure (murderer) as ego-ideal. The chief accountant is representative of the real ego, as is the woman.

Form of identification: Hidden

Depth of identification: Both employer and murderer are assimilated

Principal figure of the story: Employer

  (I) principal figure: (a) standing figure, (b) sitting figure
  (II) bed is for the principal figure
  (III) leaning against lamp post: secondary figure (murderer)
  (IV) principal figure: onlooker

Appearance of the principal figure: Speaking and being murdered

Time quality: Final with relationship feelings, mixture of times of figures

Space quality: Daily surroundings, spaces of figures mixed

Life of principal figure: Businesslike

Mood of the story: Suspicious

Conflicts in the story {
Types: interindividual, filial, social, and intra-individual
Starting conflicts: suspicion
Subsequent conflicts: murder and theft
Chief conflict: nothing ends satisfactorily
}

Themes: Fraud, suspicion, overwork, checking, excuse, eavesdropping, disguise, murder, theft, waiting in vain

Objects not included in pictures {
Things: securities
Persons: none
}

Make-up: Remained close to pictures

Structure: Conclusion and proof given

Amplitude: Story kept short

Manner: Ease of expression of subject

Behavior of subject towards examiner: Little bit inhibited

Indications from formal analysis: Differentiation, imagination, opposition, need of self-punishment, restrained agressiveness, need of control, father-complex, cautiousness, insecurity, emotionalism, need for contact, overintellectual attitude, guilt feelings, suspicion, fear, introversion, lightly hypochrondriac

Psychological Analysis. The pictures are explained with differentiation and combined to a consecutive story, which is rendered in a few compact, sober sentences. All adornment is absent: there are hardly any superfluous adjectives or other additional circumlocution. Nevertheless, the contents of the story are differentiated, which points to a well-differentiated intelligence.

The writer of the story has held close reckoning with all the details in order to construct as acceptable a story as possible. The story has stayed very close to the pictures and is carefully sealed off. (The accountant is sent away, the director murdered, the booty achieved, and the state of the wife noted.)

Ronald is undoubtedly serious and conscientious; his rather lively imagination is not given free rein, but checked by logical standards. Everything must tally.

By repeated control, the *speed* of thought is probably not great. In agreement with this, the written efforts are but little spontaneous. Everywhere there is doubting and waiting, weighing of pros and cons at the expense of direct decision and energy.

The characters in the story are clearly borrowed from Ronald's own calling, and so is the imported article that is not in the pictures (securities). The characters scarcely think and act as officials, but chiefly as social individuals (tennis, fraud, undermine health, murder, theft, vigil for partner), from which appears Ronald's social interest. But not only interest appears: social-psychological insight is evident, too. The director suspects his accountant *because of his industry,* a combination that can only be understood via a special kind of living in the thoughts of the dishonest person. A similar living in the thoughts of another appears (among other instances) in the connection made between the murder of the director and the useless vigil of his wife; another, in the choice of excuse of the director toward his accountant.

In the first case, Ronald's marked ability to put himself in another's place probably comes from his suspicions, with which the whole of the story is permeated. His paranoid constitution is repeatedly projected in a convincing manner: the director whispers, distrusts his inferior, and uses an excuse; the accountant works overtime (seen from Ronald's standpoint, so that his fraud shall not be detected); the employee eavesdrops and disguises himself. In this connection, notice the mixture of the time-factors of the different figures (see the Manual [16], analysis of Michael's story). The plans of the actors cross each other. The same holds good of the space factors: it is not usual for a bank employee to sit next to the wife of his director. All of these mixtures strengthen the paranoid element.

These numerous indications make us suppose that suspicion is the kernel of Ronald's character. Meanwhile, it is remarkable that this suspicion is not at all an efficient weapon. Indeed, the director is murdered when at last he is going to act. His plan has leaked out exactly through all his precautions. His distrust is even trumped by the suspicion of the employee.

The accountant allows himself to be sent off; his precautions not to be discovered were useless. The employee, in his turn, is not seen to taste the satisfaction of his well-thought-out plan: the end of the protocol suggests a depressed, unhappy mood. In short everything ends unhappily for everyone, in spite of the fact that everyone has tried to avoid every risk.

The disappointing results of Ronald's suspicion stimulate his carefulness and distrust; he finds himself, as it were, in a vicious circle. He becomes already less sure of his business, will check it still more carefully, be still better informed of everything, and make more and more efforts not to be seen through himself. The mental insecurity in the story is diametrically opposed to the correct intellectual finish of it.

Notwithstanding all his mental effort, Ronald can not clarify his turbid worrying. He suffers the constriction of his lack of freedom in thought and deed. He wastes his energy by always considering how everything is going to turn out, which unforseen possibility there may yet be; he directs his attention too little to the finding of a constructive solution of the problems as they arise. He finds it difficult to hack the knot through. With everything, he wants to be precise and responsible; he has no flair.

It is easy to understand that Ronald lives under the impression of the pressure of a strong superego (the director). For the ego-ideal (the murderer), such a pressure is unbearable, and in the story the ego-ideal makes an effort to free himself from the superego. But the deed, executed after many precautions (among others, waiting till the accountant leaves in order to put the blame on him), does not bring the desired result. No pleasure, but remorse is projected afterwards. In fact, the superego is still the master, and furthermore, other new feelings of guilt are added to the already existing conflicts.

Both the chief figures show clear identification and sympathy. The parts of the secondary figures are also assimilated, and in a way that shows great knowledge of human nature, but there is apparently no question of identification. The figure of the woman is brought in by Ronald chiefly to display *Ronald's* remorse for the murderer's deed. The remorse and the scruples against hurting the director are no signs of the ego-ideal, but of the writer of the story himself, of his real ego. On the subject level, Ronald has need of being alone, isolated from the director: he not only leaves the woman lying lonely, but all the actors in their dealings are kept at as great a distance as possible from each other. This impulse to be alone is continually crossed by the thoughts concerning the others.

Seen in its broad outlines, the protocol gives a reflection of an extremely complicated phase in Ronald's development, in the center of which stands the process of liberation from the tight bonds of the superego. Very obviously, this phase is not yet sealed off, which completely agrees with reality.

SUMMARY

In this chapter, by way of introduction, an explanation of the conception of projection is given, based on the meaning Freud gave to the conception when he first used it as a psychological technical term in 1894. The author protests against the wide meaning the word has acquired of late, chiefly in American writings, and fixes the frontiers with regard to expression and with regard to the choice of the correlate object in the outer world. The essence of the projection phenomenon must be seen in the fact that the projecting person does not see the other, upon whom he projects, in his own character, but rather as an analogon of himself; with this, the projection is a noncommunicative behavior because to the extent that a man is in communication with another, he is open to the "different-ness" of the other. Regarded anthropologically (that is to say, from the standpoint of philosophical anthropology), projection is rendered possible by the ex-centric position of man, that is to say, by the fact that the being of man implies that he is never fully identified with himself, and also, cannot take up a position at a sufficient distance from himself. While projecting, the person makes an effort to get completely away from himself by getting away from the other person, who makes an appeal to him to communicate with him. Projection is not a *result* of displacement, but projection and displacement are two symptoms of one and the same defense-psychism.

The FPT, composed in 1930, is a projection test by which an

almost inexhaustible polyvalence is achieved. The person tested makes a story combining and arranging, according to free choice, four vaguely drawn pictures that portray four states of existence (I: being together with one other person; II: being personally alone; III: being socially alone; IV: being together with many others in a group). Since the test can best be given in writing after the pictures have been shown for one minute, the administration is brief. Therefore, the test lends itself admirably to clinical examination where only limited time is available. It is chiefly the subject's general attitude toward life, emerging from the protocol, that may be interpreted formally as well as according to the content. This chapter deals also with the history of the FPT, with its administration, and with the analysis of the different variables.

REFERENCES

1. Aeppli, E., *Lebenskonflikte.* Erlenbach-Zurich: Rentsch, 1942.

2. Allport, G. W., *Personality.* New York: Henry Holt and Company, Inc., 1937.

3. Bellak, L., "The concept of projection." *Psychiatry,* 1944, 7, 353–370.

4. Berg, J. H. van den, "Du silence et de la réticence." *Psyche,* 1950, 5, 39, 53–68.

5. Binswanger, L., *Gründformen und Erkenntnis menschlichen Daseins.* Zurich: Niehans, 1942.

6. Ferenczi, S., "Introjektion und Uebertragung." *Jb. Psychoanal. Psychopathol. Forsch.* 1909, 1, 422–457.

7. Fleischman, "History of the analytical theories of instinct," course held by the Department of Law and Police of the Canton de Vaud, in Lausanne, 1948, March 18–24.

8. Freud, S., *Ueber die Berechtigung von der Neurasthenie einen bestimmten Symptomencomplex auf Angstneurose abzutrennen, Ges. Werke,* Vol. 1. Leipzig: Int. Psychoanal. Verlag, 1925, p. 306–333.

9. Freud, S., *Ueber einige neurotische Mechanismen bei Eifersucht, Paranoia und Homosexualitat, Ges. Werke,* Vol. 5. Leipzig: Int. Psychoanal. Verlag, 1924, 387–399.

10. Freud, S., *Ueber den Gegensinn der Urwerte, Ges. Werke,* Vol. 10. Leipzig: Int. Psychoanal. Verlag, 1924, 221–228.

11. Heidegger, M., *Sein und Zeit.* Tübingen: Neomarius, 1949.

12. Hoop, J. H. van der, "Ueber die Projektion und ihre Inhalte." *Int. Z. Psychoanal.,* 1924, 10, 276–288.

13. Janet, P., "Caractères de l'hallucination du persécuté"; in *Miscellanea Pyschologica Albert Michotte.* Louvain: Inst. Sup. de Phil., 1947.

14. Jaspers, K., *Allgemeine Psychopathologie.* Berlin: Springer, 1948.

15. Lennep, D. J. van, *Psychologie van projectieverschijnselen.* Utrecht: Ned. Stichting voor Psychotechniek, 1948 (English translation in press).

16. Lennep, D. J. van, *Four-Picture Test.* The Hague: Martinus Nijhoff, 1948.

17. Maier, N. R. F., *Frustration.* New York: McGraw-Hill Book Company, Inc., 1949.

18. Mounier, E., *Traité du caractère.* Paris: Editions du seuil, 1947.

19. Murray, H. A., "The effect of fear upon estimates of the maliciousness of adult personalities." *J. Soc. Psych.,* 1933, 4, 310–329.

20. Perls, F. S., *Ego, Hunger, and Aggression.* London: George Allen & Unwin, Ltd., 1947.

21. Piaget, J., *La représentation du monde chez l'enfant.* Paris: Presses Universitaires de France, 1926.

22. Plessner, H., *Die Stufen des Organischen und der Mensch.* Berlin: de Grüyter, 1928.

23. Sanford, R. N., "The effects of abstinence from food upon imaginal processes." *J. Psych.,* 1936, 2, 129–136, and 1937, 3, 145–159.

24. Sartre, J.-P., *L'être et le néant.* Paris: Gallimard, 1943.

25. Sears, R. R., "Survey of objective studies of psychoanalytic concepts." *Social Sci. Res. Counc. Bull.,* 1943, No. 51.

26. Wolff, W., *The Expression of Personality.* New York: Harper & Brothers, 1943.

CHAPTER 7

The Thematic Apperception Test[1]

Robert R. Holt, Ph.D.

Le style c'est l'homme. Writers, from the creators of classics to the comic strip hacks, put their own values, their own personalities into their works. Who would doubt that Dickens was a moralistic, sentimental person, or that Swift was bitter and lonely? It is a commonplace of literary criticism to point out, as was widely done, for example, of Thomas Wolfe's *Look Homeward, Angel,* that the story has much of autobiography in it; the somewhat subtler psychological exegesis of a man's less obviously autobiographical works is also frequently found in contemporary letters. When we go beyond the step of reading simply to be distracted or to lose ourselves in the excitement of a yarn, we turn to a new novelist or poet to see what aspect of experience he has found most vivid and has passed on to us; we try to get a fresh perspective on the world—and we seldom hesitate to assume that this perspective is the author's own. The more we read of his work, the more we can see what remains constant while individual stories change; through the nature of these constancies we get a feeling for the author as a man.

From an extensive and expert acquaintance of this kind with literature and literary criticism, Murray and Morgan asked themselves why the same kinds of deductions could not be drawn from study of a series of stories written or told by anyone. They hit upon the happy idea of developing a set of 20 pictures around which tales could be constructed. The pictures stimulate the imagination;

---

1 Published with permission of the Chief Medical Director, Department of Medicine and Surgery, Veterans Administration, who assumes no responsibility for the opinions expressed or the conclusions drawn by the author.

181

they give definite grist for the less imaginative person's mill, so that he does not soon run out of ideas. They permit more or less systematic exploration of specific areas of potential conflict or motivational importance. And the subject's perceptual reactions to the pictures yield an added source of valuable data about the ways he looks at his world. The result, then, was the *Thematic* (in reference to the themes that are elicited) *Apperception* (in reference to the perceptual-interpretative use of the pictures) *Test,* or TAT, for short. Experimental use revealed that Murray and Morgan had created a multidimensional instrument that elicits from a subject a rich source of data about himself. In spite of the difficulties in recording, scoring, and interpreting the TAT, the test today ranks second only to the Rorschach in widespread clinical use.

The difficulties mentioned and the lack of a generally accepted scoring scheme have given the test, in some quarters, a reputation for slipperiness or even mystery that it hardly deserves. One of the purposes of this chapter is to show that the TAT story is no more inscrutable than any other product of human thinking. The plan of the chapter is, first, a discussion of rationale, an attempt to outline nine important classes of psychological determinants that are operative in the creation of a TAT story; second, a section on some problems of administering the test; and finally, an introduction to some methods of interpreting the responses to it.

RATIONALE

The late Kurt Lewin was fond of remarking that nothing is as practical as a good theory. In the field of clinical psychology, intuitive ingenuity and accumulated practical experience have considerably outstripped theoretical development. One can go a long way with purely empirical rules for interpreting specific constellations in psychological tests, but rules of thumb always tie one to concrete patterns and give no help at all when the particulars of known significance fail to appear. There are very few such "signs" with anything like invariant meaning in TAT stories; furthermore, the flexibility that a good theoretical grasp can give is particularly necessary for the successful use of the test.

A good way to approach a rationale for the TAT is to try to understand what takes place, psychologically, as a story comes into being. To unravel a knot, it is helpful to know how it was tied; to decipher hieroglyphic traces of the unique person in his stories, it helps if one can first get some clarity about the ways in which stories come about. Unfortunately, we do not have much empirical knowledge about this kind of problem. We have a number of insightful hypotheses, however, and it is worth while to review them, remembering always that what follows is not as well established as one should like for proper scientific rigor.

Some Propositions from Freud's Theory of Dream-Formation. Perhaps nothing will be so useful in this connection as some speculations about the mental processes involved in a somewhat different kind of phenomenon, written about 50 years ago. In the monumental seventh chapter of his *Interpretation of Dreams,* Freud [*14*] gives a hypothetical reconstruction of the mental alchemy of dreams, from which the following points may be abstracted.

1. Some event of the preceding day (the *day-residue*) starts a train of unconscious reactions going.

2. *This train of associations usually leads to a repressed wish or conflict.* More exactly stated, it communicates with ideas or memories that are the cognitive representatives of an unsatisfied (usually repressed) need, which may be involved in an unresolved conflict or traumatic experience. A need is conceived to be a driving force, biologically rooted, which finds conscious expression through its *derivatives:* ideas of the need-satisfying situation, experiences of wish or desire, and affects or emotional experiences. As long as it is unsatisfied, it tends to keep propelling these derivatives into consciousness. But it may be opposed by strong forces. Direct expression may be intolerable to the conscious mature personality, whose standards would require guilt, shame, or mortification (loss of self-esteem) if the person were to have the thoughts or commit the acts he secretly wants to. Or, he might become anxious, fearful of being overwhelmed by his own dangerous impulses. Therefore, direct expression is closed off by repression and other *mechanisms of defense.* The motivating force is still unreleased, however; it continues to press for expression through any channel that is innocent-seeming enough not to be blockaded.

3. The events represented by the day-residue, having been present in ordinary consciousness, need not be repressed. Thus, *the day-residue offers to the beleaguered unconscious forces an opportunity for partial discharge.* But how can the idea of an ordinary event play such a role for an unacceptable impulse? It is one of Freud's important discoveries that a need can obtain some partial discharge through the agency of an act or thought *that is related in some way* to the need. Thus, checkmating an opponent's king may offer some discharge for the necessarily unconscious wish to

murder one's father; taking part in a revolution, dreaming about it, or telling a TAT story on the subject may all likewise give some gratification to this same need (though, of course, to different degrees).

4. The need and its associated ideas still cannot usually find any direct route to the semiconsciousness of the dream state, and must take a variety of devious by-ways, undergoing certain kinds of distortions and transformations.

5. Under the influence of directing ideas, the nascent dream undergoes *secondary elaboration*—is fashioned into a more or less coherent, usually dramatic, form.

This is not intended to be an exhaustive summary of Freud's formulations; to mention only the most obvious omission, for example, nothing explicit is said about wish-fulfillment. The reason is that only the generalizable aspects of the Freudian account have been reported here. A dream is not a TAT story, and it cannot be maintained that consciously framed stories are always wish-fulfillments.

If we consider an actual story, it will be easy to see the extent to which these formulations help in understanding how it came into being. In card 8 BM, an adolescent boy looks straight out of the picture. The barrel of a rifle is visible at one side, and in the background is the dim scene of a surgical operation, like a reverie-image. Here is a story told by a young college man, called Nailson, to card 8 BM.

Gee, it looks like a young fellow. (Pause.) Oh, fellow is about fifteen, I guess. It's (pause). He's either seen or read about some operation in which the patient had gone through all kinds of tortures, and he decided he's going to become a doctor. He's going to fix things, they're not going to happen like that any more. These are old doctors, very old, long time ago, I guess. They're going to town, probably no ether or anything else. The kid was probably just a young baby at the time, maybe. Looks like he had a nightmare or two. And (pause) that determined his life for him. He's going to spend his whole time trying to be a doctor and not have any more operations like this. He's going to (pause). Well, it could be that he's something like Bliss or some one of the great doctors that invented anaesthetics, something to bring ease to the patient during the operation. Probably spend his whole life trying to develop something like that. Anyway, he's going to be a doctor, he's not going to have anything like this happen again.

If we take the story as analogous to the finished dream, what corresponds to the day-residue, the original stimulus that set going a process resulting in the story?

1. Surely the picture, or part of the picture, must stand in the same relation to the story as the day-residue does to the dream. Neither is wholly responsible for the finished product, yet the influence of the originating content can be seen in the final product in both cases. The story is less personal than the dream in that the picture is not a personal experience in the same sense as the day-residue, but there is the compensating advantage of greater inter-individual comparability.

2. Now, it is true that the perceptual impact of a TAT picture may or may not touch off very important underlying motives or problems; some stories (like the one quoted here) go right to the heart of the subject's important formative experiences; others remain superficial and reveal little of the deep forces for which the psychologist usually searches. But the contrast to dreams is not such an exaggerated one, after all: not all experiences in daily life result in dreams, either; only the ones that have some kind of relatedness to emotional needs. Just so, only pictures the contents of which give tongue to the silent forces of the unconscious result in psychodynamically significant stories. Fortunately, the range of vital human problems is not so wide that one cannot find a few important gaps in almost any subject's defenses with a set of 20 pictures. It obviously becomes important just what the content of the pictures is; they have been chosen to touch on the basic human situations and sources of conflict that are important to most people in our culture.

Let us return to Nailson and the operation scene. The great and strikingly repeated emphasis on preventing the recurrence of scenes of torture like this primitive attempt at surgery, the event's decisiveness in the life of the story's central figure, or *hero*, the use of language, which (for this subject) is vivid—all point to the conclusion that *the perceptual process has made contact with important configurations in his emotional and conative life, which are using it to come to indirect conscious expression.*

3. If we are to adhere to a dynamic point of view, we must assume always that *some motives are at work determining the particular content chosen*. In the case of the TAT story, one cannot dogmatically say that the needs that find some partial outlet are necessarily unconscious. When the subject-matter of the picture is relatively indifferent, *and* when the inner pressure of unsatisfied,

repressed, or conflicted needs is *not* great, relatively peripheral conscious motives may be chiefly involved.   Of course, if an emotionally disturbed person is under great pressure of a psychic conflict, the latter may be foisted upon any picture, worm its way into any story —for that matter, into the content of Rorschach responses or almost any other test given to the patient.

In any event, since the subject is not personally responsible for the content of the picture, he can usually allow himself at least to describe it, or to tell a story in which there is little apparent deviation from what is objectively given.   Thus any repressed force that can become implicated can escape censorship to some degree.   In the present instance, the repressed traumatic incident was determined with fair certainty to be the shock at an early age ("a long time ago . . . just a baby at the time") of seeing his mother brutally mistreated by his father (or so he thought).   It may even have taken the form of the *primal scene* (observation of parental intercourse). It is by no means to be assumed that any such deep interpretation could confidently be made on the basis of this story alone.   It is a conclusion reached by Nailson's biographer after careful analysis of many other sources of data, including interviews as well as tests.[2] A great deal of the subject's life actually has been organized around this very slogan: "he's not going to have anything like this happen again."

4. It is clear, however, that *the basic complex remains unconscious,* in spite of its being stirred by the picture.   Instead of its being a sexual scene that "determines his life for him," it is an operation in the story.   Now, one may argue that no distortion is involved here, that, in fact, there would be gross distortion if the pictured scene were called a rape.   Of course there would be *perceptual* distortion in such a case; one would have good evidence for the hypothesis that someone who disregarded reality to such an extent was psychotic. But it is characteristic of psychotics that material related to childhood traumas does sometime break through directly, *with little distortion,* into consciousness, warping perceptual contact with reality in doing so.   In this case, then, the picture both arouses the

---

2 A sketch of Nailson containing most of the relevant data may be found in Bellak and Jaques [7].   Under another pseudonym, Nack, he is also discussed at length in Murray and Morgan [24].   In the latter monograph, there is a report of an interview in which the subject himself confirmed the hypothesis of exposure to the primal scene.

traumatic material and furnishes it with a respectable disguise, so that the distorting effect of the ego defenses on the latent content is hard to see.

5. The similarity in the final steps has already been referred to. The perceptual data, the cognitive associations, and the feelings and drives that are activated are all organized by the set to satisfy the instructions of the test, and are synthesized into a relatively orderly story. The result in this case is a great deal more coherent than most dreams, because it is mainly the product of the *secondary process* (rational thinking) rather than the *primary process* of dreams (unconscious, nonrational thinking). This is not the best place to go into an examination of differences between TAT stories and dreams; suffice it to say that the two mental products have very important differences as well as similarities, and that it is far from the author's intention to give the impression that TAT stories are to be analyzed just as if they were dreams.

Categories of Determinants. Do the above five stages exhaust all that we know or can reasonably hypothesize about how a story comes into being? Not at all. There follows a set of nine different categories of determinants that shape TAT stories. They are presented in approximately the order in which they seem to come into operation as the mental process corresponding to a story develops. In tracing the operation of these determinants, Nailson's story will be used further as an example.

1. The Situational Context. One must go back beyond the point when the first picture is presented if he is to understand the important determinants of a story. Any dynamic psychology must work with some equivalent of Lewin's formula, $B = f(P,E)$: all behavior is a function of the nature of the person and of his environment. In psychological testing, we sometimes overlook the effect of the E in this equation, because of our concern with the nature of P. A person will make up different stories for a friend who is doing some research, for a prospective employer, for a psychiatrist who is treating his neurosis, or for a prison psychologist who is investigating his motives for a crime he has committed. A different side will be turned to each, in all likelihood; somewhat different attitudes, sets, defenses, and motivations will be called up by each situation.

To understand Nailson's story, it should be realized that he was a healthy college man who was serving as a subject in a research program in order to earn some extra money.[3] Furthermore, he was being tested by a friendly, informal examiner who liked him and put him at his ease. There were therefore no pressing personal reasons for Nailson to reveal himself, and no strong pressure from the outside either, though there was plenty of encouragement. It is reasonable to suppose that he might have been much more cautious or guarded in another situation. As it was, he felt free to speak quite informally, and his use of slang (as in the phrase, "going to town," with its perhaps important *double entendre*) is not as inappropriate as it would be coming from a patient.

2. *The Directing Sets.* Another determinant closely related to the situational context and in large part growing out of it is the group of anticipations, guiding ideas, or directing sets that the subject forms. They are made up of his preconceptions of what the test and tester are like, his subjective interpretation of the instructions, and his conception of what it means to be tested. His motivation for participating may be considered a part of this group of determinants, which make the difference between such extremes as his passively giving minimal compliance to a red-tape routine, and his being challenged to maintain his self-esteem and the examiner's approbation by telling as interesting, dramatic, and finely-wrought stories as possible. This understanding of "what it's all about" has a pervasive influence throughout the formation of a story, and is naturally something the examiner must do his best to understand and influence. Since it is a function of the nature of the subject as well as of the setting and the examiner's efforts, it is often difficult to modify.

A reading of Nailson's stories gives the impression that he felt he ought to do the best he could; that he saw the task primarily as finding the best interpretation of the picture rather than telling a plotted narrative; that he did not find it much of a threat to his self-esteem or to his revealing anxiety-laden unconscious material.

3. *The Perceptual Impact.* With these more or less conscious anticipations in mind, Nailson was handed the card. The consensus of most healthy, intelligent persons is that this picture contains four

---

[3] A cooperative research program, in which the writer was involved, at the Harvard Psychological Clinic under the direction of Dr. Henry A. Murray, during 1941–1943.

figures: a youth looking straight out of the picture, and behind him, the dimly-seen figures of a man lying on his back, a bearded man leaning over him cutting into his abdomen with some kind of knife, and another man holding a lantern. A window is visible in the background, and a rifle is sharply delineated on the other side of the picture from the boy. The instructions do not specify that all of this be brought into the story, but most subjects get the definite implication (*set*) that they are to take some note of everything important in the picture. Unconscious violations of this implied requirement are, however, fairly common; Nailson commits one. He does not mention the gun.

From his first remark, it is plain that the normally most salient figure, the boy, first caught his eye. Then he probably saw the operation, and was so taken up by the associations it aroused that he did not turn his attention to the gun. We cannot assume, however, that he did not see it. On the contrary, *we must almost always assume that the subject does see and, on some level of awareness, recognize everything in the picture,* unless we have good evidence to the contrary. What he omits or interprets idiosyncratically becomes very important, for it is a clue to the kinds of dangers against which he has erected important defenses. If one prefers a less elaborate explanation, it is possible that Nailson saw the gun well enough but could not see how to fit it into the story. Since he had recognized the gun in another picture at once (3BM) when it was presented, and since the gun in 8BM does not fit well into this particular story that he practically *had* to tell, this explanation is plausible. It is unfortunate that there was no inquiry. It would have been simple enough for the examiner to have asked afterwards, casually, "Did you notice anything else in the picture that you didn't bring into your story?" The answer would have told at once whether repression or a conscious decision was responsible for the omission. Actually, this is not a very important deviation. The various elements of the picture are so difficult to integrate that the rifle is often left out.

In one other way, we learn about Nailson from our speculations about the perceptual impact. In their very useful table of apperceptive norms, Rosenzweig and Fleming [29] note that 66 per cent of normal men see the patient being operated on as a man; it is usual for the sex to be specified if there is any reference to the patient. Nailson leaves the sex indefinite. Here, as before, it is only because acquaintance with a long series of other cases tells us what to expect that we notice anything amiss. The Rosenzweig-Fleming norms are very helpful as far as they go, but they do not deal with all of the pictures, nor with all aspects of the 16 cards that were included in their study. Until satisfactory norms have been published on all such matters as these, the TAT worker has to accept the fact that his facility in using the test must, and will, grow as he tests more and more persons and builds up his own, largely unconscious, norms.

But what if he does say just, "the patient"; what then? Ordinarily, we might not assign it much significance; in Nailson's case, it is congruent with the hypothesis that in his unconscious memory or fantasy, the victim of an attack such as this is seen to be is more likely to be a woman than a man. Possibly, he would even have said that the patient looked like a woman if during the inquiry, after the card had been taken away, he had been matter-of-factly asked whether or not he noticed the sex of the patient. From other evidence, it seems a little doubtful that he would have called the patient a woman, but ordinarily the possibility would be worth looking into. (Of course, not in such a way as to make the subject overalert to all features of subsequent pictures.) More emphasis has been given to this point, for illustrative reasons, than it deserves from a practical standpoint. As in the case of the omitted rifle, this is a rather slight clue that requires the support of more evidence before it can carry interpretative weight.

4. The Arousing of Needs and Affects. It is only conceptually possible to separate the perceptual impact of the picture from the logically subsequent phase, the touching off of motivational forces and their derivatives. When we examine a series of stories told by different subjects to the same picture, they can be seen to differ in a number of ways, but often outstandingly in the kinds of motives that actuate the characters in the stories. We assume that such differences must be due to the differential importance of the motives for the subjects themselves.

In discussing the parallel to dreams, above, we touched on this fourth phase, but only so far as it involves the deeper, unconscious needs and complexes. The story we are using as a reference point may be misleading because it clearly involves motivation of this basic sort so much more clearly than do most TAT stories. Indeed, interpretation of the test would be vastly simpler if one could always assume that the strivings of the heroes represented unconscious urges of the subject.

The truth, however, is complex. The writer once tried, with a small group of very thoroughly studied subjects, to test the hypotheses that (1) when a need was actually stronger in a subject's overt behavior than he admitted, and when it involved a form of behavior that was relatively unacceptable to him, it would then be prominently present in his TAT stories; and (2) when a need was weaker in a subject's overt behavior than he judged it to be, and was considered by him to be relatively desirable, it would then likewise be found in unusual strength in his stories. The data tended to support both hypotheses (which were derived from the concepts of *projection* and of *wish-fulfillment,* respectively), but the important point is that there were many exceptions, many needs whose frequency and intensity in the stories were not explained. Take, for example, the need for sex ideation. It was found most prominently in the stories of subjects who had the strongest sexual drives in overt behavior, who felt that sex expression was quite acceptable, and who might therefore be supposed to be in little need of any fantasy outlet or projection. In the college population being studied, it seemed that when superego controls were strong enough to restrain the sexual need in the everyday lives of the more inhibited subjects, they kept it out of their TAT stories to a large extent, while in the case of the "emancipated" subject, the letting down of the barriers so far that he could engage in considerable sexual activity also made it easier for him to talk about it, but left him with enough residual need tension so that he was impelled to do so.

It is necessary to assume, therefore, that any motivational force present in a person may be aroused sufficiently in the course of the test to enter into a story, provided that stronger *restraining* forces are not present. Beyond that statement, it does not seem to be possible to lay down any very helpful laws about the kinds of needs that will be expressed most strongly.

There is one other important principle regulating the incitement of needs, and many other aspects of the stories as well: *identification.* One of the differences between the perceptual process set going by a TAT card and by a day-residue is that the subject is not directly

involved in the former, as he is in the latter.   Fortunately for man's
social existence, most persons do have a natural tendency to identify
with others when there is no important barrier in the way.   So
when they are confronted by card 1, showing a boy and a violin,
the great majority of subjects unconsciously and unhesitatingly think
about a story from the point of view of the boy, identifying themselves with him.   This patch of grays and blacks on a piece of paper
becomes implicitly a projection of oneself, and is thereby naturally
endowed with attributes of the self-concept, on some level: what one
is, what he wishes he were, or what he fears he may become.

Many of the cards present more than one person, however, and
some of them present persons of different ages and sexes.   It is
easiest for anyone to identify with someone else who has important
attributes of his own ego-identity (E. H. Erikson [11]), so the subject
usually adopts the point of view of the figure who is most like him
in some crucial way, and makes this person the central character,
or *hero*, of his story.   In fact, if there is no apparent identification
with any of the pictured figures, we have good reason to suspect
that the subject is unusually narcissistic or has strong characterological defenses against forming interpersonal relationships of any emotional depth.

As was mentioned above, *affects* make up a class of derivatives of
needs, one that has not yet been dealt with.   Depending on the
nature of a person's defenses, as soon as he looks at a picture he may
be flooded with emotional feeling that spills over into exclamations,
weeping, or other direct display; or he may completely isolate and
repress all affective experience, never varying his delivery or tone of
voice a whit; or his affective experiences and expressions (for example, silly giggling) may be inappropriate to the situation—or a
number of other possibilities might obtain.   Whatever a person's
mode of dealing with affects, they may show up in two ways: either
directly, as just described, or indirectly, through attribution to the
characters in the stories.

How did Nailson react to the perceptual impact of the picture?
First, it stirred up his aggressive need (which we know from other
sources was strong but well-controlled); but this force did not obtain
direct outlet in the story, nor was there any overt affective display.
The unconscious presence of strong destructive wishes can be in-

ferred from his dwelling on the patient's tortures and the doctors' apparent zest in inflicting them. But he could not allow himself to identify directly with the sadists (who were, incidentally, put at a great remoteness in time, so that Nailson could all the more dissociate himself from their deeds); he did, however, have his hero take over an approved version of their role, in which the aggression was subordinated to nurturance (tender care).

The needs that are directly expressed in the story are *dominance: nonpersonal* (strong efforts to master the situation), and *achievement* (hard and persistent work). Less prominent are the related pair, *cognizance* (the need to see, find out, know) and *construction* (to invent, create). The former two make an interesting comparison: Nailson considered himself to be very dominant, but actually made few efforts to lead or influence others, so that this need was not actually manifested much in overt behavior; but the need for achievement was quite strong. Nailson was an effective, hard worker, who liked to solve difficult mathematical problems for fun (cf., needs cognizance and construction), and who put successful effort into mastering the nonhuman aspects of his environment— breaking horses, shooting rapids, and so on. Thus, his behavior reflected a kind of dominance directed toward the mastery of difficult situations, rather than people, and this is the very kind of dominance expressed in his story. The example shows how difficult it is to generalize about a need from one form of its expression in a story. Assuming that dominance in general was strong would have been incorrect; so would the assumption that dominance was expressed only in the effort to solve this one personal problem.

The nature of the situation as Nailson perceived it caused the needs above mentioned to be aroused, and to shape the courses of action attributed not only to the hero but to the other characters in the story. As usually happens, the hero was not endowed with needs that were unconscious and unacceptable, fictitious shadow though he be; such needs appeared instead as actuating other characters. We have not been able to talk about these motives, it seems, without discussing what logically belongs in the next stage.

5. *Defensive Circuiting.* As has been indicated, the developing story-process enters into some devious by-ways as soon as motivational forces have been set going by the perceptual material. In-

stincts know many vicissitudes; the important needs can rarely be expressed directly, even in dream or in provoked fantasy of the kind the TAT elicits.   The transformations and long-circuits the socialized human being must force upon his needs are called mechanisms of defense.   They are defensive because, as above indicated, they serve the purpose of warding off the anxiety, shame, guilt, or loss of self-esteem that would result from unmodified exercise of one's primitive potentialities.

Historically, Nailson went through a period of overt sadism, torturing animals in his early childhood: thus, his first defense against the anxiety caused by his early trauma was *identification* with the aggressive father.   Then he began to take over some of his mother's softer ideals, and made a dramatic about-face: through *reaction formation* he became determined to defend the weak against the strong, to care for his ailing mother and all animals.   He then became a great lover and defender of animals, and decided on medicine as a career.   At the same time, his aggressive need got an indirect outlet, because one of his measures in instituting a new era of kindliness on his father's farm was to take over the butchering of the calves himself—"so that it would be done in the most humane manner."

In his story, we can see the same kind of course being taken by the aggressive need.   First, it was given a remote (in Tomkins' [*40*] sense of the term) expression through the description of the brutal doctors.   That it was a source of unconscious anxiety is hinted at in the statement, "he had a nightmare or two."   Then the hero identified himself with the aggressors, but he did so in order to bring about a denial of aggression at the same time, in the *prevention* of pain (reaction formation).   Thus we may assume that there was a series of partial releases of (unconscious) aggressive tension, as the story-process was shunted about, developing according to the defense mechanisms characteristic of the subject's life history.   Likewise, the desire to look (which must have taken on great importance if Nailson was exposed to the primal scene) could not be expressed in its most direct form.   Instead, it led to a preliminary, remote, and passing reference to seeing or reading about an operation; then it reappeared in the *sublimated* form that the need had actually taken in Nailson's life: an intense interest in scientific knowledge and discovery.

6. The Associative Elaboration. The next (only conceptually separate) stage is the accretion to the story-process of a variety of associative material. So far, logically, we have only the content given by the picture as the subject interprets it, the motivational forces that it stirs up, and the defensive routes these forces must take in order to achieve expression. But as has been indicated, it is characteristic of the emotional urges that drive us that they tend to bring their derivatives into consciousness, including the goals toward which they propel us and the associated means (objects, situations) of getting to them. Of course, the specific nature of these derivatives is determined by the individual's past history; so that here already we have one important kind of associative material, personal-historical content, being made ready to be included in the stories under the organizing influence of the existing sets.

A. PERSONAL-HISTORICAL CONTENT. One of the most common errors of beginners in TAT interpretation is the assumption that all stories are autobiographical, and that interpretation consists merely of changing names and tenses here and there, leaving the content essentially as the subject gives it. There is a perfectly good reason for such an error: frequently the content of the stories *is* derived entirely from personal history. The story we are using for an example is considerably more autobiographical than most; it happens that Nailson gave us a barely-disguised account of what is perhaps his life's most central theme. Yet for every story of this kind, there are several others in which the manifest content has little to do with the teller's past. For the content is usually determined primarily by the picture and certain socially shared meanings that each picture tends to have. Only if events and sentiments from one's own personal past are particularly fraught with emotional meaning are they likely to be worked into stories when the picture does not have some direct associative link to them.

Here we must reconsider the importance of the anticipations, or sets, under the influence of which the constructive aspects of thinking take place. The raw materials for this constructive work are the ones we have considered so far (the perceptual givens, the needs and affects), plus all the storehouse of memories available to consciousness. While the arousal of the aggressive need in Nailson might conceivably lead him to think of hunting, an activity he has frequently enjoyed, he has the set to tell a coherent story consistent with the picture; so the set operates to activate only *relevant* memories.[4] This is true, at least, in intact, healthy persons. Various kinds of breakdown in this function can be seen in stories that wander, proceed by sudden jumps, or become bogged down in a mire of many possible associations; and corresponding kinds of pathology can be inferred therefrom.

However effective the set, a person has only his own experiences, direct or indirect, to call on to put flesh on the skeleton story-process we have so far conceived. And unless he is unusually suspicious, creative, or evasive, it is far easier for the subject to think of his own direct experiences. They are not only more interesting and more vivid to him, but they may be involved in dynamic complexes like the traumatic early experience of Nailson. In such a case, the person has a positive need to bring the repressed memory back to consciousness in some form, so that it can gradually be "decontaminated" and mastered. For reasons like these, the contents most likely to be brought into the story in addition to what the picture suggests directly are autobiographical.

But it may also happen that nothing in the picture moves the subject, either because of the neutrality of its contents or because his defenses are so strong that they prevent communication between the perceptual process and latent emotional forces. In such a case, the story will be relatively stereotyped, containing no evidences of personal involvement, little by way of motives for the action, and that little all drawn from external experience—stories he has read or observation of others. Stereotyped stories of this kind usually differ very little from the bare "popular" interpretation, are not long, and have little life in them. They exist in pure form only rarely; actually, most records contain a few more or less stereotyped stories in which there is little involvement, but very few protocols are devoid of any involvement of the subject's own needs and strivings. Learning to distinguish between what is stereotyped, indicating merely that a person participates in a certain subculture,

---

4 Actually, one of the popular stories told to this picture does integrate all of the perceptual givens into a story of a man injured (often accidently shot by the boy) while hunting. Why did Nailson fail to give this better interpretation? Very probably because he could not fantasy killing his father and because of his tendency to see the person in pain as equivalent to his mother. He solved his Oedipal conflict by identifying himself with his strong, brutal father, not by a fantasy of killing him. For these reasons, the popular hunting-accident story was probably not available to him.

and what is indicative of more personal material, is essential to skilled use of the TAT. Unfortunately, it is not quickly learned. Like any other projective technique, the TAT must be worked with patiently, and with a sustained interest in learning, if one is to exploit its real usefulness.

B. SENTIMENTIVE CONTENT. Another important part of the associative storehouse that a person has to call on derives from personal experience, yet is not exactly autobiographical. That is his fund of sentiments and attitudes. As Nailson rounded out his story, he expressed very clearly his sentiment about suffering and medical ignorance: they would not recur if he could help it. There was a surgeon in the picture, so he talked about doctors; but having such strong positive sentiments toward skilled medical men, particularly the discoverers of "something to bring ease to the patient," he could not talk about doctors without expressing these attitudes. Of course, if he had been suspicious and evasive, or had thought that he stood to lose something by betraying his true feelings, he could fairly easily have disguised them and put in the stories expressions of attitudes that were not his own. In practice, however, deliberate attempts to mislead are so infrequent that the possibility of their occurrence may be ignored most of the time. Such defensiveness usually makes itself known obviously enough, and is typically expressed by a refusal to give anything beyond the bare essentials.

The most important kind of sentimentive content in the TAT, for most purposes, is the attitudes toward other persons. Here the subject's characteristic *interpersonal relationships* make their nature known, since they too are a function of basic sentiments toward classes of people: older males, older females, competitors, love-objects, the weak and helpless, and so forth. Something about the warmth and importance to the subject of his relationships with others is likely to get into his stories as sentimentive content of this sort. Nailson's interpersonal ties did not seem, on the basis of this story, to be particularly intense, though his ambivalent respect for authority figures and his tender feeling for those who are suffering were obviously determining elements of the story's content.

C. GENERAL INFORMATIONAL CONTENT. As long as a story sticks very closely to the picture, with little real invention, it may contain a minimum of any kind of content. Since it is always possible for a subject to take the test in such a meager, constricted way, the TAT cannot be thought of as a test of information. Yet it is obvious that a person must use his fund of general information even in recognizing the contents of the pictures, as well as in introducing further ideas to make complete stories. If a subject calls the monster in card 11 a diplodocus, then we clearly know that he either has a general store of information indicative of a high educational level, or that he probably has special interests and attainments in geology or paleontology. (There are implications of a different sort in the fact that he chooses to use such a word; they will be considered below.) Nailson's reference to Bliss is rather obscure. Since there is actually no such "great doctor" in the history of medicine, he hit upon an obscure figure by dint of very specialized reading, or was confused and inexact in his memory, or else was merely being pretentious and arbitrary, counting on the examiner's not looking up his apparently erudite reference. Inquiry would have helped here; without it, the second possibility seems the most likely, from internal evidence.

It has been implied in the above three subsections that a person's possible associations are patterned in personally revealing ways. But they are also more subtly patterned, as are his needs, defenses, and other aspects of personality, by the culture in which he takes part. Only what is known to his culture will be known to the individual, and the values and goals he expresses will be determined in large part by the culture, either directly or through his protest against them. This brief and inadequate treatment of an important kind of determinant will not be further expanded, since it is discussed by Henry in Chapter 8.

7. *The Enabling and Limiting Effects of Abilities.* We have by now accounted for the appearance of most of the elements of a story, and have a number of ideas about influences that shape the content into particular forms. One rather silent influence not so far spoken about is that of abilities. To a large extent, what goes into a story is fixed by the range of a person's experience and by the nature of his defenses; and, indeed, we have to think about most of these influences in terms of their interactions. But the marks of one ability—intelligence—are sometimes plain to see. No matter how favorable the defensive structure, no matter how great the exposure to a variety of experiences, if native wit is at a low

enough level, TAT stories will be primitive in their structure. They may be very useful, may contain a great deal that is of value; but that is not the question. In explaining any one story, one must take into account the author's level of intelligence—and of other abilities. Nailson's story, for all its simplicity, could hardly have been told by a very dull person. Likewise, his somewhat limited *verbal facility* set an upper limit on the literary quality of the stories he turned out. Without *creative imagination,* ingenious and original stories cannot be written, though of course one may have imagination and not exercise it.

One may infer that Nailson had an average degree of *observational ability* from this story, since his interpretation was largely in line with popular trends. On another picture, card 15, Nailson took note of small gray blemishes near the left corner of the top margin, interpreted them as running men, and brought them into the story, an interpretation requiring an observational ability apprehensively sharpened to pathological acuity. On the same picture, a paranoid schizophrenic actually saw the gray blemishes as two figures pursuing the hero.

It was mentioned that card 8 BM puts some strain on the *organizing ability* of most subjects; a number of other cards likewise picture disparate elements or a variety of them, so that something of what constitutes a "good *W*" in the Rorschach test is required to integrate what is given in the picture into a consistent story. Even such features of the stories as the interpersonal relationships between characters can be looked at from the standpoint of abilities, too. Without *empathy,* the ability to feel with others, one cannot describe in detail in a story about card 2, for example, the point of view of more than one of the persons pictured.

The effect of abilities, then, in producing a TAT story, is first, to set upper limits for a number of the production's dimensions. Second, a modicum of certain abilities is necessary for the development of real stories sufficiently rich and extensive to allow other influences on a story to make their weight felt.

8. The Internal Milieu. The TAT story is the end product of the operation of a complex mental process that takes place not in an indifferent medium, but in the mind of a person. In the subjective life of a human being, there are characteristic and pervasive states that subtly and indirectly affect whatever is transacted. They may be spoken of as the prevalent emotional tone, the emotional climate, or the *internal milieu* of the subject.

Nailson's story gives a distinct impression of forcefulness, or determination, perhaps even zest for activity and effort.   They are, in fact, qualities that are ubiquitous in his behavior.   So is optimism, a generally hopeful outlook.   These prevailing winds in the inner climate of his mind have their effects in quite an unconscious way; they are hard to measure, but they are highly reliable.   In other subjects, anxiety, depression, euphoria, or fatigue may be present in consciousness or just below its surface, as the by-products of a variety of dynamic configurations of more genotypical variables. Whatever their origin, there they are; they help to set the tone of the stories.   One of the marks of the experienced interpreter of the TAT is his sensitivity to this atmospheric quality.   It helps to give a basic orientation to the understanding of a person.

9. The Personal Style.   With all of the above categories, we still need to invoke another group of determinants, referred to as personal style, in order to explain how Nailson told just this story in just this way.   Take his choice of words, for example; how unpretentious, simple, even naive it was at times.   Even though we might ultimately be able to derive it from a complete understanding of defensive structure, it is simpler at the present stage to consider what Allport calls *stylistic traits* [1] as determinants on their own emergent level.   Whenever we can see that a hasty *tempo*, for example, is a result of anxiety, or that a slow one is a means of expressing passive hostility, then there is no reason not to interpret it as such.   But it is safe, and legitimate enough, to refer things to the level of personal style as a useful first approximation.

One feature of Nailson's personal style that emerged quite clearly in the operation story is an uneven rhythm.   Note that he made two somewhat abortive starts before he finally got into his story.   One hypothesis would be that he had trouble starting because of the intense emotional nature of his associations to the picture.   He did about the same thing, however, with every story.   Also, examples from his everyday life could be cited to show that he was a slow and uncertain starter, who nevertheless usually made a strong finish.

The matter of verbalization deserves more emphasis than it has received above.   The appropriateness, felicity, prolixity, primitivity, conventionality, and many other qualities of the way a person uses words reveal much about him.   F. H. Sanford [*30*] has shown how faithfully the characteristics of a person's verbal style may reflect basic aspects of his personality.   More of this later, however, when we consider the implications of each determinant for interpretation.

Summary.   In trying to understand how a particular TAT story came to be just the way it is, we have distinguished nine classes of determinants: the situational context, the directing sets, the perceptual impact, the arousal of needs and affects, defensive circuiting, associative elaboration, the limiting and facilitating effect of abilities, the internal milieu, and personal style.   Some of these headings are more inclusive than others, but all of them are to some degree operative in every story.   The relative importance of these determinants may vary greatly in the responses of different subjects to the situation.   When there is complete blocking and rejection, for example, the statement "I can't make up a story this time," can be explained without necessarily invoking associative elaboration any further than to say that there is none.

The subject's reaction to the test may involve all, most, or only a few of the nine kinds of determinants, depending on the kind of ego-structure the subject possesses.   A complex phenomenon such as the TAT story is produced differently in different persons. Therefore, we must not expect to get the same things out of one person's TAT that may be inferred from another's.   The stories of an intelligent, cooperative, inwardly free person will often contain an inexhaustible wealth of materials for various kinds of insights about him, permitting an extensive description and analysis of personality to be written, covering diagnostic considerations, personality traits and structure, developmental trends, relations with important persons in his life, motives and defenses, sentiments, qualities of intellect, vocational adjustment, and other areas.   Just because this is often possible, it is not fair to claim that the TAT is a test of all these regions of personality, any more than such a claim can be made for any other projective technique.   We must recognize the fact that inhibited, constricted personality structures often lead to results with projective tests that tell us that the subject has such a structure, and little more.

It may be said further that frequently a great deal more can be interpreted from a set of "cliché stories," or from a protocol obtained question-by-question, almost by a process of extraction, than is frequently claimed.   It is more difficult; it requires more experience and more sensitivity to subtle ways in which a stereotyped story differs from dead average; but, as Freud once said about the interpretation of difficult dreams, it is always possible to make some progress.

ADMINISTRATION

The Test.   The third revision of the TAT [22], which is the one in current use, consists of 30 pictures and a blank card.   The pictures have been selected and marked in such a way that there are four sets of 20 cards each: one for boys, one for girls, one for males over 14, and one for females over 14.   A card marked "BG" is used for both boys and girls; one marked "BM" is used for both boys and men; one marked "GF" is used for both girls and women.   A card number not followed by a letter designates a picture used for both sexes and all ages.   The serial number and letter designations are printed on the backs of the cards.

The following description of each of the pictures is adapted from the manual by Murray [22]: [5]

1. A young boy is contemplating a violin that rests on a table in front of him.
2. Country scene: in the foreground is a young woman with books in her hand; in the background a man is working in the fields and an older woman is looking on.
3 BM. On the floor against a couch is the huddled form of a boy with his head bowed on his right arm.   Beside him on the floor is a revolver.
3 GF. A young woman is standing with downcast head, her face covered with her right hand.   Her left arm is stretched forward against a wooden door.
4. A woman is clutching the shoulders of a man whose face and body are averted as if he were trying to pull away from her.
5. A middle-aged woman is standing on the threshold of a half-opened door looking into a room.
6 BM. A short, elderly woman stands with her back turned to a tall young man.   The latter is looking downward with a perplexed expression.
6 GF. A young woman sitting on the edge of a sofa looks back over her shoulder at an older man with a pipe in his mouth who seems to be addressing her.

---

[5] Henry A. Murray, *Thematic Apperception Test*.   Cambridge: Harvard University Press, 1943.   Reprinted by permission of the publishers.

7 BM. A gray-haired man is looking at a younger man who is sullenly staring into space.

7 GF. An older woman is sitting on a sofa close beside a girl, speaking or reading to her. The girl, who holds a doll in her lap, is looking away.

8 BM. An adolescent boy looks straight out of the picture. The barrel of a rifle is visible at one side, and in the background is the dim scene of a surgical operation, like a reverie-image.

8 GF. A young woman sits with her chin in her hand looking off into space.

9 BM. Four men in overalls are lying on the grass taking it easy.

9 GF. A young woman with a magazine and a purse in her hand looks from behind a tree at another young woman in a party dress running along a beach.

10. A young woman's head against a man's shoulder.

Pictures of Second Series

11. A road skirting a deep chasm between high cliffs. On the road in the distance are obscure figures. Protruding from the rocky wall on one side is the long head and neck of a dragon.

12 M. A young man is lying on a couch with his eyes closed. Leaning over him is the gaunt form of an elderly man, his hand stretched out above the face of the reclining figure.

12 F. The portrait of a young woman. A weird old woman with a shawl over her head is grimacing in the background.

12 BG. A rowboat is drawn up on the bank of a woodland stream. There are no human figures in the picture.

13 MF. A young man is standing with downcast head buried in his arm. Behind him is the figure of a woman lying in bed.

13 B. A little boy is sitting on the doorstep of a log cabin.

13 G. A little girl is climbing a winding flight of stairs.

14. The silhouette of a man (or woman) against a bright window. The rest of the picture is totally black.

15. A gaunt man with clenched hands is standing among gravestones.

16. Blank card.

17 BM. A naked man is clinging to a rope. He is in the act of climbing up or down.

17 GF. A bridge over water. A female figure leans over the railing. In the background are tall buildings and small figures of men.

18 BM. A man is clutched from behind by three hands. The figures of his antagonists are invisible.

18 GF. A woman has her hands squeezed around the throat of another woman whom she appears to be pushing backwards across the banister of a stairway.

19. A weird picture of cloud formations overhanging a snow-covered cabin in the country.

20. The dimly illumined figure of a man (or woman) in the dead of night leaning against a lamp post.

In the administration of the TAT, the examiner should strive to create a situation that will be as therapeutic to the subject, or at least as nontraumatic, as possible. Some of the pictures carry strong implications of aggression (especially 8 BM and 18 GF), others of sexuality (13 MF; less strongly 10), or suicide (3 BM, 17 GF, and to some extent, 14). Sometimes 12 M, 7 BM, and 18 BM are an unconscious homosexual threat to the subject.

The examiner should neither shrink back overcautiously from exposing emotionally sick persons to such sights, nor press too hard for a story if the patient is obviously upset by one of them. Patients sometimes experience a kind of "black shock" on cards 14 and 15, comparable to that seen in the Rorschach test. The examiner must guard against the possibility of doing the patient more harm than good by being too insistent on a story, or by forcing a patient to recognize something that for very good reasons he has distorted or omitted.

What can the examiner do to create a situation in which the subject will respond in the most useful ways? The most general answer is that the methods of administration must vary according to the examiner's purpose. For research in personality, especially when healthy college students are the subjects, Murray's suggestions, given in the manual that accompanies the printed pictures, are appropriate. With the reclining position, the challenge to the university man's claim to intelligence and imagination, and other devices, Murray succeeded in obtaining unusually long, detailed, rich, and revealing stories. For diagnostic use, such elaborated stories are neither needed nor wanted. The number of cards used and the particular ones chosen, as well as the nature of inquiry, also vary according to the purpose for which the test is being given. Most of the differences in styles of administration can be reconciled by reference to this one principle.

Some Specific Suggestions. The procedure of administration may best be considered in relation to the nine determinants of TAT stories already listed.

1. The Situational Context is affected by the way the test is administered. Of course, certain aspects of the situational context cannot be changed by the examiner; the subject may be anxious because the test he is taking will help to determine whether or not he gets a job or an educational opportunity, and not because of anything the examiner himself says or does. Nevertheless, the examiner should always be aware of the situation from the subject's viewpoint. With such awareness, he can offer appropriate molli-fying explanations, or assume a role of warm friendliness, disinter-ested impersonality, or whatever will be most supportive and con-ducive to a letting-down of defenses. In general, he should try to arrange for a minimum of distractions and a maximum of relaxa-tion.

One fortunate thing about the standard arrangement of the pic-tures is that card 1, the boy and violin, usually brings out the sub-ject's reaction to an imposed task. Sometimes the examiner can advantageously avoid in the test situation the kind of behavior attributed to the "bad parents" who are making the boy do some-thing he hates, or can emulate the attitudes of the "good parents" who foster the boy's talent. In any event, he must usually maintain a neutral, accepting attitude, no matter what the subject says. The most important aspect of the situational context is the interpersonal relation between examiner and patient, and the emotional attitudes of the examiner are far more important than the exact words he uses. If one dislikes a difficult patient, and is not skilled in self-control, he can use the most neutral and nondirective wording in everything that he says, and yet, because of inflection and emphasis, make the patient feel dominated and hounded. Conversely, if rap-port is good, if the subject feels basically not threatened by the examiner's approach to him but recognizes that the examiner is try-ing to help him or is genuinely interested in him as a person, the examiner can often make extensive demands on the subject.

2. Directing Sets. The purpose of the instructions is to produce the particular kind of *directing sets* that the examiner wants. Broadly speaking, one wants to motivate the subject to do his best; one wants stories with a plot having a beginning, a middle, and an end, and with characters whose thoughts and feelings as well as ex-ternal actions are described. Again, the particular words that are used in the instructions are not as important as getting these ob-jectives across to the subject in his own terms, and in such a way as to motivate him to cooperate—or, for some patients, in such a way as to arouse only a minimum of resistance. The TAT requires a rather complex set for many subjects to maintain over a period of an hour, and they forget part of it. It is necessary both to take note of any difficulty in maintaining a set, and to remind the subject as tactfully as possible of the parts of his task that have been forgotten. Efforts to challenge the subject's self-esteem by intimating that one is going to test important abilities are out of place for most patients in the clinical setting; the test is better introduced simply as something else one wants him to do in order to get information necessary to help him.

As to the other kind of sets—those that guide the development of particular stories—they must be determined by the subject himself, his own needs, defenses, and abilities. It follows that directive inquiry, when used, should be employed very deliberately, under special circumstances, and with full understanding of what one is doing. If a subject cannot be led into an important area of potential conflict in any other way, structured questions may be asked after the spontaneous story is over; they should always be written out in full, in parentheses, so that it is clear in the record that the examiner departed from the nondirective approach. Suppose, for example, a subject tells a story to picture 6 BM, in which the son tells his mother that he is going to another city to take a job, and she disowns him. The examiner has reason to know that it is important to find out what the subject's reaction to maternal rejection is; so he asks a nondirective question: "What are his thoughts and feelings?" If the answer is, "He is wondering how his new job is going to turn out," the examiner has only indirect evidence on the crucial point. It is then permissible to ask, "How does he feel about his mother's saying that she has disowned him?" Of course, one should never ask, "Does he feel bad?" or in any other way put words in a subject's mouth. Generally, one should avoid questions that can be answered by a simple yes or no.

With some subjects, the examiner need say nothing after the initial instructions except to praise the stories, though not too lavishly. The occasions that call for him to intervene actively as Rapaport [26] says, are lack of clarity (verbal, perceptual, and meaningful); failure to include one of the specified aspects of the story; and running far over or far under the average time allotted per story. The principal disagreement among writers about TAT administration concerns this matter of inquiry. It is the writer's judgment that inquiry is frequently useful and that it works best if done immediately after the picture is taken away. It is not necessary to get *all* aspects of every story. For example, if the thoughts of the characters in the stories are persistently omitted and not very revealing when inquired into for the first few pictures, it is better to abandon this line of inquiry. Done with the proper attitude and in the manner referred to above, the inquiry can be fairly extensive without upsetting or inhibiting the patient and his later productions. It is better for the examiner to underinquire than to overinquire, and in case of doubt, to save his question until after the test is completed.

3. *The Perceptual Impact.* Since the perceptual impact of specific pictures is important in determining the stories, it is a matter of concern which pictures are used. There is much to be said for each of the pictures in the published set, and for each of those in the most widely used earlier revision, but this is not the place to discuss the special merits of particular pictures. Whenever possible, all 20 pictures should be administered, in two or more sessions. Often the pressure of work in a busy clinic does not allow the time required for the complete test, but it is generally inadvisable to use fewer than 10 cards. The 11 most frequently used (for adult males) seem to be the following: 1, 2, 3 BM, 4, 6 BM, 7 BM, 8 BM, 12 M, 13 MF, 15, 18 BM. There is nothing final about the selection of pictures devised by Murray and Morgan; other workers have used other pictures with very good results. The blank card, 16, particularly deserves wider use, in the writer's opinion. For practical reasons, however, it is best to build up experience with a set that is widely used, so that one can make use of the recorded experience of others.

4. *The Arousal of Needs and Affects.* The arousal of affects by the pictures and their associations may be quite apparent in the patient's behavior and tone of voice as well as in what he says. A very important part of a complete protocol therefore is a description of the patient's behavior, changes or breaks in the tone of voice, and somatic signs of anxiety such as sweating and heavy breathing, particularly as these things change in relation to story content.

5. *Defensive Circuiting.* We have seen above how defenses play a dual role in TAT stories: they may disguise or prevent the emergence of hidden content; and yet from the defenses one learns about the ego structure of the subject. Like the early psychoanalysts, one may be impatient with the subject's defenses as resistances that

merely impede the work; one may want to find technical means in administration to avoid them. If so, he may reflect on the later experiences of psychoanalysts, which showed that often these defenses and resistances were most worthy of the analyst's attention because they were the most crippling aspects of a personality. For this and similar reasons, psychoanalysis has turned from preoccupation with the id to increasing interest in the ego via analysis of resistances. When allowance is made for this consideration, it still remains true in some cases that defenses are so rigid and ubiquitous that they prevent the production of anything more than barren descriptions of pictures. When this happens, one can try to see the subject at another time when there is reason to think he will be less threatened. Or, after exhausting one's wiles in efforts to induce the subject to relax and to respond to the first two or three cards, a strategic retreat may be made: the test may be turned into a perceptual one by showing each card briefly and asking what the situation was, or what was pictured. Then, at least, one gets the perceptual impact of the whole set of cards in a brief time.

6. *Associative Elaboration.* Sophisticated subjects sometimes start giving *personal-historical content* directly, without more than a gesture or two at putting it into story form. If one is sure that the subject has interpreted his task as merely to produce short segments of his remembered past, it is appropriate to stop him (usually only if there are slips into the use of the first personal pronoun or other unmistakable evidence) and ask if that is not what he is doing. The examiner may explain that the test calls for *stories,* that the subject is to use his imagination rather than his memory, and make them up. The reason is that the TAT is not—except in unusual cases—an efficient way of taking a personal history. The TAT's special usefulness comes in eliciting attitudes, needs, and aspects of personal experience that are *not* readily accessible to conscious efforts at remembering. It is much more feasible to gain access to these levels when the subject has the set to make up an imaginative story, not to tell a chapter of his autobiography.

7. *Abilities.* It is similarly necessary, with an occasional patient, to remind him that a coherent story is wanted, not free associations. Again, this step is taken not because free association is not a valuable method; it is just a different method, yielding different kinds of results. Only when the subject tries to tell a regular story with

a plot is one able to find out about certain *abilities* that are relevant to this kind of task. Of course, the principal way in which abilities concern the examiner in administration is that he must tailor his instructions and questions to the subject's intellectual level.

8. Internal Milieu; 9. Personal Style. The last two categories, the internal milieu and personal style, carry no particular implications for administration that have not already been covered. It might only be mentioned that the subject's style is likely to be visible in his stories more clearly, the less interference there is with his natural tempo, phrasing, and architectonic sense. The exigencies of the examiner's writing stories by hand, when no recording equipment or other special aids are available, will sometimes cramp the subject's style (as well as the examiner's hand), but the advantages of this simple method outweigh the loss, for practical use in the clinic. If the patient is told ahead of time that the examiner is going to try to write down everything that he says, and is occasionally reminded not to go too fast, he will usually match the tempo of the writing. It should go without saying that for the TAT, as in almost all psychological testing, *verbatim recording is an absolute essential.*

This section on administration has been intentionally selective in its coverage of the problem. The intent here has been, primarily, to delineate the principal attitudes and points of view from which the individual examiner may derive specific procedures that are most congenial to his own personal style of testing; and secondarily, to present certain points about administration that are not already covered in other easily available sources.

INTERPRETATION

Books have already been written on the interpretation of the TAT, and enough has been left unsaid for many a volume more. A part of one chapter in one book cannot pretend to do more than open up the topic and attempt a general orientation.

There is a great deal to be said for a set of fixed variables to be scored for each story, after the model of the insightful formulae of Rorschach, but there are many difficulties in applying such a plan to the TAT. A number of systems have been worked out; almost all of them are useful for some purposes, chiefly for research and for training in sensitivity to easily-overlooked aspects of stories. The better known scoring systems have been developed by Murray [22], Stein [36], Tomkins [40], Wyatt [42], Henry [17], Bellak [4, 5], and Aron [2]. None of these, however, is more than an aid to systematic observation, and none can be recommended for routine clinical use, though they are very helpful in research.

Strictly speaking, there are scarcely any generally applicable rules for analysis and interpretation of the TAT. One general statement can be made, however: one's skill in interpreting the TAT is greatly enhanced by, and can proceed no further than, his *thorough under-standing of dynamic psychology*. Specifically, most TAT workers have found that their insightfulness in interpretation has been en-riched most by a knowledge of psychoanalysis.

Different specific approaches are appropriate to different pur-poses for which the test is being used. The vocational counselor will seldom find it helpful to indulge in speculative reconstruction of basic dynamics; the psychodiagnostician may be quite uninter-ested in exploring the patient's sentiments; the researcher on the emotional springs of prejudice will care little to trace indications of the abilities for which the psychologist looks when consulted about the selection of highly-trained professional personnel.

The first step in interpretation is to get straight just what one's aims are. If one is working for an institution, or as part of a clinical team, that will usually involve finding out *exactly* what service one is expected to supply, and perhaps, working out a realistic compromise on the basis of what he is able to deliver. All too often, dissatisfaction with the clinical psychologist's con-tributions arises out of unrealistic expectations and the lack of a common understanding of the purpose of the testing.

The next step is to decide, on the basis of the detailed purposes of testing, what kinds of data are needed to satisfy those purposes. Suppose the setting is a psychiatric one, the job is diagnostic testing, and the specific problem is the differential diagnosis of paranoid schizophrenia vs. psychotic depression. One has given the Ror-schach test, which is meager, suggestively peculiar in spots, but not decisive. What other kinds of data will be needed? An answer to this last question requires a knowledge of psychopathology. To name a few things, one will want to try to distinguish between de-pressive blocking and paranoid caution; perhaps between delusions of unworthiness and delusions of persecution; between constriction and projective distortion of the perceptual field. These then are some specifications of the kinds of information one will want to get from a test, or from a whole battery of tests. Depressive blocking and paranoid cautiousness may both produce meager stories with long reaction times, but the latter may make itself known through an inferential, descriptive approach that *derives,* often by explicit steps, everything in the story from details of the picture itself. As far as the different types of delusions are concerned, neither will necessarily be reflected in the test, but the plots of the stories may give direct hints about one or the other kind of delusion. And by paying attention to the perceptual impact of the pictures, one can see paranoid influences at work in distortions, particularly misidentifications of sex, while the effects of depression are more likely to be seen in inert omissions of the less obvious aspects of the pictures.

Excerpts from the case of Harris, a 31-year-old, white, divorced veteran, will illustrate the use of the TAT in clinical practice, with the following objective: the patient's doctor referred him for a "full battery work-up" as an aid to long-term intensive psychotherapy that he was about to begin. The psychiatrist was interested in anything the tests might reveal—anything, that is, that would be revelant to a full understanding of the patient's personality and his illness, and that might help plan the course of therapy. The psychiatrist said that Harris had been diagnosed "schizophrenia, paranoid type." What, then, are the kinds of helpful information that the TAT can give?

Seven types of data relevant to this problem are often yielded by the TAT, namely, information about: (1) thought organization; (2) emotional organization (responsiveness and control); (3) needs: their strengths and levels on which manifested; (4) the subject's view of the world; (5) interpersonal relationships (object attachments); (6) the subject's conception of and attitudes toward himself; (7) dynamics of development and illness. Some information of all of these kinds was extracted from Harris' TAT stories. Limitations of space allow us to look at the protocols for only three pictures.

13 MF (10"). They got some lulus here don't they? (sigh; 48") Well this is a boy and girl, they've been going together. They started going together, he was very . . . she was very pretty and he was attracted by her pulchritude. This boy was jumping around from one place to another, had no goal in mind seeking what pleasure he could find, and he carried on with her to the point of sexual intercourse. (sigh) . . . . All this time he was beginning to become, well, he was becoming more nervous and uncertain. Because of that he continued to carry on relations more frequently, and the girl was unfortunately in love with him but he wasn't in love with her, in fact he wasn't in love with anybody. Finally he gets to the point where he stays all night with her . . . and even though he, let's see (sighs) he—this particular night he stays all night with her for the first time. He wakes up in the morning, realizes the seriousness of the situation because she was a nice girl and it's his duty to go ahead and marry her whether he loves her or not. He feels very guilty, shameful about the situation as far as her and his family is concerned, but he goes ahead with the marriage, which is an unhappy one. (7 minutes).

18 BM (76″). Could be the story of a fellow who was at one time a very happy man, satisfied with things in general. Then he started to stop in the local bar occasionally with a friend or two. It became more frequent as time went on till it got the best of him, that is he started drinking heavily, got the habit. He got to the point where he depended upon liquor to get along. It had a firm grip on him then. Because of his liquor why his family life got broken up which aggravated his condition still more. Eventually wound up in an alcoholic institution. I believe that's all. (4½ minutes). (What is the scene shown in the picture?) Well that could be a scene when he was very drunk and the hands represent the hold liquor had on him.

10 (40″). A story of a middle-aged woman who never married. Very active in community affairs, sewing circles, etc. She had always avoided men up to—well up to quite ah—well quite a long time, because she was picking out, she was waiting to pick out the perfect husband. When she got to the point where she was rather elderly, middle-aged, she saw she was aging, saw that she had waited too long, so she sought outlet by entering into all these so-called activities. So during the course of the meeting they decided to have a noted lecturer give a talk on, oh something or other, and he was invited to, well, lecture before the club, a woman's club, and he was, it happened he came and gave a lecture. The fellow himself was very scheming, rather handsome sort, with an eye for a wealthy widow or someone he could finangle money from. So after the lecture he does his usual casing of the members to find the most eligible and he decides upon this woman because of her wealth, etc., and so he starts laying it on thick, and the spark in her returns. She thinks that this would be her last chance to ever marry and all the time she was believing all his words, etc., and all he was thinking about was ways of getting some of her money. The romance continues and by some means or other he—gets some money from her, the period before the marriage takes place. So as soon as he gets his money he skips out and she is left at the church. She realizes then that he was no good, that her only satisfaction in life was the community affairs that she had been pursuing, in helping others. I guess that's all, kinda corny. (9 minutes).

Using the Categories of Determinants in Interpretation. We have seen at the beginning of the chapter how nine different classes of determinants may be considered to play a part in shaping a story; let us see what we can figure out about Harris by studying the impress of each kind of determinant on these stories.

1. The Situational Context. Little that is directly revelant to interpretation ordinarily comes from the first class of determinants. One is, of course, trying to interpret the nature of the person from his stories, not the nature of his environment, so that the latter becomes important mainly in a negative way: one does not want to make the mistake of thinking that a certain reaction is generally characteristic of the subject if it is determined primarily by this particular situation. For example, some male patients have violent aversions to women, which seriously distorts the results of tests given them by feminine examiners. (Female patients sometimes react similarly to male examiners.)

2. The Directing Sets. There is one way in which the situational context may tell us much about the person himself; that is through the patient's own interpretation of the situation. We are considering this factor under the second class of determinants, however, since it comes into play almost entirely in terms of general sets and motivation for cooperating with the examiner. If a patient's interpretation of the examiner's efforts to help him is that the examiner is trying to prove him insane, for example, he must be called suspicious, perhaps even paranoid. To return to Harris—knowing that the author of the above stories is confined in a mental hospital with a diagnosis of paranoid schizophrenia, one might expect that he would be suspicious, evasive, or otherwise difficult to test. Yet from these stories one can see that he is not only compliant, telling unusually long and excellent stories, but even *self*-derogatory. ("Kinda corny," he said of his own story to picture 10; elsewhere in the test he had remarked, "I'm not very good at this.") When the situation of being sent from a locked ward to take some strange tests produces only this kind of set (the rest of the stories are similar in set), it is unlikely that the patient is a paranoid schizophrenic of the usual contentious, suspicious, rigid kind. If he is a paranoid schizophrenic at all, he is much more likely one of the very different, meek, intropunitive sort, who often seem very similar to depressives.

There is another important aspect of sets that must be noted by anyone who is testing for schizophrenia. One of the characteristic impairments associated with this disease is a breakdown in the ability to maintain appropriate sets long enough for any significant achievements. Of course, like almost any other specific deficit attributed to schizophrenia, this impairment does not necessarily appear in every case. But when a patient is as unusually well able to maintain continuity and smooth development of an idea as was Harris, one may begin to wonder just how psychotic he is. At least, the TAT suggests that there was no impairment of this function; the lack of any significant drop in the Picture Arrangement subtest score in his Wechsler-Bellevue profile supports this interpretation.

3. The Perceptual Impact. In this area, too, Harris' stories were almost more remarkable for what they were *not* than for what they were. There were no serious perceptual distortions; he was not even overimpressed by details of the pictures, but usually seemed to have good average percepts (cf., in the Rorschach test, $F +$ per cent, 70; no small or rare areas chosen; average proportion of popular responses). There was, however, one important deviation. In his story to 18 BM there was something about the way he said, "It had a firm grip on him," that made the examiner suspect that there might be some symbolic, overliteral apperception of the three hands in the picture. Note that the inquiry used was completely nonleading and gave no hint of this suspicion, yet it did bring him to verbalize the autistic idea that was woven into his perception of the card. (At this point, the Wechsler-Bellevue scatter pattern offers some support for the assumption that this was in part a perceptual deviation, since the lowest subtest score of all—four points below Vocabulary—was for Picture Completion, a perceptual test.)

Of course, the significance of what Harris did here is not wholly in the realm of perception; the fact that he gave an explanation of the kind he did suggests the encroachment of symbolic modes of thinking on his otherwise good thought organization. It is mentioned here largely because it was the concern of the examiner to establish just what Harris' perception of the scene was that led to the psychotic-like idea. It is perhaps worth digressing here for a moment to point out that there is very little inquiry in these stories; little was needed. Yet in this one instance, waiting until the end of the test would very likely have meant losing the opportunity to test the hypothesis—that is, the hypothesis on which the inquiry is based, for questioning must always have a definite purpose.

4. The Arousal of Needs and Affects. The three stories quoted above, and Harris' others, are unusually rich in hints about his motivational life. Many interesting subtleties of interpretation could be illustrated by reference to them, but a full analysis would take a number of pages. Only a few interrelated themes can be considered. One that pervades all of the stories is passivity. When one reads these stories looking to see how adequate the heroes are in achieving satisfaction of their needs, one is struck by the fact that not one of the heroes made an effort to struggle against the fate that was imposed upon him; all were caught in the grip of circumstance or inner compulsion (of guilt, or of depedence on drink). That this passivity represented an actual (though unconscious) goal is strongly suggested by the definite self-defeating (and in other stories, self-destructive) tendency of the actions Harris was able to think of for his characters. For picture 13, the young man got himself more and more embroiled so that he finally felt compelled to enter into a marriage that was foredoomed to failure; in 18, the hero's responsibility for his eventual failure in life was carefully not seen. In 10, the woman did not seem to bring defeat on her own head, though she certainly was the victim of what was almost a persecuting villain. The consistency of these themes, and their deviation from the usually given stories for the several pictures, must lead to the conclusion that there was in fact a strong passive masochistic need in Harris that forced such themes into his consciousness.

Another unconscious force that we can assume with some certainty to be unusually strong in Harris, as well as related to his passivity, is a homosexual need.[6] It seems quite certain, at least, that there was a high degree of feminine identification, which almost always connotes latent homosexuality. Card 10 offers an excellent opportunity for a subject to identify himself with either of the two, equally prominent figures. There can be no doubt that Harris identified himself with the victim in this case, and his ability to create a picture of her yearnings and feelings is additional evidence of his having experienced many things in a "feminine" way himself. Then

---

[6] It is assumed that all needs such as the ones so far mentioned are present to some degree in everyone, and that the interpretative problem is to gauge their relative strengths and their interrelationships.

there was the slip at the beginning of the story for picture 13, when he nearly said that *he* was very pretty. (Actually, the patient himself was very handsome.) Although in the story Harris identified himself with the man, the heterosexuality was clearly unsatisfactory and compulsive in quality; that is, the motivation for more frequent sexual relations was directly stated to be because of the man's nervousness and uncertainty; "he wasn't in love with her, in fact he wasn't in love with anybody." In none of Harris' productions was there a happy marriage or any other satisfactory heterosexual relationship; in 10, the underlying conviction that there is no real love between man and woman must be particularly clear. This picture is almost always seen as a loving couple. In the writer's experience, only patients who are under the pressure of strong homosexual needs, usually paranoids, and neurotic characters who cannot conceive of a genuine tender relationship between any two persons, think that the scene is a sham, that there is really no reciprocal affection. There is nothing to indicate that the homosexual needs were conscious; in fact, the heterosexual acting out of a denial of homosexuality in 13 was striking.

The needs that have been discerned in these stories are quite consistent with paranoid developments of some kind, and so contribute to confirming the diagnosis. In addition, the examiner has learned much about the patient's personality and has established the severity of his underlying emotional sickness, even though his formal thought functioning may be good.

As far as affects are concerned, Harris said little about the feelings and emotions of the characters. The anxiety and guilt of the man in picture 13, however, and the disappointed yearning of the woman in picture 10 were expressed so clearly that we may justifiably set up the hypotheses that these were his own feelings. The only affect that broke through his defenses into overt manifestation during testing was *depression,* in the many sighs that punctuated his story to card 13. Another important negative statement deserves to be made: there was little that could be called disharmonious or inappropriate affect. In the affective realm, as well as in the intellectual, there was little evidence of a schizophrenic process.

5. *Defensive Circuiting.* In discussing a case, it is almost impossible to discuss motivational forces without saying something about the defenses against them, or about the ego-mechanisms

through which their expressions are controlled. The fact that certain needs seemed to be unconscious implied the operation of repression in keeping any direct recognition of them out of the stories. The self-defeating, masochistic trend implied that Harris turned aggression against himself, as did also the stress on guilt. Projection, which is certainly expected in a paranoid case, was less apparent than usual, though it was undoubtedly involved in the symbolic idea of the hands as representing "the hold liquor had on him."

One of the most significant contributions to the understanding of Harris that came from looking for evidences of his defenses was the uncovering of the character disorder that antedated his schizophrenia. In respect to this important feature of the case, the diagnosis was as blind as one could wish; if anything, one's attention should have been called *away from* characterological difficulties by the diagnostic impression given. Yet the efforts Harris made to avoid coming to grips with his true feelings and to avoid responsibility were quite striking. When he looked at the scene in card 13, his story revealed that strong feelings of guilt, shame, and anxiety were aroused, yet he tried at once to laugh off these feelings with a feebly facetious comment which was in vivid contrast to his later gloom. When he voiced some rather poignant feelings indirectly in the last of these three stories, he had to devaluate them by calling his story "corny." His heroes likewise were conspicuously avoidant in their behavior—"jumping around from one place to another, had no goal in mind"; "she had always avoided men"; "he skips out." In story 18, the denial of the hero's personal responsibility for his alcoholism is striking. The other typical defense of character disorder, acting out, has already been indicated in the discussion of picture 13. When the specific content of alcoholism was present so blatantly, one is justified in a strong hunch, at least, that the premorbid personality structure had many of the features of character disorder. In this case, it was particularly important to establish the nature of the basic adjustment, because the therapist was prepared for what happened when Harris became almost entirely free from schizophrenic symptoms: he showed a tendency to turn to alcohol, which the therapist was able to forestall fairly well.

6. *Associative Elaboration.* A number of determinants, including the associative elaboration, can be considered from the standpoint of *form* as well as content: that is, not just *what* are the needs,

but *how* appropriately, impulsively, and so on, are they expressed; not just *what* are the memories that are awakened and brought into the story, but *how* the associative process works. Is it rambling, chain-like, going off the point (as in many manics)? Is it brought almost to a standstill by depression? Does it proceed by jumps and by obscure idiosyncratic associations, so that the listener cannot easily follow the trend of thought (an indication of a schizophrenic process)? Harris' associative thinking passed this kind of inspection fairly well; it seemed to be intact. By now we have found so many aspects of his personality that were untouched by schizophrenia, so far as we can see, that we must consider the possibility that he was not psychotic in spite of story 18 and one confabulation (in Rapaport's sense) in the Rorschach. The final conclusion reached was, in fact, that there was very substantial remission from a schizophrenic episode.

A. PERSONAL-HISTORICAL CONTENT. To what extent did Harris draw on his own life and his present problems in making up his stories? To a very large extent, undoubtedly, varying considerably from one story to another. It would seem very unlikely that anything in story 10, for example, was directly autobiographical, though the story in 13 turned out to be almost entirely a condensed account of circumstances leading to his marriage. How does one decide? Certainly, plausibility and internal consistency must play a considerable role. It would not make sense for so passive and helpless a fellow as Harris obviously was, to have swindled any wealthy maiden ladies. Yet we can take something from that very secondary character, put it together with the other "lover" in 13, and piece together a generalization that does hold true of his past: that he was psychosexually immature, incapable of a real love relationship, and that there was a parasitic undercurrent in his affairs with women. It is rarely safe (and rarely does it contribute anything to the study of a case) to try to be much more specific than this. Interpretation of personal-historical material, then, is confined to a rather general level, and is concerned principally with the nature of the emotional relationships between the subject and important kinds of figures in his life.

B. SENTIMENTIVE CONTENT. One of the easiest ways to approach the analysis of a TAT is to look for indications of the subject's sentiments, his basic emotional attitudes towards certain classes of objects. From these, one can often set up hypotheses that can be tested out on other levels. Or certain sentiments themselves may have diagnostic significance. For example, in the story Harris told to picture 18, he clearly expressed a utilitarian attitude towards liquor—that it was something to depend on, in order to get along —which seems to be necessary for the development of alcoholism.

C. GENERAL-INFORMATIONAL CONTENT. Nothing particularly significant on this level emerged in the three stories under consideration. As an indirect indicator of intelligence, the kind of information a person is able to call on is sometimes helpful in questioning an impression of mental deficiency, just as may be a patient's spontaneous use of unusual words (cf., "pulchritude").

7. *Abilities.* Taken as a group, these three stories are better than average in construction and in interest. It is reasonable to infer that intelligence and imaginative ability were considerably better than average, though of course no one would attempt to use the TAT to get an IQ. Certain kinds of abilities, however, are indicated more directly by the TAT than by any other test. One thing the psychiatrist obviously wanted to know about Harris was, would he respond well to psychotherapy? A case of schizophrenia with character disorder also involved would seem, on the face of it, to be particularly unpromising. But in his stories, Harris showed a noteworthy ability to empathize, to take the point of view of more than one character in a story, and to create a convincing picture of feelings [*10*]. Furthermore, his recognition that nervousness and uncertainty may be causally related to sexual activity represented an insight considerably above the average level. These slight indications point to a capacity for psychological mindedness, an ability to examine his own behavior in psychological terms and to accept psychological explanations. This ability was not invariably present (there were no indications of it in some of his other stories) but it existed as a potentiality that might be very helpful in psychotherapy.

8. *The Internal Milieu.* Three stories are enough, in Harris' case, to give the tune of the whole test. An atmosphere of hopelessness, of fatalism, of being caught in a vicious circle of some kind, pervades his stories. It bespeaks an inner pessimism that was quite deep-rooted and was cause for some qualification of the hopeful prognosis suggested by his abilities. One infers that Harris had

had his spirit broken, that his feeling of validity and worth as a man had been so severely damaged that he might have great difficulty in ever making a successful adjustment. That there is danger in letting oneself go too far in speculations about a person on the basis of the atmosphere of the stories, which could have been a function of temporary mood, was brought home clearly by a retest of Harris after one and one-half years of therapy. Once he had achieved a better control over his passive needs, he was able to take a more positive and optimistic outlook on life.

9. *Personal Style.* Harris' way of talking, judged from this sample, seemed to be rather easy, informal without being disrespectful, generally fluent, and free of schizophrenic peculiarities. A stilted word crept in once in awhile, and he blocked to some extent when he came up against emotional difficulties. Perhaps the most noticeable feature of his style was his tendency to become vague at points during a narrative when more mental effort would have enabled him to produce a definite idea that in turn would have made a better story. In picture 10, this trait was particularly outstanding: the lecturer is to talk on "oh, something or other"; "by some means or other he gets some money from her"; note also the liberal use of *et cetera.* Here is a clue to the intellectual laziness that is very clearly seen in contrast between a Wechsler-Bellevue IQ of 126 and the meager Rorschach: 26 responses, half of them animals, with only one good whole response other than popular and near-popular responses.

The style of verbalization is very often one of the best sources of evidence for important defenses and types of pathology. From the lack of pedantry, rumination, and intellectually ambitious references, one can see that Harris was not a very obsessive person. If he had used more slang, particularly of the flippant and rather callous sort into which he slipped in describing the schemer of story 10; if he had joked with the tester, or, in general, had tried to make it plain that he was not going to get personally involved, the character disorder would have been considered much more severe and ingrained. As it was, the negative evidence of the lack of schizophrenic autism in speech was used to buttress the conclusion that the schizophrenic process had not seriously undermined the patient's intellectual and emotional functioning.

So much for the interpretation of Harris' stories. The abundance of material about Harris has been very thinly sampled here; but some of the ways it can be used in interpretation are evident.   Occasional references to other tests have been included as a reminder that cross-checking between tests, as well as from one aspect of the TAT to another, is a necessary method in clinical work.

A few final words about Harris: he had been kept in a state of exaggerated passive dependency by an overpowering mother and strict father.   After some rather nomadic years following high school, he impregnated a girl and then entered into a rather brief and unsatisfactory marriage.   While overseas in the service, he became involved in a heterosexual affair that occasioned guilt that went to delusional extremes.   He was an airplane pilot, and completed a number of missions while actively deluded about the harmful effect of his glance upon other persons, which he attributed to his own sinfulness.   He finally turned himself in to a hospital, was cooperative and seemingly in good contact with reality in spite of his delusions, though he was easily embarrassed.   After a year and a half of intensive psychotherapy, his delusions had left. Though he still had some difficulty in looking directly at anyone he talked to, he made an excellent social adjustment, and was able to obtain and hold a job.

RELIABILITY AND VALIDITY

The TAT is not a test in the same sense that an intelligence scale is, and consequently the usual canons of reliability and validity cannot be applied without considerable qualification.   The TAT affords a segment of human behavior that may be analyzed in a tremendous variety of ways, and that may serve as the basis for inferences about a myriad of personal characteristics.   Almost as well ask: What is the reliability or validity of everyday behavior?   These questions begin to make sense only when we consider a particular method of abstracting from the data that are provided.

The problem of reliability may be restated for the TAT: to what extent do the stories reflect transient and fugitive states of the person, such as moods or the traces of recent experience, and to what extent are they determined by more slowly-changing dynamic and structural features?   The reliability of the TAT has never been investigated in quite these terms, so an answer is not presently available.   Relevant data are furnished by Coleman [8]: the TAT stories told by 41 children soon after they had seen a movie showed insignificant evidence of influence by its content.

Some data are available on the stability of need-press scorings (according to Murray's scheme) of repeated TATs. In the best extended discussion of these problems in print, Tomkins [40] reports that the repeat reliability of the test, as scored in this way, may be as high as .8 or .9, depending upon the lapse of time between administrations and upon the fluidity-rigidity of the particular subjects concerned.

A second important aspect of reliability is the agreement of different scorers or interpreters working with the same protocols. The simpler and grosser the scoring scheme, the easier it is to obtain good reliability. As a result, the observer reliabilities of complex and highly differentiated sets of categories like Aron's [2] are usually not high, while those obtained by investigators who have worked with a few simple categories have been as good as anyone would wish [15, 20]. In some unreported work at the Harvard Psychological Clinic, Murray demonstrated that a highly differentiated analytic scheme (his need-press categories) could be used with high interobserver reliability. By training two other raters intensively, he was able to bring them to the point where their ratings correlated consistently around .9 with his.

The validity of any particular set of statements based upon the TAT must be a function of at least the following factors: (a) the ability, experience, and the like of the interpreter; (b) the system of scoring and interpretation he uses; (c) the particular kind of statements, predictions, or ratings the interpreter is called upon to make. The interpreter is inseparable from the test when the validity of a technique like the TAT is in question. It is unfortunately true that the ability of Harrison [16] to make blind diagnoses of psychiatric patients with 82.5 per cent accuracy using his own method of analysis, says exactly nothing about the likelihood that anyone else's diagnosis of a case, prediction of a subject's success in a vocation, or statement about personality dynamics will be accurate.

Reported studies indicate that in the hands of competent interpreters using a variety of analytic techniques, the TAT may form the basis for valid inferences about a wide variety of personality traits and abilities [16, 17] and facts of personal history [9, 19]. It may lead to valid predictions of leadership ability in officer candidates [25] or of psychotherapeutic ability in psychiatric candidates (unpublished study by L. Luborsky and the author), predictive ratings in both studies correlating above .6 with criterion ratings. TAT results have been found to agree well with the results of psychoanalytic investigation, other tests, and a variety of sources for case data [16, 17, 21, 23]. Meaningfully and statistically differentiating characteristics have been found in the TATs of known groups ranging from prejudiced and nonprejudiced normal persons [13] to various nosological groupings [3, 27]. The limits of the possible kinds of valid inferences from the TAT are yet to be explored, but by the same token, its validity for any particular task, as applied by any particular clinician, remains unknown until it has been tested.

It should be stated in all frankness that neither the reliability nor the validity of the method of interpretation advocated in this chapter has been rigorously tested, though clinical experience supports the contention that it is teachable and that it yields a variety of statements about personality that agree with independent sources of data.

RELATED TECHNIQUES

Most of what has been said in the preceding sections on rationale and interpretation can be applied to a number of related thematic techniques that are available. There have been too many modifications of the TAT for all to be mentioned, and the trend seems to be towards more, rather than fewer of them. For the most part, these modified TATs are not generally available, are not standardized, and do not require our consideration here, but a few words should be said about several sets of pictures besides Murray's.

Van Lennep [41] has discussed his *Four-Picture Test* (FPT) in Chapter 6. He began working in 1930 with a set of four rather vague water-color pictures, which were published in 1948. It is apparent from the structure of the test that it calls for a higher degree of organizing ability than does the TAT; and projective material may more easily be obtained from some subjects from the transitional material they must introduce to provide continuity between the four pictures. There are richer possibilities for formal analysis in the FPT than in the TAT, while the latter provides more by way of personal content. When satisfactory norms become available, the FPT may prove, for many purposes, to be the most useful brief thematic test, if one wishes to take no more than fifteen minutes of the subject's time.

Chronologically, next comes the *Make A Picture Story (MAPS) Test* of Shneidman [*35*]. In taking the test, the subject constructs his own pictures from a set of 67 separate cardboard figures, any number of which may be superimposed on any of 22 backgrounds, presented one at a time by the examiner. The fact that the subject is led into more active participation and construction often produces greater personal involvement in the MAPS test than in the TAT, with longer and richer stories. The test performance has numerous formal aspects, and Shneidman has shown that many of them have potential diagnostic usefulness [*34*]. The principal drawbacks of the test seem to grow out of its very fluidity and unstructuredness: with an almost infinite number of possible background-figure combinations, it will be very difficult to build up useful norms, almost none of which exist at present. For many purposes, furthermore, there seems to be value in having pictures with definitely structured content, presenting problems that the subject must face somehow.

More closely related to the TAT itself in structure are three cognate techniques, all of which are variants for use with special groups. *The Symonds Picture Story Test* [*37*] consists of 20 pictures of adolescents in various emotionally relevant situations. It is designed expressly for use with adolescents, and contains many doubtless useful pictures. Since the regular TAT has been used successfully for years with persons in this age group, however, there seems to be no reason to adopt another test (again, presented without satisfactory norms) for this specific purpose until it has been proved to be superior to Murray's pictures.

Proof of this kind is offered by Thompson for his *Thompson Modification of the Thematic Apperception Test* [*38*]. After having the original pictures redrawn with Negro figures instead of whites, but otherwise unchanged, he compared the effectiveness of the two sets of pictures in eliciting fantasy material from Negro college students. The results definitely favored his own pictures, which offer more suitable identification figures [*39*]. The similarity of the pictures to the originals means that they can be used without starting completely afresh in building up an experimental background for interpretation.

The Children's Apperception Test (CAT) has been designed by the Bellaks for use with the age group from three to 11 years [6]. Though the TAT contains a few pictures specifically for young children, and though it has been shown to be useful even with nursery school youngsters [33], preliminary experience with the new test suggests that it can evoke longer and more vivid stories. There are 10 pictures in the CAT, each consisting of animal figures only; the authors claim that children can identify themselves more easily with animals than with persons. An additional advantage of the CAT pictures is that they adumbrate most of the commonly important problems of childhood (for example, feeding conflicts, sibling rivalry, toilet training, and Oedipal problems).[7] Though considerably more experience will have to be accumulated before this new instrument can be evaluated in more than a tentative way, it looks promising enough to be recommended for work with preadolescent children.

The Michigan Picture Test, the most recent and in many ways the most carefully constructed variant of the TAT, has been reported by Hartwell, Hutt, Andrew, and Walton [16a]. Under the auspices of the Michigan Department of Mental Health, an extensive project began with a careful preliminary use of about 1,000 pictures with children. The 20 most promising pictures (divided into two parallel and overlapping sets of 12) have been selected, and have been administered in a standard way to 303 school children between the ages of eight and fourteen years, as well as to several score of clinic referrals. Only preliminary normative data were available, but the test's usefulness in distinguishing well- and poorly-adjusted children has been demonstrated. It looks as if this extensive development project is going to provide a test more thoroughly

---

[7] Mention may be made of another test using cartoon pictures of animals designed to portray either a stage of psychosexual development or a type of object relationship within that development, including oral eroticism, oral and anal sadism, Oedipal intensity, masturbation guilt, castration anxiety, and penis envy. The Blacky Pictures [7b] is a set of 12 cards containing cartoon drawings that depict the adventures of a dog named "Blacky." Blum [7a], the originator of this test, called the test a modified projective technique and used it as a medium to study the psychoanalytic theory of psychosexual development. Blum administered the Blacky Pictures to 119 male and 90 female students in elementary psychology classes. He pointed out that the test is not a clinically validated instrument, and that the findings for his sample must be regarded as tentative and suggestive, but that his data strongly suggest that some aspects of psychoanalytic theory have demonstrable validity [Eds.].

grounded in careful research and better provided with norms than any of its competitors. The areas of conflict it samples only partially overlap with those in the Bellaks' CAT, and the identification figures are children, not animals. The two instruments appear, therefore, to supplement each other, the CAT being perhaps more useful with younger children, the Michigan Picture Test with older children.

In addition to picture-story methods, there is the whole area of the closely related story-completion tests. Incomplete stories, to be finished either orally or in writing, have been used for many years by a large number of workers; Sargent's *Insight Test* [*31*] may be singled out for special mention as perhaps the best-standardized. It is reviewed in Chapter 18.

SUMMARY

The *Thematic Apperception Test* (TAT) is best approached through a consideration of the psychological processes involved in the production of the test protocol. The operations of nine classes of determinants is described: (1) situational context; (2) directing sets; (3) perceptual impact; (4) needs and affects; (5) defensive circuiting; (6) associative elaboration, subdivided into personal-historical, sentimentive and general informational content; (7) abilities; (8) internal (emotional) milieu; and (9) personal style.

Principles of administering and interpreting the TAT are presented with reference to those categories. The problems of reliability and validity are discussed with special reference to the concept of the TAT as a sample of complex behavior in contrast to a structured test performance. Related techniques are briefly noted, with recommendations about their special uses.

It has not been the author's intent in this chapter to provide a complete manual for the clinical use of the TAT. Rather, the attempt has been made to introduce the test in such a way that the reader can turn with profit and understanding to the starred works in the following list of references, and begin the use of the TAT with an orientation that may help him to grow in its application.

REFERENCES

1. Allport, Gordon W., *Personality, a Psychological Interpretation.* New York: Henry Holt and Company, Inc. 1937.

*2. Aron, Betty, *A Manual for Analysis of the Thematic Apperception Test.* Berkeley, Calif.: Willis E. Berg, 1949.

3. Balken, Eva R., and Masserman, Jules H., "The language of phantasy. III, The language of the phantasies of patients with conversion hysteria, anxiety state, and obsessive-compulsive neuroses." *J. Psychol.*, 1940, 10, 75–86.

4. Bellak, Leopold, *A Guide to the Interpretation of the Thematic Apperception Test.* New York: The Psychological Corporation, 1947.

5. Bellak, Leopold, *Bellak TAT Blank: for Recording and Analyzing Thematic Apperception Test Stories.* New York: The Psychological Corporation, 1947.

6. Bellak, Leopold, and Bellak, Sonya S., *Children's Apperception Test.* New York: C. P. S. Co., P. O. Box 42, Gracie Station, 1949. (Set of 10 cards and manual.)

7. Bellak, Leopold, and Jaques, Elliott, "On the problem of dynamic conceptualization in case studies." *Character & Pers.*, 1942, 11, 20–39.

7a. Blum, Gerald S., "A study of the psychoanalytic theory of psychosexual development." *Genetic Psychology Monographs*, 1949, 39, 3– 99.

7b. Blum, Gerald S., *The Blacky Pictures.* New York: The Psychological Corporation, 1950.

8. Coleman, William. "The Thematic Apperception Test: I. Effects of recent experience; II. Some quantitative observations." *J. Clin. Psychol.*, 1947, 3, 257–264.

9. Combs, Arthur W., "The use of personal experience in Thematic Apperception Test story plots." *J. Clin. Psychol.*, 1946, 2, 357–363.

10. Dymond, Rosalind, "The relation of insight and empathy." *J. Consult. Psychol.*, 1948, 12, 228–233.

11. Erikson, Erik H., "Ego Development and Historical Change," in *The Psychoanalytic Study of the Child,* Vol. II. New York: International Universities Press, 1946, 359–396.

12. Frank, L. K., *Projective Methods.* Springfield, Ill.: Thomas, 1948.

13. Frenkel-Brunswik, Else, "Dynamic and cognitive categorization of qualitative material: I. General problems and the Thematic Apperception Test." *J. Psychol.*, 1948, 25, 253–260.

14. Freud, Sigmund, *The Interpretation of Dreams,* in Brill, A. H. (ed.), *The Basic Writings of Sigmund Freud.* New York: Modern Library, 1938, 181–549.

15. Garfield, Sol L., and Eron, Leonard D., "Interpreting mood and activity in TAT stories." *J. Abnorm. Soc. Psychol.*, 1948, 43, 338–345.

16. Harrison, Ross, "Studies in the use and validity of the Thematic Apperception Test with mentally disordered patients. II. A quantitative validity study. III. Validation by the method of 'blind analysis' " *Character & Pers.*, 1940, 9, 122–138.

16a. Hartwell, Samuel W., Hutt, Max L., Andrew, Gwen, and Walton, Ralph E., "The Michigan Picture Test: Diagnostic and therapeutic possibilities of a new projective test for children." *Amer. J. of Orthopsychiatry.* 1951, 21, 124–137.

*17. Henry, William E., "The thematic apperception technique in the study of culture-personality relations." *Genet. Psychol. Monogr.,* 1947, 35, 3–315.

18. Holt, Robert R., and Thompson, Charles E., "Bibliography for the Thematic Apperception Test." *J. Projective Techniques,* 1950, 14. Also in *TAT Newsletter,* 1950, 3, No. 4.

19. Markmann, Ruth, "Predictions of manifest personality trends by a thematic analysis of three pictures of the Thematic Apperception Test." Unpublished undergraduate honors thesis, Radcliffe College, 1943.

20. Mayman, Martin, and Kutner, Bernard, "Reliability in analyzing Thematic Apperception Test stories." *J. Abnorm. Soc. Psychol.,* 1947, 42, 365–368.

21. Morgan, Christiana D., and Murray, Henry A., "A method for investigating fantasies: the Thematic Apperception Test." *Arch. Neurol. Psychiat.,* 1935, 34, 289–306.

22. Murray, Henry A., *Thematic Apperception Test.* Cambridge, Mass.: Harvard University Press, 1943. (Set of 30 cards and manual.)

*23. Murray, Henry A., and others, *Explorations in Personality.* New York: Oxford University Press, 1938.

24. Murray, Henry A., and Morgan, Christiana D., "A clinical study of sentiments." *Genet. Psychol. Monogr.,* 1945, 32, 3–311.

25. Murray, Henry A., and Stein, Morris I., "Note on the selection of combat officers." *Psychosom. Med.,* 1943, 5, 386–391.

*26. Rapaport, David, Schafer, Roy, and Gill, Merton M., *Diagnostic Psychological Testing,* Vol. II. Chicago: Yearbook Publishers, 1946, pp. 395–459.

27. Renaud, Harold R., "Group differences in fantasies: Head injuries, psychoneurotics, and brain diseases." *J. Psychol.,* 1946, 21, 327–346.

28. Rosenzweig, Saul, "Apperceptive norms for the Thematic Apperception Test: I. The problems of norms in projective methods." *J. Personality,* 1949, 17, 475–482.

*29. Rosenzweig, Saul, and Fleming, Edith E., "Apperceptive norms for the Thematic Apperception Test: II. An empirical investigation." *J. Personality,* 1949, 17, 483–503.

30. Sanford, Fillmore H., "Speech and personality: A comparative case study." *Character & Pers.,* 1942, 10, 169–198.

31. Sargent, Helen D., "An experimental application of projective principles to a paper and pencil personality test." *Psychol. Monogr.,* 1944, 57, vi+57.

*32. Schafer, Roy, *The Clinical Application of Psychological Tests.* New York: International University Press, 1948.

33. Schafer, Sarah, and Leitch, Mary, "An exploratory study of the usefulness of a battery of psychological tests with nursery school children." *Amer. J. Psychiat.*, 1948, 104, 647–652.

34. Shneidman, Edwin S., "Schizophrenia and the MAPS Test: A study of certain formal psycho-social aspects of fantasy production in schizophrenia as revealed by performance on the Make-A-Picture-Story (MAPS) Test." *Genet. Psychol. Monogr.*, 1948, 38, 145–223.

35. Shneidman, Edwin S., *Make-A-Picture-Story ("MAPS") Test.* New York: The Psychological Corporation, 1949. (Set of cards, figures, figure location charts.)

*36. Stein, Morris I., *The Thematic Apperception Test: An introductory manual for its clinical use with adult males.* Cambridge, Mass.: Addison-Wesley Press, 1948.

37. Symonds, Percival M., *Symonds Picture-Story Test.* New York: Bureau of Publications, Teachers College, Columbia University, 1948. (Set of 20 cards and manual.)

38. Thompson, Charles E., *Thompson modification of the Thematic Apperception Test.* Cambridge, Mass.: Harvard University Press, 1949. (Set of 18 cards and manual.)

39. Thompson, Charles E., "The Thompson modification of the Thematic Apperception Test." *Rorschach Res. Exch.*, 1949, 13, 469–478.

*40. Tomkins, Silvan S., *The Thematic Apperception Test.* New York: Grune and Stratton, 1947.

41. van Lennep, D. J., *Four-Picture Test.* The Hague: Martinus Nijhoff, 1948. (Pictures, testblanks, and manual.)

*42. Wyatt, Frederick, "The scoring and analysis of the Thematic Apperception Test." *J. Psychol.*, 1947, 24, 319–330.

*43. Wyatt, Frederick, "The interpretation of the Thematic Apperception Test." *Rorschach Res. Exch.*, 1947, 11, 21–25.

---

* References selected for the introductory use of the TAT.

CHAPTER 8

The Thematic Apperception Technique in the Study of Group and Cultural Problems

WILLIAM E. HENRY, PH.D.

INTRODUCTION

The dynamic interrelationships of interaction-feeling units that are characteristic of one individual and of his relations to his social life-space are that individual's personality.

In studies of the *individual,* the most apt analysis involves the discovery of those *interaction-feeling* units assumed *by that individual* and *the analysis and interrelation of these units within the individual.* Since the basic datum is not the individual *per se,* but rather the interaction-feeling unit, it is possible to relate and analyze the interrelationships of these units when one is dealing with a number of cases. Thus, the problem of the use of projective instruments in group and cultural studies is basically identical with that of the analysis of the individual; that is, the analysis and discovery of those interaction-feeling units that are characteristic of the group being studied, the interrelations of these units both within the group and in the characteristic social life-space of the group. Therefore, *projective techniques become relevant to all of those problems in which the feeling assumptions that people make about basic interactions are an important element.*

In order to make explicit the theory involved in this statement and in the studies described in a later section, the two following sections will explain a relevant point of view about the personality-culture interaction, and the basic nature of the projective instrument.

THE NATURE OF THE PERSONALITY-CULTURE INTERACTION

The end-products of the interaction of personality and culture may be said to be two: the process of *individuation* and the process of *socialization*. The first of these, individuation, is that process of experiencing life events in which the individual develops his unique features and organizes his own idiosyncratic way of interpreting himself, his associates, and his relationship to the wider universe. The process of socialization is that aspect of the experiencing of life events that develops in the individual sufficient conformity to group expectancies to permit him to get along amicably and to be thought a proper member of the group.

The forces that urge toward socialization are those subsumed under the concept, "culture." In terms of the persons who live in it, and especially of the children who are just learning it, culture and the demands of society consist of *day-by-day interactions with other persons.* These day-by-day interactions, in which the individual learns what his society expects of him (and, as a matter of fact, learns what he will later expect of himself), have two special characteristics. First, they teach him the skills, techniques, and other objective features of proper behavior in his group. Second, and probably more important, they teach him feelings. They teach him not only how to *behave,* but also how to *feel.* Thus, each experience, whether private (in the sense of being unique to that person) or public (in the sense of being a common, to-be-expected event), is an experience with both rational and emotional aspects. Above all, each of these experiences that serve to mold and motivate are personal experiences. Whether an event or feeling is unique in its occurrence or whether it is public, it is still a personal event. It matters not to the individual that others have had the same experience; it is still *his* experience and *his* feeling. It may alter the feeling somewhat to know that he is not alone, that others have experienced similar events, but this will not alter the essentially personal nature of the experience.

From the point of view of the social scientist, it may be agreed that each society can be analyzed in terms of four basic concepts:

1. Its pattern of *material relationships* and its physical surroundings: the high degree of emphasis on *things* and the complexity of material objects in our society as opposed to the reduced emphasis on property and physical change in some nonliterate societies; the abundance of food and a protective environment as opposed to scarcity and a physical environment that is threatening and depriving.

2. Its pattern of *formal institutions,* which give the basic structure to the society and set the framework for interpersonal relations: the monogamous family unit as contrasted with the institution of plural wives; the social isolation of the city apartment dwelling unit as contrasted with the formal social cohesion of the family group and the clan in certain nonliterate groups.

3. Its pattern of *symbol systems,* which serve to give people the rationale for the relationship of man to the universe and to explain and interpret interpersonal relations in that society.

4. Its pattern of *child training* and *adult control devices,* which insure the continuance of the structure and beliefs of the society.

But from the point of view of the child learning or the adult behaving in the patterns set by his society, the basic directives that give consistency to his behavior are essentially emotional in nature and consist of two generalizations: *what we feel and believe the world around us to be like,* and *what we feel and believe ourselves to be like.* Thus each of the societal continuities that are relevant to the life of any given individual have their substructure in the emotional life of that individual. Presumably, then, each major patterning of societal expectancies receives a major portion of its sustenance and coercive power from the partly conscious and partly unconscious emotional beliefs that individuals accord it. Thus, it is apparent that societal expectancies, which for the individual are essentially personal and emotional in nature, are an integral part of the personality of that individual. This very fact makes the personality of the individual an integral part of the society, since it is the individual's feelings and convictions that give to the societal expectancies much consistency and coercive power.

In this interaction of the individual and his society, the individual person is seen as an active human organism possessing certain physical characteristics typical of all organisms of his type, and possessing, further, certain psychological needs demanding fulfillment.[1]

The individual is viewed as attempting the completion and satisfaction of these physical and psychological needs within the society of which he is a part, using for this purpose the most effective available social groups, occupations, and social institutions. In the most extreme sense, the individual attempts to fulfill his needs with whatever means his society provides and at whatever cost to that society.

On the other hand, the society makes demands and has needs that must be fulfilled. It demands conformity to its values and modes of living and it punishes, by ostracism or social disgrace, those individuals who fail to attain a sufficient degree of that conformity. The task of the society, in a sense, is to perpetuate that society by a continuance of values and modes of living that have been found satisfactory in the past. And to this end it will coerce and distort the individual, and, if necessary, sacrifice him.

The needs of the individual and those of the society, however, are not necessarily opposed. The individual requires a social framework and a series of reasonably certain rules and codes by which to guide his behavior. And the society requires active belief and participation of the individuals within it and the spark of individually creative minds. Yet, the process by which the society gains the individual's conformity and by which the individual gains the satisfaction of his personal needs is a process largely of coercion and distortion, of partial conformities and partial uniquenesses. During this process, the society attempts to mold the individual to the pattern of the society's dominant values, and the individual attempts to achieve a satisfying uniqueness within the bounds of social comfort. For the individual, this attempt is one of strain and of continual adjustment and readjustment, out of which he develops and organizes his own personality, this personality representing the psychological counterpart and residue of the individual's life history of experiences.

THE NATURE OF PROJECTIVE DATA

The symptomatic nature of projective data,[2] in the light of the framework of the personality-culture interaction developed above,

---

[1] The remainder of this section is adapted from Henry [*11*], by permission of the *Journal of Aesthetics and Art Criticism.*

[2] While the remaining discussion will deal almost exclusively with the technique of the Thematic Apperception Test, it is believed that the points made are applicable to most projective instruments.

has two important implications.   First, it means that the data from the projective instrument are in part determined by the idiosyncratic psychologic aspects of the individual.   Second, it means that projective data are in part determined by the emotional counterparts of cultural communalities.   Since this is the case, analysis of the end-product—the projective data—will reveal both idiosyncratic and cultural elements.   The crude schema in Figure 1 will illustrate this point.

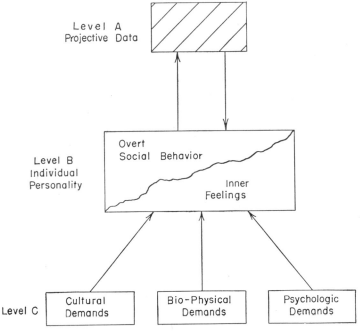

Fig. 1.   Diagram of source of projective data.

Level *A* of the diagram represents the raw data from the projective instrument.   Level *B* represents the personality of the individual, the source of the raw projective data.   This level is split in the diagram to imply that at least two major (though obviously interrelated) aspects of the personality are to be considered, the overt socially observable behavior, and the inner dynamics of feeling and emotion. The nature of the personality is such that its determinants, as represented in Level *C,* are cultural, biophysical, and psychological.   The two-way arrows between Levels *A* and *B* imply that since the projective data (*A*) are derived from and directly reflective of the personality (*B*), therefore, the reverse is true: the personality (*B*) may be derived from the projective data.   This also clearly means that since the personality (*B*) has its social, biophysical, and psychologic determinants (*C*), these three major elements will be interpretable from the projective data.[3]

The TAT may be said to be an appropriate aid in the study of any system of human interaction that has a substratum of dynamically related emotions and a consistent social life-space.   The interaction-feeling units are the interrelations existing within the complex of dynamically related emotions and between this complex and the social life-space.

One logical problem that comes to mind is that of the small group. The small, coherent group of stated purpose has almost as clear-cut a system of dynamically related emotions as does the individual. Like the personality of the individual, small face-to-face groups tend to have relatively persistent, interrelated characteristics that are consistent within the emotional substructure of the group and serve to differentiate the functioning of one group from another.[4]   Similarly, larger groups that have persisting and internally consistent emotional relationships and overt social characteristics will be appropriate problems for the use of projective instruments.   The Rorschach test, doll play test, and Thematic Apperception Test, in studies of nonliterate groups, are all examples of the application of projective instruments to such problems.[5]

It should be emphasized that the use of the TAT in studies involving large homogeneous groups may have at least three general features.   First, the instrument may be used to study specific individuals within a group [*4, 9*].   This procedure, of course, is not essentially different from the usual clinical use of the TAT.   Second, it may be used to deduce the common personality features of the members of such groups [*4*].   Third, it may be used to analyze the

---

[3] This statement also implies that biophysical data may be derived from projective data.   While we are primarily concerned with culture problems in this chapter, the not inconsiderable success of predicting psychosomatic symptoms in clinical practice may suggest that this aspect of the logic is also correct.

[4] In the last section of this chapter is a description of the use of these principles in the development of the Test of Group Projection.

[5] See especially, Du Bois [*4*], and Schachtel, Henry, and Henry [*24*].

pattern of feelings and assumptions toward various aspects of overt social behavior and common social experience [29, 11, 9, 6, 7].

The use of the TAT to investigate personality communalities and to study the internalized emotional concomitants of certain social events raises several specific problems. First, the problem of the homogeneity of the group studied; second, the problem of methods of analysis adapted to the concept of studying social phenomena; third, the problem of the conceptual framework. Each of these will be discussed below.

The Problem of Group Homogeneity.   The group to which the TAT will be relevant will have three general characteristics:

1. A substructure of dynamically related emotions
2. A persisting and consistent social life-space
3. A consistent pattern of feelings and assumptions toward the elements of the social life-space.

The TAT seems most useful when the subjects studied have the greatest amount of psychologically and socially common elements structuring their personality and social behavior.   In the study of the conference groups [15] to be described in the last section, for example, the consistent life-space was assured, since the subjects in the groups studied were well known to each other, had participated jointly over a considerable period of time, had a common previously defined goal, and had in general agreed upon the overt techniques of group procedure and the manner of attacking their joint problem. It is also probable that conference groups of this sort are made up of persons of quite similar social class backgrounds, thus increasing the communality of both social and psychological elements.   Further, groups of this sort soon develop dynamics that consist of informal, interpersonal relationships and emotional assumptions (assumptions about the nature of the relationships between group members and about the manner of approaching the group goal).

Similarly, in the study of the daytime radio serial [29] reported later in this chapter, the relevance of the TAT (in addition to the sample study of the individual case) lay in the fact that it could reveal the common personality features of the group and the common feelings and assumptions that the group made about certain elements of external reality, specifically, the daytime serial and the interpersonal relationships and moral attitudes portrayed in it.   In this instance, the relevance of the TAT was suggested by the fact that the group selected was, first, one of common social habits and expectancies, and second, one in which the common psychological elements might be expected to be great.   It was a group of lower-middle-class housewives, a group highly consistent and circumscribed in psychology and in social experiences.[6]

At this stage it is difficult to set up precise criteria for the selection of homogeneous social groups.   The points that should be made, however, are:

1. The cohesive social group is an important unit of study to which the TAT is relevant;

2. The TAT will reveal significant data about the basic psychology of such groups and about the emotional function of various overt behaviors and institutionalized social practices of the groups;

3. In the selection of such groups, attention should be paid to both the persisting pattern of social habits and the presence of internally consistent patterns of feelings and emotions that underlie and give motivational force to the social habits of the group.

The Problem of Methods of Analysis.   The analysis of an individual's TAT record to reveal data on the personality of that individual has been discussed in the preceding chapter and has been documented by Tomkins [26], Stein [25], Aron [2] and others.   For purposes of clarifying the problem of the analysis of groups, the methods of analysis there reported will be called *vertical-individual* analysis.   The references there are to the analysis of the TAT protocols for a given person, story by story, the objective being an understanding of the personality structure and dynamics of that individual. The methods described, while varying in techniques and in theory, are essentially designed for the analysis of the individual.   We shall consider here several other types of analysis that give the TAT wider applicability.

First, a simple modification of the *vertical-individual* analysis approach might be called the *vertical-group* type.   In this method, the subjects for study are all selected from some homogeneous social group, the group selected obviously depending upon the particular

---

6 It is beyond our purpose here to document the communality of the lower-middle-class housewife.   Evidence will be found in Warner and Henry [29], Warner and Lunt [30], Warner, Meeker, and Eels [31], and Warner Associates [28].

social psychological problem being studied.   The analysis of each individual TAT record is then made, as in the *vertical-individual* type.   All of these analyses are then organized into the same general conceptual framework, which has been explicitly stated and defined in advance.   Upon the completion of the individual analyses, one is then able to relate all of the cases and to determine features that all have in common.   This should be done through the segments of the conceptual framework already being used.   Thus, at this stage of the analysis, the *individual as a unit* is dropped, and the units of the conceptual framework are adopted.   One is then no longer talking about the *individual,* but about the group.   One becomes concerned about the characteristics of the group, in the terms of whatever units are included in the conceptual framework adopted.

Assume that one unit of the framework deals, for example, with *maternal image.*   In a study of a group of Hopi Indians [9], one might discover a preponderance of data suggesting the mother image to be one of authority, but of impersonality and of low emotional tie. On the other hand, collated data under the rubric *mother image* for a group of upper-middle-class white school boys might show a preponderance of feelings emphasizing a highly personified, ambivalent image in which elements of idealism and sexuality are fused. Such findings in two groups of records would be clearly important to the understanding of the dynamics of each group.   They would, however, at this stage of analysis, be characteristic of the group rather than of the individual.   One of the particular advantages of securing data on groups in this fashion is that the significance of any item of analysis, any one TAT response, may be evaluated in terms of the differences between personality dynamics of the individual who produced the response and the dynamics of the group.

The *horizontal* type of analysis is another approach to data on the group.   In this approach, one analyzes each picture of the TAT series for all cases, rather than analyzing the whole series of pictures for each case.   Thus, if there are 100 cases in the group studied, one would concentrate first upon the analysis of all 100 responses to picture 1, then all 100 responses to picture 2, then to 3, and so on through the series of pictures used.   One analyzes into a conceptual framework in this fashion when one is more directly concerned with the concepts of the framework, and does not care to pass through the individual record analysis stage, as in the *vertical* approach.

In the horizontal approach, one is primarily concerned with securing data on a number of specific areas, defined in advance or determined during preliminary analysis of the responses. One sorts out all responses that bear upon the particular concepts set up, thus securing more precise data on these given points, though slighting the dynamic interrelationships of elements within a single story.

This method has the advantage of being far less laborious than the *vertical-group* approach. The danger lies in mistaking the psychologic significance of certain responses. This can be partially circumvented by first analyzing a number of records in the usual *vertical* fashion to secure an image of the interrelationships of the various elements.

A modification of this approach is the *horizontal-thematic,* in which the whole collection of responses to each individual picture are analyzed as though they were one dynamically interdependent unit. For this method to be effective, it is particularly important that the group studied be of consistent social characteristics and be of highly similar psychological structure.

The Problem of the Conceptual Framework. It is extremely doubtful that there is any particular single framework of concepts that is inherent to the TAT. On the other hand, there can be no question of the necessity of developing frameworks of analysis that will permit cross-case and cross-group comparisons. The problem in developing such frameworks has at least two parts: first, the framework must be composed of concepts on which it is reasonable to suppose that data may be provided by the TAT; second, these concepts must be relevant to the particular problem being studied. There seems to be considerable tendency to attempt to develop for the TAT *the* conceptual framework, in terms of which all future analyses will be made. The assumption seems to be made that somehow the framework of analysis is identical with the instrument of data-collection. Once this logic has been established for a given instrument, it is extremely difficult to use different concepts in the analysis of the data. This is a most unfortunate limitation to place upon the flexibility of the projective instruments.

In the case of the Rorschach, for example, the very legitimate effort to develop a conceptual framework that would permit a clinician to analyze a protocol has jelled, and each new clinician finds himself presented with an increasingly inflexible set of variables in which he is expected to analyze a Rorschach record. This gradual petrifaction of the conceptual framework then tends to be identified with the data themselves, and we begin to hear comments implying that the Rorschach cannot reveal data beyond the range of the concepts habitually used in its analysis. Thus, for example, there is a tendency in clinical thinking that the "Rorschach reveals structure and the TAT the content of personality." In the writer's experience, this is both practically and theoretically inexact. If it were suggested that the Rorschach revealed structure *more easily* or *more accurately* than the TAT, or if it were *easier* for the clinician of medium skills to deduce structure in this manner, then it might be a reasonable statement. But theoretically, it seems completely untenable to make this distinction. Practically, also, it is an un-necessarily rigid distinction. The framework of analysis for the Rorschach, for example that created by Klopfer [20], may be used with equal utility in the analysis of the TAT.

If concepts of structure are used in analysis of the TAT, then the TAT will reveal data on structure. If concepts of content are used with the Rorschach, then the Rorschach can reveal content. I would suspect that this is fairly general practice among clinicians of advanced skills in these instruments. Certainly, no advanced Rorschach analyst would fail to work a so-called "content analysis" of a protocol. If he does work a content analysis, he can hardly avoid securing data, not only on the content of personality, but also on life experiences and value-attitudes. Similarly, no TAT analyst should neglect a systematic analysis of the *form* characteristics of TAT responses. If he makes such an analysis, he can hardly fail to secure data that may reveal the so-called structural elements of personality as traditionally seen in the Rorschach. This distinction represents a rigidity that springs from assuming that one useful framework is identical with the full range of utility of an instrument, and from the tendency to feel that there can be only one really proper framework of analysis for a given instrument. In a field still as flexible as the field of projective instruments, it seems strange that we should seek safety and respectability by prematurely crystal-lizing the one area in which our great hope of real contribution lies, that of the constant manipulation of concepts to reveal the complicated and many-faceted nature of human behavior.

In a research project dealing with the relationships of personality to social role, Henry and Tryon [*16*] were faced with the problem of integrating data from some 15 different instruments (interviews, objective tests, projective tests). Rather than assuming that each instrument had an inherent framework of analysis, it was decided to devise a framework that took its cues, first, from the conceptualization of the problem, and second, from the data of the instruments. In order to devise this framework, preliminary analyses of selected cases were made, in which data gathered by all of the instruments being used were analyzed with whatever framework the analyst of that instrument felt at home in. Through a series of conferences, a general framework was developed from the concepts that seemed most relevant to the problem and from data that were forthcoming in the preliminary analysis of cases. The final framework was considerably larger than either the concepts derived from a logical analysis of the problem or from the preliminary analyses of instruments.

Two final frameworks were used: one for the first analysis of raw data gathered by all instruments, and one for the interpretation of already derived data. Thus the first framework, presented below, served as the outline of analysis for the interviews, the Rorschach, the TAT, the free line drawings, the free essays, and so forth. While it is, of course, apparent that not all instruments revealed data on all points, such a common framework provided a method of comparing data and, at the same time, served markedly to extend the range of concepts previously used in the analysis of any one instrument. The first of these frameworks was used in the first analysis of all instruments. It is as follows:

CLINICAL CONFERENCE OUTLINE

I. SOCIAL INTERACTION
   A. *Peer Group Relationships*
      1. Extent and nature of participation
      2. Quality of interpersonal relations
      3. Time trends in relation with age-mates
   B. *Community Relationships*
      1. Subject's contacts with community institutions (church, school, clubs, commercial recreation, public agencies, and so on)

2. Subject's relationships and reputation with adults (teachers, ministers, neighbors, employers, and so on)

C. *Family Relationships*
  1. Family constellation (name, birth date, age and sex, education, occupation, residential movement, and marital history of each member of the immediate and closely related family)
  2. Family in the community
     (a) Family social characteristics and participation
     (b) Family social status and social mobility
  3. Intrafamily dynamics
     (a) Appearance and personality of parents and parent surrogates
     (b) Organization, routine, and emotional tone of family living
     (c) Nature of training routines
     (d) Affectional dynamics
        (1) Father-mother relationships
        (2) Parent-subject relationships
        (3) Parent-sib relationships
        (4) Sibling relationships
        (5) Subject relations to extended family

II. PHYSICAL CHARACTERISTICS
  A. *Appearance*
     1. General physical appearance
     2. Personal grooming
  B. *Health*
     1. Disease history
     2. Nutritional status
     3. Physical defects and assets
     4. Health habits
  C. *Energy Output*
     1. Characteristic rate and/or fluctuation
     2. Pattern of expression (athletic, social, verbal) and degree of organization (directed, random)
     3. Endurance (fatigue and rate of recovery)
  D. *Growth Pattern*
     1. Growth history
     2. Physical type (size, body type)
     3. Estimated place in the growth cycle
  E. *Sexual Maturation*
     1. Secondary sex characteristics (include data on menarche)
     2. Consistency and sex-appropriateness
  F. *Motor Pattern*
     1. Management of body
     2. Physical skills (by test and observation)

III. CHARACTERISTICS OF THE SELF
  A. *Mental Function*
     1. Level
        (a) Intelligence
        (b) Achievement

    2. Efficiency (extent of interference)

    3. Organization and logic of mental processes

B. *Imagination*

    1. Creativity (originality, constructive utilization of imagination)

    2. Fantasy (escapist use of imagination)

C. *Pattern of Emotional Adjustment*

    1. Basic emotional attitude (active-passive; strength of drive toward solution of emotional problems)

    2. Attitude toward impulse life, acceptance or rejection

    3. Evidence of anxiety

        (a) Signs of insecurity, guilt, hostility

        (b) Sources of anxiety, for example, sexual insecurity, hostility to mother, and so on

    4. Mechanisms of adjustment

        (a) Ego defenses (overt attack, defense mechanisms)

        (b) Positive ways of self-comfort (sensuous and aesthetic pleasures, seeking sympathy or affection)

        (c) System of control of behavior

            (1) Inner (preference for inner stimulation)

            (2) Conscious (conforming to standards set by other people)

            (3) Integration of (1) and (2) into overt behavior (outer control)

    5. Emotional reactivity

        (a) Drive toward outer world (inner-outer balance)

        (b) Nature of emotional ties to other persons

    6. Sexual adjustment   acceptance of impulse; progression into social-sex roles)

    7. Maturity levels

        (a) Inner life maturity

        (b) Development of age-and-sex-appropriate behavior

D. *Ideals, Identifications, and Content of Conscience*

    1. Identifications with persons, principles, and moral values (strength, direction, and content)

    2. Resolution of conflict into one or more value systems guiding behavior

The second framework of analysis was used following the initial summary of data from The Clinical Conference Outline. It is used to interrelate already derived data. It is as follows:

FRAMEWORK FOR INTERPRETATION [7]

This framework is used during the second Clinical Conference, and follows the two steps:

---

[7] These frameworks were worked out in connection with the Midwest Research of the Committee on Human Development of the University of Chicago. In addition to the writer and Caroline Tryon, many others participated in the development of these outlines, particularly R. J. Havighurst, J. Carson McGuire, Robert F. Peck and Hilda Richards.

I. Analysis of raw data

II. Organization and presentation of data during the first Clinical Conference

The various areas of the framework are described below. Within the first three categories, the details presented are determined by the *idiomatic pattern* of the particular case.

I. *Realities: Biological, Social, Psychological*

This is a summary and integration of all pertinent factors whose resultant effects influence, direct, and limit the individual's behavior. These factors are derived from biological, social, and psychological data. This section *excludes* the subject's view of these factors and his conception of himself.

II. *Self-Concept*

This is a summary and integration of the individual's concept of himself. It consists of generalizations about the motivations, anxieties, needs, and fears that define the individual's inner world.

III. *Concept of External Realities*

This is a summary and an integration of the individual's conception of external realities. It consists of generalizations about the individual's interpretations of the outer world and his feelings about how it is treating him.

IV. *Behavioral Dynamics*

This section integrates the material in I, II, and III into an explanation and interpretation of the individual's motivation and behavior. In this area, the following basic questions are asked:

A. What is he trying to do?
   1. His goals, needs, motivations
   2. His feelings, both overt and covert

B. What are the realities influencing his adjustment?
   1. External realities, positive and negative
   2. Internal realities, positive and negative

C. What is the nature of the resulting adjustment?
   1. The resulting adjustment
   2. His evaluation of it
   3. Others' evaluation of it

V. *Prognosis*

A. Peer relationships
B. Heterosexual adjustment
C. Academic adjustment
D. Intra-family dynamics
E. Community relationships
F. Philosophy of life and ideology

The writer holds no particular brief for these frameworks. It is only claimed that they were especially relevant to the particular problem under study and to the particular instruments being used. In problems differently conceptualized, different frameworks would be relevant.[8] The important points seem to be:

1. Frameworks of analysis for the projective instruments are many and varied.

2. The basic data are flexible and may be properly analyzed with reference to a wide range of concepts.

3. Experience suggests that the adaptability of these instruments becomes increasingly apparent as they are used to attack new problems and hence, as their data are analyzed in terms of new concepts.

4. The assumption that the concepts relevant to the projective data are exclusively psychological in nature seems unnecessarily limiting.

5. The utilization of sociological concepts dealing with various aspects of social life and group behavior seems particularly relevant.

STUDIES OF GROUP AND CULTURAL PROBLEMS

Some of the problems and techniques of the use of the TAT in group and cultural problems can probably be best illustrated with actual studies. In each of the studies reported below, the TAT has been employed, with varying degrees of success, in the effort to secure data on one or all of the following points:

1. Specific individuals representative of a given culture group.

2. Common personality dynamics of the members of a group or subculture.

3. Dynamics of the small group.

4. Emotional function and psychological substructure of various institutionalized forms of behavior.

5. The psychological concomitants of certain well-defined social roles in modern society.

For purposes of easy presentation, each of the studies will be reviewed in general outline, mainly to illustrate the type of technique and conceptual problem involved. In most instances, the reader will be referred to the published report for greater detail. These studies will be presented under four general rubrics:

1. The Test of Group Projection—a method for the study of the dynamics of small groups.

---

[8] See especially the framework under the Test of Group Projection outlined later in this chapter.

2. Studies of Cultural Groups—with special reference to the adaptation of the TAT pictures.

3. Studies of Institutions of Modern Society—with special reference to the psychological function of mass communication.

4. Studies of Social Roles—with special reference to the psychological substructure of certain stereotyped roles in modern society.

The Test of Group Projection.[9]   Small, coherent groups have an internal consistency and a pattern of emotionalized interpersonal relationships.   Similar to the personality of the individual, the consistent pattern of interpersonal relationships and feelings in a group is a set of dynamics that must be studied in order adequately to understand the behavior of groups.   The currently used techniques, while clearly significant, are laborious and time-consuming and often inept in revealing the dynamic aspects of the group structure.

The basic conception of a projective method for diagnosing group properties was developed at the Research Center for Group Dynamics by Horwitz and Cartwright [*18*].   The technique, involving a projective picture test with slightly modified TAT instructions, was first employed at the National Training Laboratory for Group Development, at Bethel, Maine, in 1947 as part of a project on group productivity sponsored by the Office of Naval Research.   The way the interacting group phrases a relatively unstructured stimulus configuration, the kind of relationships it sees, and the feelings it deems relevant—all revealed in the story the group tells about the picture—may provide important insights into the group's structure and internal processes.   This projective instrument is also directed to the problem of analyzing the structure and dynamics of the small face-to-face group.   It is designed, too, for work with groups of adults, meeting for purposes such as decision-making, training, formulating advisory opinions, and exchanging information.

The development of instruments of this type is based on the assumption that the nature of the group processes may be revealed by a projective device that (1) permits analyses of both the formal, structural characteristics and the informal relationships; (2) permits and encourages expression of nonrational feeling elements in the group process; (3) fosters projection of the group's characteristic mode of behaving; (4) allows considerable freedom of choice in

---

[9] This summary is adapted from Henry and Guetzkow [*15*].

interpretation to group members; (5) does not directly reveal to group members the possible significance of their responses; and (6) provides a task of delimited proportions that would challenge the group to immediate action.

The sketches for the Test of Group Projection, shown in Figure 2, are presented consecutively to the group being studied, with request for composition of a story about each picture by the group— a story upon which there is some general agreement. At the end of an hour, the group usually has written a story about each of the five pictures. Analysis is focused upon the final written stories, thereby avoiding the need for recording devices or observers. This is to be contrasted with the Horwitz-Cartwright method, which involves a scoring and analysis system utilizing all the content— including the final story—produced by the group in arriving at a story.

The five sketches are designed to educe different, though clearly overlapping, aspects of group processes. A series of pictures is used to increase the possibility of describing all important facets of the group's process. Employment of more than one picture reduces opportunity for accidental distortion by atypical reactions to the particular content of a single picture. The pictures are described below, together with the rationale for their construction and a tentative indication of each picture's primary use in the interpretation of group processes.

I. *Conference Group.* A group of seven men assembled around a conference table.

This picture elicits information about the more formal characteristics of groups, especially about the group's structure, goals, and productivity. It is particularly useful in revealing the group's:

(a) ability to deal with complex situations.

(b) feelings about the relation of work output to interpersonal relations.

(c) feelings toward the division of labor and the distinctions between various roles within the group.

II. *Man in Doorway.* A man is standing in the doorway of a house, his back and partial profile visible to the observer. He is looking out on a landscape.

This picture is designed to reveal:

(a) the feelings of the group toward a lone individual, and toward a single individual's relation to the world of forces around him.

(b) the group's feelings toward the source of motivation in an individual's behavior—does this come from the outside and exert unwelcome

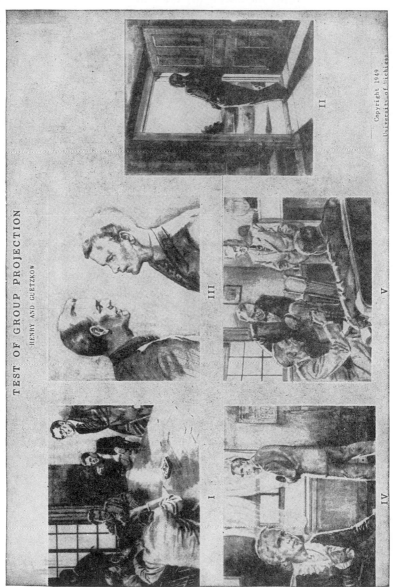

*Fig. 2. Test of group projection.**

* Reproduced with the permission of the authors, William E. Henry and Harold Guetzkow, and of the University of Michigan Press.

pressure, or from within the individual, directed outward toward influencing the world around him?

(c) the group's feelings toward inactivity—the seeming lack of direct action involved in contemplating a problem and in arriving at a starting point.

III. *Two Men.* Two men are facing each other, the older man on the left and the younger man on the right.

This picture presents a somewhat more complicated task for the group in that the relationship of two figures must be explained. The picture is designed to disclose:

(a) the group's feelings about relationships between two people.

(b) ascendant and submissive interrelationships.

(c) feelings toward authoritative pressure directed toward it and also its own use of authority.

IV. *Woman and Man.* An older woman sits in a wing chair. To her left, by a window, is a younger man looking at the woman. There is an object in his hands.

This picture is primarily designed to reveal the group's:

(a) feelings toward assertion and dependence.

(b) potential for breaking established frameworks and relationships.

V. *Informal Group.* Four men are in a room that looks somewhat like a clubroom. Two are seated on a small sofa, their backs to the observer; two other men are standing in front of them, one with his foot up on the seat of a chair.

This picture deals directly with group relationships, and especially with the informal, interpersonal relationships. It is useful in disclosing the group's:

(a) feelings toward formality or looseness of group structure, and toward the development of new procedures.

(b) sincerity and emotional involvement in the group task.

Sample Responses. The following stories produced by real groups indicate the type of material obtained and illustrate interpretations that can be made without prior knowledge of, or contact with, the group.

GROUP *A* (an industrial group)

I. *Conference Group*

Group *A* agreed that it was a daytime scene representing a fraternity meeting. The fraternity group had met to discuss the general financial situation of the fraternity. Included among the officers of the fraternity were several alumni advisors. The financial report had been submitted by the treasurer and had been discussed.

The older man on the left (the man whose neighbor's arm is around his shoulders) is being encouraged to accept the chairmanship of a fund-raising campaign to get the fraternity in better financial condition.

The fellow in the dark suit standing up in the back of the picture is excusing himself for a few minutes.

As a result of this meeting, the older man will accept the chairmanship of the financial committee and will secure enough money to put the fraternity in better shape and get the new furniture and other equipment that had been needed.

II. *Man in Doorway*

The group felt this to be a farm scene.   The man in the door pensively looking at the sunset is contemplating his future.   He had just returned from college where he had been graduated and had to decide whether to take graduate work, stay on the farm, or accept a job in the city.   It is this problem that he is thinking about.

His decision will be to travel during the summer and then take up graduate work in the fall when school opens again.   He is a thoughtful, serious individual.

III. *Two Men*

This is a college situation.   The young person on the right has just finished his sophomore year.   He has been a student during the past semester in the class of the young professor on the left.   The professor is a young but very outstanding member of the college faculty.   They have had a very friendly relationship.   The professor is encouraging the young student to continue his studies and to enter medicine.   The young man has a lot of respect and admiration for the professor.   The professor feels very kindly toward the young student and is encouraging him and inspiring him to continue.   There is a good feeling about this picture.

As a result of this meeting, the young man will enroll in school of medicine next fall.

IV. *Woman and Man*

This represents a nonfamily relationship.   The sixty-year-old woman in the picture is a kindly woman and has lost her son during the war.   She lives on a farm.   The man in the picture with his hat in his hand was a very good friend of her son.   He has returned and is calling on the lady to tell her some of the things she would like to know about the boy.

The situation is not a relaxed one at the moment because of the memory of her son's loss.   However, it is believed that after the initial tension, things will relax and they will sit down and have a long, friendly talk. They both look very nice.

It is expected, in the future, that the man will continue to keep in touch from time to time with the older lady and attempt to offset the loss of the son.

V. *Informal Group*

The scene is in a fraternity house.   It is the 25th annual reunion of the class.   It is the homecoming.   The four men in the picture are classmates and have not seen one another for some time.   Homecoming has brought them together again.   The man with the pipe is recounting some of the experiences that the class had together back in the good old days.   The man standing up to the right of the picture is half listening and half sort of dreaming of the past.

As a result of this meeting, they will all have a very enjoyable time living over the old days and will, as a result, promise to see one another more often. Just how effective this promise will be is not certain.

In order to illustrate an analysis, the following picture-by-picture summary is made of the stories presented by Group A. After each assertion, the evidence presented in the story that served as the basis for the analysis is indicated in parentheses.

I. The group that told this story was task-oriented (daytime fraternity meeting, discussing financial situation). It was involved in staff functions. Its task was to improve the functioning of the organization through persuading others in the productive side of the organization to change their behaviors (fund-raising campaign to better condition of fraternity). The group was confident and expectant that the plans it made would aid the organization in operating more effectively (will secure money).

In carrying out its decisions, this group operated through the offices of one or more of its members rather than through any authority inherent in the group itself (older men—alumni advisors). The group felt itself somewhat impotent (action taken by alumni rather than fraternity officers), and sought to accomplish its persuasive missions through involvement of out-of-group authorities who had operating power within the organization. This lack of real power within the group was also expressed in the story by omission of emotional elements in the story's plot, as well as by the fact that one member of the group felt free to excuse himself for a few minutes. The group did not seem very positively motivated toward its goal, yet it felt no fear of failure, even though it would not put out its best effort.

The affective atmosphere of the group was bland, but very friendly (fraternity). The use of neutral, descriptive titles to identify particular figures in the pictures (fellow standing—old man) indicated relatively superficial ties between members of the group. The fact that the story involved a social fraternity committee further evidenced the congeniality of the group, and indicated that the group was tied together more or less superficially.

The two or three levels of hierarchical relationships that existed within the group (officers—alumni) were not very clearly delineated. The interrelationships among the members at different levels within the organization were friendly and benevolent (advisors—arm around shoulder). There were differences in authority, age, and experience among the group members.

II. The task-orientation theme already noted in the first picture recurred (making vocational choice). The story re-emphasized the staff-function of the group (he takes school work rather than working on farm or in city). The work of the group consisted in making plans that would be executed by the individual (contemplating his future). Again, there was evidence that the group reached decisions (definite conclusion to story, as in Picture I). Yet, it was not too well motivated (pensively looking, thinking about— indirect statements, "It is this problem that . . ."—and the leisure evidenced in "when school opens again"). It allowed itself time for enjoyment while pursuing its goal (travel during summer—similar to social fraternity setting in Picture I). The relative youthfulness and inexperience of the group was again evidenced in the reference to "just returned from college," and its felt need for further training (take up graduate work). The lack of intense conflict and emotionality indicated that the group was free from intensive internal friction or strife

III. Many of the themes with respect to the authoritative and affective interrelationships pointed out in analyzing the first picture were again evidenced in this picture. The general group atmosphere was warm and congenial (friendly—feels kindly toward—good feeling), but not intimate (no names used in describing figures). The hierarchical relationships were again indicated as benevolent (encouraging and inspiring). The subordinates viewed their superiors with respect. The story suggested that the inexperienced subordinates were receiving training from their superiors (student—professor). The repetition of the "go-to-school" theme suggested that the group might not only be regarding its own sessions as ways of educating its members, but might itself be engaged within the industrial organization in planning an educative task. The ability of the group to come to decisions was again indicated in its clear statement of an outcome of the meeting of the professor and student.

IV. The content of this picture dramatically illustrated the fact that the personal interrelationships among the members of the group were not very intimate (nonfamily relationship). It indicated that in addition to its planning function, the group used a considerable proportion of its time for information exchange and communication (tell her some things). Note that the hierarchical relationship again was expressed (mother—son— friend). The subordinates within the group used their meetings at times to defend their own shortcomings (attempt to offset loss—things she would *like* to know). On occasion, the meetings were unpleasant (initial tension —not relaxed), but usually ended up with a restoration of the congeniality and easy-going pace characterizing the over-all behavior of the group (things will relax—long, friendly talk). There was to be a fair amount of time devoted to the social amenities by the participants (both look very nice). The group was clearly a continuing one that met periodically (keep in touch from time to time). Note that our description of the group's functioning was greatly enriched by the story provoked by this picture—its informational exchange and ego-defending characteristics were elicited for the first time.

V. There was very little new information obtained through the final picture. Almost all of the important themes were reproduced again —the training function of the group (classmates), its relative lack of cohesiveness (man half-listening), the relative absence of motivation (living over old days, dreaming of the past), its lack of authority (how effective is *not* certain), its pleasantness and congeniality (homecoming, enjoyable time), its ability to reach decisions (promise to see), its lack of personal intimacy (fraternity house, not seen one another for some time, four men), its continuing periodicity in meeting (25th annual reunion), and its ostensible lack of internal conflict (no reference to disagreement).

Even with more sophisticated groups, the projection technique was found to be valuable in providing insights into group functioning that neither members nor leader had possessed prior to the test.

Note how often the same themes were repeated in two or more of the pictures.   It is for this reason that a series of five pictures was considered sufficient to reveal the central aspects of the group processes.   On occasion, the authors witnessed the group's formulation of the group product.   We found the discarded stories as diagnostic of what the group was *not,* as the final stories were representative of the way in which the group did function.   Even groups in which one or two members played dominating roles were found to make modifications in the originally proposed stories, which significantly increased the accuracy with which they reflected the group's process. Perhaps the high rate of theme repetition in the group projections, as contrasted with that found in individual TAT's, is due to the fact that each story proposal must be strained through the same group-process sieve.   This tendency makes it possible to demonstrate the versatility and richness of the instrument by presenting single stories told by different groups, as follows:

Group *C* told this story about picture III, the picture of two men:

The younger man, Fred, has failed on a promotional campaign that he attempted to run in his capacity as an account executive in a large advertising firm.   His superior has long regarded Fred as his protege, an up-and-coming advertising executive whose ideas are generally good.   But the superior still retains his confidence in him and doesn't want Fred to be too discouraged.   He's consoling him and telling him to keep his chin up and to try a new tack.   The older man has no doubt things will work out satisfactorily.   Fred goes back much encouraged.

The analysis of this story emphasizes the group's cooperative accomplishment, its friendly and close personal relations (reference to the nickname Fred, protege, consoling, faith in eventual good outcome), the implication of a long-term task not completed but in which everyone had considerable personal involvement, and the presence of one benevolent but directing person.

The above story was one told by a research team that had been in repeated conference on a common problem. The interpersonal relations were both friendly and cooperative. It was clearly a group interested in achievement and willingness to submerge the unique interests of individuals to the group goal. Though essentially non-hierarchical in structure, the research director clearly exerted influence and pressure upon the group.

In contrast, the response of Group *D* to picture I reflects a group working on a common goal, greatly emphasizes the lack of personal involvement in this goal, and shows the highly individuated nature of the group participation. Group *D*'s response was:

An informal graduate seminar in social science. Objectivity in Social Science is the subject; the standing man at the table doesn't believe there is any. A mutual respect exists among the students, but the man insists on his point, and the bald man sitting at the left is formulating his answer and will presently refute his argument. After weekly meetings through the school year, they will expend much academic energy in writing a report of their discussions, which no one will read. The ash tray is full; the meeting is a long one; and they will go out for coffee in a few minutes.

Several other features are readily apparent in this story. The group was oriented toward a common goal that was secondary to their primary interests. Further, while each group member participated in the common goal, individual glory was most vital. In this connection, note especially the reference to a seminar discussion (common goal) in which each member was obliged to assert his individuality (one man does not believe in the point under discussion, one insists on his point). In this group, the interpersonal relations, while not hostile, were stormy, and the members felt their joint efforts to be somewhat futile (no one will read their report).

Group *D* was the editorial staff of a newspaper noted for its mutually respectful but nonetheless vibrant and stormy staff conferences. It was interested in group endeavor in the sense that the whole group was obliged to participate to turn out the paper. However, the more important goal was the individual by-line that each saw in print once the paper was out.

The two following stories are of particular interest since they reflect entirely different group processes. They were told independently by two matched subdivisions of a single group. The group consisted of branch-office managers in a civil service organization.   They met regularly, primarily to discuss various state and national regulations and procedures relating to their work.   The group had very little power of its own.   The branch managers met merely to clarify their understanding of the regulations and to take directions from their superior.   In response to picture II, the lone man, subgroup X reported:

Young man with time on his hands.   April.   Undecided as to whether he should leave or not.   Waiting for something to happen to make up his mind.

The reliance upon external authority, the lack of interest, and the feeling of indecision as to their own efforts and their future are amply apparent in this story.   In picture III, the two men, the subgroup reiterated its concept of hierarchy, its feeling that the subordinate person must accept authority.   They reported:

Father and son.   Telling the son the conditions on which he will send him to college.   Boy agrees to the terms.   Boy goes to college and is very happy about the decision.

The other half of the same group of branch managers showed startling similarity in its feelings.   In response to picture II, subgroup Y wrote:

Feeling and thinking: lost, empty, relaxed, pensive, wondering what to do, indecision, waiting.
What led up to scene: expectancy, waiting for someone or something to happen.
What he's waiting for will happen.

The same lack of vitality and flexibility characterizes this story. If anything, this group was more bound by rule and hierarchy than the previous one.   In response to picture III, they wrote:

Think or feel: father giving son advice or information.
What led up to scene: lack of knowledge on the part of the younger.
Outcome: acceptance on part of younger.   Older will leave.

What kind of stories are given by a number of individuals without previous acquaintance, who do not constitute a "group" in the psychological sense?   Four persons selected at random from a club lounge were invited to tell a set of stories about the pictures.   None was previously known to the others.   Their lack of common purpose and their feeling of the temporary nature of their group task are amply illustrated in their response to picture II, the lone man:

The man is young, about 25 or 30.   He is contemplating about something (can't agree what).   This is a moment out of his life—he probably will go back into the house and continue in his daily routine.

In response to picture III, the two men, they wrote:

The two men are separating.   They were in service together, were bosom buddies.   Their way of life is different, despite a common bond.   They have shared many experiences and respect each other, but each is going his own way.

Both a clinical summary and a rating system have been found productive in the analysis of group stories.   The following categories all seem relevant to an analysis of these stories.

Categories of Analysis and Rating.   The following categories represent the variables presently thought to be useful in the analysis of the stories.   Each of these variables, while not independent of the others, is capable of separate description and rating.   We believe all of them to be useful in the description of the group.   For convenience, the categories have been grouped into three classes:

I. *Sociodynamics,* wherein we are concerned with several variables dealing with the interrelationships of persons and actions within the group, with the emotional atmosphere within which these processes take place, and with the directness and intent with which the group proceeds with its task.

II. *Group structure,* wherein we are attempting to describe the more formal and structural aspects of the group that seem crucial in understanding the way in which a group carries on its activities.

III. *Outcome of group process,* wherein we wish to assess the quality of the result of the group action, and the emotional investment of the group in this result.

RATING CATEGORIES

I. SOCIODYNAMICS

A. *Communication Clarity:*   the extent to which there is present in the group clear understanding of one another's arguments and points of view. Group members need not accept one another's arguments, but must comprehend what the other members of the group are trying to say.

B. *Content-Procedure Ratio:* the ratio of time the group spends on discussion of the common group problem at hand (content) to the time it spends on discussion of procedural matters.

C. *Information-Providing:* the amount of factual information the group provides for itself in the course of its activities.   This variable is particularly relevant for decision-making groups.

D. *Goal Concentration:* the extent to which the group keeps directly to the point of the group problem, or to which it wanders onto tangential topics and loses sight of the original goal.

E. *Problem Source:* the source of the problem with which the group is dealing.   To what extent does the group feel the problem to be integral to its activities or imposed upon it from some external source?

F. *Value Orientation:* the orientation of the group toward the kind of task thought appropriate, the kind of goal it thought worth while.

G. *Tension Level:* the amount of tensions or energy present in the group.

H. *Tension Direction:* the emotional direction of energy and tension— whether the members are supportive of each other or whether the tension is largely oppositional in nature and is expended in conflict.

I. *Pacing Level:* the speed with which the group approaches its topic of discussion.

J. *Interpersonal Relations:* two aspects of interpersonal relations are treated here:

1. *Personal interdependence:* the extent to which there exists emotional interdependence among members of the group (whether friendly, supportive, antagonistic), and how much each individual feels the need for other group members.

2. *Personal affect:* the nature of the personal affect existing among group members.

II. GROUP STRUCTURE

A. *Participation Spread:* the extent to which all members of the group participate in the group activity, or whether participation is limited to a few group members.

B. *Role Differentiation:* the extent to which there is much variety and differentiation among the roles within the group.

C. *In-Group Feeling:* the in-group awareness of the group, and the extent to which it considers itself distinct from other groups.

D. *Individuality of Members:* whether each member of the group considers himself primarily as an individual in his dealings with the group, or whether he sees himself primarily in his role of group participant.

III. PROCESS OUTCOME

A. *Quality of Group Product:* the quality of the outcome of the group's activity, especially with regard to its reality-orientation, its organized qualities, and its originality.

1. *Reality orientation:* the extent to which the group activities are based on reasonable observation of fact and the realities of the group's situation.

2. *Organization of outcome:* the extent to which the outcome of the group's activity is well organized and coherently presented.

3. *Creativity of group product:* the originality of thinking about group activities and the creativity of outcome.

B. *Group Satisfaction with Outcome:* the extent to which the group feels satisfied and pleased with the outcome of its activity.

C. *Motivation to Execute Outcome:* the extent to which the group is motivated to go into action on the outcome of its acivities.

Studies of Cultural Groups.   The effort to understand the behavior of cultures other than our own has been greatly aided by the addition of psychological data and insight to the usual anthropological approach.   The projective instruments, particularly the Rorschach [4] and the Thematic Apperception Test have played an important role in this development.[10]   The discussion here will be limited to the TAT.   The first major study using the TAT in other culture groups will now be reviewed [9].

In 1942, the United States Office of Indian Affairs and the Committee on Human Development of the University of Chicago inaugurated the Research on Indian Education. This program was designed to investigate and compare in a number of Indian communities: (a) the development of personality from birth to adulthood; and (b) the relation of the child-training patterns to the social structure.   About 1,000 children from six to 18 years old in eleven Papago, Zuni, Zia, Hopi, Navaho, and Sioux communities were studied.   In addition to the TAT records collected on these children, there were also available extensive life-history material collected by psychiatrists, anthropologists, and school teachers on each child and his family; psychometric examinations; Rorschach technique records; a series of free drawings; and a battery of psychological tests designed to reveal the official ideology and moral values of the group and the dominant fears and anxieties of the children.

The Thematic Apperception Test used was a series of 12 pictures drawn by an Indian artist and representing people and social situations presumed to be within the everyday experience of all Indian children: a picture of two boys facing a man; two adults, one leading a horse; an adult woman with baby in arms and with two other children seated before her; a group of children and adults around a grinding stone; several young men in dance regalia; a landscape scene, of fields, fences, dried animal bones; and the like.   The people in the picture were Indians, of course.   All of these materials

---

10 Reports combining the various techniques are given in [*19, 22, 23, 27*].

were used in the broader study of personality development among these Indian groups. The TAT functioned in this total study of the general psychological characteristics of the groups.

In developing the methods and procedure for this investigation, the personality process, as stated at the beginning of the chapter, was regarded as the interaction between certain individual needs and demands and certain cultural demands and sanctions. Following the scheme of Kluckhohn and Mowrer [21] in order to clarify this process, we may distinguish certain aspects or components of it: the universal, the communal, the role, and the idiosyncratic components.

The universal component consists of those attributes, behaviors, and facts that are common and accepted as normal in all human beings. They spring from the commonness of certain characteristics of the physical organisms and social environments of all humans.

The communal component refers merely to the fact that members of any one society tend to share more behavioral and personality characteristics with other members of that society than with members of other societies. These characteristics spring not only from a common cultural set of demands and trainings, but also from the commonalities of physical and biological equipment.

The role component refers to the distinctions that obtain between various kinds of personalities within any one society. Thus, not only the personalities of the sexes but even those of some professional groups have a certain communality that enables a person to distinguish one from the other. These role components of personality are some of the factors that identify various subgroups within one society.

The idiosyncratic component refers to those purely individual, unique characteristics that the individual shares with no one, those that are not determined by the training characteristic of his particular social group. This component is the "private world" of meanings and feelings referred to above.

With this in mind, consider the two uses made of the TAT in this study.

A. Individual Personality Study. The first objective in this research was to investigate to what extent the TAT would be of use in the study of individuals of other societies. For this purpose, the

TAT records of 50 cases, selected by the anthropologists as representative of the various communities studied, were analyzed. In each case the records were analyzed blind—that is, the analyst was given only the age and sex of the subject and his verbatim responses to the pictures. No other information was known about any of the children studied when their TAT records were analyzed. After these records had been analyzed and written up, each was compared with all of the other data available on each child and the extent of agreement between the TAT analysis and all other data was considered. While it is beyond our purpose here to report in detail the nature and extent of these data, it will suffice to say that the vast majority of all analyses of these cases were validated in their general tone as well as in the specific details. Among the 16 Navaho cases so studied, for example, 451 interpretations were made, about 28 points for each of the 16 cases. When these 451 points were compared with all other sources of data, 375, or 83.1 per cent of them, were found to be substantiated and only 10, or 2.2 per cent, were found to be incorrect statements.

During the preparation of these TAT analyses, it soon became evident that there were certain kinds of information that the TAT could be expected to provide on individual cases. For purposes of uniformity in the study, these areas of data were defined as follows, and all records were prepared according to these areas.

1. *Mental Approach.* A description of the level and organization of the intellectual processes and their functioning.

2. *Creativity and Imagination.* The extent, freedom, and nature of imaginal processes; the manner in which they are used intellectually and emotionally.

3. *Behavioral Approach.* A description of overt behavior as observed socially and a report of its emotional background.

4. *Family Dynamics.* The emotional relationships within the family and their influence upon the individual.

5. *Inner Adjustment and Defense Mechanism.* The characteristics of the emotional life and personality structure and adjustment of the individual; his manner of meeting problems emotionally; his approach to interpersonal relations.

6. *Emotional Reactivity.* The spontaneity, reactivity, and general nature of the individual's response to emotional stimulation; his desire for contact with or withdrawal from the outer world; the extent to which his reactions to stimulation are free from anxieties or unresolved conflicts that warp his objectivity.

7. *Sexual Adjustment.* The maturity, stage, and general adequacy of his sexual adjustment.

8. *General Summary.* The patterning and integration of the above areas; final diagnosis.

This aspect of the study was directed at an investigation of the *idiosyncratic component* of personality, at a delineation of those peculiarly private and individual experiences and orientations that characterize the individual. Nevertheless, it soon became apparent that the TAT analyses were giving much more than this. *The universal component* of personality soon became obvious—it was quite clear that, precisely as we should have expected, more outstanding than the characteristics that made a given child Hopi rather than Navaho, were those characteristics of his personality that made him a human being of given age and sex. In addition, data on the *communal* and *role components* of personality were revealed—the extent and manner to which the individual fit into the general demands of his culture and into the demands of his particular role.

B. General Psychological Characteristics of Culture. The second major use of the TAT was directed at investigation of the *communal* and *role components* of personality. Rather than study the individual's relationship to his general cultural demands as in the individual studies, here we were interested in seeing what the communal and role characteristics were—the psychological characteristics that made one a Hopi, a Navaho, or a Sioux, and that differentiated a member of one tribe from a member of another. Among the topics discussed in these reports and the areas of importance in the study of primitive character patterns are the following:

1. *Physical World.* The emotional orientation to the physical world, the feeling and anxiety toward it and toward the manner of earning a living.

2. *Adult Pressure.* The extent and nature of pressure that the adults put upon children, and the children's reaction to them.

3. *Authority Systems.* Related to this is the system for the control of authority—as in the females in Hopi society and the males in Sioux—and the areas in which males and females do have authority in a given society.

4. *Interpersonal Relations.* The characteristics of the interpersonal relations and behavior: the Sioux striving for fame and individual glory, the Hopi striving for an inconspicuous place through conformity, the presumed harmony and smoothness of Hopi social relations.

5. *Sex Roles.* The roles of the two sexes and the emotional atmosphere characteristic of it.

6. *Family Role.* The unity of the family group and the emotional atmosphere characteristic of it.

7. *Spontaneity vs. Restraint.* The extent to which individual spontaneity is given freedom and the extent to which it is restrained—the nature of the outlets and sublimations allowed.

8. *Acculturation Processes.* The extent and nature of White contact and the manner in which this is accepted and integrated into the native culture pattern.

9. *Age Trends.* The relationship of the impulse-life to the culture trainings and demands over time. The characteristics of the psychological development during three major life periods, infancy, childhood, and adolescence.

10. *Intratribal Variations.* The variations of these factors among various areas of each tribe.

These categories represent at least some of the things that the TAT can provide data upon for various societies. In general, it is to be stressed that in each instance, the TAT is investigating the emotional and affective aspects of life. It is concerned with the objective material aspects only insofar as these are given affective connotations and hence are reflected in the fantasy of the individuals in that society. The use of techniques such as the TAT for individual personality study gives data on the particular personality and upon the theoretically important area of the effect of a given cultural pattern upon personality dynamics. The group use provides data for study of the communal and role components of personality and provides a methodology for delineating character patterns of primitive societies. It also yields data that check with and supplement the anthropologists' formulation of a culture, and it provides important material for the consideration of a societal personality structure. Consideration of these kinds of data in the light of the anthropological knowledge of various societies should give a firmer basis for study of the development of human behavior and the functioning of primitive and modern societies.

Several other studies have been initiated. Each has used the TAT in its original form or in a form modified from the series used in the American Indian Study described above. Examples are:

1. The Study of Mexican Indian Groups initiated by the U. S. Office of Indian Affairs under John Collier and by the Mexican Institute of Indian Affairs.

2. The Study of the Ojibwa, an American Indian group located in Wisconsin, by William A. Caudill, of the Department of Anthropology, University of Chicago.

3. A study of the Social Organization, Personality Structure, and Acculturation of the Japanese-American by William A. Caudill and Setsuko Matsunaga Nishi, under the auspices of the University of Chicago.

4. A Study of a South West African Community by Boris Iflund, of the Department of Psychology, University of California, a member of the University of California African Expedition.

5. Two Studies of South Pacific Micronesian Groups—one by Francis Mahoney, of the University of Chicago, and one by William A. Lessa, of the University of California at Los Angeles.

For our present purposes, these studies will be discussed only insofar as they are relevant to the use of the TAT.

The first problem in the setting up of these studies, including that on the six American Indian communities, was that of the selection of TAT stimulus material. It was felt that the Harvard TAT series was inadequate in one crucial respect, namely, the pictures used were representative of a culture that was not sufficiently familiar to the subjects to permit ready identification with the content of the pictures. Experience with these studies has suggested several criteria that are important in the selection of pictures for such studies:

1. The test selected should contain a number of pictures that
   (a) represent a number of basic interpersonal relations; mother-child, father-child; person alone, a heterosexual scene, a group scene, an authority scene, a scene representing the usual physical environment, scenes of some characteristic cultural economic activity,
   (b) one or two pictures representing an illogical arrangement of reality events (such as 8 BM in the Harvard set),
   (c) one or two pictures representing unreal or bizarre events (such as 17BM or 19 in the Harvard set).

2. In addition to the above basic set, additional pictures should be selected to represent special scenes characteristic of the culture or of the particular problem under study; for example, women's huts in certain groups, older persons in Indian groups, homosexual

scenes, caste groups in pictures for India.   In general these scenes must be selected in consultation with an anthropologist familiar with the culture.   The set of pictures for the study of race prejudice, of religious conflict in Jewish groups, of special attitudes toward physical incapacity in paraplegic patients, and so forth, should contain, first, the basic set of pictures, and second, a number of pictures specially slanted at the problem under study.   Basically, it is still personality that is being studied in these problems.   Therefore, by selecting a dual set of pictures, one has a greater chance of seeing the attitudes toward special problems in their proper setting of total personality dynamics.

3. Such pictures as are selected should be sufficiently stimulating in content to intrigue the subject and demand that he propose some sort of solution to it, but they should be sufficiently flexible and ambiguous to

(a) permit a full range of emotions that may be attributed to the picture,

(b) permit a full range of possible solutions to the emotional problem presented.

4. Such scenes as are selected should be pictorially appropriate to the culture of the group being studied.

For purposes of illustration, a number of samples of parallel sets of pictures may be given.   The first picture, and its accompanying stories, is used for American Indian groups.   It represents two young men and an older man.   It is generally diagnostic of feelings toward adult authority and toward paternal figures, of the spontaneity-control balance of the subject, and of the nature of passivity or assertiveness of the personality structure.

Sample stories to this picture, given here as examples, are, first, stories told by a 15-year-old Hopi Indian girl and by a 15-year-old Hopi Indian boy; second, two stories by Sioux Indians, boys of 11 and 15 years old.

Hopi girl, aged 15: This man is telling them what they should do.   He is their grandfather.   They will do what he tells them because they are listening.

Hopi boy, aged 15: Indians, they are Zuni, the father is telling the other two to go work in the field.   They will go.

Sioux boy, aged 11: They are talking Indian.   They are all Indians. They are talking about catching horses.   "Get the ropes and bridles and saddles," the old man says. They go get them. They ride them. They get the cows first. Then they go buying something—bread and like that.

Sioux boy, aged 15: Two kids back from school ready to make a living. Old man gives them a few pointers. He tells them the best way to buy cattle. Probably these kids are getting Benefit Money (from government). Put out on the range and by and by they increase the cattle.

Reproduced by permission of Robert J. Havighurst.

Fig. 3. TAT for American Indian groups.

Perhaps some of the differences between the two cultures can be sensed from these few samples. A clear contrast is afforded by the story of a 10-year-old Mexican Indian boy. The picture is the parallel one from a set made for the study of Mexican Indian groups.

Mexican Indian boy, aged 10: One day a father had two sons and he sent them to the fields to take care of his milpa so that the cattle would not enter. They took their shoulder blankets and their hats and went to the fields to watch the milpa and at night they came back. The father was satisfied and gave them each one peso and told them the next day to take care of it again and so they went. There at the milpa they met a man who was begging. The children told him they didn't have any money.

Reproduced by permission of National Indian Institute.

Fig. 4. TAT for Mexican Indian groups.

The next picture is one adopted by Boris Iflund, of the University of California, for use on the University Expedition to South Africa. The stories are those of the first and third sons of a native chief. The first son was attempting to move into closer relations with the White community, with only moderate success.

South West Africa, first son: I think these are two boys and this might be their father. . . . They look afraid and they might have done something wrong . . . and I can tell because this old man is pointing to them and in our country when someone points like that they must have done something serious and I think he will never beat them again because he is already pointing at them . . . therefore he is telling them that they should never do it again . . . and then he will leave them alone . . . (what did they do?) . . . (laughs) . . . They might have run away perhaps from work and that isn't good when people are working . . . or I'll chase you out of my kraal . . . but I think the old man will go away and leave them alone.

South West Africa, third son: To tell what they say or what . . . (whatever you like) Yes this is people . . . Is this an old man or what . . . I think these two men met with . . . with this . . . I think this one is

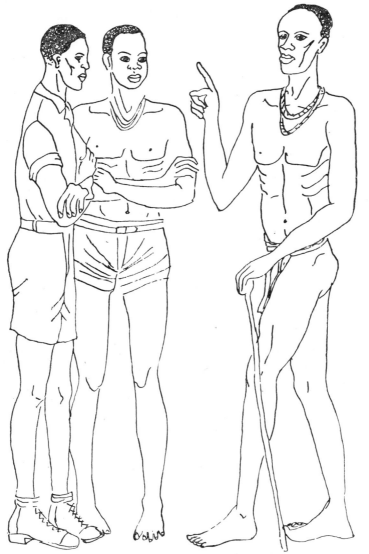

Reproduced by permission of Boris Iflund and Ella Marie K. Loeb.

Fig. 5. TAT for South West African native.

pointing something to them . . . and these are standing listening to him with interest . . . and I think this is a native . . . (what will happen?) I think this is a witchdoctor and he is pointing the direction of his treatment.

The next two pictures are taken from sets used in Micronesia. They were selected to represent special problems thought by the anthropologist to be useful in studies of the South Pacific. The first is a scene of the women's hut, used by William A. Lessa in Ulithi; the second, a picture of a hurricane-swept terrain, was used by Francis Mahoney in Palau.

Reproduced by permission of William A. Lessa.

Fig. 6.   TAT for South Pacific-Micronesia.

These studies, in addition to the data they reveal on the societies under study, have several important findings for the use of the TAT. From them, the following conclusions seem justified:

1. The TAT is of considerable utility in the study of persons in cultures other than our own, both in the analysis of individuals, and in the analysis of basic personality characteristics of the culture.

2. The adaptation of the TAT in the manner described and illustrated above is a useful procedure.

3. Adaptation of the TAT to better conform to cultural symbols of the society under study has considerable advantage in heightening the identification of the subject with the story-telling task and in securing useful data. It is probably not too necessary to have the subjects clothed to look exactly like the people in that society, or to have them of identical physical type. Rather, if the scenes are of fairly basic human interpersonal situations and consist of symbols of dress and physical surroundings that are not unrecognizable by the subject or grossly different from his own, then he will be able to identify with them and tell revealing stories.

Reproduced by permission of Francis Mahoney.

Fig. 7. TAT for South Pacific-Micronesia.

In this connection, it is of interest that White adolescents, when presented with the American Indian series, have no difficulty telling stories that may be validly interpreted to reveal basic personality data. They do not tend to tell "Indian stories." The basic stimulus in Figure 3, for example, may be said to be two young men and an older man, rather than three Indians.

In two other studies, one of the Ojibwa (Lac du Flambeau, Wis.) American Indian groups by Caudill, and one of the Japanese-Americans, by Caudill and Setsuko Nishi, the original TAT series has been used. It was felt that both of these groups were sufficiently acculturated to make the original pictures appropriate.

In the Ojibwa research, Caudill used the Harvard pictures numbered 2, 13 B, 12 F, 3 BM, 12 BG, 7 BM, 18 BM, 4, 19, and 17 BM. In the Japanese group, the following were used: 1, 2, 6 BM, 3 BM, 7 BM, 4, 6 GF, 18 GF, 13 G, 12 F, 17 BM, 16, 17 GF, 19.

The importance of the Japanese-American study lies partly in the extension of TAT material to this cultural group, but perhaps more crucially, in the conception of the method of analysis of the TAT. About his approach, Caudill says:

All TAT stories will exhibit a *press situation* and a *solution* (a lack of ending being one kind of solution). These two categories are *highly definable* in terms of culture and society. If a person's ego is strong and functioning well, one gets a story in which both press and solution are handled easily and realistically by the ego and largely at the conscious level.

If, however, the press is "fumbled" by the ego—if it activates, or creates, a *conflict* in the personality (unresolved basic drives of sex, dependency needs; or, unresolved interpersonal conflicts between mother-son, father-son, other authority relations, etc.) then *defense mechanisms* are brought into play in an attempt to resolve the conflict and bring about a solution (good or bad, realistic or magical, etc.).

It seems probable that the *conflicts* are more idiosyncratic (pertaining to a particular individual's special life situation) and less influenced by culture. In *any* society one would expect a very wide range of kinds of conflict. However, if the person is to operate successfully in the society (i.e. not leave the society physically, or go off into neurosis or psychosis) then the *defenses* available are of a narrower range than the conflicts, and the *defenses* are influenced by the culture (one cannot use a defense of physical aggression and certain kinds of acting-out and remain in white middle class society).

A development of these notions would add to, and sharpen, our understanding of basic personality theory. That is, it seems likely that much of what we now call basic personality structure is actually a pattern of common defenses, and integrative mechanisms of the ego, the range of conflicts still remaining wider and more idiosyncratic. Also, these notions, while developed for TAT analysis, are *not confined* to use with projective techniques, but constitute a frame of reference for viewing and analyzing any body of systematically gathered samples of such behavior.

Press situation of course can come from the outer world, or inner reactions—usually it is a combination of both. What happens then depends upon the ability of the ego to handle the *press* [3].

This four-part analysis, *press situation, conflict, defense* and *solution,* constitutes the framework for the analysis of TAT stories.   Its particular merit for work with cultural problems is that it integrates the cultural process and the culturally defined defenses and solutions directly into the analysis of the individual case, and does so at the level of raw data.

STUDIES OF MODERN INSTITUTIONS

Since TAT data are essentially symptomatic of the personality-culture interaction, the TAT seemed an appropriate instrument for studies on the *organized behavior* in a given society.   Two such studies have been made.   The first [29] dealt with the question: What is the emotional and social function of the modern daytime radio serial?   The second [11] dealt with the question: What is the emotional and social function of the greeting card as currently used? Only the first of these two studies will be mentioned here to illustrate further flexibility of method in using the TAT.

The daytime serial, like many other dramas, is primarily a verbal symbol system that stimulates its audience as individuals and as members of society.   Drama is always "an idealized representation of human life—of character, emotion, action—under forms manifest to the sense."   The individuals composing the audience have, as members of society, a common body of understanding through which they interpret what they see and hear in terms of the customary symbolic behavior making up the common life of the society.   But each individual in the audience has a whole body of emotions and unconscious feelings and ideas that the serial must also satisfy.   These emotionally charged private symbols, combined with those customarily used by all members of the group, are always present in every radio audience.   Therefore, to understand how a daytime serial functions and how it is used by its audience, one needs to know the symbolic content of the serial and how its symbols stimulate the woman both as a member of society and as an individual with a private world and private fantasies.

The research workers formulated four questions:

1. What is the symbolic content of the daytime serial?
2. What are the social characteristics of its audience?
3. What are the overt and covert psychological characteristics of its audience?
4. How does the daytime serial, as a symbolic system, stimulate the women (a) overtly, as members of American society, and (b) covertly and privately, as separate individuals? Or, to ask this question another way, what does it mean to them, and how does it function in their public and private lives?

The use of the TAT in this research was concentrated primarily upon questions 3 and 4 above—in describing the basic anxiety systems and defense systems of the listeners, and in clarifying their value systems. By so analyzing the personality structure of the homogeneous social unit of listeners, it was possible to relate and explain the function of the program. Such an approach adds material to one's understanding of social institutions and shows the emotional groundwork upon which they rest. From the point of view of TAT method, the study also illustrates another point—that the framework of analysis of the TAT is extremely flexible and should be shifted to highlight the particular problem under study. In this instance, the main focus of analysis was on:

1. Freedom versus restraint of the imaginative spontaneity
2. The expectancies about basic interpersonal relations
3. The morality concepts
4. The major areas of anxiety, especially as they relate to interpersonal relations
5. The habitual methods of anxiety defense

Other concepts, as indicated before, could as readily have been used with the TAT. These, however, seemed more relevant to the conceptualization of this problem and were equally relevant to the TAT.

STUDIES OF SOCIAL ROLES

Another area to which the TAT seems particularly apt is that involving the psychodynamics of social roles. These roles, having many highly stereotyped aspects and being consistent in external social appearance, are also characterized by internally consistent patterns of recurring psychological features. Research on these common psychological characteristics should aid materially in problems of selection for these roles as well as in the more general problems of the understanding of role behavior in modern society.

One such study involved the psychodynamics of the modern business executive [13]. The business executive is a central figure in the economic and social life of the United States. His direction of business enterprise and his participation in informal social groupings give him a significant place in community life. In both its economic and its social aspects, the role of the business executive is sociologically a highly visible one. It has clearly definable limits and characteristics known to the general public. These characteristics indicate the function of the business executive in the social structure, define the behavior expected of the individual executive, and serve as a guide to the selection of the novice.

Social pressure and the constant demands of the business organization of which he is a part direct the behavior of the executive into the mold appropriate to the defined role. *Success* is the name applied to wholehearted adoption of the role. The individual behaves in the manner dictated by the society, and society rewards the individual with success if his behavior conforms to the role. It would punish him with failure should he deviate from it.

Participation in this role, however, is not a thing apart from the personality of the individual. It is not a game that the person is playing; it is the way of behaving and thinking that he knows best, that he finds rewarding, and in which he believes. Thus, the role as socially defined has its counterpart in personality structure. To some extent, too, the personality structure is reshaped to be in harmony with the social role. The extent to which such reshaping of the adult personality is possible, however, seems limited. An initial selection process occurs that reduces the amount of time involved in teaching the appropriate behavior. Those whose personality structures are most readily adaptable to this particular role tend to be selected, whereas those whose personalities are not already partially adapted are rejected.

It became clear from the research that the "successful" business executives studied had many personality characteristics in common.

(It was equally clear that an absence of these characteristics was coincident with failure within the organization.) This personality constellation might be thought of as the minimal requirement for success within our present business system and as the psychodynamic motivation of persons in this occupation. Individual uniqueness in personality was clearly present; but, despite these unique aspects, all executives had in common a personality pattern.

The areas of personality in which strong common features exist for the executive are: achievement interests, social and job mobility drive, concepts of authority, the concept of the necessity for organization, decisiveness, strength of self-structure, basic personality aggression, apprehensiveness of failure, reality orientation, the nature of personal relations to subordinates and superiors, parent images, and the nature of dependency feelings.

From this research, it was apparent that the successful executive represents a crystallization of many of the attitudes and values generally accepted by middle-class American society. The value of accumulation and achievement, of self-direction and independent thought and their rewards in prestige, status and property, are found in this group. But they also pay the price of holding these values and of profiting from them. Uncertainty, constant activity, the continual fear of losing ground, the inability to be introspectively leisurely, the ever-present fear of failure, and the artificial limitations put upon their emotionalized interpersonal relations—these are some of the costs of this role.

The TAT was of particular utility in this research, not only in illuminating the psychodynamics of this role, but in predicting behavior. This latter use, of course, is the central problem of personnel selection. The key to successful prediction of behavior in this area seems to lie in the concepts of the structure of the social life-space of the executive. In other words, knowledge of the psychodynamics must be interpreted in terms of the formal and informal social organization of the job into which the man is to be placed [5, 14].

The framework of analysis of the TAT that developed from this research is somewhat different from those previously described. It is different because the basic problem being studied had different variables and because the study was slanted at the prediction of overt behavior. This general framework is given below:

OUTLINE FOR TAT ANALYSIS OF EXECUTIVES

A. *Individual Characteristics*
   Driving, tense, ambitious, thoughtful, persevering
   Conservatism, sensitivity, to social demands
   Anxiety and methods of control
   Reactions under pressure
   Motivations: achievement, activity, recognition, money, promotion, power, attainment of ideals
B. *Intellectual Characteristics*
   Intellectual level—efficiency
   Intellectual approach: planning, concrete goal relations
   Judgment: egocentric, critical capacity, response to advice
   Originality: resourceful, egocentric
C. *Working Relationships*
   Relation to total organization: loyalty, sensitivity to rank—in others and in himself
   Superiors: attitude, cooperation, acceptance of close supervision, qualifications on relationships with superiors
   Associates: cooperation, informal or when indicated, attitudes, competitive, detached
   Subordinates: kind of supervision, social distance, work standards, independence (protégés)
D. *Placement Pattern*
   Summaries: separate operating functions, line, staff, policy-making or immediate decision
E. *Potential Adjustment*
   Level of aspiration, social and professional
   Any indication of break-up
F. *Summary of Strong Points and Weak Points*

SUMMARY

The TAT is an instrument particularly appropriate to those studies of social behavior that attempt to take account of psychological factors and the relevance of social modes to personal behavior. In a sense, the TAT is an intermediate instrument, since its basic data reveal both idiosyncratic elements of individual personality and psychological features common to groups.

Much productive research has been done on the use of the TAT in diagnosis of the individual. It seems unnecessary, however, to limit its use to this field. Rather, we should focus our attention not upon the individual as such, but upon interplays of emotions in personal interaction. When the unit of our study becomes the emotions that accompany varieties of human experiences, it is possible to move readily from the individual as such and to encompass the broader field of interpersonal action in groups. Here we have available to scientific scrutiny a more varied and inclusive range of human events, and, it would be hoped, a richer area for the formation of psychological laws of a more comprehensive nature.

More specifically, it is suggested that the range of problems to which the TAT is thought relevant be extended to include:

1. The analysis of a variety of individuals in many subgroups of our own and other societies
2. The analysis of dynamics common to social groups
3. The analysis of dynamics underlying the unifying factors in the operation of small, cohesive groups
4. The analysis of the psychological function of various institutionalized modes of behavior and the pattern of feeling and personal assumptions that people attribute to them

A necessary correlate, if not a prior qualification, of this broadened scope of the TAT, is the abandonment of purely individual-oriented concepts and the adoption of conceptual frameworks that include sociological concepts. A special implication of this is that we also abandon the effort to develop any single framework for the analysis of the TAT. It seems doubtful that there is any one framework inherent to the TAT. Rather, we should experiment with concepts and problems, adapting the quite flexible data of the TAT to the problem at hand. Otherwise we will soon find that we limit the range of our scientific problems by assuming that a once-successful framework is the only appropriate one.

It is further urged that we do not regard our studies that *use* the TAT as studies *of* the TAT. Otherwise, we will soon find that we are becoming more fascinated with our techniques than with the scientific problems. While there is no doubt of the necessity of research upon the TAT as an instrument, it is imperative that we focus continually upon the scientific problems and treat the instruments as of secondary import.

In sum, the TAT is an appropriate aid in the study of any system of human interaction that has a substratum of dynamically related emotion and a consistent social life-space. In such studies, the principal feature of the TAT that makes it useful is its flexibility in terms of varying conceptual frameworks. It is suggested especially that researchers experiment with the conceptual frameworks of variables appropriate to the scientific problem of their interest, and with the adaptability of the TAT to those concepts. It is felt, particularly, that the inclusion of sociological concepts and the abandonment of the notion that the TAT is relevant only to idiosyncratic elements will prove of inestimable value in human relations research.

REFERENCES

1. Alexander, Theron, "The prediction of teacher-pupil interaction with a projective test" (Ph.D. thesis). Committee on Human Development, University of Chicago, 1949.

2. Aron, Betty, *A Manual for Analysis of the Thematic Apperception Test.* Berkeley, Calif.: Willis E. Berg, 1949.

3. Caudill, William A., in a letter to the author. Institute of Human Relations, Yale University.

4. Du Bois, Cora, *The People of Alor.* Minneapolis: The University of Minnesota Press, 1944.

5. Gardner, Burleigh B., *Human Relations in Industry.* Chicago: Richard D. Irwin, Inc., 1945.

6. Hallowell, A. I., "The Rorschach as a tool for investigating cultural variables and individual differences in the study of personality in primitive societies." *Rorschach Research Exchange,* 1941, 5, 31–34.

7. —————————, "Acculturation processes and personality changes as indicated by the Rorschach technique." *Rorschach Research Exchange,* 6, 1942, 42 50.

8. Havighurst, Robert J., and Taba, Hilda, *Adolescent Character and Personality.* New York: John Wiley & Sons, Inc., 1949.

9. Henry, William E., "The Thematic Apperception Technique in the study of culture-personality relations." *Genetic Psychology Monographs,* 1947, 35, 3–135.

10. —————————, "A Study in the application of socio-psychological research to the problems of business and industry." *Journal of Social Psychology,* 1948, 27, 37–61.

11. —————————, "Art and cultural symbolism: A psychological study of greeting cards." *Journal of Aesthetics and Art Criticism,* Vol. VI, No. 1, September 1947.

12. —————————, "Executive personality and job success." *American Management Association,* Personnel Series No. 120, 3–24, September 1948.

13. —————————, "The business executive: The psychodynamics of a social role." *American Journal of Sociology,* Vol. LIV, No. 4, January 1949.

14. Henry, William E., and Gardner, Burleigh, B., "Personality evaluation in the selection of executive personnel." *Public Personnel Review,* Vol. 10, No. 2, April 1949.

15. Henry, William E., and Guetzkow, Harold, "Group projection sketches for the study of small groups," Publication No. 4 of the Conference Research project at the University of Michigan. *Journal of Social Psychology,* 1951, 33, 77–102.

16. Henry, William E., and Tryon, Caroline, Unpublished research.

17. Hollingshead, A. B., *Elmtown's Youth.* New York: John Wiley & Sons, Inc., 1949.

18. Horwitz, M., and Cartwright, D., "A projective method for the diagnosis of groups." *Human Relations,* 1951.

19. Joseph, Alice, Spicer, R. B., Chesky, Jane, *The Desert People.* Chicago: University of Chicago Press, 1949.

20. Klopfer, Bruno, and Kelley, D. M., *The Rorschach Technique.* Yonkers, N. Y.: World Book Company, 1942.

21. Kluckhohn, Clyde, and Mowrer, O. H., "Culture and personality—a conceptual scheme." *American Anthropologist,* January–March, 1944, Vol. 46, No. 1, 1–29.

22. Leighton, D., and Kluckhohn, Clyde, *Children of the People.* Cambridge, Mass.: Harvard University Press, 1947.

23. MacGregor, Gordon, *Warriors Without Weapons,* Chicago: University of Chicago Press, 1946.

24. Schachtel, A. H., Henry, J., and Henry, Z., "Rorschach analysis of Pilaga Indian children." *American Journal of Orthopsychiatry,* 1942, 12, 679–712.

25. Stein, Morris I., *The Thematic Apperception Test: An Introductory Manual for its Clinical Use with Adult Males.* Cambridge, Mass.: Addison-Wesley, 1948.

26. Tomkins, Silvan S., *Thematic Apperception Test. The Theory and Technique of Interpretation.* New York: Grune & Stratton, 1947.

27. Thompson, Laura, and Joseph, Alice, *The Hopi Way.* Chicago: University of Chicago Press, 1944.

28. Warner, W. Lloyd, and associates, *Democracy in Jonesville.* New York: Harper and Brothers, 1949.

29. Warner, W. Lloyd, and Henry, William E., "The radio day time serial: A symbolic analysis." *Genetic Psychology Monographs,* 1948, 37, 3–71.

30. Warner, W. Lloyd, and Lunt, Paul, *Social Life of a Modern Community, Yankee City Series,* Vol. 1. New Haven, Conn., Yale University Press, 1941.

31. Warner, W. Lloyd, Meeker, M., and Eels, K., *Social Class in America.* Chicago: Science Research Associates, 1949.

32. Wyatt, Frederick, "The scoring and analysis of the TAT." *Journal of Psychology,* 1947, 24, 319–330.

CHAPTER 9

Word Association and Sentence Completion Methods

JULIAN B. ROTTER, PH.D.

I. THE WORD ASSOCIATION METHOD

The word association method, sometimes called the free association method, is perhaps one of the oldest procedures used in personality study and may well be considered a forerunner of the more recent projective techniques. It consists of presenting a stimulus word to a subject and having him answer quickly with the first word that comes to mind. Galton [2], as early as 1879, and after him, Wundt [25], experimented with it to study the association process. Kraepelin [10] adapted it for use in a study on the nature of abnormal behavior, and began a line of investigation that is still active. Soon after this, Münsterberg [14], following a different line of investigation, used the method in the detection of guilt. In 1906, Jung [5] applied it to the study of *complexes,* or areas of emotional disturbance. Although the technique is less popular now in comparison with some of the newer projective methods, word association finds many applications in present-day experimental and clinical work.

From this method, clues to the personality of the subject are usually obtained in three typical ways: (1) By analyzing the stimulus words on which the subject "blocks"—that is, words on which his reaction time, nature of response, or behavior deviates from his usual reaction; (2) By analyzing the associations or actual responses to stimulus words on which the subject shows some emotional disturbance, blocking or otherwise; and (3) By analyzing the commonness or unusualness of the subject's responses as compared to norms for his culture or for a diagnostic group.

A variety of word lists have been used in the association studies. Jung's list, one of the earliest, contained 100 words specifically chosen to sample common or frequent complexes. The Kent-Rosanoff list of 100 words, on the other hand, was designed to avoid emotionally loaded stimuli. It has been suggested that words of double meaning be avoided; however, for certain kinds of studies, particularly those concerned with determining the subject's interests, such double entendres are the key words of the list. In the detection of guilt or for some clinical purposes, the investigator may construct a different list for each subject. The Kent-Rosanoff [17] list is given below.

KENT-ROSANOFF WORD LIST [1]

1. Table	26. Wish	51. Stem	76. Bitter
2. Dark	27. River	52. Lamp	77. Hammer
3. Music	28. White	53. Dream	78. Thirsty
4. Sickness	29. Beautiful	54. Yellow	79. City
5. Man	30. Window	55. Bread	80. Square
6. Deep	31. Rough	56. Justice	81. Butter
7. Soft	32. Citizen	57. Boy	82. Doctor
8. Eating	33. Foot	58. Light	83. Loud
9. Mountain	34. Spider	59. Health	84. Thief
10. House	35. Needle	60. Bible	85. Lion
11. Black	36. Red	61. Memory	86. Joy
12. Mutton	37. Sleep	62. Sheep	87. Bed
13. Comfort	38. Anger	63. Bath	88. Heavy
14. Hand	39. Carpet	64. Cottage	89. Tobacco
15. Short	40. Girl	65. Swift	90. Baby
16. Fruit	41. High	66. Blue	91. Moon
17. Butterfly	42. Working	67. Hungry	92. Scissors
18. Smooth	43. Sour	68. Priest	93. Quiet
19. Command	44. Earth	69. Ocean	94. Green
20. Chair	45. Trouble	70. Head	95. Salt
21. Sweet	46. Soldier	71. Stove	96. Street
22. Whistle	47. Cabbage	72. Long	97. King
23. Woman	48. Hard	73. Religion	98. Cheese
24. Cold	49. Eagle	74. Whiskey	99. Blossom
25. Slow	50. Stomach	75. Child	100. Afraid

---

[1] Rosanoff, A. J., *Manual of Psychiatry and Mental Hygiene.* 7th edition. Copyright 1938 by John Wiley & Sons, Inc. By permission of the publishers.

Methods of administration also vary.   Although the administration can be visual, for the most part the list is presented orally, and the test must be given individually to assure an accurate measure of the response or reaction time.   In some procedures, the test is repeated after a standard interval and the subject is asked to recall his original responses.   The difficulty of giving the test to more than one person at a time while securing accurate measurements is one of the basic limitations of the method.   Also, the tenseness of the test conditions, with stop-watch recording of every response, interferes with rapport in certain clinical situations.

Schema for interpretation of the subject's behavior on the test have been proposed by a number of investigators.   These have been reviewed in more extensive surveys published by Symonds [18], Kohs [9], and Rapaport [15].   Here, the intention is to describe only some typical present applications in the experimental and clinical study of personality, where the concern is mainly with (1) clinical diagnosis, (2) determination of areas of emotional disturbance, (3) detection of guilt, and (4) description of interest patterns and attitudes.

DETERMINATION OF AREAS OF EMOTIONAL DISTURBANCES

Following his work with Freud, Jung [5, 6] began exploration of the association test as a method of determining *complexes,* or areas of emotional disturbance.   With the development of psychoanalysis, interest appeared in determining complexes, strongly or emotionally toned related attitudes requiring active repression. Stimuli associated with the complex would lead to blocking or other evidences of disturbance.   A word association test requiring an immediate response was a logical method of diagnosing the presence of such complexes.   Jung placed considerable emphasis on the reaction time and made a study of typical reaction times for different kinds of stimulus words.   He also recorded sex differences and the differences between groups of subjects, finding women to have longer reaction time than men, and educated or intelligent subjects to have a shorter reaction time than uneducated ones.   These studies are based on relatively few cases.   Jung also found that concrete words provide the shortest reaction time, verbs next, and abstract words, the longest reaction time.

Longer reaction time, or blocking to a stimulus word, has been found by a number of investigators to be associated with emotional disturbance or affectivity. However, a variety of other signs of emotional disturbance have been described. Hull and Lugoff [2] tested several of these and were able to verify the validity of many of the common signs or indicators. In his excellent survey, Symonds [1] has given the following list of complex signs or indicators frequently found in the literature.[2]

1. *Long reaction time.* This is the only quantitative measure available. Any reaction requiring over 2.6 of a second is usually considered significant.

2. *Inability to make any response whatever.* Occasionally no response will be elicited even though time up to a minute may be allowed. Such failure to respond may be due to a number of factors, among which may be mentioned inhibition of any response; articulatory block; attention diverted by copious or diverting imagery; absorption in trains of imagery or reverie; competition of reaction words, or no meaning found in the stimulus.

3. *Extremely short reaction time.*

4. *Repetition of the stimulus word itself.*

5. *Apparent misunderstanding of the stimulus word.* The psychoanalytic explanation is that in such cases there is a strong desire not to understand. But this explanation need not be assumed. In some cases, it may well be true that there was a definite misunderstanding due to faulty learning, or indistinct or strange pronunciation on the part of the examiner. Perhaps in all such cases the prepotency of any part of the word is also influenced by competing ideas or images perseverating from previous associations.

6. *Defective reproduction of original reaction at second presentation of the stimulus word.* In the reproduction experiment, if the second response differs from the first, suspicion of a source of irritation arises.

7. *Response with the same reaction word to two or more different stimulus words.* This is sometimes called perseveration. Perseveration may be due to a certain complex or constellation which dominates consciousness, or to a poverty of ideas or to other more significant causes. In some cases where the subject suspects the nature of the experiment he may avail himself of perseveration to assist in concealment.

8. *Strange or apparently senseless reaction.*

9. *Perseveration of ideas.* In this case, though the exact word may not be repeated as in number 7, the same idea perseverates in two or more responses. A variety of other complex signs have been noted, especially peculiarities in the response and uneasiness in the behavior of the subject. Even when the response itself seems to have peculiar significance, unless the experimenter is confident of his judgment he should be alert to prevent his imagination from imparting significance where it does not really exist. Suspicion of emotional irritation may be aroused by

---

2 Symonds, P. M., *Diagnosing Personality and Conduct.* Copyright 1931 by Appleton-Century-Crofts, Inc. Pp. 378–379. By permission of the publishers.

such mannerisms as whispering the response, bodily movements, nervous movements of the hands, reddening of the face, coughing, clearing the throat. In all probability many valid psychological indices could be determined by laboratory instruments such as changes in the pulse, blood pressure, breathing, knee-jerk, strength of grip, etc. Giving more than one word in response is a very suspicious sign. Kohs lists such types of response as quotations, titles, sentences, addition of the article (example, *the person*), or responses in a foreign language, as being significant. A familiar subterfuge may betray the presence of a complex in the naming of some article in the examiner's room.

Wells [23] has also described a list on indications of emotional disturbance in the association test.

Although there are many clinical and experimental uses of the test for determination of emotional disturbance (such as the studies of Huston, Shakow, and Erickson [4] on hypnotically induced complexes), it is usually necessary for clinical purposes to use interviews or additional tests to determine the origin of the emotional disturbance and its meaning and significance to the individual.

APPLICATION TO CLINICAL DIAGNOSIS

Like other methods of personality study, association tests have been tried as a means of separating abnormals from normals, and types of abnormals from one another. Kraepelin began such efforts, but the first systematic attempt based on large normative samples was made by Kent and Rosanoff [7] using their own standard 100-item list. Compiling frequency tables of the responses of 1000 normal adults, Kent and Rosanoff developed a system of classifications, dependent entirely upon content of responses. This system is given below [17].[3]

In the examination of a test record obtained by this method the first step is to compare it with the frequency tables and thereby distinguish the *common* reactions which are to be found in the tables and which are for the most part normal, from *individual* reactions, which are not to be found in the tables and which include the great majority of those that are of pathologic significance.

For the sake of accuracy, any reaction word which is not found in the table in its identical form, but which is a grammatical variant of a word found there, is classed as *doubtful*.

---

[3] This system, together with Table 1, reprinted from A. J. Rosanoff, *Manual of Psychiatry and Mental Hygiene*, 7th ed. Copyright 1938 by John Wiley & Sons, Inc. By permission of the publishers.

From amongst both common and individual reactions a fairly definite group can be separated out, the *non-specific* reactions. In this group are placed words that are so widely applicable as to serve as more or less appropriate reactions to almost any of the stimulus words. In the standardized procedure any of the following words, occurring as a response to any stimulas word, is classed as non-specific: *article, articles, bad, beautiful, beauty, fine, good, goodness, great, happiness, happy, large, man, necessary, necessity, nice, object* (noun), *people, person, pleasant, pleasantness, pleasing, pleasure, pretty, small, thinking, thought, thoughts, unnecessary, unpleasant, use, used, useful, usefulness, useless, uselessness, uses, using, woman, work.*

It has been shown by Woodrow and Lowell that children often furnish reactions which, though not found in the standard frequency tables and therefore classifiable as individuals by this technique, are in many instances common for children. These may be designated *juvenile reactions. . . .*

Inasmuch as the frequency tables do not exhaust all normal possibilities of word reaction, a certain number of reactions which are essentially normal are to be found among individual reactions. In order to separate these from the pathologic reactions an appendix to the frequency tables has been compiled, consisting mainly of specific definitions of groups of words which, occurring as individual reactions are to be counted as normal.

Derivatives of stimulus words. Under this heading is classed any individual reaction which is a grammatical variant or derivative of the stimulus word: *eating, eatables, short, shortness, sweet, sweetened.*

Sound reactions. In the standardized procedure an individual reaction is placed under this heading when 50% of the sounds of the shorter word of the pair are identical with sounds of the longer word and are ranged in the same order.

Among sound reactions are occasionally found neologisms; for these a separate heading is provided.

Word complements. Here is included any individual reaction which, added to the stimulus word, forms a word, a proper name, or a compound word.

Particles of speech. Under this heading are included articles, numerals, pronouns, auxiliary verbs, adverbs of time, place and degree, conjunctions, prepositions, and interjections, occurring as individual reactions.

The phenomenon of *perseveration* occurs in cases in which there is abnormal lack of mobility of attention. The names of the different types of reactions attributable to perseveration are given below in the classification table and are sufficiently descriptive; we shall refer here only to those which require further definition.

Association to preceding stimulus. Here is placed any individual reaction that is shown by the frequency tables to be related to the stimulus preceding the one in question.

Association to preceding reaction. If an individual reaction in question, or the reaction preceding it, happens to be one of the stimulas words on the list, and a relationship between the two be found to exist by reference to the frequency tables, the reaction in question is classified under this heading.

In cases in which neither the reaction in question nor the preceding reaction happens to be one of the stimulus words, but a relationship between them may be judged to exist without considerable doubt, the reaction in question is also classed here. Example: *priest, father, ocean, mother.* The latter is an individual reaction; neither *father* nor *mother* is among the stimulus words; but the association between *father* and *mother* may be judged to exist without considerable doubt; therefore in this case *mother* is classed as an *association to preceding reaction.*

Repetition of previous stimulus. Here is placed any individual reaction that is a repetition of any previous stimulus from amongst the 10 next preceding, *repetition of preceding stimulus* being placed, at the same time, under a separate heading.

Neologisms. Here are placed the newly-coined words, so commonly given by psychotic subjects, excepting such as possess a sound relationship to the stimulus word, for which, as already stated, a special place in the classification has been provided.

Unclassified. Into this group fall over $\frac{1}{3}$ of all individual reactions, it having been found impossible to find objective criteria for their more definite differentiation.

The responses of several groups of subjects, classified according to this schema, are given in Table 1, from Rosanoff [17].

TABLE 1

ASSOCIATION IN SELECTED GROUPS OF SUBJECTS, NORMAL AND ABNORMAL

Subjects	Common Reactions		Doubtful Reactions (per cent)	Individual Reactions (per cent)	Failures of Reaction (per cent)
	Specific (per cent)	Non-specific (per cent)			
1000 normal adults	85.5	6.2	1.5	6.8	
247 insane adults	66.4	4.3	2.5	26.8	
253 defective children aged over 9 years	75.2	8.2	2.1	13.0	1.5
125 normal white children, 11–15 yrs.	82.0	7.2	1.6	8.6	0.6
175 normal white children, 4–10 yrs.	62.7	4.2	3.2	18.8	11.1
125 normal Negro children, 11–15 yrs.	75.3	7.2	2.5	14.9	0.1
175 normal Negro children, 4–10 yrs.	54.1	3.5	2.5	33.2	6.7

One difficulty with this method is that normative frequency tables become dated as test words take on meanings from colloquial usage, new songs, and so on. It is also extremely difficult, if not impossible, to obtain frequency tables that can be interpreted the same way for subjects of different cultural backgrounds. For example, should a hospital patient who has lived in hill-country be tested and show a large number of individual responses, it would not be possible to determine whether they were a function of mental pathology or cultural background.

A somewhat different approach to the use of word association tests in clinical diagnosis is presented by Rapaport, Gill, and Schafer [*16*]. They used a 60-item list including words of "familial, home, oral, anal, aggressive, and quite varied sexual connotations" [p. 14]. They also used Jung's reproduction method, repeating the test and asking the subject to give the same responses to each word, and added an inquiry to obtain further information regarding the meaning of relationship of responses to the stimulus word. The inquiry may be conducted immediately after the stimulus word or at the end of the test. The authors distinguish between formal and content aspects of the responses, as has been done on other tests such as the TAT and Rorschach. Content analysis tends to be an individual clinical tool not easily tested by statistical means. In considering the nature of the responses, the authors hypothesize that the responses are determined by memory ("dynamically" interpreted in psychoanalytic theory), concept-formation ("conventionally-conceptually related reaction words"), and anticipation (preparatory set). A variety of different methods of analyzing the responses are used. Associative disturbances are classified into two major categories: *close reactions* are disturbances in the analytic phase of association, where the subject is unable to free himself from the specific stimulus. Examples of close reactions are multiword definitions, clang associations, or repetitions in different form, like *fire* . . . fireman, and *doctor* . . . "doc." *Distant reactions,* on the other hand, appear unrelated to the stimulus word. The subject may unconsciously reject "the first word that comes to mind" but accept an association to the rejected word. Distant reactions were found to be usually related to "schizophrenic pathology." In addition to a list of 25 associative disturbances, diagnostic groups were compared in terms of frequency of popular responses. Popular responses were defined in terms of frequency of occurrence in the experimental groups studied.

The kinds of associative disturbances employed by Rapaport, Gill, and Schafer [*16*] are given below: [4]

(a) Blocking—offering no reaction word.

(b) Object-naming—naming objects in the examiner's office. This is usually an expression of blocking, but sometimes of evasiveness.

(c) Definitions—a *multi-word* definition of the stimulus-word.

(d) Attempted definitions—subjects inclined to offer definitions sometimes, in their haste, offer poor ones (*rug*—"to walk on").

(e) Repetitions—of the stimulus-word (breast—"breast").

(f) Partial repetitions—the stimulus-word is included in, or part of it constitutes, the reaction (*boy friend*—"boy"; *farm*—"farmer").

(g) Clang associations—only where no sense-relationship can be established. Thus *breast*—"chest" is not considered a clang association, while *man*—"tan" or *beef*—"weef" is so considered.

(h) Phrase completion—the reaction completes a word or phrase of which the stimulus-word is part, usually the first part. These may vary between two extremes: from *table*—"cloth" and *fire*—"place", to *taxi*—"dermist", *spring*—"is here", and *city*—"a large."

(i) Close reaction proper—no significant departure from the stimulus-word, and relevant only if the stimulus-word is kept in mind (*screen*—"through"; *women*—"other"; *breast*—"two").

(j) Attributes—an adjectival association modifying the noun stimulus-word, or naming a component of the object referred to by it (*woman*—"pretty", *table*—"wood").

(k) Images—the first and sometimes only reaction to the stimulus-word is a visual image, spontaneously reported by the subject or elicited by inquiry.

(l) Suspected images—the reaction-word, and sometimes a delay in reaction, suggest the presence of an image which is not confirmed by the subject.

(m) Self-references—such as *son*—"mine", *girl friend*—"I have none."

(n) Perseveration—(1) repeating the same reaction inappropriately on successive stimulus-words; (2) repeating the same reaction on most or all stimulus-words having some link between them (*father*—"person," *boy friend*—"person," *mother*—"person"); (3) reacting to one stimulus-word with a word appropriate to the previous stimulus-word (*beef*—"food," then *nipple*—"roast"); (4) reacting to one stimulus-word with a word appropriate to the previous reaction-word (*water*—"spring," then *suck*—"autumn").

(o) Multi-word reaction—excluding multi-word definitions, which are classified separately (*social*—"lots of friends").

---

[4] David Rapaport, Merton Gill, and Roy Schafer, *Diagnostic Psychological Testing: The Theory, Statistical Evaluation, and Diagnostic Application of a Battery of Tests.* Chicago: The Year Book Publishers, 1946. By permission.

(p) Unrelated reactions—no connection can be established between the stimulus- and reaction-words (*book*—"turkey").

(q) Distant reactions—related to the stimulus-word in a far-fetched manner (*masturbate*—"loss"; *dark*—"hour"; *party*—"funeral"; *depressed*—"sex"; *city*—"policeman"; *breast*—"frankness"; *man*—"creation"; *boy friend*—"strength").

(r) Mildly distant reactions—not far-fetched but outside the usual run of reactions (*trunk*—"lock"; *bowel movement*—"passage"; *rug*—"dirt"; *laugh*—"jaw"; *intercourse*—"breed").

(s) Neologisms—such as *suicide*—"wooicide", or *orgasm*—"reproduct".

(t) Affective reactions—value-judgments, usually adjectives (*mother*—"nice"; *bowel movement*—"disgusting").

(u) Alternatives—more than one reaction (*suck*—"baby or bottle").

(v) Proper nouns—*boy friend*—"John", or *city*—"Topeka".

(w) Vulgar reactions—ranging from more acceptable colloquial reactions (*homosexual*—"fairy") to socially altogether unacceptable ones (*intercourse*—"fuck".

(x) Mishearing the stimulus-word—hearing *bold* for *bowl*, or *gladiator* for *radiator*.

(y) Not knowing the stimulus-word—either spontaneously admitted by the patient, or established by inquiry into peculiar-appearing reactions. Some of these are standard, such as *orgasm*—"organs".

We have also distinguished the following types of *reproduction* disturbance:

(a) False unrelated recall—in any of the following forms: (1) great distance between the original reaction and the recall, such as *love*—"life", then "woman"; (2) a reversal of the sex implied in the original reaction —mostly on the familiar and inter-personal words such as *father, mother, women, man, son, daughter;* (3) a shift in the interpretation of ambiguous words such as *breast*—"shirt"—"woman"; *spring*—"flexible"—"water"; (4) a reversal of mood, such as *laugh*—"cry"—"smile"; (5) abandonment of a multi-word reaction, or a definition, or any other type of reaction which is highly singular; (6) abandonment of, or switch to, a vulgar word, such as *bowel movement*—"shit"—"toilet," or *penis*—"man"—"prick."

(b) False related recall (*chair*—"sit"—"table," *depressed*—"sorrowful"—"despondent").

(c) No recall.

(d) Delay in recall.

(e) Partial recall (*cut*—"healing"—"to heal").

(f) Spontaneously corrected false recall (*dog*—"cat"—"animal . . . No! cat").

In scoring associative reactions for the purpose of statistical treatment, we did not hesitate to give more than one qualitative score to a reaction. Thus *father*—"our father in heaven" was considered as a multi-word, repetitious, distant reaction. The significance of such reactions for disorganizations of thinking is such as to warrant highlighting the reaction with every score applicable to it.

This approach to word association analysis, which is both imaginative and fruitful, appears to contain many stimulating hypotheses regarding the nature of the association process in abnormal and normal behavior and some new methods of classifying association responses. Differences among a variety of diagnostic groupings were found through this method of analysis. Since, however, all the groups were small in number and the method of analysis was developed on the same subjects with which it was tested, the studies will have to be repeated before the results may be considered stable.

A test of some diagnostic measures was made by Tendler [*19*], employing the K-R list. He used four measures that preliminary experimental work had suggested might be useful for diagnostic purposes. These were: (1) The number of adjective-noun or noun-adjective responses. For example, *deep* . . . hole, *blank* . . . book, or *man* . . . great, *moon* . . . red; (2) The number of responses with over a three-second delay in reaction time; (3) The number of individual responses as calculated from the K-R Frequency Tables; (4) The number of failures to recall or repeat the same response in the reproduction experiment. Reliabilities of the four measures were determined by the odd-even, split-half method. He found these to be .88 for adjective-noun responses, .80 for delayed time responses, .95 for individual responses, and .80 for failure to recall responses. The measures of time delay and recall correlated moderately with intelligence as measured by the Stanford-Binet. Diagnostically, he found adjective-noun reactions to be characteristic of psychotics. Since the number of both of these types of responses is related to the number of contrast responses that are numerically most frequent, contrast responses had to be considered in determining the relationship between individual and adjective-noun responses. By partial correlation analysis with contrast responses held constant, Tendler found that individual responses and adjective-noun responses were negatively correlated, giving further support to the finding that they differentiate between patients classified as neurotic and those classified as psychotic.

These studies of differences in response in various psychiatric groups indicate definite utility of this test for diagnostic purposes. In evaluating the test in this function, however, it must be considered that like any diagnostic test, the method can be no more useful than the diagnostic scheme itself. Since it is difficult, if not impossible, to find two selections of subjects belonging to the same "disease entity" that are reasonably alike, any test is limited in its usefulness in this area.

THE DETECTION OF GUILT

On the theory that a person trying to hide knowledge of guilt or a person fearful of detection will show emotional disturbance, it is natural that the association test be used for detection of guilt. By making up lists of words pertinent only to someone aware of the circumstances of a crime, it should be relatively easy to differentiate guilty from innocent people by using all the usual indicators of emotional disturbance. For example, in a house burglary where entry and exit had been through a window, a dog had been pacified with raw meat, and a necklace had been stolen, a guilty suspect who denied all knowledge might show disturbance at the words *window, meat,* and *necklace,* while an innocent person would not. Although Leach and Washburn [*11*] had remarkable success in guilt detection with naive subjects, such evidence cannot be relied on too greatly. Marston's [*13*] study suggests individual differences in relation to guilt and reaction time. Symonds concluded that reaction time was the safest indicator for lie detection but that this was not too reliable with sophisticated subjects, and Wells [*22*] found that the effectiveness of the association test for determining affectivity decreased with practice.

The association test can be combined with other measures of affective disturbance to give a more reliable indication. With complex apparatus and sometimes additional persons recording, one can give the association test and at the same time observe other signs of disturbance. For example, observations of muscle tension can be made by the Luria technique [*12*], breathing can be recorded on a pneumograph, changes in electric skin potential can be measured with a psychogalvanometer, and changes in systolic blood pressure can be detected with a sphygmomanometer. Frequently these physiological measures are used together with direct questioning in police work, with the association method omitted.

Lie detection is a practical application of the association test. If used cautiously and in combination with other evidence, there is no doubt about its usefulness. Frequently, evidence from lie detection techniques is useful in providing leads that can then be investigated along other lines. A more detailed description of the utilization of the association method in guilt detection is given by Burtt [1].

APPLICATION TO THE STUDY OF INTERESTS AND ATTITUDES

In general, the utilization of association methods for studying interests and attitudes has been little explored. The groundwork for such use began with some of Jung's observations of differences between men and women in association responses. A present-day application of the test is made by Terman and Miles [20] in their test of masculinity-femininity. Utilizing the procedure of Wyman [26], who demonstrated differences of associations in groups representing the extremes of intellectual interests, social interests, and activity interests, Terman and Myles attempted to develop a test to differentiate masculine from feminine interests. They first presented by a visual group administration, 220 stimulus words to large groups of high school children of both sexes, then weighted responses in terms of the amount of sex difference shown. Some typical common responses for boys and girls are given below in Table 2.

TABLE 2 [5]

TYPICAL COMMON RESPONSES OF BOYS AND GIRLS

| | Responses Given More Often | |
Stimulus Word	*By Males*	*By Females*
Blue	spectrum	dress
Flesh	meat	pink
Closet	door	clothes
Garden	weeds	flower
Home	house	happy
Powder	bullet	rouge
Charm	snake	beauty
Arm	leg	limb
Fair	weather	blonde
Religion	God	church
War	soldiers	hate
Stout	strong	fat
Gentle	horse	mother
Hunt	shoot	find

Terman and Miles discarded the free association method for a multiple choice test, based on the association techniques, utilizing

---

5 Terman, Lewis, and Miles, Catherine, *Sex and Personality.* Copyright 1936 by McGraw-Hill Book Company, Inc. By permission of the publishers.

responses shown to have discriminated between the sexes. Each form of their test contains 60 such multiple choice reactions. Their data indicate that for the purpose of separating the sexes, the multiple choice test is as efficient as the free association method.

Their instructions require the subject to draw a line under the word that seems to go best or most naturally with the stimulus word. Examples of some items are given below. Each item contains two male choices and two female choices.

Muffler	car	silence	silk	warm
Decay	apple	corpse	rot	tooth
Needle	compass	eye	pine	sew
Thin	air	lady	paper	skin

In a recent study, Vicary [21] reported a use of the test for public opinion and market research. His study was a preliminary investigation of the value of the method for these purposes. Vicary asked 162 New York city respondents to write the first four associations to the word advertising. He found it possible to classify his response into the categories favorable, neutral, and unfavorable. Analysis of his results, he felt, would be helpful in getting at hidden and unconscious reactions to brand names, trademarks, company names, slogans, and so on. Perhaps the same method might be applied to social attitudes as an indirect measure when taboos or other conditions resulting in unwillingness to be frank produce unreliable answers to direct questions.

Although little has been published about it, application of the fact that individuals with different interests will respond differently on the word association test can be used to study diagnoses. Utilizing ambiguous words, one meaning of which is likely to be known to only a limited number of individuals, it seems possible to discover something about the background of subjects. This is a function of the special argots that may be known only to individuals within a narrow group. For example the words smoke, hop, and needle would produce different associations and behavior from a drug addict, or someone with a long association with drug addicts, than from other individuals. Similar special argots exist for practicing homosexuals and habitual criminals. Word lists containing such words could be used both in lie detection work and in psychiatric hospital diagnosis. Experimental studies evaluating this method for the above purposes, or perhaps as a measure of change in attitudes, are greatly needed.

SUMMARY

The word association method has been less frequently used in recent years with the advent and popularization of many new projective techniques. For general clinical use, the method is limited in that: (1) It gives insufficient material for a description of the personality as a meaningful whole, while still requiring uneconomical individual administration; (2) It creates a rather tense testing situation that may not be conducive to establishment of good rapport; and (3) It frequently provides indication of the presence of emotional disturbance without indicating the precise nature of that disturbance. However, the test can be of considerable value, particularly when the subject is not readily willing or able to discuss his problem, and for the detection of guilt. As an experimental measure of personality changes in which objective measures are desired, or for use as an indirect measure of interests and attitudes, the method has not been fully explored. Further research in these applications may well prove fruitful.

REFERENCES

1. Burtt, Harold F., *Applied Psychology.* New York: Prentice-Hall, Inc., 1948, Chapter 13.
2. Galton, F., "Psychometric experiments." *Brain,* 1879, 2, 149–162.
3. Hull, C. L., and Lugoff, L. S., "Complex signs in diagnostic free association." *J. Exper. Psychol.,* 1921, 4, 111–136.
4. Huston, P. E., Shakow, D., and Erickson, M. H., "A study of hypnotically induced complexes by means of the Luria technique." *J. Gen. Psychol.,* 1934, 11, 65–97.
5. Jung, C. G., "Diagnostiche Assoziationsstudien." *J. f. Psychol. u. Neur.,* 1906, 8. 25–60; 1907, 9. 188–197.
6. ———————, *Studies in Word Association.* New York: Dodd, Mead and Company, 1918.
7. Kent, G. H., and Rosanoff, A., "A study of association in insanity." *Amer. J. Insanity,* 1910, 67, 37–96, 317–390.
8. ———————, *Free Association Test. 2 forms.* Chicago: C. H. Stoelting.
9. Kohs, C. H., "The association method in its relation to the complex and complex indicators." *Amer. J. Psychol.,* 1914, 25, 544–594.

10. Kraepelin, E., *Ueber die Beinflussung einfacher psychischer Vorgange durch Arzneimittel; experimentelle Untersuchungen.* Jena: Gustav Fischer Verlag, 1892.

11. Leach, H. M., and Washburn, M. T., "Some tests by the association reaction method of mental diagnosis." *Amer. J. Psychol.,* 1910, 21, 162–167.

12. Luria, A. R., *The Nature of Human Conflicts, or Emotions, Conflict, and Will. An Objective Study of Disorganization and Control of Human Behavior.* New York: The Liveright Publishing Corporation, 1932.

13. Marston, W. M., "Reaction time symptoms of deception." *J. Exper. Psychol.,* 1920, 3, 72–87.

14. Münsterberg, H., "The third degree." *McClures Magazine,* 1907, 29, 614–622.

15. Rapaport, D., *Emotions and Memory.* Baltimore: Williams and Wilkins, 1942.

16. Rapaport, D., Gill, M., and Schafer, R., *Diagnostic Psychological Testing: The Theory, Statistical Evaluation, and Diagnostic Application of a Battery of Tests.* Chicago: Year Book Publishers, 1946.

17. Rosanoff, A. J., *Manual of Psychiatry and Mental Hygiene* (Seventh Edition). New York: John Wiley & Sons, Inc., 1938, Chapter 38.

18. Symonds, P. M., *Diagnosing Personality and Conduct.* New York: Appleton-Century-Crofts, Inc., 1931, Chapter 10.

19. Tendler, A. D., "Significant features of disturbance in free association." *J. Psychol.,* 1945, 20, 65–89.

20. Terman, Lewis, and Miles, Catherine, *Sex and Personality.* New York: McGraw-Hill Book Company, Inc., 1936.

21. Vicary, J. M., "Word association and opinion research: 'advertising' —an illustrative example." *Public Opinion Quarterly,* 1948, 12, 81–98.

22. Wells, F. L., "Practice effects in free association." *Amer. J. Psychol.,* 1911, 22, 1–13.

23. ————————, *Mental Tests in Clinical Practice.* Yonkers, N. Y.: World Book Company, 1927, page 211.

24. Woodrow, H., and Lowell, F., "Children's association frequency table." *Psychol. Monogr.,* 1916, 22, No. 5, 110.

25. Wundt, W., *Grundzuge der Physiologischen Psychologie.* Leipzig: Engelman, 1911, Vol. 3, pages 436–456, 519–543.

26. Wyman, J. B., "Tests of intellectual, social, and activity interests," in Lewis Terman (ed.), *Genetic Studies of Genius.* Stanford, Calif.: Stanford University Press, 1926, Chapter 16.

II. THE SENTENCE COMPLETION METHOD

In the sentence completion method, the subject is asked to finish a sentence of which the first word or words are given by the examiner. In some ways, this method is related to the word association technique, the major difference being in the length of the stimulus; some applications of the method, however, demand only a single word or brief response. As in the word association method, tendencies to block or to twist the meaning of the stimulus word may appear, and responses are categorized in a somewhat similar fashion. However, even in the tests where quickness of response is encouraged, there is no attempt to measure speed of reaction and no real pressure for *immediate* association. The response tends to provide information that the subject is willing to give, not that which he cannot help giving, and analysis is usually more similar to that used with the Thematic Apperception Test than to the word association method. As in other projective devices, it is assumed that the subject reflects his own wishes, desires, fears, and attitudes in the sentences he composes, but this method differs in that the subject's production does not depend so much upon his interpretation of the standard stimulus as upon what he is able and willing to write under the test conditions.

In contrast to the usual objective tests, the method has the distinct advantage of providing freedom of response instead of forcing the subject to answer Yes, No, or "?"; he can respond to the stimulus as he wants. In addition, the nature of the test is somewhat disguised and it is less clear to the subject what constitutes "good" or "bad" answers, even though the intent of the test may be known or easily guessed. It is as easily administered in group form as the objective tests but does not have the potential advantage of machine scoring or of scoring by nonprofessional personnel.

The technique has, when compared with other projective methods, certain assets and liabilities. In addition to the fact that it is readily administered in group form, there is no necessary special training for the person administering it nor is particularized training requisite for its clinical interpretation, which rests instead on the examiner's general experience. Though many of the published articles on the method do not report attempts at objective scoring, it has been found that the technique lends itself readily to such efforts with results that are most useful in experimental or screening situations. The quickness with which it can be administered, scored, and analyzed, has also proven to be of special use.   On the other hand, the purpose of the test is less disguised than in other projective techniques, and the sophisticated subject may tell the examiner only what he wants him to know.   Also, illiterate, disturbed, or uncooperative subjects may produce insufficient material.   And the group test requires writing skill, nor has it been evaluated for potential clinical usefulness below the adolescent ages.

Two types of instructions are generally given with the sentence completion tests.   One stresses speed—the subject is urged to complete the sentences as quickly as possible with the first thought that comes to mind; the other set informs the subject that he should complete the sentence to express his own personal feelings.   Any given test may combine these aspects or emphasize one rather than another of the instructions.

Sentence beginnings vary.   Included are third-person references such as *he, she,* or the use of common names such as *Mary, James;* a personal pronoun is frequently used in relation to verbs: *I like, I suffer, I wish;* neutral stimuli in which no pronouns are used are also presented.   The sentence beginnings may be highly structured, such as "The most fun we had last summer . . ."; or highly unstructured, as in the sentence beginning "Sometimes . . .".

In a recent study, Sacks [13] constructed two forms of a sentence completion test in order to compare the value of items stated in the first person with similar items stated in the third person.   Six of the seven psychologists participating in the rating found the form of the test employing the first person to be superior.   Interpretations from this form of the test were also found to be significantly more predictive of the criterion (psychologist's rating) than the form of the test employing proper names and third-person pronouns.   Sacks felt that the use of proper names tended to arouse associations with specific people.

When used for clinical purposes, the sentence completion method is very similar to the Thematic Apperception Test.   That is, it tends to give information of personality content rather than personality structure [3].   It deals with feelings, attitudes, specific reactions to people and things, rather than providing a so-called underlying personality structure. However, analysis in terms of structure is possible from any kind of content material.

TEST FLEXIBILITY

It might be desirable for usual clinical purposes to have only a few regular, well-standardized tests, but a word should be said here about the flexibility of this particular method of studying personality. This flexibility gives it utility in studying a variety of problems clinically, experimentally, or for specific practical or screening purposes. Sentence beginnings can be tailored to fit any particular situation, using language familiar to any group of individuals. So, for example, test items might be concerned with attitudes toward the Army or toward sex; a test could be constructed for foremen in a given plant to determine their attitudes toward their fellows and the workers under them. In the OSS Assessment Program, when it became desirable to apply assessment techniques to Chinese officers, the sentence completion test was one of the most easily transferable to the new language and culture situation. A further description of some possibilities of this method will be presented later.

CLINICAL AND EXPERIMENTAL EVALUATIONS
OF THE SENTENCE COMPLETION METHOD

Many sources contribute to the origins of the sentence completion method, a number of authors looking upon their developments of it as extensions of the word association method. As a measure of language ability, the technique has a long history in psychology. Direct study of personality characteristics with this method probably began with Payne [8], who developed a test used in vocational guidance procedure, but no general publication in the psychological literature described or evaluated his method. Tendler [18], in the first published report on the subject in 1930, called it "A Test for Emotional Insight." He used 20 items, for example, *I feel happy when* . . . , and *I tell lies* . . . All of his sentences begin with the word "I" except the very first one. Tendler in many ways anticipated some of the more recent developments in projective techniques; he wanted a test that would determine "trends, fixed attitudes, attachments to persons, conflicting desires, satisfactions, and annoyances . . . ." His criteria for such a test were that it should directly evoke emotional response, allow freedom of response, and not provoke discrimination or choice. He rejected personality inventories and the free association technique on these grounds, but felt that the sentence completion method corresponded more closely to the criteria. In addition, he found the test to be of considerable clinical value and felt that informal comparison of the sentence completion with autobiographical sketches was a promising method of validation. His quantitative study indicated significant differences between subjects grouped according to their adjustment on the Woodworth Personal Data Blank.

Wheeler utilized a variation of the method, described in *Explorations in Personality* [20], referring to his form as a *similes test*. Subjects were asked to provide similes of an original nature for a series of adjectives, such as, *"As pathetic as . . . , As dangerous as . . . , As delightful as . . . .* Responses were analyzed in terms of thematic content, following the principles of H. A. Murray's theory of personality. Though the test differs from other sentence completion methods, it contains many similar characteristics.

In 1938, Cameron [1, 2] published some studies of sentence completions of 29 normal children, 20 normal adults, 22 deteriorated seniles, and 25 disorganized schizophrenics. He was primarily interested in the nature of language and the thinking process in abnormal patients and in contrasting these processes with normal subjects. He used 15 sentence beginnings such as, *I am in the hospital because . . . , A man fell down in the road because . . . ,* and analyzed the completions for logicalness, integration, distortion, and fixed thinking. Administration of the test was oral, as were the subjects' responses. The thinking of the schizophrenic patients, as well as their idiosyncratic type of associations, differed from that of seniles, normal adults, or the group of children who ranged from 7 years, 2 months to 11 years, 5 months in age. Cameron analyzed these data qualitatively but did not present quantitative results.

Lorge and Thorndike [7], in 1941, published the results of a study on a group each of whom answered 240 items. The subjects were asked to finish the sentences as quickly as possible, and most of their productions tended to be short one-word completions. The authors' items are of several kinds—the majority relatively impersonal in nature. Examples are *Women want . . . , Etchings are . . . , George wanted to know . . . . On the main street she met a* . . . . Results were interpreted in terms of a long list of traits and interests, the responses of the individuals being rated on some 70 variables. They found low reliabilities by the split-half method and felt in general that the test was not productive for studying individual differences in personality. Their method, however, was closer to the word association technique without benefit of reaction time measurements, and did not yield the personal attitudes of the subject regarding his problems.

Sanford [4], in 1943, described a 30-item incomplete sentences test somewhat more structured than others used for clinical purposes. The Sanford test illustrates the adaptability of the method for a variety of purposes—in this case, specifically for obtaining measures for a need-press analysis according to the Murray need-press system of personality description. Sanford had three types of items. The first were a series stating a press, such as, *Seeing that he was ignored* . . . (*P* rejection). The objective was to determine what reaction the subject made to such a press. The second group of items stated an action pattern of some need; for example, *she almost choked with rage when* . . . (*N* aggression). In this case the objective was to see what press the subject would associate with this particular need action pattern. The third group of items consisted of ambiguous statements for which the subject would supply the need. For example, *Jean's purpose in going there was to* . . . . Sanford gave the test to students from grades 3 to 8. He had only a very small number of subjects from the various grades, and did not make a quantitative analysis of his results.

In 1946, Rohde [9] published a study using the sentence completion method with high school children. Rohde and Hildreth had revised Payne's original test and published a 64-item test in 1941. The 1946 article was a description of the research that had been carried on for some time. Rohde's items were short and generally fairly unstructured. Typical items are: *My school work* . . . , *I want to know* . . . , *There are times* . . . , *My greatest longing* . . . , *My father* . . . , *I become embarrassed* . . . .

The instructions were general and required the subject only to complete the sentences: "Any response is entirely acceptable." Rohde analyzed the responses in terms of the Murray schema using needs, press, inner states, and cathex objects. The validation study was done on 50 cases selected randomly from a large number of cases. The test items were scored in terms of the need, press, or inner states indicated, and over-all ratings were made for each of 33 variables on a scale of 1 to 10. The rating was based on the judgment of the experimenter. As a criterion teachers and counselors were interviewed regarding the personality of the 50 subjects, and these judgments were likewise translated into quantitative terms on a scale or 1 to 10, presumably by the author. It is not clear in the report whether or not the potential bias in determining the criterion was eliminated, since the experimenter's judgment entered into both the scoring of the test blanks and the criterion rating. Rohde obtained very high validity coefficients for a projective test of this type. The Pearson product correlations for all variables combined were .79 for girls and .82 for boys. The range of correlations was from .95 to .30. Reliability coefficients obtained from test-retests based on 21 girls and 23 boys were .82 for girls and .76 for boys. It is not clear, however, whether the reliability coefficients referred to the individual scorings of the items or to over-all ratings on the variables used. Rohde also attempted to obtain an interscorer reliability by having four judges rate the same 12 papers. She apparently had 78 per cent agreement on the scoring for the individual items. That is, delineating what needs, press, or inner state are present in any given item response. Her final judgment or over-all rating, however, was dependent also upon frequency and intensity. The interscorer reliability presumably does not extend to these over-all judgments. In both her clinical evaluations and her quantitative results, Rohde has indicated that the test can be quite valuable for personality analysis at the high school level.

Use of the sentence completion method was greatly accelerated during the war; Hutt [5], Holzberg [4], and Shor [15] describe its use in Army general hospitals. Shor considered his test an adaptation of the word association method, while Holzberg used items from Tendler's original test as well as from Shor's. Shor worked extensively with this technique, describing it as the "self idea completion test." Instructions were specifically stated to encourage freedom and spontaneity of response. They were: "Complete these sentences to express your real feelings. Write down the first idea that comes to your mind. Each person will give different answers." He had 50 items in his test, such as: *I want to know . . . , I feel . . . , I hate . . . , The future . . . , My nerves . . . , My most important decision was . . . .*

Some of the gross variables he used for clinical interpretation were: (1) areas of rejection, indicated when there was a refusal to respond or a sentence was left blank; (2) areas of resistance, where there was blocking or evasion by responding with some conventional or impersonal association; and (3) other methods of evasion. In general, free clinical interpretation in relation to the examiner's psychological training was advocated, and no quantitative evaluation of the test was presented.

Rotter and Willerman [12], working originally with the tests used by Hutt, Shor, and Holzberg, re-evaluated items on a clinical basis with the purpose of avoiding those that elicit stereotypes and cut down the range of individual response. They were also interested in eliminating duplications, since they wanted as economical a test for group screening purposes as they could get. A final test of 40 items was developed, including many changes to make the test as little structured as possible. These included such unstructured items as *I . . . , Sometimes . . . , Back . . . ,* and *Boys . . . .* They also changed their instructions, feeling on the basis of their earlier experience with the tests that instructions that call for the subject to respond as quickly as possible tend to produce associations rather than content statements regarding the individual's personal feelings and attitudes. Their instructions read, "Complete these sentences to express your real feelings. Try to do every one. Be sure to make a complete sentence."

Since Rotter and Willerman were interested in a screening test, they attempted to develop a method that could be used by relatively untrained scorers and provide high interscorer reliability. They devised individual scoring standards for each item, using the scoring by example method, and set up for each item seven categories of response that could be placed on a single numerical scale. All responses were grouped into three categories: (1) conflict or unhealthy responses; (2) positive or healthy responses; and (3) neutral responses. An earlier method of scoring included separate consideration of "avoidance reactions," which were defined as responses in which the subject failed to relate the stimulus to himself as instructed, but made a neutral reply. Examples of such responses are: *Back . . . is the opposite of forward,* and *What pains me . . . is this test.* An original hypothesis that such behavior, along with humorous and flippant remarks, might be correlated with maladjustment was quickly dispelled. In fact, such answers appeared with greatest frequency in the best adjusted subjects. It was also thought that the omissions indicated great conflict, but again, higher frequency of omissions in the more maladjusted subjects was not found. It would appear that many of the best adjusted subjects were saying, in effect, that their private feelings were "none of your business."

Conflict, neutral, and positive reactions were located on a single dimension so that each test response could be given a numerical score of $+3$ to $+1$ for conflict responses, 0 for neutral responses, -1 to -3 for positive responses.

A scoring booklet with examples of typical responses for the numerical scoring of each item was developed. Two types of criteria were used in selecting examples for weighting responses to the different categories. The first type of criterion material was obtained from the responses of 45 patients whose behavior was easily classified. Fifteen of these patients were serious psychiatric cases with evidence of premilitary maladjustment, 15 patients gave no evidence of premilitary maladjustment, and their current psychological disturbances followed severe combat experience, and 15 patients were considered to have no serious psychological problems. Most of the latter had been hospitalized for orthopedic difficulties. The second type of criterion for classifying responses was based on general principles of adjustment and on the experience of the authors. An illustration of scoring examples for one item is given below.

Item 19. Other people . . .

C_3. laugh at me; are no good
C_2. talk too much; should mind their own business; annoy me; irritate me; I envy; get on my nerves; just have worries; are happier
C_1. have their worries too; are in the same boat
N. are different; some good and some bad
P_1. are entitled to their own opinions; get along with me; usually like me; amuse me
P_2. are OK; are friendly; are interesting
P_3. are swell.

To investigate the validity of the scores, Rotter and Willerman divided the 200 patients studied into three groups: (1) those considered psychologically fit for immediate return to duty; (2) those considered psychologically unfit for immediate return to duty, but who should benefit from convalescent care; and (3) those patients considered too disturbed for further service in the Army and those so seriously disturbed as to warrant recommendation for immediate psychiatric attention. The judgment for placing cases was based upon case-history information, analysis of health and personality inventories, admission diagnosis, a test of mental disfunctioning, and a psychological interview. The classification of cases into the groups was done by one of the authors, who did not enter into the scoring of the records so that no bias was present. Data used to establish scoring standards were not included in the criteria or cross-validation groups. Reliability of the test was obtained by an equivalent-halves method and yielded a correlation of .85 (corrected by the Spearman Brown-Prophecy Formula). Interscorer reliability, which the authors considered more important, was obtained by having seven judges score the same 50 records and correlating final or total scores. The average interscorer reliability coefficient was .89; validity of the test using a triserial r was .61.

An opportunity was present in this study to compare over-all clinical evaluations, as made by two experienced clinical psychologists in a second convalescent hospital, with the validity and reliability obtained from the objective scoring method. One hundred forty-eight cases were rated on a scale of *no, mild, moderate,* and *severe* disturbance. A biserial correlation of .41 for one rater and .39 for a second rater was found with the criterion of psychiatric or nonpsychiatric admitting diagnosis. The interscorer reliability of the two raters was .68. Although the criterion of the admitting diagnosis was probably weaker than the validity criterion used for evaluation of the objective scoring, the lower interscorer reliability suggested that validity would be lower than that of the objective scoring even if the same criterion had been used.

Rotter, Rafferty, and Schachtitz [10], applying the same general method as Rotter and Willerman, adapted the Army test for college students and developed objective scoring manuals [11] for a measure of maladjustment, or more specifically, for a measure of the degree to which the individual was in need of personal therapy or counseling. Separate scoring manuals were developed for male and for female college students. An example of the differences in response of the two groups is given for one item below.

Item 35.   My father . . .
Males

    C_3. promises many things and never keeps them; is the male responsible for my existence; wasn't very good; was a fool; and I have many arguments; is an alcoholic.

C_2. and I never were buddies; is in pretty bad shape; is hard to understand; is stern.

C_1. is in bad health; is good to me, but we have little spiritual communion; cannot supply me with everything; never had much of a chance; lived in——; is proud; is sensitive.

N. is home; is a salesman; is dead; had all his teeth pulled; is a hard worker; is living.

P_1. is good to me; is very intelligent, though not highly educated; is an idol to me; is an excellent mechanic; is a good hard-working man; is the kindest, most honest man I have ever known.

P_2. is extremely caustic and reactionary, but I love him; is OK; is all right; is a good man.

P_3. is the greatest dad in the world; is a swell guy; is a good joe; is a good companion.

Females

C_3. hasn't been home since I was 12 years old; still frightens me; is a stranger to me; is alcoholic.

C_2. isn't going to change and I wish he would; is not ambitious enough; is pretty strict; and I were never too close; has always made us work very hard at home; is (was) so good to me; antagonizes me; is angry with me; isn't sociable at home; is dead but I think of him a lot.

C_1. is really a good person but does not know how to warm up to people; seems more understanding than my mother; I wonder if I'll ever meet anyone as grand; worries about me too much; is a very quiet man; is the best man I know; is dead (with no feeling expressed about father's death).

N. is a successful businessman; is a——(occupation); raised a large family; is hard-working; is in——(place).

P_1. is quite a character; cultivated my interests in sports; (activity with father, such as, and I discuss current events daily); is OK; is all right; has my respect and admiration; is a good man; is wonderful.

P_2. is a very handsome and intelligent metallurgist; has a complete head of hair—hurrah! is very nice.

P_3. has a wonderful sense of humor; is very congenial; is a lot of fun; is a good guy.

As in the previous study, the authors found that the number of avoidance types of responses and omissions, as such, are not diagnostic of maladjustment. A similar validation study made with 82 females and 124 males resulted in a biserial validity coefficient of .64 for females and .77 for males. The higher validity coefficient for male subjects was believed to be a function of somewhat better criteria for male subjects. Interscorer reliability for two experienced scorers was .96; split-half reliability for the female manual was .83, and for the male manual, .84. It was considered that split-half reliabilities were not strictly applicable to this type of test because of the nonequivalence of items. A conception of how the manual was used for scoring can be obtained from some of the general principles for scoring, given below.

1. The scoring manual is to serve as a guide to be followed *as closely as possible*. It is not to be expected that all responses will be found in the scoring manual, but typical responses for each of the different numerical weights are given.
2. Each response is to be scored and evaluated independently of all others, except where there is a clear-cut reference to the previous statement.
3. Responses that start similarly to an example in the manual but are differently qualified are scored with a consideration of these qualifications.
4. Unusually long responses should be scored one point closer the conflict end of the scale than their essential meaning would place them.
5. Examples are not given for extreme weights (-3 or $+3$) in some items, usually because extreme responses to those items are rare. These weights may be assigned, however, if clearly warranted.
6. Where precedent for scoring a given response cannot be found in the examples for that item, scoring for a similar response to another item may be used.
7. Humor, clear-cut and good-natured, is generally scored as P_2 or P_3.

A 100-item incomplete sentences test usually given in two parts is described in the literature from three sources. The test was used in the OSS Assessment Program and is described in "Assessment of Men" [*19*], by the staff of that program. Separate reports evaluating the test have also been made by Stein [*16*] and by Symonds [*17*]. In developing the test, an attempt was made to include phrases whose completions would shed light on at least 12 areas of personality. These were the areas of: (1) family; (2) the past; (3) drives; (4) inner states; (5) goals; (6) cathexes; (7) energy; (8) reaction to frustration and failures; (9) time perspective; (10) optimism-pessimism; (11) reaction to others; and (12) reaction of others. The items were revised in order to obtain ones that had a low index of stereotyping or a high index of uniqueness. Sentence beginnings were of two types: those including the word "I," and those in which a third person was referred to. Stein [*16*], in his report, accumulated usual or frequent responses for the items based on 40 male subjects. Some of these items and their usual responses are given below.

SENTENCE COMPLETION TEST WITH USUAL RESPONSES

4. *Nothing annoyed Bob more than* . . . mosquitoes, profanity, noise, teasing, terrible dreams.

13. *Joe was uneasy because* . . . he was worried, he feared discovery, he was late for an appointment, he hadn't slept well, he was alone.

20. *I try hard* . . . always, but fail, not to worry about things, to succeed, to please.

28. *I usually feel awkward when* . . . in the presence of ladies, I feel that I am being watched, I speak in public, I am badly dressed, people are arrogant.

40. *What they liked about him most was* . . . his manner, his frankness, his courtesy and consideration, his ability to cope with any situation, his personality.

56. *Bill is afraid of* . . . horses and dogs, falling, the news from home, taking a chance, himself.

69. *I often* . . . dream about the war, repeat myself, pray, sit and think, daydream.

Stein gives the following seven aids to clinical evaluation of the test:

(a) The clinician's knowledge of the dynamics of behavior and personality, which is utilized to infer the crucial factors in the personality structure of the subject under observation. For example, in the case of the individual who completes item No. 99, "When he thought that the odds were against him, Bill . . ." with "fought harder," this completion suggests that we are dealing with an individual who has a high energy level, a strong need for achievement and who does not yield easily in the face of obstacles.

(b) The frequency with which a response has been made by other individuals. The rare responses are more critical than the usual ones. Since formal norms have not yet been established, the clinician should develop his own on the basis of experience.

(c) A subject's reaction time to the individual sentences and to the test as a whole. Most subjects complete each part in approximately ten minutes. The records of those who take less time are usually sterile insofar as a complete analysis is concerned, as they respond with only single words.

(d) The length of the completions. Lengthy responses are frequently found in records of individuals who wish to mask their true feelings or who have a strong desire to indicate to the examiner the precise nature of their reactions.

(e) Behavioral manifestations during the course of the test. The tensions and anxieties of some subjects increase during the course of the test. It is as if they were aware of the fact that they were revealing themselves, but lacked sufficient psychological insight to realize that their emotions were being stimulated by the test items or their answers to these items.

It is valuable to observe which items stimulate a subject's anxieties and his techniques of reacting to tension, i.e., tics, increased restlessness, refusal to continue with the test, etc.

(f) Erasures and omissions.   Erasures and omissions frequently appear where individuals feel that their responses have been too revealing or when an item has touched upon a critical area.   When erasures and omissions are present it is valuable to question the subject, after he has turned in his paper, as to what it was that he erased or the reason for the omission. At times such questioning may reveal significant material and at times it may show that the subject wanted to correct an error in spelling or did not understand a word in one of the sentences.

(g) The intensity of the language used in the response.   Strong and colorful words are frequently employed by individuals who are very definite about certain reaction patterns or who attempt to bend over backwards to fool the examiner.

Symonds [*17*], in evaluating the tests against OSS records, did not find that a psychometric approach distinguished adjusted from maladjusted subjects.   He felt that the test was descriptive but not evaluative; however, no carefully worked-out psychometric scoring method was described in his report.   In the test, the basic hypothesis for including a large number of third-person items apparently was that the subject in such items may more readily project unconscious trends or those that he is unwilling to ascribe to himself.   Although this assumption may be correct for some items, it may not be correct for all, and the problem remains of determining which of these responses refers to some important or central characteristic of the individual.

Application to Assessment of Therapeutic Improvement.   Morton [1] has used the Rotter Incomplete Sentences Blank, College Form [*10*], to measure improvement in therapy.   In one of the few studies of treatment efficacy in which a matched control group was used, Morton found significant gains in the direction of better adjustment on the incomplete sentences test in his treated group of 19 cases as compared to the control group.   Three criteria for improvement were employed three months after the cessation of brief psychotherapy.   These included the Mooney Check List, ratings of three experienced judges from recorded interviews, and the Incomplete Sentences Blank.   The incomplete sentences correlated .53

---

[1] Morton, Robert, "A controlled experiment in psychotherapy based on Rotter's Social Learning Theory of personality," (Ph.D. dissertation).   Columbus, Ohio: The Ohio State University Library, 1949.

with the ratings and .40 with the Mooney Check List. The biserial correlation between incomplete sentences and treated or untreated groups was .50. Since the tests were scored blindly by someone other than the investigator, these results suggest a profitable employment of the incomplete sentences method for appraisal of degree of maladjustment and efficacy of treatment.

APPLICATION TO THE STUDY OF SOCIAL ATTITUDES

On an a priori basis, the incomplete sentence method seems well suited to the study of social attitudes. It seems to combine desirable features of projective testing and the open-ended question advocated by Lazarsfeld [6]. Up to now no published report of the technique as applied to the study of social attitudes has been made, but Brown [2] has a study in progress that appears to be yielding promising results. Using the same instructions as those of Rotter and Willerman, she has developed a 40-item test for the study of attitudes towards Negroes. The test combines personal statements that are not obviously related to attitudes toward Negroes with sentence beginnings that are clearly related to such attitudes. Some items are neither personal nor obviously related to Negroes, and the subject may or may not express his attitudes in these completions. Sentences directly associated with Negroes are separated by the personal or neutral items. The first 20 items of this test are given below.

1. I feel ....
2. Skin color ....
3. I hate ....
4. Maybe ....
5. Some lynchings ....
6. The future ....
7. The K.K.K. ....
8. I ....
9. Georgia ....
10. Sometimes I wish ....

11. It seems to me that segregation .
12. Sometimes ....
13. The poll tax ....
14. If only ....
15. Negro body odor ....
16. Some people ....
17. Slums ....
18. Some of my friends ....
19. Harlem ....
20. Sometimes I worry ....

In the prospectus for this study, Brown states

In comparison with many projective techniques, the incomplete sentence test appeared to have possible advantages in ease and reliability in administration and scoring. As set up it would also present the advantages

---

[2] A Ph.D. dissertation in process at The Ohio State University under the direction of the author.

of not only a "Pro-con" type of measurement which appears the sole function of most attitude tests, but also the measurement of other dimensions. One of these has been tentatively labeled an "Emotional involvement" scale which would indicate the amount of concern, stress, and feeling which the individual demonstrates in his attitudes. Another scale, which has been termed "Self-consistency," will be concerned with the variability of the attitude expressed by the individual. The need or interest expressed of "action taking," or "doing something about it" would be the subject of inquiry for another scale and the amount of "optimism or pessimism" concerning the Negro situation may be another measure obtainable on the test. These scales are hypothesized subjects of inquiry.

Scoring for the various scales is done from scoring examples.

SUMMARY

While yielding less information, perhaps, than some of the more widely used projective tests, such as the Rorschach and TAT, the incomplete sentences method has demonstrated clinical value in a variety of different situations. It seems well adapted to an analysis of problem areas and useful for giving the clinician a set or orientation toward a subject so that he may structure his first interview in advance. A reasonable degree of objectivity in scoring has been obtained and it has served in some instances as an adequate screening device. One investigator feels that the test is most useful for determining unconscious trends. For the most part, however, its value for diagnostic purposes or for analysis of basic personality structure is less emphasized than its usefulness in providing information regarding the content of the subject's thought and feelings.

Two major types of instructions seem to produce different types of results: one of these types emphasizes frankness and freedom to respond in any way, and the other, speed of response. Different types of results also appear when the sentence beginnings are structured so that they are easily referred to the subject himself, as contrasted to the third person. The purpose of the speedy response and third person sentence beginning, apparently, is to get at material that the subject himself is not aware of or does not wish to express in the testing situation. However, these kinds of sentences and instructions may also produce more stereotypes and shorter responses, bordering on word associations, or responses that may not refer to the more important aspects of the subject's problems and attitudes.

The method is quite flexible, since sentence beginnings can be altered to suit a variety of purposes. In addition to its clinical uses, it has been used as an experimental method in studies of personality—specifically, for the study of the thinking process in certain abnormal types. It has been applied to the study of social attitudes and used as a measure of improvement in therapy. It seems a feasible method for investigation of a variety of situations in industry, for the study of group attitudes and opinions, and for special experimental problems in the field of personality. The fact that it can be administered to a group and still retain many of the individualistic advantages of the projective tests, suggests that it can be profitably employed in many areas as yet untapped.

REFERENCES

1. Cameron, N., "Reasoning, regression, and communication in schizophrenia." *Psychol. Monogr.*, 1938, 50, 1–34.

2. ————————, "A study of thinking in senile deterioration and schizophrenic disorganization." *Amer. J. Psychol.*, 1938, 51, 650–664.

3. Harrison, R., "The Thematic Apperception and Rorschach method of personality investigation in clinical practice." *J. Psychol.*, 1943, 15, 49–74.

4. Holzberg, J., Teicher, A., and Taylor, J. L., "Contributions of clinical psychology to military neuro-psychiatry in an army psychiatric hospital." *J. Clin. Psychol.*, 1947, 3, 84–95.

5. Hutt, M. L., "The use of projective methods of personality measurement in army medical installations." *J. Clin. Psychol.*, 1945, 1, 134–140.

6. Lazarsfeld, P. F., "The controversy over detailed interviews—an offer for negotiation." *Pub. Op. Quart.*, 1944, 38–61.

7. Lorge, I., and Thorndike, E. L., "The value of the responses in a completion test as indications of personal traits." *J. Appl. Psychol.*, 1941, 25, 191–199.

8. Payne, A. F., *Sentence Completions.* New York: New York Guidance Clinic, 1928.

9. Rohde, A. R., "Explorations in personality by the sentence completion method." *J. Appl. Psychol.*, 1946, 30, 169–181.

10. Rotter, J. B., Rafferty, J. E., and Schachtitz, E., "Validation of the Rotter Incomplete Sentences Blank for college screening." *J. Consult. Psychol.*, 1949, 13, 348–356.

11. Rotter, J. B., and Rafferty, J. E., *Manual for the Rotter Incomplete Sentences Blank, College Form.* New York: The Psychological Corporation, 1950.

12. Rotter, J. B., and Willerman, B., "The Incomplete Sentences Test as a method of studying personality." *J. Consult. Psychol.*, 1947, 11, 43–48.

13. Sacks, J. M., "Effect upon projective responses of stimuli referring to the subject and to others." *J. Consult. Psychol.*, 1949, 13, 12–21.

14. Sanford, R. N., and others, "Physique, personality and scholarship." *Monogr. Soc. Res. Child Devel.*, 1943, 8, no. 1.

15. Shor, J., "Report on a verbal projective technique." *J. Clin. Psychol.*, 1946, 2, 279–282.

16. Stein, M. I., "The use of a Sentence Completion Test for the diagnosis of personality." *J. Clin. Psychol.*, 1947, 3, 46–56.

17. Symonds, P. M., "The Sentence Completion Test as a projective technique." *J. Abnorm. & Soc. Psychol.*, 1947, 42, 320–329.

18. Tendler, A. D., "A preliminary report on a test for emotional insight." *J. Appl. Psychol.*, 1930, 14, 123–136.

19. U. S. Office of Strategic Services, Staff, *Assessment of Men*. New York: Rinehart and Company, 1948, pages 71–75.

20. Wheeler, D. R., "Imaginal Productivity Tests," in H. A. Murray, *Explorations in Personality*. New York: Oxford University Press, Inc., 1938, pages 545–550; 680–684.

CHAPTER 10

The Rosenzweig
Picture-Frustration Study [1]

HELEN JANE CLARKE, M.S.

DEFINITIONS

Frustration has been defined as occurring "whenever the organism meets a more or less insurmountable obstacle or obstruction in its route to the satisfaction of any vital need" [2]. The obstructed needs that primarily concern us here are the so-called defense needs: those "concerned with protection (of the organism) against loss or impairment of structures or functions" [2]. The obstacle or stress may be of internal or external origin and may be of an active or passive sort. Thus, the range of frustrations may be seen to include (1) those of a passive external sort, such as an inanimate object that stands between the individual and his goal; (2) active external ones, such as a physical threat separating the person from his objective; (3) passive internal ones, usually the individual's own inadequacies; and (4) active internal ones, in which intrapsychic conflict results from contravalent needs. If one thinks of functional disorders as involving inability to cope adequately with the various frustrations and conflicts inevitable in a complex environment, the reason for emphasizing this area of personality reactions is apparent.

In his outline of frustration theory, Rosenzweig advances the notion that reactions to frustration may be classified according to the economy of the need frustrated: reactions are a response either

---

[1] The writer wishes to acknowledge the assistance received from Dr. Saul Rosenzweig in the preparation of this chapter.

to the threat against the particular need frustrated, or to the implicit threat against the personality itself. The former type of reaction is termed *need-persistive,* and involves some goal-directed activity or thinking. The second type, *ego-defensive,* ignores all else in defense against the threat to the ego involved in the frustration. In later writing, Rosenzweig has described another type of reaction in which the individual responds solely in terms of the problem itself and, unable either to defend his ego or to pursue the original goal, expresses only his awareness of the fact that he is frustrated. Such responses have been called *obstacle-dominant.*

Since most or all reactions to frustration are presumably aggressive in character, Rosenzweig also categorizes such reactions in terms of how the frustrated individual handles the aggression thus engendered. In many responses, aggression is clearly directed against the environment; these are referred to as *extrapunitive* responses. The individual may show his anger in more or less subtle fashion: he may express concern and irritation over what has blocked him, or demand that others take steps to solve the difficulty, or he may become obviously hostile and blame some other person in the situation for the problem.

In another sort of response, called *intropunitive,* the frustrated person turns his aggressive feelings inward upon himself. He may do this simply by blaming himself for the frustration, or he may initiate some attempt to solve the problem, express mortification at having caused it, or even completely deny its existence in an apparent effort to punish himself by precluding sympathy.

A third group of responses includes those that appear to be motivated more by social and less by aggressive drives than those in the other categories. These reactions, referred to as *impunitive,* show an attempt to gloss over the problem, usually in a somewhat conciliatory manner. Thus, the individual may emphasize that the difficulty was unavoidable, minimize the importance of the frustration, conform to the limits it sets him, or hopefully assume that time will erase the problem.

One must also emphasize the importance of what has been termed *frustration tolerance:* "the capacity of the individual to withstand frustration without resorting to inadequate modes of response" [2]. Responses are considered adequate if they are appropriate to the situation; thus, any particular sort of reaction would be inadequate if it appeared too consistently in an individual's responses to frustration and without due regard for the demands of the environment. The concept of frustration tolerance is related to the psychoanalytic distinction between the pleasure and reality principles in its emphasis upon the capacity of the individual to delay gratification. Inadequate modes of response to frustration are thus seen as attempts to protect the personality from such discomfort. From the point of view of its intellectual aspects, frustration tolerance may be thought of as requiring the capacity for abstract thinking as a basis for gratification delay.

DEVELOPMENT OF THE P-F STUDY

The Rosenzweig Picture-Frustration Study (P-F), illustrated in Figure 1, is a controlled projective technique designed to assess patterns of reaction to typical stress situations. It may be considered projective in the usual sense, in that the subject is assumed to express something of his own personality and pattern of reaction by the manner in which he interprets and deals with ambiguous stimulus material. As a controlled technique, however, it is designed to evaluate only one particular aspect of personality—reactions to frustration. The picture association technique in general is said by its author to derive in part from the word association approach: it is similar to the word association test in its relative objectivity and in that it demands the subject's immediate association to stimulus situations, though both stimulus and association are somewhat more complex than in the earlier device. It also resembles the Thematic Apperception Technique in its use of the medium of pictures of people. The P-F differs from both of these procedures, however, in the specificity of its goal and the easily quantifiable nature of the data obtained.

Though the stimulus situations are all of an obviously frustrating nature, the characters in them are shown without any facial expression or posture that would suggest particular reactions. It is therefore assumed that in his response, the subject identifies with the frustrated character, for whom he speaks and into whom he projects his own typical pattern of reaction. Rosenzweig confesses himself still unable to answer the question as to the projective level of responses to the test; that is, it is somewhat uncertain whether they represent the subject's self-critical opinion of what he would say,

Fig. 1. Rosenzweig P-F Study, Form for Adults.

a projection of what he actually would respond, or perhaps even the deeper and/or unconscious bases of his reactions to frustration. At this point, the second of these hypotheses seems probable; in the absence of evidence to the contrary, P-F records are interpreted on the assumption that a subject's responses are a projection of what his overt reactions would be in such situations as those depicted.

The Study was originally designed to fill the need for an instrument to aid in research concerning reactions to frustration. However, since response patterns of an aggressive or hostile sort naturally play a large part in the conflicts and problems of emotionally disturbed persons, the P-F is of clinical use in amplifying and corroborating material of this nature obtained from other personality measures, particularly from the Rorschach test and the TAT. Used clinically, the P-F undertakes to answer several questions about the subject's pattern of reaction to everyday frustration: In what direction does he most often turn his aggression? What is his most frequent type of reaction? Does he choose or avoid any mode of response to an extent beyond the range of the average group? Are his responses to particular situations in conformance with those of the average group? Does he change his mode of response as frustration continues or increases, and if so, how?

Experience with the Adult Form of the P-F led to the development of a form for children (Figure 2), using pictures of children in various stress situations. The hypotheses and assumptions underlying this form are, of course, the same as those of the original test. It seems probable that children regard the test more naively, and thus project themselves more readily into the pictured situations than do adults. The two tests are felt to be readily comparable, and certain of the situations in the Children's Form directly parallel some of those in the Adult Form. The choice of which one to use depends on the age and social maturity of the subject; the Children's Form is usually indicated for youngsters under 14.

Each form of the Study consists of a series of 24 cartoon-like drawings representing incidents of everyday life; in each case, one character is shown saying something of frustrating significance to another. The subject is asked to write in the reply that would be made by the second person. In the Children's Form, an especially careful effort has been made to include a representative sample of the frustrating circumstances apt to be met with in actual life. Thus, the test items may be classified as to what need is frustrated, and whether the frustrating person is a parent figure, another child, or someone else. Situations in both tests may also be divided into *ego-blocking* and *superego-blocking* frustrations. The former of these categories includes those situations that are in themselves

Fig. 2. Rosenzweig P-F Study, Form for Children.

directly threatening to the central figure. Superego-blocking situations are those in which the central figure is being criticized for or made to recognize some mistake he has made that has provided frustration for the other person in the situation.

ADMINISTRATION

The procedure of administering the P-F is relatively simple and is carried through with as much precision as possible. The subject is given the test booklet and the examiner reads over the instructions with him: "In each of the pictures in this leaflet two people are shown talking to each other. The words said by one person are always given. Imagine what the other person in the picture would answer and write in the blank box the very *first* reply that comes into your mind. Work as fast as you can." (These are the instructions for the Adult Form; those for the Children's Form are equivalent in content, but the wording is adapted to younger subjects.) The booklet is then opened, the first situation read and explained, and the subject asked to tell the first thing he thinks of that the frustrated person might say. When he has answered, he is told to write his reply in the balloon over the frustrated character's head, and then to proceed to deal with the other items in the same way. In repeating the instructions, emphasis is placed on the importance of giving the first answer thought of, and that it is to be what the person in the picture would say, in an effort to encourage identification and projection.

The subject is discouraged from making any changes in his responses once he has written them; if he feels that he must, he is told to cross out rather than erase his original words. The length of time he takes to go through the test is recorded. After the subject has completed the 24 items, he is asked to read aloud to the examiner both the printed speech of the frustrating character and the response he has written. The examiner takes note of any significant inflection or tone of voice that might influence the scoring. If any of the responses seems ambiguous, the examiner inquires into its meaning; as a rule, the most appropriate questions are, "What does he mean?" and "How does he feel?" Leading questions, of course, are to be avoided. If the subject has misinterpreted any of the situations, they are explained to him and he is asked to make another response; his original answer is also noted and, like other errors, may be of qualitative interest in interpreting his record.

Group testing with the P-F is easily possible with persons who can read and write without difficulty. In this circumstance, the instructions and introduction to the first item are given aloud to the group. The inquiry phase of the examination must, of course, be omitted; as a result of this change in procedure, some responses may be too ambiguous to score and thus will not be included in the quantitative evaluation.

SCORING

The scoring of the P-F follows Rosenzweig's original outline of frustration theory rather closely. Responses are considered for the *direction* in which aggressive reactions are made and for the *type* of reaction displayed, and may be classified under nine scoring factors. In scoring a given response, it is necessary to decide whether aggression is expressed toward the environment (extrapunitive), is turned inward against the self (intropunitive), or is suppressed and glossed over (impunitive). At the same time, it must be considered whether the response represents blocking at the point of the frustration itself (obstacle-dominance), defense against the ego-threatening qualities of the situation, usually in the form of assignment of blame (ego-defense), or drive toward solution of the problem (need-persistence). Obstacle-dominant responses are conventionally designated by E', I', M'; ego-defensive responses by E, I, M; and need-persistent responses by e, i, m.

These nine scoring factors are considered in detail in the two scoring manuals, and examples are given of their appearance in each of the test situations [6, 7].

THE RECORD BLANK

In considering interpretation of the results of the P-F, it is necessary to go back to the questions that the Study undertakes to answer. The direction of aggression and type of reaction that the subject characteristically demonstrates can be seen from a profile and patterns on a record blank that summarizes his test scores. The extent to which his responses to particular situations are of the same sort as those of other people is secured from the Group Conformity Rating, based on "popular" scores for the various items. The question of whether changes in the subject's mode of response occur as frustration continues may be answered by determining what trends exist in his response record.

After the subject's responses have been scored, the scores are tabulated in the record blank form. The number of times each of the nine factors occurs in the record is then counted, and these sums are entered in the profile on the summary sheet. In the case of combination scores, each of the factors concerned is credited with one-half response. The totals for each of the six categories are then converted into percentages; ordinarily this is the proportion of 24, though if any responses have had to be omitted as unscorable, the total is naturally lower.

INTERPRETATION

To evaluate and interpret a subject's P-F record meaningfully, it is necessary to compare it with available norms for comparable subjects. These are presented separately for the two forms of the Study [6, 7]. In each case norms are expressed in terms of means and standard deviations for each of the nine scoring factors, for the six major scoring categories, for the Group Conformity Rating, and for certain patterns of defensive reactions which appear when the frustration is of a super ego-blocking sort. The norms for the Children's P-F are based on the records of 256 children from four to 13 years of age. The differences between boys and girls were not great, but differences among various age groups were outstanding, and the tables are accordingly arranged by two-year levels. The most recent norms for the Adult Form are based on the records of 460 normal adults, 236 males and 224 females, ranging in age from 20 through 29; this age group is felt to be representative of a reasonable adult standard. The mean educational level of the total group was somewhat beyond the first year of college. Separate norms are given for men and women.

While there is no need to give the norm tables in detail here, certain general patterns stand out and should be mentioned. As far as direction of aggression is concerned, extrapunitive responses are shown to be the most frequent both in the Adult P-F and for the various age levels of the Children's Form, while intropunitive reactions are with equal consistency the least common on most records. Ego-defense appears to be the most often used type of reaction, while need-persistent and obstacle-dominant scores follow in that order for all groups. Furthermore, there appear to be several fairly systematic changes with increasing age in the proportions involved in this typical pattern of response. These are not marked in regard to type of reaction, though there appears to be some tendency for need-persistent responses to be more frequent in the records of older children. In regard to direction of aggression, however, all factors change markedly: extrapunitive responses become less and less frequent as children grow older, while both intropunitive and impunitive reactions are seen more often. Thus the mean number of extrapunitive responses for the 4–5-year-old group is equal to 56 per cent of a total record, while at the 12–13-year-old level, only 40 per cent of the responses fall in the extrapunitive category, and intropunitive and impunitive reactions are correspondingly more frequent than for the younger groups. The norms for the 12–13-year level are fairly close to those for adult subjects on the Adult Form. Some preliminary exploration with the Adult Form has suggested that certain changes in patterns of reaction to frustration continue to take place even after maturity is presumably reached.

In evaluating the utility of any test, some information regarding its reliability and validity is necessary. These aspects of the P-F Study are still under investigation, and little is actually known about them, apart from what may be inferred from actual clinical experience with the instrument. Because of the difficulty of establishing a consistent and objective scoring system, the first work of this sort was done to determine the reliability of scoring, using a comparison of independent judgments of experienced scorers. After final revision of the scoring samples had been made, it was found that such scorers agreed in 85 per cent of their judgments; this figure was felt to meet a reasonable standard for reliability in scoring this type of test. Rosenzweig also reports test-retest reliability coefficients of .60 to .80 on the Adult Form, and he states that preliminary results with the Children's Form seem to be at about the same level.

Even less has been done to establish the validity of the P-F Study, though certain minor investigations have been conducted. In the absence of definitive data, it appears that the validity of this instrument must be thought of in terms of its usefulness in clinical practice, and must be measured by the extent to which it serves to corroborate and amplify the findings of other clinical tools. As has been found in the case of other projective techniques, one major problem in establishing the validity of the P-F has been the difficulty in finding a criterion against which to measure it. The most satisfactory standard may be the results of other personality tests. In one study along this line, a correlation of .74 was found for expression of extrapunitiveness independently derived from the P-F and from the Thematic Apperception Test.

FURTHER RESEARCH

Investigations on various normative aspects of the P-F Study are obviously required before this test can be an entirely satisfactory instrument. Certain ones have been and are being conducted; they will be summarized in a publication by Rosenzweig. However, they should probably be mentioned briefly at this point.

Beside the attempts to validate the P-F using the criterion of other projective techniques, studies have also been made using as a criterion descriptions of the subjects (psychiatric patients) by the doctors and nurses who attended them, and employing a matching technique. Investigation of this sort has been made to determine the meaningfulness or validity of the total P-F record, and of the actual responses and the record-blank material taken separately.

As was mentioned above, study of the reliability of the P-F has been approached through the test-retest method. Some of this work has been conducted in connection with a study of the effects on test patterns of various instructions. The latter investigations, however, were primarily concerned with the question of what changes, if any, would occur when the instructions were so altered as to lead to an orientation at least superficially different from the usual projective one. Thus certain of the experimental instructions contained the suggestion to be self-critical, others to be humorous, and so forth.

There has also been considerable study of changes in reactions to frustration that occur with increasing age. The completion of this work would be of theoretical interest and would also help to establish more adequate norms, thus rendering the Study more generally useful. Preliminary investigation into the patterns of aggressive reactions in certain special groups, such as mental patients, delinquents, and deviant cultural groups, has also been made and should be of interest when completed.

REFERENCES

1. Clarke, H. J., Rosenzweig, S., and Fleming, E. E., "The reliability of the scoring of the Rosenzweig Picture-Frustration Study." *J. Clin. Psychol.,* 1947, 3, 364–370.

2. Rosenzweig, S., "An Outline of Frustration Theory," in J. McV. Hunt (ed.), *Personality and the Behavior Disorders.* New York: The Ronald Press Company, 1944, Vol. 1, Chapter 11, pages 379–388.

3. —————————, "The picture-association method and its application in a study of reactions to frustration." *J. Pers.,* 1945, 14, 3–23.

4. —————————, "Revised norms for the Adult Form of the Rosenzweig Picture-Frustration Study." *J. Personality,* 1950, 18, 304–305.

5. Rosenzweig, S., Clarke, H. J., Garfield, M. S., and Lehndorff, A., "Scoring samples for the Rosenzweig Picture-Frustration Study." *J. of Psychol.,* 1946, 21, 45–72.

6. Rosenzweig, S., Fleming, E. E., and Clarke, H. J., "Revised scoring manual for the Rosenzweig Picture-Frustration Study." *J. of Psychol.,* 1947, 24, 165–208.

7. Rosenzweig, S., Fleming, E. E., and Rosenzweig, L., "The children's form of the Rosenzweig Picture-Frustration Study." *J. of Psychol.,* 1948, 26, 141–191.

CHAPTER 11

The Bender Visual Motor Gestalt Test

FLORENCE HALPERN, PH.D.

The perceptual motor test most widely known and used by clinical psychologists is the Bender Gestalt Test [2]. As its name implies, the theory underlying the test depends to a considerable extent upon gestalt concepts; and its content, a number of gestalt figures, is derived from Wertheimer's [7] configurations. Definite dynamic concepts, however, have been added to the fundamental gestalt tenet of total reaction to total situation. Thus, not only are what and how the individual perceives considered, but the way in which the perceptions are used is also evaluated. In this manner, the test ties in with the basic concepts underlying all projective techniques and permits of personality description and diagnosis.

PROCEDURE

The test consists of nine geometric forms or designs, drawn in black on a piece of white cardboard of about postcard size. These are shown in Plate I. In her original monograph, Bender [1] gave no instructions for administering the test, but in 1946 she published a pamphlet [2] with instructions that read, in part: "Here are some figures (or designs) for you to copy. Just copy them as you see them." The examiner should discourage rotation of the test cards by replacing a card in its original position when such turning occurs. If rotation continues, however, it is best to let the subject go his way, although such reactions should, of course, be noted. Similarly, attempts to turn the sheet on which the subject is copying

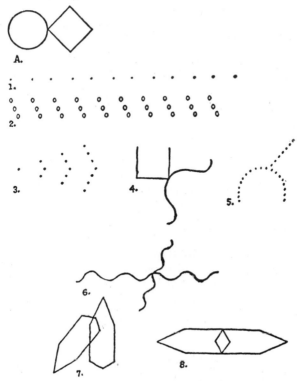

Plate I. Test figures adapted from Wertheimer.

should also be stopped, if possible. Bender suggests, "It is well to encourage the placing of the first figure near the upper left-hand corner of the paper, although if the suggestion is not readily accepted, it should not be insisted upon." Other examiners, including the writer, have found it of some value to allow the subject complete freedom in his placement, since this gives the examiner insight into the way he orients himself in a given frame of reference, and into the way he handles spatial relationships. For this reason, somewhat modified directions may be employed.

The subject is told that he will be presented, one at a time, with nine cards with simple designs on them. He is to copy these designs as well as he can on the sheet of *unlined* paper lying before him.   The subject is permitted to erase as much as he pleases, but no ruler or other mechanical aids are permitted.   Subjects frequently ask questions about where they should begin; whether the number of dots in their drawings must be identical with those on the design; whether their copies should be the same size as the test figures, and so on.   The examiner's answers should be noncommital, as on other projective tests.   "That's up to you," or "Do as you like," generally covers the situation.   The fact that the subject has appealed to the examiner for guidance gives some clues to the way he approaches new tasks, and should therefore be taken into consideration in the total personality evaluation.   It is well to have a few sheets of paper on the table, so that a subject may take another if he cannot get all the figures on one sheet.   The cards are presented in definite order, beginning with figure *A*, then figures 1, 2, and so on, and finishing with figure 8.

The examiner should unobtrusively watch the manner in which each design is reproduced and record it on a sheet of paper.   Numbers to show the order in which the various parts of the figures were made and arrows to show directional sequence are quite helpful in this respect.   Questions, verbalizations, and any other significant behavior, such as blocking or resistance, should be noted.

INTERPRETATION

Interpretation of test results depends on an understanding of gestalt principles, maturational factors affecting visual motor activity, and personality dynamics, especially as they manifest themselves in graphic media.   In perceiving, the individual organizes the stimulus in terms of his own experiences.   The end-product consists of the "original pattern in space (visual pattern), the temporal factor of becoming, and the personal-sensory-motor factor. The resulting gestalt is also more than the sum of all these factors. There is a tendency not only to perceive gestalten but to complete gestalten and to reorganize them in accordance with principles biologically determined by the sensory-motor pattern of action. This pattern of action may be expected to vary in maturation or growth levels and in pathological states, organically or functionally determined.

"There is a tendency for continuous experimentation with the external stimulating pattern and the action tendencies of the sensory-motor-conceptual person. The final pattern may represent a momentary point of equilibrium between the balancing function and is liable to change." [*1*, p. 5.] The test product is, then, an indication of how the stimulus is perceived, organized, what it means to the subject, what he does to simplify it, and what he adds to it. Likewise, his capacity to reproduce his percept, the level of his visual motor coordination, and his action patterns stand revealed.

Analyzing visual motor activity in children from the maturation aspects, Bender found that the child's first efforts consisted solely of scribbling. This apparently represents pleasure in motor play and little, if anything, more. Percepts are not yet organized as they are in the older child and the adult. In highly arbitrary fashion, any production is assigned meaning. When visual motor patterns develop, they are "organized about the primitive enclosed loop." [*1*, p. 9.] This enclosed loop is the simplest visual motor gestalt relationship. All other relationships require more control and inhibition, and develop later.

Bender's investigations show that until about the age of four, the child uses the first experienced form, namely the enclosed loop, and this, in various elaborations, constitutes his responses to any figure. In this connection, Bender says:

The more primitive sensori-motor patterns are dependent on the principles of constant motion, which seems to be largely a whirling movement in a vortex in clockwise and counter-clockwise direction,[1] with an associated radiating directional component and with a tendency to emphasize horizontal planes. Fixed points are difficult to obtain, and straight lines are not accomplished as the shortest distance between two fixed points, but as an expression of the radiating tendencies. [1, p. 24]

These facts in the development of visual motor reactions are stressed because without them, test performance cannot be evaluated.

According to Bender's study, in which she standardized her test as a performance test for children, the average child of seven should be able to reproduce with accuracy figures *A* and 5. By the age of nine, the child adequately handles figure 1, and by the age of ten, all the others, with the possible exception of figure 7. The findings here correlate with findings on standard intelligence tests as

---

1 Bender has suggested that in the schizophrenic child, a spontaneous whirling around a longitudinal axis beyond the age where such a pattern is appropriate is frequent in the illness. See the discussion of circular movement or whirling in the drawings of schizophrenic children by Montague, in Chapter 13.

to the maturational age for various visual motor patterns. In this connection, there are special cases where the test results must be treated somewhat differently than they are for the majority of subjects. In this group are left-handed subjects, especially children, illiterates, and those with very limited experience with pencil and paper. Likewise, people who have had special training with spatial and motor activities of a graphic order, such as draftsmen, are able to handle the test with an ease and facility that, to an extent, conceals some of their underlying difficulties. As in the interpretation of figure drawings by artists, their special training warrants more careful and qualified interpretation of the test results.

Finally, the way an individual handles any experience depends not only on the degree of biological development in the visual motor area that he has achieved, but on all the behavioral patterns he has developed. Emphasis on repression, rigidity, and withdrawal, as opposed to ready indulgence in emotional expression; dependency attitudes in contradistinction to self-assurance; tendencies to elation or depression; compulsive reactions; and exaggerated anxiety all play their part in the individual's motor patterns and can, therefore, be discerned in his test productions.

Keeping in mind that visual motor reactions are total reactions between the individual and the configurational stimulus, determined by the subject's age, ability, emotional stability or degree of equilibrium, habitual adjustive mechanisms, and mood of the moment, the test figures can now be approached from the clinical point of view. As in all psychological testing, it cannot be too strongly emphasized that no one deviation should be considered as having diagnostic significance. True, there are a few signs that may be considered pathognomonic, and will be discussed below, but even these should never be interpreted without further supporting data.

As with other tests, there should be no jump from test data to diagnostic label; rather, the material should be evaluated in terms of personality description that, when full enough and well enough understood, lends itself to diagnostic categorization. Likewise, neither personality description nor diagnosis should be made on the basis of any one test. However, as part of a total battery, the Bender Visual Motor Gestalt Test gives rich returns in terms of the amount of time and energy expended and has become an almost indispensible part of psychological test batteries everywhere.

Disturbances in personality integration manifest themselves in the test productions in a variety of ways. These disturbances may run the gamut from mild uncertainty regarding the adequacy of the performance (as indicated when the subject has a need to go over some lines he has drawn, reinforce angles where they meet, and so on) to clear evidence of serious regression and personality disruption.

The grosser the manifestations of serious disorder, the more clearly can they be recognized and diagnosed. In this category are included *fragmentation* and even *complete destruction of the gestalten, rotation, elaboration,* treatment of the material as if it had *concrete* significance, definite *motor difficulties,* and *primitivization* and *over-simplification* of the patterns. Again, it cannot be too strongly emphasized that the presence of any of these deviations does not in and of itself acquire diagnostic significance, but simply describes personality traits and trends.

Fragmentation occurs when the individual is incapable of treating the gestalt as a unit, but rather sees it as a number of separate entities. This can happen when organizational disturbances are present and/or when motor difficulties exist. Thus, some subjects do not perceive the circle and the diamond of figure *A* or the two polygrams of figure 7 as parts of one gestalt, but treat each detail as though it were a unit in itself. This points to a splitting or disassociative tendency. Sometimes, however, such splitting occurs not because the subject perceives inadequately, but because motor difficulties make it impossible for him to reproduce the figures as a unit. In such instances, the subject often spontaneously verbalizes his limitations or, if at the end of the test he is asked if his figures are correct, makes a statement that indicates that his is a motor disturbance rather than a disorder in perceptual organization. These latter cases, especially if other evidence of motor disturbance is present, are usually suffering from organic disorders, while those subjects who have difficulty in perceptual organization may be either organic or schizophrenic patients.

Finally, there is evidence that some subjects reproduce with a fair degree of accuracy without any realization of the fact that the details they are copying constitute parts of a total unit. This is perhaps best illustrated in figure 2, where an individual faithfully reproduces three rows of dots, but if he comes to the end of his

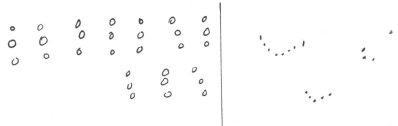

(P) Organic boy, aged 10 years	(Q) Schizophrenic boy, aged 12 years
(R) Man with organic disorder. aged 42 years	(S) Schizophrenic girl, aged 8 years

Plate II.   Examples of fragmentation.

sheet of paper before he has the correct number of dots, will simply place additional ones on a line below the initial figures. (See figure *P*, Plate II.) Here, too, the gestalt is not conceived of as an integrated, related whole.

A different kind of fragmentation may be the result of a need to handle the gestalten on a *concrete* level and ascribe to them specific meanings. For example, one subject saw figure 3 as a flock of birds flying, and so proceeded to split up the figure into three distinct parts. (See figure *Q*, Plate II.) Such efforts at meeting things on a concrete level are generally indicative of pathological thinking and are found in the reproductions of organic and schizophrenic patients. Which diagnostic label applies depends on the nature of the other reproductions. Thus, in the case of a man who interpreted figure 2 as musical notes, there was a serious disturbance in visual motor coordination, as indicated by his inability to copy a diamond. (See figure *R*, Plate II.) On the other hand, the subject who made birds out of figure 3 showed comparatively good motor coordination, as indicated by his copies of figures *A* and 7. The first case (figure *P*) was an organic patient with a localized brain lesion, the second (figure *Q*), a 12-year-old schizophrenic boy. In general, tendencies to treat material in concrete fashion point to serious regression.

Displacement occurs when the various parts of figures are related in deviant fashion. Here, it would seem that while the subject is able to separate a figure into its component details, he shows distortion in the resynthesizing process. Gestalten are handled in this fashion by individuals with atypical, bizarre, and possibly negativistic reactions to the task. Such disturbances are most common where there is organic impairment or a schizophrenic process.

Rotation of the entire figure shows disturbances in spatial orientation. This is not uncommon in young children, in some left-handed subjects, and in children with reading disabilities. In adults who have had adequate educational opportunities, such rotation shows a far-reaching disturbance. Again, to quote Bender, "This can be understood if we realize that all form arises from motion, which is vertical." It follows, then, that where there is a fundamental disturbance in motion, it will be reflected in the handling of the test patterns. Organic and schizophrenic patients show this most commonly. In this motility disruption, figures tend to become disassociated. On the other hand, particularly in cases of schizophrenia, they may adhere to one another in a sticky, "unwieldy conglomeration." Rotation of a slightly different order, which stems from a subject's inability to adhere to the horizontal position, also occurs. (See figure *S*, Plate II.) This is likely to be found in copies of figure 2, where the horizontal direction is lost and the figure acquires a curve either above or below the initial base line. Some such subjects seem to be unable to maintain their own center of gravity and therefore cannot fix themselves in space. In others, such deviations appear to be reflections of marked intensification of elated or depressed moods with resultant loss of control.

Primitivization and *over-simplication* occur: where there is (1) retarded, immature mental and emotional development, or (2) marked regression resulting from psychosis or organic damage. Differentiation can often be made on the basis of the degree of motor coordination manifested and the presence or absence of bizarre elements. Thus, the mental defective and the organic subject are likely to use the enclosed loop in practically every instance and to show difficulty in motor coordination, rotational disturbances, and possibly some tendency to employ the stimulus in concrete fashion. The organic subject may also try to conserve energy by substituting a continuous line for the more effort-consuming task of making separate dots. The psychopathic patient also simplifies his task in this fashion, being unwilling to exert himself. His performance, however, will not show difficulties in motor coordination other than those associated with impulsivity. That is, his lines will not meet accurately, but will run on beyond the limits of the pattern. His performance will be an impulsive, hasty one. Lack of inhibition will show itself in the enlarged size of his productions, and he frequently will need several sheets of paper to complete the test. Hutt [4, 5] has discussed the large amount of space these subjects leave between parts of the figures, and has interpreted this in much the same way that the use of the white space is interpreted in the Rorschach. The writer's feeling is that the presence of so much white space is the result both of the impulsive, unstable, psychopathic subject's lack of effort at holding himself in—as it were, the absence of inhibitory trends—and very weak interrelationships. Thus, for him, parts of any pattern are only tenuously linked, if at all, and so he has no hesitation about keeping them at a distance.

Elaboration occurs in those cases where the presented stimulus simply acts as a springboard for the individual's preoccupations and needs, and he proceeds in highly arbitrary fashion to use the situation accordingly.

Roughly, two kinds of *perseveration* occur on this test. One is present when the individual continues to repeat a pattern. This is particularly true in figures 1 and 2, where the dots are carried on indefinitely, but other designs are also sometimes repeated. The other type of perseveration is found when a pattern or parts of a pattern influence the succeeding ones. Again, figure 2 at times is given a single line as a result of the influence of figure 1.

Disturbances in visual motor coordination show themselves most frequently in the patient's inability to copy angles. This is similar to the difficulties some subjects have in reproducing the diamond at Year VII on the Stanford-Binet. Such patients, likewise, often have trouble with the bell-shaped form on figure 4. Achieving the angular effect on figure 3 also constitutes a problem for these persons. This type of motor difficulty is most conspicuous on figures *A*,

3, 4, 7, and 8, and in many instances, would seem to be the result of some organic disorder. Lack of motor control shows itself in sweeping, uninhibited lines, carried on beyond the point where they would ordinarily end. The substitution of dashes or complete lines for dots and exaggeration or minimization of curves may have an organic basis, but very frequently are a reflection of emotional instability.

Some subjects show a tendency to leave a little space at the point where the lines should meet. They seem unable to complete a task or to permit closure of anything with which they deal. Hesitancy, self-doubt, and anxiety are all suggested here. Behind this may lie a need to leave themselves a way out of a situation.

Alterations in the nature of the lines is frequently encountered. Curves can be either exaggerated or flattened and angles can be sharpened or rounded. In general such exaggeration and flattening are found in individuals who have difficulties in emotional control. Exaggerations sometimes occur because an individual cannot inhibit his impulses easily. If the figures are too precisely drawn, but yet remain exaggerated, efforts at inhibition that are not too successfully achieved may be inferred. An individual with such a performance is likely to show an alternation between impulsiveness and rigidity. Flattening of curves is generally associated with a kind of flattening of affect, a shallowness of emotional experience, and when the flattened line is prolonged, it may also tie in with a kind of indifference to the demands of the environment and an overimpulsivity.

The same is true of the *rounded* or *sharpened angles*. The rounded ones show emotional impulsiveness, while the sharpened ones show efforts at control bespeaking an underlying disturbance and conflict, and a sense of insecurity.

The *quality of the line* that a subject uses in making his copies of the figures is also of considerable significance. There is a vast difference between a relatively firm, unbroken line, a hesitant, timorous, sketching kind of line and a very heavy, sweeping, impulsive stroke that presses so strongly on the paper as almost to tear it. If the paper is the framework in which the individual is expected to adjust and perform, the quality of the line reveals something of his feeling toward his environment as well as his attitude toward himself. The heavy, impulsive line that almost destroys the paper shows considerable aggression and possibly even hostility toward his environment, while a sketching, faint line points to considerable anxiety, timidity, and general lack of self-confidence. Such an individual moves hesitantly from one point to another. The smooth, firm line falls roughly at a midpoint between these two extremes.

The *size of the figures* should also be evaluated. Very small figures would seem to reveal a tendency to pull back on the self and inhibit spontaneity and outgoingness. Such individuals fear to release their emotions or give them direct expression. In contrast to this are those productions already discussed that sometimes cover several sheets of paper and show a general lack of control and inhibition. Interesting variations in reactions are often obtained from ambivalent individuals who start out impulsively, suddenly inhibit themselves, go along in constricted fashion for a time, and then again show a release. This is sometimes very clearly manifested in figure 2, where the loops are more or less of average size in the beginning, then sudden expansive tendencies occur with increased size in the loops and in the space between them, only to be followed by a sudden tightening up again in the size of the loops.

The way the individual *places the figures on the paper* can also reveal a great deal about his general orientation to his environment. Many persons place the first figure right in the middle of the page with succeeding ones below it. When there is no more room at the bottom of the page, they then fill the upper half. This seems to be one of the most frequent ways of meeting the task, and if there is no crowding together of any two figures, it cannot be considered significantly different from what the average person will do. However, when crowding or actual overlapping of figures occurs, gross disregard for the limits of an entity can be inferred. This is found in individuals who are not sensitive to others, who have an aggressive, abrupt way of dealing with their environment, and also in schizophrenics and organics who do not recognize patterned relationships or who lack clear concepts as to their own body limits. Again, the differential will depend upon the nature of other factors in the test.

Some subjects place their first figure in the upper left-hand corner of the page, place the next figure directly under this and so on, in very neat, precise order. An exaggerated meticulousness can be inferred in many of these cases. When each figure is separated from the other by lines that enclose it in a separate little box, this meticulousness can be seen as an exaggerated search for security, with efforts at compensating for extreme insecurity and anxiety.

Some subjects place the figures in such a way that they seem to cling to the edges of the paper. This suggests the need for whatever additional support the environment can afford and a fear of coming out into the center of the stage in independent, self-assured fashion. Such uncertainty and insecurity are also found when the subject places all his figures on the upper half of the paper. This necessitates small, tight reproductions, crowded close to one another, and points to an effort at attaining security through contiguity.

There is one other aspect of a patient's performance that is seldom noted in interpretative efforts. This is what Bender calls the "too perfect performance." There are times when one gets copies of the gestalt figures that can hardly be differentiated from the originals, so exact are they in every detail. It is apparent that unusual control and care has gone into their execution. Interestingly enough, such productions are sometimes obtained from incipient schizophrenics or cases with a beginning organic disturbance. The unusual care they exercise reflects their efforts at holding themselves together against the impact of their imminent disorganization. In this writer's experience, such performance has been most frequent in early paretics.

ILLUSTRATIVE CASE

In order to clarify some of these concepts, the gestalt figures drawn by a 33-year-old white male of good intelligence are reproduced on Plate III. They are interpreted as follows: over-all inspection indicates that aside from the splitting of figure *A*, the total gestalten are relatively well perceived and not too poorly reproduced. The significant deviations are: figure *A*, splitting and lack of joining, and unevenness in the quality of the line; figure 1, the use of dashes instead of dots; figure 2, the flattening of the angle of the loops and the variability in the spaces between the rows of loops; figure 3, the use of dashes instead of dots and the failure to achieve accurate angulation; figure 4, the tendency to place the bell shape below the open square and the slight difficulty in having the two figures meet;

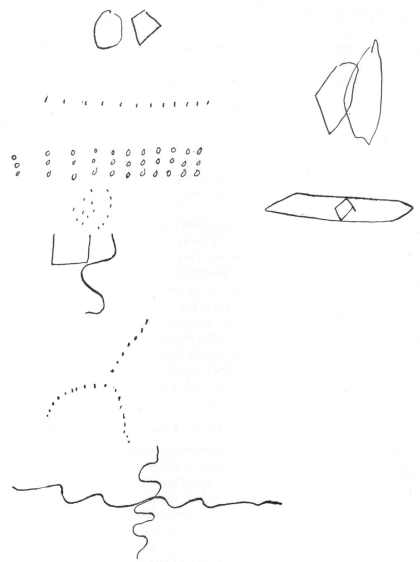

Plate III.   Thirty-three-year-old white male of good intelligence.

figure 5, the use of dashes instead of dots and the tendency to prolong the right-hand side of the figure below the base line; fig-6, the exaggeration of the curves of the vertical line and the flattening of the curves of the horizontal line; figure 7, the tendency to curve what should be straight lines and the failure to reproduce the angles correctly; figure 8, a slight tendency to prolong the left-hand side of the figure, and a running-over of the lines forming the small inner diamond.

The alternating exaggeration and flattening of the curves as seen on figures 6 and 7, together with the variability in spacing on figure 2, point to a high degree of instability and suggest that the patient will be unpredictable in his behavior. The prolongation of the right-hand side of figure 5 and the tendency to drop the bell shape in figure 4, as well as some very slight inclination for figure 1 to dip downward, point to depressive trends. The substitution of dashes for dots argues for lack of motor control and inhibition. The failure to relate the two parts of figure *A*, together with the poor angle formation on figure 7, raised the question of a possible organic difficulty. However, in view of the well-executed diamond on figure 8, doubt was cast on such a diagnosis, and when the subject was later asked to repeat some of his formulations taking a great deal of time, improvement in angulation was achieved. The difficulty on figure 7, therefore, would seem to be a function of his emotional impulsivity, pointing to vacillation between withdrawal and impulsiveness. Such impulsiveness, as has already been indicated, is also evident in the use of dashes for dots. The general placement of the figures on the page suggests an orderly method of dealing with a situation and indicates that the patient can handle spatial relationships effectively.

To summarize: these copies of the gestalt figures give the picture of a highly ambivalent, unstable, unpredictable individual who vacillates between inhibition and impulsiveness. At the present time he is depressed and is showing some mild withdrawal tendencies. Hutt has suggested that disturbances noted in the elongations and deviations of figures 7 and 8 not infrequently tie in with homosexual disturbances, and in this case it would appear that the patient's maladjustments are in part, at least, on such a basis.

History: the patient is the younger of two siblings coming from a good middle-class home. He is a high school graduate and is of at least average if not better intelligence. He had been engaged in various types of artistic work since he left school. He is constantly fighting against his homosexual tendencies and has had two overt homosexual experiences, because of which he suffers a great deal of anxiety. His adjustment is very variable, going along at times in conforming, acceptable fashion and at other times being of a decidedly asocial order. Recently, in an effort to satisfy the material wants of a man to whom he was very much attached but with whom he claims he had no sexual relationships, he forged a number of checks and finally was arrested. His present obvious depression would seem to be the result of this experience. Subsequent to his arrest, he attempted suicide by slashing his wrists. The Bender Gestalt figures, along with other tests, were obtained from the patient while he was in the prison ward of a psychiatric hospital. Psychiatric diagnosis is severe psychoneurosis with homosexual trends and some depression.

Several people have worked with the Bender Gestalt test in past years, varying somewhat both the procedure and the interpretation. Hutt used the test extensively in the Army and has added some concepts that were not present in Bender's original formulations. Thus, Hutt suggests that it is sometimes helpful to have the individual comment on each of the figures when he has completed it or possibly, at the end of the entire test. Another technique that he has employed is to ask the subject to tell him what the drawings remind him of and to modify them in any way he feels will make them "nicer." Symbolic material and fantasy content is evoked in this manner.

Billingslea [3] has devised a method for measuring angles and curves and figuring out spatial deviations. This method requires a great deal of work on the part of the examiner and consumes more time than the end-result would seem to justify.

Many years of experience with the test, used more or less as Bender originally formulated it, have convinced this writer of the clinical value of this approach. Its reliability can be established by repeated administrations to individuals without gross personality deviations. That there is a consistency in the test performance of subjects who are making a relatively stable and harmonious adjustment is thus manifested. Similarly, the validity of the test as a measure of sporadic or long-term deviations can be and has been demonstrated through various research procedures. In a study of marihuana [6], the effects of the drug were revealed through the medium of this test. Normal performances could be obtained before a subject was given marihuana, and within an hour, his productions reflected all the release of impulse and/or anxiety that result from drug ingestion. Similarly, where test productions have been obtained before and after brain injury or other traumatic experiences, the disturbances in personality found expression through the resulting distortions of the gestalten. Here, then, is a clinical instrument of reliability and validity, and ease of administration and interpretation. Finally, it appears to most subjects as a relatively innocuous task, so that even the most resistive ones respond to it. It therefore constitutes an excellent opening wedge or ice-breaker.

The discussion in this chapter by no means exhausts all the possible types of deviation found in gestalt productions of varying kinds of subjects. New anomolies are constantly being reported. Thus, Bender gave the test to a schizophrenic who added little "shadow" figures to the usual ones, that is, besides several of his gestalten he placed small, faint duplicates of his drawings. If the examiner using this test has an understanding of the gestalt and dynamic principles underlying interpretation, he will, after an initial period of experimentation and exploration, be able to interpret test performance adequately and will find that it adds considerably to his total understanding of his subject and serves to clarify certain points in differential diagnosis.

REFERENCES

1. Bender, Lauretta, *A Visual Motor Gestalt Test and Its Clinical Use.* Research Monograph No. 3. New York: American Orthopsychiatric Association, 1938.

2. ————————, *Instructions for the Use of the Visual Motor Gestalt Test.* New York: American Orthopsychiatric Association, 1946.

3. Billingslea, Fred Y., "The Bender Gestalt: An objective scoring method and validating data." *J. Clin. Psychol.*, 1948, 4, 1–27.

4. Hutt, Max L., "The use of projective methods of personality measurement in army medical installations." *J. Clin. Psychol.*, 1945, 1, 134–140.

5. ————————, *A Tentative Guide for the Administration and Interpretation of the Bender Gestalt Test.* U. S. Army, Adjutant General's School, 1945 (restricted).

scrutiny is best accomplished by coordination with other established personality instruments. This does not mean that personality appraisal through drawings cannot yield extensive and detailed integration—in innumerable blind studies and in known clinical context, it has done so. In research, too, although the method can be and has been used independently, it has been most fruitful in combination with other techniques. Figure drawing has been used to investigate pubertal through adolescent growth patterns of urban girls,[1] and to study personality determinants of perception of the body in space. It is being used as a screening device for professional occupations and in the evaluation of the progress of and terminal gains in of therapy. Norms for all developmental phases, sex differences, and various clinical categories are being accumulated, in terms rather of common characteristics than of rote signs or numerical standards.

The method has many advantages. It is simple to administer, requires no materials beyond a pencil and paper, may be completed in less than an hour even if the supplementary associations to the figures be given, and is interpreted directly from the figures that are drawn, without intermediary scoring or coding. Sources of error are thus reduced considerably. The product may be preserved indefinitely and analyzed at leisure, and it offers direct testimony of the subject's projection, rather than verbal description of it. As a motoric medium, it is often welcomed by the verbally shy or inhibited child. Also, it may be applied to the foreign or illiterate. It has almost no limitations of age, intelligence, or artistic skill. For the fantasy-laden subject, it offers a safe opportunity for release, frequently with therapeutic effects. The task as defined is ambiguous enough so that it is not easily malingered over. Although some structuring is introduced in the request for the figure of a person, the infinite choices that may be involved, and the variety of dynamic patterns of self-expression that may be evoked, give ample confirmation of its potentialities as a projective test. Actual administration consumes only the partial attention of the examiner, and it may be applied to groups of any size, if seating is spaced.

Interest in the projective significance of painting and drawing, which stems from a variety of motivations, is recorded in a wide

---

[1] *The Adolescent Girl,* auspices of Caroline Zachry Institute for Human Development (manuscript in preparation).

range of literature and is discussed from both psychological and artistic angles. That all art contains some element of the intimate personality patterns of the artist has long been recognized. The human figure representation as a basic vehicle for projection of these patterns in specific and subtle body language, however, is new to publication, despite the verification and support that the method has received in more than 20 years of clinical application to a vast variety of personalities and clinical problems. The bizarre, symbolic, and often highly artistic productions of the insane led many investigators, here and abroad, to attempt to classify graphic features common to particular psychiatric categories. The art of the insane was further studied for its likeness to that of the primitive and the child. From the case study of a patient came the analysis of art productions for the specific meanings imposed by the patient. Thus, the problem of unravelling graphic communication was attacked both from the case-study angle and from the focus of psychiatric diagnosis. The results, however, were so diffuse, so lacking in a stable point of reference, that Anastasi and Foley [2, 3, 4, 5], in their exhaustive survey of the literature, were forced to conclude that drawing as a psychological technique could not be developed as a tool that would give reliable differentiation.

In developing a systematic approach to the language of the body, the writer has provided an interpretative key, which, though incomplete, has already more than vindicated the drawing of a person as a basic psychological technique. In the drawing technique, more than in other projective methods, theory followed successful practice: empirical validation preceded the construction of a theoretical framework. The fact that the drawings of "a person" revealed wide dimensions of the personality and clinical condition of the subject was quite established before the "why" was considered. Personality theory weaves the "why" into all systems of dynamic psychology, with particular reference to the principles underlying expressive movement, depth analysis, and psychoanalytic thought.

Understanding of expressive movement owes much to Mira [32], Wolff (Chapter 16), and Harms [20], among others, while Alschuler and Hattwick [1] have contributed to the psychological appreciation of children's paintings. Bender [6, 7] and Despert [8] have pioneered in the psychological interpretation of the art of disturbed children, giving rich clinical illumination. Waehner [39] has given consideration to the formal characteristics of painting and drawing. It was the work of Goodenough [17, 18], however, in focusing on the human figure *(Draw-a-Man test)*, that led to the construction and development of the test described here. Goodenough, in scattered references, recognized the potentialities for personality analysis that her test held, although she concerned herself primarily with the human figure as an IQ index. The many studies that followed, either to confirm or to dispute Goodenough's contentions, contained new and original suggestions regarding personality variables.

The writer's technique of personality evaluation through the drawing of a human figure originated in the routine application of the Goodenough test to children for measurement of intelligence. It became increasingly apparent that children receiving the same IQ on the Goodenough Scale were telling different things. The irrepressible and spontaneous comments of the children, subsequently substantiated and elaborated by guided associations to the figures, testified repeatedly to the validity and richness of the language of the body. Most of the years that followed in the development of the drawing technique were devoted to systematization and decoding of this private, ideographic communication. These efforts were rewarded with comprehension of an ever-extending horizon of graphic detail and variety of projection. Progress became possible only after the basic key was developed—the projection of the body image in its functional implications.

ADMINISTRATION

Administration consists of giving the subject a medium-soft pencil with an eraser on it, and a sheet of blank paper, 8½ x 11 inches in size, with the instructions to "draw a person." With young children, the direction to "draw somebody" may be more easily comprehended. As a last resort, the very young child may be told to "draw a boy or a girl." Whatever the modification, the directions should be as unspecific as possible. If the subject protests that he cannot draw or that he has no talent, he is reassured that the matter of skill does not enter into consideration, since interest is primarily in what people do when they *try* to draw a person. If the subject offers the drawing as completed after he has drawn only a head, he is asked to draw the whole figure, note being made of his reaction.

Except for the possible explanation to draw a full figure, all preliminary questions asked by the subject are answered with a non-
committal "just as you please."

If the test is given individually, the examiner makes unobtrusive
notes of the comments and drawing procedure on another blank
sheet of paper. Upon the completion of one drawing, the subject
is given the blank side of the sheet on which the notes pertaining to
the first drawing were made, with directions to draw a figure of the
opposite sex, as, "now draw a male," if he has already drawn a
female. A set of two drawings, male and female, is thus obtained,
with record of which was done first. Notes regarding comments
and procedures pertaining to the second drawing are made on the
back of the first drawing, now in the examiner's hand. In group
administration, such observations are necessarily sacrificed. In that
case, the subjects are given two sheets of paper and told to make
a drawing on each sheet, one of a male, and the other of a female,
and to indicate which they drew first. If there is time, the subject
is asked to draw "yourself," "a child," or "two people." Children
draw their "family."

As an optional part of the administrative procedure, the examiner may add an inquiry after the pictures are drawn. Figure
1 illustrates a form of inquiry that has been used with children;
Figure 2 shows a form for adults. The subject is requested to
make up a story about this person as if he were a character in a
play or a novel. Questions concerning the age, schooling, occupation, ambition, family, preference for which parent, attitudes toward the body, toward friends, the family, school, sex, and marriage
guide the inquiry. This verbal and more conscious aspect of the
procedure is not an intrinsic part of the drawing technique, but it
offers an opportunity to obtain valuable indirect clinical information about the subject, and it serves for validation of features
graphically portrayed. Most often, the drawings proper are interpreted separately from the verbal associations, and frequently without any associations.

INTERPRETATION

Principles of interpretation have evolved slowly out of the study
of particular drawing traits in coordination with the clinical history
of a subject, supplementary test data, and psychiatric and psycho-

MACHOVER FIGURE-DRAWING TEST (CHILD)

Name_____Birthdate_____Date_____Grade_____

Make up a story about this figure as if she (or he) were a character in a novel or a play
by making up answers to the following questions about her (or him) as well as you can.

1. What is (s)he doing?_____2. How old is (s)he?_____

3. Is (s)he married?_____4. Have children?)_____
                                                    Boys or Girls?)

5. What is her (his) work?_____6. Grade in School_____

7. What is her (his) ambition?_____

8. How smart is (s)he?_____9. How healthy is (s)he?_____

10. How goodlooking is (s)he?_____11. Best part of her (his) body?_____

12. Worst part of her (his) body?_____

13. How happy is (s)he?_____

14. What does (s)he worry about?_____

15. When does (s)he lose her (his) temper?_____

16. What nervous habits does (s)he have?_____

17. What are her (his) 3 worst habits?_____

18. What are her (his) good points?_____

19. Many friends?   )_____
    Older or younger?)

20. What do people say about her (him)?_____

21. How much does (s)he enjoy her (his) family?_____

22. How much does (s)he like school?_____

23. How often does (s)he go out with boys?_____

24. What does (s)he call a good time?_____

25. Will (s)he marry?_____26. At what age?_____

27. What kind of a boy (or girl) will (s)he marry?_____

28. What are her (his) 3 main wishes?_____

29. Of whom does (s)he remind you?_____30. Like to be like her (him)?_____

31. Write anything you wish to add_____

Note: Mark the number 1 on top of the page of the figure that you drew first. Put a check
       mark next to any of the answers that describe you as well as the figure.

Fig. 1.   Inquiry form used with children.

logical opinion. A substantial library of drawings, annotated in
detail as to history, test data, observations, and diagnosis of the
subject, comprised the basic group for study of the meaning of
specific drawing features. Examination of the record of each of
the individuals in which a particular trait occurred helped to deter-

MACHOVER FIGURE-DRAWING TEST (ADULT)

Male-Female

Name_____ Age_____ Date_____ No._____I-II___
Problem_____Diagnosis_____

(Make a drawing of a person) Remarks and Procedure_____
_____
_____
_____

Associations (Make up a story about this person as if he were a character in a
            novel or a play)
What is he doing?_____How old is he?_____Is he married?___
How many children does he have?___With whom does he live?_____Does he prefer
Does he have brothers and sisters ? _____ his mother or his
What kind of work does he do?_____How much schooling   father?_____
                                      has he had?
What is his ambition?_____How smart is he?_____
How strong is he?_____How healthy is he?_____How goodlooking is he?___
What is the best part of his body?_____What is the worst part of his body?_____

Is he a nervous type?_____What's generally on his mind?_____
What fears does he have?_____What is he sad about?_____
What gets him angry?_____What are his 3 main wishes?_____
What are his good points?_____What are his bad points?_____
Does he prefer to be alone or with people_____What do people say about him?
Is he a suspicious type?_____

How does he get along with his wife (or parents, if unmarried)?_____
Was he ever separated?_____Does he run around with other women?_____
Does his wife run around?_____How does he feel sexually about his wife?_____
When was his first sexual experience?_____Does he have a steady girl
Does he expect to get married?_____(if unmarried)?_____
What type of girl does he like?_____
Did he ever have sex with boys?_____Was he ever approached by a man?_____
How often does he masturbate?_____What does he think about it?_____

Of whom does he remind you?_____Would you like to be like him?_____

Ask subject directly
What is the worst part of your body?_____What is the best part of your body?___
What's good about you?_____What's bad about you?_____

Note: All questions to be adjusted for age and sex of the subject. Positive answers
of clinical interest should be followed with inquiry. Mark doubtful features of
figure and clothing of the person drawn. Ask subject if any of the traits given
the characters could be applied to himself (last question useful, if time permits).

Fig. 2. Inquiry form used with adults.

mine the meaning that that particular drawing trait had for the
particular individual. Through such detailed clinical study, it was
possible to arrive at a fairly extensive system of interpretation.
These interpretations have met and are continuing to meet rigorous
standards of specific clinical validation in each case studied.

Throughout this period, the "draw-a-person" method was extended to subjects of all ages and clinical conditions. Male and female figures were obtained from each subject, and thematic associations (Figures 1 and 2) supplemented the drawing records.

Underlying the drawing technique is the wide and basic assumption that personality develops not in a vacuum, but through the movement, feeling, and thinking of a specific body. It is because the body, with its visceral tensions and muscular strains, is the battleground for the warring factions of needs and presses (to use Murray's terms), that it provides the focus for the study of personality. In general terms, the drawing of a person represents the expression of self, or the body, in the environment. What is expressed may be characterized as a *body image,* a term that has been described variously by different authors. Briefly put, the body image may be regarded as the *complex reflection of self-regard— the self-image.* Woven into this concept, as Kubie says, is "the body, its parts, its products, and its needs." Schilder [37], who has contributed most to the understanding of the body image, particularly in its pathological manifestations, stressed the fact that early libidinal fixations, attitudes toward openings and excretions, and anxiety about body functions, may be its main determinants.

Expanding knowledge of psychosomatic medicine reveals that organs tend to have emotional meaning specific to them. Minor body insults may be recorded in the drawings of body-concentrated narcissists, long beyond conscious recall of the incident that produced them. Orthopedically handicapped persons show complex reactions to their damaged body images. The body image—in broader terms, the self—tends to develop slowly. It is plastic and responsive to disease, trauma, emotional regression, and treatment. Old, primitive, and regressed individuals, who are no longer plastic, give the same drawing from one time to the next, while young and growing persons, as well as persons who are responding to treatment, tend to give variations of drawing projections consistent with the variations in their personality. The body image may be altered not only by injury, but also by tattooing, cosmetics, or clothing. In the phenomenon of depersonalization, the body image becomes confused with the environment, and the self as a unit of reference loses its boundaries. This is often expressed in drawings by a compensatory effort to reinforce and bind body walls in order better to contain and delineate ego boundaries. Strong emotions like hate, fear, aggression, or love, tend to bind the body image into a unique postural model that sets the tone of a drawing, even in the most unskilled.

When someone sets out to "draw a person," he must necessarily refer to all of the images of himself and of other persons that crowd his mind. Since the organization of the self in terms of central focus and attitudes is essentially selective, that is, it is a product of experience, identifications, projections, and introjections, it follows naturally that the composite image that constitutes the figure drawn is intimately tied to the self in all of its ramifications. Individual "persons" known to us are legion, and in the process of creating the figure, some conscious and some subliminal determinants are at work to guide us through a fluent unit representation of the body. It has been found that various sources are tapped. Morphological, age, and sex determinants constitute the more general sources from which we draw aspects pertinent to ourselves. Images of cultural and social stereotypes make their contribution to our conception of a "person." Tall, lean, asthenic persons are associated with certain psychological attributes in our minds, while persons with other types of physique are identified with other temperaments. Strong arms, thick necks, long noses, small hands, cosmetics, and the infinite details that constitute the person, are weighted with their social meanings. Combining with these social images are the images arising from our own private experience, unique to ourselves. All of these images intermingle to produce the subtle and complex projection of the self. On a more unconscious level are added the symbols that have universal meanings—symbols that have been analyzed in psychoanalytical literature and popularized in folklore.

That the task of drawing a "person" is a creative experience has been attested by all introspective accounts. The motor and expressive aspects, which, for purposes of analysis, are regarded as the formal and structural characteristics of a drawing, are inextricably woven into the content of the drawing. It is at this point that the drawing of a human figure departs from some of the principles derived from expressive movement in other contexts. *How* we say things graphically, which is the expressive aspect, depends upon *where, in what part of the figure,* it is being said, and upon *what is* being said in terms of content of the figure. The expressive aspect, that is, the distribution of graphic energy, as indicated by omissions, disturbance of line, perspective, reinforcements, erasures, or shading, must be interpreted in light of the meanings that one attaches to the various parts of the body. The drawing gives location of conflict.

Whether the organs that are stressed are related to the functions of social communication, to ideation, to nourishment and dependency needs, to brawn, to sexual potency, to fertility, to growth, to mobility, or to contact of one's body with the world about him, depends largely upon his system of aspiration, his needs, and his frustrations. Take, for example, the burly and powerful lumberjack who gives an uncertain, tiny, and shrunken figure. On the other extreme, a frail, undernourished, and effeminate male may sustain his fantasy with a graphic image of manliness and virility.

In another instance, a girl expressed glamour aspirations in the head area while giving the figure an obese and ungainly body. This girl was a severe feeding problem, as was confirmed by the treatment of the mouth, among other parts of the figure. The drive for compensatory weight in this underdeveloped girl forced her to an obese body projection although it was inconsistent with the glamour inclinations suggested by the face treatment. Then again, concern about actual obesity may produce overslenderization of a figure, and at other times it may be expressed by the fuzziness of the body walls, or a double effect given to those walls. In any case, the body image projected may refer to the subject's deepest wishes, to a frank exposure of defect, to vigorous compensation for defect, or to a combination of all three factors. When rational control is weakened, either by virtue of organic brain disease or of functional psychosis, any kinds of distortions, inconsistencies, or disproportionate organ emphasis may emerge, often creating bizarre effects. Further, when the drawing projection is markedly different from the race, age, and sex of the subject, some difficulty in normal indentifications may be assumed. Thus, when a white person projects a Chinese figure, when a pyknic, squat type, gives a tall, asthenic person, when an old woman gives a relatively youngish drawing, when a young person gives the figure of an older person, when a female gives the drawing of a male first, or vice-versa, instability of role in the sphere in which the deflection occurs is indicated.

Young people generally draw similarly to the way they express themselves in other mediums. Their patterns are larger, firmer, and richer in detail than those of old people. Individual exceptions do occur. A young child, who has not yet fully differentiated the sense of self from apperception of other parts of his environment, will most frequently give a head with some facial features interpreted as having social connotations contained in it, and with many appendages issuing from it. While this type of representation of a "person" accords with the experience determinants and needs of a child, it would be interpreted, depending upon context, as regression or low-grade defective development if offered by an adult. In hysterical and infantile adults, similar to children, the body, that is the trunk, is conceived of as a container of vague, mysterious, and silent organs. The head, as an organ of dependency and social communication, receives central attention, while the body is underplayed. With the increasing individuation, consolidation, and stability of the sense of self, body image projections become more stable and elaborated. Variations in drawing from test to test are therefore greater in the young than in the older person. Such variations are also more frequent with the ambivalent and vacillating person than they are with the self-confident individual. In adolescence, the crystallized child-self undergoes much reorganization, and the toying with many selves that is seen in this period is reflected in variability of drawing projections.

Among the many types of body image projections possible, a type that often appears more pathological at first glance than it really is, is the empty, abstract, oversimplified, geometric version of a "person." These drawings are often produced with indifference, giving concession only to the essential parts of a figure. They are diagrammatic and remote, and in those terms, may be regarded as a blueprint of the subject's emotional constriction. They represent egocentric persons whose social participation and warmly responding aspect of personality are blocked by concentration on their own needs. Interest in concrete, objective, and neutral detail is minimal, except as it fits in with the subject's immediate preoccupation. Again, in a child, such drawings may be appropriate to normal growth phases, while in an adult of average intelligence, they are generally significant of neurosis, hypochondriasis, depression, psychotic regression, or proneness to psychosomatic disorders. Hys-

terics frequently give this body-concentrated, infantile type of drawing. From the expressive movement standpoint, the circle is
considered to be primitive, effeminate, submissive, and narcissistic,
while the more angled forms imply aggression, masculinity, and
critical traits. Occasionally, a subject may offer such simple drawings evasively, in the same spirit as he offers a line or peanut-man
drawing. In most instances, the flippancy is noted, and the subject
can be encouraged to give a more sober representation of the human
figure. In any case, any stylistic drawing, whether it be simplified,
facetious, or cartooned, lends itself to detailed analysis despite the
intent of the subject to clown. No two persons evade or fool in the
same way. Individuals who give such drawings tend to handle
their problems in concealed and exhibitionistic ways. The simplest
arrangement of lines intended to constitute a "person" may be
revealing, since such factors as placement, size, pressure, joining,
proportions, differentiation of detail, and general distribution of
graphic energy can be immensely revealing.

In analyzing a drawing, impressions gained from the first glimpse
are largely determined by the postural model of the figure, to which
facial expression contributes greatly. Is the mood and tone of the
figure vigorous, is it collapsed, active, bewildered, or inconsistent?
The type of line and strength of appendages add much to the over-
all impression. The figure may be rigid or tense, or may show
undue emphasis of symmetry, armatures, or artificial props. Expansiveness, constriction, depression, vanity, daydreaming, or hate
may be the central expressive core around which authentic unit
impressions crystallize.

Conflict may be expressed in a variety of ways. A subject may be
reluctant to draw, draw only parts of the body, ask many preliminary questions, or draw the opposite sex first. Conflict may be
expressed in drawing the sex, age, or body type inconsistent with
the subject's own, or in forcing an area into view by bold disproportion or strained perspective. More direct and conscious expressions of conflict are manifested in the dissatisfaction shown by
erasures and by temperamental and aggressive reinforcement of line.
On a deeper level, conflict may emerge as shading, which is indicative of anxiety. This shading may be random and feverish in its
release of psychomotor tension, or it may be the more rationalized,

designed, and socially sublimated type of shading, which is usually identified by the subject as coloring or clothing.

The most pathological form of conflict expression is transparency. In transparency we see the ideoplastic and concrete thinking of childish and primitive mentality. Its behavioral equivalent is poor judgment. If it is confined to a specific functional area of an adult drawing, the poor judgment relates to that functional part. However, when it is characteristic of the entire drawing, the likelihood is that we are dealing with profound disturbances in judgment, which, if not consistent with the IQ and cultural background of the subject, may signify schizophrenia.

The task of unravelling the graphic communication contained in a drawing involves the study and integration of many aspects of the figure. Space limitation prohibits detailed theoretical and interpretative discussions covering all the considerations. Although it is possible to classify large areas of interpretations of both structural and content factors, it is not logically feasible to cover the multitude of possible graphic treatments in every detail. The system of interpretation that has been devised, and is continually under scrutiny and refinement, covers the meanings of most of the common details. A psychologist with understanding of projective processes can, with this basic orientation, work out the meanings of unusual details. Experience and research have proven that the basic key to understanding the human figure projection has now been forged. Among the structural features that are considered are size of the figure, pressure of line, placement on the page, theme, stance of figure, background, exactness, degree of completion and detailing, symmetry, midline emphasis, perspective, proportions, shading, reinforcements, and erasures. Of equal importance is the content of the drawing. This consists of all the individual parts of the body, the clothing, and the accessories, functionally interpreted, as well as the facial expression and postural tone of the figure.

Head. The interpretative significance of the figure drawn may be divided into large functional categories. Considered in general terms, the head and facial features are expressive of social needs and responsiveness. In the treatment of that area, we find projection of intellectual aspirations, a drive for rational control of impulses, and/or fantasy elaboration of the personality. The head is the first part of the body drawn by children, and often all that remains in the senile or deteriorated person. The body, reservoir of rejected and conflicted drives, of growth and activity potentials, and equally of decline possibilities, is more changeable with age and accident of life than the head. Most frequently, it is the head that is articulated with detailed skill and care, while the body is fragmented, schematized, or broken. The head is the most consistently exposed part of the body, and according to many investigators, is the locus of the "self."

A disproportionately large head may appear for a variety of reasons. In one subject, it may reflect over-valuation of the brain because of frustration due to mental retardation. Or it may appear because an educational disability in a person of normal intelligence has marred adjustment. Another individual gives the head emphasis because organic injury has left it painful and oversensitive to stimulations. Still another gives prominence to the head because of intellectual or perhaps moral vanity. Fantasy preoccupations may also produce a large head, because the person "lives there." The large head is favored by children and dependent persons because it is the central organ of social communication and dependence. Pronounced bulge of the forehead or the occipital region may signify emphasis on brain power. Oddly shaped heads are common in organic cases whose brain functioning is "oddly shaped."

Eyes. Facial features refer primarily to social communication. Large eyes may absorb the world visually, while small or closed eyes may exclude it. They may be "popeyed" with sexual excitation or voyeurism. The eyes may be the reservoirs of uncertainty, of bewilderment, or of fear. They may be paranoid in their wariness, or crossed out in guilt for what they have seen. Display and sexual appeal values of the eyes may be accomplished by cosmetization with long lashes. As "windows of the soul" they may reveal a life of autism and self-absorption. The pupil, as the seeing portion of the eye, may be omitted in the egocentric, hysterical individual who feeds parasitically upon what he views, but never uses the eye as an instrument of objective discrimination. The opposite is seen in the sharp dot for the pupil without benefit of an eye orbit. This denotes the penetrating wariness, and limited range of vision of the paranoid personality, where the eye is used primarily as a tool of defense, and everything that is seen has a self-referred and circumscribed meaning.

Ears. The ear, though a less conspicuous and less esthetic organ, nevertheless occupies an important role in the vigilant economy of the body. In the paranoid individual, or the person who suffers from acquired deafness *(frequently with paranoid irritations)*, the ears are the central organs of functional concentration. Disturbances or distortions of ear treatment may mean anything from mild sensitivity to social criticism, to systematized paranoia, depending upon the degree of irregularity. Gross distortion of the form of the ear, marked displacement, or odd detailing and "activity" in the ear, are usually more pathological than emphasis by size or reinforcement.

Nose. The nose, which is less important than the eyes and more important than the ears in the esthetic constitution of the face, carries the weight of sexual symbolism. Since, except for the penis, it is the only protrusion in the midline of the body, and since, like the penis, it is an "emitting" organ, the nose receives frequent attention in the sexually conflicted male. It is primarily a male symbol. A strong nose is masculine and assertive in our social stereotypes. Conflict treatment of the nose may involve shading, crossing out, or cutting a part off in a sort of castration. It may, as a symbol of restitution in the impotent male, be overextended, sometimes to a ridiculous length.

Hair. In the sphere of sexual symbolism, the hair also plays an important role. Folklore, psychoanalytic investigations, and the associations of individuals who are conversant with unconscious meanings, abound with references to nose and hair symbolism. Hair relates to sensual needs, and perhaps indirectly, to sexual vitality. It is more primitive and childish as a sexual projection than the nose, tie, or primary sex features. The pubertal girl is constantly concerned with hair on the head, as well as with the hair on less exposed parts of the body. As an expression of sexual preoccupation, hair emphasis is seen mostly in drawings of infantile or regressed adults. Hair "excitement" refers to arousal of infantile sexual drives.

Mouth. Another erogenous and frequently conflicted area is the mouth. It is an organ of early fixations and lends itself to numerous

sublimated forms of concentration.   We see mouth emphasis associated with feeding difficulties, speech disturbances, profane language, intemperate outbursts, alcoholism, excessive eating, and the
more subtle form of verbal sadism.   Graphically, it may be presented in concave and dependent forms, or in more compensatory
aggressive forms.   Not infrequently, it is projected as an organ of
specific sexual perversion, and in more moderate form, as an erotic
and sensual zone.

Other Body Features.   Proceeding further down the figure, we
find *chest* emphasis, broad shoulders, and/or large muscles, the
major concern of those preoccupied with physical power.   It may
be a frail, undernourished, effeminate adolescent who is compensating, or it may be a true self-portrait of the "body beautiful."   As
a phase of development, this treatment is not uncommon in adolescent boys.   Stressed in the extreme, it may represent a pathological
degree of body concentration.   In drawings of the female, the area
of the chest is related primarily to *breast* development.   Acknowl-
edgement of this sexual characteristic is important in connection
with the acceptance of the female role in growing girls.   Emphasis
upon the breasts is seen in infantile, orally deprived males who are
attached to a dominant mother-figure.   Large breasts drawn by a
female are interpreted as identification with a dominant mother.
In drawings by male subjects, when breast emphasis is combined
with focus on the buttocks, or when high heels on the male are
found with dandy clothing and other effeminate features, we may
look for homosexuality.   Hipline emphasis in the female subject,
if on the drawing of the self-sex, suggests interest in pelvic extension
and childbearing.   When males emphasize hips on the self-sex
drawing, homosexual problems are implied.   The crotch in the
male drawing is another area where sex attitudes may be expressed.
Legs, because of their proximity to genital areas, also have sexual
connotations.

The *neck,* which is a silent and not too arresting area esthetically,
is tremendously important in drawing interpretation because of its
strategic location in the body.   Functionally, it serves as a passage-
way between the impulse-laden body and the rationalizing, integrating, and sublimating "functions" of the brain.   Since the control of
impulses, particularly in prohibitive cultures, is a central problem
of ego integration in most individuals, the neck is a frequent area

of conflict expression.   The neck may be disturbed as a locus for fellatio, strangulation impulses, or even of asthmatic difficulties.

In the tight *waistline,* we may see more evidence of restraint and inhibition.   The waistline is the line of demarcation between what in the male is the chest area of physical power (and in the female, the area of nourishment) and the genital region of the body.   Because of its importance as a boundary, it may receive emphatic treatment, or the subject may refuse to proceed beyond the waistline.   At other times, the area below the waistline may be dimmed out, or it may be reinforced in aggressive reaction to conflict.   The neckline, and overdetailing in that area, may also serve as a line of demarcation.   It may be an effort to zone the body so that it can be mastered in small, regulated, and departmentalized sections.

Restraints and efforts at control may also be conveyed by the "mittening" of the hands, special parts in the hair, barrettes, bows, laces on shoes, and other restraining yet socially decorative devices. Blunting or inhibition of aggression may also be effected by encasement of aggressive fingers or toes.

In the *stance* of a figure, we see the subject's security of footing. Stance may also refer to attitude toward movement, activity, self-assertiveness, and even sexual activity, since the stance involves the legs, which functionally touch upon all of these problems.   In addition to maintaining the spatial stability of the body, the legs also represent contact with the environment.   The *foot* touches the ground, and it may be extended in contact with the horizontal environment outside of the body axis.   Because the feet touch the earth, they may be involved in ideas of germophobia, which are often associated with guilty sexuality.   As an extensive and protruding organ, the foot tends to have some sexual connotations. In drawings, we find foot symbolism frequent in the impotent male and in the sexually undeveloped adolescent male.   Analysis of fetishisms, common anecdotes, and introspective meanings given by tested subjects, testify to the sexual symbolism of the feet.   The foot has aggressive implications, insofar as taking a step is an act of assertion involving the movement of the whole body.

Most involved in contact with persons, with objects, and with our own bodies are the *arms* and the *hands.*   They are the primary extensive organs, and it is with them that we master the physical environment.   When arms are long, and supported by graphic indication of power, they indicate a reaching out, or ambition.   If long and weak, they may indicate a wide horizon of need for support from the environment, but no active manipulation of it.   In the treatment of the arms and hands, we may get information about such personality components as aspiration, confidence, efficiency, aggressiveness, or perhaps, guilt regarding interpersonal or sexual activity.   In the direction of the arm, as well as the vigor and robustness of the extension, is implied the direction of energy output.   It is important to note whether the arms are glued to the body, which can occur to the extent of being "built in" to it, whether they extend out, or whether they extend out and return back to the body.   Hands and feet are most common areas of conflict expression, for reasons that may be understood in social terms. As extremities and points of contact, they bear the weight of guilt, insecurity, and fear, reactions that in our culture have invaded almost all personalities.   *Fingers* vary in their expressiveness.   They may be childishly round, petal-like, and unmanipulative; they may be primitively aggressive, as in stick-fingers; or they may have long, speared, sophisticated, and aggressive qualities.   They may be compressed, expanded compulsively, or one digit may be either overlengthened or cut off, reflecting guilt regarding masturbation.

Clothing.   The significance of clothing that is drawn on the figure is similar to clothing on the live person.   It is interpreted as a need for appearances, for covering up, as a social facade, since basic body-protection, in our civilized world, is only a minor clothing incentive.   Clothing represents the surface level of the personality, either how the person actually is in appearance, or how he would like to appear to others.   It is the socially conventional and sublimated aspect of the drawing.   Conflict expressed in the clothing layer of the personality is usually less deeply hidden than in the body proper.   Nudes offered in response to "draw a person," are relatively rare, and must be distinguished from simple, unelaborated geometric forms.   Frequency of nudes among art students leads one to suspect that they are a psychologically selected group.   Nudes are distinctly individualistic and egocentric.   Children and adolescents almost never give nudes, since they are too dependent upon social support for the definition of their environmental role.   Genital organs, especially on a male, are seldom exhibited except in primitives, schizophrenic adults, and persons in analysis.   Experience with innumerable drawings indicates that such display challenges ordinary social decorum. Sexually preoccupied young children may show genitals.

Hats appear frequently in young children's drawings, when both social presentability and some phallic awakening are acutely at issue. Ties, which constitute one of the few adorments of male attire, are generally regarded as symbols of sexual adequacy, expressed on a social and clothing level. They are favored most in adolescent and young male adult drawings. Belts serve to demarcate the sexual area and fancy buckles "socialize" the dependency inferred from emphasis on the navel. Buttons and pockets are common in the drawings of the mother-dependent and the affectionally or materially deprived, this deprivation serving to prolong dependency. Pockets are also seen as the child's representation of "breasts," and appear precisely in that area before breasts are indicated, suggesting the dynamic connection of pockets and affectional nourishment. The pipe, cigarette, and gun are manifest sexual symbols, and when given particular emphasis and made active, usually represent acute sexual preoccupation. The cane is generally seen as a support or restitution for the impotent. Before the symbol value of an accessory was accepted, it had usually been verified repeatedly in specific case histories.

Structural and Formal Aspects. One could discuss at considerable length the structural or formal phases of a drawing. Mention of only some of the formal traits will be given here, with examples in the illustrative case studies.

Bilateral symmetry, which is stressed to the point of producing rigid effects, denotes an obsessive-compulsive system of emotional control, usually associated with repression, emotional distance, and overintellectualization. Emphasis on the midline of the figure, either in a row of buttons that may be added after completion, or in a body axis line, indicates body preoccupation and feelings of inadequacy. Undue attention to *body joints* suggests extreme somatic preoccupation, while the surfacing of *internal organs* is generally evidence for somatic delusions. The *size of the figure* relates to the fantasy involvement, the degree of realistic self-esteem, or the expansiveness of the subject. *Perspective* indicates the degree of self-exposure, the side that a person presents to the world. *Profile* presentation, regarded as evasiveness, is generally a male characteristic. *Front view,* with its implications of exhibitionism, naivete, and social communicability, is favored by females or socially dependent persons, such as children. Twisted or confused perspective may be seen in individuals who are virtually going in different directions at the same time. Pressure of line, thickness, flow, constancy, direction, and length of strokes, yield judgments regarding confidence, self-assertiveness, withdrawal, stability, and degree of conflict in a person. Disproportion, or any form of disturbed treatment, is interpreted as meaningful in terms of the functional significance of that area.

In comparing the male and female figures done by the same subject, we obtain information regarding the subject's attitude toward the opposite sex, toward his own sex role, toward parental figures insofar as they represent the basis of sexual identifications, and toward the wider sphere of authority. Drawing the opposite sex first, in response to "draw a person," is evidence of confusion of sexual identifications. Preliminary questions about which sex to draw, or any change of goal in that respect while in the process of drawing, are also suggestive on that point. The procedure or succession of drawing, which can only be noted in individual administration, may show irregularities so pronounced as to indicate psychotic disorganization or scattering of thought processes. The number of times a subject returns to alter or otherwise emphasize a particular area, should be noted as an especially significant indicator of conflict at the given point.

Theme or background is rarely active in adult drawings. When theme appears or movement is indicated in adult drawings, the problem of a too-absorbing fantasy life is raised. Often such drawings are given an abundance of detail, reflecting an overideational thought flow. Background, which is seen mostly in children's drawings, may appear in adult drawings in the modified form of a line to lean on as a sort of rest for posing, or a ground line for security of footing. Adolescents may give bus stop, crossing streets, or transportation theme and background, as expressions of their transitory state of mind. Placement on the page corresponds roughly to where the person places himself in the environment. The right side of the page is considered environment-oriented, while the left side is self-oriented.

ILLUSTRATIVE CASE

The following case is offered as illustration of the method of personality analysis through the drawing of the human figure. The detailed points will be given in a didactic rather than a literary or clinical spirit, and will, in certain respects, extend beyond the points discussed above.

Peter: Short Case History. Peter is an eight-year-old child of middle-class parents. His father, a physician, had been overseas for three years. Peter's mother has been distraught, unstable, and restless during the father's absence. She was young, attractive and health-conscious. She vacillated in her management of Peter. Being harassed by her personal frustrations, her patience was short, and indulgence alternated with harsh discipline. In this situational crisis, Peter grew increasingly restless, scattered, aggressive, and attention-seeking; he had night fears; he accused his mother of rejection; and he insisted upon acting as a father replacement, to the extent of sleeping with his mother. Sexual preoccupation, released in the telling of bawdy stories, the use of "dirty" words, and the handling of his genitals, became so extreme as to distress his mother. Superficially, Peter was socially polite; he had cultivated adult manners and had wooed adult favor. The underlying mood was always rebellious and aggressive during this period. Intelligence was superior, and Peter functioned adequately in his appropriate grade.

Drawing Interpretation. When asked to "draw a person," Peter was reluctant *(problems were too acute to face)*. He inquired if he might draw a Nazi officer *(authority-submission complex particularly rife at this time in his parental relationships)*. Peter finally placed the figure of a boy somewhat in the center of the page *(always forced himself into the center of attention)*. Succession of drawing was normal *(thinking is logical and quite conventional in its associative sequence)*. When asked to draw a female, Peter attempted to draw a figure on the reverse side of the page, but soon abandoned that idea and asked if he might draw it on the same side with the male *(must always be close to his mother physically and could not tolerate even graphic separation)*.

In the inquiry about the drawing, Peter said the boy was 12 *(4 years older than Peter—growth needs)*. He is walking through

Fig. 3.   Drawing by Peter, a normal child.

the park *(frequent walks with his mother in nearby park).* The
boy is given no sisters or brothers at first, and then corrected with
"Oh, yes, this is his sister," referring to the girl *(ambivalence about*

being an only child). The boy likes both parents, perhaps he likes the father better, "No, the mother" *(more ambivalence, note obsessive symmetry of drawings as a trait).* The boy is smart, not strong, but just enough to defend himself *(feels physically inferior, awkward in sports).* The boy likes boy friends better, although he has two girl friends. He is not too popular. The worst thing he did was "gypped" a comic book from the store *(all true of Peter).* The best thing the boy did was to save a baby from a fire *(need to do heroic deeds as the father. Also, fire connected with enuresis, now under control).* The nicest part of the boy is his tie *(interest in clothing and phallic strength),* and the worst part is his face *(feels homely, wears glasses, and uncertain of social acceptance).* The boy's ambition is to be a doctor *(like father),* "No, a chemist" *(still body-concentrated and professionally oriented).* He will marry at 25 and reminds Peter of a "dumb jerk" *(is discouraged and dissatisfied).*

The girl is described as eleven *(younger than the boy so that he could have authority over her)* She is just as bad as the boy. She likes the mother better *(Peter regards that as "sissy").* She is smart, but not strong *(true of Peter and his mother).* Nicest part is the dress *(appearances and surfaces),* and the worst part is the hair and the face *(sensual and social aspects rejected as inadequate).* She is sister to the boy in the drawing. She is not popular because she is a tomboy *(confused about masculine girls and effeminate boys).* She has only one or two friends *(feels rather friendless).* She is going to be a nurse *(aspiration lower for girl than for boy).* Nicest thing she ever did was to save a house from burning up *(again, heroism, enuresis, and perhaps his own emotions that are getting out of control).* The worst thing she did was to get mad and throw things at her mother, putting her into the hospital *(rejects his hostility against his mother and saddles it onto the female. Projection of negative traits indicates hostility toward the figure upon which they were projected).* The girl, too, reminds Peter of a "dumb jerk" *(is discouraged about himself and dislikes people at this point, so he cannot tolerate pleasant attitudes).*

In the drawing proper, the theme of walking shows a trend toward activity *(overactive).* The use of background is seen in children who are insecure, need a background for support, and also a stage on which to exhibit themselves. The items in the background are particularly interesting. The apparently tropical tree was reminiscent of a trip to Florida with his mother, at which time he had her all to himself. The tree *(mother symbol)* is drawn with force and aggression. The over-all effect of sturdiness is counter-acted by the leaning and uprooted quality of the trunk *(relationship with mother strong, but threatened with disruption)*. The tree is shaded *(anxiety)*, as are the figures. It also has the combination of masculine *(aggressive, speared branches)*, and feminine, narcissistic, and submissive features *(egg-shaped circles nestled in the center of the branches)*, in line with the theme of aggression-passivity and male-female ambivalence that is characteristic of Peter. The clouds in the sky accent the anxious, depressive, and disrupted quality of the drawings. A ground line is provided for the tree and the female figure only *(mother is now the primary source of insecurity)*. In brief, the presumably warm, tropical scene is fraught with insecurity, ambivalence, and aggressive dangers.

The stance of the male is relatively wide and assertive, but tension is betrayed in the posture of both figures, anxiety in the shaded and small feet, the shading throughout both figures, and the erasures about the chest cavity *(conflict about strength, feels weak)*. The anxiety is fairly rationalized *(in clothing design)*. Body walls of both figures are reinforced *(emotional instability and temperament)*, and smudgy *(anal-erotic interest expressed in sexual profanity)*. The male figure is top-heavy, with an oversized head *(intellectual aspiration and verbal drive in Peter and his home)*. The head con-tour is drawn with heavy pressure *(need for social participation)*, while the top of it is left open for the filling in of hair *(common in young girls' drawings where sensual needs are primary to intellectual needs in the self-image)*. The hair of the male is chaotic *(heightened sensual crisis)*. The facial features, with extra lines on the face *(maturity item)*, and large nose *(phallic symbol)*, are those of an older person *(drive for father replacement active at this time)*. The meticulous and manly clothing *(accent on social appearances and father replacement drive)* is elaborated with an oversized tie *(socialized expression of phallic symbol)* that Peter takes care to keep in place *(control)*. Buttons down the midline of the male give testi-mony to the close connection of mother dependency and body pre-occupation, which is specific for this case.

The trousers are reinforced with extra shading, only vaguely rationalized into design. Further isolating the area of sexual

anxiety and conflict is the strong belt emphasis, which cuts off the
genital area, and the shifting of that part of the figure off the body
axis line. Both figures tend toward some asymmetry and "off-base"
effect in the coordination of their parts *(a sense of disjointedness
characterized by Peter's awkward and restless movements)*. The
uneven arms and arm-pit areas contribute to this tilting effect *(confusion of lateral dominance giving a neuro-motor basis to the awkwardness)*. The feet are relatively small *(effeminate and insecure)*.
The neck of the male, contrary to that of the female, is wide, and
not long *(Peter is self-indulgent, has strong need for uninhibited
self-expression, while the bottleneck of the female, which is erased
and reinforced, is the restraining and rationalizing force of the
mother)*. The arms are strong *(aggressive contacts, energetic)*, but
they are cut off somewhat abruptly in length *(applies brakes sharply
in behavior)*. The arms do extend toward contact in the environment, but extension is very uncertain and self-conscious *(sort of
compromising between enterprise and reaching outward, and narcissistic recall)*. The hands fan out *(compulsive)*, but they are not too
well articulated *(achievement minimal)* in contrast to the meticulousness of the drawing. Ears, which are often omitted in drawings
of children, are fairly pronounced *(oversensitivity to social opinion
and criticism)*. The eyes lack the main seeing instrument, the pupil
(egocentricity). Lines are generally forceful *(aggressive and assertive)*, but are represented by many variations of pressure *(moody and
unstable behavior)*. Clothing reaches up to the neck, and the neckline of the female is stressed *(concealment of exhibitionistic and perhaps voyeuristic trends of Peter)*. Heavy lines of the skirt of the
female confirm this furtive sexual curiosity *(sleeps with mother and
is greatly interested in her body)*.

The female figure, although described as only one year younger,
is much smaller than the male *(narcissistic concentration, need for
masculine superiority, and general deprecation of the female in the
associations)*. She is close to him, but not touching him, and her
arm is very short *(need for mother, fear of rejection by her—she is
close, but not in his grasp)*. The long skirt is a maternal touch
(drawn when the style was for shorter skirts). Neither the male nor
female look like children, either in posture, clothing, or mood, although they are described as such. They appear depressed, preoccupied, overdressed, and restrained. The smallness of the figure

is in line with the unhappy and shut-out facial expressions *(repression and depressive features).* The female looks worried *(just as the mother always does),* and the eyes shut out the world *(mother is self-absorbed and does indeed shut out the world and the critical needs of her son).* The hairdress, which is empty *(lack of confidence about sensual acceptance by the mother of his sensual needs)* and overcontained, is precisely the style worn by the mother. Body shading in both figures refers to the body preoccupation and health concern of both mother and son. Head contour and facial features of the female are dimmer than those of the male *(mother is uncertain and shy).* The forehead is covered with hair in both figures *(conflict between sensual and intellectual needs),* which focuses a problem of both mother and son.

The drawings of human beings that this child makes reveal conflict, with positive elements of strength combined with his weaknesses, with maturity combined with infantility, and with dominance needs combined with dependency. Precocious intelligence, as well as an active growth drive (somewhat overweaning at this point), are manifest in the particular problems that are expressed as well as in the graphic quality of his drawings. Active shading, denoting anxiety; restless erasures, denoting dissatisfaction; modulation of line tensions, signifying emotional and expressive richness and controlled efforts to cope with anxiety; obvious alertness to detail; and good imaginative powers, constitute positive elements that augur favorable outcome for this temporary disturbance.

SUMMARY

This chapter deals briefly with the origin and history of drawings of the human figure as a device in studying personality. Directions are given for administering the drawing procedure. The theoretical framework underlying the method is reviewed and the principles of interpretation of drawings of the human figure are discussed. An illustrative case is given, which integrates the interpretation of the drawings with other case material.

REFERENCES

1. Alschuler, R. H., and Hattwick, L. W., *Painting and Personality, A Study of Young Children* (2 vols.). Chicago: University of Chicago Press, 1947.

2. Anastasi, A., and Foley, J. P., Jr., "A survey of the literature on artistic behavior in the abnormal. III. Spontaneous productions." *Psychol. Monogr.*, 1940, 52, 71 ff.

3. —————, "A survey of the literature on artistic behavior in the abnormal. II. Approaches and interrelationships." *Ann. N. Y. Acad. Sci.*, 1941, 42, 166 ff.

4. —————, "A survey of the literature on artistic behavior in the abnormal. I. Historical and theoretical background." *J. Gen. Psychol.*, 1941, 25, 111–132.

5. —————, "A survey of the literature on artistic behavior in the abnormal. IV. Experimental investigations." *J. Gen. Psychol.*, 1941, 25, 187–237.

6. Bender, L., "Art and therapy in the mental disturbances of children." *J. Nerv. Ment. Dis.*, 1937, 86, 249–263.

7. —————, "The Goodenough test in chronic encephalitis in children." *J. Nerv. Ment. Dis.*, 1940, 91, 277–286.

8. Despert, J. L., *Emotional Problems in Children.* New York: New York State Hospitals Press, 1938.

9. Dunlap, K., "The development and function of clothing." *J. Gen. Psychol.*, 1928, 1, 64 ff.

10. Elkisch, P., "Children's drawings in a projective technique." *Psychol. Monogr.*, 1945, 58 ff.

11. Eng, H. K., *The Psychology of Children's Drawings.* London: Kegan Paul, Trench, Trubner & Company, Ltd., 1931.

12. England, A. O., "A psychological study of children's drawings." *Amer. J. Orthopsychiat.*, 1943, 13, 525–530.

13. Federn, P., "Narcissism in the structure of the ego." *Intern. J. Psycho-Analysis*, 1928, 9, 401 ff.

14. Flugel, J. C., "Clothes symbolism and clothes ambivalence." *Intern. J. Psycho-Analysis*, 1929, 10, 205 ff.

15. —————, *Psychology of Clothing.* London: Hogarth Press, Ltd., 1930.

16. Freud, S., *New Introductory Lectures in Psychoanalysis.* New York: W. W. Norton & Company, Inc., 1938.

17. Goodenough, F. L., *Measurement of Intelligence by Drawings.* Yonkers, N. Y.: World Book Company, 1926.

18. —————, "Studies in the psychology of children's drawings." *Psych. Bull.*, 1928, 25, 272–283.

19. Guttman, E., and Maclay, W. S., "Clinical observations on schizophrenic drawings." *Brit. J. Med. Psychol.*, 1937, 16, 184–205.

20. Harms, E., "The psychology of formal creativeness. I. Six fundamental types of formal expression." *J. Gen. Psychol.*, 1946, 69, 97–120.

21. Kemple, C., "A comparative study of three projective methods. A case of rheumatic heart disease." *Rorsch. Res. Exch. & J. Proj. Tech.,* 1947, 11, 26–41.

22. Levy, D., "Body interest in children." *Amer. J. Psychiat.,* 1932, 12, 295 ff.

23. Lewis, N. D. C., "Graphic art productions in schizophrenia." *Proc. Ass. Res. Nerv. & Ment. Dis.,* 1928, 5, 344–368.

24. Liss, E., "The graphic arts." *Amer. J. Orthopsychiat.,* 1938, 8, 95–99.

25. Lowenfeld, V., *The Nature of Creative Activity.* New York: Harcourt, Brace and Company, Inc., 1939.

26. Machover, K., "A case of frontal lobe injury following attempted suicide." *Rorsch. Res. Exch. & J. Proj. Tech.,* 1947, 11, 9–21.

27. ————————, *Personality Projection in the Drawing of the Human Figure.* Springfield, Ill.: Chas. C. Thomas, 1948.

28. Machover, S., "Manic-Depressive Psychosis, Depressed Form," in A. Burton and R. E. Harris (eds.), *Case Histories in Clinical and Abnormal Psychology.* New York: Harper & Brothers, 1947, pages 115–145.

29. Margolis, M. F., "A comparative study of figure-drawings at three points of therapy." *Rorsch. Res. Exch. & J. Proj. Tech.,* 1948, 12.

30. Mateer, F., *The Unstable Child.* New York: The D. Appleton Company, 1924.

31. McCarty, S. A., *Children's Drawings.* Baltimore: Williams & Wilkins, 1924.

32. Mira, E., "Myokinetic Psychodiagnosis: A new technique for exploring the conative trends of personality." *Proc. Roy. Soc. Med.,* 1940, 33, 173–194.

33. Munroe, R. L., "The Case of a Mal-Adjusted College Student," in A. Burton and R. E. Harris (eds.), *Case Histories in Clinical and Abnormal Psychology.* New York: Harper & Brothers, 1947, pages 628–650.

34. Naumberg, M., "Studies of the 'free' art expression of behavior problem children and adolescents as means of diagnosis and therapy." *Nerv. & Ment. Dis. Monog.,* 1947, 71 ff.

35. Ross, N., "The postural model of the head and the face." *J. Gen. Psychol.,* 1932, 7, 144 ff.

36. Sanborn, H. C., "The function of clothing and adornment." *Amer. J. Psychiat.,* 1927, 38, 1 ff.

37. Schilder, P., *The Image and Appearance of the Human Body.* Psyche Monographs No. 4. London: Kegan, Paul, Trench, Trubner & Company, Ltd., 1935.

38. Shaskan, D., Alper (Machover), K., Yarnell, H., "Physical, psychiatric, and psychometric studies of postencephalitic Parkinsonism." *J. Nerv. & Ment. Dis.,* 1942, 96, 652 ff.

39. Waehner, T. S., "Formal criteria for the analysis of children's drawings." *Amer. J. Orthopsychiat.*, 1942, 12, 95–104.

40. Waehner, T. S., "Interpretation of spontaneous drawings and paintings." *Gen. Psychol. Monog.*, 1946, 33, 3–70.

41. Williams, J. N., "Interpretation of drawings made by maladjusted children." *Virg. Med. (Semi) Mon.*, 1940, 67, 533–538.

42. Wolff, W., *The Expression of Personality: Experimental Depth Psychology.* New York: Harper & Brothers, 1943.

43. ————————, *The Personality of the Pre-school Child.* New York: Grune & Stratton, 1946.

CHAPTER 13

Spontaneous Drawings of the Human Form in Childhood Schizophrenia[1]

J. ALLISON MONTAGUE, M.D.

INTRODUCTION

Children enjoy drawing and usually do so spontaneously, thereby making a graphic projection of the problems they are trying to solve in their struggle to mature. The problems expressed are inevitably those that concern all growing human beings: learning to achieve an active mastery of the physical, social, and emotional realities that must be constantly dealt with in every integrated adaptation. Schizophrenic children are no exception. They, too, are trying to solve human problems and to grow. They have, however, one additional reality to come to terms with—the biophysical reality of the schizophrenic process itself, a pathological phenomenon that alters the quality of their experience (especially in the sense of the German *Erlebnis,* as used by Rorschach [17] and Wittels [21]), and calls forth unique modes of mastery. At times it threatens to pinch off and obliterate all growth potentialities within the affected organism, causing sterile, circuitous, internal forms of release of energy [8].

Many types of defense are erected against the onslaught of the

---

[1] From a study made in the children's ward of Bellevue Psychiatric Hospital on a research fellowship granted through New York University College of Medicine by the Committee on Research in Dementia Praecox, Supreme Council, 33° Scottish Rite, Northern Masonic Jurisdiction, U. S. A.

370

illness. Mahler and his co-workers [*16*] have formulated and classi-fied these types. One such defense that they describe, which a suitably gifted schizophrenic child may use as a powerful coun-tertendency against the disintegrating threat of the psychosis, is a kind of hypercreativity that may lead him at certain stages of his illness to be a veritable dynamo of creative activity. At such times, he may draw and continue to draw during a large share of his waking hours, until the course of the illness changes significantly and a different mode of defense comes into the foreground of his behavior. In the height of their productivity, such children may be ravenous for opportunities to make graphic projections. The latter may be seen to cover all available exposed surfaces (as well as many hidden ones) in the child's environment. The production of a given child may be prodigious, but is seldom satisfying to him. Indeed, if such works are not rescued by an outsider, they are often destroyed by the child. It is as though significant contact could be felt only with the child's own drawing of the moment, and he tries repeatedly to create a form with which he can identify in order to feel safe from the disintegrating effects of the disease process.

Execution, in line with schizophrenic children's own motor tend-encies, is swift and fluid. It is an urgent speeded-up variety of the creative process, which Lee, in writing about poetry production in adolescence, has described as "a legitimate defense against acute in-crements of anxiety" [*15*]. Deutsch, writing on "Artistic Expression and Neurotic Illness," stated: "Art is a product of the fantasy of the artist who attempts to create the most perfect idealized form of reality. The fantasies of the artist are determined by his own relationship to reality which on the other hand depends on his pat-tern to come to terms with it" [*6*]. This describes the situation of the creative schizophrenic child. Unlike the nonpsychotic artist, however, his pattern is ultimately controlled by forces stronger than his own imaginative capacity to deal with them. Indeed, only a few specially gifted ones employ this defense at all, and it disap-pears completely under the following circumstances: (1) when puberty begins; (2) when the illness improves; (3) when the illness progresses. In the latter case, follow-up studies invariably show a picture in which Beck's [*1*] observations regarding defective percep-tion and fantasy in schizophrenia are valid.

THE BODY IMAGE

It is not surprising that the subject most commonly drawn is the human form,[2] for schizophrenic children are continually engaged in an effort to experiment actively with problems concerning the deeply disturbed development of their own body image. Schilder's concept of the body image [18] might be thought of as central to an understanding of all personality projection. He wrote:

The human figure has always been the outstanding subject of the arts. In every art production it is of fundamental importance to analyze the way in which the problem of the human form is handled. In primitive experience the human body has no definite form. Even the concept we have about our own body, the body image, is not fully differentiated. Primitive perception and the dream change the relations of the different parts of the body quite freely, and qualities which belong to one part of the body image may be transposed to other parts. . . . Since the final creation of a distinct picture of one's own body is a product of later development, the schizophrenic often experiences parts of his own body as belonging to external reality, and parts of this reality as belonging to his own body [19].

This is nowhere seen more clearly than in schizophrenic children who demonstrate an ever-present uncertainty in regard to their own ego boundaries.

Related to this problem is the manifest inability of schizophrenic children to identify themselves in time, space, or in relation to any other human being. Unable to individuate, they may openly express feelings of physical connection with the mother, often as a primitive introjection of the mother, which may be drawn in a very literal manner. Various aspects of the interwoven mechanisms of introjection and primitive identification have been dealt with by Klein [14] and Fuchs [10].

Storch's monograph [20] contains descriptions that are particularly illuminating. His quotations from August Strindberg's schizophrenic experience are another version of the problems expressed by schizophrenic children in their drawings as well as their verbalizations. Strindberg wrote, "For me the family has become an organism, such as in plants, a whole of which I am a part. Alone I could not exist, and I could not exist only with the children,

---

2 Other subjects spontaneously drawn are houses, natural scenes, and abstractions.

without their mother.   The family is a network of veins which are knit together; if one is severed my life runs out with the blood that drenches the sand. . . .   If one is exposed to the currents of a woman, which happens for the most part during sleep, one can insulate one's self; by chance one evening I threw a woolen cloth over my shoulder and neck, and that night I was protected, though I still noticed the currents."   (The cape motif, a mantle surround- ing the body, is common in the drawings of schizophrenic children.)

Storch also quotes Strindberg's statement that he had "wrapped himself in the silk of his own soul," and that "when he looked in the mirror after spending the night awake and in conversation it seemed as if he did not recognize his own face.   There were still traces of the persons with whom he had spoken during the night." Also: "Once I shared the pain of a man quite indifferent to me; he had undergone an operation; and so twice I fought the battle of life and death for him, with all the bodily and mental suffering. At another time I passed through three diseases in six hours. When the absent one was released by death, I arose sound again" [20]

An eight-year-old schizophrenic child made the drawings in Fig- ure 1 on pilfered file cards, and verbalized her identification prob- lems as follows:

Picture of me last year.   I had long braids.   I'm so sorry.   I may never have it again.   I had beautiful hair.   I never cut it in my life before last year.   This year I'm having funny days.   Last July I cut my long beauti- ful braids.   Now I'm crying for the whole day—last year my mother was smart.   My mother had long beautiful hair.   Last year was so beautiful in the sky.   This year it is not so good.   I used to wear high braids.   I don't like my name Florence.   If I had long braids I'd call myself Dolores. My mother used to faint if she saw those braids.   This year is such a funny year.   Last year was such a beautiful year.   What do you like— long hair or cut?   I like long hair winter or summer.   You can swim. You know two braids got drowned last year.   Last year we lived on the fifth floor and nobody talked about us.   Now we live on the second floor and everybody calls out about us.   Last year I was beautiful.   I had eye- lashes and lipstick and powder and ear rings and high shoes.   Oh, I was beautiful last year.   I went swimming and I drowned myself.   I want my long braids back again.   I was beautiful last year.   I had nail polish.   My mother was not smarter—I was smarter.   She was more lucky last year —I mean I was in a higher class.   Now they are making marks on me (*What is inside your body?*)   Mummie—skelepin—I rather say skelepin than Mummie.   I had brown shoes last year.   I don't like my name.   I hate it like poison.   Can you change your name?   How?   I want to change

Fig. 1.   Drawings of an eight-year-old girl.

Drawings of an eight-year-old Jewish girl who was functioning at a dull normal level of intelligence.   Her psychosis was fulminating and subsequently progressed to a state of marked deterioration.   While under observation at Bellevue Hospital, she had periods of frantic drawing in which she projected her disturbed body image problems.

---

my name—Dolores—Rose.   I want to dye my hair too.   Shall I dye my hair?   I want to be the same way I was last year.   I can pretend I'm seven and I want to go back to the other school.

DEVELOPMENTAL PATTERNS

A spontaneous drawing, like a dance,[3] a dream, or an autistic stream of thought, is a way of responding to significant inner and outer perceptions, and must inevitably bear the stamp of the prevailing sensory-motor action patterns of the originator. These patterns normally develop through progressive stages of maturation according to biologically determined growth laws. The physical aspects of their development, together with certain behavorial implications, have been most extensively studied by Gesell and Amatruda [11] at the Yale Clinic of Child Development. Their psychological counterparts in the interacting fields of visual perception and motility have been developed by Bender [2,4], who in so doing, freed classical gestalt psychology of certain static concepts by introducing genetic and temporal factors in the perception of visual form.

Bender's material has the special value of including both normal and pathological states (organically as well as functionally determined) in addition to material from a primitive culture in the process of being exposed to "more civilized" influences. Bender's work shows the basic importance of understanding the normal "gestalt function" of the growing human organism before attempting to survey the products of personality projection from the point of view of form principles. The gestalt function is defined as "that function of the integrative organism whereby it responds to a given constellation of stimuli as a whole, the response being a constellation or pattern or gestalt which differs from the original stimulus pattern by the process of the integrative mechanism of the

---

3 Franziska Boas' work on the subject of dance and personality projection is outstanding. In an article entitled, "Psychological Aspects in the Practice and Teaching of Creative Dance," she has stated: "Dance is concerned with the formulation of human fantasy and emotion as projected by the motility of the body passing through time and space. This is not merely the physical body considered in a detached scientific manner but is composed of the actual physical body structure of the dancer together with his subjective conception of that body at the specific moment or moments when it is seen or interpreted by an observer. . . . The dancer must realize the transformation of his outer physical form in relation to postures, tempo and content of his movements and his associated thoughts and emotions. He must be able to change his body image to coincide with the emotional content and physical appearance of his fantasy. . . . The borderline between dance activity as an art and as psychotic movement seems to lie in the ability to organize, consciously control and direct action towards a thematic goal, an ability which the psychotic patient lacks." (From *The Journal of Aesthetics and Art Criticism*, [5].)

individual who experienced the perception.   The whole setting of
the stimulus and the whole integrative state of the organism determine the pattern of the response" [4].

The continued passage of time and growth persistently help the
child toward drawing more "realistic" object representation.   Circular loops are found to be the most primitive unit of form perception, and prevail in the drawings of children until the age of four
years.   From four to seven, there is a rapidly growing capacity to
crystallize perceptual experience into more differentiated forms.
Schilder was especially interested in this problem when he
wrote:

After we have gained an insight into the psychological problems of the
child we must examine the basic form principles appearing in its drawings.   We shall have to ask whether the primitive perceptual units like
the loop, vortex, and curved lines, or geometrical forms which belong to
a later development are more prominent.   We must also consider whether
the forms are geometrical in the narrower sense or whether they approximate the forms which one finds in nature, as in the formation of a river
or a hill, which may be called organic forms.   We will be particularly interested in the attention given to the specific form of animate objects. . . .
In various artistic experiences we note an unquenchable thirst for experimentation and the wish to master parts of reality and reality as a whole,
but the experimentation of the schizophrenic person, the child and the
artist, is incomplete.   The child needs its growth to complete it.   The
schizophrenic reverts to primitive forms under the onslaught of a reality
which he cannot master, but he does not give up the struggle for the
richer world which he finds threatening him.   The so-called normal artist
points again and again toward new structures of reality although he never
reaches a definite end or takes a definite action.   The less he is bound
to convention the freer he is in his experimentation and the greater is his
chance for new discoveries.   A psychosis may help him to get rid of banal
everyday attitudes by opening up the way to new experiences.   He may be
a real artist, with or without a psychosis if his descent to the primitive
layers of experience contains at least a hope for another adaptation to a
world which can be shared by the community [19].

PERCEPTION AND MOTILITY

The content of the psychotic child's drawings and the meaning
of the various mental mechanisms that he employs in his defensive
struggle against his illness can be more completely understood with
the help of psychoanalytic theory (Psycho-economics, Freud [9]).
Fenichel [7], in writing on the "Dynamic, the Economic, and the

Structural Points of View," refers to mental phenomena "as the result of the interplay of forces pressing respectively toward and away from motility." It is the purpose of the present discussion, however, to focus on the endogenous forces in childhood schizophrenia as they distort the total pattern of the child's functioning, especially in the continuously interacting fields of perception and motility. The formative influences of the forces stemming from the environment will not be extensively dealt with, although, of course, they operate continuously in contributing to the total behavior pattern of the schizophrenic child.

It is the specific motility disturbance that is of key importance in understanding the expressive projection of the schizophrenic child from a formal point of view. It manifests itself by a constant appearance of primitive postural reflex responses [13]. Spontaneous or nearly spontaneous fluid whirling around a longitudinal axis, done playfully but compulsively beyond the age where such a pattern is appropriate, is nearly specific for the illness [Bender, 3]. Its presence is, in fact, essential for the diagnosis, unless (as sometimes happens in prepuberty children) it is defended by various catatonic rigidities that differ little from the pre-Kraeplinian descriptions of Kahlbaum.

Another constant accompaniment of childhood schizophrenia is evidence of deep anxiety, which occurs irrespective of the quality of the interpersonal relationships experienced. Although it is influenced by the latter and becomes secondarily entangled with them, it is not primarily caused by them. In this respect it resembles more closely the "predisposition to anxiety" described by Greenacre [12].

The human forms drawn by schizophrenic children at certain stages of their illness reflect the unending struggle with the inner impulse to whirl. Thus rhythmic action of all kinds, with emphasis on whirling, is frequently depicted, often with remarkable clarity and a technical facility that may exceed the expectations for the age or level of intellectual functioning. In such cases, the Goodenough score may be disproportionately high. Either circular movement is used directly or special techniques are applied to indicate whirling. An example of the latter are the barber-pole stripes (painted red and green in the original) shown in Figure 2.

Both primitive and more mature form principles may be seen in

Fig. 2. Drawing of a nine-year-old girl.

Spontaneous human figure drawing of a nine-year-old Negro girl of low average intelligence. Mature form principles prevail, but the underlying whirling motility is nonetheless presented by the use of barber pole stripes. Her psychosis progressed, and she is at present (five years after original period of observation) still in a state hospital.

378

the same drawing, or a circular movement may be used to such an extreme degree that all more differentiated form seems to dissolve in it. The latter process is sometimes seen to develop dramatically when the illness is progressing. More mature formal principles with heightened clarity of object representation may subsequently appear if the child improves and re-integrates at a higher level of functioning. Many of these children have an uncanny capacity to express the grace of movement and varying postures that they themselves demonstrate (varying from extreme fluidity to equally extreme rigidity).

Anxiety may be shown in the facial expression, especially in the treatment of the eyes, which may be unduly emphasized in relation to the rest of the face. Often, however, the entire facial features are vague, ghostlike, embryonic, or entirely missing. Subjective bodily sensations related to the whirling problem may be experienced and thrown out into the drawing. Thus, elongation and distortion of various bodily parts (especially extremities and projecting body parts) are common. (See Figures 1, 3, 4, 5, 6.) Hair, fingernails, ears, and eyelashes are frequently elongated either directly or by the addition of ornaments. Dismembered limbs (Figure 1) and free experimentation with gravity (Figure 3) may be interpreted as part of the same problem of schizophrenic body image disturbance. It is as though the subjects felt inwardly threatened by forces that might spiral them off into space so rapidly that body parts would be whirled off. Eyes may be seen falling out of their sockets. Attempts to counteract this force and "stay on earth" and "inside themselves" may be expressed by overemphasis on body boundaries (Figure 3), by rigid posturing (Figure 4), or, in the case of multiple figure drawings, by careful labeling of identities and ages (Figure 5). The ego boundary problem may also show itself by indefiniteness of boundaries, melting of the figure into the background so that neither stands out clearly, or having the body surrounded by or confluent with a cape, cavern, shadow, or halo, implying a preoccupation with the indefinite nature of the zone of interaction between the ego and the outer world.

Subjective skin sensations (sometimes verbalized as feelings of electricity) have been depicted by drawing fat ladies who are sunburned. Internal sensations may be shown by transparencies and direct representation of inner bodily functions (especially those con-

Human figure drawing made by an 11-year-old girl of mixed Jewish-Catholic background, high average intelligence. Shows primitive and more differentiated form principles interwoven. Boundaries are accentuated. Facial features vague. Her inner impulse to whirl (with resulting preoccupation about flying into space in whole or in part) permeated the theme of every drawing she made. Following a two-month period of observation, she improved and was maintained in the community with psychotherapy until the age of 16, when she became so flagrantly psychotic that commitment was necessary.

Fig. 3. Drawing of an 11-year-old girl.

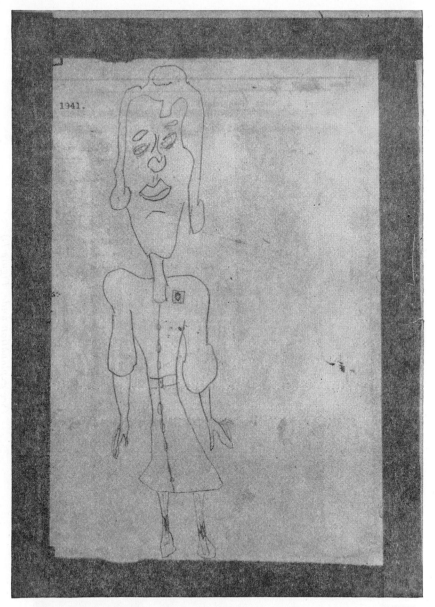

Fig. 4. Drawing of a 12-year-old boy.

Drawing of a 12-year-old Jewish boy of average intelligence. Shows schizophrenic distortion of the body image with rigid catatonic posturing. Insulin therapy was given, but the psychosis progressed rapidly and commitment to a state hospital was necessary.

Fig. 5.   Drawing by the girl who drew Figure 1.
(See explanation under Figure 1.)

Drawing by an eight-year-old girl of Protestant-Dutch background. Onset of psychosis at age of four. Observed at eight and again at 12, at which time she was committed to a state hospital. Her drawings show prevalence of primitive circular movements, schizophrenic distortion and disintegration of the body image, vivid expression of movement, and free experimentation with gravity. Much of her psychic content was related to anxiety regarding oral aggression with attending fear of retaliation. She also showed impulses to scratch the faces and hands of other children.

Fig. 6. Drawing by an eight-year-old girl.

383

nected with the gastrointestinal tract), or of fantasied introjected objects, which are often personalized and experienced as both real and influential.

Color, if used at all, is always cheerful, even when the forms are most vague and shadowy. Extremely bright color combinations are often chosen and the over-all effect may even be dazzling. At other times, pleasant pastel washes may be rapidly applied, producing a remarkable flowing dreamlike quality, which to many observers, leaves an impression of lasting charm.

SUMMARY

Spontaneous drawings constitute one device by which some schizophrenic children attempt to maintain contact with outer reality. The body image is one percept that shows distorted development. The schizophrenic child, uncertain of his own ego boundaries, seems unable to identify himself in time, in space, or in relation to other human beings. These confusions appear in his drawings.

Circular loops, the most primitive unit of form perception, are found in normal children up to the age of four years. In schizophrenic children, however, some representation of a fluid whirling around a longitudinal axis is so common as to be regarded as almost a specific for diagnosis. Examples of drawings of schizophrenic children are used to illustrate perceptual problems found in this disease.

REFERENCES

1. Beck, S. J., "Errors in perception and fantasy in schizophrenia," in J. S. Kasanin (ed.), *Language and Thought in Schizophrenia.* Berkeley, Calif.: University of California Press, 1944.

2. Bender, Lauretta, *A Visual Motor Gestalt Test and its Clinical Use.* New York: The American Orthopsychiatric Association, 1938.

3. ————————, "Childhood schizophrenia." *The American Journal of Orthopsychiatry,* January 1947, 17, 1, 40–56.

4. ————————, *Psychological Principles of the Visual Motor Gestalt Test.* Transactions of the New York Academy of Sciences, March 1949, Series II, Volume II, No. 5.

5. Boas, Franziska, "Psychological aspects in the practice and teaching of creative dance." *Journal of Aesthetics and Art Criticism,* 1943, 7, 1–20.

6. Deutsch, Felix, "Artistic expression and neurotic illness," paper read at Smith College, July 27th, 1947. Privately printed.

7. Fenichel, Otto, *The Psychoanalytic Theory of Neurosis.* New York: W. W. Norton & Company, Inc., 1945.

8. Freeman, G. L., *The Energetics of Human Behavior.* Ithaca, N. Y.: Cornell University Press, 1948.

9. Freud, Sigmund, *Instincts and Their Vicissitudes, Collected Papers,* Volume IV. London: Hogarth Press, Ltd., 1934.

10. Fuchs, S. H., "On introjection," *The International Journal of Psychoanalysis,* 1937, 18, Parts 2 and 3.

11. Gesell, Arnold, and Amatruda, Catherine S., *Developmental Diagnosis.* New York: Hoeber, 1948.

12. Greenacre, Phyllis, "The predisposition to anxiety," *The Pyschoanalytic Quarterly,* 1941, 10, 66–94, 610–638.

13. Hoff, Hans, and Schilder, Paul, *Die Lagerreflexe des Menschen.* Vienna: J. Springer, 1927.

14. Klein, Melanie, *Contributions to Psycho-analysis 1921–1945.* London: Hogarth Press, Ltd., 1948.

15. Lee, Harry B., "Poetry production as a supplemental emergency defense against anxiety." *Psychoanalytic Quarterly,* 1938, 7, 232–242.

16. Mahler, Margaret S., Ross, John R. Jr., and De Fries, Zira, "Clinical studies in benign and malignant cases of childhood psychosis (schizophrenia-like)." *American Journal of Orthopsychiatry,* 1949, 19, 295–304.

17. Rorschach, Herman, *Psychodiagnostics.* Berne: Hans Huber, 1942.

18. Schilder, Paul, *The Image and Appearance of the Human Body.* London: Kegan Paul, Trench, Trubner & Company, Ltd., 1935.

19. ————————, "The theory of art and its relationship to the psychology and psychopathology of children." To be published in Lauretta Bender (ed.), *Techniques in Child Psychiatry.* Springfield, Ill.: Charles C. Thomas, Chapter VIII.

20. Storch, Alfred, "The primitive archaic forms of inner thought and experience in schizophrenia," *Nervous and Mental Disease Monograph Series, Number 36.* New York and Washington: Nervous and Mental Disease Publishing Company, 1924.

21. Wittels, Fritz, "A neglected boundary of psychoanalysis," *Psychoanalytic Quarterly,* 1949, 18, 44–59.

CHAPTER 14

Finger Painting[1]

PETER J. NAPOLI, ED.D.[2]

INTRODUCTION

Finger painting has been known to man since ancient times. Fragments of paintings that bear the imprint of human skin have been found among the ruins of old Roman villas. A Chinese philosopher [4] reported a story of finger tip painting used in China as far back as the seventeenth century.

In the twentieth century, for the first time, record has been made of the use of finger painting as an educational device for children and of its application to recreation, diagnosis of personality, and therapy. Shaw [22] revived the use of finger painting in 1932. Since her unearthing of this medium as a recreational device, finger painting has been extensively developed and used by many others in various fields. Written reports on finger painting are distributed in the fields of fine arts, arts and crafts, recreation, education, occupational therapy, and psychotherapy. In this chapter, the primary concern is to describe and discuss the finger painting process as it has been developed as a projective technique.

Finger paints are plastic materials that the subject places with his bare hand upon a blank sheet of white paper. In this way, he creates and reacts to his own stimulus. As with other projective

1 Sponsored by the Veterans Administration and published with the approval of the Chief Medical Director. The statements and conclusions published by the author are a result of his own study and do not necessarily reflect the opinion or policy of the Veterans Administration.

2 Acknowledgment is made to the Journal Press for permission to use freely the material from the writer's previously published articles.

techniques, the subject is not usually aware of the examiner's purpose while he paints or when he later describes his painting.

The finger painting technique possesses certain advantages over other similar clinical methods. It is one of the least structured mediums, and thus has been found to reduce blocking and resistance. It lends itself particularly to very free associative processes. The freedom of color choice, which is emotionally stimulating, rarely induces rejection. Communication is enhanced because the subject verbalizes his own symbols and projections. Since the directions are simple to follow and the materials are easy to manipulate, this technique can be used by most individuals, regardless of chronological age, sex, or mental capacity. As a clinical instrument, the repetition of the process reinforces rather than invalidates the procedure as a "diagnostic test." The process involves a concept of total personality, inasmuch as the final evaluation includes the subject's physical or motor performance, his painting (the projection), and his verbalization. The technique is especially useful since it can be applied in either an individual or group situation. Finger painting is distinct from other projective techniques in that the temporal sequence of the process involves therapeutic as well as diagnostic values.

The value of finger painting in neuropsychiatry lies in several different fields. As a diagnostic tool in personality evaluation, finger painting, being basically a creative technique not bound down by any rigid forms, shows great promise as a projective instrument. There is much to be desired by way of research before one can gain full benefit from what the technique offers, but this may also be said of the other instruments in clinical practice. Finger painting can be used as recreational therapy for those patients who are relatively well and who enjoy it as they would any other recreational pastime. In occupational therapy, patients who are sick and, on the whole, rather inarticulate, use finger painting as a medium for self-expression, because it is simple and yet creative. The effectiveness with which it is so used depends to a very great extent on the skill of the therapist. In psychotherapy, finger painting is employed as an opening wedge in the patient-therapist relationship. The discussion of certain elements in a finger painting often brings up for the first time conflict-laden ideas that the patient may never have expressed before.

A FINGER PAINTING KIT

The materials necessary for the proper administration of finger painting include three standard pieces of equipment, and other items that may be easily devised. The standard equipment consists of:

1. Any standardized finger painting product, preferably the type that has some body to it in its original form
2. Standard finger painting paper
3. Finger painting record form

The other items that complete the kit include a waterproof surface for painting, a large and a small receptacle, a bucket, spatulas, rags, and newspapers, all of which may readily be purchased or obtained within any hospital or clinic.

The *colors* used, namely, blue, black, brown, green, red, and yellow, should be nonpoisonous, inorganic pigments combined with a water-soluble binder. These characteristics prevent damage to the skin or clothing. The fact that the paints can be easily washed off with clear water has understandable economic and psychological implications. Parents and teachers often forbid the use of finger paint or similar materials lest stained clothing or damaged classroom furniture result. Since this material is to be used in direct contact with the skin, which may occasionally have abrasions or open wounds, it is imperative that it should not cause irritation or infection. Moreover, this inert and water-soluble material should be harmless to the gastrointestinal tract, in case it should inadvertently be tasted or swallowed. There should be no artificial odors that may be suggestive to the individual or influence his reaction.

The *texture* of this medium must be pleasant and soothing, so as to offer a situation conducive to making use of it. The paint should contain no tactually unpleasant qualities. It should be neither tacky nor starchy, neither granular nor slimy, and it should be sufficiently resistant to the hand to initiate warming-up processes. Thus, at the same time, it causes the individual to exert pressure and movement. It is believed that the initial stage of finger painting is a critical point at which the individual begins to digress from the world of reality into his inner psychic world of imagination, creation and projection—if there is no interference during this process. The importance of this stage cannot be too strongly emphasized. Because accurate observations, recordings, and interpretations that follow the finger painting process depend upon the standardization of the essential materials, it has been found inadvisable to use finger paint of the homemade variety when this medium is utilized in either diagnosis or psychotherapy. Any material that contains the qualities mentioned above is considered a standardized medium with which to work.

A recommended *size of paper*, 16 x 22 inches, is the result of experimentation with various age groups. This size offers the small child a long reach, which is necessary because the instructions, explained later, are "to cover the whole sheet of paper and go off the sides of the paper." The young child needs this long reach; the adult, with longer arms, is happy to utilize this size for possible details, since the smaller muscles are more developed at a mature age.

The *paper* itself is impounded on one side with a clay-glazed finish to withstand the rubbing motions and pressures during the painting process. It is on this glazed side that the painting is done. The other side is dull and provides the friction necessary to hold the paper on a water-resistant table while painting.

In the order mentioned, the following materials are best for use as the *base* upon which the paper rests: battleship linoleum, varnished masonite, porcelain, and water-resistant painted surfaces. Any cracks in a surface make that surface inadequate to work upon. For the best working conditions, it is suggested that the surface be much larger than the paper used, in order to allow for going off the edge of the paper. This also permits additional portions of paint to be mixed on the side. It has been found through experience that the minimal size of this basic surface should be 24 x 30 inches.

The *height* of the working surface should vary according to the needs of the individual. A comfortable elevation for work, at which good posture can be maintained, is approximately the height of the lower part of the elbow when the painter is sitting with his arms in painting position. In actual practice, however, one cannot have a series of tables to accommodate all individuals; therefore, the difference in height can be overcome by the subject's making adjustment with the hips and knees. In this way, good posture is maintained without placing a strain on the spine. All adjustments in this regard are made from the hips down.

The *large vessel,* used for wetting the paper, is a pan 16 inches or more in length. A width of at least five inches is desirable, although wider pans make no difference. Biscuit pans, roasting pans, and dehydrators all serve the purpose equally well. A sink with a stopper may be used as a substitute.

A *small pan* about five inches in diameter and three inches deep can be used as a water supply to moisten the paper and the paint to the individual's liking. A *bucket* with a handle, half full of water, is used by the individual for washing his hands and removing all excess paint.

Spatulas, which come with the material, are used for taking paint out of containers. *Rags* are used for finishing up the job and for cleaning the table, arms, hands, and so on. For drying the finger painting, cardboards or newspapers are used.

THE TECHNIQUE OF ADMINISTRATION

All of the materials just described are arranged around the patient in a definite order. The order is the same for use with children and adults. It is best to have a table for supplies only. On this table, the paper should be placed at one end, the pan for wetting the paper at the other, and the paints in the center. This arrangement prevents the remaining paper from becoming wet. In the event that two or more individuals finger paint at the same time, this arrangement prevents individual disturbance. The technique of administration is simple to set up, easy to follow, and at the same time, emphasizes orderliness. This aspect of *order* is the first principle of organization in the performance of any job. The design that follows then becomes a manifestation of order. Have each thing in its place and very substantially fixed in the mind of the subject so that he will not be confused when he wants or needs a specific tool. Let the patient wait upon himself. This reduces the possibility of disturbance arising within the individual or with the administrator.

The table upon which the subject paints should contain only the wet paper upon which he paints and the small pan of water for maintaining the desired consistency of the paint. The bucket half filled with water is placed away from both tables. The distance does not matter, but it should be convenient to the subject when he is ready to "clean up." The newspaper or cardboard is placed in such a position that the painting, when completed, may be laid upon it to dry without its having to be moved later.

The administrator himself should be thoroughly familiar with finger painting materials and adept in their use. In his own exploration of this medium, he should become acquainted with the various parts of the hands and arms that are used in finger painting. They include the whole hand, palm of the hand, lateral aspects, clenched fist, fingers, fingertips, fingernails, arm, and so on. In the painting, the subject should be discouraged from using only one finger. Many persons are conditioned to a writing instrument and may be led to draw with one finger. If a child draws with his finger, it becomes an important indicator of his conditioning pattern.

In setting a pattern for directions for the subject, the administrator demonstrates the routine of procedure and carries on a patter of conversation about what he is doing, so that later, the subject may tell a story of what he has painted. At the same time, the administrator, having already learned to manipulate his paints, may paint a picture of an abstraction or a pattern. The writer has found an over-all pattern to be the best illustrative material to demonstrate. The story of the administrator aids in building rapport. It has been found difficult for many individuals, children or adults, to tell their story. This may be because the administrator has given them no pattern of "telling a story," or it may reflect the subject's blocking. It is difficult even for so-called normal persons to tell a story extemporaneously; one must at times, therefore, expect greater difficulty with subjects who have personality disorders. It should be explained that by story telling is not meant a definite plot with an ending or with a moral, but rather a pattern of conversation, "telling what you are doing, what you are trying to make, or identifying what has just been made."

The routing procedure is carried out in three distinct steps, each step leading into the next:
1. Preparation of the process
2. Painting through manipulation of the materials
3. Finishing the job

THE PROCEDURE

Preparation of the Process.   After the material has been arranged as previously described, the following steps are taken in the order indicated below.   The administrator takes a sheet of paper and feels it (with his skin) to determine which is the glazed side.   This side is used for painting.   The other side, being unglazed, readily adheres to the table or board, thus preventing the paper from slipping.   The unglazed side is used also for the recording of name, date, and other pertinent data.

The name, date of the painting, and serial number are the essential identifying data needed, and are usually written on the paper by the subject himself.   The subject is free to place these data on any part of the flat side he wishes.   He is told that he may choose any one of the writing instruments (pencil or crayon) he wishes to use for doing this.   If the subject cannot write, has not learned to write, or does not wish to write them, he may make his mark so that later on he may identify the paper as his own.

The paper is then rolled on its horizontal axis, with the unglazed side toward the examiner.   Using both hands, grasp the loose edge between the thumbs and index fingers, at the same time holding the roll with the other fingers.   Submerge the edge of the paper deeply into the long pan of water, at the same time releasing the roll completely, except for the edge, which is still held with the thumbs and index fingers.   Draw the paper through the water slowly, completely wetting both sides.   Lift the wet, open sheet directly over the pan, tilting it so that the excess water drips off the lowered corner into the pan.

Holding the wet paper by the edge, bring it to the work table and place it smooth side up.   Wrinkles and air bubbles are removed from the paper by placing the hand on a smooth area approximately in the center, lifting up a corner of the paper and sweeping the hand toward the outer edges.   If this is not done, the wrinkles and air bubbles will crack the paper during the painting process.   The subject then chooses whatever color he wishes.   The administrator does not suggest colors.   After the color is chosen, the paint jar is brought to the wet paper on the table.   The subject is told to take as much paint on the stick as he would like.   The subject then returns the jar of paint to its proper place so that others may use it.   Returning to his blob of paint, the subject assumes a posture that is comfortable and relaxing and permits free use of skeletal muscles.

Painting through Manipulation of the Materials. With the palm of the hand over the paint, the subject commences to move the hand, throwing the weight on the hand until the paper is completely covered with paint.   The paint is purposely of stiff consistency, so that it offers sufficient resistance to require a warming-up process.   Water may then be added to the paint by the subject in order to secure a desired texture.   The subject is instructed to cover the whole sheet of paper and to go off the sides of the paper; he should not be limited in movement by any hindrance whatsoever.   When the painting is completed, the administrator may help him to put the finger painting on the cardboard or newspaper to dry.   Drying time is about one hour, depending upon the consistency of the paint applied.   For purposes of record filing, it is suggested that the painting, after it has been dried, be ironed on the reverse side with a moderately hot iron.

Finishing the Job. The third phase, that of finishing the job, is just as important as the approach or the activity itself.   Many people begin things with enthusiasm, only to end their task inadequately and incompletely.   Avoid using the words, "clean up" or "wash up," because many people consciously or unconsciously react unfavorably to them.

The bucket, half filled with water, is used for finishing the job.   By "playing in the water the paint comes off easily."   After the subject has removed the paint from his arms and hands with the rag, he washes the paint off the table or board.   During this time of "playing in the water," subjects are often so relaxed and loquacious that it is the usual procedure for the administrator to place himself near the bucket so that he may encourage conversation by joining in it, adding to it, or listening to the individual.

There are usually three points at which one can expect to get stories: (1) while the subject is painting; (2) while his hands are in the bucket; and (3) when he volunteers to talk about the painting.   If the individual refuses to verbalize, then say nothing further about it.   The relationship should be kept pleasant.   This can be accomplished by terminating the session as a passive interview, with the administrator himself talking more fluently.   Sometimes, lack of praise and recognition causes the patient to be silent. At other times, silence is due to personality factors.

THE FINGER PAINTING PROCESS

During the finger painting process, the expertness of the administrator is of inestimable importance. Use of left and right hands, color, motion, rhythm, texture, balance, order, symbolism, and verbalization are important to note in the finger painting process. These nine categories represent responses from the inner psychic pattern of the subject because they are attributes for actual potential fulfillment value for the subject.

Through the newly aroused reaction of the subject to the administrator and to his demonstration—and all subjects are affected to some degree by the demonstration—the subject shows interest, desire, and the will to participate. This self-motivating determination to manipulate the material brings to light many facets of experiences and reactions to these experiences that are often etiological factors of behavior and adjustment. During this situation, the subject becomes the teacher concerning his inner psychic life, and directly or indirectly reveals productions pertinent to his personality. The theoretical basis of each category will be briefly explained in terms of finger painting.

Use of hands. The hand becomes significant because it is an instrument by means of which attributes are given expression. In the past, the whole of the hand as an "intaking" as well as an "outgoing" organ has been neglected. The hand is instrumental in disclosing certain clues to the pattern of the subject's behavior. These clues are manifest throughout the eight remaining categories. In finger painting data, the majority of persons show right-hand dexterity. A very small portion show ambidexterity. The remaining left-handed group can be subdivided into two groups. The first includes those who are left-handed and have been allowed to continue the use of the left hand. The second includes those who are left-handed but have been forced or conditioned to use the right hand. It is in this latter subgroup that we find a number of subjects whose present personality problems were associated in early childhood with the interference of adults. There is still another group that includes the physically handicapped, such as the spastic, the paralytic, and those with crippled hands. The successful adjustment or rehabilitation of this group depends on re-education of mental attitudes as stimulated by the therapist and the family.

Color. The colors used in finger painting are blue, green, red, yellow, black, and brown. Combinations of these give three additional colors; namely, orange, purple and "mud." In general, according to their respective color choices when compared to the clinician's description of the personality as recorded in the case records, blue and green have been found to be the dominant colors for the male, and red and yellow, dominant female colors. Black and brown have little significant difference for either sex. Black is used much more often by normal males than by normal females. Orange is rarely used and very infrequently seen in finger painting. "Mud" is not a color; rather it is a condition arrived at by mixing too many colors without any forethought, plan, or goal.

In discussing color, the writer is not considering color from the point of view of the artist's palette. He is concerned with the repetitive evidence that certain colors seem to be identified with emotional states. In this way, studies in finger painting have indicated that certain personality types show definite affinity for certain color choices and color combinations. It has also been observed in finger painting that choice of color is the result of different meanings attached to these colors. In this way, the color is to be interpreted from a polarity point of view; that is, green symbolizes security, peace, and rest at one end of the polarity arc, and jealousy, hate, and aggressiveness at the other end. Each person can find his degree of color polarity for each color somewhere between the two extremities.

Motion. One realizes the importance of the hand and its related parts as the significant instrument through which the personality is extensionalized in finger painting. The directing force behind the hand is the muscular construction of the body. The subject displays his attitudes through these muscular movements, to which he has given labels. These labels, originally coined by children, are presented and used to describe various movements. Motion in finger painting may consist of one or several of eleven general types: smearing, scrubbing, scribbling, pushing, pulling, patting, slapping, scratching, stubbling, picking, and tapping.

Smearing is the most primitive type of movement. It is the unskilled, undirected movement of large muscles. Smearing is also basic in orienting one's self to his immediate environment through muscle movement. The more skillful an individual is, the less smearing he does to orient himself.

Scrubbing is a hard rubbing motion with the whole hand in a given direction. This direction may be up or down, left or right, or in circles. Scrubbing is an advanced step over smearing; it can be called "directed smearing." This type of scrubbing is constructive in nature, since it shows mind directing representative mass. The body is relaxed and subservient to the desire to achieve. A nonconstructive type of scrubbing is illustrated by the individual who is antagonistic to the painting situation and who tenses his body because of inner drives. He will scrub, but he is sloppy and indifferent, and with undirected force often becomes chaotic in his movements.

Scribbling is isolated finger movement imitating pencil writing. Scribbling is more detailed but less directed than scrubbing. The human being first comprehends representation through mass in movement in space and not through a point in movement, which describes the extent of mass in space. Scribbling, therefore, becomes an activity with an adult tool used in the advanced art of drawing, and as a consequence, is not adequate in the development of children's skills.

Pushing out is a giving-out motion expressed by upward and downward movements away from the body, with emphasis on the up or out stroke. One type of pushing out means articulation, extroversion, accepting other people and the world of reality. With another type, this pushing out movement really means "getting rid of" or "putting out of the way."

Pulling in is a pulling-in toward the body, expressed by upward and downward strokes, with the emphasis on the pulling-in, or down strokes. At times the pulling-in motion may not be representative of the personality, but it occurs when the administrator or the environment becomes an obstacle to the subject's creation and, becoming self-conscious, he begins to pull in.

Patting is a gentle, recurrent striking with the inner surfaces of the fingers or hands. Patting means something desired or something that one is accepting. When one intensifies the patting with force, it becomes a slap. *A slap,* therefore, is a pat with a deliberate violence attached to it, and is usually motivated by anger, defiance, antagonism, or inadequacy.

By *stubbling* is meant short spring-like strokes made with the first joints of the fingers held stiffly. Many individuals who have buoyed-up emotions find this stubbling a sufficient stimulus to serve as an outlet for these pent-up feelings.

Scratching is a violent pulling-down movement with the finger-nails; it is always a pulling-down motion. The pulling-in may be directed from left to right, but it is always a pulling-in movement. The individual who scratches in his finger painting is one who has apparently had to overcome terrific emotional barriers in order to reach the position where he could so agree with himself as to have sufficient confidence in the administrator to tell him a story.

Picking is a caressing form of plucking done with the pads of the tips of the fingers. Picking is usually considered a teasing or tantalizing form of movement accompanied by guilt.

Rhythm. Rhythm in finger painting means the ability to repeat definite motion in a certain time pattern. The motion may be a single one, or motions may be in groups. Typical rhythms are characterized, therefore, in ones, twos, threes, and so on. It has been found in finger painting that the male most generally expresses himself through even rhythms and the female through odd rhythms.

Texture. By texture is meant the consistency of the paint after the subject has finished his preparatory working and smoothing it out. The ideal mixture for the paint is smooth and sufficiently wet. Smoothly prepared paint, with the correct amount of water added, is indicative of the obedient, cooperative person who wishes to excell in his desire to create. People who demonstrate this consistency in finger painting are among basic normal personalities who, if affected by strong emotional maladjustments, are amenable and respond quickly to therapy.

Lumpy and dry paint is considered to be of inadequate texture. This type of texture causes resistance to the subject. It is interesting to note that subjects who use lumpy and dry paint usually are not aware that they are the cause of their own resistance. Lumpy and very wet paint is also considered to be of inadequate texture. An individual who arrives at such a condition unwittingly causes his resistance by not working out the paint. He apparently adds too much water in a defiant manner. This type of defiance usually leads to a regrettable situation: subjects become helpless and leave the completion of the job to others. Another extreme is that of using smooth paint that has been allowed to become too dry and is therefore of inadequate texture. This is found in situations where the paint has been worked a long time and is very smooth. People who go to this extreme have spent so much time covering that the water has evaporated, leaving the paint dry. In other words, they have allowed their everyday living experiences to come to so grave a state that it may appear too late for them to cope with the situation alone.

Balance. Balance in finger painting means the equilibrium of body stance, the projective thoughts in performance, the harmony of design, the proportion, and the repetitions in composition. There is the balance that the subject experiences in his body movements, and the balance represented in the composition of the painting. If physical stance is not good but the picture itself is, then there have been certain compensations made, as in the cases of the physically handicapped and crippled. The compensation has been in terms of intellectual comprehension. One finds in therapy that if the causes of persistently bad posture can be relieved, the painting may not be so good as formerly. Yet, with re-education, these pictures progressively improve.

Order. Order is an interesting force that holds together not only the finger painting process, but the world as well. With finger painting, the individual has to be given structural sequences as contingent rungs of a ladder on which he climbs to a state of creating on a functional level. The administrator must be hidebound about giving the directions for procedure. The child more often adheres to the directions than the adult.

Symbolism. During the demonstration by the administrator, no emphasis was placed on the type of movement, selection of color, representation, or verbalization. All these are symbolic in nature. Symbolization as representation in finger painting may be abstract, a form of association, or it may approach realism. These symbols have universal usage because individuals have kindred experiences. However, the symbols have not the same universal meanings. Meanings may be different for some individuals at different times.

Typical symbolism in finger painting is portrayed according to the level of progressive development of the individual. One level of development is represented by mass, mud, under-water scenes, fish and incidentals under water, snakes, monsters, and reptiles. On a higher level of development, one sees portrayals of attempted landscapes with earth, water, sky, sun, darkness, trees, plants, and then persons and houses. In the higher levels of development, portrayals of activities of man and abstract concepts are seen. Deviations and distortions of these general symbols are interpreted according to the individual and the verbalization that he attaches to his painting. The level of functioning emotionality is usually in direct proportion to his symbolic representation.

Verbalization. By verbalization is meant the story the individual attaches to his finger painting or uses to explain it to either the administrator or to himself. Verbalization in finger painting is often difficult. It is hard to use one set of symbols (verbal) to describe another set of symbols (projections in finger painting). This difficulty is due to the fact that a vocabulary far beyond the ability of the individual is often demanded. Also, articulation is hampered by the lack of clarity of meanings of the words used (semantics) and by the lack of training on how to articulate with the symbols of language. This failure to obtain verbal responses is often deplored by the clinicians, who at times find that it hinders a fuller understanding of the subject. In the finger painting process, however, the subject has communicated on another level— preverbal or extraverbal—through his behavior and his symbols.

As the subject extensionalizes his thoughts through these media without the inhibition or deflection of adverse criticism, leading questions, suggestions, or interference from the administrator, he will break into the use of words in order to make clearer to the administrator his meanings and needs. He will, perhaps dimly at first, give short phrases to insure that the administrator understands his meanings. The vocabulary may be inadequate, the words he uses may fail to convey an adequate meaning, and his technique may be poor; yet because he has no sense of guilt about his extensionalization—finger painting—he will communicate, even if it is no more than a beginning.

Verbalization in finger painting may happen at any time during the process. It may be a running commentary during the painting or it may be in the form of expressions of pleasure, disgust, inadequacy, or boastfulness. Often a terse title is given to the finished picture before it is set aside to dry. The flow of words comes with some when their hands are in the bucket, and not necessarily while looking at the picture. During the cleaning-up period, subjects often discuss processes rather than content of their painting, reflecting their desire to establish a patient-therapist relationship.

Verbalization may take the form of one type or a combination of many types of stories or explanations—fantasy, fiction, fact, absurdity, culture, mythology, and so forth. All these stories or explanations are symbolic in their meaning insofar as they involve the projection of mental mechanisms that reflect actual conditions. At the same time, they may reveal the subject's adjustive attempts lo cope with or to justify his existing condition. The processes of finger painting, accompanied by its opportunity for verbalizations, enhances the interpretation of the personality and gives a more accurate appraisal of the subject's behavior mechanism.

THE SERIES

It has been found that a more accurate picture of the individual's total behavior pattern can be elicited if more than one painting is made. At times there arises a situation where the dynamisms at work may be suggested but not included in the same painting, and the need for confirmation is necessary through additional paintings. At such times, it is recommended that other paintings be made for confirmation of this questionable performance. At other times, though a personality pattern is formed, other paintings are necessary to make a differential diagnosis. Further, a series may be indicated when the subject cannot "tell all" during one session. This may be caused by a domination of distracting associations or a fixation as a result of the finger painting stimulus, or the subject's emotional state may be so erratic that it influences the natural and logical sequence of associations that produce the projection. Still further, because of a sense of guilt, the subject at times "rubs out" his productions so rapidly that they escape even the most discriminating observation of the administrator. Finally, and perhaps most significant of all, the series is justified because the clinician must be constantly aware that these so-called "personality tests" are being applied to the human being. The writer feels that many "experts" have been too free and too heedless in describing the behavior of human beings on the basis of one "test," be it of a few moments or a few hours' duration. Added to the fact that these findings are applied to a personality that is not completely under-stood, the error of diagnosis can be multiplied perhaps more times than has really been recognized.   Therefore, describing personality as a state of being "at a given time" makes a series of tests indicated for a more adequate sampling and verification of the clues as a definite part of the personality pattern.   This is highly important in a differential diagnosis, especially when the subject has very recently experienced emotional trauma.   Then it becomes signifi-cant in the diagnosis whether this maladjustment is transient or permanent.   Both prognosis and the therapy indicated depend in great part upon making this differentiation as accurate as possible.

Although six to eight paintings are a minimum for a given series to be reliable in the confirmation of a diagnosis, no specific maxi-mum number can be stated.   Research is beginning to show that with greater refinement of the process, we may be able to reduce this minimal number to four paintings.

Through careful observation and recording of results, it has been found that twice a week is a good finger painting dosage for op-timum results.   In this way, the subject is not fatigued by fre-quency of repetition, nor is his interest lost by too long an interval between painting sessions.   Through experience with finger paint-ing, it has been found that a group of six to eight persons constitutes the greatest number with whom adequate work can be done in personality studies, and then, only if carried out by an expert in this technique.   Larger numbers may be used when finger painting is used for either recreational or socialization purposes.

The advantages of group painting are many.   It inspires com-petition and stimulation by comparison with and comments by others in the group.   There may, however, be a tendency among the less skillful and less creative individuals to imitate a more dominant individual.   This should not be distressing, since such persons are thereby revealing their dependence upon others.   With proper therapy they can be led out of this imitative process.   Fur-ther, many movements and aspects of behavior become freer in a group situation, since the administrator's attention is necessarily divided.   The administrator, although obscure, is alert in his dis-criminating observations.

RECORDING AND INTERPRETING THE FINGER PAINTING PROCESS

Observation of the physical aspects of the subject in action is as important as the finger painting process itself. The observations to be made by the examiner include the idiosyncrasies, the actions, and the reactions of the individual during finger painting performance, from the beginning to the end of the procedure. The observation begins with the reaction of the patient during the administrator's demonstration. This preperformance observation gives the administrator cues as to what he may expect in behavior—but not in painting—from the subject. This preview of behavior serves to allow the examiner to formulate tentatively his plan of observation, thereby making for continued rapport.

All the items for the three aspects of finger painting, namely, the performance observation, the painting analysis, and the verbalization, are listed in the record form reproduced in this chapter (Figure 2). The form is presented with the aim of standardizing the method of recording the various aspects of the finger painting process. Numerical values have been used for each subdivision on a five-point scale basis, where the midpoint is considered average or normal performance. Quantitative as well as qualitative comparisons are thus made possible. A breakdown of the scale values of each item can be found in a previous publication [16].

The content analysis is empirically and experimentally derived. The following interpretative aspects will help to introduce the clinician to some of the personality insights gained from finger painting.

Refusal to write one's name could mean denial of one's own work and creativity, ignorance of the joy of possession (insecurity), the defiance of instruction and direction.

Those who show *hesitancy in choosing color* are in a state of color conflict or are disturbed by an immediate experience.

Posture often gives clues to the observant administrator. It may reflect dependency, self-consciousness, timidity, withdrawal characteristics, or embarrassment.

Slow and undirected physical motion often reflect depression or lack of motivation. Both normal and feeble-minded groups show good posture and good rhythm, form and balance. The difference, however, is in the content of their painting, and not in their posture.

Children adhere more readily to directions for procedure than do adults. *Poor performance in following the order of procedure* suggests a resentment of authority; it is also often seen in the severely neurotic and psychotic groups.

Lack of neatness has been found to be due to bad coordination, to persistent feelings of guilt or insecurity, to a disregard for the social amenities, or to resentment of authority.

Often we hear subjects say, "I don't know what to do. . . . I don't know how to do it. . . . I don't know how. . . . ," and so on. This *lack of self-confidence* is often found in maladjusted persons who show lack of skill, who have had a paucity of experience, or who show difficulty in adaptive behavior. These remarks come also from neurotics and psychotics, where they are to be interpreted as a rejection of reality.

Timid and anxious subjects often show a *reluctance to paint.* The rare incidence is the individual who bluntly refuses to paint. This is seen in the markedly fearful, guilty, or paranoid. Individuals who use large quantities of water and paint are usually anal-erotic characters who are impatient, have little or no self-reliance, are inconsiderate and wasteful, or show poor initiative. Stammerers are often found among this group. They show much enjoyment in slopping in "mud." Those subjects who use little paint are usually timid, overprotected individuals with little self-developed creative experience.

Individuals who *accept the challenge of a new situation* and who *show adaptability in exploration* usually paint longer than the average time limit. Overprotected children do likewise. Disorganized children and those with little or no creative experience usually spend a very short time in the exploratory process.

When an individual has guilt feelings, feelings of inadequacy, or fear of criticism, or when he may be ashamed of what he thinks his painting reveals, he will also *manifest displeasure at the end of the finger painting process.* Those who have not been taught an appreciation for their own achievement also do this.

The majority of people *place their paper in a horizontal position.* The few who *place their paper in a vertical position* usually have a more aesthetically developed personality.

It has been found that the *position of the first dab of paint* is a very important clue as to what may be expected of the subject. Paranoids emphasize all vertical axes and these axes are related in their verbalization of their painting. Schizoid individuals emphasize all horizontal axes, but the axes are not related in their verbalization. A few, who are usually very sensitive, emphasize diagonal axes. Figure 1 shows diagrammatically the significant finger painting areas.

The normal individual will usually utilize all parts of the hand and arm. Neurotics with bad training habits usually use their finger tips, and then only with an attitude of disgust. This is especially so with females who reject both their sex and their feminine responsibilities. The inadequate group and those with vocational or social inferiority usually paint with the side of the hand only. Those with psychosexual difficulties will paint with the palm of the hand, but with fingers turned up. Extroverts and those with little regard for conventionality will paint with their arms only. The lines or directions of movements also have their particular meanings. Normal persons will usually paint from the bottom of the paper upward, in sweeping outward, circular motions. They will also paint in up-and-down motions, accenting the upward strokes lightly. When these upward strokes are strongly accentuated, it is considered aggressive behavior. Average individuals with feelings of ambivalence usually work in horizontal motions.

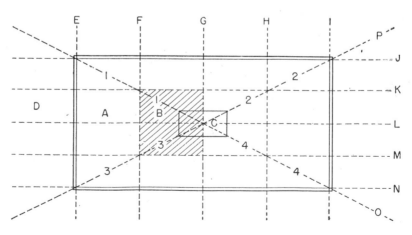

Fig. 1. Significant Finger-Painting Areas. (Adapted from Napoli [*12*, p. 97]. Used by permission.)

Color is one of the most significant categories, giving insight into the emotionality of the subject. *Blue* has been found to be the dominant color used by males. The normal use of blue denotes masculinity, security, drive, and sincerity. An abnormal use of blue (in extreme amount) denotes sadistic, impulsive, and violent behavior. When the male adds black to his blue it reflects a despondency state.

Green is a secondary dominant color for the male; it is used by those individuals who are highly developed emotionally but controlled in this emotionality. The use of green also reflects a creative potential within the individual.

When blue is used by the female in an excessive way, it shows that she identifies herself as the female complement. However, if this is the only color used by the female, it is often found that insincerity, schemingness, and rejection of her own sexuality are prevalent in the case history. The female who uses green as her dominant color also rejects her sexuality and identifies herself with the male, in a manner similar to a male's use of blue.

Red and yellow have been found to be the dominant colors for females. The use of red is normal for both sexes below the age of five or six. Above these ages, we expect to see a limited use of it in the male. Males who are overprotected, who may be under female domination, or who have difficulty in psychosexual identification, use red. The female who uses yellow in a constructive manner usually has good social values, and is aware of and accepts men. Deceptive, inadequate, and misrepresenting females use yellow in a perverted manner. The flirt or the coquettish female is also included in this group. The normal male uses yellow judiciously, and for him, the use of yellow reflects his proper values for the female. Those males, however, who are lacking in development or who cannot meet life's situations as a man, use yellow excessively.

Black is used more by males than by females. No interpretation for this difference has been found for either sex. Black is used as representing certain intellectual concepts. In a more unwholesome manner, evasion, fears, death, depression, and unexplained emotionality have been denoted by an excessive use of black.

Brown is another color that has no differential interpretation for the two sexes. This color is used by a majority of persons to represent the negative aspects of everyday living.

Purple for both sexes can represent sincere and deep depression, but with an optimistic outlook. This color is often used by persons experiencing good heterosexual relationships and adjustments. Males with good leadership qualities often use purple.

"Mud," as previously stated, is not a color but a condition arrived at by mixing too many colors together without forethought or plan. Those individuals who are destructive without remorse, who may be irresponsible, or who are inadequate, use mud. Normal individuals who are adequate but not developed in skill, and who are easily discouraged, also use mud.

Motion is another significant category in understanding the individual's behavior pattern. The immature and insecure person invariably does a lot of smearing. The more skillful a person is, the less smearing he does. Smearing is characteristic of feeble-minded or low IQ individuals. Those adults whose smearing movements dominate a picture have usually been deprived of natural infantile pursuits by overconscientious adults.

Scrubbing, although constructive in nature, is often seen in the unskilled, indifferent, or submissive person. It frequently reflects an individual's antagonism toward something. Disturbed personalities scrub. Neurotics, Mongolians and the feeble-minded scrub.

Scribbling is a motion reflecting disappointment, defiance, or lack of ability in competition. Aggressive persons, those who avoid responsibility and refuse to be imposed upon, those who show many nonsocial qualities, utilize *pushing-down movements. Pulling-in movements* are often dominant in the paintings of those who are introvertive or underprivileged. Orally deprived and selfish individuals also engage in much of this movement. Those subjects who respond to love and attention and who have been nourished with affection often enjoy *patting movements.* Defiance, anger, rejection, antagonism, and inadequacy are seen in those persons who *slap* their finger painting.

Invariably, those individuals who *stipple* in their paint—paint with the pads of finger tips only—are those who express an antagonism over their masturbatory guilt and whose case record reflects a history of enuresis.

Scratching is another method of projecting violence, defiance, and a wish to destroy that which is represented by the symbol scratched.

Normal *texture* is usually arrived at by those subjects who are cooperative and amenable, and who wish to excel in a desire to create. Normal texture is a positive prognostic sign in terms of response to psychotherapy. Lumpy and dry paint is considered inadequate texture; it offers resistance to the subject but he is not aware of the nature of his difficulty in painting. When he does become aware of it, he is usually helpless to aid himself. The uncooperative individual uses a lumpy but very wet texture. He develops this condition because he is not aware that he is not co-operative. Unable to cope with lumpy, wet paint, he becomes defiant. These situations are usually beyond his control. It has been found that these subjects indirectly enjoy a certain delight in causing embarrassment to the administrator, embarrassment really intended for the subjects' employer, parent, wife, or someone else. This condition reflects the subject's inability to absorb suc-cessfully the shock of his environmental problem, as well as a need for constant supervision and attention. This texture is most often seen in persons who may feel inferior and who very often show a history of enuresis.

Very wet texture reflects a deeper inferiority seen in the inade-quate personality. It reflects an impoverished, unskilled, and frugal attempt at creativity. At the same time, it reveals a sense of guilt about the subject's lack of productivity. This very wet texture, however, is normal for very young children and spastics. Profes-sional artists and those with latent creative potentials usually prefer a smooth, dry texture.

The interpretations of many of the symbols found in finger painting have been confirmed by the subjects in their verbal ex-planation. Fences or ladders are used as protective barriers. Bridges are indices of inadequacies. Grasses called "hairs" usually have a sexual reference. The tulip is often seen as a phallic symbol. Strong circular motions designated as wheels represent power. If the wheels are not in motion, the power or strength is potential. Roaring animals are symbolic of fear of thunder in children, and very typical of aggression in adults. Dead animals usually reflect a lack of attention and affection. Exaggerated mention of apples is seen in orally deprived individuals. Snakes are symbolic of either enemies or sex preoccupation. Crawling monsters are also symbolic of sex experience. Grass is usually significant of evasive-ness.

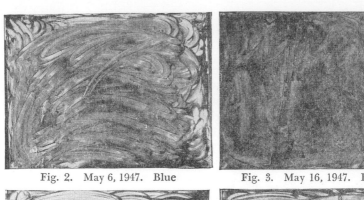

Fig. 2.　May 6, 1947.　Blue

Fig. 3.　May 16, 1947.　Brown

Fig. 4.　May 20, 1947.　Brown

Fig. 5.　May 23, 1947.　Green

Fig. 6.　June 3, 1947.　Yellow

Fig. 7.　June 6, 1947.　Brown

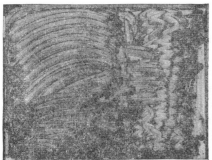

Fig. 8.　June 10, 1947.　Green

Fig. 9.　June 13, 1947.　Brown

```
                    FINGER PAINTING RECORD FORM
                          Peter J. Napoli
```

NAME:	SEX: Male	ADMITTED TO HOSP.-SCHOOL 10/46
ADDRESS: Brookly State Hosp.		WARD-ROOM 22
RACE: STATUS: single FAM.POS.: only		DIAGNOSIS: D.P. Catatonic
OCCUPATION: Musician AGE: 27		
EDUCATION: High School		
PSYCHOLOGICAL TESTS:		B.S.H. & Pilgrim State Hosp. - 9/40
		to 2/42
		Rivercrest - 8/45 to 10/46
Treatment - Insulin & E.C.T.		

PRESENTING PROBLEM:

        Patient was sensitive, brooded and worried a great deal.   Patient had

feelings of inferiority and would have frequent temper displays. He said the boys were

talking about him. He attempted to beat a girl entertainer saying she annoyed him.

Pt. sent to K.C. Observation Ward.

F.P. SUMMARY:

        Individual shows little or no initial reaction and is distracted during
demonstration. Shows much difficulty in following directions for process. Posture
manneristic. He is hesitant throughout the series. Order is loose with a tendency
toward rigidity - neatness poor - was resistant - no exploratory activity - showed
no skill - time spent in painting significantly excessive - he was pleased and
stimulated - minimal kinetic activity - does not repeat performance - does not clean
neatly.

Painting Analytics:- Right handed motions - uses one color for each painting - in
general subdued colors - smearing and scrubbing motions - Rhythm cannot be determined -
texture lumpy, dry and thick - no composition or balance - chaotic order.
First level symbolism (Mass)

Verbalization: In general descriptive, abstract, impoverished and bizarre. Dull
normal mental level.

PERSONALITY APPRAISAL:

        Behavior, painting, verbalization and patterning typical of Schizophrenia,

Catatonic type depressed.

```
                                        EXAMINER:_____
                                        Date:_____
```

Fig. 10 (above).   Finger Painting Record Form, page 1.

*Figs. 2 to 9 (at left). Series of finger paintings by male patient,
diagnosed dementia-praecox, catatonic.*

409

PERFORMANCE OBSERVATION	Number	I.	II.	III.	IV.	V.	VI.	VII.	VIII.	IX.	X.
	Date	5/6/47	5/16	5/20	5/23	6/3	6/6	6/10	6/13		
	A.T.	1 Hr.	1 Hr.	1 Hr.	1 Hr.	1 Hr.	1 Hr.	1 Hr.	1 Hr.		
A. INITIAL REACTION		1	1	1	2	2	2	1	1		
B. DIRECTIONS											
1. Differentiates sides of paper		+	-	-	+	-	-	-	-		
2. Identification (name or mark)		-	-	-	-	-	-	-	-		
3. Date		-	-	-	-	-	-	-	-		
4. Number		-	-	-	-	-	-	-	-		
5. Wetting paper		3	3	1	2	1	2	3	2		
6. Placing paper		1	1	2	1	2	1	1	2		
C. POSTURE		2	5	2	5	2	5	5	5		
D. MANNER OF APPROACH		4	2	2	2	2	2	3	2		
E. POSITION OF ATTACK											
1. First daub		•	•	•	•	•	•	•	•		
2. Horizontal or vertical		H	H	H	V	H	H	H	H		
3. Amount of paint taken		3	1	1	3	1	1	1	1		
4. Returns container		-	-	-	-	-	-	-	-		
5. Starting hand		B.	R.	R.	R.	R.	R.	R.	R.		
6. Part of hand used		T.W.H.	T.W.H.	T.	T.	W.H.T.	T.	T.W.H.	W.H.T.		
7. Line of direction of motions		←→	↓↑→	←→	←→	↻	↻	←→	↓		
8. Adds water		1	1	1	1	1	1	1	1		
9. Total amount of paint used		5	4	5	5	5	4	5	5		
F. ORDER		2	3	2	4	4	2	2	3		
G. NEATNESS		1	2	2	2	2	1	2	3		
H. PERFORMANCE											
1. Rapport		2	1	1	2	1	2	1	2		
2. Exploratory activity		1	1	1	1	1	1	1	1		
3. Skill		1	1	1	1	1	1	1	1		
4. Time painting		60	30	30	40	40	55	60	60		
5. Satisfied or displeased		3	3	4	3	3	3	3	3		
I. STIMULATED OR RELAXED		4	3	4	4	3	4	4	2		
J. CLEAN-UP		1	2	2	2	2	2	2	2		
K. REPEATS PERFORMANCE		-	-	-	-	-	-	-	-		
L. KINETIC ACTIVITY *		1	2	1	2	2	2	2	2		
PAINTING ANALYTICS											
M. HANDEDNESS											
1. Right		√	√	√	√	√	√	√	√		
2. Left											
3. Conditioned											
4. Physically limited											
N. COLOR											
1. Black											
2. Blue		√									
3. Brown			√	√			√		√		
4. Green					√			√			
5. Red											
6. Yellow						√					
7. Mud											
8. Verbalized											
9. Other:											

Fig. 11.   Finger Painting Record Form, page 2.

410

	I.	II.	III.	IV.	V.	VI.	VII.	VIII.	IX.	X.
O. MOTION										
1. Smearing	1	1	1	1	1	1	1	1		
2. Scribbling	2	2	2	2	2	2	2	2		
3. Scrubbing										
4. Pushing										
5. Pulling		3								
6. Patting								3		
7. Slapping										
8. Scratching										
9. Stubbling										
10. Picking										
11. Tapping										
12. Other:										
P. RHYTHM	?	?	?	?	?	?	?			
1. 2/4								✓		
2. 3/4										
3. 4/4										
4. 6/8										
5. 5/4										
6. 7/4										
Q. TEXTURE										
1. Lumpy-dry										
2. Lumpy-wet										
3. Average										
4. Smooth-wet										
5. Smooth-dry **	✓	✓	✓	✓	✓	✓	✓	✓		
6. Variable										
R. COMPOSITION	1	1	1	1	1	1	1	1		
S. ORDER	2	2	3	2	1	2	2	2		
T. SYMBOLISM										
First Level:										
1. Mass	✓	✓	✓	✓	✓	✓	✓	✓		
2. Mud										
3. Under water incidentals										
4. Prehistoric life										
5. Fish										
6. Snakes										
7. Reptiles										
8. Monsters										
9. Birds										
Second Level:										
10. Portrayals of seascapes										
11. " " landscapes										
12. " " vegetation										
13. " " animals										
14. " " people										
15. " " houses										
Third Level:										
16. Activities of man										
17. Abstractions										
18. Ethereal concepts										

MISCELLANEOUS REMARKS: *   Kinetic activity — Although there was some effort it was at a minimum

**   Although the paint was smooth and dry the texture was very heavy because of the excessive amount of paint used.

Fig. 12.   Finger Painting Record Form, page 3.

411

4.

VERBALIZATION

	I.	II.	III.	IV.	V.	VI.	VII.	VIII.	IX.	X.
1. Type		desc.	desc.		desc.			fiction		
2. Content		abstract	abstract	None	abstract	None	None	abstract		
3. Character		impov.	impov.		impov.			impov.&biz.		
4. Level		2	2		2			1		

I. Title.

    None

II.   " A Brown Design "

       Pt. seemed to be hallucinating quietly during the session. He was talking and would often grimace and nod. This diminished as the session continued.

III.   "Just a Finger Painting".

IV.   None

V.   None. "I'm just drawing ovals – circles --- There's so much paint on there --- I don't know it resembles something."

VI.   None

VII.   None

VIII.   "The Flag"   "The American Flag"

      (What are the colors of the American Flag?)

        "Red, white and blue"

      (What is the color of your painting?)

        "Brown"

      "I like to work with both hands – it's a reflection of the other things you know – dead people can't do those things."

Fig. 13. Finger Painting Record Form, page 4.

ILLUSTRATIVE CASE [3]

To illustrate the method of recording and interpreting the finger painting process, a series of eight finger paintings is reproduced in Figures 2 to 9. These paintings were made by a male patient 27 years old, whose illness had been diagnosed as dementia praecox, catatonic type. The recordings of the examiner on the Finger Painting Record Form are reproduced in Figures 10 to 13. There, it can be seen that the subject used only one color for each of the eight paintings; that he used mainly smearing and scribbling motions; that it was impossible for the examiner to identify the rhythm, except on the eighth picture; that the texture was consistently smooth-dry, and the symbolism consistently at the first level of mass representation. The numerical ratings on the record are based on a five-point scale of values [16].

SUMMARY

Finger painting as an amusement or as a form of artistic expression is of ancient origin. Its use as an educational device or as a diagnostic or therapeutic method is quite recent. It has clinical application as a projective technique for the understanding of personality, but it has scarcely been subjected to the rigors of scientific method.

This chapter describes a kit of standard finger painting equipment for clinical use, explains the technique and procedure of administration, and presents a method for recording and interpreting systematic observations during the finger painting process. A Finger Painting Record Form devised by the writer is used with an illustrative case.

REFERENCES

1. Allen, Frederick H., *Psychotherapy with Children.* New York: W. W. Norton & Company, Inc., 1942; "The Child's Participation," Chapter 5, pages 132–138.

2. Allport, Gordon, "The psychologist's frame of reference." *Psych. Bull.,* January 1940, 37, 1, 1–28.

3. Arlow, J., and Kadis, A., "Finger painting in the psychotherapy of children." *Amer. J. Orthopsychiat.,* 1946, 16, 134–146.

---

[3] The writer is grateful to Clarence H. Bellinger, M.D., Medical Superintendent, Brooklyn State Hospital, for permission to use the illustrated case record.

4. Chang, Y. K., "Finger painting at the Guy Mayer Gallery." *Art News,* January 14, 1939, 37, 16.

5. Fleming, Joan, "Observations on the use of finger painting in the treatment of adult patients with personality disorders." *Character and Personality,* June 1940, 8, 302–310.

6. Hutt, Max, "The use of projective methods of personality measurement in army medical installations." *Journal of Clinical Psychology,* April 1945, 1, 2, 134–140.

7. Lyle, Jeanette, and Shaw, Ruth F., "Encouraging fantasy expression in children." *Bulletin of the Menninger Clinic,* January 1937, 1, 3, 78–86.

8. Mosse, Eric, "Painting analysis in the treatment of the neuroses." *Psychoanalytic Review, January 1940,* 27, 65–81.

9. Murphy, L. B., "Art technique in studying child personality." *Rorschach Research Exchange and Journal of Projective Techniques,* September 1949, 13, 320–324.

10. Napoli, Peter J., *Finger Painting and Personality Diagnosis.* Doctoral thesis, New York University, 1945, pages v+160. (Microfilmed by University Microfilms, Ann Arbor, Mich., 1946.)

11. ——————————, "Finger painting and personality diagnosis." *Genet. Psychol. Monogr.* 1946, 34, 129–231.

12. ——————————, "Interpretative aspects of finger painting." *J. of Psychol.,* 1947, 23, 93–132.

13. ——————————, "Finger painting . . . a bibliography." *School Arts,* 1947, 46, 208–210.

14. ——————————, "A finger painting record form." *J. of Psychol.,* 1948, 26, 31–43.

15. Napoli, Peter J., and Gold, B., "Finger painting in an occupational therapy program." *Amer. J. Occup. Ther.,* 1947, 1, 358–361.

16. Napoli, Peter J., and Harris, W., "Finger painting for the blind." *J. of Psychol.,* 1948, 24, 185–196.

17. Napoli, Peter J., and Wholl, I., "Finger painting and the educative process" (in preparation).

18. *Newsweek,* "Finger-tip painter; Chinese finger-tip painting." January 23, 1939, 20–21.

19. Obrock, Irene, "The therapeutic value of finger painting." The Crippled Child, April 1936, 13, 6, 172.

20. Pennington, L. A., and Berg, I. A., *An Introduction to Clinical Psychology,* New York: The Ronald Press Company, 1948, page 427.

21. Rosenzweig, L., and Durbin, L., "Finger painting as an investigative approach to therapeutic techniques." *Occupational Therapy and Rehab.,* February 1945, 24, 1, 1–12.

22. Shaw, Ruth F., *Finger Painting.* Boston: Little, Brown and Company, 1934, pages xiii–232.

23. Stone, L., "Finger painting: children's use of plastic materials." New York: *New York University Film Library,* 1944. (A 16 mm. 2-reel silent film in color.)

24. Spring, W. J., "Words and masses: A pictorial contribution to the psychology of stammering." *Psychoanalytic Quarterly,* April 1935, 4, 244–258.

25. Symonds, Percival, and Krugman, Morris, "Projective methods in the study of personality." *Review of Educational Research,* February 1944, 14, 1, 81–98.

CHAPTER 15

Graphology

Rose Wolfson, Ph.D.

HISTORICAL BACKGROUND

Handwriting, as a product of human activity, has occupied the interest of many persons in diverse fields.   As early as the second century, Tranquillius saw peculiarities in Octavius Augustus' handwriting; and in the eleventh century, the Chinese were noting the relationship between handwriting and character.   In the nineteenth century, Galton and Pearson came to the conclusion that handwriting is a mental characteristic, and Darwin wrote: "On what a curious combination of corporeal structure, mental character and training must handwriting depend!".   During this century, too, Disraeli, Gainsborough, Madame de Staël, the Brownings, Leibnitz, and others studied handwriting for characteristics of the writer that it supposedly conveyed.

The points of emphasis and departure in the study of handwriting have also varied, usually in accordance with the individual attitude toward the writing act.   Broadly, there are five points of orientation from which handwriting can be considered: (1) characterological, (2) pedagogical, (3) forensic, (4) experimental, and (5) psychological.   Often, different orientations overlap, as the pedagogical and the forensic, or the experimental and psychological; at times, they are clearly discrete, as the characterological and the forensic.   The techniques and methodologies developed by one have frequently yielded results helpful to all.

Briefly, *the characterological approach* has its roots in the "old graphology," and ranges from an acceptance of specific graphic "signs" as indicators of definite personality traits to the broader

416

psychological theory that a "central core" permeates all the individual's acts, including his handwriting.

Writers with a characterological orientation include Camille Baldi [*3*], who in 1622 published the first treatise on the characterological meaning of handwriting; the Abbé Michon, who gave graphology its name and its first systematic approach, that of fitting isolated signs to character traits; the famous graphologist Jamin-Crépieux, Michon's critic and the originator of the "theory of resultants"; and the entire French School, which never freed itself from Michon's emphasis on isolated "signs" [*44*]. The dilettantes—Goethe, Poe, Gainsborough, and others—come under this classification as well.

The pedagogical view stresses the quality and legibility of a handwriting, and sees both as the outcome of handwriting instruction and drill, although lately there has been some change in the pedagogical view. Some recognition is accorded emotional factors in the student's ability to improve his writing [*47*].

Experiments by Thorndike [*51*], Ayers [*2*], and Freeman [*16, 17*] have resulted in various scales for evaluating handwriting quality and for analyzing the fine movements involved in the writing act. Freeman's investigations, especially, have added to the understanding of the relationship between handwriting speed and types of handwriting strokes, between speed and pressure, pen hold, and arm and finger movements [*16, 17*].

The view of *the forensic, or court expert,* is closely allied to that of the earlier pedagogues. The expert sees writing as the product of trained mechanical movements, of the kinds of learning systems acquired, and of the amount of practice attained. For him, the variability observable in writing is due to casual rather than causal factors, that is, quality of paper, light, haste, and the like. His contribution to the understanding of handwriting is considerable, for he has demonstrated the limits of variability and disguise in handwriting [*37*]. For graphology, this information throws valuable light on the crucial question of voluntary and involuntary control by the individual writer.

The experimentalists are of two kinds: (1) those interested in the various aspects of the mechanical movement per se, and (2) those interested in handwriting as an activity influenced by physiological, mental, and hereditary factors. Among the "mechanical" experimentalists, McAllister [*32*], Dearborn [*7*], and others have established certain writing movements, such as centripetal (towards the body), and centrifugal (away from the body), and the relative speed of performing each. These experiments have demonstrated not only types of movements but also the comparative ease of execution, and how they tend to vary from person to person. Experimentally, Diehl [*8*] discovered a pressure curve characteristically different for each individual, a discovery that was later confirmed in observations by Osborne [*37*] and the graphologist Saudek [*44, 45*].

Among the second group are such pioneer workers as Downey [*9*], Starch [*48*], and Gesell [*18*], who investigated handwriting from the point of view of heredity and intelligence. Their findings were inconclusive but serve as landmarks in the scientific treatment of handwriting.

Roman's work [*43*] is a fusion of the mechanical-experimental and psychological approaches. Roman used the "graphodyn," a mechanical device designed by her to determine the varying degrees of pressure, the time expended, and the interruptions that occur in writing flow during the execution of assigned writing tasks, for instance, single words or a standardized series of continuous wavy lines.

The graphodyn is a stylus attached to a light rubber tube that allows comparatively free movement. "The apparatus is worked with a lever, the writing lead at its shorter end while its longer end is fixed to a small tambour" [*43*].

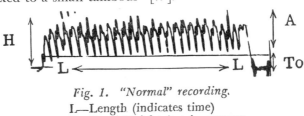

Fig. 1. *"Normal" recording.*
L—Length (indicates time)
H—Total Height (total pressure)
A—Amplitude (motor activity)
To—Residue (tension)

Fig. 2. *Hypertension and slowness.*

Fig. 3.   Hypertension and irregularity.

Fig. 4.   Total blockage.

Roman's assumption is that the graphodyn gives recorded evidence of the muscular interplay between relaxation and contraction, and shows how one phase passes into the other.   What is recorded according to this assumption is (1) total energy reserve, (2) output in motor activity, and (3) the energy retained in the form of muscle tension.   Figure 1 illustrates a recording by the graphodyn of a "normal" tracing.   Figures 2, 3, and 4 indicate characteristically "disturbed" tracings.[1]

Clinical use of the instrument with organically disturbed patients reveals consistently characteristic curves.   Work with arthritics and manually skilled subjects like art students has uncovered significant data on psychological as well as physiological problems.[2]

Roman concludes from her findings that the contraction and relaxation of the muscles, as well as their tonus, are symptomatic not only of the physical functioning of the individual but also of his emotional and psychological state.   In her interpretation of the results obtained through the graphodyn, Roman spans the bridge between the mechanical and psychological orientation.   For handwriting analysis, the tracings may be important as tangible evidence of the tensions frequently referred to by graphologists when analyzing specimens.

The psychological approach is an outgrowth of the characterological in that the psychologist studies handwriting for possible

[1] Grateful acknowledgment is made here to Dr. Klara G. Roman who contributed illustrative and expository material.   Figures 1 to 4 appear by permission of Grune & Stratton, Inc.

[2] Gottschalk, L. A., Serota, H. M., and Roman, K. G., Handwriting in Rheumatoid Arthritics, *Psychosomatic Medicine,* Nov.–Dec. 1949. 11. 6. 353–360.

clues to the writer's personality. Unlike the pure characterological, the psychological stresses not the handwriting as such, but the record contained therein of the movements that directed the pen through the writing performance. This orientation of studying handwriting as a record of inner and outer movements began in Germany with Klages [24], who stands midway between the characterological and psychological approaches.

Preceding Klages had come Preyer's experiments [40], which demonstrated that handwriting is actually "brain writing"; and Meyer's investigations [33], which resulted in the distinction between spontaneous and unspontaneous forms of writing, and the points in the specimen where each expressed itself. Klages gave due consideration to all these findings, and formulated a graphological system that broke completely with the French School of signs. The Klages system and its influence on graphological thinking and experimentation will be considered more fully under the discussion of related studies.

Although all five orientations discussed above have had their adherents here as well as abroad, in the United States psychological interest in graphology was slow and reluctant to develop, in contrast to Europe, where graphological formulations, psychological investigations and clinical application were closely interrelated. Now and then, in the United States, came sporadic investigations of one or more claims made by graphologists, but regardless of whether findings tended to support or to refute such claims, American psychologists in the main remained highly skeptical and largely indifferent to graphology as a testing device. Charlatanic and unscientific intuitive practices had given it a bad start, and there were very few psychologists who were willing to consider for investigation so debatable and questionable a technique.

Watson [53] described graphological claims as a "tissue of exaggerations," and Symonds [50] concluded from the Hull and Montgomery study [21] that the average correlation of —.016 found in the study was "about the amount of assurance that one should give to the claims of graphologists."

Yet, despite the opposition, there has been a gradual rise in interest in handwriting as a record of the individual's pattern of functioning. The rise in interest began with Downey, probably American psychology's most astute and versatile graphological investigator. Allport and Vernon concluded from their extensive inquiries into expressive movement that "graphic movement is not activity . . . dissociated from complexities of personality . . . but . . . seems to be intricately woven with deep-lying determinants of conduct" [1].

More recently, Murphy, in summing up the evidence for and against graphology, found that "much of the theory of expression offered by contemporary graphologists makes sense and is eminently reasonable. . . . The most pressing problem today is not the level of validity but how sound judgments are made and the ways in which they can be extended" [36].

EXPERIMENTAL STUDIES

Graphological investigations in the United States, clearly influenced by European concepts, have followed one of two main assumptions: (1) specific graphic elements and single individual traits are directly related, and (2) handwriting *expression* and personality functioning have a psychological relationship. The formerly much-quoted Hull and Montgomery study [21], in which a correlation of —.016 was found between the measurements of such graphic signs as slope of lines, width of stroke, lateral narrowness of *m*'s and *n*'s, and so on, and ratings on traits—ambition, pride, bashfulness—is an example of studies under the first assumption. Brown's study [20] of the relationship between specific graphic elements like alignment or a writing form, and rankings on ambition, neatness, and the like, follows a similar course.

This approach to handwriting, which supposes a one-to-one relationship between graphic signs and a specific personality feature, is psychologically naive and graphologically anachronistic. It overlooks all the experimentation and changes that have occurred in graphology since the Abbé Michon, not to mention the unreliability of the criteria on which ratings are made, that is, trait names that might mean one thing to one rater and something else to another.

A somewhat more satisfactory procedure, but still fragmentary in that which it investigates in handwriting, is the technique of correlating the measurements of specific graphic variables with objective test scores. Thus, Land [26] found a significant relationship between extreme backhand, most downward alignment, and "normal" slant and alignment, and "emotional" scores on the Pressey X-O test.

Harvey [19], in a comparable attack, concerned himself, however, with many more aspects of the writing. His treatment was wider and more thorough. He asked questions regarding (1) graphic elements that can be measured objectively, (2) their reliability, and (3) their relationship to scores on "recognized personality scales." His subjects were 50 college girls with an age range of 19–24. Scores were obtained for each on the Thurstone Personality Schedule and the Allport Ascendance-Submission Scale. The reliability test was based on specimens from 20 of the original 50 subjects, written under entirely different and noticeably less adequate writing conditions. Harvey used calipers and microscope to measure 26 graphic variables, and obtained reliability coefficients that ranged between .4 and .8; the median coefficient for direct measures was .77; for ratio measures, .71. Seven types of measures involving height yielded an average correlation of .54; three involving space had an average correlation of .33. Harvey regarded these findings as important, since his intention had not been "to obtain a measure of reliability but merely to discover whether any similarities existed at all between the handwriting measures" [19].

Only two measures, line overlap and capital ratio, correlated with ascendance above .4. Correlations with the Thurstone Scale were higher, from .4 to .6, and could be raised by throwing out certain variables whose validity of measurement was doubtful. On the basis of a multiple correlation coefficient involving the three highest dependable variables, which showed a relationship of .8 to psychoneurosis and .6 to ascendance, Harvey concluded that he had obtained a very high correlation between his handwriting measures and the scale scores.

Though he had begun his study by assuming nothing, "as though the field of research were still untouched," he ended with two tentative conclusions: that personality characteristics as recorded in handwriting issue from extremely complex patterns of behavior; and that single handwriting measures with little relation to measures of psychoneurosis and ascendance when combined in their optimum relationships, yield high indexes of considerable predictive value.

As the shortcomings of the method of correlating measurements from fragmentary parts of handwriting specimens with ratings on specific traits became more obvious, and graphologists became more and more disposed to consider the specimen as a whole, cooperative psychologists devised matching and sorting procedures as a fairer means of evaluating the validity of graphology. This innovation, naturally, moved investigations away from assumption (1), above.

Handwritings were matched by graphologists to case histories; psychologists matched graphological analyses to known persons; from a study of handwritings, graphologists ranked persons as to top or bottom position on given tests and scales [1]. One of the more recent studies using the matching method, published by Eysenck [13], has come from England; it is reported here because of its rich implications for future research. The handwritings of 50 neurotic male patients were analyzed by a graphologist, and matched in 10 five-by-five matchings to several indexes of personality: character sketches prepared by the psychiatrist, diagnoses by the psychiatrist in charge of the cases, intelligence ratings, and questionnaires answered by the patients. Ten psychologists and psychiatrists were required to match sketches prepared by the graphologist to the patients' handwritings.

The questionnaire answered by the patients was in the nature of a self-assessment on major temperamental traits defined by Eysenck and his collaborators. Each question contrasted opposite attitudes, ways of feeling and acting, or general preference. The patients' answers were carefully reviewed by the psychiatrist and psychologists in charge and found to be clinically accurate and essentially honest. The graphologist, Marum [14, 31], was required to answer each question for each patient on the basis of his handwriting specimen. Answers by graphologist and patients were then compared. Out of 1350 judgments by the graphologist, 62 per cent ± 1.4 per cent S.E. were correct. Chance was 50 per cent. Out of 152 judgments on which Marum felt very confident, 68 per cent ± 3.5 per cent S.E. were correct. Chance was 50 per cent. She did not predict intelligence ratings successfully except for those of superior intelligence. The average coefficient of contingency for the 10 five-by-five matchings of handwritings to character sketches and other personality indices, however, was 0.46. The matchings by the 10 psychiatrists and 10 psychologists showed less than chance success.

Eysenck concluded from this study that, "taken altogether, these results seem to show fairly conclusively that it is possible for a skilled graphologist to diagnose personality traits from handwriting with better than chance success" [13]. At the same time, Eysenck raised some pertinent points: the "visibility" of some traits as against others in handwriting; the probability that the handwritings of some individuals are more readily analyzed than those of others; and the great necessity of closer collaboration between graphologist and psychologist if headway is to be made in the field of personality assessment and "expressive movement."

Despite the general positive results for graphology in this study, it seems to this writer that its more important aspect for graphology and psychology lies in the implications from the results of the carefully prepared questionnaire. An analysis of the type of questions most successfully answered by the graphologist is highly suggestive of the areas or levels of functioning that graphology can most accurately tap. For example, Marum scored her highest success with question 17: When something unexpected happens, are you easily startled or do you remain quite unaffected? Her next-highest score was with question 12: Do you get rattled easily in exciting situations (examinations or maneuvers, for instance), or do you usually remain calm, cool, and collected? Her third-highest score was on question 25: Are your feelings easily hurt or do you remain unruffled in general?

Contrariwise, she had least success with question 6: Are you inclined to think things over before acting or do you often act on impulse? Her second-lowest score was on question 3: Do you usually "kick up hell" when you are not getting a square deal, or do you usually just shrug your shoulders and say: "Oh, it doesn't matter"? Her third-lowest score was on question 15: When you are working, are you easily distracted by things that are happening around you or do you usually concentrate wholeheartedly on your work? Questions of highest success appear to relate to the inner experiences of emotional stability and variation by the individual, with little difference as to how the question is put. Questions of lowest success appear to relate to the translation of some of these experiences into manifest behavior. However, in this regard, analysis of all questions with relatively low scores suggests a more consistent failure to get at individual likes, preferences, and rational oscillations (intellectual functioning). Loosely, questions appear to form clusters as to content, and the graphologist's success appears to depend on the extent to which questions fall under emotional, social, personally preferential, intellectual, and physiological areas.

It is highly possible that graphology can indicate accurately that an individual has extreme likes and dislikes without being able to indicate them specifically. To that extent, the questions in the Eysenck study may be too specific to the group tested. At the same time, the questionnaire method, if carefully controlled to cover specific behavior and reactions in broad categories of functioning—emotional, social, occupational, and so on—may ultimately lead to a methodology for relating specific behaviors to handwriting constellations. Naturally, much depends on the type of question asked, its meaning for subject and examiner, and the method chosen to study the handwriting.

Allport and Vernon earlier conducted a matching experiment that concerned itself with the question of graphic movement as expressive movement [1]. Kymographic records, much like Roman's, of pressure curves in drawing parallel lines and writing a sentence, and the sentence itself were matched with better than chance success to thumbnail sketches of the writers by graphologically uninformed judges to whom the writers were unknown. Analysis of the results indicated that the graphic movements apparently had meaning for the judges whether they matched correctly or not. Agreement among the judges was high, even when matchings were incorrect.

The Allport and Vernon experiment, the Eysenck study, and other studies that use the matching method give substantial evidence that handwriting expression and personality expression are subtly related, but they leave untouched the central question of handwriting determinants and their relative importance in a handwriting analysis.

Clinical validation as a method of attack on graphological claims is older than the matching method. Clinical validation, which does not yield easily to satisfactory statistical treatment, was utilized more frequently abroad than here. It has been used repeatedly in studies of mental and physical pathology such as cancer [52], tuberculosis [46], arthritis [4, 27], and various ego disturbances [41]. Lately, it has been re-adopted by numerous clinics and institutions for the practical purpose of seeking out techniques useful for personality testing though not yet standardized or fully validated. It is essentially a method of inquiry into mental life that aims at more refined, differential analyses than are usually obtained by quantified procedures. The amount of agreement or nonagreement among the members of a team, working blind and independently with their respective clinical tests on a given subject, is technically a matter of opinion. In actuality, however, it is entirely possible with this method to arrive at an easily recognizable similarity or dissimilarity of results from the various tests applied [6].

In a study by Munroe [35], results from the Rorschach, graphology, and spontaneous drawings (art technique) were compared to demonstrate the practicable appropriateness of these techniques for student appraisal. Eleven students out of considerably larger groups studied by the Rorschach, the art technique, and graphology were selected for intensive examination by all three techniques. The cases were to be grouped under one of two categories: "adjusted" or "maladjusted." Quantitative methods of counting up gross deviations from "normal" scores were established for the Rorschach and graphology, and applied to unknown cases with statistically significant accuracy [34]. Munroe, however, reported that the quantitative studies gave little evidence about the value of the methods for the type of refined individual diagnosis she had in mind. She suggested that complex descriptive approaches used for revealing configurations of trends within individuals "can perhaps be evaluated fairly only in reference to the particular case and in qualitative terms" [35]. Descriptive findings by the three approaches were compared with a given case history based on known historical data, objective test findings, and teacher observation and opinion. Excerpts from Munroe's findings, which described qualitatively various aspects of the subject's functioning, illustrate the method of comparison:

1. *Intellectual Aspects*
   Rorschach (1940)
   This student seems to be a well-adjusted pedant. She is intelligent...
   and ambitious...methodical, accurate, acute....
   Graphology (1941)
   She is by no means brilliant but she has good average intelligence...a
   diligent worker who is good in routine performance....
   Art Technique (1942)
   A highly constricted person...intelligent and reliable....

After comparison of the qualitative results with scores on various objective tests, Munroe stated: "It would seem that the projective tests offered not only a more complete qualitative picture . . . but also a more sober prediction of . . . academic standing than might have been legitimately derived from other data. . . ." [*35*].

In this study, although the graphologist, Lewinson, used a specific system for examining her variables [*30*], there is no indication of which variables influenced her judgments or to what extent. Munroe reported, however, that headway was made in working out a common methodology for the three techniques by the graphologist's use of her specific system.

Agreement among independent clinicians on personality functioning is of obvious practical value. In relation to graphology, however, clinical validation like the matching method requires graphological accuracy of description without inquiring into graphological assumptions and specificity of criteria. Clinical validation, however, attains a greater degree of specificity than the matching method in that areas of functioning are usually better defined and refined. More important, perhaps, than any degree of validity the clinical method can achieve for graphology is the invaluable opportunity it affords to graphology for comparison between hand writing variations and individual behavior—an indispensable requirement for the development of any device that seeks to relate human behavior to certain descriptive scores, not just for graphology.

Altogether, research findings appear to favor as psychologically most tenable and fruitful the hypothesis that handwriting *expression* and personality functioning are intricately related, but the problem of handwriting as a testing device persistently raises obstacles to quantification and interpretation. The assumption that handwriting is a potential personality "test" is based on the fact of individual variations from the prescribed school standard and the constancy of these variations as a characteristic and identifiable expression. Essentially, the problem is twofold: (1) objective evaluation of the variables or writing elements, and (2) interpreting the objective evaluations once they have been obtained.

The difficulty of evaluating handwriting resides in the two different kinds of elements inherent in writing itself: one kind of element (like slant, height, and width) can be measured physically; the other kind (style or form of the letter, the diffusion or sharpness of the borders of the stroke [pastiness], and so on) can be evaluated only qualitatively or descriptively. Unless reference is made to objective criteria, the second kind of element plainly leaves room for considerable subjective judgment. Psychology's criticism of graphology takes most of its substance from the uncertain use graphologists have made of this second kind of element.

However, even when the qualitative aspect is scientifically controlled, interpretation of the script as a whole cannot proceed objectively until some common unit of value is found for both the measurable and the qualitative elements.

Historically, those interested in handwriting "solved" the two-edged problem mostly by ignoring one aspect or the other, with the result that two pivotal approaches to handwriting analysis developed: (1) an wholistic or global, and (2) an atomistic or analytical. The so-called intuitive graphologists who responded to impressions conveyed by the whole script may be said to belong to the first approach, whereas the French School who counted "signs," and graphologists who measured slant, width, and the like, followed more closely the second approach.

The two different emphases influenced handwriting interpretation without producing a common viable system until Klages, in the late nineteenth century, constructed a system of analysis based on his philosophical concepts of expressive movement [28]. His orientation shifted interest from the handwriting specimen as such to the types of movement that produced the writing [24].

The Klages graphological system may be better understood if something is known of his philosophical concepts. Oversimplified, Klages postulates two forces within man: "mind," which binds and inhibits him, and "soul," which frees and develops him creatively [23]. This latter force Klages calls *rhythm,* or the natural, spontaneous tempo inherent in all cosmic phenomena, for example, seasons, mountains, plants, animals, and man. He identifies this quality in man with healthy, productive functioning, and the other, which he calls *measure* to denote its unvarying periodicity, as the destructive, inhibitory force. According to Klages, these two forces, always dynamically at variance, influence all of man's behavior and are most crystallized in his expressive movements—walk, gesture, posture, writing, and so on. It is in handwriting particularly, where the movements between the two forces are permanently caught, that they are most accessible for study and interpretation.

The variations in the writing, according to Klages, are actually indicators of one force or the other and of the dynamic relationship between them. There are no longer writing elements as such, but psychic movements recorded in the elements. In first expounding his system, he classified the indicators of the inhibitory movements under *contraction,* and those of the liberating movements under *release* [24]. Thus, each element could become an indicator of contraction and/or release movements. For example, minute writing is an indicator of *contraction,* and large writing, an indicator of *release,* but both expressions are contained in the single element *size* or *height of the letter.* At times this element can alternate between large and small in a single specimen, and so become the indicator of both contraction and release movements.

Klages' determinant for healthy functioning was rhythm, contained in release movements. He did not, however, consider all release movements rhythmic. His criterion for what was to be considered rhythm and what merely release was the level of the writing and the intensity of the struggle between contracting and releasing movements. By *level of the writing,* Klages apparently meant the aesthetic quality of the writing usually found in the general pattern of the writing. He left its evaluation to the judgment of the individual graphologist. To help determine the strength of rhythm, which is actually the dynamic relationship between contraction and release movements, he furnished a table of contrasting indicators classified as either contraction or release. Among them, however, he included "harmony" and "lack of harmony"; since harmony was considered an attribute of rhythm, Klages invalidated the objectivity of his tables with this inclusion.

In an over-all estimate, it might be said that Klages' contribution to graphology lies not in his tables, which he later withdrew [25], nor in any one single concept, but in the relatedness of his concepts to psychological theory, and to the promise they held for uncovering in handwriting indications of individual motor patterns or constellations that would be psychologically meaningful. In this relation, Downey wrote: "Such possibility as there exists of reading character from handwriting rests in appearance in handwriting of signs of the release of the motor impulses that produce writing or the reverse . . . it is possible to identify in handwriting signs of motor explosiveness and motor inhibition" [12]. Downey saw the Klages formulations as similar to James' description of the obstructed and explosive types of will, and believed that the determination of the degree to which psychic energy is freely liberated or obstructed was the central problem in the utilization of handwriting in psychodiagnosis. The distinction between the two types was an essential one to her: ". . . particularly if we recognize that an explosive type of will may result either from defective inhibition or exaggerated impulsion or an obstructed one from excessive inhibition or insufficient impulsion" [11]. It was especially within these two main divisions that Downey classified her "hands," paying attention to specific kinds of overlap in both.

Pulver both extended and elaborated the Klages graphological system by applying psychoanalytic concepts. He gave handwriting a third dimension, as it were, adding depth to the usual two graphic dimensions, height and width (breadth). Depth, he explained, referred to *pressure,* which in the language of graphic expression, employed front and back movements. These movements actually seek to go *through* the paper, he said, as contrasted with movements in the height dimension, which travel up and down or vertically, as seen in *size of writing, upper and lower loops,* and the like, or with movements in the width dimension, which travel from left to right or horizontally, as seen in *space between letters, space between words,* and so on.

He schematized the writing field—the paper—relating the various movements and dimensions symbolically to the different levels of functioning in the individual. Figure 5 shows a simplified form of Pulver's schematization of writing movements and the writing field [29, 30, 41].

A refers to movements in the breadth dimension, those that move from left to right, symbolically either toward or away from the environment.

B refers to movements in the height dimension, those that move from north to south, symbolically referrable to the individual's rational coordination.

C refers to movements in the depth dimension, those that move from front to back, symbolically referrable to the individual's instinctive and biological functioning.

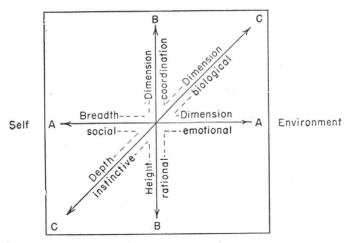

Fig. 5. Pulver's schematization of the writing field.

Pulver asserted that the multifariousness of personality allowed for no simple duality of interpretation as set forth by Klages. At each level, the expressive movement means something else, and its graphic indicator has to be interpreted accordingly.

Pulver's contribution to graphology is largely empirical. However, he called attention to the complex interrelationship of the writing elements and the nature of ambivalences as expressed in the writing picture.

More recently, Lewinson and Zubin [*30*] utilized concepts from both Klages and Pulver but sought to correct the fallacy of the Klages table by providing objective criteria for the evaluation of all aspects of rhythm. Further, though they used the concept of rhythm as a norm and that of graphic elements as indicators of tendencies toward contraction and release, they postulated rhythm as the point of balanced interplay between contracting and releasing tendencies (movements). By inference, this balance between contracting and releasing tendencies creates a third new force: rhythm, the power or energy for healthy productive functioning.

Moreover, the experimenters assumed that all graphic elements can be indicators of rhythm just as they can be indicators of tendencies toward contraction and release. Thus, for example, *size, width, spacing, slant, pressure,* and *form,* could all be indicators of rhythm. Their basic hypothesis was "that handwriting in all its aspects may be regarded as an expressive movement and that this movement may be classified on a contraction-release continuum" [*30*]. The movement is considered to be expressive in the sense that the degree of emotional control (or lack of it) is accompanied by and reflected in a corresponding control in the writing of the graphic elements. It was further assumed that the nature of this expressive movement is recorded in the structure of the writing itself. The result of the Lewinson and Zubin experiment was a "series of scales for evaluating the dynamic aspects of handwriting" [*30*]. The ultimate objective of the scales was to describe the individual's movement impulses through an analysis of his handwriting expression.

With the aid of precision instruments, illustrations, and definitions, the scales dissect the characteristics of handwriting into 16 measurable (objective) and six ratable (subjective) elements. Common units of value are then assigned to the measures through classification into seven categories. These represent the points in a seven-point scale, which is divided into three degrees on either side of a midpoint called *balance*. To the left, progressing outward and indicating increasing degrees of control, are *contraction* 1, 2, and 3; to the right, progressing outward and indicating increasing degrees of undercontrol, are *release* 1, 2, and 3. It should be noted that these terms have reference to the type of movement that produced the writing; for example, overcontrolled (*contraction*), normally controlled (*balance*), and undercontrolled (*release*).

Each element has an individual scale, and each measurement or rating can be converted into a value on the contraction-balance-release scale. Figure 6 represents the scale for the *height* or *size of the letter;* it illustrates the basic structure of the Lewinson and Zubin scales, and the means of converting measurements into their corresponding values in the contraction-balance-release continuum. Thus, a letter measuring 4.25 millimeters would have a value of *release* 1 on the continuum.

less than .75 mm.	from .76 to 1.49	from 1.50 to 2.74	from 2.75 to 3.24	from 3.25 to 4.50	from 4.51 to 6 mm.	more than 6 mm.
3	2	1	0	1	2	3
	contraction		balance		release	

Fig. 6. Scale for height or size of letters. The unit of measurement is one millimeter.

Similarly, ratings controlled by restrictive definitions and illustrations are evaluated and assigned a value on the scales. For example, the form of the letter is rated according to seven basic styles. Each style is defined and illustrated, presumably reducing the subjectivity of judgment usually attached to this graphic element. Figure 7 shows examples of the scale for *form of the letter*, with corresponding values in the contraction-balance-release continuum.

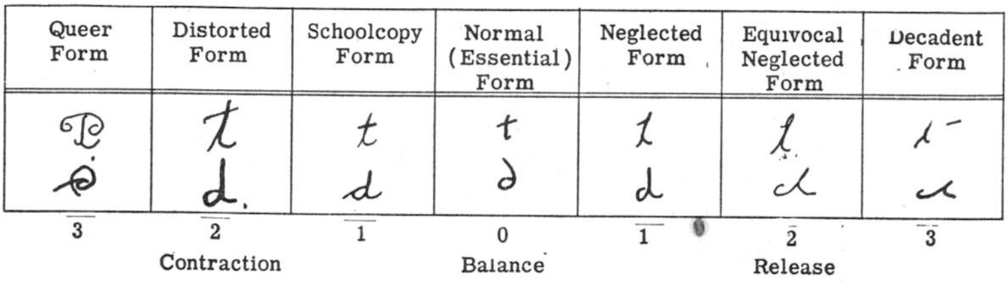

Queer Form	Distorted Form	Schoolcopy Form	Normal (Essential) Form	Neglected Form	Equivocal Neglected Form	Decadent Form
3	2	1	0	1	2	3

Contraction   Balance   Release

Fig. 7. Scale for form of letter.

The evaluations for all 22 scales are an adaptation of those used by other graphologists [22, 24, 41, 44].

The elements are grouped on the scales into four components: vertical, horizontal, depth, and form. The latter, in part, is the method used by the experimenters to synthesize the qualitative aspects of "general appearance" with the geometrically measurable aspects in the three other components. Under the Lewinson and Zubin system, the standard of judgment for the characteristics for general appearance is not the school copy form but an "essential" derivative from the school copy. Generally, it may be described as a simplified version of the school copy, optimally modified but characteristic enough in form to be recognizable if isolated from all other letters. Examples are given in Figure 7, Essential Form.

The analysis of the 22 variables in the scales results in a curve or distribution deemed to be a measure of the individual impulses that actuated the writing movements. Under the hypothesis of the scales, it was expected that the handwritings of normally adjusted individuals would have their point of highest recordings at *balance,* with diminishing degrees of recordings at the intermediate and extreme points. The theoretical distribution to approximate "the ideal distribution" for the rhythmically balanced writer was the binomial distribution $(\frac{1}{2} + \frac{1}{2})^6$ [30, 55].

The subjects tested were five normals, seven schizophrenics, five manic-depressives, one obsessive neurotic, and two undiagnosed. Statistical treatment showed the hypothesis of rhythmic balance to be untenable in all but two instances, that of the form components of two normals. Analysis, however, of the distributions for each component to determine the degree of departure from the hypothetical distribution of rhythmic balance for each subject indicated that the normals deviated less from rhythmic balance in three of the components, and in the composite distribution from all four components.

In an attempt to find another hypothesis, the assumption was made that all writings are controlled by one or more contraction tendencies, a single contraction tendency of 50 per cent resulting in rhythmic balance, one of less than 50 per cent resulting in skewness in the direction of release, and one of more than 50 per cent resulting in skewness in the direction of contraction. Analysis of the distributions of separate elements indicated that it was possible to find one consistent contraction value or a combination of two opposite values for some of the normals. Except in very few cases, it was not possible to find such values for the writings of the abnormals. The experimenters concluded, "Apparently the contraction tendency of the abnormals varies so greatly from moment to moment that no consistent contraction pattern can be found" [30]. This conclusion appeared to them to confirm the general observation that the most striking difference between normal and abnormal performance is in the consistency or variability of the act.

Except by implication in the comparison between normals and abnormals, no attempt was made to correlate personality and a subject's place on the contraction-balance-release continuum. Lewinson and Zubin's closing remark, however, touches on handwriting as a personality expression: ". . . It is reassuring to note that when carefully controlled measures and rating scales are applied, it becomes possible to discern an underlying differentiating pattern in the handwriting of an individual which may well prove to be the basis for understanding underlying personality structures" [30].

The experimenters claimed to have found an objective, specific, and unified frame of reference for handwriting that might prove useful as a testing technique. However, the subjects tested were few; such variables as age, sex, and cultural level went uncontrolled; and the degree to which differences in distributions depended on ratable (possibly subjective) elements was not indicated.

Wolfson applied the Lewinson-Zubin scales to two groups equated for sex, age, race, nationality, IQ, and socioeconomic level. The study was conducted with the general purpose of determining the usefulness of the Lewinson and Zubin approach to handwriting as a device for studying personality, and concerned itself with analysis of only the composite curve, that is, the combined results from the four components: form, vertical, horizontal, and depth. The problem of the study stemmed from the assumption made by Lewinson and Zubin that the recordings from the handwriting of the well-adjusted individual could be expected to have their greatest frequency at rhythmic balance, with diminishing frequencies at the intermediate and extreme points. Thus, hypothetically, the more perfectly adjusted the individual, the more recordings at the midpoint. Under the scales analysis, a sample population containing more normals than deviants would be expected to produce a composite distribution with its peak at *balance* and a small number of recordings at the extremes. Further, it might be expected that a special homogeneous group, limited in number, would depart in some ways from the normal. Two such homogeneous groups, similarly limited in number but differing distinctly in one respect, would be expected to show deviations from the normal group; these deviations would be indicative of the distinction between them [54].

The subjects for the test group were 33 white American males, institutionalized for delinquency. In this study, delinquency had reference not only to repeated legal offenses as such, but also to the involvement of psychological factors in delinquency as demonstrated by long-time investigators of delinquency. The nondelinquent group were 33 public school students whose social adjustment was evaluated by teachers and others to whom the subjects were known. Writing accomplishment for both groups was left to teacher opinion.

Two specific questions were asked in relation to the scales: (1) Would the two curves representative of the average distribution on the continuum for each group show any significant differences? (2) If so, in what direction?

The chi-square test showed the groups to be significantly different. Statistical analysis to determine at what points in the continuum the groups differed showed wide differences at *contraction* 3, *balance,* and *release* 3; moderate differences at *release* 1 and 2; little difference at *contraction* 1 and 2. Further, the results from analyses of the distributions with only the 16 measurable factors were not significantly different from those based on all 22. Analysis of the individual scale recordings at the three significant points indicated (1) a general tendency toward skewness in one or the other direction in both groups, the direction being the same for both groups in any single instance, but less extreme for the nondelinquent group; (2) a high discriminatory value for seven elements; and (3) problems in weighting, rescaling, and procedure.

Although the statistical results indicated that the scales actually differentiated between the two groups in the expected direction—that is, the group normally considered to be better adjusted was shown to have more balanced and fewer extreme tendencies than the deviant group—the importance of this study to handwriting analysis is not in the statistical findings as such, but in the conclusions to be drawn from them regarding the scales themselves. Wolfson concluded that despite the many problems raised by the study, "in view of the special reference to a specific type of behavior . . . the statistical results give evidence that the recordings have a meaningful relationship to psychological behavior" [54]. She considered the Lewinson-Zubin scales a promising "anatomy" or geography for handwriting, which can guide the graphologically uninformed and serve investigators of handwriting as a common, basic starting point. Most important, perhaps, the L-Z scales in their combined atomistic and global structure and their objective treatment of "rhythm" offer a scientific means of investigating how sound judgments are made and the ways in which they can be extended [36, p. 694].

As problems for future research, the Wolfson study suggested experimentation with a five-point or rescaled seven-point range, with special attention to extensive clinical data from accepted procedures for testing and interpreting personality. It was pointed out that for most elements, a relatively small portion of the entire range is associated with the midpoint, rhythmic balance, and that the inability to find consistent contraction values for the writings of subjects in both the Lewinson and Zubin study and Wolfson's study may be as much a function of the narrowness of range for balance as it is of a "disturbed personality structure." Empirical data from analyses of various handwritings and corresponding case histories suggested that the range for balance in many instances could be extended well into the measurements assigned to contraction and release 1, without violating the concept of "well-adjusted" functioning.

The emergence of seven elements with a high differential value raises the possibility of a "delinquent constellation" or of a graphic structural nucleus, containing significant indicators, in all handwritings. In this regard, however, it should be noted that the age range in the Wolfson study was 14.7 to 17 (median 15.9 and 15.7), psychologically considered as the age of physiological maturations and heightened psychic shifts and tensions. The advisability, therefore, of applying these data to adult functioning without further investigation and analysis is doubtful. At present, research is planned for application of the scales, with considered changes, to an adult population.

This presentation of the various approaches, hypotheses, and experiments in handwriting by no means exhausts the list. Space does not allow discussion of all. No mention has been made, for example, of Pascal's excellent experimental and statistical inquiries [*38, 39*], of Super's comparison of graphological diagnoses with the results from psychological tests [*49*], or of Booth's evaluation of graphology from the physician's point of view [*4, 5*]. The presentation is at best representative but by no means complete. Research studies by Wolff have been discussed in Chapter 16.

THEORETICAL AND CLINICAL CONSIDERATIONS

Turning now to consideration of some of its clinical aspects, graphology as a "test" of personality expression can be classified as a projective technique if one accepts the contention by Frank [*15*] and Rapaport [*42*] that all tests are projective in the sense that all tests reveal something of the subject's "private world." More narrowly, however, handwriting falls into the category of tests of expressive movement. As an individual test, it may be said to reflect the individual's pattern of behavior, compared with his mode of perception and association as determined by the Rorschach. Its special merit among tests similarly defined, that is, tests of expressive movement, is its comparatively easy availability, its more permanent type of record for developmental study, and its comparative freedom from falsification, conscious or otherwise. Its limitations as a test, aside from the question of the psychological functions it can or cannot tap, are similar to those connected with tests dependent on verbal performance. In other words, it is limited to subjects who have attained a certain cultural level. Whereas normally all persons can walk, gesture, stand, and draw circles, squares, and human figures, not all persons have attained a literacy level sufficient for spontaneous writing.

Also, the value of handwriting analysis in cases of severely disturbed manual motility is highly questionable. Despite accurate deductions as to anatomical areas of disturbance in arm and hand by experimental graphologists [10, 45], the amount of disturbance introduced into the writing movements by the mechanical act itself so distorts the writing picture that for usual clinical purposes the graphological technique is inappropriate. Reference here is being made to gross motility disturbances that result from infantile paralysis, palsy, advanced stages of chorea, Parkinsonism, and so on. Contrariwise, an examination of the literature and active clinical experience point to handwriting as a likely uncovering technique for diseases now considered "psychosomatic" [4, 5, 27].

Use as a clinical tool before scientific validation is not peculiar to graphology; it has its precedent in psychotherapy itself, play therapy, group therapy, the early forms of the Binet, the Rorschach, and other techniques. The issues involved in the clinical acceptance of graphology, specifically, do not differ from those involved in the acceptance of practices and theories in other psychological areas. The importance of training, clinical and psychological experience, criticalness, skill, and above all self-admissable fallibility applies to all equally. The obvious justification for its use is its practical contribution, as demonstrated by its frequent corroboration of other test findings. Another development favoring its use, and possibly more reassuring to psychology generally, is the slow emergence of a greater number of psychologists, graphologically inquisitive, experimentally wise, and practically cautious. The claims they make are in sober relation to their scientific data.

Handwriting analysis is used by clinics, psychologists, and psychiatrists as one of a battery of tests [6]. It is seldom employed alone, except in those instances where developmental phases as described through handwriting analyses of early handwriting specimens are compared with certain aspects of associative material from patients in psychiatric or psychoanalytic treatment; or when comparison of the structure of the writing before and after onset of a pathological condition is made [27, 30]. In the former instances, the questions to be answered and the areas to be explored are controlled by the kind of associative material into which the psychiatrist or analyst is inquiring.

As a test in a battery, the graphological analysis is required to confine itself to those phases of functioning also explored by one or more of the other tests in the battery, so that the graphological results can be considered in conjunction with the battery as a whole. The insights that it gives touch on the individual's patterns of behavior; considered graphological opinion recognizes graphology as a descriptive rather than a diagnostic technique.

Undoubtedly, there are still graphologists who "diagnose," and form mass impressions. Two factors, however, have militated against this type of analysis: (1) recognition by the clinical graphologist of the necessity of adapting the graphological tool to examination of the specific functions measured by more standardized tests, and (2) the critical choice by clinics, educational institutions, psychiatrists, psychologists, and others, of graphologists well grounded in psychology, theoretical and clinical, as well as in graphology.

The clinical graphologist today analyzes minutely the relationship between movements, on the one hand, and the balance and imbalance among them, on the other. The integrative process on which the total analysis hinges admittedly contains subjective judgments, but these are controlled by what is known of man's psychological processes, not by "feelings" based on wholesale impressions, as was earlier evidenced. In this sense, the clinical graphologist is no more "intuitive" than the clinical psychologist, who is told repeatedly that the accuracy of his conclusions depends on two factors: his familiarity with the technique involved, and his understanding of psychodynamics.

How the graphologist goes about analyzing and interpreting his material depends on what system or combination of systems he employs—the Klages, Pulver, Saudek, or some other. Nevertheless, barring the "isolationists" who still interpret *t*-bars and curlicues out of context, most reputable graphologists today are guided, if not by identical, at least by similar concepts and measures [*29, 39, 44*]. The elements they examine for movement tendencies are essentially the same, though nominally they may differ. There are, in all, some 20 to 25 variables, the range representing not so much an omission as a combination of graphic elements: for example, when *letter form* and *contour of the letter* are combined. A representative table of the elements handled by most practicing graphologists follows:

Common Graphic Elements

form of the letter	space between letters
form of connection	space between words
width of the stroke	width of the letter
sharpness/pastiness	slant
curvature of the stroke	fluctuation of the slant
size of the small letters	left-right tendency within letters
differences of lengths (upper and lower projections)	margins
	pressure
direction of line	placement of pressure
fluctuation of line	degree of connection between letters
space between lines	

The questions that graphologists ask in relation to the handwriting picture are similar, and are suggestive of how they arrive at an integration of their analysis. The purpose of the following discussion is to introduce the graphological method to the clinical psychologist, and to suggest some of the problems that confront the graphologist in action. It is hoped that in this way the clinical psychologist may gain some understanding of the factors involved in a handwriting analysis, and thus be somewhat better equipped to evaluate graphology and its allied problems more critically. The discussion is intended neither as instruction in graphology nor as evidence for or against its validity, and hence, may at times be arbitrary or cursory.

Before beginning an analysis, the clinical graphologist needs to know the subject's age, sex, race, nationality, and place of primary school education. Aside from the importance of age in relation to the development of the mechanical aspects of the writing act, the importance of the first three factors for an accurate psychological report is too obvious to need explanation. Nationality and place of primary school education fix the standard with which the subject began his writing expression.

The material with which the graphologist works may consist of one or more specimens written in ink. Pencil lead tends to spread too readily during the writing act and thus falsify movement relationships [*38*]. Results from single specimens usually tally so closely with other specimens from the same subject, written more or less during the same period, that single specimens are acceptable for analysis. Specimens should be at least one-half page long, should have been written with attention to content rather than the writing act, and should carry a minimum of indications of extraneous interference with the writing act (clogged ink, impaired pen, and so on).

Practically, and because the graphologist works blind for the most part, he is given specimens easily acquired from the subject— letters to the clinic, physician, dean; admissions requests; questionnaires, written reactions to tests, picture descriptions, and the like. For the most part, these are adequate for analysis if they contain sentences in running form.

In an analysis, the writing field (the paper) is considered representative of the outer world, and the writing, indicative of the characteristic involvement of the self with the world. The variations within the writing movements may be said to be a reflection of the different aspects of the individual's engagement with his environment. How the individual disposes of the writing field is indicative of the degree to which he can coordinate himself harmoniously in the face of realistic environmental limitations. The manner in which he attempts to attain a harmonious coordination is indicated by the various degrees of control (or undercontrol), as shown in the separate and total graphic movements. The writing field, in the amount of absolute area it offers to the individual, is beyond his control; he can avail himself of a larger or smaller portion of the absolute area but cannot expand or diminish it (excepting by actual physical alteration: tearing, pasting, and the like, after which he is only confronted all over again by the same basic problem). Thus, if he writes minutely, he uses less of the area per word but may use as much of the total area as the individual who writes large. Both may then be said to utilize an equal amount of space, but the manner of utilization differs.

At the beginning, it is helpful to think in four broad movement categories: (1) overcontrol, (2) undercontrol, (3) "midway" control, or a "tie" between (1) and (2), and (4) balanced or rhythmic control. Comparable clinical terminology might be (1) excessive inhibition, (2) excessive release or impulsivity, (3) extreme conflict with alternations between (1) and ((2), and (4) flexibly adaptive and productive coordination.

It should be noted that when the graphologist speaks of "overcontrol," he means, as do other psychological clinicians, *predominantly* overcontrol. There are always indicators to the contrary; though few, they must be "reconciled" to the rest of the psychological picture. Handwriting analysis is fundamentally a study of relationships as indicated by the measures and ratios of the graphic elements. Writings are neither overcontrolled nor undercontrolled because the size of the letter or the slant is of a given measurement. A handwriting is considered overcontrolled when the size, width, slant, spacing, form, and other aspects, *in interrelationship,* point in the direction of a slow, impeded execution. For example, the tendency contained in *space between letters* cannot be classified under any of the four categories until its relationship (ratio) to the tendency contained in the element, *size of the small letters,* is known.

Absolute measures, say, for *size of the small letters* or *slant,* do exist. However, these measures, like those with more dependent associations, are brought into relationship with other elements through evaluations as to the type of movements involved in producing given measures; say, for example, a slant of 115° or a letter height of six millimeters. Didactically, an analysis begins with measurements of *size of the small letters,* that is, letters that have no upper or lower projections. Some six elements are related by ratios to *size of the small letters;* thus, a cluster or nucleus of ratios is formed around this single element. Other elements, like *width of the stroke* and *pressure,* are related to each other more singularly, and integrated with the other elements (measures) through the common unit, contraction-balance-release.

Figures 8 through 11 illustrate writing pictures that fall predominantly into one or another of the four categories under discussion. If, for example, we accept the evaluations given in Figure 6 as measures for the movement tendencies in *size of the small letters,* we have a starting point for evaluation of Figure 8. Though the size of the writing is small, this in itself is insufficient to classify it as overcontrolled. It frequently happens that a writing is extremely large, yet falls into the category *overcontrol* (see Figure 12). The relationship of the measures from the other elements to size measures in Figure 8, however, indicates the predominant inhibition or restraint of most of the movements. Naturally, for such an analysis, the graphologist, like the psychologist, must be thoroughly familiar with the measures and units of values assigned to the different responses. Without detailed reference to measurements, ratios, and so on, some of the elements that categorize the handwriting in Figure 8 as overcontrolled are narrowness of the letter, wide space between words, exaggerated length of upper and lower projections, choppiness of the stroke, left-going slant, fine stroke, and elaborated lower projections.

Figure 9 demonstrates the exact opposite of Figure 8, and serves at the same time to show how measures from a single element are insufficient to categorize a writing. Beginning again with *size of the small letters,* what is noticeable at once is a variety of sizes, ranging from very small to moderately large, with the emphasis on small rather than large. The elements that carry the movements toward undercontrol, however, are space between letters, space between words, width of the letter, space between lines, width of stroke, rising line, undulation of the line, right-going slant, fluctuation of the slant, dissolution of the connecting forms, neglect of the letter forms, exaggerated curvature, and others.

Figure 10 might, in brief study, suggest overcontrol. Analysis, however, reveals almost as many indicators of undercontrol as of overcontrol. It should be mentioned in this regard that indicators in all movement categories, in all handwritings, fall at times into the balance category. In other than balanced writings, however, the tendencies tend to stay predominantly in overcontrol or undercontrol, or skip from one to the other without moving through a balanced interplay between the two. It is this lack of undulation from some overcontrol to balance to some undercontrol and back

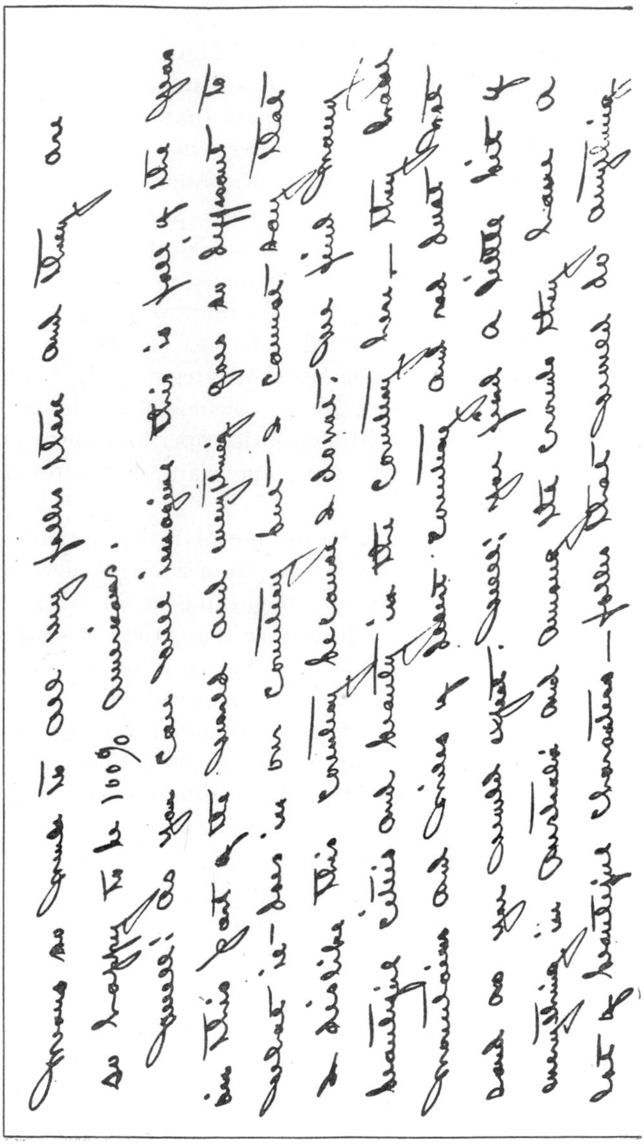

Fig. 8.   Overcontrol.   (Reduced from actual size by one-fifth.)

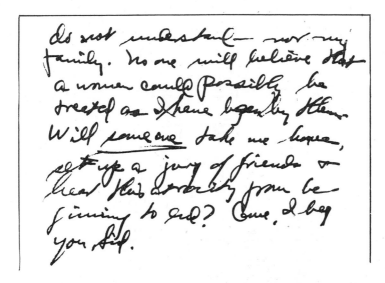

Fig. 9. Undercontrol. (Reduced from actual size by one-fifth.)

to balance, overcontrol, and so on, in an individual rhythmic pattern, that throws the movements in the direction of one pole or the other or both, as in Figure 10.

The indicators of overcontrol and undercontrol are frequently the same in this specimen; for example, curvature (jerky *and* exaggerated), length of upper and lower projections (under *and* overemphasized), space between letters (narrow *and* wide), slant (left *and* right). Elements that are indicators of predominant overcontrol are form of the letter, form of connection and margins; indicators of predominant undercontrol are width of the stroke, pastiness, and space between lines. The movements as indicated in size of the letter fluctuate regularly from overcontrol to balance to undercontrol, and so on. It is the relationship of the other movements to this balanced area that indicates imbalance.

Figure 11 illustrates a writing characterized by movements that oscillate from overcontrol to undercontrol but hover predominantly around balance. Indicators of movements predominantly in balance are width of the stroke, borders of the stroke, curvature, size of the letters, space between lines, space between letters, width of the letter, and slant.

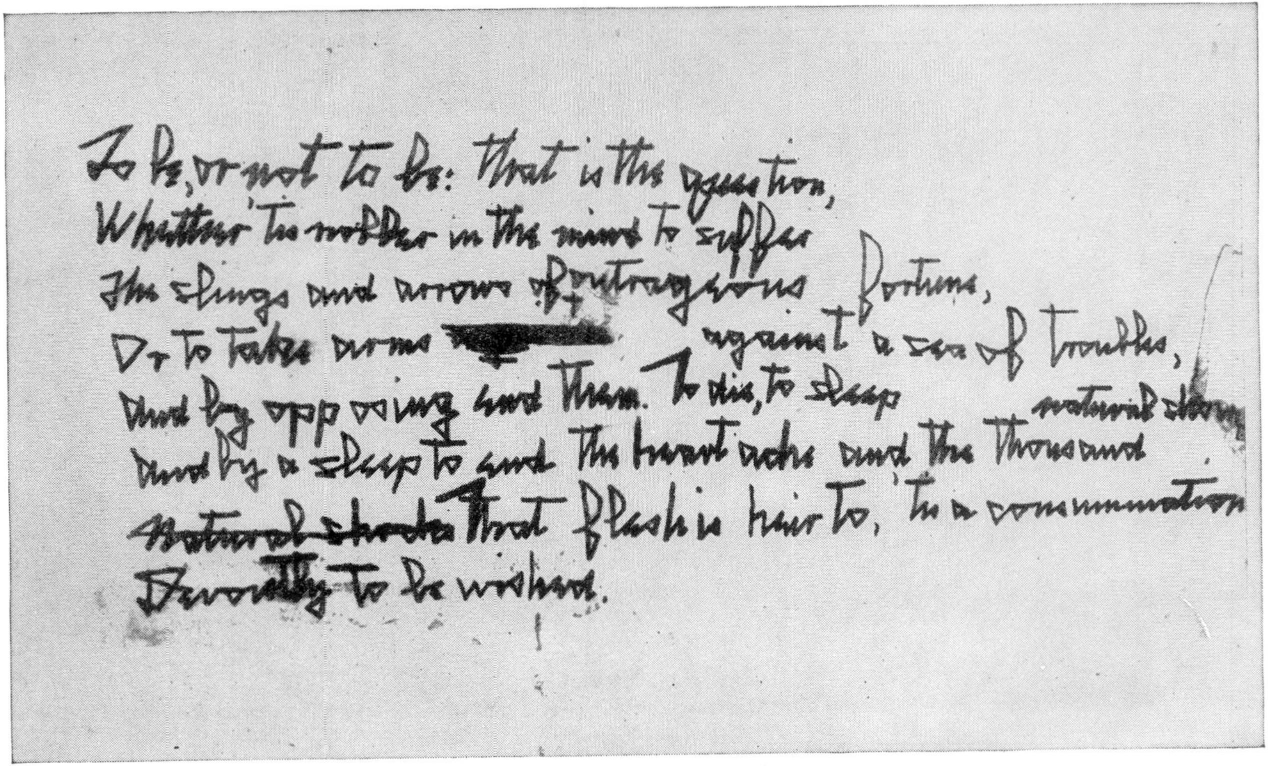

Fig. 10. "Midway" control. (Reduced from actual size by one-fifth.)

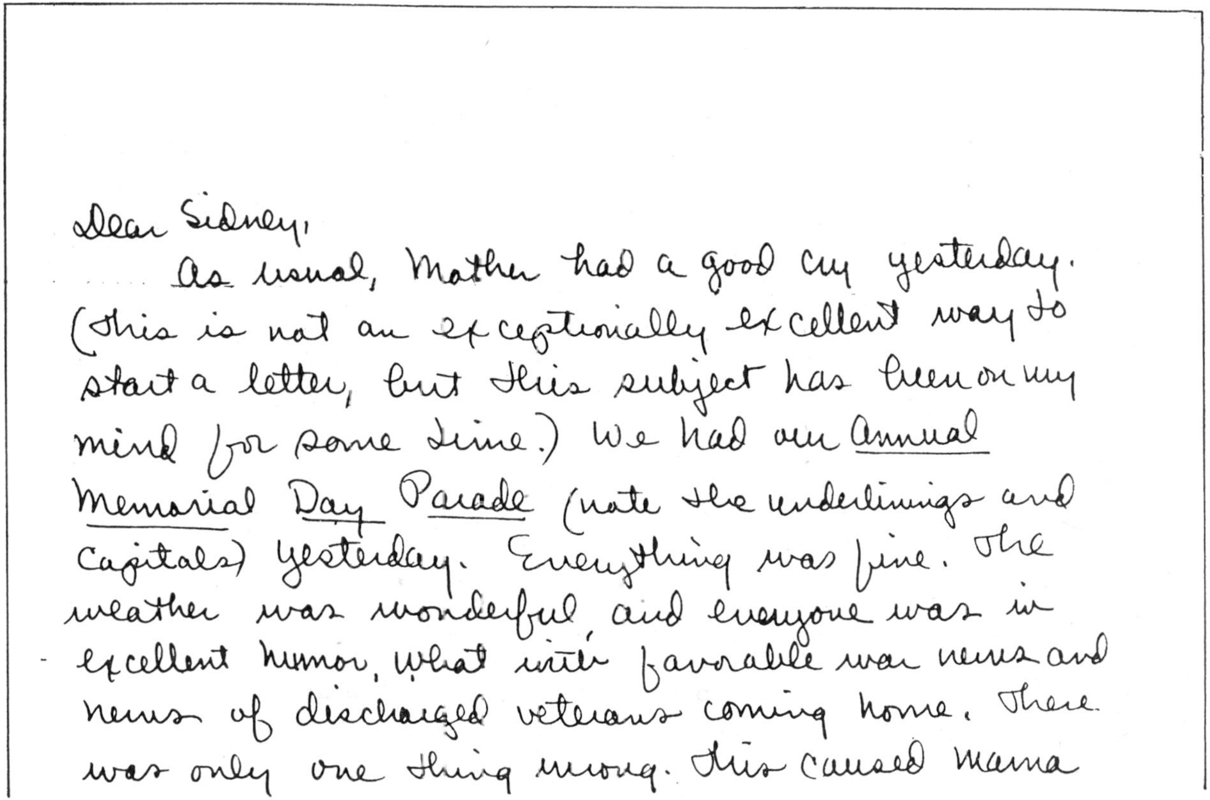

Dear Sidney,

As usual, Mother had a good cry yesterday. (This is not an exceptionally excellent way to start a letter, but this subject has been on my mind for some time.) We had our Annual <u>Memorial Day Parade</u> (note the underlinings and capitals) yesterday. Everything was fine, the weather was wonderful and everyone was in excellent humor, what with favorable war news and news of discharged veterans coming home, there was only one thing wrong. This caused Mama

Fig. 11. Balance. (Reduced from actual size by one-fifth.)

This manner of illustrating the four categories is also suggestive of the way the graphologist reduces the graphic structure to its rudiments when analyzing a specimen.   Whereas didactically, the analysis begins with *size of the letters,* clinically, it begins with those characteristics or relationships that "call attention to themselves" by dominating the writing expression.   The experienced graphologist, like the experienced psychologist, learns to recognize deviations and "norms" even before going through the formal scoring; and the likelihood is that his starting point will be where the movement emphasis takes it.   In any case, before he is through, he must take account of the whole writing expression.

Some of the questions that immediately concern the graphologist as he begins the analysis are finding the point or points of graphic emphasis, localization of emphasis to a specific graphic area or areas (height, width, depth, and so on), analyzing for spread of effect to other areas (indicated by ratios and relationships), and determining if the points of emphasis and relationships indicate balance or dynamic disturbance in the entire writing expression.

The actual translation of the characterization of a writing as overcontrolled, undercontrolled, "midway" controlled, or balanced, into a behavioral picture is rooted in a hybrid of concepts from the theory of expressive movements and Pulver's psychoanalytic analogies.   The diagram in Figure 5 is suggestive of the reference points from which indicators in the four dimensions take their meanings.   For example, to oversimplify, if a handwriting after analysis is categorized as undercontrolled, the pertinent question is: in which area predominantly?   It may be in all areas, in three areas, or in two.

Pulver's schematization indicates that movements from left to right refer to the degree to which the individual is actively involved with the environment or concentrically around himself.   If, therefore, the Pulver system is used, a predominant disturbance in the movements in one or the other direction or both (towards overcontrol, undercontrol, or "midway") establishes the finding of an unadjusted emotional relationship with the environment, and the direction in which the disturbance moves (towards inhibition, impulsivity, and the like).   How this disturbance is expressed cannot be determined from the movements in this area alone.   No disturbance in a dynamic system is single in effect; most of the time, there are related imbalances and overcompensations.

In determining the spread of effect from one area to another, the graphologist gets a more complete picture of the kind of specific expression the disturbance is likely to take. For example, if in the case above, the spread (indicated by the ratios and similar or opposite patterns of movements) is also in the direction of undercontrol in the height dimension, following Pulver, the emotional disturbance is related to a disturbance in the individual's rational organization—in the direction of dissolution (undercontrol). If the movements in all dimensions form a pattern of predominant undercontrol (again following Pulver), unadaptive, impulsive behavior in rational, social, and emotional life is indicated. If, however, the movements in only one of the dimensions—height, for example—is undercontrolled, and the rest are in balance, the individual's rational organization is troubled and uncoordinated but sustained by good emotional-social and instinctive (biological) functioning. This lack of coordination may be insufficient to throw the entire functioning out of balance, but it may also indicate a likely area of sensitivity should pressures reduce emotional and instinctive adjustment.

It should be noted that although the discussion above, in order to simplify the presentation, tended to sectionalize the writing, in practice, a meaningful graphological analysis cannot be additive any more than can a Wechsler-Bellevue scatter analysis or a Rorschach protocol. The subtleties and nuances of behavior are suggested by the different emphases of movements in the various elements. To that extent, every element is characteristically related to a single facet of the individual's functioning; this facet however is always and constantly relative, gaining added importance in one functioning, and less in another, depending on the relationships determined by the other elements. For example, didactically, *the size of the letters* refers to the individual's ego feelings. The entire height dimension, however, represents the individual's rational organization or coordination, psychologically defined as an ego function. It can readily be seen that any attempt to interpret evaluations of *size of the letters* in absolute terms, that is, without taking into account the evaluations of all those elements that determine interpretation of the many facets on which ego feelings turn, is likely to lead to a psychological potpourri. This is true for all the dimensions in relation to one another, as it is for all the elements in their relationships to one another and to the four dimensions.

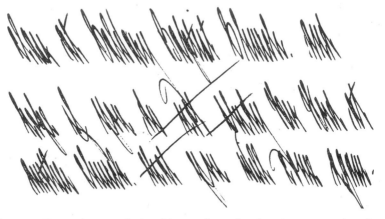

Fig. 12. Example of relationships and predominant movement expressions. (Reduced from actual size by one-fifth.)

One final example of the importance of relationships and predominant movement expressions: the dominating element in Figure 12 is the *size of the letters,* but it is not the dominant movement. Attention is called here to the difficulties one is likely to encounter in attempting to interpret by single elements instead of related movements. The dominant movement in Figure 12 shows itself in the relationships of the other elements (distance between letters and words, width of the letter, margins, slant, and so on) to the dominant element. The contradiction between the movements as determined by *size* and the movements as determined by related elements is the most conspicuous characteristic of this writing. This conspicuousness of the letter size, however, cannot be shifted about arbitrarily. It dominates the whole writing field, throwing other movements out of balanced relationship to it. At the same time, this imbalance is in the direction of extreme overcontrol. Interpretation of this conspicuous movement of undercontrol (as shown by the exaggerated size of the letters) must therefore take account of the movements of overcontrol. A domination that might otherwise be aggressively impulsive is contained and coordinated with a strong degree of control and reserve.

The problem of graphic relationships is admittedly a thorny one; the amount of emphasis given to certain relationships instead of others by graphologists is still variable—and this is the nub of the problem of objectifying graphological interpretation. It may be, however, that in the quarrel over the use of graphology, though much has been said regarding the differences among graphologists, too little has been said about their agreements. A survey of graphological literature and experiments indicates that there is considerable agreement on what are the more lasting characteristics of handwriting—for instance, spacing relationships, letter size relationships, pressure placement, and degree of connection—and a surprising amount of agreement if one thinks in ranges rather than in absolute figures on measurements for contraction-balance-release.

These converging points of agreement would appear to be the most logical starting point for inquiry into specific degrees of emphasis given the graphic variables. It hardly seems likely that in as individual a procedure as handwriting analysis, agreement by court expert, pedagogue, mechanical and graphological experimentalist, and graphologist on these different aspects is due to chance. Whatever the view, however, these agreements cannot be dismissed as coincidence until they have been systematically explored.

Throughout this chapter, frequent reference has been made in passing to the many graphological problems into which research can fruitfully inquire. It seems rather pointless at this stage of graphological investigation and clinical use to accumulate more and more studies, no matter how thorough and ingenious the methodology [1, 39], in order to present "the case for graphology."

There is already an impressive array of such studies to which the more skeptical can turn. From a practical point of view, to make graphology a more valid, uniform tool, other problems are more urgent. To list but a few: What is the correlation among graphic elements? Is the empirical division into dimensions statistically valid, and/or is it sustained by significant correspondence with specifically defined behavior? Harvey's study suggested clusterings in the height dimension and among spatial elements [19], which should be further explored.

Are all the graphic elements equally important for analysis or can some be omitted with little difference to the personality description? Closely allied to this question is the one of weighting—

What specific degrees of stress are put on the various indicators of movements of overcontrol, undercontrol, and balance? What areas of functioning are most accurately tapped by the graphological technique? What clusters or interrelationships of elements or dimensions are statistically correlated to specific types of behavior, both adjusted and unadjusted?

Clinically described constellations still await scientifically controlled investigation and treatment; clinically, constellations in arthritis [27], schizophrenia, paranoia, and so on [29], have been studied descriptively but have not yet been treated quantitatively.

Though graphology has an old history and many respected ancestors, it is still very young among quantified techniques. How it grows (possibly even *if* it grows) to productive, full maturity depends not only upon those directly concerned with applying the technique, but upon all psychologists whose primary concern is to add to the understanding of human behavior by developing more revealing, sensitive, and valid ways of probing its complexities. Graphology, like any other technique, cannot forge itself into a valid, standard tool in isolation. It needs continuous checking with the clinical picture, and matter-of-course acceptance in clinical team-work to determine how much it can contribute and where it can contribute most. Hand in hand with the problem of validating graphology is the problem of finding more valid means of testing social and emotional variables. The validations between graphological interpretation and personality variables depend as much on accurate psychological definition and valid objective criteria as they do on accurate and specific interpretation. The responsibility for validating graphology scientifically would appear, then, to be a common responsibility, not an esoteric one.

SUMMARY

Handwriting has been the object of both serious and superficial study. Generally, there have been five approaches to handwriting: characterological, pedagogical, forensic, experimental, and psychological. Experimentation by one approach frequently leads to findings useful to the others.

In Europe, handwriting as a record of personality expression has been more readily accepted than in America. European theorizing and study have led to the concept of handwriting as an expressive movement. Klages is the most outstanding exponent of this school. Pulver extended handwriting to three dimensions, and correlated them symbolically to the many intricacies of dynamic behavior.

In this country, graphology is largely held suspect by psychology; nevertheless, there has been some experimentation, noticeably influenced by European thinking. Two hypotheses predominate: isolated graphic signs equal specific traits; and handwriting expression and personality are subtly interwoven. Various researches support the latter hypothesis more strongly.

The central problem in handwriting relates to evaluation and interpretation. Evaluation is made difficult by the existence of both quantitatively measurable and qualitatively descriptive graphic elements. Valid interpretation is made difficult by the necessity of relating objective reliable criteria to specific areas or aspects of functioning. The Lewinson and Zubin scales offer experimentally a solution of the first problem; a more recent study suggests that the scales variously "adjusted" may be useful for evaluating specific behavior disorders. Considerably more experimentation is needed before the scales can be applied with standard meanings.

As a clinical test, handwriting analysis is one in a battery. Its special ability as a test is to record individual behavior patterns. To the graphologist, these are indicated by the interrelationships, balances, and imbalances among graphic elements and dimensions. Though clinical graphologists differ theoretically in the graphological systems they follow, in practice there is considerable similarity and agreement. Simple specimens can be used to illustrate broad movement categories into which handwritings tend to fall when analyzed. These categories, more or less refined, regulate the analysis.

The most pressing problem in clinical graphology today is to determine objectively what elements are most useful as indicators, and how much emphasis is to be placed on each. Working toward a solution of this problem, which is an integral part of the problem of standardizing the graphological technique, is the responsibility in one way or another of all clinicians concerned with developing and utilizing more adequate tools for personality testing.

REFERENCES

1. Allport, G. W., and Vernon, P. E., *Studies in Expressive Movements.* New York, The Macmillan Company, 1933.

2. Ayers, L. P., *A Scale for Measuring Quality of Handwriting of Adults.* New York, Russell Sage Foundation, 1915.

3. Baldi, C., *Tratto come da una lettera missiva si cognoscano la natura e qualità del scrittore.* 1622.

4. Booth, G., "The use of graphology in medicine." *Jour. Nerv. and Mental Disease,* 1937, 86, 674–679.

5. —————————, "Objective technics in personality testing." *Arch. Neurol. and Psychiat.,* September 1939, 42, 514–530.

6. Burton, A., and Harris, R. E., (eds.), *Case Histories in Clinical and Abnormal Psychology.* New York, Harper & Brothers, 1947.

7. Dearborn, G. V. N., "Kinaesthesia and the intelligent will." *Amer. Jour. Psy.,* 1913, 24, 204–255.

8. Diehl, A., "Ueber die Eigenschaften der Schrift bei Gesunden." *Psychol. Arbeiten,* 1899, 3, 1–61.

9. Downey, J. E., *Preliminary Study of Family Resemblances in Handwriting,* University of Wyoming Department of Psychology, Bulletin No. 1. Laramie, Wyo.: University of Wyoming Press, 1910.

10. —————————, "Control processes in modified handwriting." *Psychol. Rev., Psychol. Monographs,* 1908.

11. —————————, *Graphology and the Psychology of Handwriting.* Baltimore: Warwick and York, 1919.

12. —————————, *The Will-Temperament and Its Testing.* Yonkers, N. Y.: World Book Company, 1923.

13. Eysenck, H. J., "Graphological analysis and psychiatry; an experimental study." *Brit. J. Psychol.,* 1945, 35, 70–81.

14. —————————, *Dimensions of Personality.* London, Kegan Paul, Trench, Trubner and Company, Ltd., 1947.

15. Frank, L. K., *Projective Methods,* American Lecture Series. Springfield, Ill.: Charles C. Thomas, 1948.

16. Freeman, F. N., "An experimental analysis of the writing movement." *Psychol. Monog.,* 1914, 17, 4, 1–46.

17. —————————, *The Handwriting Movement.* Chicago: University of Chicago Press, 1918.

18. Gesell, A. L., "Accuracy in handwriting as related to school intelligence and sex." *Amer. J. Psychol.,* 1906, 17, 394–405.

19. Harvey, O. L., "The measurement of handwriting considered as a form of expressive movement." *Char. and Pers.,* 1934, 2, 310–321.

20. Hull, C. L., *Aptitude Testing.* Yonkers, N. Y.: World Book Company, 1928.

21. Hull, C. L., and Montgomery, R. P., "Experimental investigation of certain alleged relations between character and handwriting." *Psychol. Rev.*, 1919, 26, 63–74.

22. Jacoby, H. J., *Analysis of Handwriting.* London: George Allen & Unwin, Ltd., 1939.

23. Klages, L., *The Science of Character.* London: George Allen & Unwin, Ltd., 1929. (Translated from ed. 5 of *Grundlagen der Charakter Kunde.*)

24. —————————, *Handschrift und Charakter.* Leipzig: Barth, 1932.

25. —————————, *Handschrift und Charakter* (revision). Leipzig: Barth, 1940.

26. Land, A. H., *Graphology, a Psychological Analysis.* University of Buffalo Studies, 1924.

27. Lewinson, T. S., "Handwriting in Chronic Arthritis." *Rheumatism,* I, October 1938, London, John Bale Medical Publications, Ltd., 91–95.

28. —————————, "An introduction to the graphology of Ludwig Klages." *Char. and Pers.*, 1938, 6, 163–176.

29. —————————, "Dynamic disturbances in the handwriting of psychotics." *Amer. J. Psychiatry,* 1940, 97, 1, 102–135.

30. Lewinson, T. S., and Zubin, J., *Handwriting Analysis.* New York: King's Crown Press, 1942.

31. Marum, O., "Character assessment from handwriting." *J. Ment. Sci.,* 1945, 91, 22–42.

32. McAllister, C. N., *Researches on Movements Used in Handwriting.* Yale Psychological Laboratory Studies, 1900, Vol. 8.

33. Meyer, G., *Die wissenschaftlichen Grundlagen der Graphologie,* (2d ed.). Jena, Gustav Fischer Verlag, 1925.

34. Munroe, R. L., Lewinson, T. S., and Waehner, T. S., "A comparison of three projective methods." *Char. and Pers.,* 1944, 8, 1, 1–21.

35. —————————, "Three projective methods applied to sally." *J. Abn. and Soc. Psychol.,* 1945, 40, 215–227.

36. Murphy, G., *Personality.* New York: Harper & Brothers, 1947.

37. Osborne, A. E., *Questioned Documents.* Albany, N. Y.: Boyd Printing Company, 1929.

38. Pascal, G. R., "Handwriting pressure: Its measurement and significance." *Char. and Pers.* March 1943, 11, 3, 235–254.

39. —————————, "The analysis of handwriting: A test of significance." *Char. and Pers.* December 1943, 12, 2, 123–144.

40. Preyer, W., *Zur Psychologie des Schreibens.* Leipzig: Voss, 1919.

41. Pulver, M., *Symbolik der Handschrift.* Zürich and Leipzig: Füssli, 1931.

42. Rapaport, D., *Diagnostic Psychological Testing.* Chicago: Yearbook Publishers Company, 1946, Vol. I.

43. Roman, K. G., "Studies on the variability of handwriting." *J. Genet. Psychol.,* September 1936, 49, 139–160.

44. Saudek, R., *The Psychology of Handwriting.* New York: Doran, 1926.

45. ————————, *Experiments with Handwriting.* New York: Doran, 1926.

46. Schönfeld, W., and Menzel, K., *Tuberkulose, Charakter und Handschrift.* Brünn: Rohrer, 1934.

47. Shoen, H. H., *Improving the Handwriting of High School Students,* Teachers Lesson Unit Series, No. 52. New York: Columbia University, Teachers College Bureau of Publications, 1942.

48. Starch, D., "The similarity between brothers and sisters in mental traits." *Psychol. Rev.,* 1917, 24, 235–238.

49. Super, D. E., "A comparison of the diagnoses of a graphologist with the results of psychological tests." *J. Consult. Psy.,* 1941, 5, 127–133.

50. Symonds, P., *Diagnosing Personality and Conduct.* New York, D. Appleton-Century Company, 1931.

51. Thorndike, E. L., "Handwriting." *Teachers College Record,* 1910, 11, 83–175.

52. Vertesi, E., *Handschrift und Eigenart der Krabsgefährdenten.* Budapest: Tisza, 1939.

53. Watson, J., *Psychology from the Standpoint of a Behaviorist.* Philadelphia: J. B. Lippincott Company, 1919.

54. Wolfson, R., *A Study in Handwriting Analysis.* Ann Arbor, Mich.: Edward Brothers, Inc., 1949.

55. Zubin, J., "A proposed measure of social conformity." *Sociometry.* 1943, 6, 72–93.

CHAPTER 16

Expressive Movement and the Methods of Experimental Depth Psychology

WERNER WOLFF, PH.D.

AND

JOSEPH A. PRECKER, PH.D.

I. Expressive Movement [1]

INTRODUCTION

Increasing attention is being paid to expressive behavior as a means of understanding personality. Not only does personality function in space, it also functions in time. It is a dynamic relationship between organism and internal and external environment, with the individual as the nexus, displaying unity, consistency, and continuity.

The psychosomatic approach to disturbances of function has revealed much about the interrelationship between psychoemotional needs of the individual and the state of the organism. The study of expressive behavior makes possible an understanding of the structure and function of the individual organism as well as of the unity and consistency of personality.

Both psychosomatics and the study of expressive behavior owe much to Freud's psychoanalytic theories, which emphasized the operation of the total organism, rather than its component parts

---

[1] Part I of this chapter was written by Joseph A. Precker.

in isolation.   The *unity* of personality was stressed by Freud: the conflict of the neurotic individual was evident not only in the depth of the personality, but in every gesture, every slip of the tongue, every mannerism.   By understanding these signs, the roots of personality could be reached.   Freud's *Psychopathology of Everyday Life* extended his approach from the neurotic individual to the behavior of all.   In an interesting study, Felix Deutsch [20], an analyst, graphed the expressive behavior in terms of postural patterns of his analysands, and found distinct relationships between the motor behavior of the individual and the verbal expression of the unconscious material.   The motivations of the organism are expressed in the structure and functions of the personality.   In the words of E. B. Holt, one of the early advocates in America of psychoanalysis as a theory of behavior:

> It is clear that this *function* which behavior or conduct is of the external situation is the very same thing which Freud deals with under the name of "wish."   It is a course of action which the body takes or is prepared (by motor set) to take with reference to objects, relations, or events in the environment.   The prophetic quality of thought which makes it seem that thought is the hidden and inner secret of conduct is due to the fact that that thought is the preceding labile interplay of motor sets which go on almost constantly and which differs from overt conduct in that the energy involved is too small to produce gross bodily movements.   This is a piece of nature's economy. . . . [*38,* p. 94.]

It is these functions, these dynamic relationships, that are evident in expressive behavior, and that experimental depth psychology approaches in terms of empirical investigation.   We are all aware that each person has typical gestures.   We can recognize a friend 100 yards away by his gait.   Or we become aware, without seeing him, of the presence of a friend in a crowded room by the pattern of his voice.   The psychologist interested in expressive behavior is concerned with two questions: (1) Is this behavior consistent? and (2) What is the relationship between such behavior and the depth of personality?   The assumption that is made is that a person's movements are not accidental nor chance-determined, but are consistent under different environmental conditions, and are related to the basic motivations of the organism.

Western culture has abolished more and more the overt expression of "symbolic" gesture.   However, detailed investigation has shown that often, only the *amplitude* of such movements has decreased below our capacity to recognize it, but that the pattern itself has not entirely vanished. With proper investigation, we find that a person's gross movements or even his barely discernible movements are patterned by the scheme of his personality.

Emotional tension may be released in three basic ways, usually somewhat interrelated: expressive behavior may take the form of actual overt physical behavior, speech, or release of emotional tension in fantasy. For example, the child may kick the boy that struck him. As he grows older, he will abuse him with language rather than with physical violence. As he becomes more completely socialized, he may pass the situation over lightly, but have a fantasy in which he strikes the opponent. However, all three levels of behavior involve movements which give clues to the personality structure of the individual and his affective state. The adult who may be smiling and greeting a disliked competitor, may very well give himself away in the handshake: withdrawing muscular movements that accompany the handshake will tell the astute observer that the (affected) warm greeting is but a mask. It is these movements that are of interest to the student of expressive behavior.

The inner dynamics out of which expressive behavior emerges have two elements: the intentional, and the affective. The intentional aspect brings about the concrete form of the movement; it is often basically adaptive. The affective aspect determines the dynamics, the style of the behavior [32].

All mental activity is related to a maintenance of maximum equilibrium between the organism and its field. Whenever the equilibrium is disturbed, such disturbance is detectable in movement [51]. The analyst of expressive behavior seeks to discover the movement and relate it to the *meaning* of the shifts in equilibrium. These shifts also leave their mark on the organism: the behavior in the past establishes the foundation for present and future behavior. The lines of the face, for example, dependent on the facial muscles that are modified by habitual emotional responses, give some cues to the state of the organism [24]. In this chapter, the relationship between such cues and personality will be examined.

Schilder, in his work with the body image, stressed the gestalt concept, in which the gestalt was ever-changing, being constantly disrupted and reorganized from life situations. He also made the point, important for our study here, that expression and movement are related to processes that occur in the central parts of the brain and cannot be separated from the wishes and tendencies of the individual. He wrote:

> I have the opinion that we can in some way read from the postural model of the body what partial desires in the individual are stronger than other ones. And we expect that whenever we find the trouble in one of the partial desires, we shall find it marked in the postural model [62, p. 61].

The relationship of posture, gesture, and mannerisms with the highest brain functions, as determined by Schilder, indicates the importance to Schilder of understanding the meaning of the *gesture* in order to understand these functions. What has been at one time an expression of the entire organism is "reduced" into an automatic movement mannerism, or gesture, which may reveal the dynamics of personality if properly read.

ADAPTATION, PROJECTION, EXPRESSION

Since the time that Frank [33] coined the phrase "projective methods," practically all techniques that attempt to get below the surface of personality have been called "projective techniques." In order to understand expressive behavior, it is helpful to differentiate between adaptation, projection, and expression, which have been discussed elsewhere by Bellak [11].

Adaptive behavior is behavior that is determined by the material with which one works. If the doorbell rings, and one turns off the radiator in response to it, we call that *nonadaptive* behavior—the individual is not responding to the demands of the external world. In the same way, children can, indeed *must,* do different things with clay than they do with building blocks. *What* can be done with the materials at hand is at the adaptive level. The clearer the meaning of the stimulus, and the more ready the "set," the greater the amount of purely adaptive behavior [11].

Projective behavior involves the ascription of one's own needs and qualities to others, without conscious awareness of the process. Here, as opposed to adaptive behavior, the more exact the definition (or structure) of the situation, the *less* the projection that will occur. Therefore, the Thematic Apperception Test allows for a great deal of projection due to the ambiguous, undefined nature of the stimulus materials.

Expressive behavior, on the other hand, is one's *style* of response. Given the same materials to work with, each person approaches the situation in his own individual or characteristic way, handling the materials and organizing the situation differently. The movement patterns, the gestures, the rhythm, and the physiological bodily responses of each individual vary considerably. The expressive behavior of the individual is his *style* of response. Expression analysis deals first with the *how* of behavior to get to the basic motivations. In any cultural *milieu,* many individuals may perform the same task, but there will be manifest differences in attack, adequacy, method, and style. All of these are indications of expression. The purpose of this chapter is to discuss the relationship between expressive behavior and personality characteristics.

Adaptation, projection, and expression, although separately defined, seldom appear alone. In any situation there is a dynamic relationship among the amounts of purely adaptive behavior, expression, and projection. None of the techniques that have been developed for studying personality are pure projective techniques, pure expressive techniques, or pure adaptive behavior techniques, but rather a combination of two or three, each aspect of behavior appearing in differing degrees.

As pointed out elsewhere [11], there is another distinction that must be made: the distinction between projection and displacement. The child who kicks the cat rather than the all-powerful parent is not primarily projecting, but rather displacing emotion. Similarly, an example of displacement is found in the behavior of Miller's rats, which strike a white doll to get out of a cage when the rat they have learned to strike is not present. This *displacement* of affect is of obvious importance to the student of expressive behavior: the fearful child who suddenly attacks a doll when put into a permissive situation is *expressing* something about the structure of his personality.

There is a further distinction that must be made at this point between *expression, form,* and *content.* *Expression* deals with style of performance; *form* deals with the measurable product; *content* deals with the experiences of the individual.

In discussing various means of appraising personality, Murphy

[54] has suggested that there are five kinds of personality attributes that can be examined to a greater or lesser degree by the various newer techniques. These are kinetics, style, values, creativeness, and mental content.

However, each of the five may be revealed to a greater or lesser extent by expressive behavior. Certainly, kinetics and style are revealed in any activity. Creativeness, when not stifled by rigid definition of the stimuli, can certainly be revealed by the use of materials as well as by the finished product, for example, in the use of paints, clay, or toys. Values, too, can be expressed by the approach or withdrawal of the individual in relation to objects in the environment. Mental content is revealed less obviously by the expressive techniques.

Rosenzweig [59] differentiates among three techniques for personality appraisal: "motor-expressive" techniques (as evidenced in handwriting, voice, gait), "perceptive-structural" techniques (such as the Rorschach and the tautophone), and "apperceptive-dynamic" methods (as the TAT and the Rosenzweig Picture-Frustration method). The first two classifications obviously come under the more generic heading of expressive behavior, since they are related to *how* the individual approaches his world, or *how* the individual organizes and perceives his world. The last classification ("apperceptive-dynamic" methods) is less related to expressive behavior, unless analyzed in terms of the formal aspects.

Briefly, then, we see that the analysis of expressive behavior can be utilized in comprehending: (1) methods of perception, as in the Rorschach; (2) plastic involvement and organization [19], as in finger painting, Buhler's World Test, and the use of clay; (3) social interaction, as in the psychodrama or observation of any social situation; and (4) imaginal content (although analysis of expressive behavior is less useful here than the projective techniques).

FACTORS INFLUENCING EXPRESSION

In order to understand expressive behavior, it is necessary to understand the factors that may influence it. Allport and Vernon have set up an excellent list of such factors as follows: [2]

---

[2] Allport and Vernon, *Studies in Expressive Movement,* p. 22. Copyright 1933 by The Macmillan Company. Quoted by permission.

1. The exigencies of the immediate goal
2. Pathological or accidental deformation of the body
3. Conditions of health and disease
4. Individual peculiarities of muscular structure or bodily metabolism
5. Constitutional make-up
6. Age
7. Sex
8. Strain and fatigue
9. Conditions of the physical environment
10. Transitory emotional states or moods
11. Racial tradition (the present author would prefer to substitute *culture milieu* for the term employed by Allport and Vernon)
12. Convention or fashion
13. Special habits springing from special training
14. Temporary social environment, leading to artificial manner, or to a masking of normal expression

Recent work of anthropologists and others indicates the importance of *cultural* symbolism in expression: expression of emotions, for example, is not completely "innate" (at least not after the first few months of life), but depends on the meanings "assigned" by a particular cultural group. It therefore becomes necessary to note in detail the cultural aspects of expression. In a survey of the cultural factors influencing gesture, LaBarre [14] has demonstrated that certain expressions have almost antithetical meanings in different cultural groups, as when the Negro in Africa uses laughter to express surprise, wonder, or even discomfort.

Cultural groups might be studied in terms of the *tensions* evident in the group as a whole, individual differences, of course, being expected. An example will clarify this idea. Whereas the occidental usually has his hands in a relaxed posture when not in use, with fingers bent at knuckles and joints, the Balinese has his fingers extended in an awkward position when at rest [10]. Knowing the enormous amount of emotional strain the Balinese undergoes in his difficult socialization process, it seems quite logical that these tensions should be manifested in expressive behavior.

In extensive studies of "traditional" groups of Jews and Italians, and assimilated Jews and Italians, in New York, Efron [26] concluded that gestures are not racially inherited, but are strongly influenced by the environment, by factors of a sociopsychological nature. Does this mean that expressive behavior, individually or culturally, is inconsistent? Not at all. Wolff's analysis of African drawings and the drawings of American children demonstrates proportions that are measurable, deal with simple numerical relationships, and are *individually* consistent [77, 79]. Future analysis of expressive behavior will probably be found to be related to the individual's age and culture group [29].

Observation of the infant demonstrates that it is the whole organism that "expresses." It is the entire body, and not any particular part, that approaches, withdraws, or expresses contentment. Temperamental differences in the behavior of children a few weeks old have been reported; these differences seem to be consistent in respect to the amount and manner of their laughing and crying [16, 72, 81]. Wolff [77] also has found some correlation for parents and children in such things as pencil pressure and length of strokes in handwriting. There seem to be general psychomotor factors that maintain consistency in temperamental behavior [4]. The developmental approach to expressive behavior is important in understanding the genesis and consistency of expressive movement.

MOTOR BEHAVIOR AND PERSONALITY

What is the relationship between certain psychomotor manifestations and personality? A growing number of studies have approached this problem. As mentioned earlier, Deutsch found that there was a definite relationship between postural behavior of the patient and the unconscious material being released, or soon to be released in psychoanalysis. Deutsch reported that:

Postural attitudes reflect or substitute, precede or accompany the verbal expression of unconscious material. Every individual has a characteristic basic posture at rest to which he returns whenever he has deviated from it [20, p. 211].

Movement, whether of plant, animal, or man, is always a function of the individual in relation to some aspect of environment, internal or external [38]. Because movement is evidence of functional relationships, it has interest as an approach to personality. Schilder offered further insight through example, when he said that negativism first appears in the jaw and in the neck muscles. When we resist psychically, "we stiffen our necks and press our teeth together. We say therefore about an obstinate person, that he has a stiff neck.

Maybe we have been too little interested up to recent times in the organic problems of normal psychology" [62, p. 113].

The problem of individual rhythm has been studied in many ways. Anders [6] found that each person had a movement rhythm peculiar to himself, and that there was a personal relationship between that tempo and that of his pulse and breathing. Some of his subjects showed a one-to-one relationship between walking rate and pulse. Other rhythms have also been determined. In studying rhythm of tapping, breathing, and writing, Wolff found that *none* of his subjects recognized his own rhythm (sound) of writing or breathing; 80 per cent did not recognize the rhythm of their own tapping, which had been recorded. However, the given subject's own samples, although unidentified, were liked twice as often as they were disliked [75, p. 105].

The problem of morphology and expressive behavior has been approached by several investigators. Charlotte Wolff [73], believing the hand to be related to endocrine glands, muscular development, and intelligence, studied 115 high-grade defective boys, 9 to 16 years of age. Personality types were reported inferred correctly from hand-types in 85 per cent of the cases. Of 10 "endocrine hand-types," nine were said to be congenital. Further work in this area would be of interest.

Kretschmer [43] differentiated between the expressive behavior of his schizoid and cycloid temperaments. The cycloid temperament was said to vary between fast and slow, while the schizoids varied between tenacious and jerky. Enke [28] differentiated between pyknics and leptosomes by means of psychomotor studies. He used a number of psychomotor tests on 500 subjects. He found that pyknics were slower than leptosomes and athletics, as well as more irregular; they were "fluid, free, soft, rounded, uninhibited" in their actions; while leptosomes were "stiff and angular." He found the leptosomes to be consistently tense and cautious in any situation.

Duffy [25] studied muscle tensions and found a consistent "general factor" by means of factor analysis, which caused her to conclude that tension level is a fairly persistent characteristic of the individual and is an aspect of personality.

In a simple sensory motor task, Langer found that *motor-impulsion* (tendency to act without thinking) was correlated with aggression .52, dominance .43, exocathection .52, exhibition .40, and impulsion .38, as determined by the other measures utilized in the extensive Harvard study of personality, under Murray.   When these five attributes were considered an ascendance syndrome, the correlation was .65 between ascendance and motor impulsion [*46,* p. 515].   "Impedance" (the requiring of a disproportionate amount of time to produce the task) correlated negatively with aggression, counteraction, defendance, dominance, and impulsion, indicating feelings of inferiority, insecurity, poor integration, and self-abasement [*46,* p. 516].   Here seems to be good evidence of the relationship between motor characteristics (expression) and personality attributes.

Luria [*48*] developed a motor method to study personality, in which involuntary finger tremors were measured.   He was able to set up categories differentiating among various psychiatric classifications, such as manic-depressives and schizophrenics.   Luria found that muscular discoordination (finger tremors) could be used as a sensitive index of emotional excitement.   Other investigators [*63*] used a more convenient apparatus (the tremograph), and found the same results as Luria.

The studies cited above indicate the configuration of the organism.   Grosser movements have also been studied.   All movements in space indicate direction toward, or away from, the individual.   As Goldstein has pointed out, "The flexor movements have a closer reference to the self, the extensor movements more reference to the external world. . . .   [These movements] become a manifestation of different attitudes of the organism to the world" [*34,* p. 484].

Consistent with the work of Goldstein, one of the basic principles of Mira's Myokinetic Psychodiagnosis [*51*] is that every mental attitude implies a corresponding muscular attitude.

CONSISTENCY AND VALIDITY OF EXPRESSIVE BEHAVIOR IN PERSONALITY STUDY

Consistency.   Allport and Vernon, in their studies of expressive movement, set for themselves the problem of intra-individual consistency.   They attempted to study on the one hand the claims of specificists, who regarded personality as a *sum* of different, separately learned skills, and on the other, the claims of the configurationists, who viewed personality as an operating *unity*.   At least three-quarters of the experiments were "unequivocal in their proof of the interconsistency of expressive movements" [*4*, p. 120]. Using many measures of motor performance with 25 male subjects, the average repeat reliabilities in the same experimental session showed average coefficients of correlation of .75; those at different sessions showed average coefficients of .64. The experimenters concluded that temporary factors, such as mood, played an important but not exclusive part in determining consistency. There was clear evidence of intermuscle consistency, indicating a unity of the organism.

Allport and Vernon differentiated between two aspects of consistency:

> There are clearly two senses in which movement may be said to be "consistent." On the one hand, the term suggests that different indicators of movement must vary directly with one another; on the other hand, it suggests that even when indicators do not agree directly with one another, they may still be harmonious in the sense that both express different aspects of a single complex state.
>
> When . . . indicators are shown by a correlation to vary directly with one another they will be said to *correspond;* indicators that do not correlate, and yet are clearly related to one another through the complex medium of personality, will be said to be congruent.*

Although we use here the generic term of *consistency,* the different meanings of *correspondence* and *congruence* should be kept in mind. Consistency should be interpreted as meaningful relationships between the *same* form of expression at different times, and different forms of expression at the *same* time.

The matching methods of Wertheimer, Arnheim [*8*], Wolff [*75*], and Vernon [*69*] were designed to overcome the deficiencies of other methods. Briefly, the judge was presented with several forms of expression of several individuals, and asked which went together. In this way, evidences of congruence were demonstrated. For instance, in one of his experiments, Arnheim [*8*] had subjects match the handwritings of Leonardo da Vinci, Michelangelo, and Raphael with their names. Of 143 judges, the judgments were correct in 67.6 per cent of the cases. The matching methods allowed a quantification of qualitative aspects of personality.[3]

---

* *Op. cit.,* pp. 20–21.
[3] For a full discussion of the statistical and psychological aspects of matching, see Vernon [*68*].

The problem of consistency involves:

1. Through-time consistency of each form of expression with itself
2. Consistency of various forms of expression, one with the other (such as handwriting with profile)
3. Consistency of one or several forms of expression with personality characteristics (such as the matching of personality description with motion pictures of gait)
4. Consistency of judgments of others of a form of expression
5. Consistency of "types," or "traits" (extrovert-introvert, pyknic-leptosome, and so on) in relation to expressive behavior

In terms of everyday observation of our friends, family, colleagues, and others, we *expect* consistency. We say of someone, "He *would* act that way!" However, is there complete consistency in *all* forms of expression, or do the various expressive devices supplement each other? Two studies, in particular, point to both the *overlapping* of the meaning of various forms of expression and the *additional* insight that one technique may afford over another, depending on the individual.

The first study was one done by Wolff [74], at Vassar. Using photographs of children during a medical examination, motion pictures of children in Stone's balloon-breaking situation, paintings and drawings of the children, and pictures of the children in cold cream play, Wolff was able to make blind diagnoses that were valid when compared with the case records of the children. Of the three children used for illustrative purposes, the forms of expression of one of them were almost completely consistent one with the other. In a second child, there was some inconsistency from one form of expression to another, but still all the expressive behavior pointed in the same direction. In a third child, there was considerable inconsistency from one form to another, but with all forms of expression taken into consideration, the diagnosis pointed up *conflicting attitudes within this individual*. In this last case, using the terms of Allport and Vernon, we would find *congruence,* if not correspondence, in the forms of expression.

A second study worthy of mention here is that by Munroe, Lewinson, and Waehner [52] at Sarah Lawrence College, where Rorschach (group method), painting and drawing, and handwriting analyses were made independently. The results showed considerable *correspondence,* and even more *congruence.*[4]

---

[4] Another example of the *consistency* of forms of behavior may be seen in the film by Werner Wolff, *The Unity of Expression* [78].

The studies of Enke [*28*] revealed consistency of groups in relation to Kretschmer's "constitutional types." His purpose was to determine whether pyknic and nonpyknic types could be differentiated by motor performance or movement, such as spontaneous tapping, and pace of work. His findings were that pyknics were slower in their movements than others, were adaptable to external rhythms, and were "fluid, free, soft, rounded, and uninhibited" in their movements when compared to other groups. Thus, consistency was found within the limitations of the body-type concept.

Temperamental consistency was found in the behavior of infants, in respect to the amount and manner of their laughing and crying, indicating that developmental consistency must be considered as an important aspect of the problem [*16, 72, 81*].

The most striking findings in relation to developmental consistency are the results of Wolff's researches [*77, 79*] dealing with proportions of handwriting, drawings, and doodles. He found that there were certain proportions that were not changed by age or learning, but tended to remain the same from the first year of life. Even epileptics, persons under the influence of drugs, and psychotic patients, who might change the size of their products, maintained the same proportions as they had in their normal state. The proportions, found only after laborious measurements, were usually magnified in these abnormal states, but the magnification, again, was one of simple linear relationships, such as an increase in size by three, two, or one and one-half of the original "normal" proportions. These consistent proportions were not the same for all individuals, but rather for each individual: they illustrated an idiographic, rather than a nomothetic law.

Validity. In order to be useful in science, a technique must demonstrate validity—there must be some demonstrable relationship between the *results* arrived at and the behavior of the variable under observation. In personality study, due to the complexity of the subject, the problem of validity becomes even more difficult. According to Macfarlane [*49*],[5] the following steps represent procedures for the validation of expressive behavior:

1. Correlation with outside criteria (other expressive techniques, projective techniques, ratings, and so on).

---

5 See also Chapter 2, by Macfarlane and Tuddenham, in this volume.

2. Internal consistency of the technique. (Does it present a *meaningful* picture, in which the contradictory aspects of it are not so great that they do not fit into the total pattern?)

3. Comparison of expressive material with life history material.

4. Search for through-time consistencies (longitudinal approach to *validity*).

5. Collateral experimental approaches.

6. Degree of success in prediction.

At least the first four steps of the above-mentioned techniques for validation have been utilized in studying projective techniques, and several investigators [*15, 71, 74, 77*] present evidence of the *predictive* value of some of these expressive techniques, particularly painting and drawing.

There are special problems encountered in studying expressive behavior: possible "contradictions" between expressive values and actual behavior do not justify the conclusion that expressive forms are not revealing. A form of expression may serve as a mask, as in the blustering adolescent who is hiding a timid soul. It becomes necessary to differentiate between *surface* judgments, which display the surface appearance (or mask), and *depth* judgments, which explain the cause or motivation of the form of expression. Of course, the mask is important in revealing wish-images and ego-ideals, but this will be taken up later in the discussion of self-judgments of different forms of expression.

In the following pages, the findings of many workers in the field of expressive behavior will be briefly presented, with special attention to consistency and validity. Emphasis will be placed on studies of:

1. Facial expression and personality
2. Hands and personality
3. Voice and personality
4. Literary and artistic style, style of speech, and personality
5. Gait and personality
6. Painting and drawing and personality
7. Handwriting and personality

EXPERIMENTAL EVIDENCE

Facial Expression and Personality. In five experiments, Arnheim [*8*] judged three portraits with single character traits; the proportion of correct matchings was 84.7 per cent. In another experiment, he had judges match style of life (such as drinking preferences), with three portraits, with 59 per cent correct judgments. Vernon [67] had judges assign 30 personality traits to five photographs, six traits to each photograph. The matching was correct in 33.3 per cent of the cases. Then, using character sketches based on these photographs, written by 48 judges, Vernon had his judges match these sketches, plus "true" sketches by other judges, with the photograph. The matchings were correct in 51.3 per cent of the cases. Using the same photographs and short character sketches, but a different group of 50 judges, the correct proportion of matchings was 42.8 per cent.

In matching silhouettes with character traits, Arnheim's [8] judges were correct in 66.2 per cent of the matchings; in matching silhouettes with short character sketches, the proportion of correct judgments went up to 90.5 per cent. All of the above-mentioned matchings are better than chance.

In Wolff's experiments [75], not only were the judges able to *match* various records of expressive behavior, such as profile, voice, and handwriting, but their characterizations of them were similar for *different* forms of expression of a given subject.

The evidence presented above is brief, but illustrates both the consistency and validity of the portrait, whether it shows facial expression or silhouette, in demonstrating the value of this form of expressive behavior. The Nazis used facial expression analysis as one of their techniques of selecting officers in the last war. The analysis of facial expression seems to improve with training [35, 42]. Guilford [35] found an average gain of 51 per cent over the original ability to analyze facial expression after a 10-day period of training. Binet [12] had photographs of 10 boys and 10 girls matched with sex, and with high or low intelligence. The proportion of correct matchings was 70.5 per cent with sex, and 54.0 per cent with intelligence.

Hands and Personality. Wolff's [75] subjects were able to match photographs of the hands with other forms of expression and give personality sketches that were highly related to case histories, self-judgments, and other characterizations.

Duffy [25], using three techniques, measured the muscular tension of the hand during performance of eight different tasks. Measurements were taken on three different occasions. Scores for 25 subjects were studied and a generally consistent individual tension-level was found. Thus, in terms of appearance as well as muscular tension (perhaps related to appearance), there seemed to be evidence of both consistency and validity of the hand as a form of expression.

Voice and Personality.   In a group of experiments by Wolff [75] 30 subjects heard three voices, one their own, two of others.   They then made personality descriptions based on the voices.   Then a group of 10 judges selected the "identifying term" for each voice from these descriptions.   The "identifying term" was a term that summed up the characterizations of a certain individual's expressions.   Then another group of subjects were read the three summary descriptions (identifying terms), heard three voices at a sitting, and matched the 18 voices thus presented with an identifying term. Against a chance expectation of 33 per cent correct matchings, 77 per cent were actually correct, indicating positive results in judgments of personality from the voice.

Next, it was necessary to determine whether the personality judged from the voice corresponded to that of the speaker as known by close friends.   Ten judges were given the names of the speakers they knew, and then the summarizing terms were given to them, and they paired them with the names.   The percentage of correct matchings exceeded chance expectancy from 10 per cent to 81 per cent.

Several studies found considerable correct judgments of personality and constitutional factors from listening to the voices of speakers over the radio, particularly, voices of untrained speakers [*3, 37, 56*].   Fay and Middleton [*36*] found a significant positive correlation between the ratings as to Spranger's value type, as judged by listening to the *voices* of two representatives of each of the six Spranger "types," and the *actual* "types."

In another study, 24 judges rated the speech of 25 subjects on 46 subtests for a total of 27,600 scores.   Half the time, the judges saw the subject, and half the time, the subjects were hidden.   Personal factors (dress, appearance, physique, poise, posture, and certain biographical data) did not significantly affect the judges' ratings of speech on the subtests the author used.   A reliability coefficient of .94 was obtained by pooling the ratings of at least six judges [*17*]. Wolff [75] had above-chance success in having judges match voices with three handwriting specimens.

Again, voice seems to be another form of expressive behavior having consistency and validity.

Literary and Artistic Style, and Style of Speech and Personality. Vernon [*69*] had anonymously written essays matched by one psychologist with impressions of the subjects' personalities, derived from observing each subject engaged on performance tests for 45 minutes. The percent of correct matchings was 22.2 per cent. In another study [*67*], free designs made up from squares and triangles of colored cardboard were matched with the portraits and case studies of the subjects who produced the designs. The matchings were correct in 30.8 per cent of the cases.

In his studies, Wolff [*75*] read the same story to his group of subjects and had them repeat it. Naturally, the style of retelling varied a great deal. The personality descriptions that judges compiled from the style of retelling were successfully matched with other forms of expression of his subjects, and also agreed with the case histories of the subjects.

Balken and Masserman [*9*] devised a method of formal analysis of style of speech. Using such criteria as average number of words, parts of speech used, and certain quotients, such as total number of verbs divided by the total number of adjectives, they were able to differentiate between cases of such neurotic manifestations as conversion hysteria, anxiety state, and obsessive-compulsive neuroses. There were typical speech patterns or styles for the various diagnostic groups. For instance, conversion hysterics had a low verb-adjective quotient, while patients suffering from anxiety states had a high verb-adjective quotient. According to the authors, these language pictures corresponded to the theoretical clinical picture of these syndromes.

In a careful study of style of speech and personality, Sanford [*60*] employed a rigorous formal analysis of the speech of two subjects, and came to the conclusion that "the characterizations of style appear also to be characterizations of the persons." Although the evidence presented here is merely the most clear-cut, it seems to corroborate the general opinion of this author that the *style* of behavior, whether in speech or in literary or artistic style, is a reliable and valid means of studying personality.

Gait and Personality. Anders [*6*] found that each person had a movement rhythm peculiar to himself. This tempo was related to pulse and breathing rates.   Some of his subjects showed a one-to-one relation between walking rate and pulse.

In his study of gait, Wolff [75] found that his subjects eventually recognized their gait, when compared with the gaits of others through motion pictures taken unawares, even though the face was blotted out and coveralls obscured the contours of the body.   The character sketches that were made by various judges viewing the motion pictures were consistent with each other, and compared remarkably well with judgments of the other forms of expression of the subjects and with their case records.

The total movement of the body, walking and working, was studied by the German selection officers [51], by our OSS [55], by Enke [28] in his study of psychomotor types, by Blake [13], although he used a *static* photograph for judgments, and by Stone [47] in his balloon test.   The investigation of body movement and gait in these studies indicated the consistency and validity of gait as an expression of personality.

Painting and Drawing and Personality.   The rationale of painting and drawing as an expressive technique deserves consideration here.   If we accept the assumption that the individual's movements are expressive of personality, we are struck with the difficulty of capturing these movements to study in the confines of an office.   Painting, drawing, and handwriting, however, allow for the capturing, recording, and measuring of the transient qualities of overt movements.   Not only may conscious thought or ideas be communicated in paintings, drawings, and handwriting, but also, biopsychological patterns of which the individual may be unconscious are revealed.   While the *content* of painting, drawing, and handwriting may be consciously determined, very often the style, or manner "just happens."   However, there is considerable experimental evidence to indicate the relationship between style of performance and personality characteristics.   Although several workers in this area have used different classifications of criteria for formal analysis, the present author has established five major categories, each divided into many subgroups.   The principal categories are:

1. Content
2. Use or avoidance of color
3. Use of space (in size of product, format, and relationship of elements within the picture)

4. Form and pattern (this category includes forms and shapes, and the arrangement of forms and shapes within the picture)
5. Use of the media (this category includes characteristic handling of materials, quality of strokes and lines, pressure, and so on)

Wolff [74] successfully matched the posture, finger paintings, brush paintings, drawings, balloon play motion pictures, and cold cream play motion pictures of three children, and analyses were made. The analyses were then checked against teachers' remarks concerning the children's behavior. There was considerable accuracy in the analyses.

Waehner [70, 71] studied 760 pictures made by 38 children (ages 8 to 11) in various mental homes and hospitals. She was able to discriminate between various psychiatric classifications through the use of specific criteria, utilizing statistical methods. In another study, Waehner [71] was able to present analyses of the paintings of 55 girls of college age that were in close agreement with the Rorschach findings of Munroe and the handwriting analyses of Lewinson. Also, in analyzing the children's drawings that DuBois [23] brought back from Alor, Waehner was able to make predictions, such as a minimum of movement responses on their Rorschach records, that were confirmed by Oberholzer's Rorschach analyses [23]. Waehner's criteria are elaborate and resemble the Rorschach criteria.

Brick [15] studied qualitatively the art products of 200 children. Some blind diagnoses were made that were successful when compared with data from teacher and parent conferences. The meanings of various formal elements were presented. Elkisch [27] found that content did *not* differentiate between adjusted and maladjusted children, as determined by sociometric and teachers' ratings on the Haggerty-Olson-Wickman Behavior Rating Schedule *B*. She found that analysis of various formal elements *did* differentiate. Alschuler and Hattwick [5] made a careful quantitative study of the easel paintings of 149 children of nursery school age. Case studies, overt behavior, and teachers' and observers' ratings were compared with each formal element. The results showed close relationships between various formal elements and certain personality characteristics. Only those results in which the chances were 85 or more in 100 that the observed tendencies would be found in a similar sampling were presented as indicative.

Wolff's discoveries [77, 79] of consistency of proportions in the drawings of American and African children, and of blind and epileptic children, seem to be a good indication of the reliability of certain aspects of graphic movement. Space does not allow presentation of the detailed criteria for the interpretation of paintings and drawings, but readers are referred to the works cited above and to the work of Precker [57] in addition to chapters of this book, which present further material relevant to the reliability and validity of this technique, as well as the meanings of various formal elements. The use of space and form are particularly revealing.

Handwriting and Personality.[6] The extensive literature on handwriting and graphology is vast. A few significant studies will be cited, however, to indicate the value of this technique, which has been largely overlooked and even condemned by American psychologists, because of the inadequate use to which it has been put by a few lay "graphologists." Extensive reviews of graphological studies may be found in Eysenck [30, 31], Vernon [69], and Wolff [79].

Arnheim [8] asked judges who had never seen the handwritings of Michelangelo, da Vinci, and Raphael, to match the handwriting specimens with the concept of their personalities. He obtained 83.6 per cent positive results, instead of the 33.3 per cent expected by chance. Bobertag [14] obtained 80.7 per cent correct matchings with 450 matchings of 30 personality sketches to handwriting specimens. Downey [21] obtained agreements of judgments based upon gait, gesture, and handwriting in about 70 per cent of her cases, out of a chance expectancy of 50 per cent. Theiss [66], in Dresden, obtained positive results in 80 to 90 per cent of the judgments of handwriting, made by over 700 "naive" interpreters.

Most of the negative results in handwriting analysis have been found in studies in which *single elements,* such as slope of line and long *t*-bars, rather than the total patterns, have been studied. An example of such a study is the one made in 1919 by Hull and Montgomery [40]. More wholistic methods of analysis of handwriting have produced results well above chance [30].

In recent studies by Eysenck [30], a graphologist filled out a questionnaire as she thought a person with a particular handwriting would have filled it out. While chance would have allowed 50 per

---

6 See Wolfson, Chapter 15 in this volume.

cent correct answers, actually, 62 per cent agreed with the actual questionnaires filled out by 50 hospital patients. The same graphologist also matched the 50 handwriting specimens with psychiatrists' personality sketches in 10 groups of five each. By chance, one matching out of five ought to have been correct. In this experiment, correct responses averaged 2.4 matchings out of five. In a more recent study [*31*], 176 army hospital patients were rated by a graphologist on a five-point scale of neuroticism from short essay handwriting samples. The ratings correlated significantly ($r = .21$) with a battery of objective tests indicating neuroticism, but not with psychiatric diagnosis.

The most important findings in relation to the consistency of handwritings are the studies of Wolff [*79*], which indicate that there are unlearned, unconscious proportions in handwriting that are usually in simple mathematical relationships. Studies of the blind, of epileptics, of African children, of mentally ill, and of normal subjects, indicate considerable consistency in these proportions. Although alterations of these proportions may occur in states of illness, old age, fatigue, and so forth, the modifications are always in simple proportions—some handwritings, for instance, are reduced to one-half the original length in old age. These proportions are consistent within the *individual's* pattern, and vary from person to person.

These findings seem to establish the consistency of handwriting, in terms of both form and expression, as well as the validity of the technique as a means of personality appraisal. Carefully controlled research in the future will further establish the value of this technique.

SELF-JUDGMENTS, SELF-CONSISTENCY AND SELF-CONCEPT

The *self-concept* involves both the wishes and fears of the individual, the ego-ideal as well as the more realistic concept of self. Prescott Lecky's theory of self-consistency is of interest here:

. . . Mind is defined as a system of ideas and attitudes, the nucleus of which is the person's conception of himself. Integration of personality is normally achieved through the unification of internally consistent ideas and attitudes patterned on the person's ego-ideal or standards for conduct. Conflict is considered to be a natural function in the mental economy, whose purpose is to unify consistent ideas and cause rejection of the inconsistent [*65*, p. 162].

Can self-concept be gotten at experimentally?   Wolff [75] developed various techniques that seem to do this with great adroitness. The subject was presented with some form of his expression (voice, handwriting presented tachistoscopically, silhouette, symmetrical half-face photographs, and so on), along with the expressions of several others, and asked to characterize them.   Amazingly, the subject seldom recognized his own expression consciously, but there were good indications of *unconscious* recognition, such as greater affect in the self-characterizations (stronger feelings) and significantly *longer* characterizations.   The unconscious self-characterizations were usually much more favorable than the individual's characterizations of others and the other judges' characterizations of him. But in approximately 20 per cent of the cases studied, the unconscious self-judgments were decidedly *less* favorable than other judgments.   From Wolff's studies, and Huntley's [41] repeat studies, the percentages of nonrecognition of self are given in Table 1.   It

TABLE 1 [7]

PERCENTAGES OF NONRECOGNITION OF SELF

Expression	Wolff	Huntley
Narrative style	50	44
Voice	90	96
Handwriting (presented through tachistoscope)	85	67
Photograph of hands	73	65
Part-profile	77	62
Whole profile	62	25
Gait (motion pictures taken with subject unaware, head blotted out, all wearing same costume)	0	

is of considerable interest that gait, the only form of expression that is never completely seen by the self, was the only one that was invariably recognized by Wolff's subjects.

There are dynamic factors at work in the lack of self-recognition, demonstrated by the considerably higher percentage of recognition of forms of expression of one's friends.   In an attempt to study the dynamics in unconscious self-judgments, Wolff had his subjects determine whether the statements were "true" as they saw themselves, or not; whether they were accepted as wishes, or not.   The results are given in Table 2, from Wolff [75, p. 123].   There seems to be

---

[7] Percentages given in this table represent only complete lack of self-recognition; there were considerable percentages of uncertainty and doubt of self-recognition.

TABLE 2

<small>FREQUENCY OF ACCEPTANCE OR REJECTION BY THE SELF-JUDGE OF STATEMENTS
IN UNCONSCIOUS SELF-JUDGMENTS OF HANDWRITING</small>
(in per cent)

Accepted	*Denied*	*Accepted as Wishes*	*Denied as Wishes*
38.5	61.5	84.6	15.4

good evidence that the wishes of the individual in terms of personality characteristics can be arrived at by means of unconscious self-judgments, revealing the ego-ideal of the subject, as well as the fears of the individual. It was found that persons characterizing the self in terms of fear images (attributing to the self the qualities he fears having) were often persons driving themselves toward unattainable goals, having such high self-expectations that they could never fulfill them.

The possibilities for further use of these techniques of unconscious self-recognition could be extremely valuable in personality diagnosis.

SUMMARY

Expressive manifestations mentioned above are the result of movement. Studies of expressive movement have considerable diagnostic use in understanding personality. Those studies that have been reviewed here include facial expression, hands, voice, literary and artistic style, style of speech, gait, painting, drawing, and handwriting.

Observation of behavior in group testing situations, in individual testing situations, in life situations, in play situations, in psychodrama, and in interviews can be successfully utilized to understand the structure of personality.

II. The Methods of Experimental Depth Psychology [8]

The hypothesis that an analysis of expressive behavior may serve as a key to the diagnosis of personality involves for its validation many problems that have to be investigated experimentally.

---

[8] Part II of this Chapter was written by Werner Wolff.

UNITY OF PERSONALITY

The first task is to prove that man's behavior expresses personality. A counter-thesis states that behavior is not determined by personality but is based upon chance factors, upon imitation, or upon conditioning and learning. According to chance, expressive qualities such as those of handwriting would depend on the accidental position of the hand, or on the paper and pen at one's disposal. According to imitation, expressive behavior is a repetition of movement patterns frequently perceived, as has been argued for nationally stereotyped forms of expression. According to conditioning and learning, the individual has learned a certain way of writing, a certain way of speaking, and preserves these conditioned responses. However, if various outside stimuli are the only factors that determine expressive behavior, they must be different for each of the forms of expression, and various expressive features cannot have a common denominator of expression.

The experimental approach [75] to the problem to be discussed here was as follows: samples of various forms of expression by many persons were provided. Pictures were taken of the face, of the profile, and of the hands; the voice was recorded; the gait was filmed; handwriting specimens and samples of style of retelling a story were procured. In matching experiments, subjects were asked to match one type of expressive behavior by three individuals to another type of expressive behavior of the same persons. For instance, three voices speaking the same sentence and three standardized handwriting samples of the persons owning the voices were presented in mixed order. The subject was asked to match the handwritings to the voices. The chance expectancy for correct matchings of three pairs is one out of three. The number of correct matchings obtained in these experiments was, on the average, one and one-half to two times the chance numbers. With certain forms of expression and with certain subjects, successful results were much higher. The successful matchings indicate that a person expresses the same characteristic by different means; the expressive quality must be determined by a common denominator that cannot be sought in outside factors such as chance, imitation, or conditioning, but works from within the organism.

Even if similar expressive qualities are shown in a person's various forms of expressive behavior, it is not known whether the interpretation of these expressive qualities is uniform. A second task in the study of expressive behavior, therefore, is to prove that expressive behavior elicits a more or less uniform interpretation. The same form of expression was given to a large number of observers with the instruction to describe its expressive qualities [75]. The terms used in these descriptions were evaluated statistically; the term most frequently used was called a "summarizing term." In a following experiment [75], three forms of expression and their summarizing terms were presented in mixed order with the instruction to match the descriptive terms to the forms of expression. While chance would allow 33.3 per cent of correctness, the success obtained averaged 77.0 per cent, and in some cases, over 90.0 per cent. Detailed investigation showed that the reasons for *incorrect* matchings were not chance, but either an expressive similarity of those forms with which mistakes were made, or emotional factors in the observer that made him blind for certain forms of expression. It was concluded that in a majority of cases, forms of expression elicit a uniform reaction of the observers.

A further problem is whether the description of expressive behavior upon which different observers agree coincides with the everyday behavior of the person whose form of expression is judged. An attempt was made to answer this question by submitting the descriptions of expressive forms of several persons to subjects who knew these persons from daily life relationships [75]. The subjects were asked to identify their friends from the descriptions of their forms of expression. They were successful in 60.0 to 90.0 per cent of the cases. The results indicate that a form of expression represents personality traits that correspond to the overt behavior of the person judged.

The observation that man's behavior expresses his personality leads to another question: *What* does expressive behavior express? Overt behavior may express how a person wants to appear to others, and not to himself. For investigating the coincidence or discrepancy between overt and private behavior, the descriptions of expressive behavior by others was compared with self-ratings of the subjects concerned. The agreement between judgments by others and self-ratings was high, and the deviations could be traced to emotional factors influencing the judgment of some subjects who were looking for certain expressive qualities such as aggression and neuroticism. Other experiments indicated that such dominant characteristics had a personal significance for the judge. Upon the whole, behavior seems to express personality characteristics similarly judged by others and by the originator of expression himself.

JUDGMENTS OF SELF AND OF OTHERS

Since modern psychology has shown that a diagnosis of personality is more significant if it reaches into the depth, uncovering unconscious reactions, the analysis of expressive behavior is based upon conditions in which unconscious reactions can be elicited. Self-ratings and other kinds of conscious self-analysis have the same drawback as the judgments made by other persons, in that they deal with expressive qualities that the subject is able to control, to accentuate, or to hide. Psychoanalysis of expressive behavior is an individual procedure to detect distortions of truth and reality, but this procedure cannot be generalized or demonstrated experimentally.

In order to obtain an unbiased self-analysis on the basis of expressive behavior, a person has to judge his expressive forms without being aware of the fact that he is dealing with himself. With this aim, experiments were carried out in which a person's forms of expression were recorded without his knowledge: a concealed microphone recorded his voice; a hidden camera took pictures of his face, of his profile, and of his hands; a hidden movie camera photographed his gait. The procedures were standardized and the recordings of many persons were made under the same conditions. The subject later heard the voices of three persons speaking the same sentence. One of the voices was his own, the two others, those of friends. Would he recognize himself?

In the next series, shown in Figure 1, he was given the photographs of three persons' profile silhouettes, one being his own. In another series, also shown in Figure 1, he was confronted with three pictures of hands, one showing his own. Again, he saw a film of three persons walking; they wore similar suits and their faces were not visible. One person was the subject himself, the film being taken in an experimental situation without his knowledge. Three handwriting specimens were shown in a mirror, one the subject's own writing. Three retellings of the same story were

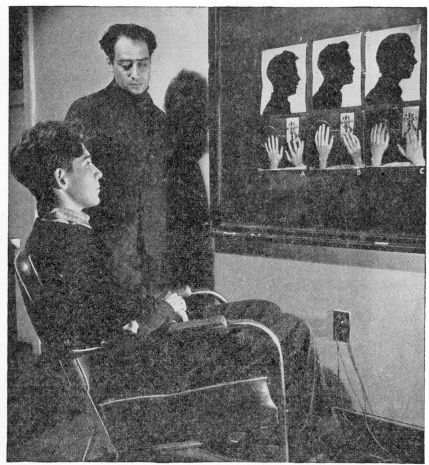

Courtesy of *Life*. Copyright by *Time,* Inc.

Fig. 1. Matching of profiles and hands.

presented to the subject, again, one his own, the others by two of his friends.

These and other similar experiments pose two questions: (1) Does a person recognize himself? and (2) If not, what is his attitude toward himself in absence of recognition and of conscious distortion of his reaction? The results were surprising. If, as it is generally believed, all recognition depends on familiarity and frequency of contacts, one should immediately recognize himself. But this was not the case. In a majority of instances, persons did not recognize themselves. Perhaps the recordings were distortions? But friends were recognized. Perhaps recognition did not succeed because one did not expect to see himself? But even if the examiner told a subject that his form of expression was recorded, he frequently did not identify himself or he believed that the forms of another person were his own and vice versa. In many cases, however, emotional attitudes were observed if a person was confronted with himself. He became nervous, he jumped up, he refused to continue.

A resistance was produced experimentally. The experimenter asked the subject to describe the personalities of the three persons from their forms of expression. A subject's self-judgments, made in a state of unawareness that they are such (these are referred to as unconscious self-judgments), deviate from all the judgments he makes about other persons and from all the judgments other persons make about him. They are especially favorable or especially unfavorable. A person overevaluates himself, for instance, by reporting "a most interesting personality," or "a genius"; or he underevaluates himself, say, as "almost a criminal," and "highly neurotic." Such self-evaluations indicate that expressive behavior is not a neutral but a very personal expression of the individual, so personal that it evokes a resistance against identification and emotional reactions, like those stimulus words that produce resistance and emotion in an association-test and become indicators of unconscious processes.

EXPRESSION OF WISHES AND FEARS

What are the unconscious processes that unconscious self-analysis detects in expressive behavior? We used the descriptive terms given in a self-analysis, mixed their order, and presented them as stimulus words upon which the subject had to give his associations. Subjects reacted to their own terms in two characteristic ways: they produced wishes or fears. For instance, a subject who has described her own unrecognized handwriting as "aggressive, clear in thinking, unclear in action," answered upon the stimulus word *aggressive:* "I should like to be more aggressive, I should like to be able to defend myself." She answered upon the stimulus words *clear in thinking:* "I should like to think more clearly, but I should also like to be less clear in my actions, in the sense of knowing less clearly, being less conscious of what I am doing." Another subject said about her own gait, which she saw in a moving picture: "A complete stranger to me, but a person full of humor. Clumsy. I should have thought that it was a 16-year-old ship's boy who intentionally shows himself to be clumsy and is then disappointed in finding that others do not laugh at his jokes." The stimulus words revealed that the subject had always wanted to be a boy, that she was a depressed person who wanted to be happy and laugh but feared to be clumsy and out of place.

EXPRESSION AND PERCEPTION

Successful matchings of handwriting, voice, or face to styles of retelling stories, and the similarity of emotional reactions to all forms of expression, suggest that all forms of expression may become indicators as complex as verbalizations, so that we may actually speak of a language of expressive behavior. The relationship between resistance against identification and the presence of wishes and fears was found equally in processes of memory and perception. In one experiment, a story was read to a subject and he was asked to retell it. The subject forgot a few data and changed others. The omitted and changed words were then given, together with an equal number of unchanged words, as stimulus words for the subject's associations. The forgotten data evoked emotional associations in a significantly higher degree than the retold data.

Similar processes worked in visual perception. Phenomena of expression and of perception seem to have common denominators, which, as deduced from former experiments, appear to be rooted in the unity of personality.

EXPRESSION AND FORM

Expressive behavior offers two distinct phenomena: expression and form. If one looks at a photograph of a person, one can distinguish the expression on his face from the pattern of that face. Similarly, an artist's drawing may reveal an expression of his moods and a form pattern in which one can recognize his style. Hands show an expression of activity, passivity, tenseness, or relaxation, and a form that may be square, elongated, or round. Handwriting shows an expression in the kind of pressure and rhythm used, and form in the size and distribution of patterns. Expression can be investigated by stimulus-response experiments; form can be measured.

We have discussed several stimulus-response experiments for an analysis of behavioral expression. We shall now give examples of an analysis of behavioral form. One principle of form is its volume, which can be measured according to the volume of response it elicits. Counting the number of words used in the self-judgment experiment, above, for a description of different expressive movement patterns, it appeared that certain forms of expression elicited, on the average, more descriptive terms than others, and that the volume was greater in unconscious self-judgments than in judgments of others. The arithmetical mean of all judgments of others was 34.4 words, on self-judgments, 66.9 words, or about double. It also was found that certain forms of expression revealed predominantly certain spheres of personality. Classifying the descriptive terms used for different forms of expression, and evaluating their distribution statistically, it appeared that the profile revealed the sphere of will to a higher degree than did the other media of expression. In the hand, the sphere of vitality seemed to be dominant; the voice seemed to show an emphasis on the sphere of attitudes; and the styles of retelling gave a clear preference to characterization in terms of intellect. Gait accentuated the social sphere.

In another experiment, full-face photographs were taken and prints were made from each slide of the negative. The dull side gave the usual photographs and the glazed side gave mirror pictures. Determining the midline of the face from the midpoint between the pupils and the middle of the upper lip, we accurately bisected each of the pictures. Then the photograph of the right side and the mirrored right side were fitted together, and the same was done with the two left halves, thus obtaining a right-right and a left-left photograph, as illustrated in Figure 2. In combined pictures of halves of the face of the same person at different ages, it was found that the expressive form was patterned at an early age and that the combination of one-half of an early age photograph—say, at 4 years old—with a much older corresponding face-half—38 years old—formed a congruent total expression [75].

By dividing the face into upper and lower parts, and into right

Courtesy of *Life*. Copyright by *Time,* Inc.

Fig. 2.   Identification and characterization of the face, shown in combinations of the right halves and the left halves and in isolating facial parts.

and left parts, the volume and characteristics of behavioral forms could be evaluated.   The lower part of the face appeared to be more expressive than the upper, and the right half of the face was,

on the average, slightly more expressive than the left. In a majority of cases, one part in a form of expression was dominant over
the other. A method of combined photographs allows measurement of the dominance of expressive forms and their development
in the life of an individual.

FORMULAS OF CONFIGURATION

Principles of formal organization in expressive behavior can be
investigated in handwriting, since handwriting is a recording of
behavioral expression and form upon paper. These graphically
recorded movement patterns can be measured in their size and in
their position and interrelation of elements. Such measurements
have led to the discovery of an unconscious formula of movement
organization [77, 79]. Lengths, distances, positions, and shapes of
graphic elements were found to be simple proportions of one movement that appears with the start, the end, or the middle of a
signature. The length of the starting stroke and of the ending
stroke, the length of first and second name, the width of curves,
the position of dots like that over the "i," each element was disclosed as part of a configurational scheme. These were lawful
interrelationships of movements, hidden regularities of forms that,
with their interdeterminateness, excluded the factor of chance.
Thus, graphic forms, as one manifestation of behavioral patterns,
were found to follow an unconscious law of organization.

The next problem was whether these configurations were related
to certain personality structures or personality traits. Studying
signatures of persons in states of elation and depression, we found
that in elation, movements tended to increase in simple proportions, and that in depressions, in states of frustration, and in old age,
they tended to decrease in simple proportions. That is, the forms
increased or decreased one, one and one-half, two, three, or even
more times as compared with their average size. It therefore
seems that one's forms of expressive movement are not only con-
figurated to unified patterns, but depend on a formula of configuration determined by the changing factors of one's personality.

Graphic movements permit the study of many principles of form
by means of measurements, and of many principles of expression by
means of stimulus-reaction experiments. The change of expression
can be studied under changing stimuli. The consistent relation be-

tween personality traits and certain characteristics of form and expression in graphic movements helps us to affirm again that an analysis of expressive behavior may serve as a key to the diagnosis of personality.

ORIGIN OF FORM IN MOVEMENTS

Since man's behavior expresses personality, which can be more or less uniformly interpreted and can be validated by information from other sources, we come now to the question of whether expressive movements are the result of maturation and sensory development, or whether they are largely an inherent part of human organization. As a *form* of expressive behavior, graphic movements may serve as an example. Although the graphic configuration as such was not learned and was never conscious to the writer, its principle could have been developed through a learning of ordered relationships. I therefore measured scribblings of young children from 10 months old on, and finding here, too, the principle of configuration according to simple proportions, could not use a theory of learning and transfer of learning for an explanation of the phenomenon.

Are these configurations of our movements a reflection of our visual perception, in which we are trained to see balance and ordered relationships? Investigations of graphic movements of persons born blind indicated that configurations of the blind are much lower than those of seeing people, but that here, also, configurations appear more frequently than chance would allow. Does the configuration of expressive forms depend on the healthy balance of the organism? Studies of graphic movements in disease, in mental disturbances, and in epilepsy indicate that the configurational scheme remains preserved. Is the configuration of expressive forms a cultural factor? Investigations indicate that they appear in all cultures, including primitive cultures. We therefore are led to the hypothesis that the principles of form in expressive movements seem to be a property of human organization.

CONSISTENCY OF FORM IN MOVEMENTS

At first glance, it seems that a person's expressive movements change considerably during his development and, even in short time intervals, according to his moods. They seem to change according to situations and conditions of expression. Measuring signatures of the same person written in childhood, adulthood, and old age, measuring them when written in normal state and in disease, comparing them when written with the right hand and with the left hand, when written with eyes open and with eyes closed, indicated that basic proportions tended to remain consistent, even if the outer appearance seemed to have changed completely. The formal principles of expressive movement seem to follow a basic formula of configuration that tends to stay with the individual during his development, during changes of his personality, and during changes in the conditions for his expression.

ORIGIN OF EXPRESSION IN MOVEMENTS

Since we distinguish the principles of form and of expression in movements we have to search not only for the origin of form but also for the origin of expression in movements. The expressiveness of movements can develop as a late product of personality organization or, as indicated by the configuration of forms, it can be manifest at a very early age. The present writer's studies of bodily postures and movements of pre-school children during their play activities, and of the expressiveness of their scribblings and drawings, indicate that laws of expression become manifest at an early age. These laws of expression seem to fall into four categories. The principle of *reflection,* according to which moods, impulses, inhibitions, and tensions find their direct reflection in expressive behavior; the principle of *empathy,* according to which the expression of movements is an attempt at imitation and identification with the object to which the movement is related; the principle of *projection,* which is manifest in movements that accompany the projection of ideas upon objects and activities; and the act of *symbolization,* in which the expression of movements is a symbolization of thoughts. These four categories of expressiveness in movements of young children suggest that the expressiveness of movements is not a late product of personality organization but is present at its early development.

According to our investigations, then, expressive movements reveal personality even at an early state of development. The question arises now whether the interpretation of expressive movements is a product of learning and training. The writer conducted several experiments to explore the question of whether a pre-school child is able to interpret the expressiveness of one medium, say, music, by another medium, say, drawings. The children heard the recorded music of a march, a waltz, and a cowboy song and, in single sessions, each child was asked to draw how the music sounded. Most of the children were able to transpose an acoustic impression into a graphic expression. They tended to interpret the expressive qualities of music by intensity of graphic movements and characteristic forms, using a heavier pressure for the march than for the waltz and preferring angular patterns for the march and round patterns for the waltz. If their drawings had any content, its choice did not seem to be accidental, but actually related to acoustic associations evoked in the child. In other experiments, young children were able to interpret social situations, in the family or in the nursery school, for example, by means of scribblings and drawings. We therefore found an indication that not only the expression, but also the interpretation of expression, is a characteristic of personality already present at an early age.

METHODS OF ANALYZING EXPRESSIVE MOVEMENTS

The finding that expressive movements are related to personality traits leads to their use in the diagnosis of personality. Since expressive movements are partly influenced by the situation under which they appear, we have to separate these outer factors from the indicators of personality. For that purpose, the author used *converging methods*. The observation of the unity of personality in various expressive movements suggested the possibility of interpreting different kinds of expressive behavior of the same person. Although forms of behavior vary in their expressiveness, there are certain characteristics that are a common denominator in the same person's different kinds of expressive movements, and thus, a personality indicator. *Differential methods* make the interpretation of expressive behavior dynamic. We study the difference between an individual's interpretation of himself and of others, consciously and unconsciously, and the differences between the interpretation of an individual and his group. *Matching methods* may allow us to detect determining tendencies in personality. The subject is asked to match concepts to expressive data such as lines, forms, or colors. He is unaware that the same expressive element, a color, say, matched to different concepts, becomes a key that opens his unconscious relationships. For instance, he may match the concept "father" to "red," "mother" to "blue," and later, "hate" to "red" and "love" to "blue," but he would not consciously admit that he hates his father and loves his mother. These relationships get their support by a network of associations established by the matchings.

Expressive movements, considered to be a reflection of the dynamics of personality, should be investigated by *dynamic methods*. Static configurations as they appear in photographs of hands or faces or in handwriting can be brought under dynamic conditions, for example, by showing different positions of photographed hands, by dissecting facial photographs into upper, lower, right and left parts, or by measuring relationships of graphic features and presenting each part in its relationship to the whole. The dynamic method emphasizes that neither form nor expression can be interpreted on the basis of single elements, but must always be considered as patterns, configurations, and expressive relationships.

EXPRESSION-ANALYSIS

Expressive movements, reflecting personality, are indicators of the *expression* of personality and of *movement* processes in personality. Expressions are produced by factors that "press out." These factors are motivations or causes of behavior, dealt with by expression-analysis. Since all movements are goal-directed, an analysis of expressive movements also reveals directions and *goals* of personality. The *method* of expression analysis, based upon a study of expressive behavior, focuses upon cause and effect in the expression of personality, considering the behavioral pattern as a configuration that results from the interplay of the more static formula of form and the dynamic direction of expression.

SUMMARY

Part I of this chapter presents a discussion of some of the more important widely scattered studies of expressive movement found in the literature.

Part II presents a discussion of methodology in the investigation of experimental depth psychology, largely devised by the author of this section. The methods employed in studying unconscious reactions were adapted for investigations of reactions to the face, the profile, hands, voice, gait, handwriting, and style of retelling a story, in each of which the subject reacted to unidentified samples provided by himself and by others.

REFERENCES

1. Allport, G. W., *Personality.* New York: Henry Holt and Company, Inc., 1937.

2. —————————, *The Use of Personal Documents in Psychological Science.* New York: Social Science Research Council, 1941.

3. Allport, G. W., and Cantril, H., "Judging personality from the voice," *J. Soc. Psychol.,* 1934, 5, 37–55.

4. Allport, G. W., and Vernon, P. E., *Studies in Expressive Movement.* New York: The Macmillan Company, 1933.

5. Alshuler, R., and Hattwick, L. W., *Painting and Personality* (2 vols.). Chicago: University of Chicago Press, 1947.

6. Anders, P., "Über den individuellen Eigenrhythmus beim menschlichen Gange und seine Beziehungen zum Rhythmus der Herz und Atemtätigkeit." *Pflüg. Arch. f.d. ges. Physiol.,* 1928, 220, 287–299.

7. Appel, K. E., "Drawings by children as aids to personality studies." *Amer. J. Orthopsychiat.,* 1931, 1, 129–144.

8. Arnheim, R., "Experimentell-psychologische Untersuchungen zum Ausdrucksproblem." *Psychol. Forsch.,* 1928, 11, 1–132.

9. Balken, E., and Masserman, J. H., "The language of fantasy: III. The language of the fantasies of patients with convulsion hysteria, anxiety state, and obsessive-compulsive neuroses." *J. of Psychol.,* 1940, 10, 75–86.

10. Bateson, G., "Cultural determinants in personality," in J. Mc.V. Hunt (ed.), *Personality and the Behavior Disorders.* New York: The Ronald Press Company, 1944, Vol. 2, Chap. 23.

11. Bellak, L., "The concept of projection," *Psychiatry,* 1944, 7, 353–370.

12. Binet, A., "Essai de chiromancie expérimentale." *L' Ann. Psychol.,* 1908, 14, 390–404.

13. Blake, W. H., "A preliminary study of the interpretation of bodily expression." *T. C.* (Columbia University) *Contr. to Educ.,* 1933, 574.

14. Bobertage, O., *Ist die Graphologie zuverlässig?* Freiburg: Hampmann, 1929.

15. Brick, M., "The mental hygiene value of children's art work." *Amer. J. Orthopsychiat.,* 1944, 14, 136–146.

16. Buhler, C., "The social behavior of the child," in C. Murchison (ed.), *Handbook of Child Psychology.* Worccster, Mass.: Clark University Press, 1931, pages 392–431.

17. Carp, B., *A Study of the Influence of Certain Personal Factors on a Speech Judgment.* New Rochelle, N. Y.: The Little Print, 1945.

18. Cleeton, G. U., and Knight, F. B., "Validity of character judgments based on external criteria." *J. Appl. Psychol.*, 1924, 8, 215–231.

19. Del Torto, J., and Cornyetz, P., "Psychodrama as expressive and projective technique." *Sociometry*, 1944, 7, 356–375.

20 Deutsch, F., "Analysis of postural behavior." *Psychoanalytic Quarterly*, 1947, 16, 195–213.

21. Downey, J. E., *Graphology and the Psychology of Handwriting*. Baltimore: Warwick and York, 1919.

22. Downey, J. E., *The Will-Temperament and its Testing*. Yonkers, N. Y.: World Book Company, 1923.

23. DuBois, Cora, *The People of Alor*. Minneapolis: The University of Minnesota Press, 1944.

24. Dunlap, K., "A project for investigating the facial signs of personality." *Amer. J. Psychol.*, 1927, 39, 158–161.

25. Duffy, E., "Level of muscular tension as an aspect of personality." *J. Gen. Psychology.*, 1946, 35, 161–171.

26. Efron, D., *Gesture and Environment*. New York: King's Crown Press, 1941.

27. Elkisch, P., "Children's drawings in a projective technique." *Psychol. Monogr.*, 1945, 58, No. 1.

28. Enke, W., "Die Psychomotorik der Konstitutions-typen." *Z. sch. f. ang. Psychol.*, 1930, 36, 237–287.

29. Erikson, E. H., "Studies in the interpretation of play." *Genetic Psychol. Monogr.*, 1940, 22, 557–671.

30. Eysenck, H. J., *Dimensions of Personality*. London: Kegan, Paul, Trench, Trubner, and Company, Ltd., 1948.

31. —————————, "Neuroticism and handwriting." *J. Abn. and Soc. Psychol.*, 1948, 43, 94–96.

32. Flach, A., "Die Psychologie der Ausdrucksbewegung," *Arch. f.d. ges. Psychol.*, 1928, 65, 435–534.

33. Frank, L. K., "Projective methods for the study of personality." *J. of Psychol.*, 1939, 8, 389–413.

34. Goldstein, K., *The Organism*. New York: American Book Company, 1939.

35. Guilford, J. P., "An experiment in learning to read facial expression." *J. Abn. and Soc. Psychol.*, 1929, 24, 191–202.

36. Fay, P. J., and Middleton, W. C., "Judgment of Spranger personality types from the voice as transmitted over a public address system." *Char. & Pers.*, 1939, 8, 144–155.

37. Herzog, H., "Stimme und Persönlichkeit." *Zsch. f. Psychol.*, 1933, 130, 300–369.

38. Holt, E. B., *The Freudian Wish*. New York: Henry Holt and Company, Inc., 1915.

39. Horowicz, R. E., and Murphy, L. B., "Projective methods in the psychological study of children." *J. Exp. Educ.,* 1938, 7, 133–140.

40. Hull, C. L., and Montgomery, R. P., "Experimental investigations of certain alleged relations between character and handwriting." *Psychol. Rev.,* 1919, 26, 63–74.

41. Huntley, W., "Judgments of self based upon records of expressive behavior." *J. Abn. & Soc. Psychol.,* 1940, 35, 398–427.

42. Jenness, A., "The effects of coaching subjects in the recognition of facial expression." *J. Gen. Psychol.,* 1932, 7, 163–178.

43. Kretschmer, E., *Physique and Character.* New York: Harcourt, Brace and Company, Inc., 1926.

44. LaBarre, W., "The cultural basis of emotions and gestures." *J. of Personality,* 1947, 16, 49–68.

45. Landis, C., "The interpretation of facial expression in emotion." *J. Gen. Psychol.,* 1929, 2, 59–72.

46. Langer, W. C., "Sensorimotor learning," in H. A. Murray and others, *Explorations in Personality.* New York: Oxford University Press, Inc., 1938, pages 508–523.

47. Lerner, E., Murphy, L. B., and others, *Methods for the Study of Personality in Young Children,* Society for Research in Child Development Monograph, Vol. 6, No. 4, Serial No. 34, 1941.

48. Luria, A. R., *The Nature of Human Conflicts.* New York: Liveright Publishing Corporation, 1932.

49. Macfarlane, J. W., "Problems of validation inherent in projective methods." *Amer. J. Orthopsychiat.,* 1942, 12, 405–411.

50. Masserman, J. H., and Balken, E., "The clinical application of fantasy studies." *J. of Psychol.,* 1938, 6, 81–88.

51. Mira, E., *Psychiatry in War.* New York: W. W. Norton & Company, Inc., 1943.

52. Munroe, R. L., Lewinson, T. S., and Waehner, T. S., "A comparison of three projective methods." *Char. and Pers.,* 1944, 13, 1–25.

53. Munroe, R. L., "Three diagnostic methods applied to Sally." *J. Abnorm. & Soc. Psychol.,* 1945, 40, 215–227.

54. Murphy, G., *Personality.* New York: Harper & Brothers, 1947.

55. OSS Assessment Staff, *Assessment of Men.* New York: Rinehart and Co., Inc., 1948.

56. Pear, T. H., *Voice and Personality.* London: Chapman and Hall, 1931.

57. Precker, J. A., "Survey of the use of the formal elements in painting and drawing as an expressive technique." *J. of Projective Techniques* (accepted for publication).

58. Rapaport, D., "Principles underlying projective techniques." *Char. and Pers.,* 1942, 10, 213–219.

59. Rosenzweig, S., "Investigating and appraising personality," in T. G. Andrews, *Methods of Psychology*. New York: John Wiley & Sons, Inc., 1948, Chap. 18.

60. Sanford, F. H., "Speech and personality: A comparative case study." *Char. and Pers.*, 1942, 10, 169–198.

61. Saudek, R., *Experiments with Handwriting*. New York: Wm. Morrow and Company, 1928.

62. Schilder, P., *Brain and Personality*. New York: Nervous and Mental Disease Publishing Company, 1931.

63. Smith, C. E., and Diven, K., "Emotional conditioning test," in H. A. Murray, and others, *Explorations in Personality*. New York: Oxford University Press, Inc., 1938, pages 523–529.

64. Symonds, P. M., *Diagnosing Personality and Conduct*. New York: The Century Company, 1931.

65. Thorne, F. C., "Directive psychotherapy: II. The theory of self-consistency." *J. Clin. Psychol.*, 1945, 1, 155–162.

66. Theiss, H., "Experimentelle Untersuchungen über die Erfassung des Handschriftlichen Ausdrucks durch Laien." *Psychol. Forsch.*, 1931, 15, 276–358.

67. Vernon, P. E., "Some characteristics of the good judge of personality." *J. Soc. Psychol.*, 1933, 4, 42–58.

68. ——————, "Can the 'total personality' be studied objectively?" *Char. and Pers.*, 1935, 4, 1–10.

69. ——————, "The matching method applied to investigations of personality." *Psychol. Bull.*, 1936, 33, 149–177.

70. Waehner, T. S., "Formal criteria for the analysis of children's drawings." *Amer. J. Orthopsychiat.*, 1942, 12, 95–104.

71. ——————, "Interpretation of spontaneous drawings and paintings." *Genetic Psychol. Monogr.*, 1946, 33, 3–70.

72. Washburn, R. W., "A study of smiling and laughing of infants in the first year of life." *Genet. Psychol. Monogr.*, 1929, 6, 397–535.

73. Wolff, Charlotte, "The form and dermatoglyphics of the hands of 115 difficult and high grade boys." *Brit. J. Med. Psychol.*, 1947, 21, 38–49.

74. Wolff, W., "Projective methods for personality analysis of expressive behavior in preschool children." *Char. and Pers.*, 1942, 10, 309–330.

75. ——————, *The Expression of Personality*. New York: Harper & Brothers, 1943.

76. ——————, "Example of a study on forms of expression." *Ciba Symposium*, 1945, 7, 32–36.

77. ——————, *The Personality of the Pre-School Child*. New York: Grune and Stratton, 1946.

78. ————————, *The Unity of Personality* (Expressive Behavior). State College, Pa.: Psychological Cinema Register, 1946. (16 mm. silent film.)

79. ————————, *Diagrams of the Unconscious.* New York: Grune and Stratton, 1948.

80. ————————, *Values and Personality: an Existential Psychology of Crisis.* New York: Grune and Stratton, 1950.

81. ————————, *Changing Concepts of the Bible; a psychological analysis of its words, symbols, and beliefs.* New York: Hermitage House, 1951.

82. Woodworth, R. S., *Experimental Psychology.* New York: Henry Holt, & Company, Inc., 1938, Chap. 11.

83. Zoepffel, H., "Ein Versuch zur experimentellen Festellung der Persönlichkeit im Säuglingsalter." *Zsch. f. Psychol.,* 1929, 3, 273–306.

CHAPTER 17

The Szondi Test

ALBERT I. RABIN, PH.D.

THEORETICAL CONSIDERATIONS

Over a period of more than a decade, the Hungarian psychiatrist, Lipot Szondi, evolved a number of genetic and psychological theories that became the forerunners of the Szondi test.

Szondi arrived at a sort of genetic determinism, which is a variety of a general philosophical theory of predestination. He himself claims, however, that his work is not philosophical but biological and biospsychological.

His first book, the *Schicksalanalyse* (fate analysis) [*10*], presents the chief tenets of his biological theory, which may be stated, briefly, as follows:

The latent hereditary factors in human beings, the recessive genes, do not remain dormant or inactive within the human organism, but exert a very important and even decisive influence upon its behavior. This latent or recessive gene theory claims that these non-dominant hereditary factors determine the *object* selection, voluntary and involuntary, of the individual. The drives resulting from these latent genes, therefore, direct the individual's selection of love objects, friendships, occupations, diseases, and forms of death. Hence, from the very beginning of the human's existence there is a hidden plan of life guided by the afore-mentioned drives. As a corollary, the process of *genotropism* is developed. Genotropism becomes manifest when two people, because of similar, identical, or related latent genetic elements—the recessive genes—become attracted to each other. Hence, this genotropic attraction determines the choice of love partners, ideals, and friendships.

A detailed psychological and psychotechnological extension of

498

the genetic formulations appears in Szondi's second major work [11]. He feels that "drives," which come forth as a result of the latent hereditary elements, constitute an intermediate layer of the unconscious. Whereas Freud dealt chiefly with the *personal unconscious,* and Jung emphasized the importance of the *collective unconscious,* Szondi has proposed another level of the unconscious— the *familial unconscious.* According to Szondi, this area has been hitherto unexplored. The familial unconscious, which lies between the personal and collective unconscious, is the source from which the "repressed ancestors" direct the selective behavior of the individual. To quote Szondi: "Freudian psychoanalysis is the ontogeny, 'Schicksalanalyse,' the genealogy, and Jung's complex-psychology, the archaeology of the deep mental processes."

Despite the voluminous genealogical material presented by Szondi, it is doubtful whether modern genetics would be willing to lend any support to his theory. At best, it may be said that the effects of the latent recessive genes upon the behavior of organisms in general and of the human species in particular is open to question. Moreover, the determination of dominance and recessiveness of psychological characteristics is a very difficult and laborious process that will require many more years of research and investigation.

Historically, the *Szondi test* is an outgrowth of Szondi's genetic and psychological theories; but it need not be bound or determined by them. It may be considered separately as an instrument of personality analysis without adoption of its avowed theoretical antecedents.

THE TEST

Materials. The Szondi test materials [12] consist of 48 cards bearing the portraits of individuals representing the following eight psychiatric diagnoses:

1. homosexual (*h*)
2. sadist (*s*)
3. epileptic (*e*)
4. hysterical (*hy*)

5. catatonic (*k*) ⎫
6. paranoid (*p*) ⎬ Schizophrenia
7. depressed (*d*) ⎭
8. manic (*m*)

The total number of 48 cards is divided into six sets of 8 pictures each; in each set, all of the above-mentioned diagnoses are represented. The majority of pictures were obtained from German textbooks on psychopathology. Some of them are of Hungarian patients, and a few others are of Swedish criminals. Thus, the portraits are presumably of a representative group of western European patients. On the back of each card is the initial (see above) of the diagnosis of the patient depicted in the portrait, together with a number from 1 to 8, indicating the order of presentation of the card in that particular set, and a Roman numeral from I to VI, indicating the number of the set.

Fig. 1. Set of pictures from the Szondi test. (Reproduced from L. Szondi, *Experimentelle Triebdiagnostik,* Testband, Copyright 1947 by Verlag Hans Huber, Berne, Switzerland. By permission.)

Administration. The subject is seated facing the examiner. The cards of the first set are laid flat on the table in front of the subject, in two horizontal rows of four each, and in the order indicated on the back of the cards as shown in Figure 1. The subject is then instructed as follows: "Pick out the two pictures you like best (or most)." After the selection is made he is told:

"Now, select the two you *dislike* most!" The examiner then records the numbers of the cards (or the corresponding initials of diagnosis of the cards) that are "liked," and that are "disliked." The same procedure is repeated with the remaining five sets. The same instructions are usually repeated with every set presented. The results of the selections and rejections are recorded for each set, as described above.

Occasionally, further amplification of the instructions is necessary. Some meticulous subjects wonder what frame of reference they should use for liking or disliking the pictures. They may be told, "Suppose you were to enter a room and meet all these people, which two would you be likely to talk to?"

For some psychiatric patients, the task is quite difficult. Some may say, "I don't like any of them," while others (paranoid or depressed) may state, "But I don't dislike any of them. They are all nice people." In those instances, a modification of the instructions is in order. In the first situation, the subject may be asked to select the two he "dislikes least," rather than the two he likes most. In the second situation, the patient may be requested to choose the two he "likes less" than the rest of them, assuming he likes them all.

The time required for a single administration of the Szondi test varies with the subject. Some subjects may require as little as 10 minutes, while others may take one-half hour or longer.

The Profile. At the end of each testing period, a profile based on the choices and rejections of the subject is constructed. The profile is a graphic representation of the results and gives the total picture at a glance. It also facilitates comparisons with other profiles obtained on the same or other individuals.

The profile record form, illustrated in Figure 2, is made up of 96 equal squares. It is divided in the middle by a heavy horizontal line. The space above that line is divided into eight vertical columns, corresponding to the eight diagnoses. There are 6 squares in each column. This upper area is the one where all the "liked" responses are recorded. An identical area below the heavy horizontal line is reserved for the "disliked" responses.

The procedure for constructing the profile is as follows: The pictures liked and disliked in the first diagnostic category (homosexual) are counted. Then, the number of squares in the appropri-

SZONDI PROFILE

S		P		Sch		C	
h	s	e	hy	k	p	d	m

Fig. 2.   The Szondi profile record form.

ate column corresponding to the number of likes are darkened, *above* the middle horizontal line, which is used as a base line. Similarly, the number of squares corresponding to the number of dislikes are darkened *below* the horizontal base line.   The full profile can be obtained by following this procedure through each of the eight columns.

Traditionally, and for the sake of distinguishing the areas easily, the upper part of the profile (likes) is darkened with a red pencil, and the lower (dislikes), in blue.

Profile Analysis.   In general, the area of positive choices (likes) is given a plus sign (+), while the area of negative choices or rejections (dislikes) is given a minus sign (—).

These generic designations of positive and negative are not altogether sufficient for the recording of the final results in any one column. It is necessary to designate the extent to which pictures of a certain category were selected; to what extent and in which category the genotropism, negative or positive, manifested itself. The simple designation of the number of pluses and the number of minuses in any one column is too cumbersome and does not give a clear indication of the "balance of forces" or their direction. Consequently, four categories of choices have been evolved. These categories are as follows:

Positive (+)
Negative (—)
Ambivalent (±)
Open (O)

The first two categories are self-explanatory. Not all of the choices in a column designated as positive need be above the midline of the profile blank. However, the balance of choices needs to be overwhelmingly in the positive direction in order to achieve this designation. Similar reasoning is behind the negative category. The ambivalent category consists of a minimum of four selected pictures, evenly or almost evenly divided between likes and dislikes. It is a designation of a situation in which the positive and negative choices balance or nearly balance each other. The open category indicates a paucity of "loading" in that particular column, that is, when a maximum of two choices is made, one on either side of the midline; one choice; or none at all.

TABLE 1

SZONDI SCORING CATEGORIES

Positive (+)	*Negative* (—)	*Ambivalent* (±)	*Open* (O)
+2;0	0;—2	+2;—2	0;0
+3;0	0;—3	+3;—3	0;—1
+4;0	0;—4	+2;—3	+1;0
+5;0	0;—5	+3;—2	+1;—1
+6;0	0;—6		
+2;—1	+1;—2		
+3;—1	+1;—3		
+4;—1	+1;—4		
+5;—1	+1;—5		
+4;—2	+2;—4		

A list of the numbers of positive and negative choices (likes and dislikes) that fall in each of the categories described is given in

Table 1.   The first figure in each column of the table gives the number of likes (positive) and the second figure, the number of dislikes (negative).

The Meaning of the Scoring Categories.   Each column in the test profile represents one of the eight test factors or drives.   The nature of those drives will be discussed in the latter part of the present chapter.   The maximum number of pictures that can be selected or rejected in any one diagnostic category is *six*.   Only three pictures would be the number selected and rejected in any one category by chance.   When the total number of pictures selected and rejected in a diagnostic category is four or greater, the factor corresponding to that diagnosis is said to be *loaded*.   From the viewpoint of Szondi interpretation, it is indicative of a tension within the personality—a need for satisfaction in this particular area.   By definition, those factors receiving an ambivalent score are loaded.   According to Szondi, the *ambivalent* score is indicative of a subjectively felt tension in the corresponding area.   It is the experience of opposing drives counteracting each other.   Conversely, the *open* score indicates the absence of tension in that particular area.   It is a sign that the drives corresponding to that factor are able to find some avenues for their discharge.   The *positive* score, representing a predominance of likes of pictures of some particular factor, shows an identification with the drives represented by the pictures of that factor.   The *negative* score, on the other hand, is indicative of a rejection or alienation of those drives.

The Series of Szondi Profiles.   Szondi and his co-worker [3, 10] believe that a valid personality diagnosis may be obtained only when the test is administered several times—from six to ten times. They recommend the administration of the test every other day until the desired number of profiles is obtained.   The basis for these recommendations is mainly empirical.

Since the Szondi profile represents a complex balance and the dynamic relationships of various drives, it is sensitive to delicate, day-to-day changes in the personality.   Single profiles obtained may be inaccurate, for they may represent or overemphasize a temporary interplay between the drive factors.   Therefore, a larger number of profiles is needed for the achievement of a more valid description of the personality and for the detection of the various areas of stability and comparative fluidity.

If the interval between test administrations is less than a day, it is found that such factors as memory and the need to be consistent with previous choices may distort emergence of the true drive-relationships at the time of administration. The experience of Szondi workers justifies a minimum interval of one day, after which the presumably vitiating influences are no longer in operation. To be sure, before the successive administrations of the test, the subject is to be instructed to select and reject the pictures that he likes or dislikes at that particular instant, without regard for his own previously expressed opinions.

SZONDI'S TYPOLOGY

The first section in this chapter dealt with Szondi's more general genetic and psychological theories. These theoretical assumptions, as we have already stated, are not essential to the use of his test. His psychological typology, however, *is* essential, since the test is based on it. Accordingly, a brief exposition of the *Vector-factor theory* is in order.

The following four *drive-vectors*, each subdivided into two constituting factors, are identified by Szondi and allegedly represent the entire scope of driving forces imbedded in the human personality, "normal" or abnormal:

   I. *S-Vector:* the sexual drive
  II. *P-Vector:* paroxysmal-surprise drive
 III. *Sch-Vector:* the self-drive
 IV. *C-Vector:* the contact drive

Each vector represents a certain personality area that appears in an extremely exaggerated form in pathological conditions corresponding to the two factors that constitute it. While the vector is a designation of a more general drive, the factors that make it up are somewhat more specific drives or need-systems. For the purposes of the test, the need-systems may be assumed, without regard for their genesis. This assumption is the main hypothesis underlying the Szondi method. Thus, the vectors and their corresponding factors are: the *S-Vector,* made up of the *homosexual* (h) and *sadistic* (s) factors; the *P-Vector,* made up of the *epileptic* (e) and *hysterical* (hy) factors; the *Sch-Vector,* made up of the *catatonic* (k) and *paranoid* (p) factors; and finally, the *C-Vector,* made up of the *depressive* (d) and *manic* (m) factors.

The selection of pictures of the eight diagnostic groups mentioned in the description of the materials is, therefore, governed by this choice of factors. They represent the whole gamut of the extreme manifestations of the factors and the general drives or vectors these factors constitute.

The relationship between the vectors and, particularly, between the factors within each vector, is a close one. In interpretation and personality description based on the Szondi, the interdependence of the various factors must be stressed. However, at this point, an exposition of Szondi's description of each discrete factor is warranted.

1. The h-factor. Generally speaking, this factor is an expression of the need for tenderness, femininity, motherliness, and passivity. The object is usually a definite person, family, religion, or other institutions. On a higher level, it expresess itself in "collective tenderness," the object being all of humanity. Ordinary occupational interests are in personal services—barber, cosmetician, valet, hotel keeper, dancer, and so on. On a higher level—gynecologist, sex pathologist, and so on.

The extremely pathological disorders manifested in this factor may be placed under the general heading of hermaphroditism. Spying, prostitution, and fraudulent dealings are among the criminal forms of expression this drive may take.

2. The s-factor. This factor expresses the need for masculinity, aggression, sadism, activity, and virility. It is the masculine drive, the need to be a man, a father, and the dominant (leading) partner. On a higher level of extreme sublimation, the need expresses itself in chivalry, ability of self sacrifice for the common good, and "drive for civilization." Usual occupational interests of individuals with such a drive are farming, animal taming, butchering, prize fighting, and so on. On a higher, more sublimated level, occupations such as surgeon, dentist, anatomist, and operating room nurse, may be expected.

Pathologically, this drive may appear in the various forms of sadism, sodomy, pederasty, and the like. Impulsive murder is the common form of criminality.

3. *The e-factor.* Here, the damming up of "raw" affect is indicated. There is a need to suppress such emotions as rage, hate, revenge, and anger. A "surprise" reaction via explosive discharge, intolerance of others, may be expected. On a higher level, "collective" righteousness, charity, piousness, and tolerance, may be the expression. Occupational interests are in such jobs as foreman, baker, sailor, flyer, and stoker. On a higher level are priest, monk, missionary, nurse, and others.

Various forms of epilepsy, migraine, stuttering, asthma, and enuresis are among the pathological expressions. Also found are forms of criminality: klepto-pyromania and impulsive murder.

4. *The hy-factor.* The major drive of this factor is the need for exhibitionism—to be "on the stage." Szondi calls this factor "the class of latent exhibitionism." The socially positive form of expression of this factor is seen in modesty. However, basically, the need is for showing off and for suddenness (surprise) in behavior. Higher-level expressions of this need are found in acting and in politics. As may be inferred from the abbreviation of the name of this factor—the pathological manifestations are revealed in hysteria, tics and phobias.

5. *The k-factor.* "Ego systole" is the descriptive phrase used by Szondi in the exposition of the k-factor (catatonia being spelled with a *k* in German). It is the need for "self-compression" or self-limitation. The native, basic form of the need is "to seal oneself off hermetically from the world and to spend the selfish life in the enclosure of the ego." However, since submission to the extreme form of this drive is not feasible, emergency outlets such as narcissism and depersonalization are utilized. Pathologically, the need becomes manifest through catatonic and a variety of other schizoid reactions. At a high level of social adjustment, there is a suppression of these extreme egoistic and narcissistic trends and adaptation to collectivity takes place. Occupations such as logician, philosopher, and mathematical physicist are manifestations of such an adjustment.

6. *The p-factor.* In contradistinction to the *k*-factor, there is the *p*-factor, which represents the need for "self-extension," or

what is termed ego diastole. It is a need aroused from the un-satisfied self-expansion desire for power: megalomania. There is a constant need for self-realization, for recognition of one's unknown capacities and, generally speaking, for furthering the self.

The socially positive and sublimated form of this need is through the furthering of humane needs, creativity, renunciation of the self, and the like. Obviously, the extreme pathological manifestations of this need are in the several forms of paranoia and related con-ditions.

7. *The d-factor.* Here, the basic need is that of seeking and retaining objects. It is most closely related to what the psycho-analysts term *anal characteristics.* A pressure for rivalry is also related to this general drive. There is a seeking of objects that may, in reality, have been lost, or that it is feared might be lost. Related self-depreciation and feelings of guilt are present. De-pression and melancholia are the more extreme pathological mani-festations of this drive. Its socialization at the higher positive level may occur in art or literary criticism, supervision of a museum, and so forth.

8. *The m-factor.* In the second factor of the "Contact-Vector," the need is for clinging to objects. It is an unquenchable need. Even when the object is possessed there is uncertainty about its possession. Thus, the trait is that of the *oral character,* or, as Szondi terms it, "the external suckling." Oral needs, therefore, are characteristic of this drive. Manic and hypomanic reactions, alcoholism, nymphomania, and satyriasis are some of the extreme pathological expressions of this need. A trend toward speech dis-orders is in the same category.

The socially positive expression of the drive appears through separation from objects in favor of the "collectivity." Politics and the art of speech are among the occupational areas into which this drive may be channelized.

It may readily be noted that each of the pair of factors in every vector is related to the other; in a sense, one factor of a pair is the reciprocal of the other in that pair. Thus, the *S*-vector con-tains tenderness vs. aggression, the *P*-vector, emotional control vs. emotional expressiveness, the *Sch*-vector, ego systole vs. ego diastole, and the *C*-vector, anal trends vs. oral characteristics.

INTERPRETATION OF THE SZONDI PROFILES

The foregoing discussion of Szondi's vectors, factors, and scoring categories readily indicates the complexity involved in the interpretation of the test. Its administration is relatively simple, but the interpretation, in which the interdependence or dynamic relationship between the several factors must be taken into account, is a highly complicated and difficult task.

In the single test profile, the amount of loading in each factor is determined, the positive and negative, as well as the ambivalent aspects of the loadings are noted, and the estimation of the effects of the factors upon each other yields the qualitative personality characterization. It is in the nature of a description of the intra- and interfactor "balance of power," each factor representing a need-system, as noted above.

The several administrations of the test project it, so to speak, into a temporal continuum. As a result, we obtain not only a cross-section of a constellation of need-systems within the individual, but also a longitudinal view of the changes in the constellation. Extreme changes from loaded to open vectors, from highly positive to negative vectors, are some of the important indicators of psychopathology that could not have been obtained from a single test administration. Moreover, the areas (factors) of change from one profile to the other, even in the "normal" individual, are important cues to the more significant need-systems in the dynamics of a personality.

It is far beyond the scope of the present exposition to give a detailed description of the methods of interpretation by means of the Szondi test. Information of this kind, accompanied by illustrative case material, has been presented by Deri [2].

THE SZONDI TEST AS A PROJECTIVE TECHNIQUE

In general, the Szondi fulfills two of the major requirements for a projective technique. In the first place, it purports to reveal the private world of the individual selecting the pictures. It attempts to lay bare the dynamics of his basic needs and drives. Secondly, the subject is not conscious of the fact that he is doing just that. He is not aware of the interpretations that may be placed on his test performance.

Szondi's particular typology and theoretical orientation result in personality descriptions that do not clearly overlap interpretations obtained by other projective methods. To be sure, *some* overlapping is inevitable, since they all deal with personality. However, whereas the Rorschach is primarily concerned with a cross-section of personality structure and the TAT with specific need-press relationships, the Szondi deals with more general drives as related to personality tensions, subjectively felt or objectively "acted out."

The ease of administration and the lack of need for verbal response on the part of the subject recommend the application of this technique to a wide variety of normal and pathological conditions. Whereas other projective methods yield very little in the case of the constricted, rigid, and linguistically handicapped person, Szondi data may be obtained with comparative ease.

The first question concerning any new method or technique of personality diagnosis that may be raised by the critical student is that of validity. Are the personality descriptions and dynamics that result from the test's application truly distinguishing and consistent with the behavior manifestations of the person tested? Unfortunately, the available published material on the Szondi test does not permit an answer to this question. There are, to be sure, published testimonies of the efficacy of the test in personality diagnosis [2, 3, 9], but they are, for the most part, descriptive and illustrative, rather than validating studies that would meet the rigorous criteria of scientific method.

Another question that may be raised by the critical reader is: Are the four vectors and their eight factors well chosen and sufficient to account for the major aspects of personality dynamics? [1]

A third question is related to the theoretical assumptions underlying the test material itself. The assumption is that the subject's reaction to the physiognomies of patients reproduced in photographs taps the deeper layers of personality dynamics. How well is this substantiated?

These and many other questions that are closely interrelated will have to be answered by future investigators before the test can become fully acceptable to the critical and scientific clinician.

---

[1] Two studies have been completed since this chapter was prepared: Wilson H. Guertin, "A consideration of factor loadings on the Szondi test." *J. Clin. Psychol.*, 1950, 6, 3, 262–266; and, by the same author, "A test of a basic assumption of the Szondi." *J. Consult. Psychol.*, 1950, 14, 404–407.—Eds.

The clinical use of such a popular projective technique as the Rorschach preceded critical studies and investigations of its assumptions and theoretical foundations. The Szondi test is beginning its career in both directions simultaneously. There are many enthusiastic "Szondi clinicians," but at the same time, there is evidence of an experimental approach to the test as well.

A report by Rabin [7] indicated that the pictures are not meaningless stimuli. He found that students and psychologists identified more pictures correctly as to diagnosis than can be attributed to chance. Moreover, he has shown that the factor of training in the ability to identify the pictures is important [8]. The related conclusion is that the pictures have differentiated *meaning,* and that their being liked or disliked is not a haphazard event. However, it has also been shown [4, 6] that the potency of the picture stimuli in any one diagnostic category varies considerably. Thus, the diagnosis per se is not the only factor responsible for selection or rejection of the pictures. There are apparently additional factors, not accounted for by Szondi theory, related to the popularity continuum. Experimentation with the test on electric-shock-treated depressed [1] and schizophrenic [6] patients appears to be another promising avenue of research.

SUMMARY

In conclusion, it may be stated that the Szondi test is an empirical procedure at best. Thus far there are no crucial experiments that would validate the test, its personality analyses, or its predictive capacity. The present "evidence" is of the nature of private empirical proof [2]. The validation is clinical validation by those who employ the method. Future research will indicate the capacity of the test to stand up under the careful scrutiny of experimentation by the research-minded clinical psychologist.

REFERENCES

1. Deri, S., "The effects of electric shock treatment on depressive patients" (abstract). *Am. Psychol.,* 1947, 2, 286.

2. ————————, *Introduction to the Szondi Test.* New York: Grune & Stratton, 1949.

3. ————————, "The Szondi test." *Am. J. Orthopsychiat.,* 1949, 19, 447–454.

4. Harrower, M. R., *Experimental Studies with the Szondi Test.* New York: privately mimeographed, 1949.

5. Rabin, A. I., "Effects of electric shock treatment upon some aspects of personality and intellect" (abstract). *Am. Psychol.,* 1947, 2, 284.

6. —————————, "Preliminary quantitative Szondi test data in normal and psychiatric subjects" (paper read at Szondi Symposium, APA meetings, Denver, Colo., September 1949).

7. —————————, "Szondi's pictures: I. Identification of diagnoses." *J. Abn. & Soc. Psych.,* 1950, 45, 392–395.

8. —————————, "Szondi's pictures: II. Effects of formal training on ability to identify diagnoses," *J. Consult. Psychol.,* 1950, 14, 400–403.

9. Rapaport, D., "The Szondi test." *Bull. Menninger Clinic,* 1941, 5, 33–39.

10. Szondi, L., *Schicksalsanalyse.* Basel: Benno Schwabe & Co., 1944.

11. —————————, *Experimentelle Triebdiagnostik.* Bern: Verlag Hans Huber, 1947.

12. —————————, *Szondi Test (Testband).* Bern: Verlag Hans Huber, 1947.

CHAPTER 18

Other Projective Methods

WOODROW WILBERT MORRIS, PH.D.

INTRODUCTION

The past 30 years have seen phenomenal growth in a new approach to the description and diagnosis of personality. This growth has taken the form of the development, refinement, and use of projective methods of psychodiagnosis. As in any promising "movement," it appears that scientific evaluation frequently suffers in the face of the wildfire-like spread of novel ideas. Thus, the Psychological Corporation was some time ago led to warn the profession editorially, in an issue of its *Test Service Bulletin* [23], as follows:

The flowering of the projective technique of studying personality has brought to clinical psychology a somewhat dandelion-like broadcasting of seed. Almost every experienced clinician naturally develops certain knacks or "gimmicks" of his own for eliciting projections. Some of these are developed systematically and become objects for research. At this point, many clinicians encounter the urge to elaborate their methods and prepare them for publication. Among the unsolicited tests . . . projective methods of one sort or another are currently far outnumbering tests in any other category. . . .

Most of these proposals contain the germs of potential usefulness. Some are limited in applicability to only a few special situations. Some present production problems complex to the point of impracticability. Many overlap too much with the Rorschach, TAT, or other techniques already widely used; they do not afford any really new opportunities for insight. Some lack only maturity and may be expected to enter the public stage when their authors have spent more labor and thought on them. A few verge on the ridiculous.[1]

---

[1] Quotation by permission of the Psychological Corporation.

This description of the state of affairs in the area of projective techniques serves admirably to set the stage for the present chapter, designed as it is to cover a variety of techniques of the sort referred to in the statement above, that is, methods that are little-known to date but have about them the aura of promise in the future.

The great variety of this conglomerate group of methods, ranging as they do from blindfold line-drawing to the telling of stories and construction of mosaic designs, makes difficult a systematically organized presentation. In a survey of projective techniques that seemed feasible to employ with blind adults, the author was faced with this same problem [15]. While it is probable that the outline employed there would be equally applicable here, there is so much overlapping in any arbitrary division of projective methods that no attempt will be made to follow that outline here.

SARGENT'S PAPER-PENCIL-PROJECTIVE METHOD

The Paper-Pencil-Projective Method was devised by Sargent [17] in an effort to see if the theories and methods of projective techniques in general could be applied to a paper-pencil situation. The essence of the method lies in two factors: (1) very carefully worded directions to the subject, which set the stage projectively, and (2) interesting but systematically selected situations involving a person the same sex as the subject, about whom the subject is to write (or relate) answers to the questions: *What did he (or she) do and why?* and *How did he (or she) feel?* Since these are important aspects of the method, Sargent's instructions to the subject will be given in full: [2]

Test of Insight Into Human Motives

Insight into others helps us to get along with them. This is a test of your ability to "see into" others. This requires both imagination and the ability to put yourself in someone else's place.

On these pages there are a number of situations which are described very briefly. After each there are two questions which I want you to answer.

Notice that the persons involved in these situations are not described. This allows you to use your imagination as to what sort of people the characters might be.

There are no right or wrong answers, but your explanations should show understanding of the characters as you see them.

---

[2] Quotations by permission of the *Psychological Monographs*.

The subject is then presented with a set of 15 situations, which Sargent calls "armatures." There are separate sets for men and women. The interests of the average college man or woman are reflected in the types of situation chosen by the author. To put it simply, they are typical college fraternity or sorority "bull session" topics. In order to illustrate the nature of some of these situations, two are reproduced below:

Armature VI: A young man discovers that a girl to whom he is engaged has had a very bad reputation in the past.
   (a) What did he do and why?
   (b) How did he feel?

Armature XI: A young man gets the impression that others are discussing him. On several occasions he thinks the conversation has stopped or the subject changed when he entered the room.
   (a) What did he do and why?
   (b) How did he feel?

The total group of 15 situations are categorized as tapping such diverse areas of adjustment as family, opposite sex, social and friendships, religion and opinion, and vocations and health.

A somewhat involved and subjective scoring system is employed, which consists in analyzing each response production with respect to the types of emotional expressions used (for example, "he felt sad"), various cognitive expressions (qualifications, elaborations, and the like), and the conflict solution.

Figure 1 illustrates another of the armatures, with the response scored. The underscorings and other marks show how each of the 15 responses are scored. Here, the conflict solution is underlined: "He began to avoid those who had been razzing him," which we have labeled an avoidance or escape solution. The next clause is an elaboration of the original situation and contains as well a feeling-expression concerned with feelings of frustration. Feelings of anxiety, conflict, and inadequacy are easily identified in the next clause, which is followed by another elaboration, accompanied this time by a feeling-expression again suggestive of avoidance and escape. The last element is obviously expressive of depressed feelings. The scoring summary in Figure 1 is for this one situational response only; with a full administration, this procedure is followed for each of the 15 armatures.

Armature IV—A young man gets a good deal of razzing because he spends his week-ends at home instead of dating.

Solution = *avoidance, escape*

Sample response and scoring—He began to avoid those who had
elaboration   Feeling = *frustration*
been razzing him.   [He did this because he could not afford to date]
Feeling = *anxiety, conflict, inadequacy*   elaboration
and <felt unable to cope with the razzing.>   [He also spent more
Feeling = *avoidance, escape*   *Feel-*
of his time at home in reading and solitary pursuits.]   <He felt
ing = *depression*
very much alone and depressed.>

Scoring summary: Conflict solution: avoidance, escape.

Feeling categories:	Frustration	— 1
< >	Anxiety	— 1
	Avoidance	— 1
	Depression	— 1
	Submission	— 0
	Satisfaction	— 0
	Negative attitudes	— 0
	Positive attitudes	— 0
	Rationalizations	— 0
Cognitive scores:	Elaboration	— 2
[ ]	Evaluation	— 0
	Qualification	— 0

Fig. 1. *Sample response, scoring, and scoring summary to Armature IV of Sargent's Test of Insight into Human Motives.* (Reproduced by permission of *Psychological Monographs.*)

The Sargent Test seems to fit the criteria for a projective test rather well. The directions immediately veil the true character of the test, both by stating a different purpose and by flattering the subject's vanity that he is able to "see into others." At the same time, the material is kept general, relatively free from the production of clichés and social stereotypes, and yet allows the subject freedom in responding in his own idiosyncratic ways.

With respect to other important problems involved in the development of a new technique, it may be stated that scoring is a rather arbitrary and highly subjective procedure, very involved and time-consuming. Much more work needs to be done in this area before the technique is ready for general clinical use. Reliability has yet to be determined. Sargent originally devised "parallel" sets of armatures, but the fact of their parallelism is questionable. In addition, if the proposed scoring approach is to be used, studies need to be done on the level of scoring reliability in answer to the general question: If scored by several psychologists, with what consistency will the various elements be scored the same? Normative standards for various age levels, socioeconomic groups, and the several psychopathological types need to be made available. Finally, interpretative values must be discovered, organized, and carefully validated.

Some of these problems have been touched upon by Sargent [*17*], and more recently, by Fassett [*8*]. Thus, while Sargent found equivocal results with regard to reliability, Fassett employed test-retest methods using a single form and found fairly promising coefficients of reliability. Sargent originally reported satisfactory interjudge agreements and agreement by repeated scorings by the same judge. Since Sargent's scoring system was complex, Fassett set herself the task of developing a simpler scoring system. The latter was developed "out of consideration of what could be identified in brief, easily scorable, communicable form." Each answer was scored according to four classifications: *interpretation,* the central character's conception of the problem; *approach,* the method of considering the problem, steps followed, or conclusions reached in coming to a solution; *solution,* how the problem is solved; and *effect,* the result of the solution on the central figure's actions or thinking. Interpretation may be either *interpersonal* or *extrapersonal.*

It may be concluded, then, that the Sargent Test is one of the more promising of the newly proposed methods but that much careful, systematic work remains to be done before it can, or should, be used clinically.

STORY-TELLING AND COMPLETION METHODS

Creative story-telling is a task that seems to have universal appeal, especially to children. Psychologists and psychiatrists have for many years taken advantage of this appeal in obtaining data that they believe to be of clinical utility in delineating the child's special areas of conflict, anxieties, wish-fulfillment fantasies, fears, cathexes, needs, modes of response, and many other adjustment items. The primary theory behind story-telling seems to be similar to that of dream theory, as proposed by Freud and elaborated by his followers. Briefly stated, it is felt that given a relatively unstructured topic, the story told will reveal this kind of information where direct questioning would not. In addition, story-telling behavior is so common a phenomenon among children that it becomes the most natural approach to their fantasy lives.

Topics assigned as story-telling stimuli range all the way from very structured, retelling *The Big Bad Wolf* and *Goldilocks,* used by Despert and Potter [6], and relatively structured topics, like *The Story of a Boy, The Story of a Hero, The Story of Two Children,* and similar subjects, to unstructured stimuli, such as asking the child simply to "tell or make up a story for me."

Despert and Potter's results are similar to those reported by Hall [10] in an analysis of dream productions. Hall found that dreams were especially valuable if examined in series, and that this sort of approach led easily to the recognition of a "spotlight" dream that seemed to state the essential problem, other dreams in the series being interpreted in the light of this dream. In his treatment he found what Despert and Potter referred to as a common theme running through children's stories, and what Murray [16] called common themes in TAT productions.

In general, the use of stories or story completions may be regarded as involving the same principles that apply to other fantasy productions of the TAT type. The only important difference lies in the character of the stimuli employed (a title in the one case, and a picture in the other). This general principle may be stated simply as follows: given a stimulus that allows freedom of association, the individual will draw upon his own background of experiences, wishes, needs, conflicts, and so on, in organizing and constructing his response insofar as he is willing and able to cooperate in the activity proposed. In this, the stimulus is of great importance. For example, children will give one kind of story in response to the title, *My Brother,* and quite a different kind to such a relatively vague title as, *A Story About A Boy.* The former is more likely to elicit stories that are highly specific and primarily descriptive; the latter, in the instance of boys, may well produce significant information with respect to ego-ideals and wishes; in girls, it may produce stories that reveal their attitudes toward boys, toward their brothers, and so forth. It is important, therefore, to obtain a *series* of stories, thus attempting to elicit, say, boys' attitudes toward themselves, other boys, parents, and girls, or whatever other information one may desire for specific purposes.

As far as the writer knows, there have been no reported attempts to "score" story productions, nor has reliability been estimated. Validity has been estimated only to the extent that it has been assumed that the fantasy material produced is autobiographical, or that symbolic expressions are used that are interpreted in much the same fashion that other fantasy productions are interpreted.

In summary, we quote from Despert and Potter's conclusions [6]: [3]

1. The story is a form of verbalized fantasy.
2. The child reveals his inner drives and his conflicts through this channel of expression.
3. A recurring "theme" is usually found which indicates the main object of concern or conflict.
4. Anxiety, guilt, wish-fulfillment, and aggressiveness are the main trends expressed.
5. The fantasies thus expressed check well with material obtained by other means (such as dream material).
6. The "story" approach is most valuable when complete freedom of subject matter is left to the child, but it is also of value when a popular subject is used instead.
7. The "composition" form is in itself inhibitory and free flow of expression is to be preferred.
8. The dull children yield less information than the more intelligent ones, although there is no absolute relation between I.Q. and productivity.
9. The story can be used as a means, not only of resolving a difficult emotional situation, but also of checking on the development of the problem while under treatment.
10. A good rapport between child and examiner is preferable, *but not essential.*

THE H-T-P TECHNIQUE

The H-T-P Technique proposed by Buck [2, 3, 4] derives its designation from the fact that the subject is requested to make freehand drawings of *House, Tree,* and *Person.* Buck describes his method as a two-phased approach: the first being nonverbal, creative, relatively unstructured, and requiring a rather primitive form

---

[3] Quotation by permission of the *Psychiatric Quarterly.*

of expression, drawing; the second, verbal, apperceptive, and somewhat more structured.

The subject is first asked to make drawings of the three objects and is allowed almost complete freedom in the manner in which he performs the tasks. Following this, the subject is asked to define, describe, and interpret the objects drawn and their respective environments and to associate concerning them.

According to Buck, "The specific items, House, Tree, and Person, were chosen because: (1) they are items familiar to even the comparatively young child; (2) they were found to be more willingly accepted as objects to be drawn by subjects of all ages than other items suggested; and (3) they appeared to stimulate more frank and free verbalizations than did other items." [4]

The technique itself is based on a series of postulates that set forth the basic theory of H-T-P as a projective device:

1. Each of the drawn wholes (House, Tree, and Person) is to be regarded as a self-portrait as well as a drawing of the specific object named, since subjects are believed to draw only those characteristics of a given whole that they somehow regard as essential.

2. A subject may indicate that a given detail or combination of details, or the method of their presentation, has special significance for him in two ways: positively and negatively.

Positively:

(a) by overtly exhibiting emotion immediately before, during, or after drawing a given detail or combination of details

(b) by presenting the detail or detail-complex in sequential order deviant from the average

(c) by exhibiting unusual concern over the presentation, as by erasing or by repeatedly returning to the detail during the performance

(d) by presenting the detail or detail-complex in a bizarre fashion

(e) by perseveration

(f) by his frank comment concerning a whole or any part or parts thereof

Negatively:

(a) by presenting a detail or detail-complex incompletely

(b) by omitting altogether one or more so-called essential details

(c) by commenting evasively or refusing to comment at all upon a whole or any part or parts thereof

3. Interpretation of these "significant" details, detail-complexes, and/or the method of their presentation, will provide information concerning the subject's needs, fears, strivings, conflicts, and the like.

4. It is essential that the subject be afforded every opportunity to aid

---

[4] Quotations from Buck are made with the permission of the *Journal of Clinical Psychology*.

in interpretation of his productions because of the clinically observed fact that the so-called universal and absolute meaning of certain symbols may be radically altered in certain configurations if the subject is not given ample opportunity to express it.

5. Adequate interpretation of a specific point can be made only when it is considered in its relationship to the total configuration.

6. Interpretation must be made with great circumspection and in the light of as complete a knowledge as possible of the subject and his environment.

Buck postulates further that the H-T-P is a valid measure of adult intelligence, for the reasons that: (1) the H-T-P appraises intelligence from the standpoints of elemental information (details), spatial relationships (proportion and perspective), and concept formation (organization and quality of the completed whole, and the subject's spontaneous and/or induced comments concerning it); (2) the problem presented to the subject in the nonverbal phase involves the reproduction in two-dimensional form of a memory image of a three-dimensional form; and (3) because of the relatively primitive method of expression, subjects who find verbalization difficult may reveal the presence of a hitherto unsuspected intellectual ability or potential.

With regard to the latter set of postulates, Buck proceeds to a method of estimating adult intelligence that is unique, to say the least. The exact mode of approach employed in this series of steps is much too involved and complicated to describe in detail here, and the reader is referred to the *Qualitative and Quantitative Scoring Manual* [*3, 4*]. Suffice it to say that fairly acceptable correlations seemed to exist between H-T-P scores and standardized intelligence tests (range of r's was from .41 to .75), although few of the 356 subjects were normals [*3*, Tables 8 and 9].

Another complicated series of instructions is presented for qualitative analysis and interpretation, in which Buck assigns psychological values to certain designated characteristics of the drawings. For example: "If the tree is tiny, the subject is believed to feel inferior and inadequate, to be indicating a desire to withdraw" [*3*, p. 370]. For more detailed instructions and suggestions on this aspect of the method, the reader is again referred to Buck's manual.

The summary for this portion of the assessment of personality by means of the H-T-P Technique is quoted from the manual [*3*, p. 395–396]:

After the examiner has completed his analysis of the subject's productions, and after he has completed his synthesis of the analytic points, he should be in a position to draw certain specific deductions concerning the subject's total personality and the interaction of that personality with its environment. To aid in the facilitation and systematization of the recording of these deductions and in their expression in commonly used clinical terminology, the following general outline is suggested:

A. Test Situation Observations: (1) Cooperativeness; (2) stress symptoms; (3) physical disabilities; (4) mannerisms; (5) attention span; (6) empathy; (7) reaction time; (8) orientation; (9) other.

B. Intelligence: (1) H-T-P derived IQ's (The examiner will wish to comment briefly upon the consistency or disparity of these IQ's, and if they are markedly disparate to attempt to account therefor); (2) present functional level as measured by the H-T-P and basic intelligence level as suggested by an analysis of the factors of internal construction; (3) H-T-P derived IQ's vs. IQ's derived from standard intelligence tests; (4) artifacts possibly affecting H-T-P IQ scores, such as physical disability, artistic training, etc.; (5) evidences of concreteness of thinking.

C. Affect: (1) Tone (depressed, elated, etc.); (2) intensity; (3) appropriateness; (4) control; (5) consistency.

D. Verbalizations: (1) Flow (scant, free, etc.); (2) spontaneity; (3) modulation (monotonous, dual, etc.); (4) idea content (perseverative, bizarre, inferior).

E. Drive: (1) Level; (2) control; (3) consistency (fatigability, etc.).

F. Psychosexual: (1) Satisfaction levels and their relative dominance; (2) conflicts and their probable sources (for example, subject unable to adjust satisfactorily at heterosexual level because of fixation at oral level, or religious beliefs, or physical disability, etc.).

G. Inter-environmental: Under this rather broad heading the examiner will wish to comment concerning certain aspects of the subject's general behavior from the following standpoints: (1) *satisfaction sources:* (a) reality-fantasy; (b) extratensive-intratensive, does the subject tend more to respond to external (extra) or internal (intra) stimulation; (c) extracathection—intracathection, does the subject tend to seek external or internal sources of satisfaction (a paranoid subject, for example, would presumably exhibit extratensivity and intracathection); (d) range (are satisfaction sources, for example, restricted to the home, to the reality level, etc.); (2) *goal attainability* (are goals realistic or fictive) and *intensity* (how avidly are they sought); (3) *temporal dominance* (here the relative roles of the psychological past, present and future, are to be considered); (4) *adaptability* (is the subject in general flexible or is he stereotyped and rigid); (5) *accessibility* (is the subject relaxed, friendly, sociable, or is he tense, hostile, withdrawn).

H. Inter-Personal Relationships: (1) *Intra-Familial:* (a) affective tone; (b) intensity; (c) permanence; (d) flexibility; (e) identification; (f) felt role (subject's conception of his position within his family, including his sexual role); (2) *Extra-Familial:* (a) affective tone; (b) intensity; (c) permanence;

(d) flexibility; (e) parental substitute reaction; (f) felt role (the subject's conception of his position in society in general, including his sexual role.

I. Intra-Personal Balance: The subject's view of the balance of the factors making up his personality as expressed in his drawings and in his verbal comments.

J. Major Needs: (As autonomy, achievement, sexual satisfaction, etc.).

K. Major Assets: (As above average intelligence, flexibility, accessibility, etc.) *A word of caution:* In his zealous efforts to identify the factors of actual or potential weakness in a subject's personality, the examiner must be very careful lest he lose sight of the factors of strength within that personality, the positive factors which determine the potential-danger weight that may be assigned to the so-called negative or weak factors.

L. Impression: (Inadequate as the present classificatory systems are, the examiner must classify; as, psychoneurosis, mixed type, average intelligence, etc.).

It should be noted here that the H-T-P as a projective technique for psychodiagnosis is not a refined method ready for general clinical application. It is encouraging that Buck stated his basic hypotheses at the outset, but it must be noted that as far as the writer could detect, in no case (with the possible exception of measuring intelligence) did Buck clearly and experimentally defend any of these basic postulates. For instance, it has not been demonstrated "that each of the drawn wholes may be regarded as a self-portrait," and, hence, all of the subsequent inferences relating the emotional reactions of the subject to the figure or any of its parts, which hang on this assumption, would seem to stand or fall on the demonstration of the acceptability of this basic premise.

With respect to H-T-P as a device for estimating adult intelligence, a paper by Sloan and Guertin [22] presents data based upon the findings obtained by correlating the various Wechsler-Bellevue IQ's with H-T-P IQ's on 54 mentally defective adults ranging in age from 16 to 30 years. Their results reveal correlations ranging from .165 with the Wechsler Verbal Scale to .412 and .472 with Wechsler Full Scale and Wechsler Performance Scale respectively. The latter two were statistically significant, being more than four times their probable errors. It was also noted that there were wide discrepancies between H-T-P scores and Wechsler scores, the former rating the subjects consistently and significantly higher than the latter. Moreover, the range of H-T-P scores was found to be *three times* that of the Wechsler-Bellevue. Sloan and Guertin are thus led to conclude that in its present form, the H-T-P is not comparable to the Wechsler-Bellevue as a measure of intelligence in a sample of adult high-grade mentally defective males.

In summary, the H-T-P technique, as proposed, stands in need of (1) experimental verification of its basic postulates; (2) substantiation of the postulate that it may be used to measure adult intelligence with validity; (3) objective scoring standards (both of intellectual and personality factors); (4) objective norms for both normal subjects at all age levels and abnormal subjects of all types; and finally, (5) careful validating studies with reference to the several psychological values assigned to the various patterns. Hence, it must be concluded that although the H-T-P technique shows promise of eventual clinical usefulness, it is not yet ready for general application in clinical psychology.

THE WORLD TEST

In this country, most of the experimental work done with the World Test has been by Bolgar and Fischer [1]. The materials and their application in psychology are not new, having been used by Kerr [13] and Buhler [5]. Much of the use of the materials by these writers and by subsequent students has had a psychoanalytic orientation and has been employed in psychotherapeutic situations. The materials and the application are reminiscent of Doll Play techniques (Chapter 22).

The present account will be limited primarily to the work done by Bolgar and Fischer [1]. The "Little World" set, adapted for use by them, consisted of 232 pieces distributed in varying proportions over the following 15 categories: houses, trees, fences, common people, uniformed people, dogs, farm animals, wild animals, bridges, automobiles, trains, boats, planes, soldiers, and details such as lamp posts and soft drink stands. The pieces were made of wood or metal; they were simple but colorful and attractive.

In application, the subject is presented with the materials and asked to do with them whatever he likes, to use as many or as few as he wishes, and to feel entirely free to act as he pleases. Time for the experiment is unlimited.

A complete record of behavior and verbalizations is kept. Questions are answered nondirectively. The construction period is followed by a brief inquiry to supplement the subject's spontaneous explanations, observations, and comments. At the conclusion, a schematic drawing of the construction is made.

Six distinct areas of reaction are delineated as factors worthy of noting for analysis and as a basis for interpretation.
They are:

1. *Choice:* What objects are first chosen for the construction? It is pointed out that this first choice is important because it frequently sets the stage for the rest of the construction. House or bridge predominated as most frequent first objects.

2. *Quantity:* Each construction contains three quantitative or measurable items—amount, variety, and space. *Amount* refers to the absolute number of pieces used. The average observed by Bolgar and Fischer ranged from 35 to 120 pieces, or roughly 15 to 50 per cent of the available pieces. The *variety* measure is determined by the number of categories rather than the mere number of pieces. The following 10 categories were used in the majority of constructions: houses, trees, fences, common people, uniformed people, dogs, farm animals, automobiles, bridges, and details. *Space* is measured in terms of the portion of the available area that the construction actually occupies. On the average, it was found that half of the surface of the table was used.

3. *Form:* Five types of formal elements may be discerned in each construction. These include: (1) geometric shape, (2) view (perspective), (3) use of the foundation, (4) direction, and (5) symmetry.

The remaining three categories are more behavioral than related specifically to the World Test itself; they are *content, behavior,* and *verbalizations.*

From experience with several hundred subjects, both men and women, and including three different clinical groups: psychotics, feeble-minded patients, and psychoneurotics, these authors were able to reconstruct a hypothetically normal construction (designated by the scoring symbol N) and hence, were able to note deviations from this norm (designated for scoring, D). A scoring sheet was used on which all quantitative deviations were scored, ($+$) for more, and ($-$) for fewer than N. Qualitative deviations were scored D and described. Relative emphasis by the subjects was categorized under the designations: practical (P), logical (L), social (S), vital (V), and esthetic (*E*).   Some of the latter, however, may be judged unrealistic, and these were designated, *p, l, s, v,* and *e,* respectively.   In the scoring, the latter may be subtracted from the former, giving values for the excess of realistic emphases over unrealistic ones (*P', L', S', V',* and *E'*).   These scores for their experimental groups were weighted and percentile ranks determined.

Norms have been established and made available [*1*] for the theme and type of construction, choice and motivation, form, quantity, realism of representation, and relative emphasis on five selected aspects of life.   Comparison of interpretations with biographical data indicated high validity and seemed not to be influenced by cultural differences.   Further investigations with abnormal groups reported recently reveal even greater promise for the test, especially because these authors seem to have evidence that within clinical groups, the method allows discrimination of differing clinical pictures, so that we can hope that further investigation will yield new insights into the processes underlying different clinical syndromes.

The World Test seems well on its way toward proper scientific standardization and validation.   Like the TAT and similar methods, it can yield information on the content of personality processes, and like the Rorschach method, it seems to give information regarding the structure of personality.   Perhaps when much more work is done with the method, the best points of both types of method may be combined in this one approach.

THE MAKE A PICTURE STORY (MAPS) TEST

The MAPS Test, introduced by Shneidman [*18, 19*], is a test in which the subject uses cardboard cut-out figures as actors against a stage background to tell a story of his own devising.   There are 67 cut-out figures, among which a six-foot human figure is represented by a cut-out $5\frac{1}{2}$ inches high; the other figures are scaled proportionately.   With few exceptions, the figures are standing.   There are 21 back-drop pictures, to be used as a stage, which are $8\frac{1}{2}$ x 11 inches in size.   They represent highly structured situations like a bridge or a bathroom, and less structured situations like a dream cloud or a blank card.   Any of the figures may fit realistically on any of the backgrounds.   The nature of the task itself is, in a sense, a variation of psychodrama in which the stage and cast are provided and the subject is left to project onto the stage whatever personnel in whatever action he may wish.

The complete MAPS test materials include:

Background pictures

Living room	Street	Medical scene
Bathroom	Dream	Bridge
Bedroom	Blank	Forest
Closet	Camp	Doorway
Cellar	Landscape	Cave
Raft	Attic	Shanty
Cemetery	Nursery	Schoolroom
Stage		

Figures: The figures are identified by number and by a letter symbol, such as *M* for male adult, and *F* for female adult, *C* for children. They include the following numbers and groups:

19 Male adults (*M*)
11 Female adults (*F*)
12 Children (*C*)
10 Minority group figures such as Negroes, Jews, Orientals, Mexicans (*N*)
 2 Animal figures (*A*)
 2 Indeterminate sex (*I*)
 6 Legendary and fictitious characters (*L*)
 5 Silhouettes and figures with blank faces (*S*)

In the administration of the test, the subject is seated at a cleared desk or table, with the examiner behind or beside the subject. The following are the directions used by Shneidman:

What I am going to do is show you pictures like this one, one at a time. (Living room scene presented.) You will have figures like this (figures removed from envelope onto table) and your task is simply to take one or more of *any* of these figures and put them *on* the background picture as they might be in real life. We might start by sorting the figures so that you can see each one. Spread them out on the table and place them so that they appear standing up. (At this point the examiner may take three or four of the figures and lay them on the table with the feet of the figures toward the subject.)

Normal subjects may be told: This is a story telling test to see how imaginative or creative you are. *Hospitalized mental patients may be told:* This is to give us information about you to give your doctor who will be working with you, so that he can help you to get well sooner.

After all the figures are placed on the table by the subject, the examiner should state:

I would like to go over the instructions in a little more detail. As I said, all you are to do is take one or more of these figures, put them on the background as they might be in real life, and tell a story of the situation which you have created, or of what you have done there. In telling the story, tell me, if you can, who the characters are, what they are doing and thinking and feeling, and how the whole thing turns out. Go ahead.[5]

As each story is completed the examiner conducts an inquiry regarding: (1) any important aspect of the instructions omitted in the stories, such as how it turned out; (2) any part of the story not clear to the examiner; (3) the age, sex, or personality of any of the characters in a story with whom the examiner feels the subject is identifying; and (4) the title of the story.

As might be judged from the preceding account, the examiner's tasks are twofold: (1) to record verbatim the story related about a given construction, including other verbalizations; and (2) to complete a *Figure Location Sheet* [6] as a permanent record of the figures used and their placements.

Shneidman [*19*] has reported a study in which he used these materials with a group of 50 male schizophrenics and a control group of 50 normal males. The results of this study indicate that certain test "signs" could be regarded as "normal" and others as "abnormal." These "signs" were found to differentiate between the two groups to a statistically significant degree.[7] Suggestions for qualitative interpretations are given by Shneidman.

This technique, combining features of the World Test, Thematic Apperception Test, and Psychodrama, is a most interesting and promising method, but certainly, one that requires much work to be done in the areas of scoring, reliability, norms, and validity, before it should be given general clinical application.

THE MOSAIC TEST

The Mosaic Test was introduced in 1929 by Margaret Lowenfeld, of London, as a technique for the study of personality through the

---

[5] Quotations by permission of the *Journal of Consulting Psychology* and the American Psychological Association.

[6] The MAPS Test Materials and Figure Location Sheets may be obtained from the Psychological Corporation, New York.

[7] At this point it should be noted that the statistical technique used is questionable (that is, significance of differences between medians), and that the groups being differentiated were apparently the same groups used to delineate the "signs" in the first place.

spontaneous productions of subjects, both normal and emotionally and mentally disordered. Lowenfeld used a set of 465 small wooden pieces in varied colors and shapes. The subject was instructed, "Make anything you like out of the pieces."

Diamond and Schmale [7] reported on an evaluation of the clinical application of the Mosaic Test in which the test materials are described in greater detail. Lowenfeld employed six colors: black, white, red, blue, green, and yellow; and five shapes: squares, diamonds, and triangles of right angle, isosceles, and scalene form. Wertham and Golden [25] used a wide variety of shapes and all shades of colors; they did not, however, report the details of either the shapes or the colors used. Diamond and Schmale used the same colors as Lowenfeld reported; their shapes were identical except that the scalene triangles were replaced by rectangles. The following measurements of the pieces are given by these authors: the squares measure 1 inch by 1 inch; the right triangles are exactly half the squares; the isosceles triangles measure 1 inch along each edge; the rectangles are $1\frac{1}{2}$ inches by $\frac{1}{2}$ inch; the diamonds are $1\frac{1}{2}$ inches by 1 inch. All of the pieces are $\frac{3}{16}$ inch in thickness. The pieces are painted in bright, saturated, enamel colors over which a coat of flat varnish is applied to prevent photographic glare. There are 10 pieces of any one color and shape, 300 in all. A board on which construction is to be done is provided; this measures 18 by 26 inches, and is painted a dull, muddy, cream color, as a good photographic background. These materials were hand-made and are not available.[8]

Wertham and Golden [25] reported their findings from a study of over 1,000 cases, including adults, children, normals, psychotics, neurotics, and criminals. On the basis of these informal studies, the authors listed 23 characteristics that they found useful in differential diagnosis. Diamond and Schmale [7] approached the evaluation of the method in a somewhat more systematic manner. Their basic assumption was stated as follows:

The basic assumption is here made that important defects in the achievement of a recognizable gestalt in the Mosaic Test situation correlates with

---

[8] The Psychological Corporation, New York, imported a few sets of Lowenfeld's version and materials in the form of 456 plastic pieces as described above. The materials are packed in a carrying case which contains a tray, manual and supplementary notes.

*and reflects significant defects in the basic personality structure of the
subject* [7, p. 240].[9]

In order to evaluate and compare the performances of subjects
from the standpoint of personality structure, Diamond and Schmale
graded mosaic performances as follows:

Normal Mosaics: Any pattern demonstrating that the subject has
spontaneously thought up an idea for a pattern and that he has executed
that idea within the limits of the test materials, utilizing both color and
form to produce an objectively recognizable gestalt. Any pattern so constructed is assumed to be "normal."

Mildly Defective Mosaics: The behavior and mosaic patterns demonstrate
minor defects in gestalt. These would include poor but recognizable form
configuration; use of color, but in a poor or otherwise unsatisfactory
manner; multiplicity of unrelated designs; peculiarities of emotional
reaction or other behavior in relation to the construction of the pattern;
preoccupation with certain technical aspects of construction to the detri-
ment of the completed pattern; and others.

Moderately Defective Mosaics: Patterns demonstrating a major defect,
yet in which there is still some definite evidence of achievement of an
organized gestalt. These would include patterns constructed with disregard of color; rejection of color by using only black and/or white pieces;
or satisfactory color with very defective form.

Severely Defective Mosaics: Mosaics seriously defective in manner of
construction, ideation, color and form, showing none or only slight
evidence of organization of a conventional type.

Unclassified Mosaics: Those patterns which by reason of feebleness of
production, lack of cooperation, or some other factor cannot be accurately
classified or evaluated as above [7, pp. 240–241].

Table I summarizes the classifications of first mosaics of Diamond
and Schmale's group of 141 patients.

From their study, Diamond and Schmale were led to conclude:

1. Evidence is presented to support the assumption that the ability to
produce spontaneously an idea for a pattern and to execute the pattern
within the limits of the test materials, correlates with and reflects the basic
personality integration of the subject.

2. It is emphasized that the mosaic performance is an integrated whole
and must be interpreted and evaluated as an entity. A system of grading
the Mosaic performance upon the basis of achievement of a well-organized
and satisfactory gestalt is suggested.

3. When so graded, the mosaic performance tends to correlate with the
degree of personality disturbance manifested in various clinical disorders.

---

[9] Quotations are made with the permission of the *American Journal of
Orthopsychiatry.*

TABLE I

CLASSIFICATION OF FIRST MOSAIC PERFORMANCES WITH REFERENCE TO
ACHIEVEMENT OF SATISFACTORY GESTALT *

Diagnostic Group	Normal Mosaic	Mildly Defective	Moderately Defective	Severely Defective	Unclassified	Totals
Schizophrenia	6		10	18	5	39
Manic depressive			2	5		7
Psychosis unclassified	1			2		3
Organic brain syndrome (severe)			2	8		10
Psychopathic personality			2	4		6
Special organic group		6	4	7		17
Psychoneurosis, ?schizophrenia	1	1	2	3		7
Psychoneurosis	4	8	3		1	16
Juvenile behavior problem	8	2	1	2		13
Organic brain syndrome (mild)	2	4	1			7
Normals	14	1	1			16
Totals	36	22	28	49	6	141

Those conditions in which the personality is most severely disordered, such as schizophrenia, psychopathic personality, and severe organic brain syndromes, reveal the severest disturbances in the mosaic gestalt. Those conditions in which the personality structure is least disordered show much less abnormality.

4. There are indications that abnormalities in the mosaic patterns appear very early, are profound and consistent, and are little affected by superficial changes in attitude, cooperation, affectual status, and social adjustment.

5. Significant differences between the color responses of schizophrenics and those of subjects with organic and affective disorders were observed.

6. Specific diagnostic interpretation, with particular reference to schizophrenia, is possible with a reasonable degree of statistical validity.

7. The Mosaic Test is simple and rapid to administer, although its interpretation requires much experience. It is worthy of a definite place in the clinical evaluation of the neuropsychiatric patient [7, pp. 249–250. Quoted by permission.].

By way of comment, it should be noted that thus far in the history of the Mosaic Test, the sole use of the technique has been in arriving at a diagnostic label, while little has been demonstrated regarding the ability of the test to delineate the more subtle nuances of

---

* From Diamond and Schmale [7, p. 242]. Used by permission of the *American Journal of Orthopsychiatry*.

personality structure and dynamics. While diagnosis is an important and useful function of the clinical psychologist, it is only a minor step in the more difficult and important problem of the description of personality as a dynamic, functioning whole.

MIRA MYOKINETIC PSYCHODIAGNOSIS

The approach to personality study that employs essentially expressive motor behavior is not a new one, but previous studies have been more narrowly oriented toward specific mental attitudes, as in the work on lie detection. Mira [14] [10] states as his basic working hypothesis that "every mental attitude . . . is accompanied by a muscular attitude, owing to the unity of the living subject." His aim in devising his Myokinetic method was "to provide an objective measure of dominant conative trends of personality as expressed in the individual's basic attitudes of reaction."

The test procedure may be described in brief as follows:

The subject is asked to sit at a rectangular table in a comfortable chair. A wooden board 12 by 15 inches is set before him, on which is pinned a white sheet of paper. The instructions are as follows:

I am going to ask you to draw some lines in order to detect the accuracy of your movements. Hold this pencil in your right hand and draw ten lines like this one (E draws a horizontal line 5 cm. long). Before you start, I must tell you that you are to draw all of them the same length, parallel and as close together as possible, starting and ending on the same level like this (E draws two more lines below the model). You are not allowed to draw these lines as if you are writing, resting your wrist on the table. Your hand must be free and should move loosely, with its movement directed by the forearm just as I am showing you now. You can, if you want to, move your hand along the paper when drawing, provided you do not fix it and you do not attempt to make movements with your fingers like this. Of course it would be very easy for you to do it just as I have told you, but in order to increase the difficulty, you are not allowed to see what you are doing. So, I will blindfold you with this handkerchief and you will have to keep on drawing merely guided by your feelings and without any possibility of visual control. Remember, you will draw the lines from left to right, one beneath the other, and as close, equal, and parallel as possible.

Forty lines are obtained in this manner, 20 by each hand, 10 going from left to right and 10 from right to left. Similar sets are ob-

---

10 Quotations from this article are made with the permission of the Royal Society of Medicine.

tained in the vertical and sagittal planes. Other drawings are obtained of "zigzag" lines, interlocking chains, staircases, and a top of a castle with four battlements. Only the first set will be discussed here, the others being left for the reader to investigate in the original source.

Mira standardized his method on 145 subjects of known clinical diagnoses, including normals, epileptics, depressed patients, schizophrenics, elated patients, psychopaths, organic brain syndromes, and others. The data obtained by the method described above were quantified in the following seven categories:

1. Length of lines drawn.
2. Average length of lines corresponding to each hand in different planes, and all together.
3. Variability of lengths of lines drawn.
4. Sense and amount of general variation for each hand (obtained by adding all of the differences algebraically and dividing by N).
5. Absolute and relative shifting of sequence of the 10 lines (This operation is described as the most significant one. It entails determining the centers of all the lines and drawing the perpendicular from the first line and measuring the amount of shift from the perpendicular for all the succeeding lines in millimeters).
6. Corrected averages of these shiftings as compared with those that should occur had the subject been able to keep the length and separation of lines according to instructions.
7. Coefficient of coherence (obtained by dividing the average relative shift by the average absolute shift).

In interpreting these measurements, Mira hypothesizes some rather esoteric and unvalidated assumptions. He states, among other things, that for him the right hand expresses what is actually present in the person's mind (hence, conscious control), and the left hand is more related to the constitutional trends of the individual. Other notions include such assumptions as that upward movements are related to elated moods, and downward movements, to depression; that outward shiftings are correlated with extraversion, hetero-aggression, and liberality; that inward shiftings are indicative of introversion, auto-aggression, and selfishness.

According to Mira's hypotheses, the best discrimination psychodiagnostically might be expected between the elated and depressed as compared with normals. It is noted in Mira's data that the patients described as depressed and retarded showed a negative shift in the lines in the vertical plane (–10.9 Rt., and –7.0 Left), whereas elated patients showed a more positive shift (12.3 Rt., and 23.9 Left). This is a marked and probably significant difference. The normals showed no such marked deviations. Further data revealed apparently significant deviations among other patient groups, especially those designated as suicidal. In the vertical plane, these patients on the average showed a much greater downward shift in the left hand than did the depressives. These few illustrations serve to indicate the possibilities of the test in a screening type of diagnosis. Again, it must be emphasized that Mira's hypotheses are all in need of experimental study and validation. The empirical results look promising; nothing is known about the psychological rationale nor do the test results give us any insight into the dynamics and structure of personality.

THE TAUTOPHONE METHOD

Audition is a receptive sense that has been utilized in the perception of stimuli, the responses to which may be interpreted in keeping with the projective hypothesis. One approach of this type is that suggested originally by Skinner [21] in a quite different context: testing certain hypotheses related to the development of speech sounds. Skinner called his device a "verbal summator." The apparatus employed is a phonograph record that repeats patterns of vowel sounds including the sounds *ee, ay, ai, ä, oh,* and *ö.* A seventh neutral vowel, *uh,* was added as a sort of leaven. The first-mentioned vowels were used throughout as accented syllables, with the *uh* element inserted as an unaccented sound.

Shakow and Rosenzweig [20], working on the hypothesis that these materials offered projective possibilities, changed the name of the device to "tautophone," feeling this to be a more descriptive title. They also changed the mode of presentation to fit their purposes. Thus, they show the subject the apparatus, saying:

Here is a phonograph. On it is a record of a man's voice saying different things. He speaks rather unclearly so I'll play over what he says a number of times. You will have to listen carefully. As soon as you have an idea of what he is saying tell me at once.

One experimenter operates the player while the other records responses and other pertinent information, the whole experiment taking approximately 30 minutes, on the average.

Shakow and Rosenzweig worked out a somewhat subjective but systematic scoring system in which they take cognizance of such variables in the responses as complexity of structure of the response (for example, responding in syllables, words, phrases, or sentences); the similarity of the response to the stimulus sound (designated as either "close" or "remote"); non-English responses; and personal references (concerned with the kind of personal reference contained in the response, thus: first person, second person, and third person pronouns and references to nonhuman characters). When sentences are used, sentence structure is recorded—declarative, interrogative, or imperative. Each response is also classified for predominant content, as is done in Rorschach content categories.

These response scorings are then combined in various ways to produce total and pattern scores. Indices are proposed for suggestibility, contact, human reference, self-reference, subjectivity, and interrogativeness. Also observed are such factors as sequence of various types of complexity, closeness, and content.

Shakow and Rosenzweig conclude with an analogy to the Rorschach method, pointing out several obvious likenesses. Since no reliability, validity, or normative data are furnished, this method is in need of further research and experimental investigation before it can be classified as an applicable technique. In the investigations reported by Grings [9] and Trussell [24], in which the tautophone was used, no very promising or encouraging results were found.

SUMMARY

The foregoing review of several diverse projective methods includes only the few that have appeared on the psychological horizon that seem promising enough to warrant further consideration. There appears to be a tendency, referred to in the opening remarks of the chapter, for many to devise their own novel and interesting methods. Those presented above have in common the fact that *some* careful, scientific steps have been taken prior to publication. The danger is that many uncritical readers will accept them as reliable, valid techniques, when in most cases, reliability and validity have not yet been demonstrated or claimed.

There are some psychologists (fortunately, they are in the minority) who will object that standardization, the establishment of norms, and the statistical treatment of projective methods will destroy the nature of the method. This is not necessarily the case. While much depends upon the clinical acumen of the psychologist and his background of training and experience with many different types of personalities under varying conditions, it is also true that the method must supply the examiner with sufficient stable, valid information so that his interpretations are communicable and defensible. Such is the character of scientific enterprise.

In summary, eight new and promising projective methods have been reviewed briefly. Two are relatively more conceptual or ideational (story telling and the Sargent Test) in that they require the subject to respond to stories or situations with his own organized, verbal response, much in the manner of TAT response. The H-T-P combines the features of drawing and projective associations. The World Test and the MAPS Test remind one of psychodrama, TAT, and doll play. The tautophone utilizes projective associations to auditory stimuli. Mira's Myokinetic method relies completely on a theory of expressive movements.

As has been said repeatedly above, *these are only promising methods;* all of them, in one way or another, need further work in the areas of standardization, collection of norms, studies in reliability, studies in interjudge agreement on interpretation, and, above all, studies on the validity of interpretations.

REFERENCES

1. Bolgar, H., and Fischer, L. K., "Personality projection in the world test." *Amer. J. Orthopsychiat.,* 1947, 17, 117–128.

2. Buck, J. N., "The H-T-P test." *J. Clin. Psychol.,* 1948, 4, 151–158.

3. ————————, "The H-T-P technique: A qualitative and quantitative scoring manual," Part one. *J. Clin. Psychol.,* 1948, 4, 397–405.

4. ————————, "The H-T-P technique: A qualitative and quantitative scoring manual," Part two. *J. Clin. Psychol.,* 1949, 5, 37–76.

5. Buhler, C., and Kelley, G., *The World Test. A Measurement of Emotional Disturbance.* New York: The Psychological Corporation, 1941. (Test materials, manual, and record forms available.)

6. Despert, J. L., and Potter, H. W., "Technical approaches used in the study and treatment of emotional problems in children. I. The story, a form of directed fantasy." *Psychiat. Quart.,* 1936, 10, 619–638.

7. Diamond, B. L., and Schmale, H. T., "The Mosaic Test. I. An evaluation of its clinical application." *Amer. J. Orthopsychiat.*, 1944, 14, 237–250.

8. Fassett, K. K., "A preliminary investigation of the Sargent Test." *J. Clin. Psychol.*, 1948, 4, 45–55.

9. Grings, W. W., "The verbal summator technique and abnormal mental states." *J. Abnorm. Soc. Psychol.*, 1942, 37, 529–545.

10. Hall, C. S., "Diagnosing personality by the analysis of dreams." *J. Abnorm. Soc. Psychol.*, 1947, 42, 68–79.

11. Hertz, M. R., "On the standardization of the Rorschach Method." *Rors. Res. Exch.*, 1939, 3, 120–133.

12. Kelly, G. A., and Bishop, F., "A projective method of personality investigation." *Psychol. Bull.*, 1942, 39.

13. Kerr, Madeline, "The validity of the mosaic test." *Amer. J. Orthopsychiat.*, 1939, 9, 232–236.

14. Mira, E., "Myokinetic psychodiagnosis: A new technique for exploring the conative trends of personality." *Proceedings of the Royal Society of Medicine,* 1940, 33, 173–194.

15. Morris, W. W., "A Survey of Projective Techniques for use with the Adult Blind," in *Psychological Diagnosis and Counselling of the Adult Blind.* New York: The American Foundation for the Blind, Inc., (in press).

16. Murray, H. A., "Techniques for a systematic investigation of fantasy." *J. Psychol.*, 1937, 3, 115–143.

17. Sargent, H., "An experimental application of projective principles to a paper and pencil personality test." *Psychol. Monogr.,* 1944, 57, 5, vi + 57.

18. Shneidman, E. S., "The Make a Picture Story (MAPS) projective personality test: A preliminary report." *J. Consult. Psychol.*, 1947, 11, 315–325.

19. ——————————, "Schizophrenia and the MAPS test: A study of certain formal psycho-social aspects of fantasy production in schizophrenia as revealed by performance on the Make a Picture Story Test (MAPS)." *Genet. Psychol. Monogr.*, 1948, 38, 145–224.

20. Shakow, D., and Rosenzweig, S., "The use of the tautophone ('verbal summator') as an auditory apperceptive test for the study of personality." *Char. and Pers.* (Duke University Press), 1940, 8, 216–226.

21. Skinner, B. F., "The verbal summator and a method for the study of latent speech." *J. of Psychol.*, 1936, 2, 71–107.

22. Sloan, W., and Guertin, W. H., "A comparison of H-T-P and Wechsler-Bellevue I.Q.'s in mental defectives." *J. Clin. Psychol.*, 1948, 4, 424–426.

23. *Test Service Bulletin,* No. 36.   New York: The Psychological Corporation, 1948.

24. Trussell, M. A., "The diagnostic value of the verbal summator." *J. Abnorm. Soc. Psychol.,* 1939, 34, 533–538.

25. Wertham, F., and Golden, L., "A differential—diagnostic method of interpreting Mosaics and colored block design." *Am. J. Psychiat.,* 1941, 98, 124–131.

PART IV

General Intelligence Tests in Personality Appraisal

Interpretation of the Wechsler-Bellevue Intelligence Scale in Personality Appraisal

MARTIN MAYMAN, M.A.

ROY SCHAFER, PH.D. AND DAVID RAPAPORT, PH.D.

The inclusion of a chapter on intelligence testing in a volume on projective techniques represents an advance in the theory and methodology of clinical psychology. Recently, the Wechsler-Bellevue Intelligence Scale was classed among the nonprojective personality tests at a professional symposium [1]. In the intervening years, more and more clinical psychologists have recognized the advantages of this test for the analysis and assessment of personality organization.

Part I of this chapter will suggest a tentative rationale for the projective application of intelligence tests. Part II will present briefly an analysis of the specific intelligence functions tapped by the various problems in the Wechsler-Bellevue Scale, and will touch on some instructive ways of analyzing test records. Part III will illustrate how personality descriptions and differential diagnostic analyses may be derived from patterns of scores and qualities of performance on this test.

I

A brief review of the principles underlying projective techniques in general should clarify the theoretical problems involved in applying intelligence tests to the problem of personality assessment. Following this review, we shall elaborate the sense in which an intelligence test may be considered a projective technique. We shall then outline a general point of view regarding the place of intelligence and thought functioning in personality development. This discussion will lead to suggested modifications of the principles underlying projective techniques.

PRINCIPLES UNDERLYING PROJECTIVE TECHNIQUES

Projective testing achieved its first explicit definition and rationale in an article, later expanded into a monograph, by L. K. Frank [2, 3]. Frank showed that implicit in the concept of projective testing is a dynamic orientation and approach to the analysis of personality. There are several necessary principles or propositions underlying projective testing.

1. Projective testing deals with the *structure or organization of unique personalities.* Unlike traditional psychometric procedures, projective testing conceives of the personality as a configuration of interrelated processes rather than as a checklist of abilities or traits. It does not seek to determine for each individual his position within a larger normative group with regard to his scores or ratings on each discrete trait.

2. The personality so studied is viewed as a relatively stable configuration of *dynamic processes* organized around the needs, feelings, and personal experiences of an individual, and serving to maintain and defend his private world, actively molding the present internal and external pressures in the light of past experiences. Projective testing techniques are used to bring into focus the deep-lying motives, organizing principles, and defensive processes that influence the way in which an individual enters into new situations and deals with broad life problems.

3. This configuration of basic dynamic processes is constantly operative in the life of an individual, "patterning, warping, bending, distorting and otherwise converting every situation or experience into the configuration of the individual's private world . . ." [3, p. 43]. Every new act, expression, or response of an individual— his gestures, perceptions, feelings, verbalizations, motor acts—in some way bears the stamp of his personality. This third major assumption in projective testing, that *an individual patterns his*

personal productions in accordance with the dispositions of his active personality matrix, has been referred to specifically as the "projective hypothesis" [4].

EXTENDING THE PROJECTIVE PRINCIPLES TO INTELLIGENCE TESTING

The major criterion that psychological tests have had to meet in order to be considered *projective* tests has been that they be relatively unstructured problem situations that permit the subject wider latitude of responses than do the standard psychometric procedures. Unlike aptitude and intelligence tests that call for conventionalized, "correct" responses, or personality questionnaires that ask direct, pointed questions to which the subject is expected to give *yes* or *no* answers, the projective tests place the subject in a situation where he may exercise considerable freedom in developing the form and content of his response. Wittingly or unwittingly, he must select the raw material around which he will develop his final response, and he must organize this raw material into a meaningful whole. This brings into play the directing motives and organizing principles that determine his modes of coping with *all* life situations. In so doing, he provides an abundance of clues to his dynamic personality organization.

We should expect that the whole person will manifest his individual characteristics, not to the same degree, but to different degrees in different activities. For example, he would express himself with varied uniqueness in handwriting, in projective tests or problem-solving situations. With this qualification, not only the thought processes should bear the stamp of the person's organizational matrix, but perceptions, feelings and motor-acts as well [10, p. 654].

This type of analysis of the directly expressive aspects of a subject's responses, of his "style" of adjusting and behaving, concerns itself with only one aspect of personality—currently active, expressive structuring of situation and response. That such active projection occurs in *all* test responses, stereotyped or not, has long been recognized by clinical psychologists. Thus, the subject's reaction to the test situation, the qualities of verbalization, the impulsiveness or affect-charge even in simple responses on the Wechsler-Bellevue Scale, are in this respect revealing of a subject's underlying personality structure. However, inasmuch as the relatively unstructured projective test situations are so much better suited for eliciting active projection than is a test like the Wechsler-Bellevue Scale, it would hardly be justified to consider the Wechsler-Bellevue Scale a projective test on this basis alone.

To validly include a so-called non-projective test in the category of the traditional projective techniques, we must consider the relevance for personality analysis of a subject's aptitudes and skills, language and concepts, attitudes and achievements, which are as much a part of his personality as are the underlying dynamic processes and adjustment patterns shaping his productions on the relatively unstructured projective tests. A large part of a person's life involves such stereotyped, habituated functions or responses. An individual's repertoire of motor skills, his relatively fixed attitudes, interests and beliefs, and his range of abilities as measured by tests of intelligence, all are quasi-stable, quasi-autonomous processes that together make up the peripheral layer of his personality. They are, in a sense, the more or less well-established and easily available contents of the ego, the concrete techniques and tools stored up to help the individual deal economically with routine demands of reality.

These more peripheral, more stable psychological processes, tapped by a so-called non-projective test like the Wechsler-Bellevue Scale, differ from the usual projective test responses in one major respect: they are not new products of current conflicts and adjustment efforts; rather, they are habituated functions and responses that developed *earlier* in the life of the individual and are expressions of *earlier* adjustment efforts. The kinds of capacities nurtured by the individual, the kinds of functions and achievements neglected or actively avoided, the level and range of development of capacities and modes of functioning, and the current efficiency of these processes, all may be used as indicators of the individual's distinctive course of development, and as such, may be as revealing of personality dynamics as are the usual projective test findings. *The characteristic patterning that has taken place in the development of an individual's cognitive-attitudinal field is as essential an aspect of his personality as are the underlying dynamic processes and organizing principles.*

We may therefore distinguish two approaches in the projective analysis of personality: (1) the usual approach, consisting of an analysis of the current expressive manifestations of the personality matrix; and (2) the approach, through "nonprojective" tests, to the pattern of quasi-stable ego contents and functions that are the crystallized end-products of personality development. This dis-tinction implies that there is no such thing as a projective test per se, but only "projective testing." If approached with appropriate methods and a well-organized set of hypotheses about the place of a particular response-process in the personality organization, then any test datum, even the most conventionalized response, may be used to uncover significant features of the subject's personality. It has been possible to make such projective inferences from the patterns of achievements on the Wechsler-Bellevue Scale.

THOUGHT PROCESSES AND PERSONALITY ORGANIZATION

A recognition of the dynamic significance of patterns of developed functions and acquired skills is necessary in order to account for those correlations between specific patterns and personality charac-teristics that have been observed in testing practice (see Part III). From a more general point of view, such recognition is required by contemporary clinical understanding of the longitudinal and hier-archical aspects of personality development. Pertinent elements of this contemporary clinical conception will be outlined in the following paragraphs.

We may, for the sake of conceptual clarity, mark off schematically four levels of differentiation and stability of the psychic processes.

On the deepest level, we find the basic motivating forces of the personality—the drives, the deep-lying fears and anticipations that have become associated with these drives, and the expression of these drives in a diffuse, unorganized stream of ideation normally unconscious but apparent in the conscious thought processes of schizophrenics [11].

On the next higher level, we find basic modes of adjustment and control that begin very early to exercise a selective influence on the perceptions, activities, responses, and directions of the individual's psychological development. These modes of adjustment and con-trol have been referred to in the psychoanalytic literature as "char-acter structure," prominent aspects of which are the "defense mechanisms" (repression, intellectualization, denial, and the like); the defenses define the limits of freedom to exercise or develop available or potential modes of functioning and avenues of perception and expression. They also serve to keep the underlying diffuse stream of ideation out of consciousness.

On the third level are the differentiated thought functions [1] and capacities that emerge in the process of selective development. These functions help the individual effectively to organize his experiences and cope with his reality. They cannot be sharply separated from the components of the personality farthest removed from the core of the personality, that is, the acquired contents, the specific ideas or acts that are crystallized manifestations of these thought processes. The range, level, precision, and other aspects of intellectual and psychomotor acquisitions and skills are, in fact, our principal objective indices of the kind of selective differentiation of thought functions that has taken place in the development of any individual. For schematic clarity, therefore, we may distinguish as a fourth level of personality structure these highly differentiated, quasi-stable products of the less finely differentiated, underlying thought functions.

These four levels of the psychic processes must be viewed as always in some dynamic interdependence. The individual's deepest motivating forces are, quite early in life, subjected to repressive checks. The particular pattern of controls that is established in an individual shapes the subsequent lines of his development and ego crystallization. One pattern of control, for example, may be a generalized attitude of denial and avoidance of any situations that are potentially dangerous in that they might stir up unacceptable impulses or painful memories. A person following this pattern of control seems to adopt the guiding motto: Hear no evil; see no evil; speak no evil. Curiosity, free and vigorous play of the intellect, forceful exploration of new modes of self-realization, all may be markedly hampered by such controls, whereas other functions such as learning what is the "proper" way to behave may be enhanced. In such a case, we may expect the long range effects of such selective development to be reflected in unevenness in the level of attainment on various tests of intellectual and motor functioning. In another case, where the pattern of controls has been quite different (for example, vigilant alertness and restless explora

---

[1] In Part II-B we shall develop the specific denotations of this term.

tion), the resultant patterning of skills will be quite different and will be meaningfully correlated with other differences in the personality development and organization.

How may this conception of the relation between patterns of thinking and personality development be applied specifically to the problem of individual variations in intelligence? The following framework of propositions concerning intelligence is offered as the one most in accord with the point of view thus far elaborated and with the experimental literature. (1) It is necessary to abandon the idea that a person is born with a fixed "intelligence" that remains constant throughout his life. (2) Every individual is born with a potentiality for intellectual development that may be referred to as his natural endowment. This potentiality unfolds through a process of maturation within the limits set by this endowment. (3) The maturation process is fostered or restricted by the wealth or poverty of intellectual stimulation in the environment during the early formative years. (4) This maturation process is one aspect of personality development and is fostered or restricted by the timing, intensity, and variety of emotional stimulation and by the resulting course of emotional development. If the kind of emotional development is that in which every item of new knowledge carries a threat, the natural potentialities for intellectual growth may remain underdeveloped; on the other hand, the emotional development may be of a kind that accelerates the assimilation of all possible knowledge as a protection against danger. (5) Emotional disorder or brain injury may cause a slow-down, arrest, or regression in the maturation of an individual's potentialities. (6) In the course of development, natural endowment differentiates into various functions that can be tapped by intelligence tests in which these functions underlie achievement. (7) The functions that develop unhampered will automatically pick up and assimilate facts and relationships from the environment and organize them into a frame of reference that is then brought to bear in assimilating new experiences and molding creative achievements. (8) Formal education that provides the individual with systematically presented ideas plays a role in this development, helping to enlarge the individual's repertoire of facts and relationships (within the limits of his emotional receptivity and his endowment). (9) Wealth of late adolescent and adult life experience may further enlarge this repertoire. (10) Special cultural predilection and intense intellectual ambitiousness may lead the individual to seek out unusual facts or areas of information, and they may play a role in the development or acquisition of highly complex ideas and skills.

SUGGESTED MODIFICATIONS OF THE PROJECTIVE PRINCIPLES

The foregoing discussion of the relation of intelligence testing to personality appraisal suggests two modifications of the basic propositions underlying projective testing.

(1) Personality must be conceived not only as a configuration of dynamic processes, but also as a hierarchic organization that includes quasi-stable processes that have emerged in the longitudinal development of the individual.

(2) The "projective hypothesis" must be applied with the full recognition that a person reveals himself not only through creative, self-expressive behavior, but also through his quasi-stable achievements—that is, his pattern of selective development and application of thought functions. This recognition establishes the importance of a test of intelligence (and, for reasons to be advanced below, particularly the Wechsler-Bellevue Scale) in any battery of projective personality tests.

II [2]

STRUCTURE OF THE WECHSLER-BELLEVUE SCALE

The Wechsler-Bellevue Scale [12] is an adult intelligence test organized into 11 subtests, each containing relatively homogeneous, but increasingly difficult, items. The subject's achievement on each subtest receives an independent score from 0 to 17,[3] based on the subject's level of achievement with reference to the standardization group. The scores on all subtests are therefore commensurable, and it becomes possible directly to compare a subject's achievement on one subtest with his achievement on another. Thus, a score of 15 on one subtest and a score of 9 on another represents a definite

---

[2] In this section, we shall draw freely from previous publications of two of the authors, Rapaport and Schafer. We are grateful to the Year Book Publishers for permission to reproduce material from *Diagnostic Psychological Testing* [6], and to the International Universities Press for permission to reproduce material from *The Clinical Application of Psychological Tests* [8].

[3] The study [6] on which this chapter is based used the second edition of the Wechsler-Bellevue Scale.

discrepancy in the subject's level of achievement on the two types of items.

The scale includes six verbal subtests, including the *Vocabulary* subtest, and five nonverbal or performance subtests. Recognition is thereby accorded to the fundamental differences between the thought processes underlying achievement on items requiring verbal response and those requiring visual and/or motor performance. Of the verbal subtests, four (*Vocabulary, Information, Similarities* and *Comprehension*) may be designated as *essentially verbal* subtests, since they require a fund of essentially verbal memories and concepts for adequate response. In contrast to these subtests, which call verbal intellective ability directly into play, *Arithmetic* and *Repetition of Digits* (Digit Span) do not tap essentially verbal functions. While requiring vocal responses, they deal essentially with numbers and numerical relationships.

Of the performance subtests, three (*Block Designs, Object Assembly,* and *Digit Symbol*) require not only visual organization of the material, but also a close integration of the visual organizing process with motor manipulation. These *visual-motor* tests may be distinguished from the two other performance subtests (*Picture Arrangement* and *Picture Completion*), in which motor performance is not a significant factor in achievement. These two performance subtests may therefore be designated as tests of *visual organization* primarily.

In the verbal part of the test, the only timed subtest is Arithmetic. In the performance part, all of the subtests have time limits, and on all but Picture Completion, the speed of performance contributes to the score. The timed subtests vary in the rigor of their time limits, and hence, in the extent to which the subject is under pressure. Finally, it should be noted that some subtests allow part-credit for responses that are not fully acceptable, while others do not. All of these features of the Wechsler-Bellevue Scale demonstrate the variety of situations and the range of pressures with which the subject is confronted.[4]

---

[4] Space does not permit a discussion of procedures in administration and scoring. Readers interested in using the Wechsler-Bellevue Scale for clinical personality evaluation should acquaint themselves not only with the standard procedures described in the test manual [*12*], but also with the suggested additions and modifications in administration and scoring outlined in *Diagnostic Psychological Testing, Vol. I* [*6*], and, more concisely, in *Manual of Diagnostic Psychological Testing, Vol. I* [*7*].

THOUGHT FUNCTIONS TAPPED BY THE WECHSLER-BELLEVUE SCALE SUBTESTS

In Part I, frequent mention was made of the various thought functions that develop with psychological maturation and serve the organism in its effective adaptation to reality.   In each individual, some selective development or retardation of intellectual capacities occurs.   With the onset of maladjustment or pathology, we may observe a further selective encroachment upon thought functioning; certain capacities or thought functions may be severely disrupted, others less so.   The pattern of functions impaired and functions left relatively undisturbed in any subject varies significantly with the maladjustment syndrome, and may be reflected in the unevenness of achievement on the different subtests (see the discussion of methods of analysis, below).   To draw from such patterns of scores meaningful inferences regarding the pattern of maladjustment requires an understanding of the specific thought functions underlying achievement on each subtest.   Personality-oriented research in this area is sorely needed to clarify the workings and ramifications of these thought functions.   A tentative rationale or working hypothesis for each of the subtests will be presented in this section.

In working with the Wechsler-Bellevue Scale, it has proved helpful to postulate several basic thought functions: *memory* and *concept formation,* which come into play in the accumulation and organization of memories and experiences; *attention, concentration,* and *anticipation,* which operate in the selective orientation of the individual in every reality situation; and *visual organization* and *visual-motor coordination,* which deal with perceptual processes and their integral role in directing motor processes and manipulations.   Of the available intelligence tests, the Wechsler-Bellevue Scale, with its 11 distinct subtests, seems best suited for the appraisal of the efficiency of these thought functions in any subject.

Each subtest of the Scale is considered to reflect the level of development and efficiency of functioning of one or, at most, two functions.   It is understood, however, that not one or two, but *many* functions play a part in achievement on any subtest.   Thus, although Similarities may be considered a test of verbal concept formation (as we shall see below), there can be no doubt that the subject must also *attend* to the questions asked; he must make a correct *anticipation* about what kind of response is required so that he does not give opposites or descriptions of the objects mentioned; he also implicitly performs a *memory function* in calling to mind essential characteristics of the named objects; yet, despite the subsidiary functions of attending, anticipating, and remembering, verbal concept formation remains the crucial function. It is in this sense only that each subtest is considered a test of one or two particular thought functions.

The *Vocabulary* subtest reflects the range of ideas, memories, and relationships that an individual has unwittingly picked up and organized into verbal meanings. The *memory* and *concept formation* aspects of thought functioning are focal in the acquisition and organization of the experiential contexts that give words their meanings. The wealth and precision of a person's vocabulary depend partly upon his natural endowment and partly upon the wealth and stimulation of his early educational environment (granting, of course, the individual's emotional receptivity, or inclination to accumulate and organize his experiences in this way). There is reason to believe that if a meager natural endowment or a poor initial educational environment have limited the development of vocabulary early in life, then neither subsequent good schooling nor a great variety of later life experiences will effect any radical elevation of the level of vocabulary development [6]. Emotional development enforcing "cultural" ambitions, and ego defense by intellectualization, usually lead to the active use of functions underlying vocabulary and tend to enlarge the scope of vocabulary. If emotional development sets restrictions on those aspects of thought functioning that underlie the development of vocabulary, it will interfere with the acquisition of a wide range of words.

The *Information* subtest may be considered a test of memory development and functioning. The concept of memory used here is not that of the rote learning and naive conditioned response theories; it rather considers that the experience of words, objects, facts, and relationships becomes *integrated,* in the course of unhampered development and functioning, into the individual's unique frame of reference, by virtue of their appeal to his needs, strivings, interests, or affects. This concept of memory further implies that experiences are delivered into consciousness when a new situation again appeals to the same needs, strivings, interests, or affects with which the experience is linked in the subject's frame of reference. Like Vocabulary, though to a lesser degree, the wealth of information eventually acquired depends on the natural endowment and the early educational (cultural) stimulation; but information can be more easily enriched by schooling and experience. For this reason, the Information subtest is also a test of *intellectual ambitiousness*.

The vicissitudes of the functions underlying achievement on the Information subtest are correlated with the individual's basic modes of adjustment and control. As with Vocabulary, so with Information: the acquisition of knowledge is hindered in a person who uses as a primary method of adjustment the defense of pushing out of consciousness (repressing) facts that are even remotely connected with conflict-laden ideas and feelings; and, in contrast, that person who finds comfort and safety in escaping to, and arming himself with, intellectual knowledge will develop a rich fund of information. In Part III we shall see clinical groups that are characterized by one or the other of these preferred modes of adjustment.

The recall of previously acquired information is not, as a rule, facilitated by voluntary effort. Subjects who try hard to recall a piece of information they "know so well," will soon give up: "I can't think of it now." There is no answer on the Information subtest that can be "thought out." Rather, automatic and effortless recall makes for successful achievement. Excessive reliance on repression may interfere with recall during the testing, just as it may limit the extent to which information is acquired.

The *Similarities* subtest requires for successful achievement the function of *verbal concept formation*. If we look at an idea or object from the point of view of its being similar to, dissimilar to, or belonging with other ideas or objects, we are studying concept formation. Inquiry into the similarity or commonness of two things is also a search for the conceptual abstraction or generalization under which the two objects or ideas can be subsumed. We shall consider that a concept has a *realm*, which consists of all the things that possess the qualities denoted and connoted by the concept, and a *content*, which is the statement of the commonness of the objects in the realm. Thus, in Similarities, two given objects or ideas constitute the realm of a conceptual category whose content must be discovered. The hierarchical organization of ideas in terms of realm and content is what is referred to here as concept formation.

Experience shows that there are, roughly, three different levels on which subjects seek this content: the concrete, the functional, and the abstract. On the concrete level of concept formation, either a specific common feature of the things in question is considered to be the content linking them (an orange and a banana are similar because "they have peels"), or the content linking them is a concrete situation in which they are frequently encountered together (a fly and a tree are similar because "they are found outdoors"). On the functional level, it is the function the two things perform, or what one does with them, that is selected as the content that may serve as the basis for a conceptual categorization (an orange and a banana are similar because "you eat them both"). On the abstract conceptual level, it is a general term connoting or summing up *all* the essential common characteristics of the two objects that is considered to be the content linking the two (an orange and a banana "are both fruits"). The conceptual content arrived at on the first two levels, in contrast to that on the abstract conceptual level, is too limited and does not imply all the essential content common to both things.

The process of actively deriving a concept from given material may be interfered with in many forms of maladjustment. It is possible to derive valuable diagnostic clues from a study of the flexibility, appropriateness, and level of a subject's active conceptual thinking. Vocabulary refers to denotations of facts, and Information to memory of specific facts—these two frequently shading into each other imperceptibly; but Similarities refers to relationships of facts, and through this subtest, the examiner may glimpse how the subject sees his world and relates things in it to each other.

The *Comprehension* subtest tests *judgment*. The concept *judgment* implies the effortless and automatic sizing up of a situation and the mobilization of such information as will lead to an appropriate and relevant response. The very wording of several Comprehension questions, *What should you do. . . . ?* implies the

judgmental character of the problems.[5]   A wealth of factual information is not in itself helpful here, and may rather contribute to
hesitancy and doubt.   The concept of judgment implies—beyond
intellectual, logical, and informational factors—an emotional-atti-
tudinal orientation that automatically picks out what is appropriate and what is relevant in the situation.   Thus, judgment is
a borderline concept between the areas frequently referred to as
intellectual and emotional.   A stable balance of emotions is prerequisite for the selection of the appropriate information making
for good judgment; hence, maladjustment often lowers the Comprehension score.   It must be noted, however, that many of the
particular items in the Comprehension subtest call for highly conventionalized responses; to a large extent, then, the subtest deals
with the grasp of conventional judgments rather than with independent, creative judgment.

Digit Span achievement is considered to rest primarily on the
function of *attention*.   Attention is here defined as a relatively
effortless, passive, and nonselective registering of stimulation in
consciousness.   Attention is at work in everyday life when we are
able to follow the flow of a lecture or a book without a sense of
special effort.   Attention disturbance is evident when, while listening to a lecture or reading a book, we discover that we are repeatedly
losing the train of thought.   Experience shows, and inquiry with
subjects confirms, that a subject does well only if he can take in
the series of digits with a sense of effortlessness.   Most subjects
who must make great effort to listen to the digits, to enforce their
retention, soon begin to fail; in this subtest, voluntary effort can
not replace the optimal condition of automatic, effortless attention.
Attention is disturbed by the intrusion into consciousness of over-
charged ideas, anxieties, and affects, and these have been found to
be special disrupting factors in Digit Span achievement.

The *Arithmetic* subtest is here considered a test of *concentration*
primarily.   Concentration, which is closely related to attention, is
defined here as an active focusing of attention to facilitate the
meaningful intake of complex material or the meaningful manipulation of complex thought patterns.   Concentration becomes neces-

---

[5] The "why" questions evaluate a subject's comprehension or understanding
of the essentials of a situation without calling for decision as to appropriate
action, but may still be viewed as judgment items in terms of our definition.

sary when the smooth, automatic functioning of attention is disrupted or inadequate to the occasion. Arithmetic is a test of concentration primarily in that it requires a directed focusing of attention, an extracting of the essentials of the problem, and a working through of the relations involved. To do all of this, the subject must direct himself to the abstract continuum of numbers and the pattern of the four basic arithmetical calculations. These ideational structures have usually been acquired and become ingrained in the course of ordinary life experiences. To turn back upon these internalized patterns in order to structure and solve a particular problem is the task of concentration. The concentration factor is further emphasized by the time limits on each item. The time-pressure forces the subject to apply himself actively to the problem, avoiding and suppressing as many distractions as possible. Arithmetic is thus unlike Vocabulary and Information, which depend primarily on memory organization and efficiency; it is unlike Similarities, where abstractions are to be derived from specified objects or ideas; and it is unlike Comprehension, where logical selection by concentration leads rather to doubt than to quick, unequivocal judgments.

The *Picture Arrangement* subtest is a test of *anticipation* and *visual organization*. In it, several series of sketches must be arranged into meaningful sequences. Visual organization is required here for the accurate grasp of the essentials of each sketch. Organizing the separate sketches into a meaningful whole—a story—requires *anticipation*. Poor performance on this subtest may usually be traced to an encroachment on smooth anticipatory thinking. In our everyday activities, we always anticipate events and their consequences, and we plan our course of action accordingly. Anticipation is also present in any listening and understanding; we do not understand if we do not "get set for," or anticipate, what is to come next. Thus, if someone starts a sentence with "Though," we anticipate a sentence of coordinate clauses the two parts of which will be in an antithetical relation to each other. The meaningful continuity of everyday experiences is largely dependent on anticipations that make it possible to understand an event in the context of its antecedents and consequences. Similarly, in Picture Arrangement the subject draws from each sketch an anticipation of the meaning of the whole series as well as of its possible antecedents

and consequences.   Guided by these anticipations, he proceeds to
arrange the sketches sequentially.

Picture Completion, like Picture Arrangement, involves *visual
organization,* but the most important function it taps seems to be
concentration.   This subtest requires deliberate focusing of attention, an active searching of the picture, and the checking of this
sketch against internalized patterns.   In Arithmetic, concentration
involved essentially the turning back on internalized arithmetical
patterns; in Picture Completion, the subject must consider, in addition to internalized patterns, the external patterns that are set before him.   He must discover how the incomplete patterns put
before him deviate from the internalized patterns mobilized by the
stimulus material.   Systematic, voluntary, selective effort is thus the
prerequisite of successful performance.   As with Arithmetic, the
strict time limit accentuates the concentration character of the
test; the subject must actively apply himself if he is to succeed.

The *Object Assembly* subtest, like Block Designs and Digit
Symbol, is basically a test of *visual-motor coordination.*   In these
three subtests, motor activity guided by visual organization is
essential for successful performance.   Such coordination has not
been sufficiently well explored by psychologists, probably because
it is concealed in everyday life by two factors: (1) the space and
goals of movement are usually familiar to us; it appears as though
we first organize visually the space of our motor actions, and then
decide upon their course; thus, motor action seems only a servant
executing a decision; (2) many everyday actions are performed by
habituated and stereotyped motor actions, giving the impression
that no visual guiding function is at work.   Neither of these kinds
of action is as simple as it appears.   Our motor actions at all times
necessitate constant visual reorganizations of the space in which
they occur; this, in turn, necessitates progressive reorganization of
the motor action.   The essence of visual-motor *coordination* lies
in the fact that we do not experience in a jerky fashion these mutually dependent reorganizations and reorientations; on the contrary, this coordination makes for smoothness of performance.
Accordingly, we do not become aware of its shifts until difficulties
of a motor or visual nature are encountered.

Two specific features of the Object Assembly subtest that distinguish it psychologically from Block Designs and Digit Symbol, are

that little or no information is given to the subject as to what the final product will be, and that each jigsaw piece has a fixed relationship to the other pieces and to the completed pattern. Accordingly, visual organization in this subtest consists of trying to grasp the whole pattern by means of anticipations from its more or less meaningful parts. On the *mannikin* item, the anticipation of the final pattern is usually immediate unless the subject is profoundly disturbed; on the more difficult items, the anticipation may or may not be immediate, depending on the subject's capacities for anticipation and visual organization. If the proper anticipation has been formed, motor action appears to be a mere duplication of a discovered pattern. If visual organization is absent or vague, trial-and-error motor action begins; pieces are brought into random or near random relationships to each other until two pieces are recognized as belonging together—a process that leads to progressive clarification of the visual pattern. In such procedures, the progressive reorganization and reorientation implied in visual-motor coordination can be easily recognized and observed. Good performance on this test, therefore, requires both adequate anticipations and smooth visual-motor coordination.

Block Designs is also a test of visual-motor coordination, but it differs from Object Assembly in that the subject, knowing beforehand what the final pattern is going to be and trying to construct it out of identical, interchangeable blocks, does not make anticipations from the meanings of the component parts. Instead, this subtest calls for thought processes analogous to those involved in concept formation. Before the visual pattern can direct the process of reconstruction, the complex design must be broken down by the subject into units equivalent to faces of the blocks. This visual analysis and synthesis involves a steady interaction between the presented pattern and the available blocks. On the very simple items, the visual analysis is usually immediate and precedes any motor action. On the more difficult items, visual organization achieves a partial differentiation of the design; the role of motor action is to juxtapose the block faces, guided by the visual differentiation already obtained. This constructed part, in turn, initiates further differentiation of the original design. In Block Designs as well as in Object Assembly, the speed of motor action must be geared to the acuity and speed of visual analysis and organization for most efficient performance.   Too rapid or too slow motor performance gives no chance for visual organization to direct the placing of the parts or to recognize correct trial-and-error placements.

The *Digit Symbol* subtest also requires smooth visual-motor coordination for successful performance.   Whereas in Object Assembly, the performance takes the form of anticipation and placement, and in Block Designs, the form of analytic-synthetic reproduction, in Digit Symbol it takes the form of imitative activity.   This subtest differs from the other two in three other respects: (1) speed is especially essential for high achievement; this makes Digit Symbol a test of concentration as well as of visual-motor coordination; (2) the motor manipulations required are more complex: they consist of eye and head movements involved in finding the symbol to be copied, locating the space into which they are to be placed, writing the symbol, shifting the eyes to the following number and then to the key above, repeating the entire complex sequence of acts with as few hesitations and interruptions as possible; (3) there is a learning factor involved: the subject becomes familiar with the nine symbols; the association of a digit with its more or less meaningless symbol may be learned, although few subjects rely on memory alone in filling in the symbols; and learning of the spatial position of the numbers and symbols on the key-line—which occurs most frequently—facilitates their speedy location.   The amount of learning appears to depend largely upon the adequacy of concentration.

Thus, the three subtests of visual-motor coordination require in common a fine tuning-together of visual organization and motor action; however, the type of situation in which this occurs is different in each subtest, and the secondary functions tapped by each are correspondingly different.

Only with the aid of a rationale such as that which has been tentatively advanced here, will the clinical psychologist be able to draw inferences from his test data as to the warping or encroachment of maladjustment on ego functioning.   However, before one can apply such a rationale to specific test findings, he must have analyzed the test record and extracted the significant aspects of the subject's performance.   In what follows, some helpful analytic methods will be described.

METHODS OF ANALYSIS

Characteristics of personality and maladjustment are indicated in the Wechsler-Bellevue Scale results in three main ways: (1) by the relative impairment or superiority of a function; (2) by its temporary inefficiencies; (3) by the subject's manner of coping with the problems—the way he verbalizes his responses, reacts to difficulty, and so on.

Impairment or Superiority of Functions. The impairment or superiority of the different thought functions tapped by this intelligence test is established by *scatter analysis.* Scatter analysis, as used here, is analysis of the quantitative differences between the weighted subtest scores. Since all raw subtest scores in the Wechsler-Bellevue Scale are converted into commensurable Z-scores, it is possible to compare an individual's level and efficiency on one subtest with his performance on any other subtest. It is assumed, and has been borne out by experience, that a well-adjusted person will have developed relatively evenly in the various areas of functioning explored by this test. It follows from this that any significant deviation of one subtest score from the general level of subtest scores indicates some distinguishing feature of the subject's personality organization or maladjustment.

Several different types of comparison are possible: a comparison of the verbal score-level with the performance score-level; a comparison of the achievement on any verbal subtest with the general level of the remaining verbal subtests, and the achievement on any performance subtest with the general level of the remaining performance subtests; a comparison of the achievement on subtests vulnerable to maladjustment with the relatively sturdy Vocabulary score; and those intercomparisons of specific subtest scores that clinical experience has indicated to be a fruitful source of diagnostic indications.

Scatter analysis is dependent upon establishing baselines from which to estimate impairments or superiorities. Our experience shows that three main baselines may be profitably used.

1. Vocabulary Scatter. Of all intelligence test scores, the Vocabulary score is usually the last to reflect impairment by maladjustment. In almost all clinical cases, it is the Vocabulary score from which the premorbid level of intelligence development (before pathology impaired intelligence-functioning) can best be inferred. The remaining scores show greater or lesser vulnerability to maladjustment, and, therefore, comparison of these scores to the Vocabulary score as a baseline will indicate the extent of impairment. A slight amount of variability of the subtest scores below the Vocabulary score is frequent even in the normal range, but in this range, the Comprehension, Information, and Similarities scores generally stay close to the Vocabulary level.

2. *Mean Scatter.* It is also necessary to see how the more vulnerable scores compare with one another. Mean scatter measures the difference between the scores on any subtest and the general level of the scores on the remaining subtests. Thus, if all the scores excepting Vocabulary are pushed down markedly, mean scatter may demonstrate that the Comprehension score, for example, is especially impaired, as it is frequently in chronic schizophrenics. Analysis of mean scatter should be pursued separately for the six verbal subtests and the five performance subtests.

3. *Specific Subtest Comparisons.* Also crucial to scatter analysis are the specific comparisons of pairs of subtest scores other than the Vocabulary score. These comparisons aim at answering such questions as: "How does the subject's judgment compare with his fund of information?" "How does his attention efficiency compare with his capacity for concentration?"

Thus, scatter analysis compares the score on one subtest with the general level of other scores, in order to find special impairments; with the Vocabulary scores, in order to estimate extent of impairment; and to single other scores, for the pattern of selective impairment, which may afford revealing data for the understanding of the subject's personality or maladjustment.

Temporary Inefficiency. Inasmuch as each of the Scale subtests comprises homogeneous items of varied degrees of difficulty, item analysis of the sequence of passes and failures within each subtest clarifies the smoothness and efficiency of the function or functions underlying achievement on that subtest. It is important to know whether the final subtest score derives from failures on some relatively easy items and successes on some difficult ones (in which case we usually speak of temporary inefficiency), or whether the failures first set in on difficult items and mark the point where the subject's development is no longer adequate to cope with the new items. The difficulty of items can be established statistically by the incidence of failure on each in the general population.

Inefficiencies may be due either to anxiety of noteworthy intensity or to a psychotic process. When anxiety is their source, the inefficiencies are characterized by uncertainty, wrong choices between correct and incorrect alternatives, and quick or delayed correction of wrong answers. Furthermore, these failures on the relatively easy items will tend to be few and to occur on those items that, although ordinarily easy, are frequently missed by other cases showing inefficiency. For example, in the Information subtest, the capital of Italy may be "Naples," the average height of American women may be "5 feet 2 inches," there may be "4 pints" in a quart, "48 weeks" in a year, and so on. Intense anxiety can prevent knowledge or ideas, once acquired, from emerging into consciousness, and may lead to wrong or inaccurate responses. Anxiety alone, however, can never account for answers so incorrect as to be absurd. Such extremely deviant answers, especially when accompanied by a degree of bland confidence, usually indicate a psychotic process. Furthermore, if the subject knows what ethnology and the Apocrypha are, and yet does not know where Brazil is, this, too, suggests psychosis; the discrepancy between retained and lost information in such cases is too great to be accounted for merely on the basis of anxiety determined, temporary inefficiency.

Qualitative Analysis. Thus far, we have seen that an advance beyond gross statements about IQ is accomplished by scatter analysis; that scatter analysis is amplified by item analysis. We can now consider how amplification of the test findings in general is accomplished by qualitative analysis, particularly of the subject's verbalization of his responses. In his verbalizations, we can follow the subject's intelligence *at work* and thus, we can often see clearly in both correct and incorrect responses expressions of the subject's maladjustment or personality make-up. This analysis is concerned with *how* the subject failed or passed the test items. Were doubt and indecision characteristic? Were more or less bizarre ideas expressed? Was impulsiveness prevalent?

It must be remembered that, although the correct responses to the test items are fixed by common agreement, the routes to these, as well as to the incorrect responses, are not fixed. Thus, the subject's manner of reasoning out Comprehension, Similarities, or Arithmetic items, his speed and confidence in delivering his responses, his anxiety or blandness about incorrect responses, are all revealing of him. For example, when an otherwise intelligent subject blandly states that the capital of Italy is Constantinople, or that a dog and a lion are alike because both have cells, psychosis is strongly indicated. When a subject lists five alternative courses of action or explanations on some of the Comprehension items, mentions three similarities on some of the Similarities items, and gives extensive and quibbling definitions on the Vocabulary items, an obsessive character make-up or obsessive pathology must seriously be considered. If wild guessing occurs on every "difficult" item, no matter how obviously beyond the subject's level of ability it may be, we may anticipate other manifestations of bland impulsive behavior, probably asocial or antisocial in character.

Furthermore, on a number of the Scale items, a greater range of possible responses is permitted, and here, verbalization may become especially revealing. This is true, for example, of the difficult Picture Arrangement items, where distorted anticipations may be verbalized in explaining the sequence of pictures offered. In one of these sequences, a paranoid subject saw a woman rejecting a man's attentions by signaling to another man, although objectively, it is the same man in both pictures and there are no indications of signaling.

In the course of experience with any test, an examiner becomes familiar with the usual forms of verbal expression used by subjects, with the usual errors or failures, and with the usual ways of passing or failing items. It is against this subjectively-retained experience as a baseline that he may detect deviant verbalizations or qualities of performance, the form or content of which stems from a specific maladjustment type or personality organization. To date, however, qualitative analysis of verbalization and test behavior is the least explored and systematized of all the analytic methods applied to intelligence tests, or, for that matter, to tests in general.

III

This last section is a review of those scatter patterns and qualitative features that have been found to be characteristic of various types of maladjustment syndromes.[6] The validity of the brief personality and diagnostic sketches that may be derived from Wechsler-Bellevue data has been discussed elsewhere [6]. Here, we shall confine ourselves to descriptive summaries of test findings without reference to supporting data. The major purpose of these summaries will be to show how a variety of personality maladjustment types may reveal themselves in the Wechsler-Bellevue protocol. We shall forego the opportunity of using the summaries to demonstrate the validity of the rationales tentatively advanced in Part II. Such demonstration has been attempted in *Diagnostic Psychological Testing* [6].

Although the findings are reported here in terms of specific maladjustment syndromes, the evidence for any particular diagnosis consists of descriptive interpretations of test findings. Such interpretations, strictly defined, do not commit themselves to any diagnostic scheme; they refer always to behavior or thinking that can be immediately and concretely apprehended. An interpretation may, for example, state that the thinking of a subject characteristically tends to be concerned with fine detail, that it lacks a wealth of reference, or that it suffers from an insufficient grasp of the essentials of a situation. These characteristics may point toward a particular diagnosis, but they are not the exclusive property of any one diagnostic category. Therefore, the indications summarized below under the various diagnostic labels should be understood to refer to characteristics of behavior and maladjustment first, and to diagnoses only secondarily.

The patterns to be described will, no doubt, require modification as further research and further diagnostic advances are made. They are useful as leads, not as final answers, and they are most useful when surveyed in the context of the results from a battery of tests.

Each maladjustment syndrome will be characterized briefly before the test findings are summarized. These descriptions are not meant to be definitive. Rather, they emphasize those aspects of the syndrome that are most influential in determining the patterns and qualities of test responses.

---

[6] The remainder of this chapter is drawn from *The Clinical Application of Psychological Tests* [8]. Omitted from this discussion are the following maladjustment syndromes: hysteria, mixed neurosis, neurasthenia, neurotic and psychotic depression, unclassified schizophrenia, and incipient schizophrenia.

OBSESSIVE-COMPULSIVE NEUROSIS

Those persons who rigidly and pervasively resort to the defenses of isolation, reaction-formation, rationalization, and intellectualization in their efforts to cope with their impulses and the demands of the world about them are in the category of obsessive-compulsive neurosis. The bulk of their thought processes, whether elicited by everyday situations or by test items, almost invariably reflect excessive reliance on this defensive structure.

It is difficult, on the basis of test results, to distinguish obsessive-compulsive *character* neurotics without classical symptoms from obsessive-compulsive neurotics with symptoms (obsessions, compulsive rituals). It is also difficult to distinguish cases whose symptoms tend more toward the obsessional side from those whose symptoms tend more toward the compulsive side. Finally, it is often difficult to draw the line between normal and pathological obsessive-compulsive characteristics. The best, though not infallible, rule to apply is the following: as the incidence or extremeness of the indicators to be described increases, the chances that a character or symptom neurosis is present also increase. There is, however, little point in trying to predict the presence of clear-cut symptoms; delineation of personality make-up is the crucial job.

The chief characteristics to be sought out are pedantic intellectualizing (perfectionism and ostentatious, circumlocutory, circumstantial display of erudition), rationalizing and doubting (rumination, excessive qualification, overcautiousness), and rigidity (inability to be casual when casualness is appropriate, inability to permit full-bodied emotional experiences to develop, inability to be flexible and spontaneous in responding).

The Wechsler-Bellevue Scale scattergram usually shows the excessive reliance on intellectualization in conspicuously high Information and Vocabulary scores, frequently with a relatively (but rarely absolutely) low Comprehension score and a relatively (but rarely absolutely) low performance level. It is unusual to find an IQ in an obsessive case that falls below 100: the Total IQ is generally 110 or more; the Verbal IQ is frequently in the superior or very superior range. The low Comprehension score takes on special diagnostic significance if it is the outcome of a doubt-laden casting about among alternative reasons or courses of action and of pedantic rejection of popular beliefs; the high Information and Vocabulary scores take on special diagnostic significance if they are achieved through, or in spite of, overdetailed, often ostentatious factual reference, qualification, or specification; the relatively low performance level takes on special diagnostic significance if it is clear from the observation of the performance that tension and resulting inefficiency, rather than depressive retardation, are pulling down the scores on the visual-motor subtests. When the Digit Span score remains on the general verbal level, despite indications elsewhere of acute anxiety, obsessiveness is suggested, especially if the score is achieved by active organization of the numbers into groups. Occasionally, the Similarities score is slightly lowered by doubting and pedantry interfering with the selection of the most appropriate and adequate response.

There are a fair number of cases whose Comprehension score remains on the Information and Vocabulary level; however, the qualitatively obsessive features usually persist. In these cases, impairment of judgment is still indicated but is not as extreme as when the score drops. There are also a fair number of cases whose performance level does not drop, although the rest of the record is clearly obsessive-compulsive; in these cases, it is usually safe to assume some degree of chronicity and "adjustment" to the neurosis, so that the patient is not in a state of incapacitating tension at the time of testing. The obsessive-compulsive character neurotics frequently have this pattern.

The most reliable indicator of obsessive-compulsive features in the Scale is the quality of verbalization: if verbalization is overdetailed and doubt-laden, obsessive-compulsive features are likely to be conspicuous in the character make-up, if not in the pathology itself. We have seen obsessive-compulsive neurotics whose performance level exceeded their verbal level and whose Comprehension score exceeded their Information score, but whose obsessive-compulsive characteristics were nevertheless identifiable in the quality and expressive aspects of their verbalizations. This pattern is observed most often in obsessive-compulsive women.

Examples of qualitative features. "There is a good deal of dispute as to who invented the airplane but the Wright Brothers get credit for it." "If I were lost in the forest in the daytime I might follow the sun . . . or go by the moss on the north side of the trees

. . . or maybe follow a stream.   Do I have a compass?   If I had one, I'd . . . (etc.) *(Which would you do?)* It depends on the terrain: if . . . (etc.)." "A cedar is a coniferous tree, yields fragrant wood, generally used to make chests." "A diamond is a carboniferous stone, formed deep in the earth under high pressure, mined and sold as a gem or for industrial purposes; also a baseball diamond." "A dog and a lion are alike in that they are four-legged mammals, possessed of fur, tails . . . meat-eating . . . can be tamed."

ANXIETY STATE

The chief symptom of an anxiety state is acute, free-floating anxiety, manifested in restlessness, apprehensiveness, tremulousness, and other bodily expressions of anxiety, and impaired attention and concentration.   Low mood and striking inhibition are often present.

Some of these cases yield records that do not adequately distinguish them from normal subjects.   In general, however, the patterns to be described occur with strikingly high regularity.   Because acute anxiety is outstanding in most neuroses and many psychoses, many other types of clinical cases frequently manifest patterns resembling those described below.

The most conspicuous features in the Wechsler-Bellevue Scale are, usually, a markedly lowered Digit Span score (impaired attention), a less markedly but still noticeably lowered Arithmetic score (impaired concentration), and a lowered performance level (tension and resulting inefficiency).   Qualitative analysis generally reveals easily mobilized tension, many temporary inefficiencies, usually quickly followed by corrections, and anxiety disrupting both intellectual and fine motor manipulations.   The motor awkwardness and fumbling, as well as the impaired ability to plan and later to check the Block Designs and Object Assemblies for accuracy, lower the performance level but make it clear that tension, and not depressive retardation, is responsible for this lowering.   Word-finding difficulty, impulsive blurting out of unfinished or unchecked responses, and fumbling for proper formulations are also typical.

Anxiety-ridden verbalizations: "There are four pints in a quart . . . No!   Two!   Wait a minute . . . That's right!   Four!"   "If I was the first to see a fire in a movie I'd . . . er . . . I'd . . . get out as fast as I could . . . that is, I'd tell the . . . what do you call them? . . . oh! . . . ushers . . . first and then I'd . . . er . . . I'd get out."

Acute anxiety and depressed mood are frequently the presenting symptoms in cases where decompensation of compulsive defenses is under way. In these instances, the scatter usually reflects both the anxiety state and the compulsive character make-up. Qualitatively, obsessive-compulsive features are outstanding: the record is dominated by pervasive but ineffective attempts at precision, stilted verbalizations, and cumbersome pedantry. For example: "A microscope may be defined as a visual instrument designed to optically enlarge and thereby make visible to the naked eye minutiae." Although the symptomatic diagnosis may be anxiety state or anxiety and depression, the characterological diagnosis will be obsessive-compulsive character make-up.

NARCISSISTIC CHARACTER DISORDER

Cases characterized by striking egocentricity, extremely low anxiety-tolerance, a rigid tendency to avoid anxiety-arousing situations, solicitation of the affection and assistance of others with minimal return of affection and assistance, and a weak capacity for empathy, are called narcissistic character disorders. Emotional lability is a frequent feature and tends to be exploited in shallow histrionics; overdemonstrativeness is frequently superimposed on the basic coldness and distance. Aggressively demanding behavior may also be prominent.

The chief personality features to be watched for are the rigid tendency to forestall, minimize, negate, or otherwise avoid anxiety-arousing, emotional situations; superficial outgoingness and spontaneity, but basic anxiety and solicitousness, relating to the examiner; fleeting histrionic reactions, changing from problem to problem, test to test, and day to day. The avoidant tendency will be particularly apparent in attempts to evade responsible, introspective thinking. Some of these patients will have developed a good deal of charm and wit, and will try to show the examiner a good time; the aim of all this, however, is avoidance and denial of serious problems rather than the expression of genuine friendliness or good spirits.

It is most usual to find the performance level equal or superior to the verbal level. This discrepancy takes on special diagnostic significance if Picture Arrangement is relatively high and if Arithmetic is relatively low. The discrepancy between the verbal and performance levels usually refers to the characteristic emphasis on action or "doing things," and the avoidance of serious, rational application to problems. The high Picture Arrangement indicates the typical facile social anticipations. The low Arithmetic indicates the inability to maintain goal-directed activity in the face of acute anxiety, and the attempts to avoid the anxiety that is so readily stimulated in most patients by these problems. A relatively low Arithmetic score is most frequent in narcissistic women. The typical woman in this group protests vigorously that she has always been unable to do such problems, that she has been out of school too long, and so forth. Further, by histrionics, charm, or sudden rigid negativism, she will attempt to eliminate the necessity for doing the problems. If the examiner inquires how wrong answers have been arrived at, these patients are prone, after brief floundering around, to say that they guessed. The examiner is usually able to see that the answer is not a guess—for example, "48 men" on Problem 10—and is able to infer that the patient would rather fake inadequacy than apply herself responsibly to a more or less introspective and anxiety-arousing problem. Usually, this evasiveness is most clearly seen in the Arithmetic subtest, but it is often present throughout the Scale. Another frequent qualitative indicator is the attempt to flaunt a social sophistication, which may vary from the smart-alecky or roguish quality to utter disdain, ennui, and even horror at the examiner's naivete. The response to *Why should we keep away from bad company?* is particularly instructive in these cases: eyebrows are arched, the concept is disputed, chuckles precede the response, or self-references are made. In Picture Arrangement, the *flirt* and *taxi* sequences may elicit impish or hilarious laughter or a bored, supercilious look. The front varies, but the underlying message is the same: "I refuse to respond to this situation with any sincerity of feeling!" In the Vocabulary subtest, impulsive guesses, sometimes based on clang-associations, are often present.

Some of these patients, especially if they are retested during the course of psychotherapy, take the test with an air of utmost seriousness, diligent application, and carefulness. The resulting record may resemble that of an obsessive-compulsive. Careful observation and detailed analysis of verbalization usually reveals, however, that this application and thoroughness is ostentatious rather than genuine—an attempt to "look good," impress the examiner, and win his approval. In contrast, the true obsessive will be as thorough as his own demands on himself require. The narcissist, if encouraged to be brief, can usually change his style easily; the severe obsessive does not know what brevity means.

Because of their relatively high performance level and their labile affectivity, many of these patients often resemble hysterics. Hysterics, however, are generally more passive and less actively solicitous or demanding, more naive and less "sophisticated" or crassly egotistical, and generally more restrained, although their sporadic affective displays may be much more intense. This same differential diagnostic problem arises in nearly all the other tests, so that the tester cannot pass the buck to the Rorschach test, for example, but must try to solve the problem in each test by careful qualitative analysis. Many patients with narcissistic character disorders create an atmosphere of being easy to test; unless they are continuously pinned down, however, the examiner will be left with records full of evasions and ambiguities.

PSYCHOPATHIC CHARACTER DISORDER

As used here, the diagnostic term, psychopathic character disorder does not apply indiscriminately to overtly aggressive persons, nor to those who commit crimes on the basis of particular neurotic conflicts. It is meant to be applied in a narrow sense to persons who are characterized by the following features: (1) a long history of coming into conflict with legal or social rules, or both; (2) blandness with respect to antisocial acts and to the absence of any long-range goals or organized life pattern, although in individual situations, remorse or anxiety may be felt or feigned; (3) a general lack of time-perspective; (4) minimal capacity for delay of impulses; (5) a superficially ingratiating, overpolite, and deferential manner of relating to other persons.

The chief personality features to be sought out are weak integrative ability and underlying primitiveness of thinking, blandness, ostentatious overcompliance covering a basic callousness and inability to empathize with others, impulsiveness, fabulizing, and preoccupation with antisocial behavior. The patterns to be described have been seen mainly in the records of adolescent psychopaths, but appear to represent adequately the test results of many older psychopaths.

The characteristic pattern is a superiority of the performance level over the verbal, low scores on Comprehension and Similarities, and high scores on the tests of visual-motor coordination and speed. Frequently, the Digit Span score does not drop, reflecting the characteristic blandness. Picture Arrangement is often conspicuously high; this is especially true for shrewd "schemers" who can quickly size up a social situation and manipulate it for their own ends. If Picture Completion is high, overalertness or watchfulness is probably characteristic. The over-all pattern will indicate that this is a bland, unreflective, action-oriented person whose judgment is poor, whose conceptual development is weak, but whose grasp of social situations may yet be quick and accurate.

Qualitatively, the chief feature is usually blazing recklessness in guessing at answers. This is particularly apparent in Information and Vocabulary: "George Bernard Shaw wrote *Faust*." "Magellan discovered the North Pole." "Chattel means a place to live (chateau)." "Ballast is a dance (ballet)." "Proselyte means prostitute." These smack very much of the naive guesses of some hysterics or narcissists with low intelligence levels, but the high Picture Arrangement, the low Comprehension, the blandly high Digit Span, the consistent brazenly pretentious or ostentatiously compliant quality of the verbalizations, and the remaining test results will facilitate the differential diagnosis. It is rare to find a psychopath with a Verbal IQ above the average range; the Performance IQ, in contrast, may reach the superior or very superior range. If the Verbal IQ is high, but the other features persist, the clinical diagnosis is likely to be narcissistic character disorder. The responses to *Why should we keep away from bad company?* and *Why are laws necessary?* are likely to be perfect.

SCHIZOPHRENIA

It is important that a discussion of schizophrenia take into account the many different schizophrenic syndromes that occur clinically and underlie characteristic differences in test productions. Some of these syndromes will be treated separately in the following pages. First, however, it may be of some advantage to summarize some findings and considerations that hold for schizophrenics in general.

The test responses of almost all schizophrenic subjects are greatly shaped by enduring, non-schizoid aspects of premorbid character make-up. Thus, a person who has relied heavily on obsessive defenses, and who has ultimately developed a schizophrenia, will most likely yield patterns throughout the test that are clearly indicative of past achievements and present qualities referable to obsessiveness. The same holds for a person with a pronounced premorbid emphasis on repressive defense. Now, we have already seen that the diagnostic Wechsler-Bellevue Scale patterns of the intellectualizing obsessives and the repressive hysterics are, as a rule, markedly different from each other. Psychologically, there is no reason to expect that the development of a schizophrenia represents a *complete* abandonment of premorbid adjustment efforts and a *complete loss* of associated achievements; and, on the basis of empirical test results, it is clear that there is no such complete break with the past. Consequently, if the scatter patterns of a premorbidly hysteric-like schizophrenic and a premorbidly obsessive-like schizophrenic are compared, it is likely that in the first case the score on the Information subtest will be strikingly low, and in the second it will be strikingly high. In other words, *it cannot be assumed that all variations in test results are referable to the presence of the psychosis.* Nor can it be assumed that the nonpsychotic variations are purely random. Rather, deviant responses and test results will often reflect both the persistence of premorbid adjustment efforts and achievements, and the effects of the psychosis on these achievements and adjustment efforts. The following discussion, in the incomplete way our present understanding allows, will attempt to distinguish variations referable to non-schizophrenic factors and variations pertaining directly to the effects of the psychosis on intellectual processes and achievements.

Schizophrenic disorganization is indicated by four aspects of the intra-individual and inter-individual variations of efficiency and achievement. (1) *What varies?* A relatively low Comprehension score is diagnostically more significant than a relatively low Object Assembly score. (2) *In what direction does it vary?* Variations of Digit Span upward rather than downward are generally diagnosti-

cally most significant.   (3) *How much does it vary?*   How extreme
is the deviation from the hypothetical base-line?   (4) *What is the
quality or content of the variation?*   A response may be not only
incorrect but also bizarrely inappropriate, neologistic, and so on.
It is not necessary that the indications of schizophrenia in any particular set of test results embrace all four aspects of variation.   No
one type of variation has been shown to be present in a sufficiently
large percentage of cases to be firmly established on statistical
grounds as a valid diagnostic indicator.   Nevertheless, the occurrence of two or three types, and sometimes even one type, of variation will suffice to indicate the correct diagnosis.

Extreme scatter of subtest scores is one of the important diagnostic
indicators in schizophrenia.   If one or more of the scores deviate
extremely from the Information-Vocabulary level, or if nearly all
the scores show striking, though not necessarily extreme, variability
among themselves, schizophrenic disorganization of thinking is
suggested.   The following sets of subtest scores exemplify this rule:

	Case No. 1	Case No. 2	Case No. 3	Case No. 4	Case No. 5
Comprehension	12	5	11	7	10
Information	10	11	12	10	14
Digit Span	14	6	3	11	16
Arithmetic	6	7	14	13	8
Similarities	11	8	12	8	15
Vocabulary	11	13	12	10	15
Picture Arrangement	8	10	4	8	11
Picture Completion	6	8	10	13	6
Block Designs	12	6	10	10	16
Object Assembly	12	6	11	10	13
Digit Symbol	6	13	9	6	10

The high Digit Span of Case No. 1 and the low Digit Span of
Case No. 3 can both be diagnostic; the high Arithmetic and high
Picture Completion of Case No. 4 and the low Arithmetic and
low Picture Completion of Cases No. 1 and No. 5 can all be
diagnostic.

There are, however, certain scores that tend to drop more often
and more dramatically in the records of schizophrenics than in
those of other types of cases, and these are the scores on Comprehension, Arithmetic, and Picture Completion.   Thus the characteristic impairments of judgment and concentration in schizophrenia
are often immediately apparent in the scatter.   Other scores—the
scores on Digit Span, Picture Arrangement, and Object Assembly—

drop in many types of cases, including some normals; only if there is an extreme drop of these scores (eight or more points if the general level is superior, or six or more points if the level is average or below) does the scatter of these scores become diagnostically suggestive. As is generally true, the scatter analysis must be supported by qualitative analysis and by the results in other tests.

Qualitative Indications

Information: failing a number of very easy items and passing a number of difficult ones; incorrect answers or "can't remember" on items that should be passed on the basis of special interests or training, as when a musician fails the *Faust* item, a lawyer fails the *habeas corpus* item, or a history teacher fails the *Rome* or *Tokyo* items; wild guesses in a setting of high intelligence, such as that "Marco Polo discovered the North Pole," "Rickenbacker invented the airplane," "Tom Sawyer wrote Huckleberry Finn"; stilted, neologistic verbalizations, such as, "A thermometer is an emercurated tube to measure the degrees of temperature in Fahrenheits"; impulsive, absurd answers even if corrected, such as, "Washington's birthday is July 4th." Most of these patterns reflect disorganized memory functioning and loss of previous achievements.

Comprehension: failing one or more easy items and passing the difficult ones; bringing in irrelevant preoccupation such as syphilis on the *born deaf* item; consistently egocentric responses *offered seriously,* such as neglecting the letter in the street because "it's not my business," or reading the letter because of "curiosity"; elaborating clearly inappropriate courses of action, such as singing the national anthem from the stage of the burning theater to prevent panic, or building a hut in the forest "until someone found me"; inappropriately intense moralistic reactions to the *bad company, laws,* and *marriage license* items; irrelevant intellectualizing, such as (on the *taxes* item), "It all began with the idea of no taxation without representation"; answering other questions than those put by the examiner, such as explaining why people should be "good" on the *bad company* item. In general, these types of errors reflect schizophrenic impairment of judgment.

Digit Span: clear-cut superiority of digits backward over digits forward, such as 7 backward and 4 forward; extreme superiority of digits forward over digits backward, such as 9 forward and 3 backward; arbitrary "systems" to facilitate remembering, such as "adding them up." The last is a clear instance of impaired judgment.

Arithmetic: failing most of the easy items and passing one or more of the last three difficult items; [7] approximate answers such as "about 50" or "roughly 100"; inability to profit from even the most obvious assistance on easy items that have been failed; bizarre attempts at solution; adherence to the idea of 3-cent stamps on the *stamp* items; a literal approach to the problems that is sincere and not feigned for the sake of a laugh (as is often the case with narcissistic character disorders), such as disputing that seven pounds of sugar cost 25 cents. The unusual failures appear to reflect impairment of the ability to concentrate; the literality reflects the concreteness of thinking so often seen in schizophrenia; the bizarre attempts to approximate answers reflect impaired judgment.

Similarities: failing or contaminating good answers on easy items ("Orange and banana are *citrus* fruits"), and passing difficult ones; extreme syncretistic, expansive concepts, such as "composed of cells," or "inanimate objects," or "lacking human intelligence"; extreme concrete and fabulated concepts,[8] such as, "Fly and tree are similar in that you may be fly-fishing and catch your line in the branches of a tree," or, "Egg and seed are alike because you have to feed seed to the chicken and it will be healthy and can lay eggs"; consistent, negativistic denial of similarity, yielding a low score, when the intellectual level is above average; consistent offering of differences in addition to or instead of similarities.

Vocabulary: failing easy items and passing difficult ones; blandly associating to vocabulary words, such as *fur*—"soft" and *diamond*—"pretty"; impulsive, extremely strained clang-associations as bases for defining words,[9] such as, "Traduce means three deuces when you play cards," or "Belfry means a kind of bellboy."

Picture Arrangement: distorted percepts or confusion, such as seeing the Little King as two different persons in the same story, or not being able to identify the elevator despite average or high gen-

---

[7] Certain patients with narcissistic character disorders may do the same, however.

[8] Certain patients with narcissistic character disorders may also do this.

[9] Mildly strained instances of clang-associations are not unusual in the records of narcissistic character disorders, psychopaths, and naive hysterics. The distinction is often difficult to draw. Sometimes pretentious subjects with a low intelligence level and weak cultural background also do this.

eral intelligence; *extreme* discrepancies between the sequence offered and the story told; fragmentation or blocking of anticipations on easy items to such an extent that each picture is discussed in isolation and continuity is lost; strange and arbitrary anticipations based on peripheral details or even totally extraneous considerations.

Picture Completion: failing easy items and passing difficult ones; frequently referring to attributes or details obviously not intended to be present, such as colors, designs, the rest of the body in a picture of a head, the other eye in profile pictures, food in the pig's bucket, or the captain on the bridge of the steamer; inability to recognize certain objects, such as the playing card or light bulb, despite average or high intelligence (usually occurs where confusion is a symptom).

Block Designs: using colors other than red and white, especially if red or white blocks are being used at the same time; persistent acceptance of grossly incorrect designs as correct, such as building diagonal rows of all-red and all-white blocks on *item 6* and insisting on the correctness of the result after being asked to "make sure"; persistent rendering of the designs upside down; planless but relaxed rotation and "fitting" of blocks until some solution is reached (pattern coherence); readiness to ruin a correct design at the least suggestion from the examiner that it may be incorrect. For the most part these errors reflect defective reality testing or impairment of conceptual thinking.

Object Assembly: misrecognition or lack of recognition of the *profile* or the *hand* after the object has been assembled; planless but relaxed fitting of contours, frequently leading to correct solution, but often so unresponsive to cues as to indicate defective reality testing and blocking of anticipations, say, by getting one-half of the ear correct on the *profile* after the face parts and occipital piece are correctly placed, and then trying to fit the other half-ear all around the periphery of the head; acceptance on any of the items of absurd placements, for example, accepting or even seriously attempting the reversal of arms and legs on the *mannikin*.[10]

Digit Symbol: frequent errors of copying other than changing the reversed *N;* frequent skipping of spaces and thereby entering what

---

10 Organic cases may attempt this; impulsive subjects may also attempt it, but are quick to reject it as soon as they check what they are doing.

would have been the correct symbol in the wrong box; gross distortions of symbols; marked fluctuations of rate of work.

PARANOID SCHIZOPHRENIA

Those cases who are, as a rule, not generally bizarre, but who have developed clear-cut, predominantly paranoid delusions of a grandiose or persecutory nature, and who are often confused, or apathetic and retarded, are paranoid schizophrenics.

On the basis of test results, it is difficult to distinguish some of the retarded acute paranoid schizophrenics from psychotic or severe neurotic depressives. As a rule, these cases can be detected only if a *battery* of tests is administered; the results in any one test may be quite well organized. This quality of good preservation in the tests of acute paranoid cases appears to parallel the clinical observation that the delusional structure may barely touch the system of conventional logical relations. The chief features to be sought in the test results are sporadic appearances of basically disorganized thinking and arbitrary perceptual organization in a setting of inhibition and suspicious overcautiousness, or confusion and agitation. Again, however, any of the test features mentioned in the general section on schizophrenia may be present.

The most striking feature of the scatter in the records of acute cases is likely to be a more or less general drop of the performance level; Block Designs, however, still tends to obtain the highest of the performance scores. The Comprehension score is usually not strikingly lowered—a feature distinctively paranoid in its implications once the diagnosis of schizophrenia has been established, since it reflects good preservation. Although some of these cases show extreme scatter of the general schizophrenic variety (great drops of the Comprehension, Arithmetic, and Picture Completion scores), in general, it is the *paranoid* schizophrenics who yield little scatter. The greatly scattering paranoid cases are likely to be confused; the cases with little scatter other than a drop of the performance level are likely to be apathetic and retarded. In a schizophrenic setting, a relatively high Arithmetic or Picture Completion score, or both, indicate paranoid overalertness. A relatively high Similarities score also indicates prominent paranoid features.

Qualitatively, peculiar verbalizations, particularly in the Similarities subtest, and perceptual distortions in the Picture Arrangement and Picture Completion subtests, are especially likely to be present. In the *flirt* Picture Arrangement sequence, the woman may be seen as two different women—Negro and White—or the second chauffeur in the front seat may be seen as the woman inside the car; or the bust in the *taxi* sequence may be seen as a living person.[11] Because the chronic cases often have a "good front," the Comprehension score may remain on a high level even though there may be many peculiar verbalizations within that subtest. For example, in reply to *Why are people who are born deaf usually unable to talk?* one patient said in a confidential tone: "Some people try to keep it a secret, but I happen to know that it's because they have the disease. (?) You know . . . venereal disease . . . and they pass it on to the children." With chronicity, the Similarities or verbal concept formation score usually drops and the Block Designs and Object Assembly scores often rise. Peculiarities and distortions increase. The homosexual features that are often evident in these cases may be indicated by misrecognitions of the sex of the *mannikin* and *profile* in the Object Assembly subtest. Negativistic, suspicious behavior is usually striking.

SIMPLE SCHIZOPHRENIA

Withdrawal, apathy, blandness or absence of affective display, and peculiarities of behavior and thinking are the diagnostic clinical features of simple schizophrenia. "Antisocial" acts may be conspicuous in this setting; in female simple schizophrenics, this often takes the form of promiscuity. The experience to be summarized below was largely with simple schizophrenics 25 years of age or less. Occasionally, there may be some difficulty in distinguishing simple schizophrenics from bland psychopaths or inhibited, schizoid, normal subjects of low intelligence or poor cultural background. The chief features to be sought in the test results are blocking and perseveration, "flatness," absence of indications of emotional responsiveness and efforts at rapport, peculiarities of thinking, and general loss of interest.

Typically, the scores on the three tests of visual-motor coordination are high relative to the scores on the verbal subtests, Picture Arrangement and Picture Completion. The Comprehension and

---

[11] These distortions may also occur in the records of patients with non-schizophrenic paranoid conditions.

Arithmetic scores are likely to be quite low, reflecting the basic impairments of judgment and ability to concentrate. The Digit Span score is often relatively high, indicating blandness, as do the well-retained performance subtest scores. Information and Vocabulary tend to be spotty at the low levels and the high levels are rarely reached, reflecting loss or lack of general interests. Often the Vocabulary score is strikingly low. Rarely will one of these cases obtain a Verbal IQ above the average range.

Some simple schizophrenics resemble psychopaths by guessing wildly but blandly on the difficult items. These cases are likely to behave antisocially. Misuse of words and borderline neologisms tend to occur. A few peculiar verbalizations in the Similarities and Comprehension subtests are usual. The peculiar formulations and misuse of words facilitate differential diagnosis from psychopathic character and from hysteria or character disorder on a low intelligence level. Perceptual vagueness and arbitrariness are often conspicuous: objects in the Picture Completion series may not be recognized, the bust in the *taxi* sequence of Picture Arrangement may be seen as a woman, and so forth.

The general intellectual picture will be one of pathological unreflectiveness, minimal general interests, vague reality testing, and impaired judgment.

THE NORMAL PERSONALITY

In clinical psychological testing, the important questions are these: *How can we characterize the subject's typical efforts at adjustment?* and *How effective are these efforts?* The first question pertains to characteristic reliance on particular defenses and an associated selective organization of experience; the second question pertains to the presence and degree of anxiety, emotional lability, and control and modulation of impulses. These questions can be asked for the ill and the healthy alike. *Normal* and *neutral* are not synonymous; each so-called normal person has his distinctive pattern of adjustment efforts and handicaps, and psychological testing of normal people therefore requires the same clinical orientation as the testing of any other type. Characteristic emphasis on obsessive or repressive defenses, inhibition or avoidance, and so forth, is to be sought out. The level of judgment and concentration, the appropriateness of concepts, the sharpness of reality testing, and the integration of past achievements must all be assessed. While it is true that many subjects who are apparently normal clinically, yield Wechsler-Bellevue Scale results that are indistinguishable from those of neurotic subjects with the same general type of character make-up, it is also true that many others can be distinguished from their neurotic counterparts.[12]

SUMMARY

The main thesis of this chapter is that the so-called tests of general intelligence reveal more about the subject than mere information on general intelligence as such. Performance on intelligence tests is so interwoven with behavior that is thought of as the expression of personality that the concepts of intelligence and of personality are inseparable. Tests of intelligence, then, have potentialities, still undeveloped, for appraising personality.

This chapter is divided into three parts: Part I suggests a tentative rationale for the use of intelligence tests in personality appraisal. Part II presents an analysis of the specific intelligence functions tapped by the various problems in the Wechsler-Bellevue Scale, and discusses methods of analyzing test records. Part III illustrates how personality descriptions and differential diagnostic analyses may be derived from patterns of scores and qualities of performance on this test.

REFERENCES

1. *Annals of the New York Academy of Sciences.* 1946, 46, 531–678.
2. Frank, L. K., "Projective methods for the study of personality." *J. Psychol.,* 1939, 8, 389–413.
3. ————————, *Projective Methods.* Springfield, Ill.: Thomas, 1948.
4. Rapaport, D., "Principles underlying projective techniques." *Char. and Pers.,* 1942, 10, 214–219.
5. ————————, "Principles underlying non-projective tests of personality." *Annals of the N. Y. Acad. of Sciences,* 1946, 46, 643–652.
6. Rapaport, D., Gill, M., and Schafer, R., *Diagnostic Psychological Testing.* Chicago: Year Book Publishers, 1945, Vol. 1.

---

[12] Research in this area of testing—the differentiation of normal from neurotic character make-up—is urgently needed. Allied to this problem is the problem of assessing from test results the adjustment resources or "toughness" of normal personalities.

7. Rapaport, D., Schafer, R., and Gill, M., *Manual of Diagnostic Psychological Testing.* New York: Josiah Macy Jr. Foundation, 1944, Vol. 1.

8. Schafer, R., *The Clinical Application of Psychological Tests.* New York: International Universities Press, Inc., 1948.

9. ————————, "The expression of personality and maladjustment in intelligence test results." *Annals of N. Y. Acad. of Sciences,* 1946, 46, 609–623.

10. Scheerer, M., "Problems of performance analysis." *Annals of N. Y. Acad. of Sciences,* 1946, 46, 653–674.

11. Storch, A., "The primitive and archaic forms of inner experiences and thought in schizophrenia," *Nerv. and Ment. Dis. Monog.* No. 36, 1924.

12. Wechsler, D., *The Measurement of Adult Intelligence* (2nd ed.). Baltimore: Williams and Wilkins, 1941 (3rd ed., 1944).

CHAPTER 20

Qualitative Aspects of the Stanford-Binet

GLADYS L. ANDERSON, PH.D.

The preceding chapter has presented in considerable detail a discussion of intelligence scale records and their contribution to personality appraisal. Although there is a Wechsler-Bellevue Scale for children [28], research and clinical observations with the Wechsler-Bellevue have been made almost exclusively with adults. Moreover, most of the data on that test represent performance of mentally ill persons or of other adults in difficulty. The diagnostic syndromes for adults have been much further developed than any comparable work with children. Diagnostic syndromes for children are almost nonexistent. The syndromes for adults represent cross-sectional observations of adult behavior, about the genesis of which practically nothing of a reliable or valid nature is known.

Both informal clinical observation and observational studies of a known reliability and validity support the general assumption that children are growing psychologically at a faster rate and in more directions than are adults. Studies by Reed [23] and by Anderson and Brewer [1] showed that second- and third-grade children were more flexible in their personality and behavior characteristics than were their teachers. Consistent with these studies is the further observation that adults enter in mental hospitals for a variety of reasons that seem to represent different kinds of arrested, frustrated, blocked, inhibited, or atrophied growth. There seem to be good reasons why the syndromes of mental disease (which still

have many internal inconsistencies among adults) are almost lacking
for children.

It is chiefly for this reason that this discussion of the performance
of children follows, instead of precedes, the discussion of the performance of adults, and that the Binet tests, which greatly antedate
the Wechsler-Bellevue, are now discussed in this reversed order.

HISTORICAL BACKGROUND

The two Stanford revisions of the Binet-Simon tests have constituted the most widely used individual psychological examination
extant.   The tests have been so widely used that the oversimplified
numerical IQ has become rooted in cartoons and joke books, and
has been misappropriated for commercial aggrandizement in advertising and other programs.   Even among teachers and social workers and among many psychologists, the name of Binet is associated
with IQ, and all too frequently with nothing else.

Alfred Binet (1857–1911) was a biologist, physician, and philosopher.   But judging from his numerous publications, he was primarily an experimental psychologist.   The history of any science
is a record of process, of evolution, of differentiation, and of integration.   It is a record of struggle for meanings and for the refinement of observations.   Looking back with a perspective of 50 years
on the struggles of experimental psychologists of Binet's day, one
sees two general trends of approach to the study of human behavior.
These two approaches were each valid in their way, but their contributions to the development of psychology as a science were
different.

On the one hand, there was a trend that adapted the methods of
other sciences, a trend that had as its chief procedure the control
of all variables except the one that the experimenter was trying to
measure.   This necessitated the measurement of very small variables, like the limen of tactile sensitivity, the discrimination of
weights, and the decrement of energy output of the index finger in
the repeated lifting of a known weight at equal intervals of time.
This approach was exemplified in the work of Weber, Fechner,
Wundt and others, and is sometimes thought of as a German approach.   Those investigators set up hypotheses and established
laws of human behavior that they verified by experimentation in
much the same way that laws of matter were verified by physicists

and chemists. Their admitted objective, however, was to study *simple* psychological processes, functions, and faculties.

At Columbia University, working with Cattell and with tests that he brought back from Germany, Wissler [*30*] in 1901 showed that there was an unreliable relation, or little more than could be expected by chance, between results on psychological tests, physical measurements, and college grades. Psychologists concluded that the psychological tests measured special functions unrelated to college grades. American psychological laboratories had been established for the most part by students of Wundt or of other representatives of the German approach. The reaction of these American psychologists to Wissler's findings seems to have been an abandoning of hope in mental tests and an entrenchment in further laboratory study of simple, controlled functions such as sensation, imagery, and memory. Some of these psychologists referred to their work as investigations in "pure" science.

On the other hand, there were psychologists whose admitted objective was to study not so much isolated, simple variables as the more complex behavior of the whole person. Representatives of this approach were, for the most part, Frenchmen. Itard, Seguin, and Binet were all interested in the more complex psychological processes found in the behavior of a person in day-to-day experiences. Binet, to be sure, made many studies of the so-called simpler functions, such as memory, sensation, reaction-time and sensory discrimination. From his own studies, he rejected the association theory of memory then current among psychologists and looked for more meaning in the experiences of the subject. He experimented with sentence completion tests and with the interpretation of ink blots. In one experiment, he asked children to write 20 words as fast as they could, then, by careful questioning, tried to discover from the children's own introspections what made them think of individual words and groups of words, and what they were thinking about before and after they hesitated in the middle of the test. In another, he asked children to describe objects and tell stories about pictures, and used a question period afterward to discover more meaning in the children's mental life out of which the details of the stories emerged.

Binet published books and articles on his findings, as well as interpretations of the complexities of human behavior. He did all of these things before he was asked to develop the mental tests for which, unfortunately, he is so uniquely known to Americans. Of Binet's monograph, "L'étude expérimentale de l'intelligence," (1902) [2], reporting his elaborate experimental study of his two daughters, aged 14½ and 13, Goodenough says, "In my opinion it remains the best as it almost certainly is the first example of the use of the projective approach to the study of personality differences" [10, p. 129]. Of this same monograph, Cronbach has written, "Binet described the application of the inkblot and imagery tests to his daughters, coming out with clinical qualitative descriptions of the way their intelligence functioned which read as if taken from the most modern results of projective techniques" [5, p. 104].

In 1904, Binet prepared mental tests for use in the schools of Paris. He died in 1911, the year that Goddard produced the first English translation of the tests.

American psychologists, having 10 years previously, and for good reason, rejected "psychological tests," did not receive the Binet tests with eagerness. But when Terman produced the Stanford Revision in 1916, psychologists, with their tradition of rigid controls and exact measurements, accepted the mental age and IQ because of their quantifiable potentials.[1]

The insight that was Binet's, the interest in studying the complex mental functions, and the possibilities of exploring the child's inner mental life, were slowly developed by others.

The Juvenile Psychopathic Institute was established in Chicago in 1909, to study delinquent children. William Healy, its first director, published a book on mental conflicts and misconduct [12] in 1917. Freud had published in 1913 his *Interpretation of Dreams* [9]. Healy's book went beyond Freud in revealing a dynamic relation between stealing and other social taboos, and his comprehensive methods of studying the child became the model for the Commonwealth Fund's demonstration clinics over the country in the 1920's. Healy used psychological examinations and devised many of his own techniques [3], but he also explored the inner mental life of the child. The child's "own story" was one of the most important parts of the clinical procedure. In 1921, Rorschach

---

[1] For stimulating discussions of the historical background of the development of psychological examinations, the reader is referred to Goodenough [10] and Cronbach [5, ch. 6], and to what is perhaps the best and most detailed expository review in the English language, by Peterson [20].

published his own version of ink blots and his theories about their use in psychological examination. In the 1930's, Murray and his students were working on other devices reported in *Explorations in Personality* [19].

It was Alfred Binet himself who laid the groundwork and set the pattern for the qualitative interpretation of psychological tests as revealing unquantifiable information about the inner mental life of the child.

QUALITATIVE ASPECTS OF ADMINISTRATION [2]

Rapport. A part of the report of every psychological examination should be a statement as to whether or to what extent it is judged the subject did his best. It has been assumed by psychologists that rapport is a sine qua non for a subject's best performance. The ability to establish rapport is also assumed by psychologists to be a quality of any expert, well-trained examiner.

While strict adherence to standardized procedure is essential for any examination, no examiner is thereby assured of the subject's best performance. Almost any graduate student can memorize the directions and learn to manipulate the test materials. The examiner's judgment as to whether the subject did his best may be based on few or many subtle perceptions and selective observations, and also on hunches, insights, subliminal cues, biases, prejudices, projections, and lapses of his own attention.

Observation vs. Inference. The evaluation of rapport is arrived at by inference. One cannot perceive rapport; one perceives behavior and infers rapport. It appears to be very difficult to recognize the difference between an inference and an observation. Students are not the only ones who have this difficulty. Quite generally, one tends to make an inference and then to treat the inference as though it had the same degree of reliability and validity as an observation. To the errors in reliability and validity of an observation are compounded the errors in reliability and validity of the inference. Such compounded, unwitting errors constitute a major problem of human communication.

Art vs. Science. There is another problem in the development of rapport that involves both perception and communication. Clin-

---

2 Adapted from a paper, "Rapport: Operational Definitions in a Clinical Training Program," presented at the meetings of the Midwestern Psychological Association, 1949, Chicago.

ical psychology, in its diagnostic as well as its therapeutic functions, is still said to be more of an art than a science. It is helpful to make a distinction between art and science that can be meaningful to clinical psychologists and particularly to students in training. Suppose a certain surgeon is deft and sure; he is so swift and accurate in his diagnoses as to be the envy of his colleagues. They can watch him work, but neither they nor the surgeon himself can say what he has done or how he has done it. They call him an artist. As an artist, he makes highly valid perceptions, but perceptions of such subtle similarities and differences that they are unperceived by his colleagues and uncommunicated by the surgeon himself. Until he can verbalize his perceptions, until he can communicate to others not only what he thinks he has found but also the evidence for his judgment, he is practicing an art. When he, or when some other person, learns to verbalize these perceptions, his art rises from a level of perception to a higher level of verbalization. At this level, the art can be communicated to others and become a science. The horizons of communication are pushed farther out and the activity, skills, and perceptions can be verified and taught to others.

In this sense, and to a large extent, the development of rapport is still an uncommunicated art. Terman and Merrill [25, pp. 56–58] devote only two pages to a discussion of the importance of rapport, offering a series of specific positive suggestions and cautions.

Psychologists, like artists in other fields and like human beings in general, have a problem of being articulate. The way to be articulate is first to have something to say—to have made an accurate perception. Students in training have demonstrated that they can make the distinction between their observations and their inferences and can discuss rapport on the basis of communicable perceptions.

In an effort to sharpen the perceptions of what happened during a testing situation, the writer asked students who were learning to administer the Stanford-Binet to record during the examination evidences of rapport or of lack of rapport. In the form of narration and description, they reported the dynamic process of interplay in terms of observed behavior. Herewith, for example, is a part of a report:

John (aged 8) spontaneously told the examiner his nickname; sat with both hands and forearms on the table leaning toward the examiner during most of the test; occasionally relaxed (*interpretation?*), pushed chair from table and then pulled it closer to the table; offered to sharpen a broken pencil; initiated conversation; asked examiner if he had more tests like the Verbal Absurdities; mentioned that he could give more than two reasons why most persons would rather have an automobile than a bicycle; on his own volition helped the examiner pick up paper scraps before leaving the room. At the conclusion of the test he readily accepted the invitation to stay and make a drawing of his own choice. His drawing was a crudely (*evaluative term*) drawn delivery truck. On the truck he printed his own nickname. He then asked the name of the examiner, saying "I'll put your's right here and we'll be partners."

Terman and Merrill have on their Record Booklet [26] four categories on which test behavior is rated. The students made these ratings. (Other investigators have published other lists [4, 16] of things to look for in test behavior.) After the students had written and discussed a number of their own observational records, they found that they could group their observations in a number of categories. It was believed, however, that in the training situation, it was more valuable for the students to make up their own assortment of categories as their test experience accumulated more items to sort. In this way, they had at all times the idea of an open system of classification that they could expand or modify at will. The purpose of this project was not to develop a complete checklist, but, as explained above, to assist the students in training themselves to make accurate and subtle perceptions and to communicate them.

Consecutive vs. Serial Order of Administration. The order of test administration is included here for brief discussion because it is one of the factors affecting test performance that has involved qualitative interpretation of the test results. In Binet's original batteries, the tests were presented as a series of games; when the child had played one game he turned to another. When the tests were later arranged into age-level series, the games were broken up, some, like the memory for digits, being presented at several age levels. The vocabulary test, however, which in all versions and revisions has received credit at several ages, has remained an exception; it has always been administered as one test.

There has been much discussion, considerable controversy and confusion, and practically no research, on the order of presentation of test items.   The term *consecutive order,* as used here, means the standard order in which the test items appear in the manual [*25*] and the record booklet [*26*].   *Serial order* is used here to designate a grouped order of presentation in which those tests having similar instructions, as, for example, memory for digits forward, are administered as a group.   This was the original plan of Binet and was much preferred by earlier writers on test administration: Mateer [*17*] (1924), Wells [*29*] (1927), Bronner, Healy, Lowe and Shimberg [*3*] (1927), and more recently, Louttit [*15*] (1947), and Carter and Bowles [*4*] (1948).

Terman recognized in 1916 that "the child's efforts in the tests are sometimes markedly influenced by the order in which they are given" [*24*, p. 130].   He pointed out that beginning the examination with language or memory tests might be embarrassing to the child, and recommended as initial tests those dealing with objects and objective things:

> The tests as arranged in this revision are in the order which it is usually best to follow, but one should not hesitate to depart from the order given when it seems best in a given case to do so.   It is necessary to be constantly alert so that when the child shows a tendency to balk at a given type of test, such as those of memory, language, numbers, drawing, "comprehension," etc., the work can be shifted to some more agreeable tasks.   When the child is at his ease again, it is usually possible to return to the tests with better success.[3]

Of the 1937 revision, Terman and Merrill said,

> The tests of each year group should be given in the order in which they appear in the manual and record booklet. . . .   Serial testing—that is, giving all the tests of one type consecutively (digits, sentences, etc.)—is not permissible if the test score is to be interpreted in terms of the established norms. . . .   In order to secure the child's best effort, however, it is sometimes necessary to change the test sequence.   For example, if the child shows resistance toward a certain type of test, such as repeating digits, drawing, etc., it is better to shift temporarily to a more agreeable task.   When the subject is at his ease again, it is usually possible to return to the troublesome tests with better success.[4]

Terman and Merrill pointed out that the standardization of the test in the given order presumed that the child would have an ad-

---

[3] L. M. Terman, *The Measurement of Intelligence.*   Boston: Houghton Mifflin Company, 1916.   By permission.   Page 130.

[4] L. M. Terman and M. A. Merrill, *Measuring Intelligence.*   Boston: Houghton Mifflin Company, 1937.   By permission.   Page 56.

vantage in successes on preceding items, and that to change the order would change the difficulty of the item by an unknown amount.

What Hutt [*14*] called *adaptive testing* was an experimental procedure that included serial testing.   Other features of the adaptive method were to begin four years below the anticipated mental level, to alternate easy with hard items, to establish both the basal and maximal levels as carly as possible in the test administration, and not to administer tests below the presumed basal level nor above the presumed maximal level.   Hutt had 290 children tested by the *consecutive* method, and 340 tested by the *adaptive* method.   His hypothesis was:

Any modification of the administration of an item or of items of the scale, which did not change its (or their) median age value(s) would not effect [*sic*] the norms of the test to any appreciable extent.   It was therefore possible that the "adaptive" procedure might raise (or lower) the test results for some portions of the population without thereby affecting the median result for the population even though the means might be modified.[5]

Among his findings, Hutt reported that when applied to "total populations" or to very well adjusted cases, the two methods yielded comparable results.   He interpreted this to mean that "adaptive" testing had no significant effect upon the "norms" of the test: "Analysis of our data warrants the probable conclusion that for poorly adjusted individuals and especially for very poorly adjusted ones, the 'adaptive' method yields higher IQ ratings which appear to be more valid for the cases studied" [*14*, p. 103].

Frandsen, McCullough, and Stone [*8*] have reported a study using 47 children divided into four groups of nine and one group of eleven.   They administered Forms *L* and *M* by Consecutive and Serial Order as first and second tests among the four groups, and found the results from the two methods to be "practically identical. . . .   The correlation of .93 indicates both very close general agreement between the two arrangements and also high reliability of testing with both procedures" [*8*, p. 319].   The mean test-retest difference obtained from serial and consecutive arrangements was 5.48, which they reported to be only very slightly higher than the

---

5 M. L. Hutt, "A clinical study of 'consecutive' and 'adaptive' testing with the Revised Stanford-Binet." *J. Consult. Psychol,* 1947, 11, 98–99.   With permission.

average test-retest difference of 5.09 obtained by Terman and Merrill.   They concluded that on the basis of present evidence, clinicians who favor adapting the Stanford-Binet for serial testing apparently need have no hesitancy in using Terman and Merrill's norms for interpreting IQ's thus obtained.

The advocates of serial testing have been unanimous in pointing out that any adaptation of the standard method requires more of the examiner in the way of expertness than does the administration by the consecutive order.   Carter and Bowles [4] discuss other problems of test administration in considerable detail, and at the several year levels of the test.

QUALITATIVE INTERPRETATION

The early regard for the importance of rapport in test administration was an admission that there were certain intangibles of motivation, certain inhibitions to action, certain fears, apprehensions, and anxieties that might either inhibit a response altogether, cause a lapse in attention, or otherwise effect a distortion in the perception of the problem of the test.   Although these possibilities were probably all known to Binet, they have at no time been very clearly stated.   The Binet-Simon tests have undergone several revisions.   They have been made into age-level and point scales.   The objective of all revisions, including that by Terman and Merrill, has been to produce a system for allotting to the subject's responses a classification into *pass* or *fail* or into a defined score value.

Traditionally, scant qualitative interpretation has been offered, apart from a rating of the child's test behavior, an interpretation of the child's attitudes during the test, and the expression of the examiner's judgment as to whether the results did or did not represent the child's best performance.   Supplementary scoring manuals by Pintner, Dragositz, and Kushner [21] and by Wrightstone [31] have clarified certain ambiguities but have mainly drawn a clearer line between pass and fail responses.

Yet, for clinical psychologists, the qualitative interpretation of psychological examinations, including tests of general intelligence, is not new.   In 1927, Bronner, Healy, Lowe, and Shimberg wrote:

Emotional conditions are of exceedingly great importance in their influence on test results. Yet, in spite of this they are frequently overlooked, or, if noted, not taken into account. It is a matter of primary concern . . . to know the emotional attitude of the subject. Emotions may be inhibitory, "blocking" responses. Fear, anger, or indifference may play a very important role in the psychological examination. . . . Underlying or persisting emotional disturbance about one's situation in life may be, and in many cases is, a complicating factor in test results [*3*, pp. 14–15].*

Twenty-one years later, in 1948, Carter and Bowles wrote *A Manual on Qualitative Aspects of Psychological Examining* [*4*], summarizing the available literature, which is scattered and scanty indeed, and adding many provocative ideas from their own experience. There is nothing for the Stanford-Binet, for example, comparable to the extended consideration given to the detailed analysis of responses to individual test items on the Wechsler-Bellevue by Rapaport, Gill, and Schafer [*22*], or by Mayman, Schafer, and Rapaport in Chapter 19 of this volume.

Scatter. The interpretation of scatter in performance on the Stanford-Binet has involved range of successes and failures, amount of performance at each age level, and combinations of the two. Since the age level scales were first introduced, many efforts have been made to devise a statistical or other meaningful method for evaluating scatter of performance. These methods are critically reviewed by Harris and Shakow [*11*], in a study with which any contemporary examination of scatter must begin.

Terman and Merrill make only a casual mention of scatter in 1937: "Whatever the nature of intelligence may be, its manifestations in the individual are uneven. One individual will do better with one kind of material than he does with another" [*25*, p. 65].

Hunt and Cofer conclude a discussion of qualitative results of intelligence tests, as they may reveal psychological deficit, with the statement, "The scatter approach appears now to be a blind alley" [*13*, p. 984].

The reason that the search for a scatter score on the Binet tests has led so many researches into blind alleys is probably inherent in the structure of the test battery itself. Except for the vocabulary tests, the items are not uniformly spaced at different levels of difficulty. Nevertheless, even though one does not have a scatter score, it is a source of many valuable clinical cues to note the kinds and degrees of failure, the attitudes toward failure on different

---

* Quoted by permission.

items, the excuses and explanations offered by the child for his known or even his presumed failures, and his reactions to his successes.

Studies of Individual Test Items. In 1938, Bühler [6] made a study of responses on the Ball and Field Test (1916 revision) as a help in the diagnosis of emotional difficulties. She sorted out responses into four groups: normal, confused, formalistic, and involved. She reported that normal and average children produced only two per cent of the confused, formalistic, and involved responses, and that 78 per cent of such responses were produced by children with emotional problems. The remainder of responses in these three classifications were produced by children who did not understand the directions.

In 1941, Young [32] published a one-page report of his observation of a peculiar error in the test of memory span for digits by an adult male. The subject was unable to reproduce correctly a nine-digit series containing the number "2," although he could reproduce series of 11 or 12 digits not containing the number. The subject traced the error to a previous traumatic experience.

Cruickshank [6] used the Ingenuity Test of Form *L,* year 14, to make a qualitative analysis of the responses of mentally retarded and normal subjects of the same mental age. His purpose was to study the methods of solving a problem above the mental level of the subjects. He found that the normal subjects responded more realistically to elements pertinent to arriving at a logical answer to the problem. Feifel [7] used the Vocabulary Test to make a qualitative analysis of types of response given by normal adults and to compare the responses with those of abnormal adults of similar backgrounds. He reported that an analysis of the verbatim responses showed that the abnormals significantly more often selected "the use and description types of response, and the demonstration, illustration, repetition, and inferior explanation kinds of definition" [7, p. 200]. Both of the above studies offer some contribution to the qualitative functioning of mental mechanisms, but the findings are rather remotely related to projective mechanisms as such or to an understanding of personality dynamics.

Examples of the use of responses on individual test items in the

---

6 Charlotte Bühler, "The Ball and Field Test as a help in the diagnosis of emotional difficulties." *Char. and Pers.,* 1938, 6, 257–273.

appraisal of personality are given by Murphy [*18*]. In a brief paper, she made a plea for a fuller qualitative use of the Stanford-Binet tests in approaching a better understanding of the personality problems of school children. She showed the possibility of qualitative use of content analysis, form analysis of drawings, and distribution of successes and failures.

Protocols by Students in Training.[7] All of the studies cited above represent the work of trained and experienced examiners. Even so, the studies reporting the qualitative interpretation of performance on the Stanford-Binet have shown very meager relation to the motivational and emotional life of the subject. The writer has maintained that not only expert examiners, but also student examiners in training, can give attention to the details and subtleties of behavior of the child in the psychological test situation.

To test this hypothesis, a number of devices were used in training students to administer the Revised Stanford-Binet:

1. The student examiner wrote a description of the child.
2. The student examiner wrote a description of the child's behavior during the examination.
3. The examiner made a verbatim record of the responses to the test items and of spontaneous remarks of the child.
4. The examiners were provided with 5- by 8-inch mimeographed blanks on which they could report for test items so called *unusual* responses. Most of the unusual responses were recorded under five categories:
   (a) doubtful scoring
   (b) double meaning in interpreting the test response
   (c) example of emotional blocking
   (d) subtle errors in test administration
   (e) other kinds of unusual response

The form provided space for the examiner to write the child's response and to record a description of relevant behavior. The accumulated reports of unusual responses were discussed at weekly meetings of the class.

At this stage of their training, the students had not had systematic training in the field of projective techniques. The testing was not part of a clinic study. Beyond the strict adherence to the standard test procedure of the Stanford-Binet, the students were expected to be alert for incidents in test behavior that *might* be related

---

[7] Adapted from a paper, "Projective Aspects of the Stanford-Binet," presented at the meetings of the American Psychological Association, Boston, September 1948.

to the child's problem of getting along with the world in which he lived.

The following examples of test responses and test behavior have been reported by student examiners.

Connie. C.A. 8 years, 6 months. At year X is the test item, Picture Absurdities—Frontier Days, a picture showing a white man shooting at a distant Indian when he is under immediate attack by two other Indians. The child is shown the picture and is asked, "What's foolish about that picture?"

Connie replied, "Four Indians and one cowboy. And the cowboy is shooting right at the Indians." Connie then said, "I don't see how they can fight in that lot, because somebody might own it."

On the previous Picture Absurdities Test at year VII, where a man is sawing a log with the teeth of the saw turned up, Connie had given a correct response to which she added remarks about her self: "He's keeping his leg on the log. . . . That isn't funny. No, he's got the saw on the wrong side. I guess I must be blind. That's what my mother calls me."

During the test, Connie made several references to her cousin. At year VIII, Comprehension test: "What makes a sailboat move?" Connie replied, "I can't think what that thing is. I just can't say it. You know I'm not an artist like my cousin is. That thing right there. . . . No, the wind does."

Here was a child who, in a standardized test situation, on almost every item in the test, had to work through the problem of her relationship to the outside world.

Examples of other remarks that Connie made are: "Shall I make it as wide as this?" "Shall I do it this way?" "I shouldn't have done that." "I promised not to forget, but I did." "I don't think I draw good at all."

Although no further work was done with the child, the examiner did learn from the teacher that Connie had recently enrolled in the same school as her cousin; Connie and her parents had been forced to move when their house was sold and were temporarily living with her cousin and the cousin's parents. It may be that for Connie, all the world belonged to somebody else and even the cowboys and Indians were trespassers.

Terry. C.A. 8 years, 9 months. At year XIII, there is this situation: a purse with a lot of money in it has been lost in a big field. The child is told, "Take this pencil and start here at the gate and show me where you would go to hunt for the purse so as to be sure not to miss it." If the subject fails to understand that he is to mark the path, the examiner adds, "Mark it with the pencil to show me where you would go to hunt for the purse."

Terry, with an IQ of 120, responded to this XIII-year-level test: "Here is how my father would do it." He then indicated the approved plan by moving his pencil above the paper in a perfect detailed spiral, saying as he did so, "He would go round, and round, and round." The student examiner then asked, "How would *you* do it?" Terry then marked the paper as shown in Figure 1.

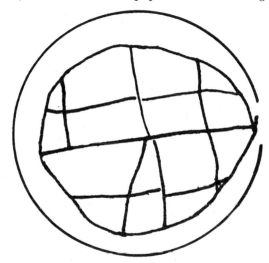

Fig. 1. Year XIII. Plan of search.

Terry understood the problem and showed that he had an intellectual awareness of how to cover the field, but for some reason, he was unable to give the popular, that is, the correct response. He had to be different from his father, even if he made his performance a failure in problem-solving.

Sam, a Negro boy. C.A. 5 years, 0 months. Pictorial Likenesses and Differences occur at year IV–6 and year VI. The examiner presents card (a) and says, "See these crosses that are just alike? Here's one *(pointing)* that is *not* like the others. Put your finger on the one that is *not* the same as the others." For each following

Fig. 2.   Years IV–6 and VI, Pictorial likenesses and differences.
Five-year-old Negro boy: "None of 'em's different."

card the child is asked to "put your finger on the one that is *not* the same as the others." When Sam was shown the card with the three white circles and one black one (Figure 2), and was asked to put his finger on the one that is *not* the same as the others, he replied: "None of 'em's different." He then looked up at the examiner, and back to the card, and very hesitatingly pointed to the black circle and said, "I guess, maybe, this one is a *little* different." All the other cards in the series were passed with no hesitation and no error.

Henry. C.A. 6 years, 1 month. The Maze-Tracing Test is presented at year VI. The problem is, "This little boy lives here, and here is the school house. The little boy wants to go to school the shortest way, without getting off the sidewalk. Here is the sidewalk. Show me the shortest way. Mark it with your pencil, but don't go off the sidewalk. Start here and take the little boy to school the shortest way."

On Maze 1 (Figure 3), Henry, IQ 121, carefully stayed within the lines. But one can notice that he did not stop at the school house.

On Maze 2, Henry did not take the "shortest" way and he did not go all the way to school. And on Maze 3, he again went past the school house. Did this child comprehend the problem of taking the boy to school the shortest way? On two of the three trials he overshot the mark. The little boy did not "stay" at school, though he did take the shortest path. At this point in the examination, the examiner noted that the child was easily distractible and talked constantly about his younger brother at home. As has been said, Henry had an IQ of 121, and it was the failure on this maze-tracing test that placed his basal age at 5 years. The examiner seriously questioned whether Henry should have been credited with a failure on this item, which purported to test his intelligence. The examiner learned later that Henry's younger brother not only was not at school, but was at home having a birthday party.

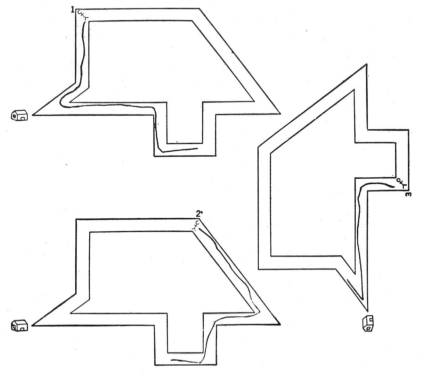

Fig. 3. Year VI, Maze tracing.
"The little boy wants to go to school . . ."

Bert. C.A. 12 years, 9 months, IQ 73, filled his test responses with projections of his own personality problems. Asked to state in what way a snake, a cow, and a sparrow are alike, he replied, "If you get 'em mad, the cow sticks you, the snake wraps his tail around you, and the sparrow eats stuff out of your garden."

Bert failed at year X to name 28 words in one minute. The student examiner noted that the words he did name related only to farming. The examiner discovered later that the father had recently lost his job. The father and the boy wanted to move to a farm, but the mother had a job in town and refused to move.

In the Verbal Absurdities Test, year XI, item 2-a, the judge says to the prisoner, "You are to be hanged and I hope it will be a warning to you." Bert commented, "The judge shouldn't have told him that he was going to hang him.   He will try to find some way to get away." In defining *obedience,* Bert said "got enemies." Defining *courage,* Bert said "get somebody mad and get 'em all mixed up."

Both in his successes and in his failures, when Bert revealed himself as a person, he revealed an unhappy boy in conflict with the world in which he lived and greatly frustrated by powers beyond his control.

At year VII, Comprehension III has the question: "What's the thing for you to do when you have broken something which belongs to someone else?" Something more than failure and success is revealed in the two answers following:

1. "Go and tell them, cry, then you won't get in much trouble."

2. "Buy them a new one with your own money."

Naming 28 words in one minute, year X, is often revealing of undisclosed conflict and tension if the words are written verbatim by the examiner and the contents studied.   It was pointed out above that this was a method of free association used by Binet.

Definitions of abstract words provide another kind of almost free association, particularly when the words are at a level too difficult for the child.   The content analysis of the child's failed responses often discloses important information concerning preoccupations and areas of misperception.

One other example of a test in which children frequently give a personal interpretation or a personal involvement in the answer is the Problem Situation at year XI.   This is a simple story about a boy who wanted a pet.   The examiner says, "Listen, and see if you can understand what I read.   Donald went walking in the woods.   He saw a pretty little animal that he tried to take home for a pet.   It got away from him, but when he got home, his family immediately burned all his clothes.   Why?" The only persons mentioned in the story are Donald and his family.   Terman and Merrill describe the test as another variation of the completion method, a method that permits unlimited elaboration.   The following responses are examples of those offered by school children:

1. He probably ran away like I did—*(told of running away from home)* —I stayed at my grandma's for a week.   My ma tried to get me to come home but I wouldn't.

2. He tried to catch a little birdie and pulled his feathers off. The little birdie told his mother and the mother took her little boy's clothes off to see how he would like it.

3. To punish him for trying to get something.

4. 'Cause he brought the animal back. 'Cause when they would give him a spanking his clothes would burn he would be so red—a red-hot whipping.

5. Because he was cruel for catching the little animal in the woods.

6. It was his step-mother who burned them—you know step-mothers are mean to kids.

In the Revised Stanford-Binet, the child's personal relations with the world are revealed in his reactions to many of the test items. The several drawing tests disclose the child's spontaneity or lack of it in his methods of work. In the reproduction of the circle, the square, and the diamond, in the Maze Drawing, the Memory for Designs test, and the Plan of Search for the lost purse, one can distinguish the deliberate from the impulsive method of putting an idea into action; one can find children who are careless and others who are meticulous perfectionists. Many of the hypotheses underlying the Bender Gestalt test (Chapter 11) are equally applicable to the drawing tests in the Stanford-Binet. In these tests are found frequent examples of retracing lines, erasing, exaggerated or open angles, distortion of proportion, inversion of design, omissions of detail, faint lines, and heavy lines.

In the Picture Completion: Man, year IV and V, are some of the same scoring and interpretation problems found in the Draw-a-Person test (Chapter 12) or in the H-T-P test discussed in Chapter 18.

Personal content from the life experiences of the child is found more frequently in some test items than in others. The child's misperceptions and projective behavior are more easily elicited by the less structured test items that require abstract symbolic expression and tolerate a wide latitude of responses. Such test items involving verbal expression and abstract thinking are found at numbers of age levels. Open-ended questions, which admit anything the child cares to say, are found in the Picture Absurdities I, year VII; II, year X; Verbal Absurdities I, year VIII; II, years IX and XII; III, year XI; Comprehension III, year VII; and IV, year VIII. The question about a statement or a picture: "What is funny (or foolish) about that?" permits a wide range of individual variation in response. It permits different kinds of expressions of exactness and of errors in perception. It reflects variations in attention with its ranges of intensity and its varieties of instantaneous or momentary diversions, and variations in logical arrangement of detail.

SUMMARY

The historical development of psychology as a science showed two trends in the early 1900's. One was the development of methods to study *simple* psychological processes, such as sensation, tactile discrimination, and memory. Leaders of this trend were mainly German psychologists. The other trend was represented by an attempt to study the more *complex* processes of day-to-day behavior of the whole person. This trend seems to have been associated more with a French influence, including that of Alfred Binet. Binet made studies using both objectives—the simple and the complex mental processes. He experimented with many methods now thought of as "projective techniques"—he developed sentence completion tests, asked subjects to interpret ink blots, used free association methods, as in the naming of words in a given time, and asked children to tell stories about pictures. This emphasis in Binet's work prior to 1902 was eclipsed in America by interest in the quantitative, numerical scores of mental age and IQ.

This chapter discusses nonstandardized, qualitative factors in the administration of the Revised Stanford-Binet and qualitative factors in the responses that, beyond being interpreted as pass or fail, yield information on the one hand about the child's very clear perceptions of the world about him, or, on the other hand, about his misperceptions of his relation to the world in which he lives.

Rapport is a sine qua non for a psychological examination. Very little has been written about it except to state that it is important. Suggestions are offered here for sharpening one's observations during the examination and for recording the evidence for or against a relationship of rapport.

Scatter has been a controversial qualitative aspect of performance almost since the age-level scales were first constructed. Although investigators searching for a numerical or statistical evaluation of scatter have ended in a blind alley, the interpretation of scatter in a child's responses still has clinical usefulness. The examiner may note the kinds and degrees of failure, the attitude toward failure on different items, the child's explanations for his known or presumed failures, and his reactions to success.

Published studies of qualitative aspects of the Stanford-Binet usually offer little interpretation through the projective mechanisms as such, or through an understanding of personality dynamics. A high level of training and experience is required for qualitative interpretation. In this chapter, responses to individual items are presented to show that even the protocols submitted by students in training can reveal much about the child's motivations and frustrations, and other aspects of his personality dynamics.

Some test items have greater potentiality than others for eliciting responses with dynamic reference. The drawing tests reveal many qualities of expressive behavior as well as degrees of clarity of the child's perceptions and of his facility in visual-motor responses.

Personal content from the life experiences of the child is found in the less structured test items and open-ended questions that require abstract symbolic expression and tolerate a wide latitude of responses. There are many such items in the Stanford-Binet, found, among others, in the successions of tests of picture absurdities, verbal absurdities, comprehension items, and definitions of abstract words.

REFERENCES

1. Anderson, H. H., and Brewer, J. E., "Consecutive studies from fall to winter of teachers' dominative and socially integrative contacts and related changes in the children's classroom behavior," Chapter 3, in H. H. Anderson, J. E. Brewer, and M. F. Reed, "Studies of teachers' classroom personalities, III." *Applied Psychology Monographs No. 11*, 1946, 101–153.

2. Binet, A., *L'étude expérimentale de l'intelligence.* Paris: Alfred Costes, 1902.

3. Bronner, A. F., Healy, W., Lowe, G. M., and Shimberg, M., *A Manual of Individual Mental Tests and Testing.* Boston: Little, Brown and Company, 1927.

4. Carter, J. W. Jr., and Bowles, J. W. Jr., "A manual on qualitative aspects of psychological testing." Monograph Supplement, *J. Clin. Psychol.*, 1948, 4, 109–150.

5. Cronbach, L. J., *Essentials of Psychological Testing.* New York: Harper & Brothers, 1949.

6. Cruickshank, W. M., "Qualitative analysis of intelligence test responses." *J. Clin. Psychol.*, 1947, 3, 381–386.

7. Feifel, H., "Qualitative differences in the vocabulary responses of normals and abnormals." *Genet. Psychol. Monogr.*, 1949, 39, 151–204.

8. Frandsen, A. N., McCullough, B. R., and Stone, D. R., "Serial versus consecutive order administration of the Stanford-Binet Intelligence Scales." *J. Consult. Psychol.*, 1950, 14, 316–320.

9. Freud, S., *The Interpretation of Dreams* (A. A. Brill, trans. and ed.). New York: The Macmillan Company, 1913.

10. Goodenough, F. L., "The Appraisal of child personality." *Psychol. Bull.*, 1949, 56, 123–131.

11. Harris, A. J., and Shakow, D., "The Clinical significance of numerical measures of scatter on the Stanford-Binet." *Psychol. Bull.*, 1937, 34, 134–150.

12. Healy, W., *Mental Conflicts and Misconduct.* Boston: Little, Brown and Company, 1917.

13. Hunt, J. McV., and Cofer, C. N., "Psychological Deficit," in J. McV. Hunt (ed.), *Personality and the Behavior Disorders.* New York: The Ronald Press Company, 1944, Vol. 2, Chap. 32.

14. Hutt, M. L., "A clinical study of 'consecutive' and 'adaptive' testing with the Revised Stanford-Binet." *J. Consult. Psychol.*, 1947, 11, 93–103.

15. Louttit, C. M., *Clinical Psychology* (rev. ed.). New York: Harper & Brothers, 1947.

16. Louttit, C. M., and Waskom, W. B., *Manual for the Indiana Psychodiagnostic Blank.* Publ. Indiana Univ. Psychol. Clinics, Series II, No. 8, 1934.

17. Mateer, F., *The Unstable Child.* New York: The D. Appleton Company, 1924.

18. Murphy, L. B., "The appraisal of child personality," *J. Consult. Psychol.*, 1948, 12, 16–19.

19. Murray, H. A., and others, *Explorations in Personality.* New York: Oxford University Press, Inc., 1938.

20. Peterson, J., *Early Conceptions and Tests of Intelligence.* Yonkers, N. Y.: World Book Company, 1925.

21. Pintner, R., Dragositz, A., and Kushner, R., "Supplementary guide for the Revised Stanford-Binet (Form L)." *Appl. Psychol. Monogr.*, 1944, No. 3.

22. Rapaport, D., Gill, M., and Schafer, R., *Diagnostic Psychological Testing.* Chicago: Year Book Publishers, 1945, Vol. 1.

23. Reed, M. F., "Consecutive studies of the schoolroom behavior of children in relation to the teachers' dominative and socially integrative contacts," Chapter 2, in H. H. Anderson, J. E. Brewer, and M. F. Reed, "Studies of teachers' classroom personalities, III." *Applied Psychology Monographs No. 11*, 1946, 15–100.

24. Terman, L. M., *The Measurement of Intelligence.* Boston: Houghton Mifflin Company, 1916.

25. Terman, L. M., and Merrill, M. A., *Measuring Intelligence.* Boston: Houghton Mifflin Company, 1937.

26. —————————, *Record Booklet—Form L. For the Revised Stanford-Binet Scale.* Boston: Houghton Mifflin Company, 1937.

27. Wechsler, David, *The Measurement of Adult Intelligence* (3rd ed.). Baltimore: Williams and Wilkins, 1944.

28. —————————, *Wechsler Intelligence Scale for Children: Manual.* New York: The Psychological Corporation, 1949.

29. Wells, F. L., *Mental Tests in Clinical Practice.* Yonkers, N. Y.: World Book Company, 1927.

30. Wissler, Clark, *The Correlation of Mental and Physical Tests.* New York: Columbia University, 1901.

31. Wrightstone, J. W., *A Supplementary Guide for Scoring the Revised Stanford-Binet Intelligence Scale, Form L.* New York: Board of Education, 1941.

32. Young, Clarence W., "The possible use of the memory span for indication of complexes." *J. Abnorm. Soc. Psychol.,* 1941, 36, 115.

PART V

Projective Techniques in Therapy

CHAPTER 21

The Use of Puppetry as a Projective Method in Therapy[1]

ADOLF G. WOLTMANN, M.S.

INTRODUCTION

"Hit him!" "Kill him!" "Watch out, he is still alive. He is going to kill you!" "Turn around quick. He is coming after you. He is going to bite you!" "Hit him again and kill him!" "You better run home to your mother. This place ain't safe!" "Kill him!"

Excited voices of children fill the room. Some children stand up with their fists in the air, ready to come to the rescue of the little character on the stage. Others sit quietly, but their flushed cheeks and heavy breathing betray their tense emotional state. A few hide their heads in their hands, as if afraid of watching the struggle between the little puppet and the crocodile. The fight on the puppet stage continues. With a stick twice his size, the little puppet boy subdues and apparently kills the fierce puppet crocodile. The animal sprawls lifelessly on the stage, but as soon as the puppet boy turns his back, it reopens its threatening mouth, lifts its head, and chases the little boy all over the stage. Another battle ensues. The crocodile is hit and killed again, only to come back to life

[1] Special thanks and acknowledgements are extended to Dr. Lauretta Bender, Senior Psychiatrist, Children's Ward, Psychiatric Division, Bellevue Hospital, New York City, for her encouragement and guidance, which made possible the exploration of the therapeutic qualities of puppetry. Her keen insight into and understanding of children's personality structures were invaluable in the formulation of basic principles of group therapy through the means of puppetry.

and to harass the little boy until finally, the puppet boy is victorious over the fierce animal. This time the killing is final. The crocodile is pushed off the stage. The puppet boy bows and acknowledges the rousing applause from his responsive audience. The tense excitement is gone, the atmosphere relaxed. The children are happy that their beloved puppet actor has escaped unharmed from this life-and-death struggle.

An examination of scenes like the one just described raises a number of questions. Why do some children clamor wildly for killing, while others hide their heads? Why do some children move their hands as if they had to fight the animal aggressor on the stage, while others shrink away from such aggression and advise the puppet character to run away and to find safety and refuge in the sanctum of the home and the presence of the mother? Why do the children relax when their puppet hero is victorious? Why do some children urge the crocodile to eat up the puppet? Obviously, these puppets have specific meanings for each child. What determines these meanings, and what do they convey in terms of the child's thinking, reaction, and participation?

It is assumed that each child identifies himself, in a manner specific to him, with the puppet characters and with the actions portrayed by them. It is further assumed that this identification leads to projections in the sense that each child projects his own feelings, desires, wishes, and anticipations into the puppet show.

Before a fuller comprehension of these complicated processes is possible, the elements that go into a puppet show must be analysed. This calls for a discussion of puppets, the stage, the play, the psychological rationale of puppet types and of the puppet plays, the combination of acting and play content into a meaningful whole, the reactions of children to general and specific puppet play situations, and the possible therapeutic influence that puppet shows have on children.

PUPPETS

Puppets are divided into three large groups: shadow puppets, string puppets (marionettes), and hand puppets.

The *shadow puppet* is used predominantly in the Orient. It is made of translucent material such as parchment or thin leather, mounted on a stick. The shadow puppet is held close behind a translucent screen, and a light behind the puppet throws its shadow on the screen, so that the audience, facing the screen, does not see the real puppet but only its shadow. Most shadow puppets have arms joined to the body and moved by additional sticks. The puppeteer sits behind the screen and manipulates these puppets above his head. The shadow puppet is limited in its movements: it can only move from right to left or vice versa across the stage; it cannot turn around on the stage because it would lose its form and appear as a thin, black line on the screen; it cannot move into the background because a retreat from the screen toward the light would cause enlargement and distortion of the shadow. Its action radius is also limited. Shadow puppets cannot put on a good, convincing fight. Finally, the use of shadow puppets in this country labors under a cultural handicap. The oriental shadow puppet is endowed with color symbolism that is strange and alien to us. A shadow puppet in blue, say, might mean that the character is good and noble. The same puppet, appearing in red, perhaps, indicates that this good person has turned into a villain. Different facial features such as a pointed or a bulbous nose, a high forehead, a protruding chin, and so on, likewise have specific symbolic meanings commonly understood by oriental audiences and not requiring verbal explanations or specific deeds.

The *marionette,* or *string puppet,* is the best known member of the puppet family in this country. It is a jointed doll with movable head, arms, and legs. Elbow and knee joints allow for human-like movements and actions. The various parts of the marionette are fastened to strings gathered above the doll in a wooden control. The puppeteer stands behind and slightly above the marionette, his body hidden from view by the backwall of the stage. He holds the control in his hands, and by shortening or lengthening different strings, endows his puppet with lifelike motion. The feet of the marionette are heavily weighted down with lead. Quick and hasty string movements interfere with gravitational forces and result in a pendular swing. If the puppeteer does not possess skill and fine muscular control, the string may become entangled and seriously interfere with the planned action.

This brings to mind an anecdote related by Charles Dickens. During his travels in Italy, he saw a marionette show portraying the death of Napoleon. Dickens found this sad scene highly amusing because the physician who was attending the dying Napoleon suffered from entangled strings and hovered over Napoleon like a vulture. These remarks should not be interpreted as a slur on the artistic potentialities of the marionette, but should simply be regarded as a warning.

The marionette is the most artistic puppet type at our command. It appears in full view of the audience, in contrast to the shadow puppet and the hand puppet, which usually show only the head and the torso. It can run the whole gamut of human actions and emotions. Yet, the appearance of two or more marionettes on the stage calls for caution. Care must be taken that they do not touch each other too closely, lest they become entangled in each others' strings. This potential danger, therefore, precludes close, lifelike, aggressive actions such as fighting, punching, or hitting. It also interferes with scenes in which puppets, through kissing, stroking the face, and dancing, demonstrate love and affection.

The third type of puppet is known as the *hand puppet* or the *glove puppet,* more commonly referred to as the Punch and Judy type of miniature actor. The anatomy of the hand puppet is very simple. It consists of a three-dimensional head with a costume or garb attached to it. The arms form part of the dress and are not joined to the puppet body as in the shadow puppet and the marionette. The hand puppet, as the name implies, is manipulated by the hand of the puppeteer, which is inserted into the puppet. The index finger moves the puppet head, the thumb and the middle finger manipulate the two puppet arms. This close connection between puppet and puppeteer allows for quick and direct action, because every move of the hand and the arm is immediately transmitted to the puppet. Neither the shadow puppet nor the marionette enjoys this intimate relationship with its master: movement transmitted through sticks or strings is indirect.

The hand puppet's simple anatomy, which makes possible easy manipulation, its immediate responses to the puppeteer's actions, and its lack of entangling strings and of sticks that inhibit free-swinging motility, makes this little actor an ideal medium for the portrayal of human problems, especially when the onlookers are children. Children do not need elaborateness and overdecoration. In order to drive home a point, a puppet show for children should consist of simple, obvious, direct, and forceful actions, so that, if necessary, a whole show can be acted out in pantomime and still be fully understood. A shadow puppet or a marionette is usually handled by one puppeteer. The hand puppet player can easily manipulate two puppets at the same time, one on each hand. This allows for closer coordination of action. In the above-mentioned scene, one puppeteer plays both the puppet boy and the crocodile. In this way, the crocodile is able to play possum when the boy looks at it, and move as soon as the puppet turns its head. This close coordination makes the actions look more convincing. The radius of puppet action is only determined by the reach of the puppeteer's arms. Movement can be as fast or as slow as desired without running into contrary gravitational forces.

The technical elements of building and constructing puppets are omitted. The reader is advised to consult *The Puppet Theatre Handbook,* by Batchelder [1], for a comprehensive, detailed, and illustrated presentation of these technical aspects.

STAGE

In order to be effective, each one of these three puppet types needs its own frame of reference, which must be in proportion to the size of the puppet. One of the main reasons that effective puppet play requires a stage is that the puppeteer must be kept out of sight; otherwise, the illusion of human-like acting on a miniature level is destroyed. Although the stage imposes limitations on the action radius of the puppet, this is necessary so that the attention of the audience may be focused on the immediate happenings. Stage props must be in proportion: a puppet twenty inches high would look ridiculous sitting on a life-size chair.

A transparent screen and a source of illumination are necessary for a shadow puppet. The stage requirements for the marionette call for a complicated structure consisting of a proper stage for the marionette with a solid backwall. A raised platform behind this wall serves as a place where the puppeteer can move and direct the puppet unseen. Curtains and illumination enhance the stage effect.

The hand puppet does not need such elaborate surroundings for good acting. Anything that keeps the puppeteer out of sight will serve. The back of a high chair, a blanket nailed between two door posts, or a screen will serve as an emergency stage. Simple stages can easily be built if greater permanence is desired. Again, the reader is referred to Batchelder's instructive and comprehensive handbook [*1*] for specific instructions that include information about draw-curtains, lights, dimmers, and other desirable paraphernalia.

This chapter deals with the therapeutic applications of puppetry. For such purposes, elaborate stages and settings are not so important as they might be for theatrical or commercial entertainment. It has been pointed out that in order to be effective therapeutically, hand puppetry in particular should be simple, direct, forceful, and obvious. This applies also to stage construction. Too elaborate and too colorful stages and stage settings are like overornamented and overdecorated frames that detract from and minimize the appeal of a picture.

PUPPET PLAYS

To write a good hand puppet play is just as hard or as easy as to write a good book for children. The great difference between the two lies in the fact that characters in a book never act. The script for a puppet play must be translatable into actions. Just as the writing of the score for a musical composition must consider the range of each instrument, so a script for hand puppets must clearly visualize the action radius of the hand puppet.

Before considering the positive aspects, a few words must be said about what should not be done. In order to appear spontaneous, puppets should employ ordinary language. Verses and rhymes may be suitable for special occasions, but they are not our everyday mode of conversation. A puppet show in verse, especially when played for a group of children, sounds very stilted and unreal. Instead of helping children, it bores them. Whenever possible, soliloquies should be avoided. Children are much more active than grown-ups; therefore, a good puppet show should contain a great deal of action. This breaks the dominance of the spoken word, emphasizes physically what the puppets try to do, and appeals to the children's own mode of working through certain situations. In order to render a puppet show effective, the stage should not be overcrowded with puppets. This is an important fact to remember in writing a puppet show for children; avoid confusion and interferences with action.

A good hand puppet play should have a plot or a central theme. The development of the central conflict should be so obvious as to be easily understood by the children. In order to give the young audience a chance to participate in the puppet drama, a good hand puppet show should consist of a skeleton text that allows for changes, interruptions, improvisations, and discussions between the puppets and the children. This keeps the puppet show alive and makes the children feel that they are part of it; therapeutic aims are much easier to accomplish in this manner. More will be said about this later on, when the interaction between script and puppet acting will be discussed. It suffices here to state that the basic ingredients for a good hand puppet show include a consideration of the nature of the conflict to be portrayed, the general level of understanding of the children for whom the show is prepared, and the absolute minimum number of puppets necessary to act out the intended plot. When the plot is put down on paper, the writer should think in terms of the puppet show. By this is meant that he should visualize each puppet's place on the stage, the entries and exits, and the actions that are supposed to take place. Care should be taken throughout the show to effect a good balance between words and actions. Everyday language should be used. Dialogue should be brief and to the point. The examples given later in this chapter will illustrate these theoretical dictums.

PSYCHOLOGICAL RATIONALE OF PUPPETRY

The following remarks are pertinent to a fuller understanding of the therapeutic application of puppetry. The three main puppet types were discussed at the beginning of this chapter. To that elaboration must now be added the fact that puppetry, regardless of geographical location and type, can be traced back to the cultural beginnings of mankind. Puppetry, like the folk song, the folk dance, the arts, and architecture, had its origin in religious rituals. It is not an artifact like the radio or the movies. Together with the other mentioned cultural manifestations, it has survived the rise and fall of nations and races. It has been modified by divergent cultural streams but has never been flooded out of existence; its survival to the present day testifies well for its inherent strength and general appeal.

Throughout its long existence, hand puppetry has retained a

very important trait that has been lost by the marionette: hand puppetry still employs *types,* rather than *characters* created for a specific play. These types developed in various cultures and were modified by changes within those cultures, so that today the type remains although the original archetype may have disappeared.

It is impossible within the brief confines of this chapter to give a full historical survey of the development of puppet types, but as each important puppet type is discussed, short historical data will be included in the description.

The hero of all the puppet shows that were used in the therapeutic puppet shows at Bellevue Hospital [*3, 8*] is a boy by the name of Casper. His pointed cap and multicolored costume render him ageless, so that he can easily portray youngsters between the ages of six and 12. The origins of this type go back to about 5000 B.C., when it appeared on the East Indian shadow stage as a servant to a rich master. Basically, he is a comedian who causes his master to become involved in all sorts of compromising situations. The same type is also noted on the Greek and Roman stage, either as a living actor or as a puppet. He has become world-famous as the English Punch, having been introduced into Great Britain by Italian showmen during the time of Queen Elizabeth. In France, he has thrived under the name of "Guignol," in Russia, as "Petrushka," and he entertained German children first as "Hanswurst" and later on as "Kasper." The Turkish shadow puppet, "Karagöz," belongs to the same family. Basically, this type represents the man on the street with all his ambitions, strivings, and desires. He stresses primarily the earthy and material things in life. Like all of us, he oscillates between courage and cowardice. He seldom is at a loss for words, but more often than not, he uses physical force to defend himself and to settle an argument. He is both clever and naive, full of hope and in deep despair, trusting and rejecting. Since he is only a puppet, he can act out his audience's innermost wishes and desires.

This type was used in the Bellevue puppet shows as the main character. The nature of the therapeutic aims and the age distribution of the audiences made it necessary to change him from a man into a boy. Right from the start, we noted the great popularity that he enjoyed among the children of the ward. An investigation into the children's responses and reactions over a period of several years gave us pertinent clues to his popularity.   We learned that most children identified themselves very closely with him. He seemed to express their wishes and desires, and his combination of words with actions was a real demonstration for them of how problems could be handled and settled.

Casper and his fellow puppets cannot simply be defined in psychoanalytical terms, but there is no question that the various sides of the total psychic structure are reflected differently in the various puppets. Casper is the expression of strong infantile desires which demand satisfaction.   He knows that he must adapt his drives to the demands of reality.   This satisfies the demands of the super-ego.   We must therefore see in Casper something of the Freudian "idealized ego" which reaches for reality without being in conflict with the "id" or pleasure principle.   The monkey, which plays an important part in some of the shows, gets his gratifications easily and corresponds in many ways to the "id" which has not been restricted. . . .   Casper's parents take over the role of the super-ego.   We believe that the child sees his parents as dual personalities.   The Good father and the Good mother love and protect the child, feed him and show him affection.   The Bad father and the Bad mother inhibit the pleasurable impulses of the child and train him in a manner not always agreeable to him [8].

In order to underline the superego function of the father, we made him appear as a plainclothes detective, connected with the police department.   He thus not only represents authority in the family setting, but also personifies the controlling force through which law and order are maintained in the community.   The Bad mother in the puppet shows is portrayed by the witch.   She is the product of folklore and fairy tales.   As such, she does not need any specific introduction because the children immediately sense what Casper or any other puppet might expect from her.   In one of our shows, she denies food and rest to Casper, makes him work hard, and belittles all of his attempts to please her by being orally aggressive to him.   In another show, she helps Casper to get rid of his baby sister.   "The part of the Bad father is portrayed by the giant, the magician, and also partly by the cannibals.   The giant, through his enormous body, is a physical threat to Casper. The magician, through his magic and clever scheming, is intellectually superior to Casper" [8].   The cannibals show hostility to Casper and threaten him with oral aggression.   They would like to cook and eat him.   Cannibals appeared on the European puppet stage about 200 years ago, probably as a result of mercantilism and colonization, which brought Europe in contact with primitive cultures.

The crocodile or alligator plays a very important part in a good puppet show. This animal represents oral aggression in a twofold way. Those children who like the crocodile identify their own oral aggression with the big mouth and the sharp teeth. The child's oral aggression against the world is frequently met by counter-aggression, directed by the environment against the child. Therefore, those children who are greatly afraid of the crocodile usually express their own fears of counter-aggression. This probably appears to them as punishment and as fear of the harsh, forbidding forces in the world about them. Occasionally, children become overwhelmed by their own aggression. Fear of the crocodile might then be expressed in the words of an eight-year-old boy who said during a group discussion about a puppet show: "I am afraid of the crocodile. It might eat me up myself." The crocodile or alligator made its appearance on the European puppet stage with the cannibals.

The figure of the devil is another puppet character of long standing. Like the witch, he is a product of folklore and fairy tales, to which have been added theological identifications. He needs no special introduction, because every child immediately knows what he stands for. How intense the projection of youngsters into a puppet show can become is best illustrated by the example of a six-year-old boy. When the devil suddenly and without any prior warning popped up on the stage, this boy bolted from the room, shouting, "Casper, pray for Jesus Christ. The devil is here."

Added to these major actors are minor characters that serve to round out any specific plot. In one of our shows, Billy, the bad boy, and his mother appear. Billy is the negative Casper in the sense that he completely rejects authority, sasses and hates his mother, beats up Casper, and is very demanding and overbearing. The contrast between the good Casper and the bad Billy has served for many illuminating discussions about various family constellations, attitudes toward parents, and the consequences that might ensue if the balance of power were shifted toward the child. Another character type, General "Hitt-'em-and-kick-'em from bang-'em-and-slang-'em," serves as Casper's Prime Minister and Chief

Executor when Casper tries to build up a government for children and finds it expedient to eliminate adult control and authority.

This enumeration of puppet types may suffice to stress that puppets are capable of representing specific personalities either directly or indirectly, or specific sides or aspects of personalities. With such an array of types, there is hardly any limit to the portrayal of problems.

Over and above the flexibility that is provided through the grouping of these various puppet types, there are other psychological factors that make hand puppetry an ideal medium for tackling and solving problems.

Puppetry Is a Make-Believe Affair. A puppet consists only of a head and a costume. The hand and the voice of the puppeteer give it a pseudo-life. A puppet might be beaten, but it does not feel real pain. It might be killed, but since it consists of inanimate material to begin with, killing is never real but only simulated. Situations may be very threatening, but puppetry carries with it the reassurance that everything on the stage is only a make-believe affair. This by no means detracts from the realness with which the children follow the actions, identify themselves with this or that character, and project their own wishes into the show. The make-believe nature of puppetry allows it to go beyond the limits of biological life. It is perfectly normal that a bad character like the crocodile is killed, comes back to life, is again killed, and so on. Children are not concerned about the killing, but clamor for the reassurance that takes place each time the bad and threatening character is killed. Solutions to problems have to be experienced again and again before complete mastery is achieved. However, should severely neurotic or psychotic children feel threatened by the show, one can easily reassure them by taking them backstage, where they can see for themselves that the puppets are not really alive, but are only doll-like characters guided by the puppeteer.

This make-believe nature of puppetry is further expressed by the combination of puppets used. A puppet show in which only realistic characters appear is too logical and does not allow for fantasy digressions. A puppet show in which only fantasy characters act is too unreal and fantastic and does not allow for identifications on a reality level. A good puppet show, like a good fairy tale, should therefore combine both realistic and fantasy factors.

This mixture of reality and fantasy makes it easier for the child to enter into the spirit of the problem presented, and aids in the identification. Since parts of the show or some of the puppets (witch, devil, giant, and so on) are symbolic expressions of attitudes, the child himself feels free to project his own attitudes into the show.

Children, by and large, enter quickly into the make-believe nature of the puppet show. Yet it will happen that very disturbed and psychotic children object to a puppet show because their own main problem consists of a severe struggle between maintaining a reality appreciation and giving in to their own delusions. One psychotic youngster felt compelled to wash not only the puppets, but also the stage. He claimed that the puppets and everything connected with them were dirty and had to be cleaned. Dirt, to this child, represented the threat of insanity, whereas clean and white stood for reality. Another one of our young patients objected to the puppet show as being too mechanical, and called me the "mechanical man." This little girl went through a rapid phase of deterioration toward the end of her stay in the ward and always went into hiding when a puppet show was given. These and similar experiences taught us that severely psychotic children might conceive the puppet show as a threat to their endeavor to hang on to reality. These children were much more aware of the make-believe nature of the puppet shows, and therefore reacted in very marked fashion. They felt threatened and had a strong desire of defending themselves against such make-believe.

Another important prerequisite for a good hand puppet show is the *close interaction between the audience and the puppets.* Several centuries ago, it was quite common for the actors on the legitimate stage to address some of their lines, and also off-hand improvisations, directly to the audience, which, in turn, talked back. This form of audience participation is no longer practiced on the legitimate stage, but it has been kept alive on the puppet stage. Before the show starts, the children are told that they are expected to enter into the show by telling the various puppets what to do, suggesting modes of action, warning of threatening dangers, and aiding the actors verbally in whatever way they can. The puppets, in turn, speak directly to the children. Casper, for instance, might ask his audience whether or not he should play hookey from school. He acts dumb, tells the children that he never did such a thing, and asks them to instruct him on how to go about it.   It is self-evident that the answers Casper receives contain valuable clues to the children's thinking and experiences.   In this way, material is produced that would be extremely difficult to extract in an individual interview.   The children are not aware of the fact that they themselves give away clues to their own behavior.   On the contrary, they feel highly flattered that Casper takes them into their confidence.   They really have the feeling that they themselves are running the show.   This makes it clearer why it was said that a good hand puppet show should consist of a skeleton-like, flexible script, because without this, such improvisations and audience interaction could not take place.   It is not uncommon for the puppets to deviate temporarily from their script to follow some suggestions from the audience, and to return to the regular plot at the proper time and continue with the play until a new interruption causes another deviation.

Puppetry Is a Group Activity.   This brings to the fore therapeutic factors beyond the willful control of the puppeteer.   The child who witnesses a puppet show is not alone, but goes through a number of emotional and social experiences as a member of a group.   The numerical strength offers protection to the individual.   He can express his own feelings because others do the same.   The child also learns to realize that others about him are interested and involved in the dramatic presentations, and that therefore, his own problems are not exclusively his own, but that others have similar problems.   This is a very reassuring insight.

In the beginning of the puppet work at Bellevue Hospital, staff members took copious notes, trying to get down on paper the reactions of various children. They soon learned that most children entered so completely into the spirit of the shows that they remembered their own participation. During the following group discussions and individual interviews, children told what they had said, what other children had proposed, and how each child had reacted to the show. The staff therefore discontinued the note-taking during the show, because all of the reactions were easily elecited during the follow-up period.

An extremely revealing device for the study of a child's reaction to a puppet show is the so-called "half-show." The child sees unveiled before him the beginning of a problem that, in true dramatic fashion, becomes involved and demands a solution. Whenever the conflict is at its height, the show is stopped with the promise that it will be continued at some other time. Then groups of children and individual children are asked what should happen. What kind of solution would they propose to the problems of the puppets? The various solutions made are colored by the child's own problems and his ability to understand intellectually and emotionally the implications contained in a particular problem. Although each child tries to unravel the conflict in terms of his own involvement, background, family constellation, and general level of maturity, he is not aware of the fact that he talks about himself. By discussing the puppets and their problems, he is spared the embarrassment of talking about himself. In this fashion, relevant material, disclosing the child's own dynamics and attempts to work through his own conflicts, is brought to the surface in an easy fashion. Children who block in individual interviews talk freely during a group discussion. Once the ice has been broken, the skillful therapist can rapidly make the transition from the problems of the puppets to the child's own conflicts. The mere fact that children are encouraged to seek solutions to problems has a great therapeutic effect, because it makes clear to a youngster that his own particular maladjustment is not a hopeless mess leading to doom and complete failure, and that there are not one, but several possible solutions. Such insights are encouraging and further the progress of rehabilitation.

PUPPET SHOW CONTENTS

In order to make the foregoing theoretical discussion more meaningful, the contents of two puppet shows are offered here as an example of how script and action blend into a puppet show.

"Casper in Africa." The presentation of "Casper in Africa" in synoptic form is taken from an earlier publication [8]. This show is very much liked by the smaller children because it contains little verbal material and stresses easily understood action. It is full of repetitions and allows for a great deal of experimentation with situations on Casper's part.

When the curtain opens, Casper appears somewhere in Africa. He is hungry and looks for food. He finds a banana, but before he has a chance to eat it, a monkey takes it away. Casper gets himself more bananas, which are also promptly stolen by the monkey. Casper is bewildered by the disappearance of his food until he finds out that the monkey is the culprit. The children, of course, have told him over and over again what this animal has done, but Casper does not pay attention to their remarks. Whenever he looks in the direction pointed out by the audience, the monkey has disappeared and pops up at the other side of the stage. Finally Casper sees the monkey and a fight ensues. Casper and the monkey become friends when they realize that they can have all the food they want if they stick together.

At the beginning of the second act, Casper is alone on the stage. He finds a trinket. While he goes off to get some wrapping paper in which to send this trinket home to his mother, an alligator appears and takes the trinket away. Casper blames the theft on the monkey and beats him up when he appears on the stage. The sudden reappearance of the alligator makes Casper realize that there are other forces to cope with in this strange environment. The alligator attacks Casper and nearly kills him, but the monkey comes to his rescue and helps him to kill this ferocious beast.

Before the alligator is finally overpowered, many amusing repetitions take place. The alligator may run away in the middle of the fight, leaving Casper and the monkey hitting each other. Or the alligator may seem dead, and while Casper is talking to the monkey, it may suddenly come back to life and attack both figures so that the fight starts all over again. All of these repetitions lead to new experimentations with the same situation, and mastery of it is achieved through trial and error.

The beginning of the third act shows two cannibals speaking gibberish and performing a wild dance.[2] The cannibals capture Casper and try to drag him off to the tribal cooking pot. Again the monkey appears in time to save him. The same repetitions as those in the fight with the alligator are brought into play. The cannibals, however, are not killed, but are taken back to America with Casper, who feels that they need training and education.

In the light of the fact that the puppets directly or indirectly represent specific persons or stress specific sides of a personality, we may say that in this show, Casper represents a very small child in

---

[2] Full credit for this gibberish, and for the spine-tingling tonal quality of the witch, goes to Harry von Borstel, my first assistant many years ago.

a strange world. His first sensation is hunger. In his attempt to satisfy his hunger, he comes into conflict with the monkey, which, as we have stated earlier, represents to a certain extent the unrestrained pleasure principle. Oral aggression is encountered and mastered. The cannibals, with their queer body movements and strange language, are perhaps the first impressions the small child has of his own parents. Repetitive action on Casper's part, composed of aggression and investigation, is necessary before he learns the true nature of these new forces. In other words, this show represents some of the basic experiments the small child goes through in his development. The small child can easily understand what happens on the stage because complicated logical word structures are absent. Simple, direct, and obvious action dominates the show.

"**Rock-a-Bye, Baby.**" The second show reproduced here is called "Rock-a-Bye, Baby." It was written originally for a nursery-school child whose unrestrained sibling rivalry had resulted in a serious behavior disorder. Through the years, the show has been altered and rewritten. We took our clues for revisions from the reactions of various children, until finally the present script seemed to be acceptable to the majority of children.

Act I

When the curtain opens, the stage is empty. Casper appears and immediately addresses the audience:

CASPER: Hello! Everybody hello! (*Speaking rapidly*) Good morning, good night, good afternoon, good morning, good night, hello!

AUDIENCE: Hello, Casper.

CASPER: You know what? I am sooo glad that school is over. Do you know why?

AUDIENCE: (*Mixed reactions. Some children say that he does not like school, others state that Casper can play after school, and so on.*)

CASPER: No, that isn't it. I tell you why I am glad that it is 3 o'clock and that I can get out of school! . . . You know, now that I am home I can play with my mother. You don't know her, but she is the best, the finest, the prettiest mother a boy could have. Let me call her, and you'll see for yourselves.

Casper calls his mother who at first answers from backstage, but at his persistent calling, finally appears on the stage.

MOTHER: Here I am, Casper. Why do you call me? What do you want?

CASPER (*running towards mother and embracing her*): Hello, mother dear. I told these children out there so much about you that I want them to meet you.

MOTHER (*towards the audience*): Hello, children. (*Towards Casper*) Casper, darling, the weather is so nice, why don't you run down and play for a while with the children in the street?

CASPER: No, mother. I don't want to play with children in the street. I want to play with you. I am so glad that school is over so that I could run home and play with you.

Before the mother has a chance to reply, Casper grabs her and whirls her around on the stage.

CASPER: Mother, we learned a new song in school. It goes like this. . . .

Casper sings "Have you ever seen a lassie go this way and that way," and dances around with his mother. The mother protests, frees herself from Casper's grip.

MOTHER (*slightly out of breath*): Casper! Stop that. I can't dance around like that.

CASPER: All right, mother. Let's play something else. Let's play choo-choo train. I am the engine and you are the train.

Casper whistles like an engine, again grabs his mother and pushes her around on the stage while he makes choo-choo-like noises, imitating a moving train. Again the mother stops him short.

MOTHER: Look, Casper, I told you once and I'll tell you again: stop this rough play. I can't play this way.

CASPER: All right then. Let's play something else. Let's play "Cops and Robbers." I am the cop. (*In a loud voice*) Hey you! Stick 'em up. You are under arrest!

MOTHER: Casper, I can't play that sort of thing. I am not feeling well, I am tired. Besides, I have to go back into the kitchen and look after the supper. If you don't want to play downstairs with the other children, sit down quietly and do your home work. (*Mother exits*)

CASPER (*watches his mother leave the stage, follows her with his eyes, and slowly shakes his head*): Children, I don't know what this means. Mother always used to play with me. We always had so much fun. But lately Mom doesn't play with me. Whenever I want to play with her, she pushes me away, tells me that my games are too rough. She is always tired, she does not feel well. I wonder what's up. . . . Could it be that mother is sick and needs a doctor?

Various answers from the audience may come forth at this point. Some of the children tell Casper that he should not be such a sissy and not to depend too much on his mother. They tell him to forget about it and to play with the other children. Some of the children seem to be concerned about Casper's mother and tell him to be kind to her and help her instead of being so rough.

CASPER: Well, I really don't know what to say. I think that maybe she should go to a doctor and find out what is wrong with her.

MOTHER (*reappears on stage*): Casper, darling, dinner is nearly ready. Daddy will be home soon. Go to the bathroom, wash your hands and face, and don't forget to go to the toilet.

CASPER: Oh, mother dear. Why should I all of a sudden wash myself? You always wash my hands and face for me. Why not do it again today?

MOTHER: No, Casper. You are getting to be a big boy and you have to learn to do these things by yourself. Now run along.

CASPER: I don't want to. You come with me. You open my pants, put me on the toilet, and then you wash me. Please!

MOTHER: Casper, I am surprised at you. Run along and do the things I told you to do. Daddy will be home soon, and we all want to be ready when he comes.

CASPER (*acting like a little cry-baby*): Ah, come on, mother dear. You always used to do these things for me. Do it again!

At this point, the children in the audience usually take Casper to task for acting like a baby. They tell him that since he already goes to school, he should be able to care for his toilet needs and be able to wash himself. Casper does not like what he is told by his audience and tells the children that they are jealous because their mothers do not take such good care of them. The more he begs his mother to wash him and put him on the toilet, however, the more firmly his mother rejects his pleas.

MOTHER: Look, my darling son. I told you several times that you have to do these things yourself. You are a big boy. You have to learn to do things yourself.

CASPER: But I don't want to grow up. I don't want to learn to do things myself. I want to be your little boy and I want you to be my dear mommy who does everything for me.

MOTHER (*laughing*): Look, my dear Casper. I am glad to hear that you like me so much. You cannot, however, always be a little boy. You are growing up and now you have to learn to do things yourself.

CASPER: But why do I have to learn these things now? Why can't you wait till next year?

MOTHER (*sighs*): Well, Casper, there is something I want to tell you and I might just as well tell it to you right now. You have noticed that lately I have been tired and not feeling well, and that I have been unable to play with you as much as I used to.

CASPER: Yes, that is true. I have been scared because I thought that maybe you were sick and needed a doctor.

MOTHER (*laughs and touches Casper's head*): You don't have to be scared. I am not sick. But there is a reason for my not feeling well and for teaching you to do things on your own. You see, before long you will have a baby brother or a baby sister!

CASPER: A baby brother or a baby sister? . . . What has that to do with you?

MOTHER: Well, I tell you. I am carrying a little baby under my heart and that is the reason why I get tired so easily and that's why I can't play with you.

CASPER: Is that all? That's simple. Just take the baby out from under your heart. Then you won't be tired any more and you can play with me again!

MOTHER (*laughing*): No, Casper. It isn't as easy as all that. The baby has to stay there till it is ready to come out. . . . But the way you talk . . . aren't you glad to get a baby brother or a baby sister?

CASPER (*sulking*): No, I am not glad. I don't want anybody else in here. Mother, I want you and you alone. I don't want nobody else around here in the house.

MOTHER (*hugging Casper*): Don't worry. I'll always be your mother and I'll always like you. But I think it would be very nice for you to have a little brother or a little sister.

FATHER (*enters*): Hello everybody. Hello, mother. (*Kisses her*) Hello, Casper. (*Pats him on the head*)

MOTHER: Hello, father.

CASPER: Hello, father.

MOTHER: Casper, quickly run upstairs and get washed so that we can eat.

CASPER: Come on, mother, you wash me.

FATHER: What do I hear? A big boy like Casper can't wash himself? Casper, you are getting to be a big boy. Don't you want to be a detective on the police force like your dad?

CASPER: Yes, daddy, but I want mother to wash me.

FATHER: Now run along and get washed while I take off my shoes and put on my slippers. (*Father exits*)

CASPER (*whispering*): Come on, mother, wash me.

MOTHER (*in loud voice*): Casper, I told you before that you are going to be a big boy. Go and wash yourself.

FATHER'S VOICE OFF STAGE: Casper, stop being a baby. Go and wash yourself before I come out and wash you. I can teach you in a hurry how to be a big boy. (*Casper exits*)

FATHER (*re-enters*): Well, darling how are you? You look tired. Suppose you take a little nap. I'll see to it that Casper gets his dinner. You go to bed and I'll bring you your food as soon as you are in bed.

MOTHER: Thank you so much, my darling. I would like to rest up a little, but the dishes have to be washed after dinner.

FATHER: Don't worry about that. Casper and I will wash the dishes after we eat. You go and lie down. Casper and I will do the rest.

Mother kisses father, thanks him for his concern about her, and exits. Father exits too. Casper re-enters. He sings in a loud voice, "The farmer in the dell." The father rushes in.

FATHER: Casper! Shhh! Your mother is not feeling well. She is trying to sleep. Be quiet. Don't make any noise, otherwise you wake her up. Sit down quietly and read until I call you in for dinner. *(Father exits)*

CASPER: Yeah! Be quiet. Don't make any noise. That's all I hear now. Mother can't play with me. Nobody washes me. Everything I have to do myself. What for? All because there will be a little baby in the family. . . . I don't want a baby brother or a baby sister. . . . See what happens? Nobody has time for me, nobody cares for me. . . . Why do I have to grow up now? Why can't I still be my mother's baby? . . .

FATHER *(off stage)*: Casper, come into the dining room, dinner is on the table!

CASPER: All right! *(Exits. Curtain is drawn at end of Act I)*

Act II

The stage is empty when the curtain opens. The mother is heard off stage singing, "Rock-a-bye, Baby." She enters the stage still singing, holding a little baby in her arms. While she finishes her song, she gently places the baby into a small doll-house bed on the stage. (The bed is important because without it, the children are very quick to criticize the mother for putting the baby on the floor.)

MOTHER: Hello, children! This is Casper's little baby sister. Isn't she sweet? Oh, we are sooo glad to have her. She really is an angel. *(Looking at the baby)* Oh, my little one is tired and wants to sleep. . . . Mother will take care of that. *(To the children)* Children, will you do me a favor and help to put the little baby to sleep? . . . . Thanks, that's very nice of you. Let's all sing "Rock-a-bye, baby!" [3]

As a rule, the children sing with the mother.

MOTHER: Thank you so much, my children. Now my little baby is sound asleep. Shhh! Don't make any noise now; let's keep quiet so that my baby can sleep and I can do my housework.

Mother exits. The audience is quiet. Enter Casper, singing at the top of his voice: "Four and twenty blackbirds baked in a pie." Mother rushes in and grabs Casper.

MOTHER: Casper, keep quiet. The baby is sleeping.

CASPER: Hello, mother. *(In a rapid way)* Hello, hello. Good morning, good night, good evening, good afternoon, good morning, good night, hello!

MOTHER: Casper! Stop that nonsense and keep quiet. Can't you see that the baby is asleep?

---

[3] The success of this show has been greatly enhanced by the rich, professionally trained voice of Mrs. Margaret Greene, who played the female roles in these shows.

CASPER: Well, it is good that the baby is sleeping. Now you will have time to play with me.

Casper grabs his mother and whirls her around on the stage while he sings, "Have you ever seen a lassie go this way and that way." The mother stops him.

MOTHER: Casper, how often must I tell you not to be so wild. I have no time to play with you. I have work to do.

CASPER: Ah, come on, mom, just a little play. *(Pleading)* Let's play "Cops and Robbers." I am the cop. *(In a loud voice)* Stick 'em up. You are under arrest!

MOTHER: Stop this, I say. Stop it right now. The baby is sleeping and I don't have time to play with you. When the baby sleeps I have a chance to do my work. You know that. . . . Suppose you take a little nap yourself.

CASPER: Who? Me? Take a nap? Who do you think I am, a little baby? I don't want to sleep. I want to play.

MOTHER *(in a kind voice)*: Come on, my little boy. You know that mother knows best. Take a little nap and rest up.

Casper refuses to comply and to lie down. The mother gently pushes him down into a lying position.

MOTHER: Close your eyes and go to sleep like a good little boy.

CASPER: Do I have to close both eyes, or can I keep one eye open.

MOTHER: Close both eyes.

CASPER *(sits up)*: Do I have to lie down or can I sleep sitting up?

MOTHER *(again puts him down into a lying position)*: Casper, I want you to sleep. Please keep quiet. Close your eyes and sleep.

Casper remains quietly lying down. The mother looks at both her children and then turns to the audience.

MOTHER *(in a soft, almost whispering voice)*: Children, both of my darlings are sleeping now. Please keep quiet so that you do not awaken them. Let's all keep quiet so that I can finish my housework.

Mother exits. Casper lifts his head a little, looks around. When he sees that mother is gone, he gets up and hollers in a loud voice.

CASPER: Hello, hello!

Casper quickly puts down his head while his mother rushes on to the stage.

MOTHER: Who made that noise? Who is trying to wake up my children?

As a rule, the audience remains noncommital. The mother cautions the children to keep quiet and exits. As soon as she is off stage, Casper again gets up and makes loud noises, singing a nursery rhyme. He quickly puts down his head when he sees his mother rushing onto the stage.

MOTHER *(somewhat annoyed)*: Children, didn't I tell you not to make noise? You surely will wake my children.

One or another child in the audience might tell the mother that Casper is the culprit, but the mother looks at Casper and tells the audience that this is impossible, because her son is sleeping. A highly amusing touch is added to this scene when Casper gets up behind his mother's back while she talks to the children in the audience. Casper dances around, but as soon as the mother turns her head from the audience towards him, he again lies down so that the mother never sees him in action. This coordination between the two puppet characters is achieved through a very simple device. The puppeteer playing Casper presses one of his knees against the leg of the puppeteer playing the mother. After Casper has his head down on the stage again, the pressure is released and the other puppeteer knows that now the mother can turn her head to Casper.

While the mother is busy talking to the audience and impressing the children with the importance of keeping quiet, the baby begins to cry.

MOTHER: You see, children, now you woke up my darling baby. (*To the baby in a sweet way*) What's the matter, my darling? Can't you sleep? (*Lifts up the baby and laughs quietly*) Oh, that's it. Baby needs a new diaper. That's all right. Mother will take care of that. Don't cry. Mother will give you a nice dry diaper.

Mother exits. Casper gets up.

CASPER: Children, did you hear that? (*Mimicking mother*) Yeah, that's all right. Mother will fix that. Mother will give you a clean diaper. . . . (*In his regular voice*) Yeah, if the baby makes number one and number two in her diaper, that's all right. I should dare to make number one and number two in my pants. Mother wouldn't say that's all right. I'd get a spanking. . . . Everything the baby does is all right. She cries at night, her diapers stink up the house, she always comes first. Everybody has time for her, but nobody has time for me. . . . Hey, I have an idea. . . . You remember how quickly mother picked up the baby when that little brat cried? . . . I have it. I am going to cry too, and then mother will come in and take care of me.

Casper begins to cry, but his mother does not come.

As a deviation from the ordinary plot we at times did let the mother come in and look at her son. As soon as she realizes that his crying is nothing but an attention-getting device, she scolds him and calls him a cry-baby. She also tells him that she is much too busy to treat him like a little baby and reprimands him for causing her unnecessary work. In the original script, Casper cries but the mother does not come.

CASPER (*in a crying voice*): You see, children, how much my mother cares for me? When the baby cried she stopped her work and right away took care of her. I am her child, too, but does she come and look at me? NO! I can cry my eyes out but she wouldn't bother. . . . I hate this little brat of a sister of mine. Everything was all right before she came, but look at the mess now. Everybody makes a fuss over her and says that she is pretty. . . . Yeah! Pretty! She has no hair on her head, no teeth in her mouth, and she can't even talk. . . . I can talk. I can write my name, I can even make a somersault, but does anybody ever look at me? . . . . Oh, here comes mother. I better make believe I'm sleeping.

Casper quickly puts down his head while mother enters with the baby in her arms.

MOTHER: Well, little darling. Everything is under control now. Mother gave you a nice clean diaper and now you can sleep some more.

Mother looks at Casper.

MOTHER: I see that my big boy is still sleeping. That's good. Now I can finish my work. Children, please be quiet and do not wake up my children.

Mother exits. With his head still down, Casper asks the children if his mother has left. When he is told that she has gone, he gets up and walks over to the baby.

CASPER: Well, little stinker. Do you feel better now with a clean diaper. . . . That's all you are good for, making number one and two in your diaper. Mother can't play with me because she always has to change and wash your diapers. . . . Don't look at me that way, stupid. Why don't you say anything? Why did you come here in the first place? Didn't you know that I was here first? Why don't you go back where you came from? I hate you. You are nothing but trouble to me. I hate you. Do you hear me? Don't look at me in that stupid way. I am going to hit you.

Casper has talked himself into a rage and slaps his baby sister. The baby begins to cry. Casper quickly puts down his head while his mother rushes on the stage.

MOTHER (*picks up the baby*): What is it now, my darling. . . . No, your diaper still is dry. . . . Why are you crying, my darling?

At this point, there will always be some children in the audience who tell the mother that Casper hit his baby sister. Since Casper pretends to be sleeping, the mother does not believe what the children are telling her.

MOTHER: Maybe the baby has some gas pains.

While the mother gently pats the baby, the baby stops crying.

MOTHER: See darling, it's all over now. Go back to sleep.

The mother puts the baby back into the crib.

MOTHER: Mmmmh! I nearly forgot. I have to do some shopping for supper. Shall I send out Casper? No, he is too small yet to buy and carry all the things I need. I had better go myself and let Casper take care of his baby sister. . . . Casper, wake up!

Casper doesn't move. The mother walks over to him and shakes him gently.

MOTHER: Come on, Casper, dear. It's time to get up.

CASPER (*yawns*): Mother, I don't want to go to school today. Let me sleep a little longer.

MOTHER (*laughs*): Come on, little silly boy. This is not school time. It is late in the afternoon. Mother has some shopping to do and she wants her big boy to take care of his little baby sister while mother is out.

Casper gets up.

CASPER: All right, I'll take care of her.

MOTHER: That's the boy. You watch while mother is out. Should the baby wake up and start crying, give her the bottle. You will find her milk bottle in the icebox. I won't be long. Good-by!

Mother exits. Casper looks in the direction of her exit as if watching her. After he is sure that she has left the house, he turns to the baby.

CASPER: Dad is working and mother is out of the house. Now is my chance to get even with you. I told you that I don't want you around. Now is my chance to get rid of you. (*To the children*) Children, what shall I do with my bratty baby sister? . . .

This is the time for the children in the audience fully to express their own feelings of aggression. Through the years, we have collected some choice suggestions, such as killing the baby with a knife, throwing it out the window, burning it up in the oven, and stuffing it down the toilet bowl. Also, each audience usually contains children who identify with the baby and who plead with Casper not to harm the baby. "You wouldn't like it if you were a baby and your sister was in your place," is usually their strongest argument. Casper listens while these various suggestions come forth from the audience.

CASPER: Thank you, children, for trying to help me out. I'd like to do what you tell me but I can't. You know that my father is a detective. If I kill my baby sister, he and all the other detectives will find out soon that I did it and they will have to take me to prison. If I go to prison I can't be with my mother and I don't gain anything. There must be some other way. . . . Let me think. . . . I have it. Before, my mother used to tell me fairy tales about witches and everything. Suppose I call the witch! When she comes, I give her the baby and nobody will know what has happened to the baby. Nobody will know where the baby is. My mother will forget about the baby and then I'll be her child again and she will play with me again. Yes, that's what I'll do. Witch . . . WITCH! . . . . WITCH!

Witch appears.

WITCH: Who is calling me?

CASPER: Oh, hello, dear witch. I have been calling you.

WITCH: What do you want?

CASPER: Come over here and take a look. See this baby? She is a nuisance and a pest. I want you to take the baby away so that nobody will know where the brat is.

WITCH: I don't take babies. Why do you want to give away your baby sister?

CASPER: I want to give you a present. Please take her. We don't need her. She is a pest. She stinks up the house with her diapers. She cries at night. She is too much work for my mother. Please take her. We really don't need her.

WITCH: No, I don't take babies.

CASPER: Please, please, take her. I give you all the lollipops I have and I give you my weekly allowance.

WITCH: MMMMMH! I see that you want to get rid of this baby. I don't take babies with me, but I can do something else. Where is the baby's milk bottle?

CASPER: It is in the ice box. I'll get it for you.

Casper exits and returns with the milk bottle.

WITCH (*moves her hands over the bottle and the baby*):
Hokus, pokus, three and twenty,
Here is witchcraft good and plenty.
Let this baby drink this milk, hick!
The milk is sour and the baby will get sick.
Ha, haha, hahahahahahah!

Witch disappears. Casper and baby alone on the stage.

CASPER: Hey, witch! Where are you? What am I supposed to do with this milk? . . . . The witch is gone, but she cast a spell on the milk. I'll give the milk to the baby and see what will happen.

Casper feeds the baby with the milk bottle. The baby begins to cry. Casper hears his mother re-enter the apartment and quickly hides the milk bottle. The mother rushes in and picks up the baby.

MOTHER (*anxious*): My darling, what happened? Why are you crying so? Oh, my goodness (*Mother begins to cry herself*) The baby is blue all over. What has happened? My baby is sick. I have to rush her to the hospital immediately. I'll never forgive myself if anything should happen to my darling. Why didn't I stay with her!

Mother, still crying, rushes off stage with the baby in her arms. Casper has been standing by silently, watching his mother's reaction.

At this point we usually draw the curtain and ask the children what should happen next. For the sake of continuity, the full show is described here.

CASPER (*after a brief period of silence*): Children, did you hear my mother cry? She is terribly upset. What am I to do now? If the doctors in the hospital find out what happened, my mother will never forgive me. If she knows that I tried to kill my baby sister, she'll never speak to me again, she'll never love me anymore. Children, quick, help me. What can I do to stop my baby sister from dying? She must live, or my mother won't love me any more. My mother might even send me away to prison or to some special school and I'll never see her again.

The children usually suggest that Casper recall the witch.

CASPER: That's a good idea. I call her and ask her to take off the spell. . . . . Witch! . . . . Witch! . . . . WITCH!

Witch reappears.

WITCH: Who is calling me now?

CASPER: I have been calling you.

WITCH: What do you want now?

CASPER *(half crying)*: I made a terrible mistake by letting you put a spell on the baby. Please let my baby sister be better again.

WITCH: You are a foolish boy. First you want me to make your baby sister sick, and now you want me to make your baby sister better again. What nonsense is that? Do you think that I waste my time just running back and forth making babies sick and healthy? Hahaha! No, young man, I don't make babies better. I only make them sick, and once they are sick, ... they DIE! Hahahahahahah!

CASPER: You mean to say that my baby sister is going to die?

WITCH: You heard me.

CASPER: Please don't let her die. I give you all the toys I have and all the candy I ever get, and my allowance too, but please don't let anything happen to my baby sister. I am sooo sorry about what I did.

WITCH *(very brusque)*: Nonsense. You heard what I said. Your baby sister is going to die.

Casper exits and quickly reappears with a stick.

CASPER: If my baby sister is going to die, you are going to die with her. *Casper beats up the witch. The witch cries for mercy, but Casper hits her relentlessly. He stops every so often and asks the witch if she is ready to remove the spell. As long as the witch refuses he continues beating her, until finally, the witch promises to remove the spell. As soon as the witch has said some magic words and Casper is reassured that his baby sister will live, he again hits the witch, and this time, he kills her.*

CASPER: Wow! That was some job. I had to kill her, because if she had gotten away, she could have cast another spell on the baby and the baby would have died. She also could have put a spell on all of us and we all could have died. This way, she is dead and she won't be able to harm us anymore. . . . I can't keep the dead witch lying around the house. I'd better get rid of her before my dad comes home. Children, are you sticking with me or are you going to snitch on me to my parents?

After Casper has been reassured that the children will not tell on him, he picks up the witch and exits.

The father enters.

FATHER: Hello, mother; hello, Casper. . . . Where is everybody? Nobody seems to be home. . . .

Before some children have a chance to tell the father what has happened, Casper returns.

CASPER: Hello, Daddy.

FATHER: Hello, Casper. Where is mother? I don't see her anywhere.

CASPER: You can't see her. She went to the hospital.

FATHER *(greatly surprised)*: To the hospital? Which one? Who is sick? Where is the baby?

CASPER: That's what I am trying to tell you. The baby took sick, so mother rushed her to the hospital.

FATHER: That sounds terrible. I hope it is nothing serious. What hospital did mother go to? I am going there myself to find out.

As the father exits, he is met by the mother, who returns with the baby in her arms.

FATHER: Oh, hello, mother. I was just on my way to the hospital to find out what happened.

MOTHER: Oh, hello, father. Hello, Casper. Don't worry, the baby is all right, but I had some excitement. . . .

CASPER: Hello, mother.

FATHER *(interrupts)*: Here, let me hold the baby while you sit down and tell us.

The mother hands the baby to the father.

MOTHER: I went out to do some shopping. When I came back, the baby was crying and turning blue all over, so I took her to the hospital right away. The doctors there examined my little darling and said that the baby had an upset stomach, probably from bad milk. They gave the baby some medicine and she stopped crying right away. Her real color came back, her temperature came down to normal, and now she is sleeping for a little while. But I really got frightened when I first saw her.

FATHER: I am very glad that it wasn't anything more serious. But where did the baby get the bad milk?

MOTHER: Oh, I don't know. Maybe our icebox needs fixing. Maybe the milk was old and I didn't notice it. I bought some fresh milk on the way home, and I got something else. Casper, darling, aren't you glad that your baby sister is well?

CASPER: Yes, mother, I am. I was scared when I saw you crying before.

MOTHER: Don't be scared anymore. Everything is all right. Casper, I brought a surprise for you. Can you guess what it might be?

CASPER: Another baby sister?

MOTHER *(laughing)*: No, no, not so fast. Let's give this little one a chance to grow up. I'll give you a hint. It has something to do with strawberries.

CASPER: Strawberry shortcake?

MOTHER: No!

CASPER: Strawberry long-cake.

MOTHER: No, Casper. It is strawberry ice cream.

CASPER (*embraces his mother*): Thanks, mom dear. That is very sweet of you to think about me.

MOTHER: Why shouldn't I? I am so happy that both of my children are all right that I feel like having a little celebration.

CASPER: Mother, may I hold my baby sister too?

MOTHER: Certainly my pet. Daddy, give the baby to Casper and please help me to fix the ice cream in the kitchen.

Father gives the baby to Casper, who holds her in his arms. Father and mother exit. Casper is alone on the stage with the baby.

CASPER: Children, I am very glad that everything turned out so well. If I hadn't killed the old witch, my baby sister would be dead by now and maybe all of us would be sick. I'll be a good boy from now on. Little babies are only little, not as grown up as I am. They can't do a thing for themselves and they need a mother to look after them. As long as mother is not cross with me, I'll be a good boy. I'll help mother so that my baby sister can grow up. . . . You aren't angry with me anymore, children, are you? . . . . That's good. . . . Oh, my little baby sister is yawning. She wants to sleep some more. Children, please do me a favor and help me sing her to sleep. Let's all sing "Rock-a-bye, Baby."

When the song is finished, the curtain closes and the mother's voice is heard off stage, calling Casper to eat his ice cream.

FOLLOW-UP IN THERAPY

This complete text might stimulate one or more readers to play this show for a group of children. Whoever undertakes such a task should be aware of the fact that he is handling dynamite that might explode at the wrong moment. This show stirs up anxieties and brings to a conscious, tangible level latent hostilities and repressed fantasies, the handling of which calls for professional skill and understanding of children's problems in general. The show should be produced only if the puppeteer is a trained therapist, or if he has professionally trained persons with him who are able to discuss and to analyze the contents with the children. Each child who has seen the show should be given a chance to discuss it and to act out, as much as possible, any particular part that seems troublesome to him. If the group or individual discussion is not sufficient, a child might be encouraged to draw pictures about the show, to model scenes out of plasticine, or to act out, either with puppets or with other children, some of the contents of the show.

In the beginning of our puppet work at Bellevue, we played the full show in a somewhat different form. Numerous changes were made, based on the reactions and recommendations of the children in the audience. Among other things, we discovered that the ending was rather flat. The children were not fully reassured that Casper's mother really loved her son. Several children remarked that their mothers bring home ice cream whenever they want to show real love and affection. This clue was incorporated in the ending with good results. The bringing home of ice cream, from then on, really demonstrated to our children that Casper's mother harbored no hostility toward her son. This little incident is mentioned to point out that most puppet shows for children, no matter how skillfully written, do not seem to be perfect unless groups of children have a chance to discuss various possibilities and to rearrange the content. This process may be repeated several times, until finally a show emerges that seems to be acceptable to children of various age levels.

The so-called *half-show* offered us an excellent opportunity to use these puppet shows as a truly psychotherapeutic measure. It was indicated that in the *full show* the curtain might be drawn when Casper's mother rushes her sick baby to the hospital. The children are told that the real ending will be played at some other time. Instead of finishing the show at this moment, the children are asked to say what they think could, should, or might happen. These discussions can be carried out with the whole group. We found it expedient, however, to break up our audience of approximately 50 children, ranging in age from 3 to 11 years, into small groups of five to eight children of approximately the same age.

In a typical *group discussion,* the therapist first gives a brief resume of the contents of the show, leading up to the part where the show was terminated. Each child is then asked to relate in his own words what he or she thinks should take place now. These endings are recorded. After each child has told his story, a more general discussion follows. The children are asked, "Will Casper's mother know that Casper was responsible for the baby's illness?" If she does know, "Will she forgive him?" If she does not forgive him, "What form of punishment will Casper receive from his mother?" "Will the father know what took place?" "Will he punish Casper or will he forgive him?" "Was Casper right in hating his baby sister?" "Was Casper right in killing the witch?" The stories the children tell and the answers they give to the diverse questions will automatically lead to the formulation of new questions.

Although the puppet shows themselves carry strong cathartic values, the real therapeutic nature of puppetry lies in the follow-up. It is here that each child will discuss Casper's problems in terms of his own knowledge or insight, his own family constellation, and his own problems and maladjustments. While discussing the problems of the puppets, the child is spared the embarrassing situation of talking about himself and his own family.[4] While he listens to others, he realizes that there might be several solutions to a problem. He also learns, sometimes with great surprise, that he is not the only one who has difficulties. The group exchange of thoughts brings the children closer together and forges them into a unit that tries to solve some very basic human problems. Most children are amazed when they learn that there is more than one solution to a problem, and that problems in general can be solved. They further realize that it is perfectly permissible to discuss deviant behavior openly. The material elicited during these group discussions also provides good starting points for follow-up individual therapy.

So far, this chapter has described puppet shows *for* children. What happens when children themselves *give* a puppet show? Education has realized the value of puppet shows in the curriculum. In these endeavors, puppetry becomes a group project in which the whole class participates. Puppets are made, stories are selected and rehearsed, and the final performance constitutes the crowning achievement of perhaps a term's work. These puppet shows in schools certainly have definite value, but they lack one prerequisite that would make them truly therapeutic devices, and that is spontaneity. Memorizing of lines and careful training in the handling of the puppets does not allow for spontaneous dramatic shows. If puppets are to be used therapeutically, there should be a minimum of instructions to a child or to a group of children and then the children should play out whatever they like. In the nursery group, there will be found a great deal of aggressive behavior. The spoken language will be at a minimum but the puppets may

_____

4 Note that the opportunity to discuss the problems of the puppets is consistent with the emphasis on anonymity of the doll characters in individual therapy with children, discussed by Solomon in Chapter 22 [Editors].

engage in endlessly repetitious hitting and beating of each other. The older the child, the more balanced his performance will become. Under no circumstances should a group of children be expected to perform a show that adheres to dramatic syntax and the developing of a problem. Since one deals with spontaneous dramatic presentations, one should analyze the contents of the show and not criticize the children for omissions or for lack of or failure to develop a dramatic plot.

In the puppet shows given by children at Bellevue Hospital, we were forever amazed to find that these children seldom repeated parts of the show they had seen. On the contrary, they usually acted out scenes that had no relationship to the shows put on by the puppeteers. Careful analysis of these children's shows revealed in every instance that the children acted out their own problems.

Puppetry is a group activity in the true sense of the word. It brings to a group of children basic human problems in a dramatic form, but unlike the movie or the theater, the child himself becomes part of the show. His suggestions are accepted by the puppets as a valid contribution. Instead of being forced to go alone through a dramatic experience, he is sheltered and protected by the group about him. The protection of the group is not valuable in childhood alone, but seems to form a soothing component throughout our adult years. The real meaning of this for adults has been described by the writer [11]. The child, within the sanctuary of the group, feels free to express himself without being singled out. He also witnesses others about him being interested in the same problems and becoming involved in the dramatic content in various degrees.

Motor tension may run high within the group. Children may disagree with one another and fight it out right then and there. Other children may run toward the stage and help one puppet to beat up another puppet. Still others may rise in their seats, flex their muscles, and imitate the action on the stage. The observance of this behavior is very valuable for follow-up interviews and therapeutic discussions.

SUMMARY

Puppets are divided into three large groups: shadow puppets, string puppets or marionettes, and hand puppets. The advantages and limitations of each are discussed.

The hand or glove type, commonly used in Punch and Judy shows, permits direct manipulation and quick action. One puppeteer can manipulate two puppets at the same time. This type of puppet is especially adaptable for use in shows for children. A suitable stage is necessary for each of the three types of puppet.

Writing a hand puppet play is as difficult as writing a book for children. Desirable and undesirable factors and characteristics are discussed.

The psychological rationale for types of characters and for plot is presented. Close interaction between the puppets and the audience is a prerequisite for a successful show with children. A puppet show for disturbed children stirs up anxieties and brings to a conscious level latent hostilities and repressed fantasies, the handling of which calls for professional skill and understanding.

Examples of two scripts used for therapeutic purposes with children are presented and interpreted. These shows should be produced only if the puppeteer is a trained therapist or if he has professionally trained persons with him who are able to discuss and to analyze the contents with the children.

Although the puppet shows themselves carry strong cathartic values, the real therapeutic nature of puppetry lies in the follow-up discussions. The material elicited during group discussions also provides good starting points for follow-up individual therapy.

The therapeutic application of puppetry, like that of so many other projective techniques, has not been evaluated statistically for validity and reliability. Future experiments may provide scientific proof for the factors that so far have been used only clinically. On an empirical level, puppetry has been found to be extremely helpful in the understanding of the etiology of maladjustment in childhood. It also constitutes a very valuable therapeutic technique through which groups of children can learn to understand the complexities of deviating behavior and to find solutions that promise a more harmonious future.

REFERENCES

1. Batchelder, M., *The Puppet Theatre Handbook.* New York and London: Harper & Brothers, 1947.
2. Beaumont, C. W., *Puppets and the Puppet Stage.* New York: The Studio Publications, Inc., 1938.

3. Bender, L., and Woltmann, A. G., "The use of puppet shows as a psychotherapeutic method for behavior problems in children." *Am. J. Orthopsychiat.*, July 1936, 6, 3, 341–354.

4. ————————, "Puppetry as a psychotherapeutic measure with problem children." New York State A. Occup. Therapy, 1937, 7, 1–7.

5. ————————, "Play and psychotherapy." *The Nervous Child,* Winter 1941–42, 1, 17–42.

6. Jenkins, R. L., and Beckh, E., "Finger puppets and mask-making as media for work with children." *Am. J. Orthopsychiat.*, April 1942, 12, 2, 294–300.

7. Rambert, M. E., "Une nouvelle technique en psychanalyse infantile: Le jeu de guignols." *Revue Francaise Psychanalyse,* 1938, 10, 1.

8. Woltmann, A. G., "The use of puppets in understanding children." *Mental Hygiene,* July 1940, 24, 3, 445–458.

9. ————————, "Puppetry as a means of psychotherapy," in *Encyclopedia of Child Guidance.* New York: The Philosophical Library, 1943.

10. ————————, "Therapeutic Aspects of Puppetry," in Paul Mc-Pharlin (ed.), *Yearbook of Puppetry 1942–43.* Detroit: 1944. Copyright by The Puppeteers of America.

11. ————————, "Life on a target." *Am. J. Orthopsychiat.*, January 1945, 15, 1, 172–177.

CHAPTER 22

Therapeutic Use of Play

Joseph C. Solomon, M.D.

INTRODUCTION

The foregoing chapters have concerned themselves primarily with the use of projective techniques as instruments for the *diagnosis* and *study* of the operations of human personality. This chapter deals with the use of the projective method as a form of *therapy*. As will be pointed out, the phenomenon of projection is not only a matter of academic interest, but is actually the sine qua non of therapeutic work with children.

Projection is a device that the human organism employs in its normal development. As the child experiences sensations or excitations that are unpleasant to him, he has the tendency to transfer these feelings into the outer world. In other words, some sensations that the ego tries to ward off are gotten rid of and experienced as being outside the ego. *Animism,* which is such an integral part of childhood thinking, is a good example of this phenomenon. The child can impart to his teddy bear, to Mickey Mouse, or to any other object, characteristics derived from his own ego. The animated objects can have emotions and experiences similar to his own, thereby eliminating to some extent the tensions that can arise within him. This device is normally employed by the child to help master anxiety.

Projection, then, becomes one of the defenses employed by the organism to relieve tension. A good example of this is the person who wants to discuss a problem relating to himself but says, "A friend of mine is having some trouble." Similarly, the projective method, by releasing hostile impulses, is used to direct aggression against representative objects and thus, by-pass the true object. This phenomenon gratifies the instinctive demands and at the same time preserves the ego from the retaliation of the victim of aggression. It also tends to establish equilibrium within the individual when there is no other possible outlet for this aggression. A case in point is the hanging in effigy of those feared or hated—Hitler, the Kaiser, or the rival college mascot. Similarly, the historical use of the scapegoat to hide one's guilt is a well-known phenomenon.

There are many examples of the use of projection for various purposes in our culture and in the cultures of other peoples, including the so-called primitive people. The ceremonial customs of other peoples appear to us as being childish, since in some respects, they exhibit many of the phenomena that children manifest in normal play in our culture. It is interesting in this respect that primitive people also look upon many of the things done by the white man as being of a distinctly childish nature. The most familiar example of ritual use of the projective method is the sticking of pins into the wax or clay image of one's enemy.

This phenomenon is so widespread among peoples of the world that to list the instances would take us through all the pages of history and to all parts of the world. We would go from ancient India, Babylon, Egypt, and Greece to the savage peoples of Africa, Australia, and the Pacific Islands, to the voodoo practices among the Negroes in some parts of this country [7]. There is a similarity between the child who releases aggressions against the effigy of a hated person and the sticking of pins in the effigy of one's enemy as practiced by primitive peoples. But there are distinct differences in the concept of the use of magic. It is true that the child's thinking has largely a magical quality. He can master his environment by magically controlling the world through his own actions in the play situation, thereby counteracting to some extent the magical powers that caused his tension in the first place. In the case of primitive people, however, it is not enough merely to feel better in this magical way; there is an actual carrying out of the complete disintegration of the hated person. For this reason, the priest or witch doctor is called upon to use his magic to help the person not only to attain some feeling of equilibrium, but also, to obtain a feeling of revenge by sometimes provoking hostility to such a point that the individual actually kills his enemy. The feelings of hostility are sometimes fortified by ceremonial dances and chants that have the added quality of releasing guilt by sharing the aggressive impulses with the medicine man and with the members of the tribe. To some extent, this happens in the therapeutic situation between the child and the therapist and in the normal situation of group play of children.

Although the practice of projective magic has generally been used in a negative fashion, there are instances where it has been used for positive benefits, dealing mainly with fertility both of humans and of the soil. The throwing of rice at weddings is symbolic: it represents an old custom among primitive people of inducing fertility. Children in playing also use symbols and dances to help approach the real world of adults.

Modern psychiatry and psychology have learned much from anthropological study. It is one of the goals of all science to explore the unknown, the magical, and the mysterious. Much scientific progress has been made in explaining the nature of the human mind and of human emotion. In our culture, we have developed the concept that human conflicts can be resolved by the use of scientific methods. In former years, human behavior was influenced by the use of applied magic. Today, we are attempting to modify human behavior by the use of scientific means, instead of by calling into play supernatural forces.

Let us proceed from this brief anthropological reference to a short history of the growth and development of play therapy. By working therapeutically with adults suffering from various forms of neurotic disorder, workers in the field of human behavior learned that the difficulties dated back to early childhood. As a consequence, they turned to an approach to the child for two reasons: to study psychic development, and to treat the nervous child in an effort to prevent adult neurosis. It was found that the classical psychoanalytic approach used with adults did not work well with children, since children do not learn the technique of free association easily. Rather, they express their thoughts and feelings by action.

Quite some time ago, Rousseau [18] tried to understand the psychology of the child through observing his play. Play therapy, as applied to the psychopathology of the child, dates back to Von Hug-Hellmuth [21]. Since then, many studies in the personality development of children have been conducted at various universities, schools, and clinics, and by private investigators.

In Europe, play technique became an integral part of child analysis. Two schools of thought grew out of the work in this field, the so-called Viennese School, built around the contributions of Anna Freud [8] and some of her outstanding disciples; and the English School, based on the thinking of Melanie Klein [10] and her followers. The essential difference between the two is in the approach to the child. Anna Freud approaches the child slowly and establishes a close human relationship before attempting to determine the child's intimate thought processes. Melanie Klein, on the other hand, is very direct in her early interviews and uses deep interpretation of symbolic material at early stages of therapy.

As the years go on, however, there seems to be greater uniformity of opinion as to the usefulness of various methods of approach. In the United States, there has been a certain amount of child analysis practiced, primarily by the followers of these two European schools. But more prominent in this country has been the development of the Child Guidance Clinic. The essential difference between child analysis and therapy in a child guidance clinic is this: in child analysis, the analyst sees the child daily or almost daily, while in the guidance clinic, the child is seen less frequently, and disciplines other than direct therapy with the child may be introduced. For example, one or both parents may be seen by the psychiatric social worker or by another therapist. There environmental changes may be made, and so forth.

The author wishes to emphasize the following point: academic interest and superficial knowledge do *not* make a therapist. Anyone who is to work with children in therapy should receive a carefully supervised training. The ideal therapist should be a child analyst. In other words, not all psychoanalysts are equipped to treat children, but all child therapists should be psychodynamically trained.

INDIRECT THERAPY

Although this chapter is devoted to the subject of play as a therapeutic device in the treatment of the emotional problems of children, the author wishes to mention the fact that this is not the only tool used for the purpose. It constitutes only one part of the therapeutic program. It is what is spoken of as *direct* therapy.

Indirect therapy refers to the therapeutic work with the parents and to other means of influencing the child's external environment.

There is no question about the importance of working out the emotional problems of the parents whenever it is possible, especially those problems that have reflected themselves in the handling of the child. In very young children, perhaps below the age of four or five years, the problems of growing up can be fairly well dissipated when more wholesome attitudes are developed by the parents. Older children, too, profit from improved parental attitudes. It is a well-known observation that even adolescents may show remarkable improvement in behavior and personality as the parent matures emotionally during psychoanalysis. However, there seems to be a critical age, variable, to be sure, when certain fairly well fixed patterns of disturbed thought seem to go on even when the parental attitudes are materially improved. This is attributable to the fact that the child suffers from the already internalized parent, who continues to give him difficulty.

An improved attitude in the child is not always effected exclusively through the relationship established between parent and therapist. It is also achieved in a subtle, indirect way when the child is placed in therapy. Parents relax to a great extent when they have called in assistance in the management of a disturbed child. Direct therapy with the child invites the parents to take serious inventory of themselves; they realize that they are objects of discussion between the child and his doctor.

There are some children who live in such disturbed environments that no amount of direct therapeutic work can overcome the constant barrage of emotional blows they are receiving. Play technique can only be useful in ridding the child of past traumatic or mistaken ideas about the world in which he lives. When the home situation is such that no amount of therapeutic work with the parents can alleviate the situation, that is, when the parent is psychotic, brutal, or alcoholic, then a major environmental change such as placement in a foster home or institution becomes necessary. The projective method of play therapy is not a panacea for all childhood problems.

With these reservations firmly established, the subject of play therapy will be discussed from two points of view—*content* and *relationship*.

Fig. 1. Food Interest: food interest is often an excellent medium of approach to the child. Through food, the child's oral preoccupation can be determined. Scenes that arise at the dinner table are often reenacted. By following leads afforded by the child, much valuable information concerning the interpersonal relationships in the home can be elicited. Interviews are kept in the third person as long as necessary.*

CONTENT OF PLAY THERAPY

It has been reported that play is the natural language of the child. An expression of early cortical development of the child is the use of symbols. This symbolization of the vectors that influence the child appears as a modified or miniature replica of the life situation (see Figure 1). It is an effective means by which the child approaches his world of reality. By dealing with things that are small or inanimate, he can master situations that to him are overwhelming. When the child is flooded with a large quantity of

---

* Figures 1, 2, 3, and 5 are from Solomon, J. C., "Active play Therapy," *American Journal of Orthopsychiatry*, 1938. 8:479–498. Used by permission.

excitation, he attempts to get rid of it by subsequent active repetition of the situation that induced it. He thereby minimizes in retrospect the omnipotence of his environment and prepares for the future, thus increasing the powers of his own ego. The child has a tendency to relive symbolically the events that caused him to develop tensions, for example, being scared by a fire engine. He repeats in his own play a pattern of burying his toy fire engine with blocks; it then has less power to scare him. In an atmosphere of comparative security, such a child will heal himself of his own tension. However, when this fear is added to other pre-existing anxieties stemming from disturbances in the interpersonal relationships in the home, the problem becomes more complicated. By utilizing the natural healing device employed by the child, the therapist has a very potent medicine with which to alleviate the child's suffering. When the disturbance is due to isolated events, particularly if they are of comparatively recent origin, re-enactment of these events in effigy has therapeutic value. In such situations, the actual *content* becomes of major importance, and desensitization to the traumatic experiences can take place by releasing the dammed-up surplus affect. This is called *release therapy* by Levy [12]. He discovered that children subjected to a recent anxiety-provoking situation could be given much comfort by recreating the situation in effigy. He found the method effective only when the symptoms followed a specific event or events, and when they were of short duration and in the recent historic past of the child. He stipulated, too, that family relationships must be normal or nearly so.

The therapist can approach the child by entering into his world and discovering the inner reactions to what is happening in his life. It is true that if the therapist allows the child to play in a specifically observed situation, the child will make himself understood through the use of his spontaneous creations. However, many therapists sit back and wait too long for something to happen in the treatment situation, and are quite unable to discern adequately what is going on in the mind of the child. Advantage can be taken of the child's solipsistic naiveté in getting him to elaborate, at great length, many details of his inner life, if the therapist employs the device of keeping the interview situation on a fairly anonymous level (see Figure 2).

Resistance and defense mechanisms are employed by the child in

Fig. 2. Use of Spontaneous Productions. This scene grew out of the construction of a play situation of a child riding the street car. The child spontaneously produced the incident of the accident, in which both the mother doll and the little brother doll were injured. The examiner observed the fantasy unfolding and afforded the child strong support, in order further to elicit the wishes of the girl doll.

order to protect himself against revealing too much of his inner mental processes. Some therapists allow the child free play and take advantage of the slipping of his defenses to reveal him in his true light. For example, when a child shows some form of aggression in doll play by allowing a boy doll to beat up a father doll, and inadvertently says, "my father," some therapists are apt to show him very promptly that that is what he would like to do to his father. Others prefer not to trap the child in this type of disclosure, but to keep the play in the third person, ignore the child's slips, and thereby allow more content to be expressed (see Figure 3). In this way, the therapist gives the child the added comfort of

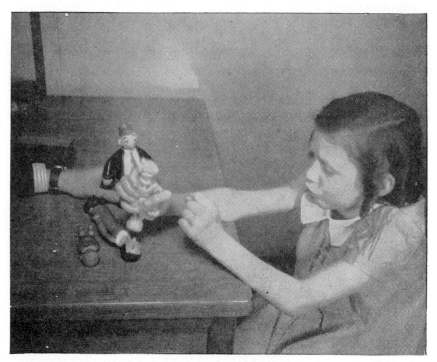

Fig. 3. Overt Display of Aggression. The overt display of aggression gives the child patient the opportunity of abreacting some of the unexpressed emotions. Care must be exercised not to provoke too much anxiety; this is done by keeping the play anonymous and by other guilt-relieving devices.

maintaining his anonymity in a defensive way. By keeping this principle in mind, great leeway of activity on the part of the therapist can be maintained. There need be no particular quarrel as to which of these two approaches is the better, inasmuch as the defenses offered by the child are maintained in both instances. In the last analysis, the child sets his own dosage. However, there is much to be gained in obtaining a great deal of information as to conditions in the home from the content, as revealed by the child when the anonymity is preserved. This enables the therapist to be much more intelligent with the parents, or with the therapist who is working with the parents, in order to help alleviate the pressures currently operating upon the child in his environment. It is the feeling of this writer that therapy with the child is greatly enhanced when the therapist knows at all times what is going on in the home. Therapeutic effectiveness is greater when this information is available, especially when it comes from the mouth of the child. When this is coordinated with the information received from the parents, a truer picture of the dynamic forces can be ascertained.

The opinion has been expressed that activity on the part of the therapist may sometimes be a bit overwhelming and frightening to the child. This criticism is not valid if one uses the activity the way children do themselves. It is not unusual, when children are playing together, to find one child suggesting to the other, "Let's make up a game about so-and-so," or, "Let's pretend such-and-such." This type of suggestion offered by one child often stimulates the fantasy of the other, and a play pattern emerges that is satisfying to both children. By the same token, in active play therapy, the therapist enters into the world of the child by working through situations partially suggested by the child himself. It is evidence of his active interest in the child and his appreciation of what the child may be thinking about. Resistances to revealing inner thought processes are much greater when the therapist waits for the child to produce something. In such a situation, the child is more likely to feel criticized for some of his interests than when the therapist himself seems vitally interested in using the material and engages the child in play on the child's level of performance.

For example, if a situation presents itself in which the therapist can engage the child's play in such things as toilet activities, a considerable freedom is attained. When the therapist participates in such play situations, by providing miniature toilets, diapers, and so on for the doll figures, the anal or urethral interests are relieved of the sense of naughtiness or shame, and normal aggressive and exhibitionistic activities can gain expression. This expression of behavior is useful not only to the child's therapist, but also to the therapist working with the parent. Thus, the statements of the parents can be coordinated with the revelations from the child, making a more complete picture.

Sears [1] and his students [*15, 16*] have been experimenting on the

---

[1] Sears, R. R., Personal communication, July 23, 1947.

relative effectiveness of different variables in doll play of children. His experiments are valid only for the first few interviews, since he rarely conducts his investigations beyond that point. Even with this limited scope, however, he has made some interesting observations. In experiments where the variable was that of high experimenter-child activity versus low experimenter-child activity (passivity), abreactions of an aggressive nature began earlier and were more pronounced in the high activity group. Also, the amount of nonstereotyped thematic play and the number of theme changes were greater under conditions of high interaction between experimenter and child. These experiments point only to greater productivity of content when the therapist takes an active interest and when there is some organized presentation of the materials. The organized presentation, however, does not go so far as to create specific situations. There is little doubt that if specific situations were created, greater activity would be shown, as Levy [11] demonstrated in his sibling rivalry experiments. Specific examples of created-play situations that can be employed are shown in Figures 1, 2, and 3.

Lippman [13] made the observation that children often show greater anxiety in direct interviews than in play. This is true because in play, the child is able to avoid verbal consciousness and communication and to hide his identity, thereby avoiding the potentially punitive actions of the therapist. The child can test out his own awareness as well as the attitudes of the adult, and feel that he is not committing or exposing himself. And yet, in spite of this safeguard, a state of tension may be precipitated. This anxiety may be the result of the child's sudden awareness of the extent of his own wishes. Small doses of anxiety may be regarded as therapeutic, especially if the therapist is kindly and accepting. It is important that when anxiety is released, it is adroitly handled.

RELATIONSHIP IN PLAY THERAPY

The next point to be taken up here is the *relationship* between therapist and child. There is little question that this is the more important aspect of therapy. Even though immediate or manifest anxiety is more easily provoked by active than by passive methods, it is readily relieved by the introduction of a doll representing the therapist, toward which the child can abreact some of his feeling, thus relieving a burden from his superego [*19*]. The therapist doll often becomes the central figure of most of the spontaneous play.

It has been the experience of the writer that a great deal of therapeutic movement can be released when the therapist actively introduces into the play situation the doll representing himself. Even when this is done, the anonymity is preserved for as long a period of time as the child desires, and emotions centering around the therapist-child situation proceed in effigy. Usually, after the therapist doll is introduced into play, it takes on a greater degree of importance in the configuration of the play than even the sibling doll or parent doll figures. Thus, the child uses a relationship much closer to the therapist to air some of the problems resulting from the disturbed interpersonal relationships within the home. As the child releases aggression, either oral or anal in character, or as he expresses tender sentiments, he comes to grips with his instinctive expressions. Guilt feelings or direct fear of punishment become living expressions in the transference situation. As the child survives his own instinctive expressions, he gains greater confidence in all of his human relationships.

The age factor in the use of play technique seems to be of comparatively little importance. Very young children are unable to use this symbolic play because of inability to use symbols, but after cortical development has reached a point where symbolization is employed, the use of doll play to reproduce the inner thought processes is a normal means of communication. The writer has used play technique for children of all ages. Adolescents will sometimes be very much interested in doll technique merely as a playlet or puppet show to illustrate some points that may be difficult to discuss directly.

The interest of children in comics has suggested to the writer the comic strip technique for eliciting the child's fantasy. The child is presented with a blank page blocked off in oblongs like a page in a comic book. He is asked to make up a story with some continuity. If he is resistant, he is shown some stick drawings of a man and lady and a child and asked to make up a story about them. Children who are resistant to the use of dolls frequently find that they are interested in making a set of drawings, and sometimes run a continuous series week after week on a family sequence. In this technique, the therapist is often introduced as another figure either by the child or at the suggestion of the therapist. A typical draw-

Fig. 4. The comic strip technique for eliciting the child's fantasy. (From Kasanin, J., J. C. Solomon, and P. Axelrod, "Extrinsic factors in the treatment of anxiety states in children," in the American Journal of Orthopsychiatry, *12:439, 1942. Used by permission.)*

ing by the use of the technique is shown in Figure 4.

The first picture shows a boy riding down the street on his bicycle (patient had just been given a bicycle, bought through the efforts of the social worker). Patient insisted that this represented another boy, not himself. In the second picture, the boy is supposed to have passed a red light on purpose. A car, driven by the therapist, is coming down the street. Patient said that he himself was standing on the corner. The car strikes the boy on the bicycle and kills him. A crowd gathers. Patient said he pointed his finger at the therapist, accusing him of killing the boy. The crowd joins in pointing their fingers at the therapist. A policeman then arrests the therapist. Patient expressed keen delight with the next picture, depicting the therapist in jail. There is a trial, he is found guilty, and is sentenced to the electric chair. The next picture shows a tombstone in a cemetery. All the other persons are sobbing, but patient shows himself laughing merrily. The next action consists of the therapist coming back to life in the form of a Zombie. It comes at patient at night with a knife, to get revenge. He was expecting something like this to happen and hid in the closet after placing a dummy in the bed. Prepared with a long knife that has poison on it, patient kills the Zombie for all time.

It must be remembered that the relationship between the therapist and child *forms;* it is not constructed. It is an outgrowth of the child's tacit admissions as well as of the interest and understanding expressed by the therapist. The child wants to be understood and is much more aware of unwholesome attitudes than he openly expresses. By bringing his thoughts into the open impersonally, the child lessens his need for concealment. Thus, new energies are released and utilized constructively by the body economy.

Erikson [5] states that deeper conflicts find their projection in formal patterns of play that complement the specific content. He has shown also that when emotionally charged experiences are brought to the surface, the child shows a disruption in the continuity of play. When play patterns are disruptive, or, as has been the writer's observation, when a child is extremely repetitious about a play configuration, the therapist should suspect that the attitudes within the home are still pathological. Well-conducted play sessions should show movement in the dynamics and behavior of the child. When lack of movement is observed, it may be that the child is being subjected to new emotional traumata. He does not get the chance to rid himself of old hurts before new insults to his psyche are perpetrated.

Enlightenment along sexual lines has been considered a major factor in the therapy of the child. In our culture, it is rare to find a child who suffers because of the lack of knowledge concerning sex differences, the birth of babies, and so on. It is only when misinformation has had a pathological effect that the question of enlightenment assumes great importance. Alexander [1] points out that if the misinformation includes the prospect of someone's being hurt, the child suffers. This is particularly true when the fantasies intensify the child's Oedipal conflict.

Considerable attention should be paid to the defense mechanisms of the child. It must be remembered that these forces are not as firmly entrenched in the child as in the adult. Some therapists feel that nothing should be done about removing defense mechanisms, but rather, that the child be encouraged to grow by building new and stronger defenses against his fears. This should not be taken at face value, especially if we consider regression to anal or oral performance, or withdrawal into fantasy, as methods of defense. Certainly, we should not strengthen these defenses, because they are the presenting symptoms for which the child may have been brought for treatment. More can be said on this subject but would distract from the purpose of this presentation.

When a child feels that he is understood and is comfortable with this understanding, the therapist becomes very important to him. This importance, in some instances, makes the therapist a *new* parent, offering *new* sets of instinctive gratifications and *new* superego values. In other cases, the therapist is invested with the qualities of the actual parent and is treated as a transference figure, as in adult analysis. In the role of the parent figure, the therapist is invested with omnipotence. This power, which formerly may have been an overwhelming punishing force, may now become a medium of protection against real or fancied dangers. Thus, the relationship between therapist and the child can become a valuable growth experience. As the child abreacts his feelings in the relationship situation, he is brought face to face with the products of his own instinctive drives and the actualities of his interpersonal relations. The therapist sets a new level of reality in which appropriate demands are placed on the ego. It must be remembered in this connection that it is not the instincts that are ill, but the ego that is called upon to handle them.

Through active play, it has been learned that much of a child's thinking is on a conscious level. However, a great deal remains unconscious and can only be uncovered through the understanding of the spontaneous play of the child. Melanie Klein [*10*], Erikson [*4*], and others have done extensive work in interpreting spontaneous play creations as though they were dream symbols. The spontaneous productions are more readily forthcoming when the therapist shows an active interest in the child, so that he will feel encouraged to reveal symbolically his areas of disturbance.

In all forms of psychotherapy, the alleviation of guilt is an important consideration. By play techniques, the therapist can actively participate in accomplishing this purpose. For example, a child reveals a great deal of aggression against the effigy of a parent, and, as a result, shows tension. The therapist then enters the play by suggesting that the injured person be taken to the hospital for care. There are, of course, many devices he can use to dilute the child's guilt.

As the child obtains release from his anxiety and hostile impulses, he is afforded the opportunity of working through his dependent and thwarted libidinal strivings. When the child obtains the support he needs to withstand the discipline, criticisms, and temptations of his parents, he is free to give expression to his tender impulses. It is difficult to offer affection when all the life functions have been previously subjected to the negating or overly seductive influences of parental authority. Furthermore, to show affection, the child must have learned to accept alternatives other than the apprehension of impending catastrophe.

As the child progresses in therapy, the following phenomena occur:

1. Contact with the child's thinking
2. Abreaction of the anxiety and aggressive impulses
3. Working through dependent wishes
4. Affording alternatives to the feeling of impending tragedy
5. Release of tender impulses in an atmosphere of acceptance
6. Alleviation of the sense of guilt
7. Crystallization of the ego structure in terms of reality

The last-mentioned phase of therapy merits further elaboration. If the therapy is carried on adequately, the child reproduces in the relationship situation the forces that caused his symptoms. By the use of the therapist doll, the child is able to localize his emotional tensions to the therapist-patient relationship, thereby bringing cause and effect closer to the surface and into the world of reality testing. He then carries this testing process into his total environment. In other words, he transfers the microcosm of the therapeutic relationship into the macrocosm of his other human contacts.

As a consequence of therapy, changes take place in the child's behavior. Since children are characteristically disposed to act their thoughts rather than to introspect, parents and teachers must be prepared for altered patterns of performance. These may sometimes take the form of wild aggressions in previously shy, anxiety-ridden children, and must be considered a stage in the ego change of the child. As the adults accept the change, so the child will learn to accept the change within himself. The major emphasis in therapy will always remain upon increase in the strength of the ego. This implies the mastery of the instincts in terms of the real world. Therapy is an enjoyable experience to the child because he derives a great deal of pleasure in the mastery of his impulses. The forces that had originally aroused anxiety are mastered by the child after he has worked through his difficulties. This consists in reproducing actively, in play and in the therapeutic relationship, the life situations that caused him trouble.

THERAPEUTIC APPROACH TO DIFFERENTIAL REACTION TYPES IN CHILDREN

Until recently, no attempt has been made to delineate clearly a differing clinical approach for different types of children coming for therapeutic assistance. McClure, [*14*] has made a noteworthy contribution in this direction. She differentiated three main reaction types in children and offered a different therapeutic approach for each of the types. Her types were: (1) hysteric, (2) obsessive, and (3) labile. It will be recognized that these types correspond roughly to the adult hysteria, obsessive-compulsive, and psychopath groupings. The author would like to offer a modification of McClure's classification and combine her ideas with others in the field, including his own, in planning the therapeutic approach for each type of problem child. The proposed grouping is as follows: (1) aggressive-impulsive, (2) anxiety-phobic, (3) regressive-reaction formation, (4) schizoid-schizophrenic.

Each of these types will be discussed in some detail. McClure states that the therapeutic program should be geared to each of the reaction types with the idea that they are fairly static. The writer's feeling is that although reaction types are quite constant in adults, they are not always static in children. Children do not necessarily remain in a given category, but can move in any direction. For example, anxiety-ridden children can become quite aggressive as their superego pressure is lessened, and compulsive children can go on to develop schizophrenia.

Aggressive-Impulsive. Those cases that show overt hostile or overt affectionate behavior constitute the aggressive-impulsive group. They may display anger, rebellion, clowning, or other strong bids for attention or affection. These children are quite contented with the expression of their own emotions but may become disturbing to the people about them. The main psychopathology is in the lack of development and integration of the superego. The id impulses are strong. The ego may be strong or weak. In the weak-ego group, the tendency toward impulsiveness becomes more marked. This group consists mainly of children who are using their aggressions as fairly successful defenses against anxiety. They are the potential delinquents, whereas children with stronger ego structures may become socially useful leaders.

The aggressive group must be handled very firmly. The therapist, of necessity, sets some carefully defined restrictive limits. If the child destroys property or attacks the person of the therapist, the therapist must make every effort to curtail such activity, but he must do so without anger or vindictiveness. The author usually tells the child that he may do anything he wants to the rubber doll representing him, but that he must not attack him in actuality. This varies with the age of the child—aggression by a three-year-old can be absorbed, whereas the problem with an athlete of 14 may be different.

Anxiety-Phobic. The second group, the anxiety-phobic, presents a predominantly emotional tone of fear. They exhibit extreme emotional responsiveness and invite emotional reactions from others. In phobic cases, the fears are attached to specific objects or situations (see Figure 5), whereas in the anxiety cases, the fears are more generalized. These cases suffer from strong superego demands and strong id impulses. Their ego structures are poorly differentiated. The punishment or guilt factor for their strong instinctive urges is

Fig. 5. Phobic Fantasy. A scene of a ghost visiting a sleeping child is reenacted after the patient had reported her fear of ghosts. In the course of play, the ghost was first identified as a man; later as the girl's father. The case history showed that the parents were separated. The child fantasied being taken away by the father. However, this prospect frightened the child because it meant loss of the mother's protection. Therefore, the father became a ghost in the mind of the child.

provocative of the symptomatology. If the anxiety is of the objective variety, in other words, due to reaction of punishing parents, much must be done to lessen the pressures at home. Cases that show superego anxiety require more direct therapy because the punitive processes have already been internalized. Anxiety caused by the instincts themselves does not seem to offer much of a clinical problem in early childhood, but can be troublesome during adolescence.[2] In the anxiety-phobic group, repressive measures are

---

[2] Reference is here made to the type of anxiety exhibited by adolescents who seem to be overwhelmed by the onrush of pubertal sexuality. Some observers have felt that maturation of the reproductive apparatus releases such forces

contraindicated. The therapist must be prepared to handle objectively the tense situations presented by the child. He must be the stabilizing force through which the child fortifies his ego. If the symptom picture changes from anxiety-ridden to aggressive, the therapist must change his tactics and set limits, just as he would if aggression were the presenting symptom.

Regressive-Reaction Formation. The third group, the regressive-reaction formation group, includes those cases where the original anxiety is replaced to a great extent by various types of defense mechanisms. They show a turning away from tension by retreating into infantile forms of behavior or to actions that are opposite in trend from the original emotional reaction. Cottrell [3] suggested

that the individual is unable to cope with them. What usually happens in such cases is that the sexual energies call into play all the superego forces that had been well established during the Oedipal phase. This calls to mind the ideas originally promulgated by Freud, who attributed anxiety to the inability of the individual to handle the sexual impulses. Shortly after his original contributions, he changed his view and considered anxiety to be the product of external threats (or seductions), which only later are experienced by the individual as internal threats. In this respect, anxiety becomes a process mediated by the ego, rather than a property of the instincts themselves.

The individual with emotional tension, says Freud, treats the instinctive demands as though they were external dangers partly because he understands that their gratification would lead to conflicts with the outside world. This concept, then, suggests that there is no such thing as anxiety due to the instincts as such. This is at variance with the opinions of other investigators, particularly Melanie Klein, who believe that tensions may arise from the instincts per se. Some of Klein's followers go as far as to say that the human mind is so constituted as to require the individual constantly to manipulate fundamentally opposed instincts; since the instincts are inborn, some form of conflict exists from the beginning of life. It is true, however, that conflicts arise in those situations where the gratification of one instinct would lead to the frustration of another instinct or instinct derivative, but these situations are bound to arise in the course of life experiences. Such a case would be a child who holds back the bowel function for fear of being abandoned by its mother. The stronger force is the need for protection by the mother, which is in turn a derivative of the self-preservative instinct. Is this not what Freud spoke of as the threat from the outside world? Furthermore, we do not see anything in animals that could be called "instinctive anxiety." Moreover, the child who fears his own aggression (for example, "I want to bite—I may be bitten") clearly shows that the tension is an outgrowth of the external threat. The formula, "I am so angry that I may burst," seems to be more nearly like the concept that the tension arises from the instinct, but this is not the case, as this formulation is derived from the previously expressed one or from an identification with the victim of one's own aggression. Mention should also be made of the anxieties that arise from conflicts in identification. A child may identify himself with his father but become fearful because this has engendered the displeasure of his mother, or the child may identify himself partially with his mother and partially with his father in such a way as to cause confusion in thought and action (conflict of introjects). A more far-reaching description of the mechanisms of human thinking appears in a paper, written by the author of this chapter, entitled "Perceptual and Conceptual Thinking in Ego and Super-ego Formation from Birth to Old Age." (Forthcoming publication.)

3 Cottrell, L., personal communication.

the term "adversive" for the group showing reaction formation. These cases show outwardly a comparatively small degree of emotional responsiveness. They are more concerned with things than people, and hence, at first appear rather distant and are difficult to reach. They show strong superego and ego structures. Their primitive urges are intense and, as McClure says, "unintegrated."

The best approach to this group is through the medium of things. The therapist must at all times maintain a warm, affectionate interest in the child and in the child's creativeness. Although doll play may be of interest to the child, at first he must be allowed to express himself through whatever medium he may choose. Clay, finger paints, crayons, or other materials may be the means of entering the child's fantasy world.

Schizoid-Schizophrenic. The fourth group, the schizoid-schizophrenic, has attracted considerable attention from the therapeutic point of view in recent years. In these cases, there is more or less complete distintegration of the ego, with relative freedom to express primitive id impulses as a part of consciousness. Patients can become so completely unemotional in relation to reality that they appear as little robots. The manifestations may vary from slight withdrawal to complete disorganization of personality, as in adult schizophrenics. The work of Sullivan [20], Fromm-Reichmann [9], Federn [6], Rosen [17], Despert [3], Betz [2], and others has brought new light to the treatment of these cases.

The recent trends in therapy for the schizoid-schizophrenic group are thoroughly in accord with the methodology of play techniques. It has been pointed out in the recent literature that it is necessary to break through the autistic barriers. In order to accomplish this, the therapist must approach the patient on a level of thinking occurring at the preverbal period. This corrosponds to the activity of a parent who makes emotional contact with an infant. Or, as a colleague said in discussing Rosen's paper, "The therapist must behave as though he were practically psychotic himself." This is exactly what the writer means when he says that play with the child should be used to enter into his world. It is only after a means of communication has been established and an affectional relationship has developed that these children can approach actual reality. It is not merely a question of re-repressing the id impulses; rather, it is that the ego structure must be formed out of the working through in the transference situation of the overwhelming emotions that caused the child to retreat from reality.

The future of play technique as a medium of therapeutic assistance for the child patient lies in the effective utilization of the patient-therapist relationship and in the planned handling of each case according to the clinical reaction type.

SUMMARY

Projection of one's feelings onto objects or other persons has been used as a therapeutic device for thousands of years. Primitive man created the image of his enemy, and then maimed or destroyed that image. The child in the play situation expresses fantasies similar to the thinking of primitive man.

In Europe, two schools of psychoanalysis have used play therapy with children. Anna Freud and her followers approach the child slowly and establish a close relationship before attempting to determine the child's intimate thought processes. Melanie Klein is direct and uses deep interpretation of symbolic material in the early stages of therapy. In contrast to both European schools, American Child Guidance Clinics depend much on modification of the child's environment and on the use of indirect therapy through treatment of parents and others.

Play therapy is discussed from the standpoint of content or symbolism, and from the point of view of the relationship between the therapist and child. Content is more readily obtained if the therapist can help the child to maintain the anonymity with which he frequently initiates the play.

The therapist is active in the interview and is often himself represented by a doll in the play situation. The strengthening of the child's ego and the alleviation of his guilt are important objectives in therapy. The therapeutic approach differs according to the type of problem presented by the child. These different approaches are discussed under four groupings: aggressive-impulsive, anxiety-phobic, regressive-reaction formation, and schizoid-schizophrenic.

REFERENCES

1. Alexander, F., "Symposium." *Am. J. Orthopsychiat.*, 1938, 8, 424–428.

2. Betz, B. B., "A study of tactics for resolving the autistic barrier in the psychotherapy of the schizophrenic personality." *Am. J. Psychiat.*, 1947, 104, 267.

3. Despert, J. L., "Psychotherapy in child schizophrenia." *Am. J. Psychiat.*, 1947, 104, 36.

4. Erikson, E. H., "Dramatics production test," in H. A. Murray and others, *Explorations in Personality*. New York: Oxford University Press, Inc., 1938, 552–582.

5. ——————, "Studies on the interpretation of play. Clinical observations of play disruption in young children." *Genet. Psychol. Monogr.*, 1940, 22, 557–671.

6. Federn, P., "Principles of psychotherapy in latent schizophrenia." *Am. J. Psychotherapy*, 1947, 129, 129–144.

7. Fraser, J. G., *The Golden Bough* (1-vol. abr. ed.). New York: The Macmillan Company, 1940.

8. Freud, A., *Psychoanalytical Treatment of Children*. London: Imago Publishing Company, 1947.

8a. ——————, "Introduction to the technique of child analysis" (L. P. Clark, trans.). *Nerv. Ment. Dis. Monog.*, No. 48, 1928.

9. Fromm-Reichmann, F., "Transference problems in schizophrenics." *Psychoanalyt. Quart.*, 1939, 8, 412.

10. Klein, M., *Psychoanalysis of Children*. New York: W. W. Norton & Company, Inc., 1932.

11. Levy, D., "Studies in sibling rivalry," Monog. No. 2. New York: Am. Orthopsychiatric Assoc., 1937.

12. ——————, "Release therapy." *Am. J. Orthopsychiat.*, 1939, 9, 713–737.

13. Lippman, H., "Section on play therapy." *Am. J. Orthopsychiat.*, 1938, 8, 518–520.

14. McClure, A. C., "Reaction types in maladjusted children; some clinical observations with reference to play therapy." *Brit. J. Med. Psychol.*, 1945–46, 20, 389.

15. Phillips, R., "Doll play as a function of the realism of the materials and the length of the experimental session." *Child Develop.*, 1945, 16, 123–143.

16. Pintler, M. H., "Doll play as a function of experimenter-child interaction and initial organization of materials." *Child Develop.*, 1945, 16, 145–166.

17. Rosen, J. N., "Treatment of schizophrenic psychosis by direct analytic therapy." *Psychiat. Quart.*, 1947, 21, 117.

18. Rousseau, J.-J., *Emile*. New York: E. P. Dutton and Company, 1925.

19. Solomon, J. C., "Active play therapy: Further experiences." *Am. J. Orthopsychiat.*, 1940, 10, 763–781.

20. Sullivan, H. S., "Therapeutic investigations in schizophrenia." *Psychiatry*, 1947, 10, 121.

21. Von Hug-Hellmuth, H., *A Study of the Mental Life of the Child*. Washington, D. C.: Nervous and Mental Disease Publishing Company, 1919, XIII.

CHAPTER 23

Psychodrama as a Projective Technique

ROBERT BARTLETT HAAS, ED.D. AND J. L. MORENO, M.D.

INTRODUCTION

The "action" approach to human interrelations has been the unique contribution of Moreno, who formulated and presented the communications methodologies now widely known as *sociometry* [10], *sociodrama* [17] and *group psychotherapy*. They are founded on a "socio-interactional" theory of personality—a conception of the self as the totality of social and private roles the individual plays in his interpersonal and intergroup contacts. The way he plays these roles in relation to the counter-roles of others, and the several kinds of status he achieves in the concrete social situations to which he is constantly responding [*18*, pp. 133–143], give him his uniqueness as a person.

For Moreno, the *roles* of the indivdual, and of the individuals who make up the groups in which he functions, are the measurable units of behavior. The ability to *read* [1] one's own roles and the roles of others, and then to produce appropriate role-responses, is the skill essential in furthering human enterprises. Many factors tend to block success. One individual may not be able to meet the unpredictable aspects of the other person's role behavior satisfactorily. The demands and taboos of our culture may interpose barriers that we cannot overcome. Highly personalized attitudes,

---

[1] The broad concept of *reading*, as it is used in this chapter, is the contribution of Dr. Peter L. Spencer, Director of the Claremont Reading Conferences, Claremont College, California.

habits, and value patterns may prevent our accurate reading of a complex situation. In order to relieve these blockages, which frequently cause us to misread and misevaluate ourselves and others, and to replace them with a process that will allow for the growth of "proper evaluative reactions," Moreno has developed the concept of *spontaneity*,[2] the basis of a therapeutic approach to interpersonal maladjustments.

Spontaneity is the ability of a subject to meet each new situation with adequacy. . . . *It is a plastic adaptation skill,* a mobility and flexibility of the self, which is *indispensable to a rapidly growing organism in a rapidly changing environment* [*11*, pp. 81, 93].

The spontaneous individual is creative in his moment-to-moment adjustments. His flexibility enables him to read concrete situations accurately and fully. He evaluates, he is aware of alternatives; he plays his roles of response resourcefully. The person low in spontaneity will reflect his lack in *stereotyped* or *conventional* role-playing, reading just enough of the situation, of himself, and of the others, to make a momentarily acceptable adjustment. The person who is impulsive rather than spontaneous will err in the opposite direction; he will misread and misevaluate, and his role-responses will be irrelevant or even irrational.

Action research has built experimental techniques out of the concepts of *role* and *spontaneity*. *The Sociometric Test* [*6, 7*], for example, allows an observer to tap the spontaneous choice and rejection patterns that pass between the members of a group and condition the psychological atmosphere in which they function. Such a test may serve as a charting of specific relationships: who in the group is unchosen; who is highly chosen; who is rejected; who depends on whom; who is independent of whom; who is hostile to whom; and so on. These data disclose the kind of status and prestige that individuals are earning through their role-playing in a real-life situation. To a degree, they disclose the subjective motivations for the behavior of individuals in the group.

The Situation Test [*11, 12*], a sociodramatic technique, allows the observer to follow the *role behavior* of individuals through a planned series of real-life or lifelike situations. In doing so, he

---

2 The reader is referred to a stimulating paper on *Spontaneity* as a psychologic and psychiatric concept, originally published in 1933 by Adolph Meyer. See Alfred Lief, *The Commonsense Psychiatry of Adolph Meyer.* New York: McGraw-Hill Book Company, Inc., 1948, pages 576–589 [Eds.].

may interpret projections of his subject's role and interactional and spontaneity processes. The observer may also discover how, and how well, the individual is reading himself and the others who function as co-actors in his life situation.

Exploration of the individual and his groups represents only one aspect of action research. Retraining and therapeutic phases follow. *Sociometric guidance* [10, 13], for example, puts group members into optimal work or play relationships. *Sociodramatic guidance* [4, 10] explores and treats, at one time, members of a group who share similar problems. *Psychodramatic guidance* [3, 11] treats the individual in relation to his group. The literature has many detailed accounts of these procedures. French [2] used psychodrama in the training of foremen. Lippitt [8] has used it in the training of leaders. The method has been used as a demonstration and research technique by Hendry, Lippitt, and Zander [5]. Perhaps the least remarked aspect of the action approach, yet one of its most frequent accomplishments, is effectiveness in stimulating that *self-other evaluation and accommodation* through which human beings in association become more insightful of one another, and, in consequence, more efficient and effective human communicators.

A SURVEY OF PSYCHODRAMATIC TECHNIQUES

Psychodramatic research has developed in many directions. Some specific techniques have been tested clinically and found reliable for exploring, diagnosing, and retraining the distortions of communication and interpersonal relations in individuals and groups.

These are *action* techniques. They may be differentiated from pencil-and-paper techniques and from interview and lecture techniques in that they consider the subjects *in action*—when they are *role-playing* [3] in real-life situations.

The action techniques that have been most frequently utilized are of wide diversity: the Spontaneity Test, Role-Playing Tests, and Interaction Tests; the Psychodrama (in both its individual and group forms), the Sociodrama, the Living Newspaper, and the Impromptu Theatre.

---

[3] *Role-playing* is a term that in sociodramatic usage refers to the private and social roles in which one functions in his interpersonal or intergroup contacts. The term has been misinterpreted on occasion to mean play-acting or otherwise pretending or behaving insincerely. See the sociological discussion of man as a role-player in Young [19, pp. 131–156].

PROCEDURES

The commonly used intelligence tests and personality tests permit the analysis of "cold material which the subject leaves behind after his excitement in the state of production has passed" [*10,* p. 122]. In contrast to the Stanford-Binet test, the Word Association test, the Rorschach, and other tests of personality and intelligence, the Psychodramatic Tests require that the subject be warmed-up to a *feeling level* in which he will release highly personalized affect material. Since the emphasis is deliberately on the *act and feeling* of the subject, the director is able to glimpse functional levels of intelligence and to detect behavioral efficiency in crisis situations. In some instances, the psychodramatist employs production methods that stimulate maximal *projection* in the testee. Thus, the dynamic aspects of the personality are revealed through role performance.

The director is usually assisted in administering the test by an *auxiliary ego,*[4] or trained role-player, who is carefully coached for the particular counter-role he is to assume. The responsibility of the auxiliary actor is to present every subject tested with the *same* basic dramatic stimulus, yet to remain alive to the subject's unique response in each surprise situation, so that he can continuously re-offer the testee a phase of the crucial dramatic motif that will take him by surprise. The auxiliary ego is, on the one hand, the research instrument of the director; on the other, he is the colleague of the subject, doing everything possible to bring him to bear upon his role-act and to promote spontaneous reactions.

THE PROJECTIVE AND EXPRESSIVE ACTION TEST

Among the group of tests psychodramatic research has designated as Interaction Tests, there is an experimental battery that has become known as the *Projective and Expressive Action Test.*

Del Torto and Corneytz, in their methodological survey of projective techniques and their evaluation of the psychodramatic method as the "comprehensive climax in the history of projective research" [*1,* p. 372], have performed a singular service for spontaneity research. They have demonstrated the practicality of using "a set

---

4 The *auxiliary ego* in sociodramatic procedures is any person who carries a counter-role to the subject. In clinical drama, the auxiliary ego is carefully trained to assist in the therapy; in didactic drama, he may be either instructed or totally free to improvise his counter-role as he wishes.

of experimentally constructed test situations which provide a norm for interpreting the differential response of subjects as a *planned operational procedure"* [*1*, p. 371] for projective *action* testing.

Their version of the test is designed to stimulate the subject to the fullest possible projection and expression of his personality in action. The emphasis is upon spontaneous expression at all psychological levels.

Through the test, we gain an intensified picture of the individual in interaction with objects and people, either imaginary or real. This projective action test combines the concepts of spontaneity and roles, and in addition, explores their relationship to the individual's fantasy and reality levels. Whereas the other action tests define the situation rigidly for the subject, and the test results are analyzed only in terms of social reality, this test in addition encourages the subject to externalize highly personalized fragments of his inner world.

Unlike other projective devices, such as the Rorschach, TAT, and Finger Painting, the Projective Action Test "does not consider it possible to analyze the individual separated from the social matrix in which he lives; therefore its very methodology of analysis includes seeing the subject in a whirl of interpersonal contacts" [*1*, p. 357]. Carefully planned situations are used to facilitate the subject's release of various levels of personality not dealt with in the Role or Spontaneity Tests. The expression of these new levels is accomplished by the introduction into the psychodramatic process of object relationship, fantasy, past and future time, and a new freedom for highly individual and unimpeded action.

The test objectives might be summarized:

1. To determine the subject's natural spontaneity levels from the character of his self-structured presentations.
2. To explore the role performance of the subject on his own level of presentation, reality, or fantasy.
3. To explore and evaluate the interactional capacities of the individual in a range of expression situations (from free to structured) and in many areas of contact.

Description. The Test consists of a series of nine situations "whose operations are pre-planned and objectified, but, in which [the subject] has latitude for the expression of his personal reaction and content ideas" [*1*, p. 368].

Before the operationally standardized portion of the test is administered, the authors propose a warming-up period for the subject, similar to that required for subjects in a formal psychodrama or sociodrama session. They recommend:

1. A short "mutual-interview" (subject-director) for building rapport and confidence and for introducing the subject to spontaneity principles.
2. A preliminary situation, defined by the subject, in which he is introduced to the action experience with the least possible psychodramatic resistance, and from which the director may get "*hints* as to the subject's interests, attitudes and manner of behavior. . . ." [1]

Following this, the subject is introduced to the test situations, of which there are nine:

Test Situations [5]

1. *The Imaginary Person Situation* (no auxiliary ego).
    Instructions: "You are on the stage with an imaginary person . . . invent this person and create a relationship with him or her. You identify the person, the time, the place, and the activity. There are no limitations except that you may invent only one person. What you do in the situation is entirely up to you. All right, begin."
    Cues for analysis of enactment:
    (a) Designed to get his personalized and unimpeded projection of what a social relationship means to him; opens up areas of interest for further intensive psychodramatic study.
    (b) How does he communicate?
2. *The Object and the Auxiliary Ego Situation.*
    Instructions: "You are on the stage with an imaginary object and another person. You are to establish a relationship with the person and the object. I shall name the object for you. What you do in the situation is entirely up to you, but you may not introduce any other objects or persons. The object is _____. All right, begin."
    Cues for analysis of enactment:
    (a) The influence of social relationships upon how the subject deals with objects. Does he monopolize, share, or surrender the object?
    (b) The study of differentials between acting with an imaginary person and with a real person.
3. *The Primary Ego: Three-Objects Situation* (no auxiliary ego).
    Instructions: "You are on the stage alone with three imaginary objects. I shall name these objects for you. You may choose one, two, or three, but you may not introduce any other objects. There are no limitations except that you deal with at least one of the objects. What you do

---

[5] Condensed and adapted from Del Torto and Corneytz [*1,* pp. 368–371]; used by permission.

with the objects is entirely up to you. They are _____;
_____, and _____. All right, begin."
Cues for analysis of enactment:
  (a) Which objects does he choose, emphasize, or reject?
  (b) Does he have a need to integrate them?
  (c) Is his interest in them functional or aesthetic?
4. *Periodic Stimulation Situation* (several auxiliary egos).
  Instructions: "You are to create a situation on the stage. In this situation you are (*director defines his role*), and your companion is (*the director defines the role of the auxiliary ego, in relation to the subject's role*). (*The director defines the situation: time and place.*) What you do in the situation is entirely up to you. All right, begin."

  At controlled intervals, the director sends in auxiliary egos who have been instructed as to the type of stimulation they are to offer. Each replaces the previous auxiliary ego. The basic situation is not changed; each stimulus fits itself to the situation in progress without interrupting the action. For example, the role of the subject is defined as an artist working in his studio. At controlled intervals, the director sends in an aggressive lover, a landlord demanding rent, and a model waiting to be posed.
  Cues for analysis of enactment:
    (a) Designed to test the subject's range of expansiveness within the role.
    (b) To test his spontaneous adaptations to surprise elements.
5. *The Hidden Theme Situation.*
  Instructions (*Given to the subject outside of the room*): "When you go on to the stage, a situation will be in progress. You are to enter that situation. What you do in the situation is entirely up to you, but you must relate yourself meaningfully to the situation in progress. All right, begin."

  While the instructions are being given to the subject outside, a defined situation with two auxiliary egos begins on the stage and is already in full progress when the subject enters.
  Cues for analysis of enactment:
    (a) How does the subject perceive the theme and situation in progress?
    (b) How does he create a role in relationship to it?
6. *The Mute Situation.*
  Instructions: "You are on the stage with another person. I shall give you a theme to act out. Neither you nor the other person may speak. All your communications are to be in terms of gestures and bodily movements only. The theme is _____. What you do in the situation is entirely up to you. All right, begin." (The auxiliary ego has been instructed.)
  Cue for analysis of enactment: designed to reveal physical resources for communication and expression.

7. *The Reversal of Role Situation.*

Instructions: "You are to create a situation on the stage with another person. In this situation you are (*the director defines a role*), and the other person is (*the director defines a role in relation to that of the subject*). (*The director defines the situation: time, place, and theme.*) What you do in the situation is entirely up to you. All right, begin."

The situation is allowed to develop for a controlled period of time, and at the end of the action, the subject is instructed to immediately change roles with the auxiliary ego and to replay the situation as *exactly* as possible.

Cue for analysis of enactment:

(a) How aware is the subject of both the content and the manner of expression of his own role and the role of the auxiliary ego?

(b) How sensitive is the subject to others in social situations?

8. *The Triple Situation.*

Instructions: "You will be given three consecutive situations. Each one will be different. You will go *immediately* from one situation to another without break, except for further instructions. I shall outline each situation for you. You must observe the given instructions, but beyond that, there are no limitations. What you do in each situation is entirely up to you."

The director then defines the first situation, and it continues for a controlled time. The action is interrupted and instructions for the next situation are immediately and briefly given.

Cues for analysis of enactment:

(a) Designed to test the subject's spontaneous adaptability to such shifts.

(b) What are the conserved portions of behavior: role lag? (We define role lag as inappropriate residues of role expression that carry over from one situation to another, a role inertia.)

9. *The Descriptive Situation.*

Instructions: "In this situation you are alone. You may choose a locale familiar to you in real life or out of your own fantasy. We would like you to describe this locale fully: your surroundings, the objects. But describe it as if you were experiencing and living in it now. What you do in the situation is entirely up to you. All right, begin."

Cue for analysis of enactment: designed to elicit a perceptive protocol.

Reading the Test Results. In a study of the procedures that have been used for gathering and organizing data from commonly used projective and expressive tests, Del Torto and Corneytz noted four major "areas of contact" with the subject:

1. Contact with the subject's *imaginal content* (as in the Free Association Test, Word Association Test, and Thematic Apperception Test).

2. Contact with the subject's *methods of perceptions* (Rorschach).

3. Contact with the subject's *plastic involvement and organization* (finger-painting, Buhler World Test).
4. Contact with the subject's *social interactions* (psychodrama).

The *Projective and Expressive Test Situations* were constructed by Del Torto and Corneytz "to contact with all these four areas, making it the most varied and intensive projection method yet developed" [*1*, p. 361]. The portions of the test descriptions labeled *cues* may already have served to indicate how these areas of contact are met with in the action test.

For purposes of illustration, [the authors] have analyzed psychodramatic procedure into fictional stages indicating how judges may gather data in terms of fantasy (Imaginal Content), perception, plastic involvement, and social interaction. This outline can be used as an analytical frame of reference for the evaluation of stenographic reports [*1*, p. 361].

The authors provide a detailed analysis of this aspect of the test, but a brief summary here may be sufficient.

PROJECTIVE CRITERIA [6]

Imaginal Content:
>   (a) The subject's definition of his surroundings in the warming-up process.
>   (b) His choice of objects.
>   (c) His definition of his own role as determined by his participation; his definition of the roles of others.
>   (d) His introduction of ideas and their development.

Methods of Perception:
>   (a) The subject's descriptions during the warming-up process.
>   (b) His perception in action.

Plastic Involvement and Organization:
>   (a) The subject's organizing of objects and his involvement with the "organic plastic field."
>   (b) His organization of themes and situations.

Social Interaction (Interpersonal Relations):
>   (a) The subject's channels of social interactions.
>   (b) His social-interaction "type" (imitative, sympathetic, demonstrative, or solitary).

It is important to realize that the psychodrama is primarily a production method, not a psychology, and that "projection" represents to the psychodramatist only one of the many techniques of production. Thus, test results might be *analyzed* from a number

---

[6] Adapted from Del Torto and Corneytz [*1*, pp. 362–367]; used by permission.

of points of view: psychoanalytically, semantically, sociologically, and so on. The psychodramatist himself would utilize another mode.

The frame of reference for psychodramatic analysis is the situation, and the roles and role relationships that evolve within a specific situation. Analysis is based on the client's self-dramatizations—on the clues that come out when he is warmed up to a spontaneity state, and on the categories that emerge from the attitudes he expresses. This method of analysis, again, is in contradistinction to those that analyze the "cold" content of the client into "lists of categories" (pre-arranged by the psychologist, or agreed upon by the jury of collaborators) that have little subjective anchorage in the motivation of the subjects.

What does the "process analysis" of a psychodramatic production include? A process analysis intends to cover as fully as possible the total counseling situation—the verbal content, temporal aspects, interpersonal or interactional character of the process, and role aspects of the process. It is obvious that a system of recording is required that will make the total process available for later analysis [3, 10].

The verbal content is recorded either electrically or in shorthand. Observers record mimetic patterns of the subject and the duration of his acts and pauses. Subsequent analysis of the attitudes, language, and roles is made. Together, these provide a more inclusive picture of the client's production than would the recording of verbal content alone.

THE PSYCHODRAMA STAGE AS A DEVICE FOR THERAPEUTIC LEARNING

Over and above the problem of analysis, the psychodramatist is concerned about the therapeutic implications of testing on the projective level. Although he believes the psychodramatic form of the projective test to be the most inclusive of all those currently used, he is more concerned with the *client tested* in a reality situation. To quote a critique of the nondirective interview that might also apply to most projective tests:

Not only is the counselor's role, because of the deliberate restrictions on the techniques employed, psychologically monotonous, but the whole counseling situation also takes on an unreality from the fact that the client's spontaneity is met with so little counter-spontaneity in the therapist. Indeed, the non-directive counselor, because of the unnaturalness of his role, produces an interview which is almost on the fantasy level. A more realistic therapeutic procedure would seem to be one which, in accord with Moreno, would leave clients "on a level which is as near as possible to the level of their natural growth;" and one in which the counselor's role, in addition to being permissive, activates the client and "stimulates his spontaneability" to immediate production on action as well as on verbal levels [3, p. 5–6].

The auxiliary ego technique introduces a significant advance in methodology. What happens, in essence, in the psychodramatic situation is that the traditional two-way counseling relationship is broken up, and a new triangular relationship (including, either symbolically or actually, "the others" of the client's world) takes its place:

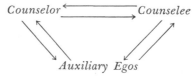

Counselor ⟷ *Counselee*

Auxiliary Egos

In this relationship, the counselor loses his autonomy; he need not fear either his directiveness or nondirectiveness as a therapist; he can stand outside the therapy, relying on the spontaneity of the client (who is warmed-up for self-direction by specific psychodramatic production techniques) and/or upon the auxiliary egos (representing "the others" of the client's world) to work through situations and role conflicts without his interference. At times, the counselor may alternate his stimuli, assuming now a directive counselor role, now an indirective one, now a nondirective one. The psychodramatic counseling relationship (in both its diagnostic and therapeutic phases) provides the context for a variety of counseling techniques, or perhaps it is more accurate to say that psychodrama provides the matrix in which the various counseling techniques so far developed can reach an intelligent synthesis.

One of Moreno's greatest therapeutic achievements has been to break the deadlock of the traditional secretive interview situation and to open the counseling session to a selected group of participant actors and participant observers who may take part in and actually facilitate the therapy. In other words, the *vehicle* in which learning takes place symbolizes the kind of learning that is contemplated.

AUTONOMY OF THE LEARNER AS A FACTOR IN TESTING

Learning is an all-inclusive process of which educational learning is only one phase. It must include learning in life itself from infancy up to old age, for subhuman as well as human organisms. It must include social and cultural institutions. It must include therapeutic learning, as on the couch or on the psychodrama stage. Once we have formulated such a broad view of the learning process, we can go a step further and evaluate all these various learning instruments as to what they accomplish for the autonomy, the spontaneity, and the creativity of the learners themselves.

One can measure the educational or therapeutic value of an instrument by the degree to which it stimulates the autonomy of individuals or groups. The degree of autonomy, for instance, that psychoanalysis permits a subject to attain is limited to the verbal dimension. Nondirective counseling may be given a still lower rating, because by itself, it does not increase the spontaneity of the therapeutic learner; on the other hand, it is so designed that it decreases the spontaneity of the counselor. The degrees to which the subject warms up to an experience and to an expression of himself and others is a measure of the autonomy of the self. It is useful to study the degrees, the range, and the intensity of warming-up that individuals attain in the course of various operations of learning. We can talk about instruments that encourage only a minimum of involvement and autonomy. Some instruments encourage the individual to warm up only to perceptions, others only to fantasies, others only to a free association of words. Projective tests are among these instruments in every case.

SUMMARY

The Projective and Expressive Action Test, as developed by Corneytz and Del Torto, not only permits the tester to gather data about the subject systematically in terms of imaginal content, perception, plastic involvement, and social interaction (areas contacted in other projective and expressive testing) but also in terms of the subject's spontaneity, role, and interaction performance within the lifelike context of a social situation. In addition, because of the wide role and situational range presented in the test, with its inclusion of both structured and unstructured possibilities for the testee, it affords an especially useful instrument for turning up clues the counselor can follow intensively in subsequent retraining or therapeutic sessions.

The action-diagnostician has at his disposal, however, more "total" forms of production which allow him to get at all aspects of the subject's personality in action. These instruments are Psychodrama and Sociodrama in their "classical" forms, and both are types of spontaneous drama in which the director encourages his subjects by means of definite production techniques (such as role-reversal, double-ego, substitute-role, mirroring, improvisation, symbolic distance, dream presentation, monologue, dialogue, soliloquy, word-less psychodrama, hypno-drama, and the like) to achieve a maximum of involvement and autonomy in self-projection. Beginning at the subject's own level of presentation, these techniques enable the counselor to explore, diagnose, and at the same time treat, on the deep-action level, individuals or groups of individuals sharing similar or common problems. Just as the role-therapist prefers to contact his subject on the *action* rather than the verbal level, so his predilections are for a *reality* rather than a projective context and for an *inclusive* form of production (Psychodrama or Sociodrama) rather than the more partial production form that the Projective and Expressive Action Test represents. Future research in action methods and group psychotherapy will probably emphasize instruments "that would mobilize and sustain in controlled fashion larger and larger areas of personality," in the quest for a reality test and a reality therapy worthy of utilizing man's spontaneous potential for achieving creative self-hood.

REFERENCES

1. Del Torto, J., and Corneytz, P., "Psychodrama as expressive and projective technique." *Sociometry,* 1944, 8, 4, 356–375.
2. French, J. R. P., Jr., "Role-playing as a method of training foremen." *Sociometry,* 1945, 8, 410–425.
3. Haas, R. B., "Action counseling and process analysis, a psycho-dramatic approach." *Sociatry,* December 1947, 1, 3, 256–285. (Also published in *Psychodrama Monographs,* No. 25. Beacon House, N. Y., 1948.)
4. Haas, R. B., Gilchrist, Robert, and Kahn, Lothar, "Building friendly relations." Columbus, Ohio: University of Ohio, University School Series No. 4, 1947, 29–34.

5. Hendry, C. E., Lippitt, R., and Zander, A., *Reality Practice as Educational Method, Some Principles and Applications.* New York: Beacon House, 1944.

6. Jennings, H. H., *Leadership and Isolation.* New York: Longmans, Green & Company, Inc., 1943.

7. —————————, in association with the Staff of Intergroup Education in Cooperating Schools, Hilda Taba, Director, *Sociometry in Group Relations.* Washington, D. C.: American Council on Education, 1948, Chaps. 9 and 10.

8. Lippitt, R., "The psychodrama in leadership training." *Sociometry,* 1943, 6, 286–292.

9. Moreno, F. B., "Psychodrama," in P. L. Harriman (ed.), *Encyclopedia of Psychology.* New York: Philosophical Library, 1946, pages 601–607.

10. Moreno, J. L., *Who Shall Survive?* New York: Beacon House, 1934.

11. —————————, *Psychodrama.* New York: Beacon House, 1946, Vol. 1.

12. —————————, "Situation Test," *Sociometry,* May–August 1946, Vol. IX, Nos. 2–3.

13. —————————, *A Sociometric Work Guide for Teachers.* Washington, D. C.: American Council on Education, 1947.

14. —————————, "Psychodramatic shock therapy." *Psychodrama Monographs,* No. 5. New York: Beacon House.

15. —————————, "A case of paranoia treated through psychodrama." *Psychodrama Monographs,* No. 13. New York: Beacon House, 1944.

16. —————————, "Psychodramatic treatment of psychoses." *Psychodrama Monographs,* No. 15. New York: Beacon House, 1945.

17. —————————, *The Theatre of Spontaneity: An Introduction to Psychodrama.* New York: Beacon House, 1947.

18. —————————, "Discussion of Snyder's 'The present status of psychotherapeutic counseling.'" *Psychol. Bull.,* 1947, 44, 6, 564–567.

19. Young, Kimball, *Social Psychology.* New York: F. S. Crofts and Company, 1946, pages 133–143.

CHAPTER 24

The Use of Projective Techniques in the Interpretation of Hostility Patterns[1]

DAVID M. LEVY, M.D.

The sibling rivalry experiments [2] offer certain special advantages in the study of hostility patterns. The children are placed in identical situations—the play of the older child and the new baby at the mother's breast. The same play material and the same techniques in encouraging and stimulating activity are used. Each child brings his particular experience and personality configuration to bear on a standardized play situation.

When the play is started in the usual manner, the child is told that the mother has to feed the baby. Clay breasts are put on the mother doll, the baby is placed in position and encircled by the mother's arms, the mother is seated in a chair, and a doll representing brother or sister is placed near the chair. The child is then told, "Now, this is the game. The brother comes and sees a new baby at the mother's breast. He sees it for the first time. Now what does he do?"

In most cases, repeated acts of hostility against one or more of the objects in the play can be observed, in a progressive series, rang-

---

[1] Reprinted in adapted form from David M. Levy, "Hostility Patterns," *American Journal of Orthopsychiatry*, 1943, Vol. 13, No. 2, pages 441–461, with permission of the author and the *American Journal of Orthopsychiatry*—Eds.

[2] David M. Levy, *Studies in Sibling Rivalry*, Research Monograph No. 2. New York: American Orthopsychiatric Association, 1937.

ing from highly inhibited to fully uninhibited forms. Comparison of the numerous patterns, in addition to careful study of the minute phases in the changing series of events, should aid in delineating psychodynamics of the hostile act in general, and, in particular, its performance in the sibling rivalry situation.

Every hostile act, as observed in the sibling rivalry situation, may be considered a true representation, or a deflection from a true representation, of a direct personal assault on a definite social object. Stated in terms of the specific play situation, the "model" act represents the child attacking the baby sibling with its teeth, hands, or feet. It may be represented graphically thus:

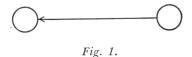

Fig. 1.

Any deviation from this play may be regarded as a modification or a complexity of the simple structure of the hostile act. Such modifications are observed at every phase. They are indicated by dashes made at various points in the graph:

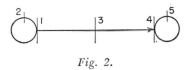

Fig. 2.

Point 1 has reference to the "impulse," that phase of the act immediately preceding the release of movement in relation to the object (muscular or verbalization of muscular movement). It is sometimes difficult to differentiate inhibition of the impulse from "getting set," or readiness to act. When the child says, "I don't know what to do," or "I can't think of anything," though actually, as later events may prove, he does do something, it is still difficult to know whether he held back the impulse to attack or was merely in the process of orientation, of adjusting to a new situation. In most instances, however, no difficulty is presented; for example, when the child says of himself (or of the doll representing the self) that he doesn't want to do anything to the baby, or punishes the self-doll for wanting to hit the baby.

Point 2 refers to deviations in the use of the self alone as the attacker. The child, for example, may use an animal to attack the baby, add another child or many children to make the attack, or ask the examiner to start it ("You do it for me").

Point 3 refers to deviations in the act, after release of movement in relation to the object, before contact with the object has occurred. The deviations at this point represent every variety of avoidance of impact with the object, blocking of movement (withholding attack after making an attacking gesture of slapping, crushing, and so on), or shunting the attack on to other objects.

Point 4 refers to forms of attack and their deviations.   The child, for example, instead of assaulting the object, may tease it, abuse it verbally, distort it, throw objects at it, or conceal hostility with evidence of affection.

Point 5 represents deviations in the object of attack; for example, instead of attacking the baby, the child attacks any other object, including the examiner, or adds other babies, attacking a crowd rather than a single object.

After he attacks the object, the child typically attacks the self, attempts to restore the object, and makes a verbal justification for the hostile act.   All varieties of the punishing, restoring, defensive maneuvers have been studied, besides numerous other forms.   The absence or distortion of any of the three typical sequelae (punishment, restoration, defense) of the hostile act, are likewise noted.

This study is an attempt to illustrate the method of investigation as applied to the sibling rivalry experiments of a particular patient. The child's fantasy as revealed in known behavior, dreams, drawings, compositions, and the Rorschach test, are investigated and compared with the patterns as manifested in the sibling rivalry play.

Since the case study is oriented to the particular manifestations revealed in the sibling rivalry experiment, only those phases of the life history that have special reference to them are depicted.   The patient was a boy 11 years and 11 months old at the time of referral. His sister, the only other child in the family, was 9 years and 5 months old.   The presenting problems were disobedient and negativistic behavior, difficulty in making friends, and undue sensitivity to criticism.

At the time of the sibling rivalry experiment, the boy was jealous of his sister and fought with her.   The fights were more in the nature of verbal spats, with occasional blows. At the same time, he confided in her frequently and asked her advice. As time went on, she assumed more and more a maternal role with him. In spite of the jealousy and quarrelling, there was a close and warm attachment.

The experiment was made in the 29th session. It was deferred because the boy had previously refused to "play with dolls." The standard material was used—a steel "amputation" mother doll, a rubber brother doll, a celluloid baby doll, and a chair. This time he made a slight protest about "playing with dolls." He criticized the clay breast I made for the mother doll. He added a second breast, and then fashioned both of them in a more pendulous form.

SIBLING RIVALRY EXPERIMENT

Trial I. Patient: "He gets jealous and runs away. Anyhow I never saw my sister at the breast."

Trial II. Patient: "He's jealous and runs away. Jealous hatred. I get that way often."

Trial III. Patient: "He gets curious, hides behind the door, so nobody can see him when he looks. Anyhow it wouldn't happen. They would never let him in the room."

Trial IV. (Usual stimulus sentence. I said, "Now the play is different. The brother comes in and says, 'That bad, bad baby at my mother's breast.'") Patient: "Brother gets mad. He says, 'You nasty mother, why do you have another baby?' He gets mad." He refused to go on. I encouraged him. He said, "It couldn't really happen." Then, "Well, you asked for it." He crumpled up the baby and put the brother to the breast. He said, "The brother drinks." (Then what happened?) "The mother catches him and gives him a spanking." He illustrated the spanking.

Trial V. He grabbed the baby, threw it away, then took the mother doll, spanked her, and said, "Nasty, nasty mother, for getting another baby. Then the brother goes away and cries. Then the mother sits down and cries and cries. Then the husband comes in and they get after the brother and send him to jail." This he demonstrated in detail.

Trial VI. Patient: "He (the brother) takes the baby away. He goes to the breast. Then the baby has a fight with the brother and the brother was what you're thinking. I'm just copying you. He marries the mother. Then the father comes and says, 'You can't marry my wife,' and beats him up." He illustrated with an imaginary father. He then took the mother apart and when I asked why, he said, "It's not what you're thinking, tearing her limb from limb because she had another baby."

Analysis of Sibling Rivalry Experiment with Comments

Trial I. An *escape* reaction. "Anyhow I never saw my sister at the breast," represents a *denial* that the play has reference to his own experience. This, though true, is a type of defense he exploits, as seen later on in the analysis.

Trial II. *Escape.* Repetition of Trial I, omitting the *denial*.

Trial III. *Escape* again, this time by hiding instead of running. The *denial* is in the form of the impossibility of such an occurrence. The fact that the escape reaction (hiding) is used to protect a guilty curiosity of seeing the baby at the breast, implies a sexual curiosity.

Note that though the patient recognizes jealousy of the baby in relation to running away, there is no "mounting" of activity in the first three trials. The play of sexual curiosity in Trial III may have diverted him from the rivalry aspect of the play, or the use of escape reactions may explain the lack of progress, since Trial II is simply a repetition of Trial I.

Trial IV. *Inhibition of impulse.* When the hostile feeling is activated, he releases verbal hostility against the mother, then comes quickly to a halt. As the sequence of the play indicates, he fights off the impulse to attack the baby. His defense against the impulse is in the form of *refusal* (he refused to go on), and *denial* ("It couldn't really happen"—a type of defense used for the third time and implying in this connection that there's no point to the whole thing, so why bother?).

Projection. The remark, "Well, you asked for it," is classified as a projection, though that is probably an elastic use of the term. I *did* ask for it, in the sense that I urged him to go on. I never told him what to do; however, my encouragement ("Go ahead," and "Let the brother do what he wants to") clearly invited him to yield to his impulse in the play. Thereafter, the attack followed, implying that the "projection" that involved sanction, facilitated the assault.

A strong assault. Crumpling up the baby is an assault, stronger than a "mild assault," like flicking the baby or dropping it, and weaker than a primitive assault, like biting off a part of the baby doll, or really crushing it with hands or feet. Primitive assaults are seen most commonly at the ages of 3, 4, and 5, after which they become much less frequent.

Regression. He "puts the brother to the breast."

Escape and punishment. "The mother catches him and gives him a spanking." The punishment seems appropriate to the act, as measured against the play of children in this situation. However, my question, "Then what happened?" made for this additional act, since he had come to a halt. Since typically, the attack and the regressive behavior, or either, are followed by punishment, I assume that the punishment was left out; further, that it was left out because the fear of punishment was greater in his case than in that of others, unless further sequences of play fail to support such an assumption. *Escape* is inferred from his statement, "The mother catches him."

Trial V. The impulse is quickly released. *Strong assault* on the baby, and a *mild assault* on the mother follow. Then an escape reaction occurs ("The brother goes away"), to be followed by tears. The boy's tears may represent *regret* at his action. The mother's constant crying represent sorrow. Then punishment of a severe type follows, through action of father and mother. The sequelae of the attack are unusually severe. They would be more appropriate to overt destruction of the baby and mother. They are exaggerated in comparison with most of the reactions of children (about 140) who experienced the sibling rivalry play. The usual punishment for "throwing the baby away" is spanking, scolding, or a similar act on the brother doll. It is also unusual for the brother and mother to be in tears.

The assumption in Trial IV is suggested by the play in Trial V. The patient withholds his aggression because his fear of punishment is great. Release of his aggression carries too severe a penalty. Hence, the escape reactions in the earlier trials and the defense against the oncoming push into activity through his *denials* are easily comprehended.

Trial VI. *Mild assault* ("He takes the baby away"). *Regression* ("He goes to the breast"). *Punishment* (a retaliation—"Then the baby has a fight with the brother"). The rivalry play then gives way to the Oedipus play. The punishment for marrying his mother is performed by an imaginary father, rather than a father doll (as in Trial V). *Assault* on the mother, by amputation, then follows the rivalry play, judging by his denial of what I am "supposed" to be thinking—a *projection*.

As compared with Trial V, the consequences are all toned down. Judging on the basis of other sibling rivalry plays, the reason may be found in his keeping the assault mild, in using a purely imaginary father rather than the more "realistic" figure-representation, and also in making an attack while at the same time denying its meaning.

The intrusion of the Oedipus situation in the sibling rivalry play is more likely to be found in the pre-adolescent, hardly at all in the younger groups. It is not usual even at this age level, the rivalry aspect of the relationship being well maintained. One reason for the mixture may be due to the fact that the sibling rivalry experiment was made in the 29th interview, and was preceded by a number of sessions in which sexual feelings toward the mother had been revealed.

In the case of this patient, as in many others, playing out a situation is more productive of anxiety, and hence, is a superior form of emotional release, than verbal fantasy. It is worth noting that inhibition of the impulse (at the point of release) occurred but once. The patient was otherwise always ready to respond to the situation in some way or other, if only to escape from it.

"The brother was what you're thinking. I'm just copying you." That is a pattern of defense, classified as *denial*, in this case a form of projection. He assumes that I, not he, have the idea that the brother has a sexual impulse toward the mother, and denies that such an idea has any reference to himself.

Now referring back to the "model" act of hostility, we may summarize the patterns as follows:

1. *Impulse.* There is little difficulty in this case at the point of release. One instance of "refusal" at the impulse occurred.

2. *The self.* Evidently he accepts himself as the one who feels "jealous" and has "jealous hatred." When the impulse is activated, he utilizes my sanction as an aid in the attack ("Well, you asked

for it," and "I'm just copying you"). Hence there is difficulty in taking responsibility for the self as sole agent.

Simpler forms of this mechanism are seen when the child, instead of attacking on his own, adds figures to represent allies, often brothers and friends, or represents an animal as the attacker. The mechanisms may be paraphrased as follows: "Not just I, all of us together are doing it" (use of allies); "I'm not doing it, he is doing it" (use of animal, fairy, witch, and so on); "I'm doing it with your permission" (sanction of grown-up); "I am doing it because you asked me to" (attack disguised as obedience to grown-up). Even young children (age 5) may protect the self as attacker through use of natural forces like winds, volcanoes, or accidents. This mechanism may be paraphrased: "It wasn't my fault, it just happened. I could do nothing about it."

All deviations from the simple assault may be regarded as devices for the protection of the self from the consequences of the act. So far, we have dealt with those phases of the act that occur at the point of release, with the self as the instrument of attack.

3. *Aim.* Escape reactions occur in five instances. They represent deflections of aim in four. In one instance, an escape follows the assault. The patient presumably feels an impulse to attack and immediately runs away. The impulse is released, so that a relationship to the object takes place, though in the form of escape. The consistency of this reaction—it occurs in five of the six trials—indicates (as determined by comparative studies, besides clinical data) a high degree of anxiety. The highest degree of anxiety overtly manifested under "deviations in direction" is seen in younger children when they actually run out of the playroom. Other mechanisms in this category are "escape into distraction" (typically, getting busy with some other form of play), "displacement" (deflecting aim of attack onto other objects), and "inhibited movement" (stopping an attacking gesture after it has started).

4. *Attack.* The attack on the baby was in the form of crumpling it (in IV), throwing it (in V), removing it from the breast without violence (in VI). The strongest attack was in Trial IV (strong assault). It became less and less violent in the trials following.

Attack on the mother was verbal in Trial IV ("You nasty

mother"), spanking and verbal in Trial V ("Nasty, nasty mother" and so on), amputation in Trial VI. In contrast with the attack on the baby, the attack on the mother increased in violence with each trial.

The strongest attack, judging by the retaliation, occurred in Trial V, when mother and baby received the strongest *combination* of violence. Excepting the two verbal attacks, some form of assault was used. None of the deviations of the assault pattern in terms of teasing, attacking from a distance, accidents, illness, operations, traps, or stealing the baby's food were employed. The patient either grappled with the object directly or kept at a distance from it (escape). There is a sort of all-or-none rule in his procedure, implying an impulsive quality. There is a flexibility in the form of his attack. The assault on the baby decreases, that on the mother increases. The attack on the baby starts at the peak and then descends—a reversal of the usual order, and a further indication of impulsive behavior. The attack on the mother, which follows, rises in a more usual manner.

5. *Object.* There is no deviation in the object. The patient does not change it to anything else, nor does he add other objects so that by attacking a group he may be protected from the implied accusation that he is attacking a specific individual.

6. *Sequel.* Sequel is not a well-chosen word to indicate the events following the attack on the object, since it implies that the act is completed. The act usually continues after the attack has been made. The word sequel, for want of a better word, is used with the understanding that it applies to that phase of the act following attack on the object.

The punishment has already been noted as unduly severe. In Trial V, when punishment appears a second time, it is related to the Oedipus situation. This complication has also been noted previously. Since the mechanisms described for the hostility pattern are generally applicable to any act involving danger to the self, the mechanisms are included as part of the sibling rivalry play.

Frequently the child punishes the doll representing the self immediately after the attack (and in some cases, before the attack is released, as an inhibition to the impulse). In this case, the father and mother figures are used to administer the punishment. In

Trial IV, punishment occurred after I asked, "Then what happened?" It appeared that the act would otherwise have ended. At this point, since the data on the sibling rivalry experiments have not all been compiled, I may only infer that there is an indication of keen anxiety, consistently found in cases when the punishment is left out. Its severity when it appeared is confirmatory evidence. In Trial VI, the punishment was not demonstrated by the use of the figures in the play.

The punishment is glossed over in the story, "Then the father comes and says, 'You can't marry my wife,' and beats him up." That type of defense, a story type of verbalization, is difficult to capture. One can only record as far as possible the manner of expression. The use of an imaginary father rather than a real father doll is a help, since by keeping the play in the realm of sheer fantasy, the patient has a strong measure of protection. Another confirmatory datum occurs in Trial IV when he represents the brother as running away after the act, then being caught and punished.

His denials (four instances) are of the same order. They are his most frequent and intensive form of defense. The expressions are used as follows: "Anyhow I never saw my sister at the breast" (Trial I); "Anyhow it wouldn't happen. . . ." (Trial III); "It couldn't really happen" (Trial IV); and, "I'm just copying you" (Trial VI). Through such tactics, he denies any relation of the play to himself, to reality, to anything logical, or to anything that went on in his mind.

The projection mechanisms were used to ascribe the responsibility of the attack to me (Trial IV, "Well, you asked for it"), and a denial that he had any idea of attacking the mother (Trial VI, while amputating the mother-doll, "It's not what you're thinking, tearing her limb from limb because she had another baby"). One of his denials ("The brother was what you're thinking, I'm just copying you") may also be classified as a projection, since thereby he ascribes his own ideas to me.[3]

---

[3] Since all projection mechanisms, as the term is used in psychiatry, contain a denial and an accusation—an implied denial that the impulse or idea or act belongs to the self, and the direct accusation that they belong to someone else— the differentiation from denial is sometimes difficult. Actually, projections are denials in which the thing denied is projected.

Regression occurs in two responses when the brother is restored to the breast from which the baby was taken away. Regressive responses at this age period are infrequent. Though complicated by the Oedipus play, they represent a strong need for protection as in infancy.

The absence of restoring behavior is noteworthy. It occurs so frequently in children after any attack that rises above a mild assault that its absence requires consideration. Some children feel the process of restoration before it occurs and say in advance of the attack, "And I won't put it together again." Whatever the explanation of its origin, restoring behavior is a valuable restorative in the equilibrium of the hostile act. The absence of this "constructive" feature is a handicap in the patient's psychic resources in overcoming the anxiety following the attack.

We may summarize the psychodynamic patterns as revealed in the sibling rivalry play by stating that our patient had a strong aggressive impulse, with a tendency to quick release of destructive behavior, withheld from execution because of an intense fear of punishment and disapproval; that in the release of his impulse, at least as manifested in the sibling rivalry play, there was evidence of strong anxiety shown by frequent "escapes" and "denials." The implication of these mechanisms in terms of his method of defense against the anxiety set off by his aggressive impulse, was that he tries to escape or avoid situations in which there is danger of actual combat. His method of defense against disapproval (an implied accusation) was by denying that his actions or motives could be interpreted as really implying any evil intention, or having any logic in them at all. The projections in the play implied also a strong tendency to divert blame from himself and attribute it to others. This would involve much argumentation in which, it is assumed, his aggression would be especially manifested. Judging by the use of "sanction" in releasing his aggression, it was implied that he would utilize the aid of others, and in argument, protect himself by recourse to authority. This implication is consistent also with the regressive behavior in the sibling rivalry play, indicating infantile dependency, a strong bid for support, yet at the same time, competitive struggle for first place.

In terms of the sibling rivalry situation, we may say that he had not quite relinquished his position as the only child at the time of the play, and that his competitive, jealous behavior was not yet modified into acceptance. The absence of restoring behavior would indicate difficulty in developing the accepting phase.

Summary of the Classifications in the Sibling Rivalry Play

I. 1) Escape
   2) Denial
II. 1) Escape
III. 1) Escape
   2) Denial
IV. 1) Inhibition of impulse
   2) Refusal
   3) Denial
   4) Projection
   5) Assault (strong)
   6) Regression
   7) Escape
   8) Punishment
V. 1) Assault (strong)
   2) Assault (mild)
   3) Escape
   4) Punishment
   5) (Regret)
   6) (Sorrow)
VI. 1) Assault (mild)
   2) Regression

3) Punishment
4) Assault (strong)
5) Projection
6) Denial

Totals

Inhibition of impulse ...	1
Escape	5
Denial	4
Refusal	1
Projection	2
Assault	
Mild	2
Strong	3
Primitive	0
Punishment	3 (+2)
(Regret)	
(Sorrow)	
Regression	2
	—
	23 (+2)

Drawings. Since the patient was facile in drawing sketches, this became a favorite activity during treatment. He produced 85 altogether in about 20 sessions. The method developed into a routine. He would start drawing as many as came to his mind, three to five per session, in all but a few instances. After he finished, I would ask him to explain what he drew, and then would use them as a basis for his associations. The drawings may be classified as follows.

Landscape (9). They deal directly or by association with violence, death, suicide, destruction, isolation. Titles of these drawings as given by him were: "Forest fire," "Fire," "People falling down a cliffy ledge," "Landscape" (associated with isolation), "Sun and cloud," "Waterfall" (associated with death), "Mountains in snow," "Ships in a storm," "Storm" (associated with death). (See meaning of cliffs and chasms in his Rorschach test.)

Drawings containing animals (14). These are concerned chiefly with the subject of the captor and the prey. In these he identifies himself chiefly with the victim. He associated a cat and dog picture with himself and sister.

Other drawings in this series deal with escape, punishment, fright, curiosity. Titles: "Angry horse left behind," "Panther and prey," "Curious dog," "Frightened rabbit," "Cat and dog," "Eagle, its eggs are stolen," "Eagle and fish," "Dog running from fox," "Fight with a whale," "A duck and a cage" (associated with imprisonment), "Hunter killing an animal," another with the same title, "Fox and chicken," "Knight and dragon" (associated with death).

Drawings of objects (5). In three, the content is violent death (train crashing into a tree, plane on fire, car hitting a rock). The fourth drawing is the "Holy Cross," associated with getting rid of his fears. The fifth is a drawing of a book, associated with his interest in reading.

Drawings of people (57). These deal chiefly with the subjects of crime and heroes. He drew one series of 12, dealing with the exploits of a gangster—his killings, final capture, and death. One drawing deals with pirates. The drawings of heroes contain mostly baseball and football players. There are three drawings of suicide and one of a funeral. All the subjects referred to under landscapes, animals, and objects are also depicted in this series.

In general, the drawings portray a competitive dog-eat-dog existence in a world full of danger and violence, in which the patient is struggling along in the form of a helpless, abandoned victim, trying to escape from the enemy, driven from pillar to post, finally resorting to suicide; and also, in the form of a great hero, winning the applause of the crowd and vanquishing all his foes.

The drawings help to illuminate his responses to the Rorschach test. The replies of chasms, steep rocks, and cliffs, as evidence of anxiety, are confirmed. They represent dangerous forces of nature, chiefly in the form of falling into depths. The Rorschach replies— the dead animals, people wearing masks, and the animal with fire shooting out of its mouth—are similar in content to his drawings.

Dreams. The patient related 20 dreams. In eight, the content was chiefly of killing (4) and crime (4). In one of these, he saved his mother from robbers; in another, dealing with spies and tortures, there is clear indication of sexual activity with his mother's breasts.

In one of the murder dreams, his sister is killed; in another she is "symbolically" killed, that is, two baby carriages appear and only one baby is present.

Five are frank Oedipus dreams in content or by ready association; for example, getting a woman away from her husband, a fight with a man for a woman, a dream in which he falls in love with an older woman, and one dealing with the parents separating. Three concern his more independent sex drive: one is a symbolic coitus (climbing up a ladder with a girl), another is symbolic of some form of sex curiosity, and a third is a direct sex exploration, a dream in which he is kissing a girl. Four dreams (including two already described) contain manifestations of rivalry with schoolmates and with his sister, and one is concerned with his offering someone a gift.

Of the 20 dreams, two were repetitions of dreams he had had many times before. They were usually frightening, sometimes nightmarish; for example, a dream of being caught by robbers, and awakening with a cry when he was just about to kill himself or be killed. (The patient said he remembered all his dreams very well, and always used them in his daydreams, turning them around, however, so that he would "best the robbers, catch Public Enemy No. 1," and so on, a control that he realized he could not exert in dreams of the night.)

The second repeated dream was one in which he saved his mother from robbers. In some of these he ran away from her. Then, he said, "she goes with her husband against me." It appears evident that at the time of treatment, anxiety engendered by his aggressive impulses was especially activated by the Oedipus situation.

Dreams and drawings are similar in content; in fact, the same type of associations was yielded by both. The dreams, in contrast, offered a greater wealth of data in terms of content and associations, and also less concealment. This contrast is true in general. Dreams are more productive of unconscious material, both in younger and older children, than are drawings. However, it should be noted that to some of his drawings associations were quite similar and as productive as dreams. In contrast with the drawings, his dreams contained very little landscape, animals, or objects. They were almost all of people in some sort of action.

Defense Patterns of the Hostile Act in Dream Structure *

Repeated dream: *Running away* from robbers.
Dream No.   1 *Hiding* from cops. *Surrender* to cops.
            3 *Accident.* Takes his girl friend up a ladder, about to tell her something, then accidentally falls down. (He was going to do something sexual to her. Accident used as disguised punishment (?) or protection against sexual impulse.)
            5 *Bribery.* Pays his way out of being tortured.
            12 *Use of allies.* In fighting with a boy, he is getting the worst of it, and a girl helps him.
            13 *Hiding and running away.*
            16 *Disappearing.*
            19 *Denial.* Death of his rival changes to "nothing serious."

Of the nine patterns, four are "escapes," one is denial of the "reality" of the act, one probably punishment. Surrender represents passive acceptance. The patterns so far are typical of those in the sibling rivalry play. The use of bribery to placate the assailant and of an ally to serve him were not used in the sibling rivalry, though in the latter instance, his use of the examiner to aid in the attack is analogous. As in the sibling rivalry, no restoring devices were used, and the punishment (attacks made upon him) was severe. Rivalry with a boy or with his sister occurred in five of the 20 dreams (6, 7, 12, 18, and 19).

Defense Patterns in Response to Associations and Interpretations.

In Session I, after reviewing his eight drawings, I said, "Now let's see what all this has to do with your life." He said, "Bet you can't. Bet you can't" (Rivalry). In Session VI, he said he likes to argue. "I am the greatest arguer in the world." He said he can always get satisfaction in his imagination. "In my imagination I can control the world."

In IX, in association to a drawing of a boy stealing bananas, I asked his association to banana. He appeared anxious, ran a pencil over his face, asked what time it was, said, "What good is it to know what banana is?" He then told me what it meant and that he was scared to say it. Then he said, "It's time to go." The secretary knocked at the door to indicate that time was up. He said, "It's about time."

In X, in association with a dream in which it became clear that

---

* Exclusive of symbolism.

his description of a woman who was supposed to be his wife fitted his mother closely, he first denied the obvious and then asked, "Do other boys have dreams like this?"

In XII, he told of a dream in which he went up a ladder of lights with a girl, was about to tell her something, then fell down. Then he was in a rich mansion, but it was in school. He started bouncing the ball and then flew into the living room where his mother was. Then he said, "Get this in your head. It was in school and it was a rich mansion. And my mom couldn't be in school. So it's flukey. Now I'll give you three guesses what I was going to say." Later he said, "You can't explain the dream. You can't explain the lights and about the girl and the mother." (Denial of meaning, by argument; use of attack by attempting to dominate—"three guesses," "You can't explain . . ."—as protection against fear of association.)

In XIII, after a typical Oedipus dream, in which he was kidnapped by a man and a woman whom he described and recognized as his mother and father, he said quickly, "I know the whole thing. The woman was my mother and the man was my father, and I wanted to marry her so she turned against me. But what has this money got to do with it?" (Defense by the quick interpretation, as though to say, "Don't tell me, I know, but explain something else." Defense by racing through an interpretation, and distraction.)

When asked the meaning of "going up and down," an item in the dream, he said, "I refuse to tell you. Anyhow it doesn't explain the money." (Refusal and distraction.)

He asked me the meaning of something in the dream, and anticipating that I would ask him its meaning, he said, "You know it already, so why waste time." (He wanted a quick interpretation so he could quickly pass to something else—a form of escape.)

Also in XIII, in association to "skushy fatty bulldogs," I repeated, "Two big skushy fatty things." He said, "Tits, but it's dumb. Why sic them after me? Anyhow why say such vulgar things? Let's get it over with. Anyhow I don't think it's right. I disagree." (Denial of meaning—"It's dumb." Projection—"Why say such vulgar things." Escape—"Let's get it over with.")

At another point in the same session, he denied his own interpretation—the horn of a rhinoceros as penis. He said, "Where did it get blue from? I got you caught there. How do you know it's all true? You got no proof for any of this." (Attack by projection, and denial of meaning.) Of another dream, "The whole thing's nuts. That's clear. Let's get to the other dream." (Escape by racing to the next thing.)

He was interested in unravelling dream and treated it like a mystery story. He was very challenging. Said, "Now what does that mean? You're stuck." I admitted it, and then he proceeded good-naturedly. Note the frequent defense—"That wasn't my idea. That was yours."

In XVI, he said after I interpreted his dream, "There, you're stuck again." (Defense by distraction and attack—competition with me.)

XX. "If you try to take away my imagination, I'll stop coming."

In XXI, he said he had three dreams and he solved them all himself. (Competition.)

In XXII, before associating a woman in a dream as his mother, he said, "I know what you're thinking of." (Projection.) Again he associated, and said, "It's nuts."

In XXIV, after my interpretation, he said, "Well, you got that right for once."

In XXVII, he said to me, before making an association, "I can always tell what you're thinking of." Regarding thoughts about birth, he said, "Don't think I think about these things all the time— just once a year." (Defense of rare event.) Then he said, "I know what you're thinking of. Want to guess?" It was coitus with mother. Then he made a face at me; asked, "What time is it?" then said, "So what! So what! Oh yes, oh yes, oh yes." Regarding masturbation, he said, "I do it once in a blue moon." He picked up a game and looked at it. (Distraction.)

In XXIX, the sibling rivalry experiments were made. After XXX, there was much dropping of defenses, but in XXXII he said, "What do the pictures mean? You're the genius around here." (Competition.)

In XXXIII, he said, "I made up my mind never to agree with you." When I replied that he hated to think I could help him, he said, "I know it. I'm the only one who can help me."

In his defense against acceptance of the meaning of the fantasies, whether of dreams or drawings, the patterns were again chiefly in the form of escapes (10 instances) and denials (eight instances). A type of rivalry with the therapist was another frequent form.

The escape patterns were simple indications of a wish to leave, in three instances ("What time is it?" "It's time to go"), and "distraction" in two instances (attempting to get my attention away from important to what he regarded as irrelevant material). A more subtle form consisted in "racing" through the "dangerous" associations, landing onto "safe" or presumably innocuous associations (four instances). After an obvious Oedipus dream, he said quickly, "I know the whole thing. The woman was my mother, and the man was my father, and I wanted to marry her so she turned against me, but what has the money got to do with it?" At another point he made this pattern more obvious by saying, "Let's get it over with." This method was used again when he said about a symbolic sexual act, "You know it already, so why waste time?" and again, when he said quickly of a dream, "That's clear, let's get to the other dream." This "chase" through the dangerous meanings is quite like the escapes in the play, and the frequent running away episodes in the dream.

His denials (eight instances) that the dreams or drawings had meanings that I, or even he, attributed to them, were chiefly in the form of arguing. He would argue that a dream couldn't mean anything because of its inconsistencies, and after an interpretation was made with his help, he would argue that I couldn't explain this or that detail. He would deny meanings by saying they were "flukey" or "dumb" or "nuts." He would even deny his own interpretation by trying to prove it was illogical because of a detail; for example, in the instance of the horn of rhinoceros as a penis. At one point, he said, "I made up my mind never to agree with you."

In spite of the arguments employed to disprove the point that interpretations had any relation to his own feelings or experience, he actually refused to give associations on only one occasion. This occurred in association to the phrase "going up and down" (Dream 6). It clearly had sexual meaning. He said, "I refuse to tell you."

In his arguments he would challenge my ability to solve the meaning of his dreams or drawings. On other occasions, his rivalry with me was quite obvious. All the activities in which he challenged my ability or was clearly competitive were classified under rivalry.

They occurred frequently (on more than 12 occasions). For example, when asked to see what his drawings had to do with his own experience in life, he said, "Bet you can't. Bet you can't. Bet you can't." He would try to make me guess what his associations were, saying, "I'll give you three guesses." He would challenge me— "You're stuck, you can't explain" this or that. Sometimes he would say, "I know exactly what you're thinking," "Well, you got it right for once. What do the pictures mean, you're the genius around here." On one occasion he said in a competitive manner, "I had three dreams and I solved them all myself."

The competitive relationship with me appeared to serve a number of functions. Besides fulfilling a competitive role, as with his sister, father, and schoolmates, it served as a defense against anxiety by putting me in the weaker position. He was the one who knew, I was the one who had to guess. He could then decide if I was right. He tried to reverse our roles so that I could not be dangerous to him. Since the main reliance of his aggression was the argument, he held tight to his intellectual weapon, afraid to release it.

The rivalry served also as a distraction. By turning the interpretive phase of the therapy into a contest, he could escape into a kind of play in which we matched wits. Actually it was a play, since the rivalry was a pattern that never really hindered the process of interpretation. It became a kind of ritualistic pattern, preceding his acceptance of the meaning of his fantasy, or a request for my help in solving the problem. The pattern was modified as time went on, but some elements of it were maintained more or less throughout.

Defense patterns in the form of projections occurred in five instances. He criticized me for an interpretation he made himself. After referring to breasts as "tits," he asked me why I said such vulgar things. On those occasions in which he said, "I know what you are thinking," the defense was evidently a projection, if also a form of rivalry.

The "defense of universality" occurred only once. After it appeared obvious that his description of his wife in a dream tallied with his mother, he denied the resemblance, then admitted it, and asked "Do other boys have dreams like this?"

A defense of the opposite variety occurred also on one occasion —the "defense of rareness," a common form in children. He evidently felt guilty in describing the process of birth and said, "Don't think I think about these things all the time—just once a year." (Defense of rarity is similar to the defense of "long ago.")

Stories and Daydreams. In his day fantasies, there were baseball and football teams in which he remembered the names and characteristics of each player. He also fantasied battles of imaginary nations, with names of generals, cities, and so on. Usually, the names of people were thin disguises for real names. Such fantasies went on for years and occurred at any odd moment during the day. They were responsible for one severe accident in which he was run over by a taxicab, suffered a skull injury, and luckily made a full recovery. The day fantasies dealt chiefly with the subject of rivalry, and involved Oedipus rivalry at the time of treatment.

At the age of 12, he had a serial story in his fantasy concerning a battle between the countries of Kesk and Zelzibar. Movran was the only city of Zelzibar. Whoever captured it would win the battle. Zelzibar was owned by a man named Rocky Smith. To quote the patient, "The people were wild. He couldn't make them do any work so the country couldn't progress. So after he revolutioned, he gave his country to the other country so he could be ruled and protected, although the other country would get a lot of money out of it." Other countries wanted to rule Zelzibar, countries called Young and Inton. One country got into Zelzibar by tunneling through its mountains. He said, "This war lasted two weeks in my imagination—a record!"

Further details had to do with war strategy. The names were definitely related to friends and family and carried through the same plots as in his drawings and dreams.

He wrote numerous stories. They concerned detectives, criminals, and boxers. He also wrote poems about crimes and similar topics.

RORSCHACH TEST

A formal study of the Rorschach test will not be presented. The responses are recorded for those who wish to study them. They indicate definite evidence of anxiety in an intelligent boy who is introverted and has a rich and very active imagination. The responses seem to confirm especially the content of the drawings. Evidence of anxiety was seen in the black-white and space responses (six)—chiefly chasms, steep rocks and cliffs.   There was color shock to Plate IX, followed by response of "rocky chasm."

Rorschach Test.   Time: 21 minutes.   Age of patient: 11 years, 11 months.

I   1) Two people holding hands. (*W*, except central portion)
    2) A little kid between them (lower ⅔ central area).
II   1) Two people wearing masks, their hands together.   They are kneeling down. (*W*) Pause. Encouraged.
    2) (Reversed) Like a cave or chasm and the steep rocks. (*W*)
III   1) Two people holding a pail.
    2) A forest. (Negro heads are trees, and light gray is the rest of the forest.)
IV   1) (Side) A dead butterfly.
    (Several turns)
    2) A big animal.   Midpart is the tail.
V   1) (Immediately to side position, then straight) Butterfly.
    2) (Reversed) A person standing on his hands. (Midsection.)
VI   1) A skeleton (top ⅓), and
    2) Left-over skin of a dead animal. (*W*)
    Pause.   Encouraged.
    3) and 4) (Reversed) A chasm and the sun.   It looks like a face and the cliffs.   (Lower midstreaks, eggs and lateral extension of them, making the bottom central angle.)
    5) (Side) A lake, trees and at the rim and sky all reflected in the lake.   (Trees on rim of lake are the whole central streak; the rest of one side is the lake, and the other side is the sky.)
VII   It looks like a lot of things.
    1) and 2) Indian children sitting on a rock, each pointing (lateral paw) to something he saw.
    3) and 4) Two rocky mountains and waterfall (clasp) running down. (*W*)
VIII   No pause. 1) A wolf. (Lateral pink)
    2) A lady with a colored dress.   She's holding two pet animals.   They're climbing up her hand.   But she has no head. (*W*)
    3) (Reversed) Like a seat with nobody in it. (*W*)
IX   1) and 2) (First long pause, 32″) I see a rocky chasm again.   There's the rainbow. (Brown area and space; rainbow is the central prongs.)
    3) and 4) (Side) Two jaws of an animal (medial brown profiles) and fire shooting out of its mouth (gray-green stalk).   It's a dragon, there's its head (green). (*W*)
X   1) Two people holding up a pole.   You can't see their heads because they're bending back.
    2) (Reversed) A rocky ledge (pink), and
    3) The blue things are men holding a can with food in it, and
    4) That green thing is a tame bird coming down to eat it (low

green). (Later said it was a wild bird and they made it tame.)
5) Spiders (Lateral blue).
6) A bug (Lateral gray).

There were five responses with content of frightening aspect:
(1) two people wearing masks; (2) a dead butterfly; (3) skin of a
dead animal; (4) two jaws of an animal with fire shooting out of its
mouth; (5) men hold a can of food and a bird comes and steals it.

CLINICAL DATA

According to the mother, the patient became a feeding problem
several months before his sister's birth. He was then two years and
a few months old. He refused food unless the maid or his mother
helped feed him. Previously he had learned to eat nicely without
the help or presence of a grown-up. The difficulty lasted for some
months, and thereafter he was a finicky eater for several years.

When he first saw his baby sister, he said, "She's cute." There
was no evidence of jealousy in the early months. When grown-ups
came to visit, he brought them to see the baby as though to show
her off. Later, when his sister was seven or eight months of age
and could get at his things, he became very angry. He would hurl
blocks at her. The baby had to be guarded from his attacks.

(Note that the so-called sibling rivalry reaction was evident before
the baby was born. The sibling rivalry reaction is primarily to
privation or change in terms of care, affection, and attention, or
to differences in the appearance or routine of the child's familiar
world. One of my patients showed the first untoward reaction
before the birth of the next baby when a bassinet was placed in his
room. The baby may not be perceived as the object of rivalry, for
months or even years, if at all, especially when the age difference is
but two years. This may be so even when sibling rivalry reactions
are not in evidence until after its birth. Note also that the patient's
response to the change preceding the birth of his sister was in the
form of regression, and, as in the sibling rivalry play, in relation
to feeding.)

According to the written observation of a school teacher who
visited the home when the patient was three years old, both parents
were "strict," though affectionate. As time went on, however, the
father became immersed in business difficulties and left the responsibility of rearing the children almost entirely to the mother. At

the time of treatment, the parental picture was clearly that of an indulgent father who needed strong persuasion to play with his children or assert occasional authority; and a mother, competent, responsible, worrisome, and affectionate, though lax in disciplining her son.   Certainly he was allowed the privilege of impudent retort and marked freedom of expression.   There were occasional tense scenes in which the mother spoke to him severely.   She tried to make him fully aware of his bad manners and lack of consideration for others.   These unfair bawlings-out according to his version, were especially reserved for him.   When the sister tore her shirt, he said to her, "Because you're the favorite, nothing will happen," and added, "She gets all kinds of credit, her beautiful little curls."

After the late infantile period of primitive jealousy, the relationship to his sister became bossy and competitive.   At the beginning of the treatment period (age 11 years and 11 months to 12 years and 0 months), he expressed his criticism of her and his feelings of jealousy quite freely.   He often "dreamed" (daydreamed) of victorious competition with her.   At that time, evidence of affection also had been apparent for some years.   A confidential relationship was established.   Toward the end of the treatment he spoke about his affection for her and his protective feelings toward her. He confided in her and asked her advice.   Her role to him became increasingly maternal, though verbal spats were still occasionally in evidence.

Careful records of his behavior were made on occasion by his teachers, beginning in the nursery school.   At 3 years and 4 months, a continuous record of his activities was kept for an hour and a half. The record contained 23 instances of activity centering on possession of objects.   They were mostly protective retorts—"No, all mine," "Don't touch that," "No, you can't have any of these dishes—mine —all my dishes—can't have any."   There were several boasts about possessions; for example, "I've got apples home.   Yes, I have, and cookies."   He made one attempt to snatch an object from another child.

The same record contained five instances of negativistic behavior: (1) a child was playing with a suit case; patient kicked it; (2) a child started walking up steps; patient pushed him; (3) a child showed the teacher a picture and said it was a duck; patient said, "No, that's not a duck"; (4) a child said, "Dollie's in there."   Patient said, "No dollies"; (5) a child said, "Asleep, asleep." Patient said, "No, not asleep."

It was noted that he was shy at first and stood behind a door. "He said No, automatically, to all suggestions, yet he yielded easily." "His attitude was very negative," yet he made approaches to the children.

After five months (age 3 years and 11 months), he became more sociable with children and grown-ups in the nursery school, though he was still considered withdrawn as compared with the others, and negativistic. Descriptions of his negativistic behavior and lack of "integration with the group" feature the school notations up to age 10. When he was nine years old, it was noted that he had "hostile" reactions to teachers, that his violence was chiefly in speech, though he would occasionally bump into a teacher and slap her lightly, as though the gesture was not intended to be taken seriously. It was noted also at this time that when visiting with other children in the toy department of a store, he was visibly frightened when a clown came near. In the period of his improved social relationship, he usually made a close friendship with one child.

Through ages seven, eight, and nine years, his vivid imagination and creative fantasy were striking. At eight years, several stories he dictated to his teachers were preserved. The first two deal with sibling rivalry situations. In the first, two parents decided to have a baby. When the baby was five years old, he went to school. "He did not know any children but he killed lots of teachers." Details of the murders were cited. The children thought the boy was so nice they gave him a choice of anything he wanted. The boy said, "I want some soldiers like as I was a king." They were his army. He was the strongest. John, who became his best friend, was next. The army marched past his home. Then he went into his house and told his parents he would never see them again. He went off with his army to the regular American army to fight the English.

In the second story, a boy, a girl, and their father and mother each fell down the stairs, which were made out of paper. The police came and arrested them all. They were next in prison, starving. Then the patient arrived with his army of 20,000 men. They burned the prison and the poor prisoners escaped by jumping out through holes made by fire. "They hung the police up on a string," and then marched back to New York.

(In terms of the sibling rivalry situation, the response to the new baby in the first story is to ignore her and attack the mother. The objects of attack, baby and mother, are changed in the story to children and teachers. The competitive struggle is solved by infantile omnipotence, and the parents are punished by his departure —an exploitation of the escape reaction.)

(The sibling rivalry solution in the second story is an attack on the entire family group. The attack, in which he also is included, changed into an accident, and to make doubly sure no evil intent can be charged against him, the stairs are changed into paper. That is similar to his "it-couldn't-really-happen" defense in the sibling rivalry play. Then the solution, through infantile omnipotence, takes both a restoring and a destructive form, and he is the hero of both actions. The use of an ally, a best friend, in both, may indicate the affectionate phase of his relationship to his sister. His best friend is put in a safe secondary status. The arrest of the entire family, presumably because they fell down the stairs, indicates that the fall represents a punishable act—an attack. It is a frequent disguise, especially in sibling rivalry play, though not often followed by punishment. It usually serves its purpose of concealment and averts a penalty. The punishment in relation to food is consistent again with food responses in the actual sibling rivalry and in the sibling rivalry play. The unusual method of escape, through holes made by fire, is a birth symbol, judging by similar representations in the treatment sessions. The hanging of the policemen, representing in the usual way an attack on the father, indicates a merging of Oedipus and sibling rivalry fantasy, as in the sibling rivalry experiments. In the stories written at the time of treatment, this merging is seen more clearly.)

At the ages of 10 and 11, interest in reading and creative writing were noticed. In contrast, he had no interest in arithmetic. His general behavior was recorded as a see-saw of shrinking and boisterous rude behavior. He was unduly sensitive, though he entered all group activities. He had a "genuine friendship" with one boy in the school. He revealed much interest in world affairs and constantly quoted his father in support of his arguments.

When he was 12, a teacher stated that he showed less evidence of absorption in his imaginary world and less anxiety in his school work. He did his own thinking, read only the best books, wrote many stories, and painted pictures of Indians, hunting scenes, and animals tearing into each other. He was very friendly with his teachers, but still sensitive and argumentative.

His relationship to boys, as revealed during treatment, confirmed the observations made by his teachers in the nursery school. There, the competitive attitude was manifested in a struggle to exclude all others—to push them away from his possessions and to keep them out of his territory. His negativistic retorts to children were presumably designed to deny that any child besides himself had a right to say anything, or could say anything correctly. At the same time, he was trying to remain in some social relationship, and his bids for friendship gave promise that he would in time make a definite alliance. Up to the period of treatment, his relationship with boys followed consistently the history of his relationship with his sister (excepting in the first seven to eight months of her life). The stages were: (1) refusal of any form of social acceptance; (2) acceptance of the presence of the rival, though at a safe distance; (3) acceptance of social contact on a competitive basis; (4) close, loyal friendship with a favorite, though maintaining superior status. At the time of treatment, he had not yet developed an easy give-and-take relationship. Friends were still rivals, allies in battle, audiences to applaud his exploits, at times even confidants, but they were never taken for granted simply as friends.

His negativistic retorts in the nursery were traceable later on as arguments in which he just had to win. They became for some years a *modus vivendi*. When pressed for facts, he used the authority of his father; later, also, of myself. He would tell me about the arguments he had at school and ask for information that would demolish his foes.

In his battle of words, he suffered from the intensity of his feelings. He was able to marshal facts well enough in class debates, but in personal arguments, he would become too excited to organize his thoughts. As a result, after the battle, he had many fantasies of the things he might have said. The subjects were anything from baseball to world events. Social and political subjects gradually played a more prominent role.

The strong rivalry relating to possessions that first appeared in response to the baby sister, and later on, in the nursery school, was manifested at the time of treatment in his attitude toward money. He watched every penny, complained about the cost of movies, and thought of various projects for making money. At the same time he was extravagant in purchasing gifts. Naturally, there were various other influences that helped shape his attitude toward money; however, the consistency of holding on to possessions, starting in the rivalry situation, appeared to be an important factor.

In the sibling rivalry play, his patterns measured against the clinical data in this section show the sibling rivalry dynamics only in terms of their operation at the time of study. It would be impossible to reconstruct directly from the play material the developmental phases of the sibling rivalry relationship. The sibling rivalry play reveals in his case, generally, the play of his aggression. It tells how he handles his hostilities. It reveals the strong aggressive tendencies, the fear of release, and the quick escape, and fits well into the pattern described by his teachers of initial attack and compliance. The competitive tendencies and argumentation with recourse to authority are easily implied from the sibling rivalry play. Furthermore, the play, more than the observation of his behavior, reveals clearly his methods of defense against the anxiety set off by the aggressive impulse.

SUMMARY AND CONCLUSIONS

A study of hostility patterns was made by determining, through a standardized play situation, the act of hostility reduced to its simplest form (the "unit act"). The act represents the child assaulting the baby, the attack being followed by punishing, restoring, and self-justifying behavior. The various phases of the act and the deviation from its simple structure were investigated. This involved a study of the impulse, that is, the phase preceding the release of movement in relation to the object; the self, and deviations in the use of the self as attacker; the aim, and deviations in the aim after release of movement in relation to the object before contact with the object had occurred; the assault, and deviations from that form of attack; the object, and deviations in the use of the object as the target of attack. Besides investigating these phases, all deviations from the usual punishing, restoring, and self-justifying behavior were analyzed.

The particular patterns manifested in the play were found to have special characteristics representing general and individual psychodynamics of hostility. The method of investigation was applied in detail to the sibling rivalry play of a particular patient. When his responses at the various phases of the hostile acts were classified and analyzed, they revealed a regressive trend to the infantile dependent state, and a strong aggressive impulse with a tendency to quick release of destructive behavior, withheld from execution by an intense fear of punishment. This pattern and others were compared with those obtained by analyzing the patient's life history, dreams, drawings, stories, associations during treatment, and the Rorschach test. The material obtained from each of these sources revealed the same mechanisms, though highlighting different aspects.

The content of the drawings revealed especially the competitive and violent struggle for position, the dangers involved in the battle, triumphant victories including death to the enemy, tragic defeats, helpless states, and even suicide. More than any other form, the drawings made use of animals and landscapes.

The defense patterns used in his dreams, revealed in their manifest content, were especially typical of those in the sibling rivalry play. In both, escape reactions were featured, punishment was unduly severe, and restoring behavior was absent. Only one defense pattern classified as denial occurred in the dreams, an instance in which the death of a rival was changed into "nothing serious." Denials occurred four times in the sibling rivalry play. In his defense against acceptance of the meaning of his fantasies, whether of dreams or drawings, the patterns were as in the sibling rivalry play, chiefly in the form of escapes and denials.

Including all forms, the escapes were seen as: (1) running away, (2) hiding, (3) disappearing, (4) distracting conversation or play, (5) indication of a wish to leave, and (6) racing through "dangerous" to irrelevant associations. The denials were seen as: (1) a denial that the fantasy was part of a real experience, (2) a denial that it could happen, (3) a denial that it had any logic in it, or (4) a denial that it was even his fantasy.

The rivalry aspects of the sibling rivalry play appeared also in drawings, dreams, written compositions, and in his relationship with the therapist. The fantasy of direct aggression, in the form of assault or murder, appeared in sibling rivalry plays, dreams, drawings, and compositions. Such fantasy appeared more frequently and intensely in the drawings and written compositions than in the dreams and sibling rivalry play. On the other hand, direct evidence of regressive behavior and of sexual fantasy appeared in the sibling rivalry play and dreams alone.

Contrasting his dreams, drawings, and sibling rivalry play, direct release of hostility was most frequent and intense in the drawings, less in the play, least in the dreams. The reverse order occurs in regard to sexual behavior. The patterns of defense against release of sexual or hostile impulses were relatively more frequent in the play and least so in the drawings. Since the patterns of defense may be considered as indices of anxiety, we may conclude that all in all, his dreams reflected more anxiety than the other media of fantasy; or, put in other words, more protective devices were utilized in his dreams in the attainment of a goal.

A study of the sibling rivalry reactions, traced through a series of observations made at home, in the nursery school, and in grade school, revealed their various developmental phases: (1) refusal of any form of social acceptance; (2) acceptance of the presence of the rival, though at a safe distance; (3) acceptance of social contact on a competitive basis; (4) close, loyal friendship with a favorite, though maintaining superior status.

The play showed the sibling rivalry dynamics only in terms of their operation at the time of study. It revealed the methods of defense against the anxiety set off by the aggressive impulse more clearly than the clinical study. It did not reveal the sibling rivalry relationship in its genetic or developmental phases.

The method of investigation was especially directed to the study of the hostility patterns. Other patterns were considered when necessary, since dynamic patterns merge. The study of special dynamics, which is, of necessity, a deliberately selective process, was aided by utilizing an experimental method, and tracing through the special dynamics in the real and fantasy life of the patient. The experimental play situation enables a certain precision of method and the possibility of new observations otherwise quite elusive.

Author Index

Subject Index

711